A GRAMMAR OF TARGUM NEOFITI

HARVARD SEMITIC MUSEUM

HARVARD SEMITIC MONOGRAPHS

edited by
Frank Moore Cross

Number 34

A GRAMMAR OF TARGUM NEOFITI

by
David M. Golomb

David M. Golomb

A GRAMMAR OF TARGUM NEOFITI

Scholars Press
Chico, California

A GRAMMAR OF TARGUM NEOFITI

David M. Golomb

Library of Congress Cataloging in Publication Data

Golomb, David M. (David Marcus), 1945–
A grammar of Targum Neofiti.

(Harvard Semitic monographs ; no. 34)
Bibliography: p.
Includes index.
1. Aramaic language—Grammar—1950– . 2. Bible.
O.T. Pentateuch. Aramaic—Versions—Targum
Yerushalmi—Language, style. 3. Codex Neofiti 1. I. Title.
II. Series.
PJ5252.G64 1985 492'.29 85-10719
ISBN 0-89130-891-1 (alk. paper)

Printed in the United States of America
on acid-free paper

PREFACE

This study represents a revision and expansion of a doctoral dissertation presented to Harvard University in 1978. The original study was prepared under the direction of Thomas O. Lambdin, and I wish to take this opportunity to thank him for his help, his advice, and his good humor, and to wish him all the best in his "retirement."

I also want to record my sincere appreciation to the editor of this series, Frank Moore Cross, for all his help and encouragement over the past few years.

This volume has been prepared with the assistance of the Melton Center for Jewish Studies and the College of Humanities at The Ohio State University.

I dedicate this book to the memory of my parents, Gilbert Golomb and Miriam Edna Golomb, who would have derived much pride and pleasure from its appearance, and to my "new" parents, Mel and Florence Rubel, who have always offered unfailing love and support, through good moments and bad.

But mostly this book is for my wife, Susha, with much love.

David Marcus Golomb
Reynoldsburg, Ohio, 1985

CONTENTS

CHAPTER 1

INTRODUCTION

1. Preliminary Remarks

The Codex Vatican Neofiti, a complete text of the Palestinian Targum, has assumed a certain amount of notoriety since its publication. In 1949, Alejandro Díez Macho, a student of Paul Kahle, found it in the Vatican Library, marked on the spine "Targum Onkelos," but with a title page that read *trgwm ḥwmš yrwšlmy hw' spr hq̣dš nq̣r' kgwm`*.

Díez Macho returned to the MS some few years later and announced its discovery in 1956. The MS has turned out to be, not a complete copy of the Fragmentary Targum as first thought, but a different Palestinian Targum. It is, however, a 16th century copy, completed in 1504 A.D., as attested by the colophon.[1] Twelve years elapsed until the first volume of the *editio princeps* appeared in 1968, the book of Genesis, and this was followed by Exodus (1970), Leviticus (1971), Numbers (1974), and Deuteronomy (1978).

The MS was copied by at least three hands, and has the additional feature of (often copious) marginal, variants and interlinear readings. There may be as many as 12 hands involved in the writing of the last two. Occasionally verses accidentally omitted from the MS (e.g. Gen 35:10) and corrections to the text (e.g. Gen 36:21 where *lbny bnyhwn b'r^{c}' dgbl'* is crossed out and *bnwy dgblh b'r^{c}hwn d'dwmyy* is written alongside in a large unpractised hand) are added in the margin. Unfortunately, Díez Macho often refers to the whole MS including marginalia and interlinear readings as though they are a uniform text. The language under consideration in this study is only that of the main text, except in those instances where occasional verses were omitted erroneously and have been added in the margins.

The edition of Madrid-Barcelona, while impressive in its binding and presentation, is not particularly easy to use (a medium-quality facsimile edition has also been published by Makor in Jerusalem). The Hebrew *lemmata* of each verse have been omitted in this edition, often obscuring for the user without access to the original an error or a misreading. Similarly, the many "false starts" in the MS are not recorded. Characteristically, when the copyist made an error, he simply left it and wrote the correct word immediately following, occasionally underlining the wrong word with dots. These false starts are often instructive for determining the correct reading and interpretation, something not always understood by the editor. More problematic is the indiscriminate use of square brackets for all kinds of corrections (including emendations), which has already been commented upon by others.[2]

Díez Macho, in a long article published in 1973,[3] lays out his ideas concerning the Palestinian Targum, and Neofiti 1 in particular. Controversy has arisen due to the fact that, following Paul Kahle, Díez Macho and his pupils (as well as, for example, Martin McNamara[4] and others) have insisted on taking the extreme position that the Palestinian Targum (i.e. Neofiti) constitutes a pre-Christian version. Other scholars, such as Fitzmyer and Jonas Greenfield[5] among others, have objected strongly to these "strident" arguments and have dealt with them on many grounds. Díez Macho's main thesis is that Palestinian Targumic Aramaic (= Neofiti 1) is close to that of Jesus and the Jews of the 1st century (in other words, it is contemporaneous with the Aramaic of Qumran and Murabba^{c}at), which itself has been "contaminated" by a popular, contemporary, spoken Aramaic, namely that preserved by the Palestinian Targum. His methodology involves examining a number of selected morphological features in Qumran Aramaic (specifically in 11 Qtg Job and the Genesis Apocryphon) and comparing them in Neofiti.

2. The Nature of Targum

Díez Macho[6] has argued strongly and convincingly against the suggestion that the text of Neofiti is a product of the 16th century editorial activity of the school of Cardinal Egidio, and the arguments need not be recapitulated here. Such obvious alterations as Gen 1:1 are indeed subsequent to the copying of the MS (the erasure of the w before wškll can be detected even with the naked eye), and probably date from the same time as the censorial erasures of references to idols, etc. that are common throughout the MS. It is a given of this study that the MS is an authentic Targum, albeit at times demonstrating conflated readings or even mixed traditions,[7] and that the language of the MS is reasonably uniform and hence amenable to analysis. However, the understanding of the nature and function of a targumic text that is offered here needs to be argued.

While this is not the place for a comprehensive analysis of the character of the Palestinian Targum, methodologically and conceptually the study of targumic materials often betrays a confusion of a number of different levels of analysis. The ideas below represent the position taken throughout this study, and are important in order to avoid argument that in essence revolves around different objects of study. Various studies (including at times the editio princeps) have confused, in the first place, the spoken and the literary forms of the language (see above, note 5); the activities of the məturgəman with the written Targum; and the chronology of the texts dealing with məturgəman and Targum in the Mishna and in the Gemara.

Despite Fitzmyer's eloquent rebuttal,[8] there persists a confusion among some scholars between the spoken and the literary forms of the language. In Fitzmyer's succinct words, "when one is dealing with ancient written texts, especially of limited number, and of (in some cases) uncertain provenience, it is a moot question whether one can say that one text is written in a literary form of the language and that another is composed in the spoken or popular form -- unless, of course, one has some independent, extrinisic evidence of such a distinction. How do we know what the spoken form of Aramaic was like in 1st century Palestine?" (p. 73). It is, of course, absurd to argue from an ancient text for evidence of the spoken form of a language. But this kind of methodological confusion has come to be used to bolster other assumptions, particularly concerning the antiquity of the targumic tradition.

It is a fundamental misunderstanding of the nature and function of Targum to even attempt to isolate and identify spoken forms. Targum is first and foremost rabbinic literature -- it is no more a collection of orally transmitted stories, random translations, recorded versions, etc. than is the Hebrew Bible on which it is based and which it purports to "translate." The Hebrew Bible was viewed as a coherent, unified text by the rabbis, one whose mysteries could be revealed if the true meaning could be discovered. The rabbis, after all, were not exegetes, and viewed their task as explicating God's word. The coherence of the entire Pentateuch was a matter of faith, and hence the vehicle in which explication was done was of necessity also coherent. Examples of textual coherence abound, and the following is merely offered as representative.

In Gen 32:7, Jacob is told that Esau is coming toward him with four hundred men. The Hebrew *'arba^c-mē'ôt 'îš* is translated *'rb^c m'h dgbryn pwlmrkyn* 'four hundred (of) men, generals' (not 'soldiers' as in the translation in the *editio princeps*). The question then arises, why did the "translator" add the word *pwlmrkyn* 'generals'? The answer lies in an understanding of the rabbinic view of the incident. Prior to the relevant verse, in Gen 31:18 Jacob leaves Laban's household with cattle, possessions, and wealth -- a well-off and powerful individual. The reasoning appears to be that it was not probable that he would be distressed by the sight of a mere four hundred men, hence each "man" must have been a general, each with his own army (cf. Bereshit Rabba, *ad loc.*), and so Jacob was "greatly afraid." The denouement of this encounter is even more interesting, however, because, when Jacob finally does meet Esau (Gen 33:1), not only is there no confrontation, but also the four hundred "generals" are now "four hundred men on foot" (*gwbryn rglyn*). What has brought about this peaceful encounter when a military one was anticipated, and why have the armies of Esau turned into a small battalion of foot soldiers?

The answer of the rabbis lies in the incident that took place between the report of the spies (Gen 32:7) and the actual encounter (Gen 33:1): the confrontation of the angel (named Sariel in the Targum) with Jacob, their wrestling together, and Jacob's transformation into "Israel" (Gen 32:25-33). Jacob is no longer afraid of Esau because Jacob is no longer the same Jacob -- having met and conquered the divine, he is now self-assured and confident, and is clearly in charge during his meeting with his brother. Thus the rabbis attempt to explain a series of apparently confusingly related incidents: the report of the four hundred; the wrestling with the angel; the non-violent encounter between the two brothers. It is clearly missing the point to suggest, then, that the targumic text somehow preserves the "spoken" form of the language -- this is a well-structured, literary account and is most definitely not an oral "folk tradition" merely recorded by the "translator!"

A second confusion, and one related to that which confounds the "spoken" and the "literary" forms of the language, is that which conjoins the oral translation of the Hebrew Bible, as well as the activities of the "translator," with the written Targum. A number of well-known mishnaic texts have been used by numerous authors in describing their view of the Targum and its relation to the Hebrew Bible.

Most scholars,[9] even those who are acutely aware of the dangers of confusing the oral translation with the Targum, begin with a premise that the unlearned masses did not know Hebrew, and could not follow the Bible readings in the synagogue service. As a consequence, the text was translated for them into the 'vernacular' Aramaic (hence the assumption that the Targum somehow represents the "spoken" as opposed to the literary language). Then a variety of mishnaic texts are cited[10] that demonstrate the system involved -- the rules concerning the interpreter; how many verses are to be translated at a time; the texts to be read but not translated, and those to be neither read nor translated, etc., etc. But there is not the slightest shred of evidence to show that the text we are considering, i.e., the "Palestinian Targum," is connected in any way with the activities of a synagogue functionary called the məturgəman, or, indeed, with the lectionary practices of the Jewish community, except that all three are concerned with the notion of "translation."

As many scholars have pointed out,[11] this identification of the Targum with the synagogue activities derives from an opinion, given by R. Ika, in the name of R. Hananel who attributed it to Rab in the Babylonian Talmud, (Meg. 3a) where Rab interpreted the word məp̄ōrāš in Nehemiah 8:8 as referring to the Targum.[12] Furthermore, what evidence there is does not seem to demonstrate that the Jews of the first century C.E. needed an Aramaic translation at all.[13] The use of Hebrew as a literary language at Qumran is well noted, and there is some indication of its use as a colloquial tongue. Fitzmyer is typically cautious when he points out "pockets of Palestinian Jews also used Hebrew, even though its use was not widespread" (p. 46). While one could, I believe, interpret the available evidence as showing a much more widespread use of Hebrew, even a conservative interpretation is sufficient to demonstrate that, whatever the functions of the Targum may have been (see below), providing a biblical text for the unlearned masses in their own vernacular was not one of them. The confusion of the oral translation in the synagogue with the written Targum is a confusion of what Sperber (1973, Vol. IVB, pp. 1-2) colorfully called The Targum as a Religious Institution and The Targum as a Literary Document. As he clearly states, "there remains a gap of about 1,200 years" between the two. Furthermore, "any attempt to treat the Literary Document as the direct successor of the Institution, or, as one might say, as the Institution transfigured from oral into written form, must be considered as a complete failure, since it has nothing even resembling a trustworthy evidence to rest upon. It is utterly unscientific!" (p. 2).

A third common confusion is a chronological one concerning the evidence found in the Mishna and that found in the Gemara. There seems to be an attitude that the Targum as Institution began sometime after the period of Ezra, and continued down intact until perhaps the sixth century C.E. However, most of the evidence cited from the Talmud refers to the functions and activities of the _məturgəman_, not to the Targum. Furthermore, the talmudic passages clearly indicate an evolution of the role of the _məturgəman_, so that one must clearly distinguish between the facts the Mishna presents us concerning the translator, and the later comments on that text in the Gemara. Even more importantly, one must not then take the final step of transferring this mixed view back into the pre-Christian period; nor can one then extrapolate from the _məturgəman_ to the Targum. In other words, if we are discussing the role of the "translator," we must distinguish (as least) three separate periods in the evolution of this official position: pre-mishnaic, mishnaic, and post-mishnaic. We must furthermore distinguish between: (i) those talmudic texts that discuss the written document we know as the Targum;[14] (ii) those that discuss the activities of a synagogue official called the _məturgəman_;[15] and (iii) those texts that discuss the lectionary activitiy connected with an Aramaic translation of the Hebrew text.[16]

One example should suffice. McNamara, as mentioned, believes that the Bible was rendered into Aramaic for the benefit of the masses who knew no Hebrew. He then continues:

> The Mishnah gives considerable detail on how this rendering into Aramaic was to be done. The interpreter (called the _Meturgeman_) had to be distinct from the reader. Any competent person, even a minor, could act as interpreter, subject, naturally, to the control of the head of the synagogue.
>
> Certain texts detrimental to the honour of Israel or the ancients, were read out in Hebrew and not rendered into Aramaic.

> The Aramaic translation had to be given orally. It was forbidden to use written texts for this purpose. One reason given for this is that the written law should be transmitted in writing and the oral law by word of mouth (Palestinian Talmud, Meg. 4, 1, 74d, 1.16). Another reason given in the Babylonian Talmud (Meg. 32a) is that of impressing on the people the difference between the sacred text and its interpretative translation (McNamara, "Targum and Testament," p. 48).

As can be seen, this is a classic case of confusion. Oral law and written Targum, a variety of historical periods and talmudic texts, all are thrown together in a bewildering account of what constitutes the Aramaic Targum.

How, then should this material be understood? Clearly, the interpreter was not "rendering" the Hebrew into Aramaic, as even McNamara hints at further along:

> By the time the Mishnah rule came to be codified, and probably long before, the task of the Meturgeman was scarcely that of rendering the Hebrew text into Aramaic for the first time. Nor was he likely to have had the liberty to render the Hebrew text at will (p. 49).

The function of the "translator" in the mishnaic period (there is no evidence for a "translator" prior to the mishnaic period) was to recite a fixed, traditional, authorized Aramaic version in conjunction with the reading of the Hebrew text (see further below). Hence even a child could do it, since it involved memorizing a standard literary translation.[17] In the post-mishnaic period, this function appears to have been performed by a low-level synagogue functionary, the məturgəman (a fairly inferior status position if we can judge from some of the negative comments recorded[18] in the Talmud).

One must similarly understand the prohibition against "written" Targumim. The restrictions clearly state that the Targum may not be read out in the synagogue,[19] and these rules certainly became hard and fast in the post-mishnaic period. But this surely implies that there is a written text![20] R. Akiba's early training involved studying Bible and Targum, and "in Sifre, Deut. 161, the Targum is mentioned as a branch of study intermediate between the Mikra and the Mishnah" (Bacher, "Targum," p. 57). The prohibition is against an activity in the synagogue service, not against writing down the Aramaic translation.

One obvious question must now be asked: If the Jews of the 1st century spoke, wrote and understood Hebrew, and did not need a vernacular Aramaic translation, just what is the Targum that we have preserved today, and what was the purpose of translating the Bible into Aramaic in the first place? The first part to this answer is that it is not a vernacular translation. Even a casual contact with the text is enough to convince the researcher that the text is a highly technical piece of rabbinic literature. There is structure to this work, cohesion, literary technique, and above all, translation technique[21] -- it is most certainly not an "off-the-cuff" rendering into colloquial Aramaic for the benefit of the illiterate. Secondly, as has been already mentioned, the Aramaic translation is an interpretive rendering, and this is the key to understanding the function of the Targum. While post-biblical Hebrew was known and used, it clearly would have been inappropriate to interpret the sacred text from one "Hebrew" to another. Aramaic was the language in which this sacred text could be commented upon, discussed, expanded, manipulated to extract meaning -- the language of interpretation; not the close reading of the Mishnah, wherein the text might be scrutinized for truths, hidden or otherwise, but rather the explanation of what the Hebrew text is trying to say. The Targum is the authorized community standard of what the words of the Torah mean -- in discussing Zechariah 12:11 in Meg. 3a, R. Joseph comments 'ilmale' targumna' dəha'i qra' la' yada^{c}na' ma'i qa'mar "if it were not for our Targum of that verse, we would not know what it means."[22]

With this view of the Targum in mind, a number of conclusions can be drawn that provide both a theoretical infrastructure for the linguistic analysis that follows, and also form a set of methodological principles:

1. A Targum is a written document, not an example of a spoken form of the language.

2. A Targum MS forms a coherent body of literature and is not a random collection of stories, homilies, translations, etc.

3. A Targum constitutes a fixed, traditional, authorized, interpretive translation.

As a consequence, certain translation conventions can be identified, and the motivations for their use, as well as for the overall translation of the text, can be explored and described (see especially Chapter 9, Syntax).

3. A Grammar of Targum Neofiti

This grammatical study differs from other Aramaic grammars in a number of ways. In the first place, it is an attempt to write a synchronic model of the language of one MS. As a consequence, the analysis (see especially Chapter 7, Nouns and Adjectives) is based primarily on the written forms as found in the MS, not on supposed vocalized forms derived from other Aramaic dialects or traditions. When vocalizations are offered, they are based on the form in Targum Onkelos, taken from Sperber, "Onkelos," and/or Jastrow, "Dictionary," and they are usually only offered to resolve a problem or to illustrate a form that is not clear in the MS Neofiti 1.

Unlike other grammars of Aramaic, there is no attempt made to suggest the historical development of forms (except when such information is essential for the understanding of a particular word in Neofiti). This constitutes a clear decision to focus only on synchronic material with the aim of finally providing the scholarly community with a useful grammar of this MS, so that further work on it, as well as on the vexing question of the "Palestinian Targum," will be able to rest on a reliable linguistic base. During the writing of this work, I often had recourse to the "standard" reference grammar for "Jewish" Aramaic, Gustaf Dalman's Grammatik des jüdisch-palästinischen Aramäisch, published in Leipzig in 1894, and like all students of Aramaic, I am indebted to Dalman for his work. However, as Kutscher pointed out over twenty years ago ("Studies in Galilean Aramaic," Tarbiz, Vol. 21, 1961, p. 192), the volume suffers from serious defects and flaws, not the least of which is the fact that Dalman lumped the language of the Palestinian Targum together with that of the Palestinian Talmud and Midrashim, and with that of Onkelos. The volume is, at best, exceedingly difficult to work with, especially so as it entirely lacks a section on syntax. In spite of Kutscher's marvellous studies, or perhaps because of them, a modern, thorough grammar of "Galilean" Aramaic still remains a scholarly desideratum. It is hoped that such studies as this present one will form a basis for a better understanding of the language until such time as a good, synthetic grammar does appear. One thing that does seem clear is that studies based on individual manuscripts will enable conclusions to be more tightly drawn. Kutscher's insistence on reliable texts demonstrates the need to thoroughly understand a particular MS idiom before general statements on the nature of a particular "dialect" of Aramaic can be formulated. This is even more the case when one wishes to discuss a concept such as "*the* Palestinian Targum," without first being able to appreciate the relationships between the various surviving representatives of the Palestinian targumic tradition.

Dalman's work provided one model for an Aramaic grammar: the volume is rich in the collection of forms to be found there (even though they are not always easily accessible). However, in the tradition in which Dalman wrote, the synchronic and the diachronic are thrown together, and the analysis is often obscure. The researcher cannot be sure where a particular form comes from, whether it is a "true" form or a postulated one, nor even whether all the necessary information has been collected. This present work is based on my Ph.D. dissertation, completed in 1978 under Professor Thomas O. Lambdin of Harvard University, which was a grammar of the language of the book of Genesis in the Targum Neofiti 1. As a consequence, much of the analysis is indeed based on Genesis, however reference is always made to the rest of the MS when this is done. As a further consequence, and unlike Dalman, there is no attempt in this study to provide a comprehensive concordance of all the forms in Neofiti, but rather to offer a schematic analysis of the forms of the language, illustrated by copious references from the text. Similarly, there is no attempt to reconcile the language of Neofiti with that of other examples of Palestinian Aramaic. Such studies must appear in another format.

Other models for an Aramaic grammar are not easy to come by. Students often have recourse to such small works as W. B. Stevenson, *Grammar of Palestinian Jewish Aramaic* (Oxford, 1924), or Max Margolis, *Lehrbuch der aramäischen Sprache* (München, 1910), however both of these are really little more than student workbooks containing paradigms (themselves not always useful or even accurate). While it is considerably more reliable, the small *Grammar of Biblical Aramaic* by Franz Rosenthal (Wiesbaden, 1963) is also aimed primarily at the student. However, I did make use of this for some comparisons, even though it deals with a completely different period of Aramaic. To the same period of Aramaic belongs Hans Bauer and Pontus Leander's *Grammatik des Biblisch-Aramäischen* (Tübingen, 1927). The model it provides is essentially that of Dalman: an analysis based on a mixture of synchronic forms and historical reconstruction. As a model for the writing of a grammar I found it wanting, however I did gain many insights into the historical development of Aramaic forms from this volume.

Even further afield is Stanislav Segert's Altaramäische Grammatik (Leipzig, 1975), which mixes Old Aramaic inscriptional material with Imperial Aramaic (in particular Biblical Aramaic). In this volume there is less mixing of synchronic and diachronic analysis, and also a much greater reliance on cited forms. While the format is very much that of 19th century German Semitic scholarship, the copious and reliable citations make this a useable book, and a good model, at least in part, for writing a grammar of one Aramaic dialect.

This present volume, then, has attempted to combine the best features of its predecessors: as little mixing as possible of contemporary and historical analysis; schematization of information coupled with numerous, reliable citations; in-depth analyses of a variety of problematic questions in Aramaic syntax (notably lacking in all Aramaic grammars); and a useful format that provides scholars with both data and suggested analysis of that data on which other scholarship may be based.

NOTES

[1]Díez Macho, "Deuteronomio," pp. 85-87.

[2]E.g., Joseph Fitzmyer, review of Neophyti 1, Tomo I: Genesis, by Alejandro Díez Macho (ed.) in Catholic Biblical Quarterly 32 (1970): 107-112 and review of Neophyti 1, Tomo II: Exodo, by Alejandro Díez Macho (ed.) in Journal of Biblical Literature 91, No. 4 (December 1972): 575-578.

[3]Alejandro Díez Macho, "Le targum palestinien" in Exegese biblique et judäisme, J.E. Ménard, (ed.) (Strasbourg, 1973): 14-77.

[4]Martin McNamara, Targum and Testament (Shannon, 1972).

E.g., Jonas Greenfield, "Standard Literary Aramaic" in Actes du premier congrès international de linguistique sémitique et chamito-sémitique, Paris, 1969, André Caquot and David Cohen (eds.) (The Hague, 1974): 280-289.

[6]Díez Macho, "Deuteronomio," pp. 84-100.

[7]E.g., the famous "Four Cases of Moses" midrash that appears in Lev 24:12, Num 9:8, 15:34, and 27:5. However, it is by no means clear that these four versions do indeed represent different traditions, and a detailed study of their language, together with their relationship to the surrounding verses, should prove instructive on this point. It must be recognized, after all, that a targumic text is viewed by its compilers as a coherent whole, just as is the biblical text on which it is based, and as such the insertion of a midrashic expansion is to be seen as having conscious literary, religious, and/or didactic intent.

[8]"The Phases of the Aramaic Language," pp. 73-74, in A Wandering Aramean: Collected Aramaic Essays, Scholars Press, 1979.

[9]See, for example, J.F. Stenning, The Targum of Isaiah, Oxford, 1949, p. vii; M. McNamara, Targum and Testament, Shannon, Ireland, 1968, p. 48; A. Sperber, "Onkelos," Vol. IVB, p. 1; even Fitzmyer cautiously assents: "There is no reason to deny that the targums came into existence as orally translated forms of the Scriptures being read in Hebrew in the synagogues" ("Phases of Aramaic," p. 73).

[10]E.g., McNamara, Targum and Testament, p. 57.

[11]Cf. e.g., W. Bacher, "Targum," p. 57.

[12]The rest of the verse is not usually quoted -- not only was məpōrāš interpreted as Targum, but also śôm śekel as the pəsuqin, and wayyābinû bammiqrā' as pisqey tə^{c}amim, or some say the masoret, which had been forgotten and was now established again. In other words, the whole verse is an interpretive attempt to plumb the depths of Scripture by attributing a variety of current divisions of the text to a famous historical character. It is certainly not a verse on which modern scholarship can base theories concerning the origins or the nature of the Aramaic Targum!

[13]Cf. Fitzmyer, "The Languages of Palestine" in A Wandering Aramean: Collected Aramaic Essays, Scholars Press, 1979, pp. 44-46.

[14]Such as Meg. 3a.

[15]Such as Moed Qaṭan 21a, Ḥagigah 14a and 16a.

[16]Such as Meg. 21b, 23b, 24a, 24b.

[17]The Mishnah from which this quote is taken (Meg. 24a) is not a description of who can or cannot be a translator, but rather lists a series of synagogue activities: reading from the Torah; "translating;" repeating the blessings before the šəma^{c}; passing before the ark; and lifting up the hands. A child may read and translate, but not pass before the Ark nor lift up his hands. Similarly, a person in rags (pôḥē^{a}ḥ) may repeat the blessing and translate, but may not read from the Torah, nor pass before the Ark, nor lift up his hands. Finally, a blind man may repeat the blessings and translate. Hence it is absurd to interpret this as evidence about the nature or functions of the Targum, or even about the role of the məturgəman. What is being discussed here is the verbatim recitation of a fixed Aramaic version of the Torah, which can be done by anyone who has memorized it, including the three cases mentioned in the Mishnah (who are restricted from performing the obviously more important functions of passing before the Ark, raising the hands, etc.).

[18]Cf. e.g., Moed Qaṭan 21a.

[19]There is no reason to doubt the authenticity of the quote in the Talmud (Meg. 32a): so that people will not say targum katub battorah 'the Targum is written in the Law'. However, I doubt that this means that the general populace will be gullibly deceived into thinking that the Targum really is to be found in the scroll of the Law. Rather this should be

understood to mean that the authorities should be wary of attributing to the Targum the same status as the Scripture. This is clearly a potential danger -- the Targum had an official role as the sanctioned community interpretation of the Hebrew text. Hence people could become convinced of the primacy of its interpretations. That this is a potential danger is apparent from the quote mentioned above (Meg. 32a). The debate between R. Meir and R. Judah centers on the order for opening the scroll, finding the place, saying the blessing, and reading. R. Meir draws a parallel to Ulla who, in discussing why the reader should not prompt the translator, explains that this is so that people will not say targum katub battorah 'the Targum is written in the Law', to which R. Judah replies targum 'ika ləmiṭ^ce 'with the Targum they might make an error', bərakot lika ləmiṭ^ce 'with the blessings they will not make an error'.

[20]Cf. W. Bacher, "Targum," pp. 57-58 for a variety of talmudic citations concerning the written nature of the Targum.

[21]Cf. Chapter 9, Syntax, especially Section Two, Parts A and B, and the literature cited there for detailed examples. The most obvious case of translation technique is the use of anthropomorphic avoidance formulae, though there are others. Cf. also M. Klein, "Converse Translation: A Targumic Technique," in Biblica, Vol. 57, No. 4, 1976: 515-537, and "The Translation of Anthropomorphisms and Anthropopathisms in the Targumim," in Supplement to Vetus Testamentum, Vol. 32, Congress Volume, 1981: 162-177.

[22]Cf. also Ḥag. 28b.

CHAPTER 2
ORTHOGRAPHY

1. The Nature of Error

The various questions concerning the production of the MS, the relationships between the copyist hands, and the presence of interlinear and marginal variants have been extensively studied. The presence of many errors in the MS has been noted, and suitable caution has been urged in dealing with this medieval copy.[1] Nevertheless, the language of this MS does display an internal consistency, and even the presence of interpolations can be detected, usually with a good degree of certainty.

One crucial distinction that must be made is that between errors that are attributable to the medieval copyist(s), probably quite unfamiliar with Palestinian Aramaic, and perhaps even unfamiliar with Onkelos, and errors that are attributable to undetermined scribes who prepared the text which provided the basis for the medieval copyists' work. At times, these two errors may be difficult to distinguish (e.g., w/y confusion is both a medieval copyist phenomenon, and one familiar from early Jewish manuscripts). However, one can often determine what is blatant copyist error, e.g., Gen 35:9, mrb^{c}yt' for mrbnyyt', with עי for ניי; and so too in many other examples.

This distinction is important, for it enables us to eliminate many of the gross infractions from our analysis of the language, or even from a consideration of the provenance, milieu, etc., of the MS. The failure to make this distinction, for instance, makes it difficult at first to follow the reasoning of A. Tal, "Neophyti 1," where he says that "the scribe was most unfamiliar with the Aramaic language" (p. 38), but then later, that a number of phenomena which he adduces constitute "sufficient proof of the presence of Onqelos in the consciousness of the scribe" (p. 42)! Clearly, by the first he means what we refer to here as "copyist," by the second, "scribe." It is difficult to argue with his assessement that Neofiti cannot be classified as a "good manuscript" (p. 38), but one cannot then extrapolate that the language of Neofiti is either inconsistent or irrevocably flawed. It is the thesis of this study that the language is reasonably consistent; that interpolations can be identified, by and large; and that, once medieval copyist phenomena are explained and considered, the language of the MS is readily amenable to investigation and analysis.

2. Types of Error

The largest number of errors in the MS are what can broadly be termed "spelling errors," namely, the unintentional replacement of one or more letters in a word by one or more other letters. This replacement creates a form that is not paradigmatically justifiable in terms of the canons of the Aramaic language, or else is justifiable but semantically it is other than that which is expected. For an immediate example of the former, see, e.g., mrb^{c}yt' for mrbnyyt', cited above; for the latter, the spelling of qimā 'pillar' as qyym', under the impact of the common qyym' 'covenant' (= qəyāmā), or the spelling of the construct of 'land' as 'r^{c}' for 'r^{c}, under the impact of the commonly occurring determined state, might both be cited. It must be stressed that it is not always possible to distinguish "scribal spelling errors" from "copyist spelling errors," as defined above. The routine replacement of certain letters by others might point to a medieval copyist phenomenon, but this must be balanced against the multitude of times the "correct" form occurs. Without doubt, the written Vorlage from which Neofiti was copied must have contained spelling conventions that made the task of the inexperienced(?) medieval copyists much more difficult, e.g., the similarity of w and y, or of final n and final k.

But beyond that, some spelling errors are considerably less common, and seem to derive from copyist inabilities, e.g., y for h, d for l, final m for ṣ, s, and ^{c}. These are often encountered in less common words that were presumably not understood by the copyist.

Letter confusion occurs frequently in the MS, the following being found numerous times:

1)	t	ת	for	ḥ	ח
				r	ר
				y	י
2)	y	י	for	w	ו
				h	ה
3)	w	ו	for	y	י
				final n	ן
4)	z	ז	for	w	ו
5)	k	כ	for	b	ב

6)		h	ה	for	ḥ	ח
7)		h	ה	for	t	ת
8)		r	ר	for	d	ד
9)		d	ד	for	l	ל
10)		g	ג	for	n	נ
11)		s	ס	for	ṭ	ט
12)	final	n	ן	for	final k	ך
13)	final	m	ם	for	s	ס
					ṣ	צ
					c	ע

As can be seen, letter confusions fall into four broad groups:

1) a group based on a single downstroke (י ו ז ן ך) ;
2) a group based on a curved single downstroke, with or without a second stroke (י ו ר ה ח ת);
3) a group based on a semicircular stroke (ל נ ר ד ג ב כ);
4) a group based on a circular stroke (ם ל ע צ ט ס).

Some letters fall into more than one group (י ו ר ל) , hence the apparent chaotic situation in the MS. However, once these conventions are kept in mind, the MS reads well. Nevertheless, it cannot be determined whether these confusions also existed in the work of the pre-medieval scribe, and hence constitute "scribal" as opposed to "copyist" error.

A second kind of spelling error occurs very frequently in Neofiti, that called "aural" in this study. By this term is meant a mistake that results from the incorrect recording of a word that was read aloud. This view of the medieval copying process, in which the text was dictated at least in part, presumably to a group of copyists, will account for such common spellings as the masculine construct plural ending in -yh rather than -y, under the impact of the common 3rd masculine singular pronominal suffix -yh; or the spelling 'r^{c}' for the construct 'r^{c} 'land of --', mentioned above; or the occasional spelling of b for w, reflecting a medieval pronunciation of w as /v/, e.g., Gen 27:41 hywby 'his life', for hywwy; or the occasional confusion of t/ṭ, k/q, ^{c}/', e.g., Deut 4:42, wbtqwp for wbtkwp 'suddenly', or Gen 4:6 (and Exod 23:2) b^{c}š (and mb^{c}š') for b'š (and mb'š'). A detailed analysis of such phenomena, including a description of their occurrence by groups of folios, will surely help resolve important questions concerning the number of hands involved in the production of the MS.

The final group of spelling errors are ligatures and letter simplifications, and these can certainly be attributed to the copyist, who either misread letters written closely together in the *Vorlage*, or else formed his own letters quickly or carelessly, and so fashioned the ligature or the simplification. See, for example, Gen 35:9 - עי - for ניי cited above, or Gen 37:2, where the suffix הון - is written over as הם, or Deut 19:5, where the form *wyzdḥp* (ויזדחף) occurs for expected *wtdḥp* (ותדחף).

Finally, note should be taken of the many abbreviations found throughout the MS. In these, one or two (rarely more) letters are left off, and the apocopated form is marked with a slanting stroke, thus `. This manuscript convention can cause difficulty in the analysis, especially in determining whether a form ends in א or ה, see, e.g., Chapter 9, *Syntax*, Part Two, Section B. At times, the expected ending (usually a pronominal suffix) has been added in the margin, and at times, the slanting stroke is absent.

3. The Use of Matres Lectionis

The use of *matres lectionis* in Neofiti, as in Onkelos, is not indicative of synchronic vowel length. The letters *h*/*y*/*w* can be used to represent various vowels, however, just as frequently, the vowel is not marked. The situation may be summarized thus:

In final position

the letter *w* can mark either o or u;
the letter *y* can mark either i or e;
the letter *h* can mark either ā or e;
the letter *'* can mark either ā or e
(the latter usually in historical spellings that are based on a root ending in *'*).

In medial position

the vowels o or u can be marked by *w* or Ø;
the vowels i or e can be marked by *y* or Ø;
the vowel a (ā) is usually unmarked
(however, cf. occasional examples such as *kl m'n d-* 'whoever', Gen 20:16, and *yt'rq* 'it shall be poured out', Lev 21:10, Ct *yittāraq* from root r-y-q);
the vowel ə (*shewa mobile*) is usually unmarked

(however, cf. occasional rare examples such as *mlk'hwn* 'their king', *malkəhon* → *malkahon*, Gen 26:1, or *z^{c}yr't'* 'the young woman', *zə^{c}irətā* → *zə^{c}iratā*, Gen 19:35, with *aleph* as internal *mater lectionis*; and the more common forms with *y* as internal *mater lectionis* for ə, e.g., *lyhwn* 'to them', *lə hon* → *lihon*, Gen 1:28, or *'^{c}ybr* 'let me pass', *'a^{ca}bar* → *'a^{c}əbar* → *'a^{c}ibar*, Deut 2:27).

The letter *y* is also used on occasion to resolve a final consonantal cluster, one that ends in *-t* for the most part, e.g., *^{c}bdyt* 'you (ms) did', *^{ca}badt* → *^{ca}badet* → *^{ca}badit*, Gen 26:10.

Finally, consonantal /w/ can be marked with either single or double *w*, e.g., *lwt*/*lwwt*; consonantal /y/ can be marked with either single or double *y*, e.g., *qym'*/*qyym'*. There appears to be a slight preference for single *w* for /w/, and for double *y* for /y/, however there are also obvious spelling conventions, e.g., *lwwt* occurs over *lwt* at a ratio of approximately 10:1.

4. Methodological Considerations

When dealing with any unpointed text, one of the main problems is vocalization, and certain factors must guide the choice of the vocalization that is suggested. First and foremost, in dealing with this MS, a general knowledge of Aramaic is assumed, including the historical development of the Aramaic forms. Many forms as they are spelled in the MS cannot reflect a legitimate pronunciation, given the fact of their historical development, and they must be accounted for in some way. For example, a few 2 ms perfect verb forms are spelled *qtlyt*. This suffix should not historically end in *-it*/*-et*, and so this spelling must be accounted for as indicating a resolution of the final cluster -Ct, where C is a dental stop, for example the word *^{c}bdyt* 'you did', as discussed above.

Secondly, a specific knowledge of the Aramaic of Targum Onkelos is assumed. Most of the lexical items in Neophyti 1 can be paralleled in Onkelos, and therefore it has been chosen as the basis for the vocalization proferred, when it is not obviously at odds with the form suggested by the *matres lectionis* or with the historically necessary form. Onkelos, however, has many problems of vocalization and is itself not at all uniform, especially in those forms where Neophyti is most difficult to interpret (e.g., the segholate nouns).

In this study emendations are proposed for many forms in order to bring them into uniformity with the Aramaic "norm" that common sense and a knowledge of the history of Aramaic demand. This is especially so when "incorrect" forms result from one of the orthographic confusions mentioned above, and this represents an intentional attempt to classify the forms of the language as effectively as possible. This approach eliminates the need for citing long lists of apparently "exceptional" forms (especially in the chapter on the noun) which are in fact not abnormal at all.

The use of matres lectionis with vowels in both Onkelos and Neophyti is not indicative of synchronic vowel length, and consequently they have been ignored in vocalized transliterations. As a result, the following transliteration for the Aramaic has been adopted:

Xִ	or	יXִ			=	i	
Xֹ	or	וֹX			=	o	
Xֻ	or	וּX			=	u	
Xֵ	or	יXֵ			=	e	
Xָ	or	הXָ	or	אXָ	=	ā	
Xַ	or	Xֶ			=	a	(the latter primarily in segholate nouns)
Xְ					=	ə	(with guttural, a = Xֲ)

On the other hand, full account of matres lectionis has been taken in the transliteration of Hebrew, as follows:

Without matres			With matres			Shewa		
Xִ	=	i/ỉ	יXִ	=	î	Xְ	=	ə
Xֹ	=	ō	וֹX	=	ô	Xֲ	=	a
Xֻ	=	ū	וּX	=	û	Xֱ	=	e
Xֵ	=	ē	הXֵ	=	ē(h)	Xֳ	=	o
Xֶ	=	e	יXֶ	=	ey			
Xָ	=	ā/o	הXָ	=	ā			
Xַ	=	a	יXֵ	=	ê			

The traditional terms for the verbal conjugations (pəᶜal etc.) have been replaced by the following terminology:

G stem - "Grundstamm," the basic form of the verb (= $\underline{p\partial^{c}al}$)

D stem - "Doppelungsstamm," the stem with doubled middle radical (= $\underline{pa^{cc}el}$)

C stem - "Causative," the stem formed with prefix $\underline{'-}$ in the perfect (= $\underline{'a\bar{p}^{c}el}$)

Gt stem - The medio-passive of the G stem (= $\underline{'itp\partial^{c}el}$)

Dt stem - The medio-passive of the D stem (= $\underline{'itpa^{cc}al}$)

Ct stem - The medio-passive of the C stem (= $\underline{itta\bar{p}^{c}al}$)

Verbs, one of whose triconsonantal radicals is a "weak" letter (i.e., w/y/h/'), are referred to in the body of this work as Primae Infirmae (or I-weak), Mediae Infirmae (or II-weak) and Tertiae Infirmae (or III-weak). When there is a further division within one of these groups, terminology such as I-y, II-w or III-Aleph is employed, indicating that the first radical of that root is y-, (e.g., y-n-q) or that the second radical is -w- (e.g., q-w-m) or that the third radical is -' (e.g., q-r-'), respectively.

NOTES

[1]See, e.g., Klein, "Printed Edition;" Tal, "Neophyti 1;" Martin, "Palaeographical Character," and the critique of this in Weil, "Le codex neophyti I;" Miller, "Type II Marginalia;" and the bibliography cited in Grossfeld, "Bibliography," I and II, and in Díez Macho, "Neophyti," Vol. 5.

CHAPTER 3
PREPOSITIONS

As in other Aramaic dialects and Semitic languages, prepositions can occur either independently or with nominal suffixes. For the actual forms of the suffixes, see Chapter 7, Nouns and Adjectives. The following list is presented as a complete inventory, and the use of suffixes is noted. References are only cited where comment is deemed appropriate.

+ 'l 'to': This non-Aramaic form appears but rarely in N, and it is probably an accidental occurrence of the Hebrew preposition which it translates. Cf. Gen 4:8 wqm qyn 'l hbl 'hwy 'and Cain rose up against Abel his brother' (MT wayyāqām qayin 'el-hebel 'aḥîw), Gen 39:10 wl' šm^{c} 'lyh 'and he did not listen to her' (MT wəlō'-šāma^{c} 'ēleyhā), and Deut 32:46 'lhwn 'to them' (MT '^{a}lēhem).
+ 'rwm 'lhn 'except', 'but rather': When translating a passage with a Hebrew Vorlage, it usually stands for MT kî-'im, however note should be taken of the unusual, misspelled form in Gen 21:26 'rwm 'lhym (sic) ywm' hdyn 'except today' (MT biltî hayyôm, 'except today',) and Deut 1:36 (MT zûlātî).
+ b- 'in', 'by', 'with', etc.
+ bgw 'inside': This translates both MT bətôk and bə in equal proportion, and occasionally for ləma^{c}an, cf. Gen 18:24. Suffixed forms usually are spelled with two ws; note also the archaizing spelling bgw' in Gen 3:8.
+ bgyn 'on account of': Usually followed by kdyn, occasionally by kn, rarely by kk, most often translating MT ^{c}al-kēn 'therefore'.
+ bgll 'because of': Usually for MT ba^{ca}bur (and rarely bə, cf. Gen 18:28), including with suffixes, as in Gen 12:13 bgllk 'because of you' and Gen 18:26 bgllhwn 'because of them'. Cf. mn bgll below.
+ byn 'between': This occurs primarily in such constructions as byn ... wbyn, byn ... lbyn, and byn ... l- 'between ... and ...', but also in an extended sense of 'whether', as in Gen 38:25 byn mkwlt' ṭb' byn mkwlt' byš' 'whether a good measure, whether a bad measure' (no MT). It also occurs with singular suffixes, cf. Gen 16:5 byny wbynk, 'between me and you' (MT bênî ûbêneykā). There are some examples of an alternate plural form as in Gen 15:17 byny gzryy' h'ylyn 'between these pieces' (MT bên haggəzārîm hā'ēlleh),

Gen 36:37 (mn) byny nhryy' '(from) between the rivers' (for the MT toponym (mē)rəḥōbôt hannāhār), and Gen 23:6 bbynynn 'among us' (MT bətôkēnû).

+ bzmn 'at the time of': Twice in Genesis (7:13 and 17:26 for MT bə^{c}eṣem hayyôm hazze, and elsewhere without Hebrew Vorlage (cf. also hyk zmn and ^{c}d zmn below).
+ bl' 'without': In paraphrase for MT ^{ca}rîrî 'childless' (Gen 15:2), bl' bnyn 'without children'. Cf. also Chapter 4, Conjunctions, mn bly d-.
+ bmṣy^{c}wt 'in the middle of: For MT bətôk.
+ b^{c}d 'for': This form occurs rarely, and is probably a Hebrew gloss, cf. Gen 20:18 'rwm mṭrwd ṭrd YYY b^{c}d kl ptḥy yldh lbyth d'bymlk 'because the Lord had indeed sealed up every birth opening in the house of Abimelech' (MT kî-^{c}āṣōr ^{c}āṣar YHWH bə^{c}ad kol-reḥem ləbêt '^{a}bîmelek).
+ br mn 'besides', 'apart from': Also appears with suffixes, e.g., Gen 14:24 br mny 'apart from me' (MT bil^{c}āday).
+ bš^{c}t 'at the time of': cf. bzmn.
+ btr 'after', 'behind': Usually translates MT 'aḥar, especially in the idiom btr ptgmy' h'ylyn 'after these things', e.g., Gen 15:1 and many others. This preposition usually occurs with plural suffixes, as in Gen 24:39 btryy 'after me' (MT 'aḥ^{a}rāy), etc., however cf. Gen 19:6 btrh 'after him' (MT 'aḥ^{a}rāyw), and others.
+ gb 'with': Rare, only twice in Genesis (22:5 and 31:32), for MT ^{c}im. Cf. ^{c}m below.
+ d- 'of': As a preposition this form is used in genitive expressions of Type 1 and Type 2 (see Chapter 9, Syntax, and Golomb, JAOS, 1982. However cf. also Chapter 4, Conjunctions). It is spelled less commonly dy, though no apparent criterion for the use of one over the other is discernible. That they are orthographic alternants seems indicated by phrases such as Gen 15:17 šbybyn dy nwr šlh⟨b⟩yn d'šh 'sparks of fire, flames of fire' (no MT). The form can also translate an MT construct; with suffixes, it is used as the possessive, usually translating MT lə + suffixes.

The form of the possessive varies. Most commonly, it is constructed on the reduplicative base d(y)d-, e.g., Deut 32:35 dydy 'mine', Gen 4:8 dydk 'yours' (no MT), Num 16:5 dydh 'his' (MT lô), Gen 34:23 dydn 'ours' (MT lānû), Gen 15:13 dydhwn 'theirs' (MT lāhem), Lev 22:27 bš^{c}t 'nngy ddhwn(!) 'at the hour of their distress' (no

MT, compare the similar phrase in Gen 38:25 š^{c}t 'nqy 'the hour of my distress'); less common are d(y) + l (e.g., Gen 47:6 dly 'mine', Gen 38:25 dylyh 'his', MT lô) and also with suffix added directly to dy, cf. Gen 26:20 dynn (MT lānû).

+ hyk 'as': Usually translates MT kə-, but is common in passages with no Vorlage, or in paraphrase. Note the defective spelling hk in Gen 31:2 l' hk d'tml wl' hyk dqdmwy 'not as yesterday nor as before' (MT ('ênennu ^{c}immô) kitəmôl šilšôm, and cf. the similar phrase in Gen 31:5).

+ hyk zmn 'at the time of(?)': Only once, Gen 7:11 hyk zmn ywm' hdyn 'on that (very) day' (MT bayyôm hazze), but note also the prefixed (!) use of the preposition in Deut 6:24 hkzmn ywm' hdyn, MT kəhayyôm hazze.

+ ḥlp 'in place of': Translates MT taḥat 'instead of', and also without Vorlage, e.g., Gen 29:22 lmsbh yth ll'h ḥlp rḥl 'to marry him to Leah in place of Rachel'. Cf. tḥwt below, which is occasionally used in error for ḥlp due to the similarity of form between Aramaic tḥwt and MT taḥat.

+ ytyr mn 'more than': Used as a form of the comparative (cf. mn below).

+ k- 'as', 'according to': Usually translates MT kə- and also in paraphrase. It is common in the technical translation idiom whwh kn kmymryh 'and it was so, according to His word', often for MT wayəhî kēn, e.g., Gen 1:7 and parallel verses. Cf. also Exod 15:3 kšmyh kn gbwrtyh 'as is His name, so is His might' (based on MT YHWH 'îš milḥāmā YHWH šəmô).

+ k'lw 'as (if)': An uncommon preposition, possibly late Hebrew rather than Aramaic. Cf. Gen 31:15 hl' k'lw nkryyn 'tḥšbnn lyh 'have we not been considered by him as strangers?' (paraphrasing MT h^{a}lô' nokriyyôt neḥšabnû lô).

+ kwwt 'like': This preposition occurs both independently, e.g., Num 12:7 l' kwwt kl nby'h hw' ^{c}bdy mš<h> 'not like any (other) prophet is my servant Moses' (based on MT lō'-kēn ^{c}abdî mōše), and with suffixes, e.g., Exod 15:11 kwwtk 'like you' (bis, MT kāmōkā), Gen 34:15 kwwth 'like him' (MT kāmōnû), Deut 1:11 kwwtkwn 'like you (pl)' (MT kākem).

+ klpy 'towards': Used with the G and C stem of the root dwq 'to look' to translate the MT idiom hišqîp ^{c}al-pənê.

\+ kl q(w)bl 'opposite': Translates the MT idiom ᶜal-pənê + toponym, and also pānîm 'el-pānîm in Gen 32:30, in the phrase 'pyn kl qbl 'pyn 'face to face'. Cf. also lqbl, mn kl q(w)bl, and qbyl below.

\+ l- 'to', 'for': This preposition occurs as a much less common alternate for yt (q.v.) to mark the direct object of a transitive verb. In most cases, counter examples with yt in similar or identical situations can also be found; the one common denominator seems to be that, in most of the cases, the direct object is a proper name, however there are, as stated, many more counter examples with yt (see Chapter 9, Syntax.) As the citations demonstrate, there does not appear to be any direct copy of the Hebrew preposition used in the Vorlage.
With Vorlage: Gen 4:4-5, wqbl YYY brᶜww' yt(!) hbl wyt (!) qrbnyh: (5) wlqyn (!) wlqrbnyh (!) l' qbl brᶜww' 'and God received Abel and his offering favorably: (5) but Cain and his offering he did not receive favorably' (MT 'el throughout); Gen 24:14 w'p lgmlyk 'šqy 'and your camels also will I water' (MT wəgam-gəmalleykā 'ašqe); Gen 27:15 w'lbšt lyᶜqb 'and she clothed Jacob' (MT 'et, cf. also Gen 27:30).
Without Vorlage: Gen 4:16, 4:24, 27:42 qṭl lhbl 'he killed Abel'; Gen 16:5 nsbyt lhgr 'I took Hagar'; Gen 34:1 (erased by censor) s'ybw btwln wplḥy (erased by censor) lbrtyh dyᶜqb ... (erased by censor) ᶜl dy s'bw ldynh brtyh dyᶜqb '(uncircumcised ones) have defiled virgins and worshippers of (idols) the daughter of Jacob ... (idolators), because they defiled Dinah, the daughter of Jacob'; Num 21:34 ḥm' mšh lᶜwg 'Moses saw Og' (cf. also Gen 28:12); Gen 18:1 lmšyzbh llwṭ 'to save Lot'; Lev 22:27 śrh yldh lyṣḥq 'Sarah gave birth to Isaac'. There does not appear to be any common feature to the selection of verbs in the examples cited but as mentioned, the fact that the direct object is a proper noun seems significant.

\+ lblḥ(w)d 'alone', 'by one's self': Always translates MT ləbadd + suffixes, and always with plural suffixes, e.g., Gen 2:18 lblḥwdwy 'on his own', etc. Note the "defective" spelling lblḥdwy in Gen 32:34.

\+ lbr mn 'outside of': For MT mi(ḥ)ḥûs lə-.

\+ lbtr 'behind': With singular suffixes, in the sense of 'backwards', as in Gen 9:23, whwwn mhlkyn lbtrhwn ... w'pyhwn hpykw lbtrhwn 'they walked backwards ... and their faces they turned backwards' (MT '^{a}hōrannît, both times). Cf. btr above, and mn btr below.

\+ lgw 'into': All examples occur in the idiom ^{c}l (G & C stem) lgw 'to enter into (a house, etc.)', for MT bā' (G & C stem) 'el. Cf. bgw above, and ^{c}l below.

\+ lw(w)t 'to', 'into', 'unto': The regular translation of MT 'el with verbs of motion, e.g., ^{c}ll, ḥzr, 'th, etc. Also occurs with singular suffixes, e.g., Gen 22:5 lwwtkwn (MT '^{a}lêkem) and note especially Gen 8:9 where MT wattāšab 'ēlāyw 'el-hattēbā is translated interestingly as wḥzrt lwwtyh ltybwth (!) 'and it returned to him to the ark.' The spelling lwwt predominates over lwt at the rate of approximately 10:1 (cf. Chapter 2, Orthography).

\+ l^{c}yl mn 'on top of': For MT mimma^{c}al lə-.

\+ lqbl 'opposite', 'in front of': Translates a variety of MT terms: lə^{c}ênê (Gen 23:18); 'el (Gen 30:40); neged (Gen 31:37); 'el mûl (Exod 26:9). It also appears in idiomatic paraphrase, e.g., Deut 5:4 mmll lqbl mmll 'speech against speech' (MT pānîm bəpānîm), or Gen 15:10 šwy kl ḥd lqbl ḥbryh 'he placed each one opposite its fellow' (MT wayyittēn 'îš-bitrô liqra't rē^{c}ēhû).

It is particularly common in the idiom sdr (sdry) qrb' lqbl 'to array the battle line in front of', e.g., Gen 14:9, Gen 15:1, Num 24:20, etc. It occurs with both singular and plural suffixes, e.g., Gen 31:5 lqbly 'towards me', Gen 31:2 lqblyh 'towards him', Exod 1:10 lqwbln 'against us' (MT bānû), but Num 24:20, Deut 2:19, etc. lqblyhwn. Note especially Gen 14:8 wsdrw lqblthwn (!) sdry qrb' 'and they arranged the battle lines before them', for the MT technical military idiom wayya^{c}arəkû 'ittām milḥāmā. (There is a not uncommon letter confusion of t for y in Neofiti, cf Chapter 2, Orthography.)

\+ lqdmwt 'towards': Only with singular suffixes, usually for the MT liqra't/liqrā't + verb of motion.

\+ m(n) 'from': This usually translates MT min. It is also used in a partitive sense, e.g., Exod 18:25 mn kl yśr'l 'from all of Israel', Lev 4:2 ḥd' mnhwn 'one of them', Gen 30:14 mn ybrwḥy (sic) dbryk 'some of your son's mandrakes'.

In general, MT min + infinitive is translated mn l- however cf. Gen 20:6 mlmḥṭy 'from sinning' (MT mēḥ^{a}ṭô). For the comparative, see Gen 4:8 w^{c}l dhww ^{c}wbdyy ṭbyn mn dydk 'and because my works were better than yours'.

It is also common in the idiom mn ... (w)^{c}d ... 'from ... to ...' (usually for MT min ... (wə)^{c}ad .... The preposition takes singular suffixes. Note occasional plene spellings, e.g., Deut 3:17 myn, Gen 44:18 mynk 'from you'/mynhwn 'from them'; cf. also the numerous compound prepositions listed below.

+ mn bgyn 'on account of': With kdyn etc., cf. bgyn above.
+ mn bgll 'because of': Usually with singular suffixes, for MT ba^{ca}bûr + suffixes, however, also independently, cf. Gen 18:24 mn bgll ḥmyšty zkyy (sic) 'because of the fifty righteous ones' (MT ləma^{c}an), etc., and numerous examples in passages without Hebrew Vorlage, or in paraphrase. Cf. bgll above.
+ mbyn 'from among': Cf. Gen 35:2 mbynykwn 'from among you' (MT bətōk^{a}kem), and byn above.
+ mn btr 'after': Usually for MT 'aḥar/'aḥ^{a}rê, cf. btr above. Note the spelling mbtrh 'after him' in Gen 22:14.
+ mn gw' 'from within': Mostly found in the technical religious idiom wmyt w'tknš mn gw' ^{c}lm' 'and he died and was gathered up from within the world' (often for MT wayyāmōt, cf. e.g., Gen 5:5 and others). It is less commonly spelled mn gw/mgw, cf. bgw above.
+ mn kl q(w)bl 'opposite', 'in front of': Usually with singular suffixes for MT minneged/ləneged. Cf. kl q(w)bl, lqbl above, and qbyl below.
+ mn lwwt 'from (the presence of)', 'by (means of)': Translates MT mē'ēt, mē^{c}im, miyyad, both with and without (singular) suffixes. The preposition is variously spelled: mlwwt, mlwt, mn lwt.
+ ml^{c}yl l- 'above': Infrequent, for MT mē^{c}al lə-, cf. m^{c}lwy below.
+ mn lr^{c} 'below': Infrequent, for MT mittaḥat, cf. mn tḥwt below.
+ m^{c}lwy 'above', 'from upon/before': This is the most common spelling -- less commonly found are m^{c}ylwy, m^{c}lwwy, m^{c}ylwwy, also for MT mē^{c}al. So too with suffixes, e.g., Exod 10:28 m^{c}lwy 'from before me' (MT mē^{c}ālāy), Gen 38:14 m^{c}lwwh 'from upon her' (MT mē^{c}āleyhā).
+ mn qdm 'from before': Most often found in the phrase mn qdm YYY 'from before the Lord', especially paraphrasing a biblical anthropomorphism, e.g., Gen 1:2 rû^{a}ḥ '^{e}lōhîm = rwḥ drḥmyn mn qdm YYY 'a spirit of mercy from before the

Lord', or Num 27:18 '^{a}šer rû^{a}ḥ bô = drwḥ qdš mn qdm YYY šryyh ^{c}lwy 'upon whom rests a holy spirit from before the Lord'. It also translates MT mippənê (e.g., Gen 16:8) and min e.g., mēYHWH = mn qdm YYY, many times. The preposition takes plural suffixes, cf. qdm below.

+ mn tḥwt (l-) 'beneath', 'below': For MT mittaḥat (e.g., Gen 1:7) and mittaḥat lə (e.g., Exod 6:7). Note Gen 35:8, where the MT wattiqqābēr mittaḥat ləbêt 'el taḥat hā'allôn is condensed as w'tqbrt mn tḥwt blwṭh 'and she was buried beneath the oak', and also Exod 20:4 where the MT wa'^{a}šer bā'āreṣ mittaḥat wa'^{a}šer bammayim mittaḥat lā'āreṣ is (mistakenly?) expanded to wdy b'r^{c}' mn lr^{c} wdy bmy' mn tḥwt l'r^{c}' mn tḥwt 'and which is in the earth below, and which is in the water beneath the earth beneath'.

+ smyk l- 'near': Paraphrasing a number of MT idioms. The example in Deut 2:19 (MT mûl) appears to be spelled smwk, but this is more likely a case of w/y letter confusion.

+ ^{c}d 'up to', 'until': The preposition is used in a directional sense and a temporal sense, in both cases for MT ^{c}ad. Note especially the common phrase ^{c}d ^{c}lm 'until eternity'. It is also found often in various constructions for some Hebrew adverbials, e.g., ^{c}d kdwn (MT 'āz, Gen 12:6, and often), and in a variety of paraphrases and passages with no Hebrew Vorlage.

+ ^{c}d zmn 'until (the time of)': Only in the common phrase ^{c}d zmm ywm' hdyn 'until this (very) day' (MT ^{c}ad hayyôm/^{c}ad hayyôm hazze). Cf. bzmn above.

+ ^{c}l 'on', 'upon': Most commonly for MT ^{c}al, and in the common phrases 'tgly (mmryh dYYY) ^{c}l '(the word of the Lord) was revealed to' and ^{c}ll ^{c}l 'to enter into' (MT bā'). Cf. lwwt above.

+ ^{c}l gby 'on (the surface of)': Uncommon, cf. ^{c}l gby mdbḥh 'on the altar' (Lev 22:27 no MT, Gen 8:20, MT bammizbē^{a}ḥ).

+ ^{c}l ydy 'by (means of/the hands of)': For MT min, bə, ^{c}al yad; note Num 21:7 ^{c}l ydyhwn d^{c}m' 'on behalf of (?) the people', for MT bə^{c}ad hā^{c}ām. Takes plural suffixes.

+ ^{c}l ^{c}sq 'concerning', 'because of': Most commonly for MT ^{c}al dəbar, ^{c}al 'ōdōt, ^{c}al, etc. Without Vorlage, often in the idiom ^{c}l ^{c}sq ptgm' hdyn 'concerning this matter'. Occasional spellings ^{c}l ^{c}ysq and once (Gen 25:21), MT lənokāḥ is translated by the plural, ^{c}l

^{c}sqy. Note also Gen 26:32 ^{c}l ^{c}sq db'yrh dḥprw 'concerning the well which they dug'.

+ ^{c}m 'with': Translates MT ^{c}im and its equivalents, occasionally spelled plene ^{c}ym, and cf. especially Gen 44:18 ^{c}myn! (no MT) 'with us' (= metathesis for ^{c}ymn?). Cf. gb above.

+ qbyl 'in front', 'before': Rare, e.g., Gen 31:32 (MT neged), cf. kl qwbl, lqbl, and mn kl q(w)bl above.

+ q(w)dm 'in front of', 'before': The usual translation of MT lipnê, and often in the paraphrase wgly qdm YYY 'and it was revealed before the Lord' (MT wayyar(') 'ᵉlōhîm). Note also the irregular use of qdmyy l-, apparently the adjective 'first' + l- in place of qdm in Gen 29:26 lmytn z^{c}yrt' qdmyy lrb<rb>nt' 'to give the younger before the older'. Takes plural suffixes, e.g., Deut 1:1 qdmykwn 'before you (pl)'/qwdmwy 'before him', etc.

+ tḥwt 'beneath', 'under': The usual translation for MT taḥat = 'beneath'; there are examples, however, of mistranslation for MT taḥat 'in place of' for ḥlp (q.v.), e.g., Gen 22:13 tḥwt bryh 'under (= in place of) his son', and Exod 21:26 tḥwt ^{c}ynyh 'under (= in place of) his eye'. Also occurs with both singular and plural suffixes, e.g., Gen 2:21 tḥwth 'under it' (MT taḥtennā), Gen 37:34 wšwy śq' tḥtwy 'and he placed sackcloth under him' (MT wayyāśem śaq bəmotnāyw).

CHAPTER 4
CONJUNCTIONS

The following list is presented as a complete inventory, and is divided into the following categories: Time; Place; Condition; Purpose; Manner; Coordination and Disjunction. Some prepositions are found in more than one category. Examples are only cited where comment is deemed appropriate.

1. Time

\+ 'rwm 'when': Always translates MT kî, at times abbreviated to 'rw. Cf. 4. Purpose, below.

\+ bzmnh dy '(at the time) when': All occurrences paraphrase Hebrew bə- + infinitive, with or without pronominal suffix; also common in passages without Vorlage.

\+ bywm' d- 'on the day when': For MT bəyôm + infinitive.

\+ bš^c^t' d- 'at the time when': Usually for MT bə^c^ēt/lə^c^ēt + infinitive.

\+ btr d- 'after': Not common, e.g., Gen 18:12, btr ds'byt 'after I have grown old' (MT 'aḥ^a^rê bəlōtî). Cf. the more common mn btr d- below.

\+ kd 'when': When translating Hebrew, it usually translates (wayhî) ka'^a^šer, however, it more usually paraphrases a Hebrew infinitive with bə-, cf. e.g., Gen 9:14 (MT bə^c^an^a^nî), etc., or it is used in passages with no Hebrew Vorlage, cf. e.g., Gen 21:33 whwwh kd 'klyn wštyn 'when they were eating and drinking' (note that here whwwh does not translate MT wayhî!).

It is also used in a technical religious idiom in Genesis, in the phrase kd npq b- 'similar to'. In 1:26 bdmwtn kd npq bn 'in our image, similar to us' translates MT bəṣalmēnû kidmûtēnû; in 5:3 a similar phrase bdmwtyh kd npq byh 'in his image, similar to him' translates the similar (but not identical) MT bidmûtô kəṣalmô--both these phrases were obviously considered identical by the targumist; finally, in Gen 2:18 and 2:20 the MT ^c^ezer kənegdô is also translated by the same idiom, zwg kd npq byh 'a partner, similar to him'. The idiom is possibly to be understood as a calque of late Hebrew kayyôṣē' bə, cf. Jastrow, "Dictionary," p. 926.

\+ kdy 'when': This "archaism" occurs often where kd is expected, usually for MT kə/bə + infinitive, with or without pronominal suffixes. Note also Gen 12:11 whwh kdy qrb 'and when he drew near' (MT wayhî ka'^a^šer hiqrîb), and especially Deut 2:16 whwh kd dy spw 'and when they had perished' (MT wayhî ka'^{a}šer tammû).

+ kywn d- 'when': Unlike kd/kdy above, this conjunction appears only in paraphrastic or untranslated passages, cf. Gen 31:22 whwh kywn d'zlw 'and when they went', Num 12:12 wkywn dmṭ' qṣh 'and when the appointed time came'. Spellings such as Gen 28:10 kwwn d- either reflect w/y confusion or "defective" spelling.

+ kl ywmyn d- 'all the days that': cf. Chapter 5, Adverbials, for nouns in the absolute after kl, and cf. also ^{c}d zmn d- below.

+ mn btr d- 'after': Usually translates MT 'aḥ^{a}rê + infinitive, with or without pronominal suffix, and occasionally in paraphrase. Cf. btr d- above.

+ mn d- 'when', 'after': Translates a number of MT idioms, and common in paraphrase, cf. especially Num 21:19 mn d'tyhybt lhwn byr' 'after the well had been given to them', paraphrasing the poetic mimmattānā naḥ^{a}lî'ēl, and Gen 4:16 where it is used in the apodosis following ^{c}d l' 'before', whwh ^{c}d l' qṭl lhbl ... wmn dḥṭ' wqṭl lhbl 'and before he killed Abel ... then after he sinned and killed Abel'.

+ mn zmn' d- 'from the time when': Uncommon, cf. mn d above, and ^{c}d zmn d below.

+ ^{c}d dy 'until', 'while': For MT temporal idioms with ^{c}ad, and also in untranslated passages. There appear also to be a number of examples of ^{c}d alone used as the conjunction especially in verses without Vorlage, e.g., Exod 14:25 ^{c}d 'ynwn yhybyn bmṣrym 'while they were (yet?) in Egypt', and Deut 1:1 ^{c}d 'ynwn yhybyn b^{c}br yrdnh 'while they were (still?) in Transjordan'. These last examples may also be ^{c}d = /^{c}ād/, the adverb 'again', cf. the discussion in Chapter 5, Adverbials, ^{c}d.

+ ^{c}d zmn d- 'until': The more common translation of MT ^{c}ad + infinitive (cf. ^{c}d dy above), and also for other MT temporal idioms with ^{c}ad (^{c}ad '^{a}šer, ^{c}ad 'im, ^{c}ad kî). Note also Gen 24:19 ^{c}d zmn yšlmwn 'until they finish' (MT ^{c}ad 'im-killû). Also common without Vorlage or in paraphrase.

+ ^{c}d l' 'before': For MT ṭerem (+ imperfect) and lipnê (+ infinitive), though much less common than qdm ^{c}d l' (q.v.). Cf. also mn d- above.

+ qdm ^{c}d l' 'before': The common translation of MT ṭerem

(+ imperfect) and *lipnê* (+ infinitive). There are isolated examples of the spelling *qdm ^{c}l l'* with assimilation of the *-d* to the *l-*, presumably the common pronunciation, the form with *^{c}d* being a standard literary spelling.

2. *Place*

\+ *b(kl) 'tr' dy* 'where(ever)': For MT *ba'^{a}šer*, *məqôm '^{a}šer*, *bəkol məqôm '^{a}šer*, etc.

\+ *l'n d-* 'whither': Occurs rarely in the MS, cf. e.g., Gen 27:8, in a mistranslation of MT *la'^{a}šer* 'according as', in which the Aramaic adds the imperative 'go!' to effect the sense 'to where', clearly as a result of the following verse, beginning *lek-nā'*, cf. MT *šəma^{c} bəqōlî la'^{a}šer '^{a}nî məṣawwā 'ōtāk* = Aramaic *šm^{c} bqly w'zl l'n d'nh mpqdh ytk*.

\+ *lkl 'tr dy* 'to wherever': Occurs once in the MS, Gen 20:13, translating MT *'el kol-hammāqôm '^{a}šer*. Note that *'tr* is not determined state to parallel *hammāqôm*, and cf. Chapter 5, *Adverbials*, for nouns in the absolute state after *kl*.

\+ *mh d-* 'wherever': The indefinite pronoun is used only once, Gen 20:15, in the phrase *mh dšpr b'pk šry* 'dwell wherever it seems good to you', translating MT *baṭṭôb bə^{c}êneykā šēb*. Elsewhere *mh d-* = 'that which', cf. Chapter 6, *Indefinite Relative Pronouns.*

\+ *mn 'n d-* 'from wherever': Infrequent in the MS, cf. e.g., Exod 5:11 *sbw lkwn tbn mn 'n dy tškḥwn* 'take straw for yourselves from wherever you find it' (MT *qəḥû lākem teben mē'^{a}šer timṣā'û*).

3. *Condition*

\+ *'y* 'if': Most uncommon, cf. Gen 37:32, translating MT *'im-lō'*, as *'y l'*. Cf. *'n* below.

\+ *'ylw* 'if (only)': Occurs mostly in passages without Hebrew *Vorlage*, always followed by a perfect tense. Also used in paraphrase of an MT narrative perfect, e.g., Gen 26:10 and Gen 31:27. For a passage with *Vorlage*, cf. Num 22:29 *'ylw hwh bydy ḥrb* 'if only there were a sword in my hand' (MT *lû yeš ḥereb bəyādî*).

\+ *'(y)lwly* 'if it were not that': Translates MT *lûlê*, *lûlē'*.

\+ *'n* 'if': Translates MT *'im*, also in the negative *'(y)n l'* = *'im lō'*. Also used in paraphrase of the Hebrew, and in passages where there is no Hebrew *Vorlage*. The spelling *'n* predominates over *'yn* at the rate of approximately 4:1. In numerous instances, the Hebrew *'im* is used where that word is found in the MT.

\+ *'rwm 'lh(y)n* 'except that', 'rather': Used occasionally as a conjunction translating MT *kî 'im* + finite verb, and other MT idioms. Cf. the same form in Chapter 3, *Prepositions*.

\+ *dl'* 'lest', 'that not': Translates MT *pen* + imperfect, and *'^{a}šer* + *lō'* i.e., 'that not', followed by the imperfect or the perfect. Also used in passages with no Hebrew *Vorlage*, and in paraphrase. Note the form in Gen 39:10 *dlh' (!) lmhwy ^{c}mh l^{c}lm' d'ty* 'so as not to be with her in the world to come', with the spelling *dlh'* apparently a copyist error.

\+ *dlm' d-* 'perhaps': Used as a conjunction, usually without Hebrew *Vorlage*; variously spelled *dylm' d-*, *dlmh d-*. Cf. *mh dylm' d-* below.

\+ *mh dylm' d-* 'perhaps', 'what if': The common translation of MT *'ûlay*, variously spelled: *mh dylm' d-*, *mh dylm'*, *mh dylmh 'm* (!), *mh dylmh d-*, *mh dylmh*. Note also Gen 24:39, *mh llm' d-* ! (= assimilation or error?).

4. *Purpose*

\+ *'lwly d-* 'because': Uncommon, cf. Deut 1:1 (no MT).

\+ *'rwm* 'because': Often, usually for MT *kî*.

\+ *'ry* 'because': Uncommon, also for MT *kî*.

\+ *'p ^{c}l gb d-* 'in spite of the fact that': Only in passages with no Hebrew *Vorlage*; note the spelling in Num 12:16, *'wp ^{c}l gb d-*.

\+ *bgll d-* 'because': For MT *ba'^{a}šer* and *ləma^{c}an*.

\+ *d(y)* 'because', 'that': For a variety of MT idioms, and also very common in verses without *Vorlage*

\+ *hw'yl w-* 'since': Uncommon, cf. Gen 18:17 (no MT).

\+ *ḥlp d(y)* 'since', 'because': For a variety of MT purpose idioms: *^{c}ēqeb '^{a}šer*, *ya^{c}an '^{a}šer*, *taḥat '^{a}šer*.

\+ *lpm d-* 'because': Rare, cf. Num 12:16 *lpm dqmt lh mrym ^{c}l gyp nhr'* 'because Miriam stood on the bank of the river' (no MT).

\+ *mn bgll d(y)* 'so that', 'because': The common translation of MT *ba^{ca}bûr* (*'^{a}šer*) and *ləma^{c}an* (*'^{a}šer*), and also in paraphrase and in passages without *Vorlage*, e.g., Gen 16:5 *mn bgll dl' yqṭlwn ytk* 'so that they should not kill you', and Gen 28:10 *mn bgll dhwh dbyr' mtḥmd lmmll<h> ^{c}myh* 'because the Word was desirous of speaking with him'.

+ mn bly d- 'because not' For MT mibbəlî, e.g., Exod 14:11, Deut 28:55, etc.

+ ^{c}l d(y) 'because (of the fact that)': Usually found in passages without Hebrew Vorlage, through cf. Gen 31:20 ^{c}l dl' tny lh 'because he did not tell him' (MT ^{c}al bəlî higgîd lô). Note also Gen 3:22 ^{c}d dy, with assimilation of the -l to the d- (no MT).

5. Manner

+ hyk mh d(y) '(just) as', 'according as': The common translation for MT ka'^{a}šer, and also in paraphrase and in passages with no Hebrew Vorlage. Note Gen 34:22, where the form is hyk d- (MT ka'^{a}šer), and especially Deut 2:14 hyk mn dy (!) (MT ka'^{a}šer).

+ kmh d- 'as': Uncommon, cf. Gen 18:5 kmh dmlylt' (sic) 'as you have spoken' (MT ka'^{a}šer dibbartā).

6. Coordination and Disjunction

+ 'w 'or'. Invariably transates MT 'ô. Twice in Genesis (24:21 and 27:21), MT 'im lō' is translated 'w l'. Otherwise it is the normal disjunction between nominal or verbal forms; it also occurs in passages without Vorlage, e.g., Gen 38:25, h' hy' prgwd' dbrk 'w l' 'is this the cloak of your son, or not?', in possible imitation of the biblical idiom. In the parallel verse in Gen 37:32, the phrase is 'y l', perhaps an error for 'w l' due to w/y confusion.

+ 'l' 'but (on the other hand)': In apposition to phrases containing l', e.g., Gen 13:7 l' hwwn zmmyn b^{c}yrhwn 'l' mbqryn w'zlyn 'they did not muzzle their cattle but let them graze and wander', and Gen 22:14 l' hwwh blby plgw ... 'l' mn yd 'qdmyt bṣpr' 'there was no division in my heart ... but I immediately arose in the morning', neither with Vorlage.

+ brm 'but', 'however': Occasionally for MT '^{a}bal and 'ûlām, otherwise, it occurs in passages without Hebrew Vorlage, and in paraphrase. Note the use in Gen 20:16, ^{c}l dy 'tksyt brm mn ^{c}yynwy dṣdyq' lyly' ḥd 'because you were hidden, even, from the eyes of the righteous one, for one night'.

+ w- 'and'.

CHAPTER 5

ADVERBIALS

Many of the adverbial expressions listed here, in particular those consisting of a preposition + nominal form, are used exclusively in paraphrastic passages or in midrashic interpolations in the text. They are often adverbial "comments" added to the text, and they are designed to provide background information on the motives, reactions, etc. of the characters, in particular those passages in which God is seen as the (often arbitrary) initiator of events. Numerous of them are indeed parts of euphemistic paraphrase to avoid either anthropomorphism or divine offense (e.g., *bb^{c}w*, *bmymr*). At other times, the comment they provide has been suggested by some word, phrase, or element in the massoretic text (cf. *brgz*, based on the MT *'ap* 'also', resembling *'ap* 'anger'). Where the use in Neofiti is exclusively or primarily in paraphrase, it has been so noted in the entry.

1. Adverbial Forms

\+ *'p* 'also': Usually translates MT *gam*, occasionally spelled *'wp*, cf. Deut 2:11. Note also Gen 24:25 *'p tbn 'p ksh sgyn ^{c}mn w'p 'tr lmbth* 'there is with us both much straw and fodder and also a place to spend the night' (= MT *gam ... gam ... gam*), for extended adverbial usage.

\+ *bb^{c}w* 'in prayer' ⟶ 'please': Only used in such idioms as the commonly occurring *bb^{c}w brḥmyn mn qdmyk*, 'in prayer, with mercy from before you' addressed in prayer to God; also the similar *bb^{c}w mn qdmyk*, in speaking with God; and simply *bb^{c}w mn*, addressing angels and human beings, cf. Gen 19:2, 38:25, etc.

\+ *bdyn'* 'it is right/just': Always in the phrase *bdyn' hw' d*, 'it is right that', e.g., Gen 4:24, Lev 1:1 (no MT).

\+ *bh bš^{c}t'* 'at that very time': Only found in passages with no Hebrew *Vorlage*; cf. also the next entry.

\+ *bhn bšnyh* 'in those very years': Primarily used in the phrase *wbhn bšny(y)h hwh mwl(y)d bnyn wbnn* 'and in those very years he begat sons and daughters', in Genesis, e.g., 5:4, 5:7, 11:13, etc.

\+ *bḥdwh* 'joyfully': Only in paraphrase, e.g., Gen 22:14, *w'qdmyt w^{c}bdyt mymryk bḥdwh* 'and I arose early and did your commandments joyfully'.

\+ bkd(y)n 'then': Usually for MT 'āz. Occasional apparent spellings bkdw/y are to be understood as due to the common confusion in this MS between w/y/final n, cf. Chapter 2, Orthography.

\+ bmymr 'by command': Usually in phrases such as bmymr mn qdm YYY 'by command from before the Lord'.

\+ bpry^{c} 'quickly': The regular translation of the MT infinitive mahēr used adverbially, e.g., Exod 32:8, Deut 4:26, and often; occasionally spelled bwpry^{c}, e.g., Deut 9:12, etc.

\+ bqwšṭ' 'truthfully', 'faithfully': Only in paraphrase, e.g., Gen 5:22.

\+ brgz 'angrily', 'in anger': Only in paraphrase, but cf. especially Gen 18:23 h' brgz 't mšyṣyy' zkyy' ^{c}m ḥyyb' 'will you in anger destroy the righteous with the guilty?' (MT ha'ap tispe ṣaddîq ^{c}im-rāšā^{c}) with a misunderstanding(?) of 'p 'also' as 'p 'anger' leading to the Aramaic addition of brgz.

\+ br^{c}ww' 'favorably': To be found in such expansions as Gen 4:4 and 4:5, wqbl YYY br^{c}ww' yt hbl wyt qrbnyh wlqyn wlqrbnyh l' qbl br^{c}ww' 'and the Lord received Abel and his offering favorably, but Cain and his offering he did not receive favorably', paraphrasing the MT verb šā^{c}ā 'el.

\+ br^{c}wt 'with pleasure' ⟶ 'it pleases': In paraphrase, in expressions such as Gen 24:42, 'm (sic) br^{c}wt qdmk lmṣlḥh 'rḥy 'if it is pleasing before you to make my way prosper', etc. Note the spelling br^{c}tkwn in Gen 24:49.

\+ bšbw^{c}h 'in oath': Used of either God or human beings, e.g., Gen 4:15, w'mr lyh YYY bšbw^{c}h 'and God swore to him' (MT wayyō(')mer lô YHWH), or Gen 21:24 w'mr 'brhm h' 'n' 'štb^{c} w'qyym bšbw^{c}h 'and Abraham said: Behold I swear and I will carry out by oath' (MY wayyō(')mer 'abrāhām 'ānokî 'iššābe$^{a c}$).

\+ bšlm 'in peace': Only in paraphrase, e.g., Deut 5:30 ḥzwrw lkwn bšlm lmšknykwn 'go back in peace to your tents' (MT šûbû lākem lə'oh^{o}lêkem).

\+ btkwp 'suddenly': For MT bəpeta^{c}, bəpeta^{c} pit'ōm, e.g., Num 35:22, Num 12:4. Note the apparent spelling btkyp in Num 6:9, probably a case of w/y confusion, or else cf. Jastrow, "Dictionary," p. 1668. Note also the case cited by the editor, Deut 4:42, which has btqwp, where MS 440 of the Vatican Library has btkwp. In this case, however, the other suggested emendation, i.e., to add rwgz' appears to be indicated, given the MT.

\+ gmyr' 'completely': For MT kālīl, and also in paraphrase of MT ^{c}āśû kolāh in Gen 18:21 klyyh ^{c}bdw gmyr' 'they did the destruction completely'.

\+ dmḥr 'tomorrow', 'on the next day': Only in Gen 30:33 wyshdn ^{c}ly zkwwty bywm' hdn wdmḥr 'and my righteous deeds will witness for me this day and the next day', expanding the MT wə^{c}āntā-bî ṣidqātî bəyôm māḥār, perhaps ellipsis for bywm' hdn wbywm' dmḥr.

\+ hdh zmnh 'now', 'this time': Always translates MT happa^{c}am.

\+ hkh 'here': Translates various Hebrew idioms, pōh, hēnnā, kōh (Gen 31:37), mizze (mn hk') and also in paraphrase, lō' hāyətā bazze in parallel verses in Gen 38:21/39:22 as lyt hk'. It is also used idiomatically in Gen 24:60 brm mn hk' wlhl' 't 'zlh 'but from here and henceforth you shall go'.

\+ zmn tn(y)ynwt 'again', 'a second time': Mostly translates MT šēnît (e.g., Gen 41:5, Lev 13:58, occasionally for MT ^{c}ôd.

\+ ḥzwr ḥzwr 'round about': For MT sābîb and its derivatives. Note also Gen 35:5 dy ḥzwr ḥzwr ythwn (with the first ḥzwr dotted out, apparently a mistake by the copyist, who seems to have assumed dittography, i.e., ḥzwr for the correct ḥzwr ḥzwr) 'which is around about them', translating MT '^{a}šer səbîbôtêhem.

± ḥs l- 'far be it from': Only in Gen 38:25, ḥs lh tmr klty hy' m^{c}br' bnyn dznw 'far be it from her, Tamar my daughter-in-law, that she conceive children of harlotry'. Cf. also Gen 44:7 (expected but missing in the text); see also mḥws below.

\+ y'wt 'rightly', 'correctly': Usually in paraphrase, though cf. Deut 13:15 (= MT hêṭēb).

\+ ywm btr ywm 'day after day': For MT yôm yôm.

\+ ywm' hd(y)n 'today': For MT hayyôm and hayyôm hazze. Note that in Gen 24:42, MT hayyôm is rendered ywm' dyn whereas Gen 25:33, kayyôm 'this (very) day' is translated as an apparent calque kywm' hdyn. Cf. also dmḥr above.

\+ ywm ḥd 'in/for one day': For MT yôm 'eḥad.

\+ kdwn 'now': Primarily translates MT ^{c}attā, but also ^{c}ôd and its variants, as well as less common idioms, e.g., h^{a}lōm. Also common in verses where there is no Hebrew Vorlage in phrases such as h' kdwn, ^{c}d kdwn, mn kdwn, etc.

\+ kd(y)n 'thus': Mostly translates MT kēn, especially in the phrase bgyn kdyn translating MT ^{c}al-kēn. Also for MT kōh, ^{c}attā, and twice, Gen 10:18 and 24:5, the idiom mn btr kd(y)n 'then', 'afterwards', translates MT 'aḥar; in Gen 6:4 it translates 'aḥ^{a}rê-kēn. Cf. also mn bgyn kdyn 'therefore' and kl kdyn 'all this'. The spelling kdn is rare.

\+ kḥd' 'together': For MT yaḥdāw.

\+ kk 'thus': Only in Gen 38:26, in the phrase bgyn kk, translating MT ^{c}al-kēn (cf. kdyn above).

\+ kmst 'worthy' ⟶ 'in accordance with': In Num 7:7, kmst pwlḥn{y}hwn 'in accordance with their service' (MT kəpî ^{ca}bōdātām), otherwise Deut 16:10/17 and Gen 20:16 and elsewhere in paraphrase or used adjectivally.

\+ k(y)n 'thus': Usually for MT kēn, and without Vorlage, especially in the phrase wkn ktb' wmprš w'mr 'and thus (says) the Scripture, and it explains saying' (e.g., Gen 30:22). The spelling without -y- is the more common.

\+ k^{c}n 'now', 'please': Translates MT nā' often, after imperatives etc., and also in h' k^{c}n 'and now', translating MT hinne-nā' (often). Also used in numerous paraphrastic contexts.

\+ lbr' 'outside': Usually translates MT haḥûṣā/baḥûṣ (e.g., Gen 19:7, Num 35:4, etc.); cf. also Gen 19:6 where the paraphrase of wayyēṣē' '^{a}lēhem lôṭ happetḥā 'and Lot went out to them to the door' is wnpq lwwthwn lbr' 'and he went out to them outside'.

\+ lhl(') 'away', 'beyond': The normal translation for MT hāl'ā (e.g., Gen 19:19, Num 17:2, etc.) and also in the common idiom mn hk' wlhl' 'from here/now and henceforth' (cf. hkh above).

\+ lḥd' 'very': Translates MT mə'ōd. Cf. the next entry.

\+ lḥd' lḥd' 'very much', 'exceedingly': For the MT extended idioms (bi)mə'ōd mə'ōd.

\+ lḥwd 'only': The common translation for MT gam, 'āk, and raq.

\+ l^{c}lm 'forever': Translates MT lə^{c}ōlām.

\+ ltmn 'thither': Translates MT šāmmā.

\+ mgn 'for nothing': Always for MT ḥinnām; cf. ^{c}l mgn below.

\+ mḥws 'grace' ⟶ 'far be it from': In the idiom (b)mḥws mn qdm 'please do not —— ', for MT ḥālilā and paraphrase (e.g., Gen 19:16). Cf. ḥs l- above.

+ mlgw' '(from) within': In Gen 6:14, translating MT mibbayit (opposed to mn lbr (q.v.) = miḥûṣ '(from) without').

+ mlqdmyn 'in the beginning': In Gen 1:1, translating MT bərē(')šît and also in Deut 33:27 mdwr 'yqr škynth d'lh' mlqdmyn 'the dwelling place of the Shekinah of God is from the beginning', based on the poetic mə^{c}ōnā '^{e}lōhê qedem. Cf. also Gen 3:24 w'šry yqr škyntyh mn mlqdmyn (sic) mn mdnh' 'and the Glory of his Shekinah placed from the beginning to the east' etc., paraphrasing the MT wayyaškēn miqqedem ləgan-^{c}ēden etc.

+ mn btr 'afterwards': Only in Gen 30:21, translating MT wə'aḥar, apparently ellipsis for mn btr kdyn (see kd(y)n above.

+ mn yd 'immediately': Only in paraphrase, e.g., Gen 22:14 mn yd 'qdmyt bṣpr' 'I immediately arose early in the morning', and Lev 22:27, also based on the Abraham story. Also spelled myd.

+ mn ywm' dbtryh 'on the next day': In Num 11:32 for MT mimmoḥ^{o}rāt; cf. also Gen 19:34, mn ywm' dbtr which is probably an abbreviation for mn ywm' dbtrh as Díez Macho emends, even though there appears to be no abbreviation mark on the word (which is the last word in the line).

+ mn lbr '(from) without': In Gen 6:14, translating MT miḥûṣ; see lbr' and mlgw' above.

+ mn l^{c}yl 'above': For MT miləma^{c}əlā, however note also Deut 3:24 bšmyy' mn l^{c}yl ... ^{c}l 'r^{c}' mn lr^{c} (q.v.) 'in heaven above ... on earth below', based on MT baššāmayim ûbā'āreṣ.

+ mn lr^{c} 'below': cf. mn l^{c}yl above, and also Exod 20:4 (MT mittaḥat).

+ mn qwšṭ' 'truly': For MT hā'umnām, 'omnā, h^{a}kî and 'ākēn, in a variety of passages.

+ mn tmn 'from there': Translates MT miššām and without Vorlage in the same sense, cf. e.g., Gen 21:33 wl' hwwn z^{c}yyn mn tmn 'and they would not move from there'. Also spelled mtmn.

+ ^{c}d l^{c}lmyn 'forever': Only in midrash, e.g., Gen 3:22 'yt hwh ḥy wqyym k'ln ḥyy' ^{c}d l^{c}lmyn 'he would live and endure as the tree of life forever' (see l^{c}lm above).

+ ^{c}d 'again', 'another': (= ^{c}ād) in Gen 29:27 for MT ^{c}ôd and in Gen 25:6 ^{c}d hwwh bḥyyn 'he was still alive' for MT bə^{c}ôdennû hay. Spelled often ^{c}wd, presumably the Hebrew ^{c}ôd introduced to avoid confusion with the preposition ^{c}d (= ^{c}ad), also translating ^{c}ôd, and frequently the combined form ^{c}wd twb. Also in verses without Vorlage with the same meaning (cf. twb below).

\+ ^{c}l mgn 'in vain': In the Decalogue, Exod 20:7, for MT laššāw' (cf. mgn above).

\+ štq 'silently': A participle used adverbially, cf. Gen 24:21 translating MT maḥ^{a}rîš, wgbr (sic) hwh šty wmstkl bh štq 'and the man drank and looked at her silently'.

\+ twb 'again': The common translation of MT ^{c}ôd, cf. ^{c}d above.

\+ tmn 'there': Translates MT šām, cf. ltmn and mn tmn above.

2. Interjections and Introductory Particles

\+ 'l(w)wy(y) 'oh that', 'would that': Translates MT interjections lû and hēn lû (e.g., Num 14:2, Gen 17:18, etc.); in paraphrase, cf. Gen 21:7 w'mrt 'lwwy mn yyzyl wtny ... 'and she said: Oh, who will go and tell ...' (MT wattō(')mer mî millēl lə'abrāhām), and especially Num 24:23 'lwwyy mn yyḥy bywmy' h'ynwn ... 'Oh who will live in those days ...' (based on the poetic MT 'ôy mî yiḥye miśśûmô 'ēl). For a similar idiom, and in particular the example in Num 23:10, cf. lwwy below.

\+ h' 'here', 'behold': Usually in translation of MT hēn, hinne, and the interrogative proclitic h^{a}-. Note Gen 24:23, where the same proclitic in the MT h^{a}yeš is translated by h'yt 'is there?'. It is commonly used in translating MT hinne + suffixes, cf. e.g., Gen 6:17 h' 'nh (= hinənî) and Gen 16:11 h' 't (= hinnāk). (Note that three times in Genesis 22, verses 1, 7 and 11, the Hebrew word hnny 'here I am' is used by Abraham in his answer to God, presumably due to the explanation advanced in 22:1 ^{c}ny 'brhm blšn byt qwdš' w'mr lyh 'brh<m> hnny 'Abraham answered in the language of the Sanctuary and Abraham said to Him, Here I am'. However, note that in Gen 27:18, in the dialogue between Jacob and Isaac, the same hnny (= MT) is used. There are also many examples of h' used in passages without Hebrew Vorlage: with verbs, e.g., Gen 3:22 h' nyṭrw<d> ytyh mn gnth d^{c}dn 'we will expell him from the garden of Eden', and Gen 15:7 h' šmš' ṭm^{c} 'the sun set'; with nouns, e.g., also Gen 15:7 wh' ghynm 'and here was Gehinnom'.

\+ hl' 'is it not that': Usually used where MT has h^{a}lō', however cf. e.g., Gen 6:3 hl' mḥtm hw' qdm<y>y sdr dyn' ddry<h> dmbwl' 'is it not that the judgement of the generation of the flood is sealed before me', without Hebrew Vorlage.

\+ wwy 'woe': Common in the phrase wwy k^{c}n ^{c}ly 'oh woe is me', usually without Hebrew Vorlage, however cf. Num 21:29 wwy lkwn mw'byy 'woe to you, Moabites' (MT 'ôy-ləkā mô'āb).

\+ *ṭwby-- 'happy is -- ': Uncommon in the Pentateuch, cf. Gen 38:25 wṭwbwy kl 'nš dmgly ^{c}wbdwy 'and happy is every man who reveals his works' (no MT), and Deut 33:29 ṭwbykwn yśr'l mn kwwtkwn 'happy are you, Israel, who is like you?' (MT 'ašreykā yiśrā'ēl mî kāmôkā).

\+ lwwy 'if only': Common in the phrase 'n lwwy, cf. Gen 23:13 lḥwd 'n lwwy 't mqbl mny 'but if only you would listen to me' (MT 'ak 'im-'attā lû šəmā^{c}ēnî), especially in 'n lwwy mn ytn ... 'if only, who would give ...' (e.g., Deut 5:29, 28:67), for MT mî yittēn. Note particularly Exod 16:3 'lwy (< 'n lwy?) my (sic) ytn, also for MT mî yittēn and Num 23:10, where there appears to be a conflated reading of the poetic passage: lwwyy tyhwy swpyh 'lwwy tyhwy 'ḥryth hz^{c}yrh dbhwn 'would that his end will be, would that his last day will be as (that of) the least among them' (MT ... ûtəhî 'aḥ^{a}rîtî kāmōhû). Cf. 'lwwy above.

3. Negatives

\+ l' 'no', 'not': Common in verses without Vorlage and also for MT lō' (and 'al) in a variety of functions:

i) as an interjection: Gen 18:15 l' 'rwm gḥkt 'no but you did laugh' (MT lō' kî ṣāḥāqt), Gen 27:21 h' 't hw' dyn bry ^{c}św 'w l' 'are you really my son Esau, or not' (MT ha'attā ze bənî ^{c}ēśāw 'im-lō'), Num 13:20 h' 'yt bh 'ylnyn 'w l' 'are there trees in it, or not' (MT h^{a}yeš bāh ^{c}ēṣ 'im-'ayin);

ii) negating an adjective: Gen 7:2 dy l' dky' hw' 'which is not clean' (MT '^{a}šer lō' ṭəhōrā);

iii) negating a noun or nominal phrase: Gen 20:12 lḥwd l' brth d'mh 'but not the daughter of my mother' (MT 'ak lō' bat-'immî), Deut 5:3 l' ^{c}m 'bhtn qyym YYY yt qyymh hdyn 'not with our fathers did the Lord establish this covenant' (MT lō' 'et-'^{a}bōtênû kārat YHWH 'et-habbərît hazzō(')t);

iv) negating a possessive; Gen 15:13 b'r^{c}' dl' dydhwn 'in a land which is not theirs (MT bə'ereṣ lō' lāhem);

v) negating a verb in the perfect or imperfect: Deut 8:4 lbwšykwn l' blwn m^{c}ylwykwn wrglykwn l' hlykw ḥpyyn 'your garments did not wear out from off you, and your feet did not go unshod' (MT śimlātəkā lō' bālətā mē^{c}āleykā wəraglǝkā lō' bāṣēqā), Gen 18:15 l' gḥ<k>t 'I did not laugh' (MT lō' ṣāḥaqtî);

vi) as a negative imperative/jussive: Gen 35:17 l' tdḥlyn 'do not fear' (MT 'al-tîr'î), Exod 20:5 l' tsgdwn lhwn 'you shall not bow down to them' (MT lō'-tištaḥwe), Gen 31:35 l' yb'š b'pwy drybwny 'let it not be evil in my master's sight' (MT 'al-yi(ḥ)ḥar bə^{c}ênê '^{a}dōnî), Exod 20:7 l' ysb gbr mnkwn 'let not any man from among you take' (MT lō' tiśśā').

l' is also used in idiomatic expressions:

i) l' ... wl' 'neither ... nor', e.g., Gen 26:35 l' mn yṣḥq wl' mn rbqh 'neither from Isaac nor from Rebecca' (no MT), Gen 30:22 l' lml'k' wl' lśrp (sic) 'neither to an angel nor to a seraph' (no MT);

ii) wl' ^{c}wd 'and no more', e.g., Gen 2:23 hd' zmn' wl' ^{c}wd 'this time and no more' (MT zō(')t happa^{c}am).

\+ lyt '(there) is not': This occurs translating MT 'ên etc., and also in idiomatic paraphrases:

i) it functions as the negative of 'yt (see Predicate of Existence, below): Gen 4:8 lyt dyn wlyt dyyn etc. 'there is no justice and there is no judge ...' parallel to 'yt dyn w'yt dyyn etc. 'there is justice and there is a judge ...' later in the same verse (no MT). As such, it translates MT 'ên, e.g., Num 14:42 lyt 'yqr škynth dYYY šry ^{c}lykwn 'the glory of the Shekinah of the Lord does not dwell upon you' (MT 'ên YHWH bəqirbəkem), Gen 37:24 lyt byh myyn 'there is no water in it' (MT 'ên bô māyim);

ii) it also translate 'ên + suffixes: Gen 20:7 w'yn lyt 't mḥzyr yth 'and if you do not return her' (MT wə'im 'ênkā mēšîb), Gen 39:9 lyt rb wšlyṭ bbyth hdyn mny 'there is none greater or more powerful in this house than I' (MT 'ênennû gādôl babbayit hazze mimmennî);

iii) it occurs as the negative of possession: Gen 15:1 lyt ly ḥwl<q> l^{c}lm' d'ty 'I have no part in the world to come' (no MT), Exod 22:1 lyt lyh ḥwbt špykt 'dm zkyy 'he shall not have guilt for spilling innocent blood'

(<MT 'ên lô dāmîm), Num 20:5 'wp l' myyn lyt ln lmšty 'even water we do not have to drink' (<MT ûmayim 'ayin ləštôt);

iv) it occurs often as the negation of a participle (for MT imperfect or participle): Deut 1:9 lyt 'nh ykyl 'I am not able' (MT lō'-'ûkal), and see also Gen 44:26 and Num 13:31 (lyt 'nn yklyn 'we are not able'), Deut 7:22 (lyt 'twn yklyn 'you (pl) are not able'), etc., Deut 1:32 lyt 'twn mhyymnyn 'you (pl) do not believe' (MT 'ênkem ma'amînim), Exod 32:1 lyt 'nn ydᶜyn 'we do not know' (MT stative perfect lō' yādaᶜnû), etc.;

v) note the following idioms: (a) Gen 18:1 lyt 'pšr lḥd mml'ky mrwm' dy ... 'it is not possible for one of the heavenly angels that ...' (no MT), and see also Gen 4:14, 29:15, etc.; (b) Num 14:16 lyt yklh qdm YYY 'there was (= is) not the ability before the Lord'⟶ 'it was not possible for the Lord' (<MT mibbiltî yəkōlet YHWH), and cf. the parallel positive phrase in vs 14:12 (and also Exod 32:10) 'yt yklh qdmyy lmmnyh ytk l'wmh rbh wtqyph mnhwn 'there is the ability before me to appoint you as a people greater and mightier than them';

vi) note also the unusual negation of an imperfect verb in Gen 19:19 w'n' lyt 'wkl 'and as for me, I am not able' (MT wə'ānōkî lō' 'ûkal), cf. (iv) above.

4. Predicate of Existence

\+ 'yt 'there is': Usually translates MT yeš, e.g., Gen 18:24 mh dylm' d'yt ḥmšyn zkyyn bgw qrt' 'perhaps there are fifty righteous in the city' (MT 'ûlay yeš ḥᵃmiššîm ṣaddîqim bətôk hāᶜîr), Num 13:20 h' 'yt bh 'ylnyn 'w l' 'are there trees in it, or not' (MT hᵃyeš bāh ᶜēṣ 'im-'ayin). It is not the usual translation for MT yeš + suffixes, where a form of rᶜwt is preferred (e.g., Gen 43:4 'n brᶜwtk mšlḥh 'if (it is) in your wish (to) send', for MT 'im-yeškā məšallēᵃḥ, etc.), however cf. also Deut 13:4 h' 'yt rḥmyn yt 'wlpn 'wryyth dYYY 'is there love for the teaching of the law of the Lord?' (<MT hᵃyiškem 'ōhᵃbîm 'et-YHWH). It is also common in passages without Hebrew Vorlage, e.g., Gen 4:8 'yt dyn w'yt dyyn w'yt ᶜlm 'wḥrn w'yt mtn 'gr ṭb lṣdyqy' w'yt mtprᶜh mn ršᶜy<'> lᶜlm' d'ty 'there is justice and a judge and another world and the giving of good reward to the just and retribution exacted from the wicked in the world to come', and many other examples.

As the possessive, it translates MT *yeš l-*, e.g., Gen 33:9 *'yt ly sgyn* 'I have much' (MT *yeš-lî rāb*), or MT *l-*, e.g., Gen 27:38 *h' brkh ḥd' 'yt lk* 'do you have one blessing?' (MT *habərākā 'aḥat hî' ləkā*), and also often in paraphrase or untranslated passages, e.g., Lev 19:18 *'yt lh zkw bdynh* 'he has innocence in the law' (no MT), and especially Gen 31:29 *'yt ^{c}my ḥyl w'wklsyn sgyn* 'there are with me many soldiers and people' (MT *yeš-lə'ēl yādî*).

It is also to be found in idiomatic and other expressions, for example in translating the common MT *'^{a}šer b-* as *d'yt b-* 'in which there is' (the same is also found without *Vorlage*, e.g., Gen 30:22 *d'yt bhwn r^{c}w'* 'in which there is pleasure'). Noteworthy also are the constructions, the negative of which were discussed above (*Negatives*, *lyt*), *h' 'yt 'pšr* 'is it possible?' (e.g., Gen 18:14) and *'yt yklh qdm* 'there is ability before -- ' (e.g., Gen 4:13, Exod 32:10); similarly to be noted is the unusual example with finite verb in Gen 3:22 *'ylw nṭr mṣwth d'wryt' wqyym pqwdh 'yt hwh ḥy wqyym k'ln ḥyy' ^{c}d l^{c}lmyn* 'if he had kept the commandments of the law and observed its precepts, he would have lived and endured like the tree of life forever, (but now, since he did not ...)' in a midrashic expansion based on the MT *wə'ākal wāḥay lə^{c}ōlām*.

CHAPTER 6

PRONOUNS

1. Independent Personal Pronouns

The following forms are attested:

	Singular	Plural
1	'n'/'nh	'nn/'nḥn'
2m	't	'twn
f	't	---
3m	hw'	'nwn/'ynwn/'nn(!)
f	hy'	'ynyn/'nwn(!)

Remarks:

1s: The spelling 'n' predominates over 'nh at the rate of about 2:1

2fs There is no orthographic difference between the 2ms and the 2fs; the latter is recognized from context e.g., Gen 24:23 brt mn 't 'whose daughter are you?' (MT bat-mî 'att), and is only found in verses with Vorlage. There are two noteworthy examples in Gen 12:13, the form is written, in a cramped line, merely as א , apparently just a copyist error for את; also, in verse 11, the MT 'iššā yəpat mar'e 'ātt is translated as 't(!) špyrt ḥzy 't 'you are a woman beautiful of appearance'. Here, the first 't should probably be read as an error for 't' 'woman', rather than as apposition, or the like.

3ms: The expected hw' often appears to be written hy' due to the common w/y confusion in the MS, cf. Chapter 2, Orthography.

3fs: In Gen 35:6, the form is written hy, probably to be understood as an abbreviation, even though the expected abbreviation mark is absent (or else, a simple spelling error on the part of the copyist).

1pl: The common form in 'nn, either for MT '^{a}naḥnû e.g., Deut 5:3 'rwm 'lhn ^{c}mn h' 'nn kwln hkh ywmh hdyn ḥyyn wqyymyn 'but rather with us, behold, we, all of us here this day are alive and enduring' (MT kî 'ittānû '^{a}naḥnû 'ēlle pōh hayyôm kullānû ḥayyim), or for MT naḥnû, e.g., Exod 16:7,8 w'nn mh 'nn ḥšybyn 'and as for us, what are we accounted?' (MT wənaḥnû māh kî tallînû ^{c}ālēnû/wənaḥnû māh lō'-^{c}ālēnû tǝlūnnōtêkem), and also Gen 42:11, Num 32:32. The "archaic" 'nḥn' occurs once, in Gen 37:7, and note also Gen 13:8 where the MT kî-'ᵃnāšîm 'a(ḥ)ḥîm 'ᵃnaḥnû is translated in error as 'rwm hyk gwbryn 'ḥyn 'n' (sic, = 'nn) 'for we are like brothers'.[1]

2pl: The 2mpl does not occur frequently in the Pentateuch; the 2fpl is expected only in Gen 31:6, but here it is missing in favor of the Hebrew lemma, viz. w'tnh ydᶜtn ('rwm) ...[2]

3mpl: The spelling 'ynwn occurs twice as often as 'nwn. The form 'nn(!) only occurs in Gen 26:20 dynn 'nn my' 'the water is ours' (MT lānû hammāyim). This form may be influenced by the spelling of the previous word dynn 'ours', or, more likely, it may be emphatic opposition, i.e., the lpl pronoun (q.v.).

3fpl: The form 'ynyn only occurs once (Gen 33:6, subject lḥynth 'concubines', MT haššǝpāḥôt); elsewhere, the 3mpl '(y)nwn is used (e.g., Gen 21:29, subject šbᶜty 'mrt' h'yln 'these seven lambs', MT šebaᶜ kǝbāśōt hā'ēlle, Gen 28:8, subject bnthwn dknᶜnᶜ'y (sic) 'the daughters of the Canaanites', MT bǝnôt kǝnāᶜan, cf. also Gen 6:2).[3]

2. Pronominal Suffixes Attached to Singular Nouns

The following forms are found attached to nouns ending in a consonant:

	Singular	Plural
1	-y	-n/-nn/-n' (!)
2m	-k	-kwn
f	-(y)k	(-kwn)
3m	-(y)h	-hwn
f	-h	-h(y)n

When attached to nouns ending originally or presently in a vowel (e.g., 'ḥ) the forms are:

	Singular	Plural
1	'ḥy	'ḥwnn
2m	'ḥwk	'ḥwkwn
f	'ḥwk	('ḥwkwn)
3m	'ḥw(h)y	'ḥwhwn
f	'ḥwh	'ḥwhn

Remarks:

1s: There are occasional apparent spellings of the 1s suffix with -w, due to the w/y confusion previously mentioned, cf. Chapter 2, Orthography. With the two kinship terms 'b 'father' and 'm 'mother', the 1s suffix is replaced by the determined state either as a term of deference or as a vocative, e.g., 'bh/'b' 'my father' or 'oh father!' This should not be confused with occasional spelling errors, such as Exod 5:1 wyḥgwn qdm'(!) bmdbr' 'and they will celebrate a feast before me (!) in the desert', MT wəyāḥōggû lî bammidbār. Note should also be taken of the unusual form in Gen 37:9 š'lyn bšlmyy 'ask after my welfare' ⟶ 'give me greeting', written with -yy. This may indeed be the plural noun šlmyn, but this word does not usually occur in the plural in Aramaic (and nowhere else in this MS). The idiom is always used elsewhere in the singular (e.g., Gen 37:10 lmš'l bšlmk, and many other examples), and hence the example in Gen 37:9 may be simple copyist error.

2ms: The form is always -k (vocalized presumably -āk after consonants), with occasional rare errors of the plural suffix for the singular, e.g., Gen 27:40 ṣww'ryk 'your neck'. In Gen 17:2, the expected ytk is written ytn (!) with orthographic confusion of final n (ן) for final k (ך), cf. Chapter 2, Orthography.

2fs: The 2fs is ideally -yk (= -ik), but it is just as regularly written defectively -k (compare qltk 'your jug' in Gen 24:43 with qwltyk in Gen 24:14, etc.).

3ms: Again, the form is ideally -yh (= -eh), but it appears as often (if not more often) written defectively -h. Nouns ending in consonantal -y are written with one -y-, e.g., Gen 11:1 šrwyh 'its beginning' (i.e., šeruyeh).

There are some examples of nouns ending in א where the 3ms suffix would be expected, e.g., Gen 27:41 blb' 'in (his) heart' (MT bəlibbô) or Gen 36:32, 36:39 qrt' '(his) city' (MT ᶜîrô), which should be seen as the determined state of the noun, rather than as -' = -eh, however cf. the impossible form in Exod 4:3, tlq yt' (!) 'cast it' (MT hašlîkēhû), and also the form in Exod 5:1 (qdm') cited above. Attached to nouns ending in a vowel, the 3ms form is written -why/-wy (with equal frequency), e.g., 'bwy 'his father' (= 'əbuwi). Cf. 3ms suffix attached to plural nouns, section 3 below.

3fs: The 3fs is always -h (= -ah), also on forms ending in a vowel, e.g., 'bwh (= 'əbuh). Forms ending in consonantal -y can be spelled with one -y- or two, e.g., ptyh 'its breadth' (Gen 6:15) vs. ptyyh (Gen 13:17) (= putyah).

1pl: Following a consonant, the normal form is -n (= -an), following a vowel, it is -nn (=-nan), cf. plural nouns, section 3 below. The historical form -n' occurs less than a dozen times, and apparently only in ln' 'to us' (e.g., Gen 20:9, 31:14, Deut 1:22, and others, always for MT lānû and once in b'r^{c}n' 'in our land' (Gen 29:26, MT bimqômēnû). It should be noted that the 1 pl perfect G verb form ḥṭ'n' also occurs in the same Gen 20:9 passage; elsewhere, MT lānû is regularly translated ln.

There are a number of unusual 1pl suffixes in Genesis: in Gen 24:23, the hybrid form lnwn (!) occurs, however it appears that this is the Hebrew lānû (= MT) with a final -n added, following some space after the word, at the end of the line. Similarly, in Gen 34:16, the form lwn can hardly be a viable form in the language (e.g., *lon ⟵ lān) and is probably due to metathesis of the Hebrew form lnw (=MT). The unexpected ^{c}myn in Gen 44:18 (no MT) is also presumably metathesis by scribal error for ^{c}ymn.

2fpl: There is no separate form attested for the rarely occurring 2fpl suffix, cf. Gen 31:5 'bwkwn 'your father' (subject = Rachel and Leah), however this could be taken as 'bwkyn due to the w/y confusion common in this MS (this is unlikely considering the spelling of the 3fpl suffix -hn, cf. below).

3mpl: The suffix is generally written -hwn, however note the defective spelling in Gen 4:6 zywhn d'pyk 'your countenance', following the parallel verse 4:5, which has zywwhwn d'pyk. Similarly, the form in Gen 6:4 gybryn mpršyn bšmhn (paraphrasing MT 'anšê haššēm) 'warriors renowned by name' could be taken as a singular noun + suffix -hn, but is more probably the absolute plural form, i.e., šəmāhān.

Other noteworthy forms (all in Genesis) are 26:1 mlk'hwn 'their king', with a rare example of א as mater lectionis for the vocalic shewa in malkəhon; 1:28 lyhwn 'to them' (= lihon ⟵ l hon), with י as mater lectionis; and 5:2 šmwn (MT šəmām) 'their name', either šimhon ⟶ šimon, with syncope of the -h-, or more probably, a scribal spelling error.

3fpl: The ideal form is -hn, e.g., bhn, etc. The form lhyn is used very rarely, cf. Gen 26:18 lhn ... lhyn (corrected by Díez Macho to lhwn). In fact, the 3mpl lhwn is used often for the 3fpl, cf. e.g., Gen 19:33, and others, and the common confusion in this MS between the letters w/y, together with the general extension of the masculine forms to the feminine (cf. e.g., the 2pl above), indicate that all spellings -hyn should probably be read -hwn.

3. Pronominal Suffixes Attached to Plural Nouns

The following forms are attested:

	Singular	Plural
1	-yy/-y	-ynn
2m	-yk	-ykwn
f	-yk	---
3m	-why/-wy	-yhwn
f	-yh/-h' (-hh)	-yhn

Remarks:

1s: The normal spelling -yy (= -ay) occurs on plural nouns and prepositions taking plural suffixes, e.g., ᶜlyy, qdmyy, etc.; there are occasional spellings with single -y. There are numerous spelling errors in the MS due to w/y confusion, so, e.g., Gen 27:20 qdmwy = qdmyy, and many other examples. One unusual copyist error should be noted in Gen 27:46, bḥy (MT bəḥayyay) for bḥyy, presumably by mistaking the -y for the suffix rather than as one of the radicals of the word, and then writing that "suffix" with one -y rather than two.

2ms: The suffix is usually written -yk, though there are many instances of the spelling -k on both plural nouns and prepositions, e.g., bnk 'your sons' Gen 22:17; 'pk 'your face' Gen 20:15+; ᶜlk Gen 15:14; qdmk Gen 3:18+, etc. (cf. the Biblical Aramaic qərê).

2fs: The 2fs suffix is always -yk, though presumably not distinguished from the 2ms in pronunciation (i.e., both = -ak, due to extension of the masculine form to the feminine of section 2 above).

3ms: The suffix is usually written -wy (= -owi/-o'i), derived from an earlier -why (= -ohi). The development of this suffix is complicated: original -ahu > -au, to which the suffix was secondarily readded, -au + hu > -awhu > -ohu, with dissimilation to -ohi. This earlier form occurs occasionally in the MS, but its distribution appears to be limited to a number of nominals: the prepositions qdmwhy and ᶜlwhy, and the nouns bnwhy, ḥywhy, ydwhy, nšwhy, ᶜwlymwhy and ᶜyynwhy, i.e., all nouns that indicate inalienable possession (see Chapter 9, Syntax). The motivation for the retention of the historical spelling is not immediately obvious, but the limited distribution of the forms argues that they are clearly retentions and in no way reflect the actual pronunciation of the suffix. (The original suffix -hu > -hi, which has not undergone the development described above for -ohi, is seen on the forms *'bw 'father' and *'ḥw 'brother', i.e., 'bwhy = 'əbuhi, Gen 22:7 etc., and 'ḥwhy = 'əḥuhi, Gen 31:46, alongside the expected 'bwy/'ḥwy, although superficially these two separate suffixes appear to have had the same development.

There are a variety of noteworthy forms in Genesis:

(a) In Gen 27:41 'his life' is written ḥywby for ḥywwy, certainly a copyist error reflecting the medieval pronunciation of -w- as [v], i.e., ḥayyowi = [ḥayyovi], written ḥywby;

(b) There are occasional examples of the 3ms suffix for the 3fs on 'b/'ḥ in Genesis Chapter 29, apparently a scribal/copyist error due to the more common occurrence of the masculine suffix;

(c) Finally, the two forms mwy (dmbwl') 'waters (of the flood)' (7:7, 7:10, 9:11 and elsewhere) and ḥwy 'his life' (11:32) for expected mywy (not attested) and ḥywy (e.g., 5:7) appear to result from a misinterpretation of the -y- of myn as part of the plural suffix and not as a radical of the word. Hence the root m- was extracted to which the suffix was then attached, i.e., mowi. This was then presumably extended to hy(y)n, even though the -y- in this word = [yy] i.e., a doubled consonant, with the resulting ḥ- + suffix ⟶ ḥwy, i.e., ḥowi.

Of course, with the noun 'ḥ, the singular and plural forms with 3ms suffix are homographous, i.e., 'ḥwy = 'his brother' or 'his brothers', but presumably differed in pronunciation as in, e.g., Targum Onkelos, singular = '^{a}ḥuwi, plural = 'a(ḥ)ḥowi.

3fs: The suffix is usually written -yh, with occasional rare defective spellings -h,. e.g., Gen 24:46 m^{c}lwh 'from above her', Gen 21:19+ ^{c}yynh 'her eyes' (MT ^{c}êneyhā), indicating a pronunciation -ah, homophonous with the suffix added to the singular noun.

There are two examples in Genesis of the archaic suffix -h'/-hh (cf. e.g., the Genesis Apocryphon for similar archaic retentions): in 25:22 the MT bəqirəbāh is translated bm^{c}h' 'in her womb' (=bimə^{c}ehā?), vs. the expected m^{c}yyh in Gen 38:27; in 33:7, the MT wîlādêhā is transalted wbnhh (= wabənehā?), vs. the expected bnyh in Gen 3:15, plus other examples.

1pl: In accordance with the rule enunciated for the singular noun, i.e., following a vowel the suffix is always -nn, the 1 pl suffix is always found as -ynn (= -enan). Note also trynn 'the two of us'.

Noteworthy also is the form in Gen 29:22 b'rnn (!), clearly to be vocalized as plural be(')renan 'our wells' with the suffix written defectively (otherwise the suffix would have been written -n, as on a singular noun).

The only other exceptional form is ^{c}ln' 'over us' (Gen 37:8), translating MT ^{c}ālênû, apparently to be vocalized ^{c}əlenā (cf. Biblical Aramaic, Ezra 4:12 etc.), an archaism as in ln' and 'r^{c}n', see above, section 2.

2pl: The normal form of the 2mpl is -ykwn (= -ekon), with occasional defective spellings -kwn, e.g., Gen 3:5 wytptḥn ^{c}yynkwn 'and your eyes will be opened'. There are no 2fpl forms attested.

3mpl: Similarly, the 3mpl form is normally -yhwn (= -ehon), with occasional defective spellings -hwn, e.g., Gen 37:25 gmlhwn 'their camels' (MT gəmallêhem) inter alia. Note also Gen 36:7, where an apparent Hebrew suffix mmwnyhm(!) appears to result from a later hand ligaturing the Aramaic ון→ם, cf. Chapter 2, Orthography.

Noteworthy is the alternation in Genesis translating MT (bi)šəmōtām '(by) their names' (i.e., written defectively without -w- in the MT), between (b)šmtyhwn (25:13, 36:40), i.e., apparently imitating the plural Hebrew houn form + the Aramaic suffix, and šmhtwn (25:16), i.e., the "correct" Aramaic irregular plural form + the singular form of the suffix.

3fpl: The 3fpl suffix is usually written -yhn (= -ehen), with occasional examples of the 3mpl suffix extended to the feminine, e.g., Gen 31:43 bnyhwn 'their sons' (subject = bnty 'my daughters', MT bənêhen).

4. Demonstrative Pronouns

The following forms are attested:

ms	dyn / dn / dnh
fs	d'
m/f pl	'lyn / 'ylyn / 'ln

Remarks:

ms: The spelling dyn is only slightly more frequent than dn, both in passages for MT ze and in passages that have no Masoretic Vorlage. There are occasional instances of the older dnh for MT ze, usually in difficult passages not always well understood by the "translator," e.g., Gen 27:36 wh' ᶜqb yty dnh tryn zmnyn 'surely this one has been on my heels twice', for MT wayyaᶜəqəbēnî ze paᶜamayim, i.e., 'for he has supplanted me these (!) two times'.

fs: The fs d' translates MT zō(')t, and also occurs in passages without Vorlage, e.g., Gen 30:15 h' zᶜyr' hy' d' 'is this a little thing?', paraphrasing MT haməᶜaṭ. As in other Aramaic dialects, this feminine form is used for the "neuter," as in Gen 30:15, and also e.g., Gen 4:10 mh hy' d' dᶜbdt 'what is this that you have done?' (MT me ᶜāśîtā, cf. Gen 26:10). There are occasional translation errors, when a masculine Aramaic noun is treated as feminine because it translates a feminine Hebrew noun, e.g., Gen 17:10 d' qymy 'this is my covenant' (MT zō(')t bərîtî). Note also the unusual mistake(?) in Gen 36:10, d' r^{c}w'l bt bśmt 'this is Reuel, daughter of Bosmat', misinterpreting the Hebrew '^{e}lîpaz ben-^{c}ādā 'ēšet ^{c}ēśāw rə^{c}û'ēl ben-bośmat 'ēšet ^{c}ēśāw '(these are the names of the sons of Esau) Eliphaz son of Adah, wife of Esau, Reuel son of Bosmat, wife of Esau' by identifying Reuel with Eliphaz, and as a woman (?), perhaps due to a misunderstanding of the term 'ēšet ^{c}ēśāw 'wife of Esau'. However, cf. Gen 36:17, where Reuel is correctly identified as a male. Finally, in Gen 2:23, the demonstrative adjective is used for the pronoun, lhd'(!) y'y lmtqryh <'t'> 'this one is worthy of being called woman', paraphrasing MT ləzō(')t yiqqārē' 'iššā (perhaps due to dittography with the preceding hd' zmn').

pl: These are used primarily to translate MT 'ēlle. The spelling 'lyn predominates at the rate of about 5:1; there are rare examples of alternate spellings, e.g., 'lyyn and even 'ln (cf. e.g., Gen 36:10). The same forms are used for both mpl and fpl, cf. Gen 15:11, 'ylyn 'ynwn mlkwwt' d'r^{c}' 'these are the kingdoms of the earth'.

It is also used in a distributive sense, e.g., Exod 14:25 'mryn 'lyn l'lyn 'saying to each other' (no MT), and especially Lev 24:17 b'lyyn wb'ylyn 'in both (sets of cases)', and cf. Num 15:34 and Num 27:5 for two other occurrences of the same midrash with the same expression.[4]

5. Demonstrative Adjectives

The attested forms are:

	Proximate	Distant
m s	hdyn/ hdn (dyn/ dn)	hhw' (hw')
f s	hd'/ hdh (d')	hhy'
m/f pl	h'lyn/ h'ylyn/ h'yln ('lyn)	h'ynwn

Remarks:

Proximate:

ms: The spelling hdyn predominates at the rate of about 7:1; the adjective commonly translates MT hazze, often in such phrases as bywm' hdyn, ptgm' hdyn, zmn' hdyn, etc. The normal position is postnominal, after all other adjectives, e.g., Gen 29:22 gbr' ḥsyd' hdyn 'this righteous man', however there are isolated preposed examples, e.g., Gen 28:17 hdn tr^{c}' 'this gate' (no MT), the motivation for which is not apparent.

There are also occasional examples of the demonstrative pronoun dyn/dn used for the adjective (cf. Section 4 above), e.g., Gen 4:14, 17:26, 31:43 ywm' d(y)n 'this day', Exod 32:1 dn mšh 'this Moses'.

fs: The fs usually translates MT hazzō(')t; the spelling hd' is twice as frequent as hdh. The form is common in the phrase bš^{c}t' hd' 'at this time', and especially in Genesis, 'r^{c}' hd' 'this land'. In one instance (Gen 2:23) the adjective precedes the noun it modifies, hd' zmn' (!) 'this time', in imitation of the MT zō(')t happa^{c}am. Cf. the ms above for the "correct" phrase. There are also occasional examples of the demonstrative pronoun (d') usd for the adjective (cf. the ms above), usually where the MT has zō(')t, but note especially Gen 24:65 mn hw' d' gbr' (sic) 'who is that man?' for the opaque archaic MT form mî hā'îš hallāze.

pl: The common spellings are h'lyn and h'ylyn, rarely h'yln, and usually for MT hā'ēlle, especially in the phrase ptgmy' h'lyn 'these things'. The normal position is postnominal, however, cf. the demonstrative pronoun used for the adjective preposed at least once, Gen 14:3 kl 'lyn mlkyy' 'tḥbrw 'all these kings were joined together', clearly based on the MT kol-'ēlle ḥobrû; for the pronoun replacing the adjective postnominally, see, e.g., Gen 19:8 lgbry' 'lyn 'to these men' (MT lā'^{a}nāšîm hā'ēl) and other examples where the Masoretic text contains uncommon forms or unusual syntax.

Distant:

ms: The form commonly translates MT hahû', especially in fixed phrases such as 'tr' hhw' 'that place', lyly' hhw' 'that night', and ywm' hhw' 'that day'. There are occasional examples of hw' for hhw', always in imitation of the MT, e.g., Gen 19:33 ballaylā hû' as blyly' hw'.

fs: Always translates MT hahî', especially in the common phrases 'r^{c}' hhy' 'that land', bš^{c}t' hhy' 'at that time', and bšt' hhy' 'in that year'.

pl: An uncommon form, usually in the phrase bywmyh h'ynwn 'in those days' (e.g., Gen 6:4, for MT bayyāmîm hāhem).

6. Interrogative Pronouns

'yy 'how': Unusual, in Deut 7:17 (MT 'êkā); cf. the more common 'ykdyn/hyk below.

'ykdyn 'how': The more common translation of MT êkā/'êk, e.g., Deut 1:12; cf. also Deut 18:21 for the unusual defective spelling 'kdn (!), and hykdyn, below.

'n 'where': The common translation for the MT idioms 'êpōh (e.g., Gen 37:16); 'ê (e.g., Deut 32:37); and 'ayyē (+ suffixes, e.g., Gen 18:9, Exod 2:20, MT 'ayyô = 'n hw'); also common in paraphrase, cf. Gen 3:9 'n hy' mṣwth dpqdt ytk 'where is the command that I commanded you (based on MT 'ayyekkā). Cf. hn, below.

hyydh 'which': fs (cf. hyydyn, below), in the idiom found in the parallel verses Deut 4:7 and 4:8 (and 4:33 based on the preceding two) hyddh 'wmh wmlkw d- 'which (is) a (= the) people and kingdom who--' (based on MT mî gôy gādôl; 4:33 = ^{c}am).

hyydyn 'which': ms (cf. hyydh above), also based on MT mî, in Deut 5:26 hyydyn kl bśr' dy 'which (is) any flesh that ...' (i.e., 'who are the human beings who ...', MT mî kol-bāśār). For examples without Hebrew Vorlage, cf. Gen 15:11 hyydyn hw' ṭyys' dn 'which (one) is this bird?', and Lev 24:12 bhydyn dyn' mqṭlyn ytyh 'by which judgement they should kill him' (note that this final explanatory sentence is missing from the other three examples of this midrashic passage, the "Four Cases of Moses", Num 9:8, 15:34, and 27:5).

hn 'where': Only once, in Gen 4:9, spelled with the Hebrew vowel (הָן), presumably to indicate the pronunciation of an unfamiliar word: hn hw' hbl 'ḥwk 'where is Abel your brother?' (MT 'ê hebel 'āḥîkā); cf. 'n, above, and lhn, below.

hyk 'how': For MT 'êk, e.g., Gen 26:9, 44:8, etc., and cf. hykdyn, below.

hykdyn 'how': Usually written as one word, e.g., Gen 39:9, Exod 6:12 (both for MT 'êk), however note, e.g., Gen 44:8 hyk kdyn ngnb 'how then shall we steal' (MT 'êk).

l'n 'whither': For MT 'ānā, e.g., Gen 16:8, Deut 1:28, and many other examples.

lhn 'whither': Only once, Num 22:30, lhn 't 'zl bl^{c}m ršy^{c}' 'whither are you going, evil Balaam?' (no MT), cf. hn, above.

lmh 'why': For MT lammā, usually in the phrase lmh k^{c}n (however, cf. Gen 12:19). Note, however, that the preferred expression for 'why' is the composite bgll mh (e.g., Gen 4:8, no MT); in addition, MT maddû^{ac} is similarly always translated mn bgll mh, e.g., Gen 26:27, Exod 18:14 (note apparent error forms in Exod 3:3, mn bgll (!), and Gen 40:7 mn bgll mn (!)).

mh 'what': Translates MT mā.

mn 'who': Translates MT mî. There are occasional spelling errors, e.g., Gen 3:11 m'n, and occasional instances of mh for mn (e.g., Gen 27:18). Noteworthy also is Gen 38:25 dmn 'ynwn 'to whom do these belong?' (based on MT ləmî).

mn 'n 'whence': Translates MT mē'ayin; note especially the unusual form in Gen 16:8 mnn(!) 't 'tyyh 'whence are you coming?' (MT 'ê-mizze bā(')t), and cf. mn hn, below.

mn hn 'whence': Only once, Num 11:13 mn hn 'yt ly bśr 'whence should I have flesh?' (MT mē'ayin lî bāśār), cf. hn, lhn, above.

ᶜd 'ymt 'how long', 'until when': The standard translation for MT ᶜad-mātay, e.g., Exod 10:7, Num 14:27 (spelt ᶜd 'mt in Exod 10:3). Note also Exod 8:5, for MT ləmātay, and Num 14:11 (twice) spelt ᶜd 'mty/'ymty, paraphrasing MT ᶜad-'ānā.

7. Relative Pronoun

The relative pronoun can be written either dy or d-. When it translates MT 'ᵃšer, dy predominates over d- at the rate of about 3:1. Otherwise, there appears to be no motivation for the use of one form over the other; however, as a nominalizer, the form d- clearly predominates (see below). Parenthetically, one should note some isolated examples where no relative pronoun occurs where it is expected: Gen 28:13 'rᶜ' 't dmk ᶜlh 'the land upon which you are sleeping' (MT hā'āreṣ 'ᵃšer 'attā šōkēb ᶜāleyhā) and, in a verse without a Masoretic Vorlage, Gen 27:27 hw' ṭwr' brk ytyh ḥy wqyym kl ᶜlmy' YYY 'this is the mountain which he who lives and endures for all eternity, the Lord, has blessed'. Other uses of the relative pronoun are:

(a) often in paraphrase of a Hebrew participle, e.g., Gen 1:11 dtyn dᶜśb dmzryᶜyn zrᶜ 'the plants of grass which produce seed' (MT deše' ᶜēśeb mazrîᵃᶜ zeraᶜ, and for a determined participle, Gen 2:13 hw' dḥzr wmqp yt kl 'rᶜ' dkwš 'it is the one that returns and encompasses all the land of Kush' (MT hû' hassôbēb 'et kol-'ereṣ kûš), or Num 24:4 (24:16, etc.) 'ymr dšmᶜ mymr mn qdm YYY 'an utterance of one who has heard a word from before the Lord' (MT nə'ūm šōmēᵃᶜ 'imrê-'ēl;

(b) introducing the apodosis of a "cleft sentence,"[5] e.g., Gen 34:41 l' y'h hw' dyhwwn 'mryn ... brm y'y hw' dyhwwn 'mryn 'it is not right that they should say ... but it is right that they should say' (no MT), and especially the example in Gen 28:16, which has no antecedent marker expressing 'it is', 'yqr škynh dYYY dšryh (sic) b'trh hdyn '(it is) the glory of the Shekinah of God that is dwelling in this place' (MT yeš YHWH bammāqôm hazze).

(c) as a nominalizer, 'the one who', 'that which', commonly (but by no means exclusively) following the direct object marker yt, often appearing to imitate MT 'et 'ᵃšer, e.g., Gen 28:15 yt dmlylyt lk 'that which

I spoke to you' (MT *'et '^{a}šer-dibbartî lāk*), and especially Num 22:6, where the copy is most obvious, *yd^{c} 'nh dy 't mbrk yhwwy mbrk wyt mh dy (!) 't lyyṭ hwwy (!) lyṭ* 'I know (that) that which you bless will be blessed and that which you curse will be cursed' (MT *yāda^{c}tî 'et '^{a}šer-təbārēk məbōrāk wa'^{a}šer tā'ōr yû'ār*.

For the accusative not based on Hebrew *'et*, see Exod 4:12 *w'lp ytk yt dy tmll* 'and I will teach you that which you shall say' (MT *wəhôrêtîkā '^{a}šer tədabbēr*) or Exod 15:26 *wdšpyr b'pwy t^{c}bdwn* 'and that which is good in his sight you shall do' (MT *wəhayyāšār bə^{c}ênāyw ta^{ca}śe*).

The relative pronoun is also used in the nominative, e.g., Gen 22:10 *dnks l' m^{c}kb wdmtnks pšṭ ṣw'ryh* 'the one who sacrifices does not hesitate and the one who is sacrified stretches out his neck' (no MT).

In a number of verses in Balaam's prophecies (Num 23:7 to Num 24:19), the often-recurring MT *ya^{ca}qōb ... yiśrā'ēl* 'Jacob ... Israel' are translated by *dbyt y^{c}qb ... dbyt yśr'l* 'those of the house of Jacob ... those of the house of Israel'. Most noteworthy are three cases (23:23, 24:5, *bis*) of *ddbyt yśr'l/y^{c}qb* '(some of ?) those of the house of Israel/Jacob' -- the first, however, may be an error for *ldbyt yśr'l*, as it follows *lbyt y^{c}qb*; the last two appear in a paraphrase of the famous verse MT *ma-ṭṭōbû 'ōhāleykā ya^{ca}qōb miškənōteykā yiśrā'ēl*, and this verse is characterized by a number of unusual forms,
transmission errors, and the like (including the final phrase *wmšknyhwn dy ḥzwr ḥzwr lh dy(!) dbyt yśr'l* 'and their tents which are round about it, those of those of the house of Israel'). The "expected" nominalized form is also found, e.g., Exod 4:13 *šlḥ k^{c}n byd dn dḥmy lyh lmštlḥ'* 'send, now, by the hand of he who is worthy to be sent' (MT *šəlaḥ-nā' bəyad-tišlāḥ*).

(d) followed by a preposition + resumptive suffix referring to the antecedent of the relative, e.g., Gen 38:25 *bmklwt' d'ynš mykl byh* 'by the measure by which a man measures' (no MT);

(e) in possessive idioms, e.g., Gen 38:25 gbr' d'ylyn dylyh 'nh m^c^brh ... dmn 'ynwn ^c^zqth wšwtp' whwṭr' h'ylyn mynyh 'nh m^c^brh 'the man to whom these belong, by him am I pregnant ...the one to whom these ring, cord, and staff belong, by him am I pregnant' (no MT), or Num 16:5 wyd^c^ (sic) YYY mn dmn dydh 'and God will make know who is his' (MT wəyōda^c^ YHWH 'et-'^a^šer-lô, cf. above).

8. Indefinite Relative Pronouns

This term encompasses a number of idioms compounded with kl, mn, mh + d (and occasionally dy), usually translated 'whoever', 'the one who', etc.

bkl d 'wherever':	For MT bəkol '^a^šer, e.g., Gen 28:15 (possibly a Hebrew calque).
kl d 'whoever', 'whatever':	Usually for MT kol + determined participle, e.g., Gen 4:15 kl dyqṭwl qyn 'whoever kills Cain' (MT kol-hōrēg qayin), or Gen 21:6 kl dšm^c^ 'whoever hears' (MT kol-haššōmē^ac^); or for MT kol ('^a^šer), e.g., Gen 7:8 kl drḥyš 'whatever crawls' (MT kōl '^a^šer rōmēš, and cf. Gen 1:30 kl drḥš, MT kōl rōmēš).
kl mh d 'whatever' 'that which':	Usually translates MT kol '^a^šer. Cf. without Vorlage, e.g., Gen 3:19 kl mh d^c^bdt 'whatever you have done'. There are occasional errors with kl mn d for kl mh d, e.g., Gen 7:5.
kl mn d 'whoever', 'the one who':	Apparently a variant for kl d (see above), e.g., Gen 3:24 lkl mn dl^c^y bh 'for whoever studies it' (no MT), or Exod 15:1 kl mn dmtg'y qdmwy 'whoever exalts himself before him' (no MT, in the midrashic expansion of the Song of Moses). Note the unusual spelling kl m'n d in Gen 20:16, with א as an internal mater lectionis (MT kol '^a^šer). Cf. the following idiom mn d, and Chapter 2, Orthography).
mn d 'whoever', 'the one who':	The most common of the three possibilities (cf. kl d, kl mn d). Usually used to translate MT determined participles, and occasionally for MT '^a^šer (= 'the one who',

'that which'), e.g., Gen 9:6 mn dšpk 'dmyh dbr nš 'whoever spills the blood of a man' (MT šōpēk dam hā'ādām), Gen 7:23 wmn dhwh ^{c}myh btybwt' (MT wa'^{a}šer 'ittô battēbā). Common in paraphrase and in midrashic expansions, e.g., Gen 2:9 mn dhwh 'kl mnh 'whoever would eat from it', Exod 3:14 mn d'mr whwh ^{c}lm' mn šrwy' ... 'the one who spoke, and the world existed from the beginning ...' (based on the name of God in the MT 'ehye), Num 24:9 mn dmbrk ythwn yhwwy mbrk wmn dlyyṭ ythwn yhwwy lyṭ 'whoever blesses them will be blessed and whoever curses them will be cursed' (based on the poetic MT məbār^{a}keykā bārûk wə'ōrəreykā 'ārûr, and cf. also Num 22:6, cited above, 7(c) Relative Pronouns, for a different idiom, and also Gen 27:29 for a translation based on the Balaam verses).

mh d 'whatever': Translates MT '^{a}šer (='that which', cf. kl mh d, above) e.g., Gen 9:24 mh d^{c}bd lyh 'what he had done to him' (MT '^{a}šer-^{c}āśā-lô), and MT determined adjectives, e.g., Gen 16:6 mh dšpyr 'that which is good' (MT haṭṭôb) or Gen 32:14 mh d'yty 'that which he had brought' (MT habbā'). For further paraphrastic usage, see, e.g., Gen 31:39 mh dhwwn gnby' gnbyn b'ymm' 'whatever the thieves used to steal during the day' (based on the difficult archaic MT form gənûbtî yôm).

9. Reflexive Pronoun

The only examples of an independent reflexive pronoun occur in the idiom mn^{c} grm- 'withhold (one)self', cf. Gen 27:40 mn^{c}yn grmyhwn mlml^{c}y b'wryyt' 'withholding themselves from studying the Law' (no MT), and Exod 32:10 mn^{c} grmk mn lmb^{c}y rḥmyn ^{c}lyhwn 'withhold yourself from praying on their behalf' (based on MT hannîḥā lî, in the story of the Golden Calf). The use of the reflexive pronoun is uncommon and appears to be restricted to this one idiom in two midrashic passages. Otherwise, the medio-passive stems regularly express the reflexive (see Chapter 8, Verbs). For grm = 'bone', cf. Gen 50:25 wtsqwn yt grmyy mn hkh 'and you will bring up my bones from here' (MT wəha^{ca}lîtem 'et-^{c}aṣmōtay mizze).

10. Miscellaneous Forms

Collected in this section are the nominal forms based on kl 'all' and the adverbial uses of the interjection kmh/mh 'how much!' etc. For the expression of the direct object, see below, Section 11.

+ kl 'everything', 'all', 'any': Always translates MT kol/kōl, and used often in verses without Vorlage, e.g., Gen 13:16 hyk mh dlyt 'pšr dy kl gbr lmymny (sic) yt ^{c}pr' d'r^{c}' 'just as it is impossible that any man count the dust of the earth'.

In the determined state kwl'/kwlh/kl'/klh 'everything', 'everyone', it either translates various forms of kol/hakkol, or is used in paraphrase etc., see e.g., Gen 20:16 w^{c}l kwl' 'twwkḥt 'and above all you have been justified', Gen 22:14 kwl' gly wydy^{c} qdmyk 'everything is revealed and known before you'. Note especially the unusual expression in Gen 34:31 kl' mn kl hdyn kl' yhww<y> škm br ḥmwr mlglg bnpšyh 'everything more than all this (?), that Shechem son of Hamor should not be proud in his soul'.

The noun is used commonly with possessive suffixes, e.g., Gen 34:16 kwln 'all of us', Exod 14:7 kwlhwn 'all of them' (MT kullô!), etc.

It is also used in partive expressions, e.g., Gen 31:39 kl ḥd mnhwn 'every one of them' (no MT). It should be noted that kl is generally not used in translating MT partitives in which the nominal form is repeated. Each expression is translated in a different manner, cf. e.g., Gen 39:10 ywm btr ywm 'day after day' (for MT yôm yôm), or Exod 36:4 gbr mn ^{c}bydth dy 'nwn ^{c}bdyn '(each) man from his work which they (!) were doing' (for MT 'îš 'îš mimməla(')ktô '^{a}šer hēmmā ^{c}ōśîm), etc.

+ kl dkn 'how much more so!': In a long midrash in Gen 44:18 based on the meeting in Egypt between Joseph and his brothers: dlm' l' 't'mr lk ... mh d^{c}bdw šm^{c}wn wlwy ... mn bgll ds'ybw bgwwh yt dynh ... kl dkn bgll bnymn 'ḥwnn 'perhaps it has not been told to you ... what Simeon and Levy did ... because they had defiled Dinah in it (i.e., Shechem) ... how much more so because of Benjamin our brother'. See ^{c}l ḥd kmh (wkmh) below for three other similar expressions in the same verse.

+ *kl mn d^{c}m* 'anything' (with negative ⟶ 'nothing'): In verses with Hebrew *Vorlage*, for MT (*kol*)-*mə'ûmā*, e.g., Gen 22:12 *wl' t^{c}bd lyh kl mn d'm* 'and do not do anything to him' (MT *wə'al-ta^{c}aś lô mə'ûmā*), or for MT *dābār*, e.g., Deut 2:7 *l' ḥsrtwn kl mn d^{c}m* 'you have lacked nothing' (MT *lō' ḥāsartā dābār*). There are also occasional positive examples, e.g., Gen 33:11 *'yt ly kl mn d^{c}m* 'I have everything' (MT *yeš-lî-kōl*). Note the variety of spellings; *kl mn d^{c}m*, *kl m'n d^{c}m* (Gen 39:6), *kl mh d^{c}m* (Gen 39:9), *klwm md^{c}m* (! Gen 30:31, and cf. Abraham Tal, *The Language of the Targum of the Former Prophets*, Tel Aviv, 1975, pp. 16-17). Cf. also *md^{c}m*, below.

+ *kmh* 'how (much)': Only one example, in a paraphrase of Balaam's prophecies in Num 24:5 characterized by a number of such forms (cf. *mh* below), *kmh ṭbn wnḥmn mmryh ^{c}tyd myytyyh ^{c}lykwn ddbyt y^{c}qb* 'how good and consoling are the words (that are) destined to come upon you, oh ones of the house of Jacob'.

+ *md^{c}m* 'anything': Usually found in the idiom *kl mn d^{c}m* (q.v. above), however see Exod 5:11 *l' mtmn^{c} mn pwlḥnykwn md^{c}m* 'nothing shall be withheld from your labors' (MT *'ên nigrā^{c} mē^{ca}bōdatkem dābār*).

+ *mh*/*m'* 'how (great, etc.)': For MT *ma(h)* 'how (great, etc.)' usually followed by an absolute state adjective, e.g., Gen 28:17 *mh dḥyl hw' 'tr' hdyn* 'how fearful is this place' (MT *ma(h)-nnôrā hammāqôm hazze*), or Gen 38:29 *mh tqpt* 'how you have become strong' (MT *ma(h)-ppāraštā*), and common in paraphrase, see, e.g., twice in the Song of the Sea, Exod 15:6 and 15:18 *ymnk mh hdyr' hy' bḥyl'* 'your right hand, how beautiful it is in strength' (based on MT *yəmînkā YHWH ne'dārî bakkō^{a}ḥ*), and *mh y'h hw' lk klyl mlkwt' YYY* 'how lovely is the crown of kingship to you, oh Lord' (no MT), or twice in Balaam's prophecies, Num 24:5 *mh y'yyn mšknyhwn dbyt y^{c}qb* ... *mh y'h hw' mškn zymn' dšry bynykwn ddbyt y^{c}qb* 'how beautiful are the tents of the house of Jacob ... how beautiful is the tent of meeting which dwells among you, oh ones of the house of Jacob (based on MT *ma(h)-ṭṭōbû 'ōhāleykā ya^{ca}qōb miškənōteykā yiśrā'ēl*).

Followed by an absolute state noun, meaning 'what a--', see e.g., Num 23:23 mh 'gr ṭb mtqn lkwn qdm YYY l^{c}lm' d'ty 'what a good reward is prepared for you before the Lord, for the world to come' (based on MT ma(h)-ppā^{c}al 'ēl).

11. Direct Object Marker

There are four methods used in the MS to mark the direct object of a transitive verb: yt, l-, zero, and by a pronominal suffix attached to the verb. The choice of one form over the other is often, though not entirely, dependent on the Massoretic Vorlage. For complete details and discussion, see Chapter 9, Syntax, Part One, Section B, below.

The most common expression of the direct object is yt. In passages with a Hebrew Vorlage, it usually translates MT 'et-/'ēt, and can even be misemployed for the MT 'et= 'with', e.g., Gen 39:2 whwh YYY yt ywsp 'And God was (with) Joseph', MT wayhî YHWH 'et-yôsēp.

The marker yt can also translate other MT prepositions, e.g., l -, Gen 29:13, etc., depending on the needs of the particular Aramaic verb, and it also occurs commonly with suffixes, yty, ytyh, ytn, etc.

Much less commonly occurring is the preposition l-, see Chapter 3, Prepositions, above. Its use is considerably more restricted than that of yt, being used with proper nouns, e.g., Gen 16:5 nsbyt lhgr 'I took Hagar', Lev 22:27 śrh yldh lyṣḥq 'Sara bore Isaac', Num 21:34 ḥm' mšh l^{c}wg 'Moses saw Og', or with nouns that are either associated with proper nouns or are substitutes for proper nouns, e.g., Gen 4:5 wlqyn wlqrbnyh l' qbl 'but He did not accept Cain and his offering', and Gen 34:1 s'ybw ... lbrtyh dy^{c}qb 'they defiled the daughter of Jacob'.

However, cf. Gen 24:14 w'p lgmlyk 'šqy 'and your camels also will I water'. As noted above, many counter examples of similar environments using either yt or Ø can be brought, and the motivations for the use of l- in these few cases (and those cited in Chapter 3) are not immediately apparent.

The use of Ø to mark the direct object is also not common, and usually occurs where the MT also has Ø. However, there are cases in passages with no Hebrew Vorlage, cf. Chapter 3, above for examples, and again the motivation for the use of this expression is not clear.

Most limited of all are those few examples with a pronominal suffix. In the books of Genesis and Exodus, twelve examples only were noted, eight imperfects, three perfects, and one participle. Most significant is the fact that in six of the twelve cases, the form attested is identical to that found in Onkelos in the same verse. However, it must be stressed that the verses are not identical in Neofiti and Onkelos, merely the specific verb form! Indeed the language of these verses is quite different, e.g.,

Exod 2:12 -- Neofiti = w'stkyl lhk' wlhk' wḥm' 'rwm l' hwwh tmn gbr wqṭl yt mṣryyh wṭmryh(!) bḥl';

Onkelos = w'tpny lk' wlk' wḥz' 'ry lyt 'nš wmḥ' yt mṣr'h wṭmryh (!) bḥl'.

'And he looked from side to side and saw that there was no one (there), and he killed the Egyptian and hid him in the sand'.

It is difficult to know how to interpret cases such as this (others can be found at Gen 21:13 'šwynyh; Gen 32:18 yš'lynk; Gen 35:12 'tnnh; Exod 3:15 šlḥny; and Exod 4:21 t^{c}bdynwn). There is no mimic of the language of Onkelos, however it is beyond the range of coincidence that these individual verbs should be identical, even in such a small sample. It is even more confusing when one realizes that, in Gen 32:18, Onkelos has y^{c}r^{c}ynk ^{c}św 'ḥy wyš'lynk, while Neofiti has y^{c}r^{c} ytk ^{c}św 'ḥy wyš'lynk 'my brother Esau will meet you and will ask you', i.e., both verbs in Onkelos have the suffixed direct object, whereas only the second verb of the pair in Neofiti has it!

NOTES

[1]Not to be corrected to 'nḥn', as suggested by Díez Macho, p. 69, given the preponderance of the form 'nn.

[2]Each verse in the MS is preceded by a one or two word quote of the beginning of the Hebrew verse. Occasionally, as in this case, the first Aramaic words of the verse are omitted, and the Aramaic continues as though the Hebrew lemma is part of the text.

[3]One might also see 'ynyn in Gen 33:6 as an error for 'ynwn, due to w/y confusion; otherwise, it is an archaic retention.

[4]In the fourth occurrence of this, the Four Cases of Moses midrash, the phrase is not used (Num 9:8).

[5]For a detailed discussion of the cleft sentence, see H. J. Polotsky, Etudes de syntaxe copte, Le Caire, 1944, p. 57-68; reprinted in Collected Papers, Jerusalem, 1971. See also Gideon Goldenberg, "Tautological Infinitive," Israel Oriental Studies I, 1971, pp. 36-85, especially pp. 50-59.

CHAPTER 7

NOUNS AND ADJECTIVES

The analysis presented here is based primarily on data collected from the book of Genesis,[1] however its results have been cross-checked and supplemented by reference to the other books of the Pentateuch in the MS.

PREFIX FORMS

A. Nouns Formed with Prefix m-

	Abs.	Det.	Cons.	Suff.
ms	mqtl	mqtl'/h	mqtl	mqtl-
mp	mqtlyn	mqtly'/h	mqtly	mqtly-
fs	mqtl'/h	mgtlt'/h	mqtlt	mqtlt-
fp	mqtln	mqtlt'/h	mqtlt	mqtlty-

1. Masculine Forms

a. Strong Roots

Common nouns are found such as mgdl/mgdl' 'tower', mdbḥ/mdbḥ' 'altar', mdnḥ/mdnḥ' 'east', m^{c}rb/m^{c}rb' 'west', mqdš/mqdš' 'sanctuary', etc., as well as some less well attested, e.g., mrḥq' 'abomination' (Gen 34:7), and m^{c}br 'crossing' (Gen 32:32). There are occasional unusual spellings, e.g., Gen 26:6, 29:1 mdynḥ', probably madnəhā ⟶ madnḥā ⟶ madinḥā, and mškynyn 'tents', presumably maškənin ⟶ maškinin, with matres lectiones for vocalic shewa. Nouns of this class are also attested commonly with suffixes, e.g., mdršhwn 'their study', mdršyhwn 'their studies', mtqlh 'its (ms) weight', mtqlhwn 'their weight', mšknyh 'his tent', mšknh 'her tent', and note also the spelling in Gen 35:21 mškwnyh 'his tent', presumably maškəneh ⟶ maškoneh.

b. Weak Roots

A well-attested set of classes:

(1) I-Weak: mymr/mymr' 'word', myšr/ myšr' 'plain', mbwl' 'flood', mtn 'giving, etc. Note the misspelt plural construct forms mšryh, myšryh, mšrh, all used in the phrase mšry ḥzw(w)h 'The Plains of the Vision', for

MT 'ēlōnê mamrē' 'The Plains of Mamre', the mistranslation and consequent misinterpretation apparently due to the homograph mmr' 'word', except in Gen 12:6, where the phrase translates MT 'ēlôn môre, which is apparently identified with 'ēlōnê mamrē'. With suffixes, e.g., mymry 'my word', etc., mṭwlhwn 'their burden', and cf. mṭlnwy 'his wanderings' in Nouns Formed with Suffix -(w)n', below.

(2) II-Weak: ml'k/ml'k' 'messenger', mmwn/mmwn' 'property', mrwm'/mrwmy' 'height(s)', mzwn 'food', mḥws 'insult'. Note also such misspellings as ml'kyh for construct ml'ky (Gen 28:12), and mdwrwnyn (!) 'dwellings', for mdwryn (Gen 6:14). Suffixes: ml'kyh 'his messenger', mzwnk 'your food', mdwryhwn 'their dwellings'.

(3) III-Weak: mr^{c}y 'pasture', and with suffixes, mšrwyk 'your dwelling', mšrwyyhw` 'their dwelling' (Gen 10:30), mštw‹y›hwn 'their foundations' (Gen 30:11, spelled mštwrhwn!).

(4) Geminate: mmll 'speech', mgn 'protection', myḥ` 'heat' (Gen 18:1), mṭlyn 'booths'.

(5) Double Weak: mytyy' 'comings' (Gen 33:18).

(6) Special Root: msq 'ascent' (Gen 19:15, root s-l-q).

2. Feminine Forms

a. Strong Roots

mptḥ/mptḥ' (sic!, in Gen 30:22, where the plural is mptḥn with femine numeral, but with other masculine modifiers), m^{c}rt' 'cave', mḥšbt 'thought' (construct), mktšyn(!) plagues (Gen 12:17, with f pl adjective rbrbn).

b. Weak Roots

(1) I-weak: mtnh/mtnth 'gift(s)', mwrkywn (presumably morkiwan)/mw‹r›kw(w)t' 'feeding troughs' (with confusion of -d- for -r-, see Chapter 2, Orthography), mpḥn (rwḥ) 'despairing (of spirit)', Gen 26:35. Suffixes: mṭrty 'my service', mynqth 'her nurse-maid', mdynthwn 'their states'.

(2) II-Weak: mklwt' 'measure' (?), three times in Gen 38:25. If this is from the root k-w-l, the form is presumably məkilutā.

(3) III-Weak: mṣwh/mṣw(w)th/mṣwwn 'commandment(s)' (Deut 7:10, mṣwwn qlylyn!. Note the misspelling in Gen 35:9, mrb<nyy>t' 'foster-mother', spelled mrbᶜyt', with a copyist error of עי for ניי. Suffixes: mṣwty 'my commandments', mṣwtyh 'its (fs) commandments'.

B. Nouns Formed with Prefix t-

This is not a well-attested class of nouns. The forms found, primarily in Genesis, are:

1. Masculine Forms

a. Strong Roots

tbšyl/tbšyl'/tbšylyn/tbšylyyh 'meal(s)', tḥmd' 'delight', tšlwmy 'payment(s)', Deut 19:21, Exod 21:24, and cf. twrgmn 'interpreter', in Nouns Formed with Suffix -(w)n', below.

b. Weak Roots

(1) I-Weak: twtb/twtbyn 'sojourner(s)'.

2. Feminine Forms

a. Strong Roots

(1) twšbḥ'/h/tšwbḥn 'praise(s)' (cf. also Exod 14:3, 15:11).

b. Weak Roots

(1) II-weak: ttwbh 'repentance'.

(2) III-weak: tḥyyt 'resurrection' (construct, Gen 25:34).

C. Nouns Formed with Prefix '-

Only occasional feminine forms are attested.

a. Strong Roots

'ḥsn'/'ḥsnh/'ḥsnt (construct) 'possession', 'rmlh 'widow', and cf. also 'rdᶜnyn 'frogs' in Nouns Formed with Suffix -(w)n', below.

b. Weak Roots

(1) Double Weak: 'wry(y)t' 'Law'.

SUFFIX FORMS

A. Nouns Formed with Suffix -w(t')

All nouns with this suffix are feminine.

	Abs.	Det.	Cons.	Suff.
fs	qtlw	qtlwt'/h	qtlwt	qtlwt-
fp	qtlw(w)n	qtlw(w)t'/h	qtlw(w)t	qtlw(w)t-

1. Strong Roots

A variety of spellings with matres lectionis w and y are included here.

a. qtlw: bqrwth 'cattle'; mlkw/mlkwwn/mlkwwt' 'kingdoms'; tpšwt (construct) 'stupidity' (Deut 10:16); plgw 'division'; pršwt (construct) 'crossing'; shdw/śhdwt'(!) 'witness' (Gen 21:30 and 31:47, respectively); (byny) šmšwt' 'twilight' (Exod 12:6, but cf. Gen 49:27 byny šmšyy').

b. qtwlw: bkwrwt' 'birth-right' (Gen 25:32).

c. qtylw: 'rykwt 'length'; knyšwt'/knyšwt (construct) 'confluence,' 'congregation'; mṣy^{c}wt (construct) 'middle'; qšyṭwt (construct) 'uprightness'; špykwt (construct) 'spilling'; tmymwt (construct) 'innocence'.

d. qwtlw: 'wmnwt (construct) 'craft'.

e. qytlw: zydnw 'wilfulness' (Lev 24:12).

f. Derived from the Gt stem: 'tpgšwt' 'meeting' (Gen 32:25), cf. 'ytbrywthwn, below.

g. With Suffixes: 'bylwtn 'our mourning' (Deut 26:14); bkwrty (sic) 'my birth-right' (Gen 27:36)/ bkwrwtyh 'his birth-right'; ṣdyqwtk 'your (ms) righteousness'.

h. With Prefixes: 'ḥsnw 'possession'; 'rmlwth 'widowhood'.

i. With Double Suffix: swkltnwtkwn 'your (mp) understanding' (Deut 4:6, and cf. the adjective swkltnyn 'clever' in the same verse); pwr^{c}nwth 'retribution' (Deut 32:35).

2. Weak Roots

a. I-Weak: 'ntw 'wifehood'; hymnw 'belief'.

With Suffixes: yldwty 'my kindred', yšrwtk 'your (ms) right conduct'.

With Prefixes: t(w)ldw(w)t' 'births' (in genealogical formulae).

With Suffixes: t(w)ldw(w)tyh etc. 'his births', etc.

b. II-Weak: ṭ'bwt(!) 'good thing', used adverbially ⟶ 'well' (Gen 30:34), apparently for ṭb'wt (e.g., Deut 9:21, the spelling ṭ'bwt apparently influenced by such words as Onkelos ṭ'b', cf. also ṭbw', however, also attested here is ṭ(y)bw 'goodness' (Exod 20:6, 34:7); śybw/sybw(!) 'old age' (the first, in Gen 15:15 and 25:8 probably influenced by the MT śêbā, cf. with suffixes, below. Contra, however, see Deut 32:25 gbryn sbyn 'old men', for MT poetic 'îš śêbā).

With Suffixes: sybwt(y)h 'his old age' (Gen 21:2, 21:7, Lev 22:27), but śybty 'my old age' (Gen 42:38, MT śêbātî).

c. III-Weak: 'sw 'cure'; b^{c}w 'grace'; dmw/dmwt (construct) 'image'; zkw/zkwth/zkwwt' 'merit(s)'; znw 'harlotry'; zpw 'loan' (Deut 23:20); ḥyzw 'appearance'; nbw 'prophecy'; ṣlw/ṣlwt' 'prayer'; ršw/ršwt' 'permission'; š(y)rw/šyrwt' 'meal'; tbw/t(y)bwt' 'ark'; thw 'regret'; ṭ^{c}wn 'idols' (Deut 4:8); l^{c}wt(!) 'toil' (Gen 3:18, cf. Onkelos for the spelling with ^{c} also, even though the root appears to be l-'-h).

Derived from the D stem: rmyw 'deception' (Gen 29:22); qšyw 'severity' (Exod 1:13,14).

Other: On formal grounds, the feminine ḥdw (=ḥedu)/ ḥdwh/ḥdwn 'joy(s)', with consonantal -w- in the determined, should also be considered here (cf. Gen 21:6 ḥdw rbh 't^{c}bd! 'a great joy has been done').

With Suffixes: dmwtyh 'his image', dmwtn 'our image'; zkwtk 'your merit', zkwwtk 'your merits', zkwwtyh 'his merits'; ṭ^{c}wwthwn 'their idols'; lwwty(!) 'my toil' (Gen 31:42, apparently ləwuti ⟵ lə'uti, cf. l^{c}wt above); r^{c}tkwn(!) 'your (mpl) favor' (= rə^{c}utkon?, Gen 24:49); (byt) šqwwtn 'our watering places' (Gen 29:22).

Other: Abstract nouns derived from other nominal forms include ṭlywty 'my youth'/ṭlywthwn 'their youth' (from ṭly 'young person'), špywtyh 'his peace' (from špy 'quiet'), and nśywtyh 'his leadership' (Num 11:26, from nśy' 'leader').

With Double Suffix: ^{c}nwwt<nw>tyk 'your (ms) humility' (Gen 35:9, spelled with an error of metathesis ^{c}nwwtwntyk, i.e., root ^{c}-n-h + n + wt).

With Prefixes: 'ytbrywthwn 'their creation' (Gen 2:4, derived from the Gt stem), twtbwtk 'your dwelling'/ twtbwtyhwn(!) 'their dwelling' (or 'dwellings'?, Gen 36:43).

d. Geminate: twrbwwt (construct) 'children' (root r-b-b), and note numerous spelling errors twrbbt (Gen 17:12), trbbt (Gen 17:23, 27), ttbbt! (Gen 17:13, see Chapter 2, Orthography).

B. Nouns Formed with Suffix -yt'

All nouns with this suffix are feminine.

	Abs.	Det.	Cons.	Suff.
fs	(qtlyt)	qtlyt'	(qtlyt)	qtlyt-
fp	qtly(y)n	qtly(y)t	qtly(y)t	qtly(y)t-

1. Strong Roots

a. There is only one example in the absolute, gpryt 'sulphur' (Gen 19:24), for the MT absolute goprît, and perhaps in imitation of it. However, cf. Deut 29:22 gpry!, for the same MT goprît. Other strong root examples have mater lectionis w, zhwryt' 'crimson thread' (Onkelos zəhoritā); qlwpyt' 'peel' (Jastrow, "Dictionary," p. 1373, qəlupitā), zr^{c}y(y)t (construct)/ zr^{c}yyt' 'progeny' (pl).

(1) Forms with Suffixes: zr^{c}y(y)ty 'my progeny', zr^{c}y(y)thwn 'their progeny', etc.

b. Strong Roots with Prefix: mrglyt'/mrglyyn (absolute = margaləyān?) 'pearl(s)'

2. Weak Roots

a. III-Weak: bkyth 'weeping'; rbyt'/h 'girl' (Note Gen 24:55 rbyty for MT hanna^{c}arā, with -y for -h or -').

(1) Forms with Suffixes: klytyh 'his wrath' (Onkelos = klwtyh, therefore perhaps w/y confusion); šryty 'my beam' (again Onkelos = šrwty, therefore perhaps w/y confusion); rbyth(!) 'her girls' (Gen 24:61, MT na^{ca}rōtêhā).

b. III-Weak with Prefix: mšryt'/mšry(y)n (absolute) 'camp(s),' (=mašrəyān?); mštyt' 'feast'.

C. Nouns Formed with Suffix -(w)n'

All nouns of this form are masculine. Adjectives formed with this suffix are either masculine or feminine, depending on the referent. Nouns derived from strong roots fall into three categories, with or without matres lectionis w/y: qtln, qwtln, qytln. There are two subcategories: Nouns with prefixes; and nouns derived from III-weak roots.

1. qtln

'bdn 'destruction' (Num 24:20); 'mtnyh 'fearful ones'; bsmnyh 'perfumes'; gzlnyn 'robbers'; sprwn 'scribe'; ^{c}lbnh 'humiliation'; ^{c}rbwn/^{c}rbwn' 'surety' (for MT (hā)^{c}ērābôn, Gen 38:17,18); qrbn 'sacrifice' (Lev 16:1); rḥmn' Merciful One; (Exod 34:6); šlṭwnyn 'rulers' (Gen 49:17).

a. With Suffixes: '<b>dnhwn 'their destruction' (Num 24:20, the b is added above the word); srḥny 'my offense'; ^{c}lbny 'my humiliation', ^{c}rbwnyh 'his surety'; qrbny 'my sacrifice', etc.; šlṭnwy 'his commanders'.

b. Feminine Adjective: ś^{c}rnyyn 'hairy' (=śa^{ca}rānəyān, for MT śə^{c}īrōt, Gen 27:23).

2. qwtln

'wlpn 'instruction'; ḥwšbn 'accounting' (cf. ḥšbnwy, below), ^{c}wrmn' 'serpent' (Gen 49:17); pwlḥn' 'worship' (Gen 21:9, but cf. plḥny etc. below, and plḥn' four other times in Genesis, plus construct plḥn, Gen 1:2, and absolute plḥn in Exod 1:14); pwr^{c}n 'avenger' (Deut 6:15, Exod 20:5); rwḥṣn 'safety'.

a. With Suffixes: kwprnyhwn 'their willages'; ḥšbnwy 'his accounts'.

b. Adjectival Forms: 'wḥrn 'other' (but cf. ḥwrn four other times in Genesis); swkltnyn 'clever' (Deut 4:6, with double suffix, -t-, -n-); swrbnyn 'rebellious' (Gen 26:35, feminine plural!); qwšṭnyn 'truthful' (Gen 42:16, Exod 18:21).

3. *qytln*

   zywtnyh 'distinguished ones' (Gen 14:5).

   a. *Adjectival*: *ryqn*/*ryqn'*/*ryqnyn* 'empty' (Gen 31:42, ms, Gen 1:2, fs, Exod 3:21, mpl).

4. *Nouns with Prefixes*

   'rd^{c}nyn/'rd^{c}ny' (!) 'frogs' (Exod 7:28ff, cf. Onkelos *^{c}urdə^{c}ān*, and once only in Neofiti, Exod 8:9 *^{c}rd^{c}nyy'*), *mṭlnwy* 'his wanderings' (Gen 13:3, root n-ṭ-l), *twrgmn* 'interpreter' (Exod 4:16, for MT *pe* 'mouth').

5. *III-Weak Roots*

   b(y)zywn 'disgrace', *mnyyn*/*mnyynh* 'counting', *nsywnh* 'temptation', *qny(y)n* 'possession', *rbbnyn* (!) 'chiefs' (Gen 25:16, perhaps a copyist error for *rbrbnyn*).

   a. *Suffixed*: *qnyynwy* 'his possessions'.

6. *Other*

   šwpnynyn 'turtle-doves' (Num 6:10, with suffix *-yn-*).

OTHER NOMINAL FORMS

Unlike those nouns formed by the addition of prefixes or suffixes, the following categories are marked by internal vowel patterns, at times spelled with *w* or *y* as *matres lectionis*, but not necessarily so. In general, the vocalizations offered are based on Targum Onkelos, except where a *mater lectionis* indicates a clearly divergent form. In those cases, a vocalization is suggested and the Onkelos is also given. In the following analysis, a noun is vocalized only the first time it appears, the other forms being easily derived, so for example, the vocalization of the absolute singular of *lbwš* 'clothing' is given as *ləbuš*, but not that of *lbwšyn* or *lbwšykwn* etc.

A. *Nouns of the Form qtwl*

These include the following vocalizations:-
(qətulā:) qətul; (qutlā:) qətol; (qātolā:) qātol; (qitolā:) qitol; (qittulā:) qittul; (qattulā:) qattul; (qittolā:) qittol.

1. *qətul*

   The largest category attested in the MS, in both the masculine and feminine, with no special discernible meaning.

a. Masculine Forms

lbwš/lbwšyn/lbwšy (construct) 'clothing'; lḥwš 'red'; qrḥ(:)/qr(w)ḥyn/ qrwḥy' (without -w- in Gen 30:32 and 31:8); blwṭ (construct) 'oak'; gbwl' 'border'; ḥbwš' 'imprisonment'; tḥwm' 'area'; krwbyh 'cherubs', etc.

(1) With suffixes: tḥwmh 'her area', tḥwmhwn 'their area', tḥwmyhwn 'their areas'; ḥbwšwy 'his prisoners'; lbwšwy 'his clothes', lbwšykwn your (m pl) clothes', etc.

b. Feminine Forms

btwlh/btwln 'virgin(s)'; khwnth 'priesthood', Exod 28:3 (abbreviated khnt` in Gen 14:18); ktwbh 'marriage contract'; nmwrt' (pl.) 'speckled'; qbwrh/qbwrt' 'burial-place'; qṭrt (?) 'incense' (construct, Gen 27:27); qrwḥt' (pl) 'white-spotted'; rṣw^{c}h 'strap'; šbw^{c}h/šbw^{c}th 'oath'.

(1) With suffixes: ybwmtyh 'his brother's wife' (cf. however, Onkelos yəbimtā, Deut 25:7,9); qbwrt` 'her burial-place' (Gen 35:20, for MT qəbūrātāh); šbw^{c}ty 'my oath'.

2. qətol

A common category with masculine nouns and also adjectival forms; no special meaning discernible

a. Masculine Forms

bkwr'/bkwrh 'first-born' (however, cf. Onkelos bukrā, therefore this may be a Hebraism, Gen 10:15 and 38:7 respectively -- also the form bkyr, below); ḥšwk' 'darkness'; lṭwm (absolute) 'a resin' (Gen 37:25); nhwr/nhwr'/nhwryn/nhwry' 'light(s)'; nmr(:)/nm(w)ryn 'speckled' (five times without -w-, twice with); ^{c}<bw>ry' 'passers-by' (?, in Gen 21:33 spelled ^{c}wbry', without Hebrew Vorlage, but perhaps nevertheless influenced by Hebrew ^{c}ōbərîm, or otherwise an assimilation to the bilabial, i.e., ^{ca}borayyā ⟶ ^{c}oborayyā, or most likely, a combination of these two); qṭwlyn 'slayings' (?, in Gen 37:33, qṭwlyn 'tqṭl ywsp 'Joseph has truly been slain', attempting to render the MT cognate infinitive ṭārōp ṭōrāp yôsēp; cf. qāṭolin 'murderers' below, with the same spelling);

qšwṭ 'truth' (Exod 34:6, Deut 22:20, cf. qwšṭ', Segholates, below); rḥwb' 'open place'; šḥwd 'bribe' (Deut 10:17); thwm' 'the Deep'.

(1) With suffixes: bkwrk 'your (ms) first-born', bkwr(y)h 'his first-born' (the forms spelled bkwrh may also be determined state).

b. Feminine Form

qṭrt (construct) 'incense' (Gen 27:27).

c. Other

Perhaps śm'lh (= śəmo(')lā) 'left' in Gen 24:49 (MT śəmō(')l), śm'l(y)h 'his left', Gen 48:13,14 (MT śəmō(')lô), and śml'hwn (?) 'their left', Exod 14:22 (MT śəmō(')lām) should be considered here also. Note that elsewhere MT śəmō(')l is translated by drwm (q.v , in (3.) below).

3. qātol

As in other Aramaic dialects, this category is used primarily as a nomen agentis (however cf. also dārom and pātor). Only masculine forms drwm'/drwmh 'south' (for MT negeb, śəmō(')l, and in Gen 36:34 ('ereṣ) hattêmānî, cf. śm'lh above); ḥmwdyn/ḥmwdyh 'covetors' (Deut 5:21); yrwt 'inheritor'; mtwly (construct) 'poets' (Num 21:27, mtwly mtlyyh, for MT hammōšəlîm); nṭwr' 'keeper'; prwq 'redeemer' (Exod 6:7); ptwrh/ptwr' 'table' (Exod 25:23,27); qṭwl/qṭwlyn 'murderer(s)', cf. 2. qaṭol 'above'.

a. Suffixes: ptwry 'my table' (Num 28:2, see Kaufman, "Akkadian Influences," pp.81-2).

b. Other

Perhaps 'dwnyh 'his lord', only in Gen 39:20, for MT 'ᵃdōnê (yôsēp) should be included here. This appears to be a Hebraism, for the expected rbwnyh (q.v., in (7.) below).

4. qitol

An obscure class. The only possible examples may indeed by classifiable elsewhere: 'šwn/'šwn' 'exact time', spelled thus everywhere except in Gen 18:5, in a midrashic expansion of the text, where the construct form b'yštwn(!) occurs, in 'rwm bgyn kdyn b'yštwn šyrwt' ᶜbrtwn 'for because of this at the time of the meal you have passed by', clearly for b'yšwn, the confusion apparently due to the similarity with b'yštwn 'you have done evil'. Furthermore, this is the only occurrence of the word in any form spelled with -y-, presumably also adding to the copyist's confusion. However, given the alternate Onkelos form '^{a}šun, see, e.g., Jastrow, "Dictionary," p. 60, perhaps this belongs in the category qətul, above (see also Kaufman, "Akkadian Influences," p. 59, especially n. 134); qyṭwr'/qyṭwr (construct) 'smoke', only in Gen 19:28 for MT qîṭôr, therefore perhaps a Hebraism (or possibly qiṭṭurā in Aramaic). Cf. Pseudo-Jonathan ad loc., quṭrā.

5. qittul

A well-attested class, primarily of abstract nouns. Only masculine forms are attested: yḥws (construct) 'genealogy' (=yeḥus<*yiḥḥus), usually used in Genesis in the phrase yḥws twldwwth, etc. for MT tôldōt (note Gen 37:2, yyḥws), however cf. forms with suffixes, below; nswkyn 'libations'; sdwr 'arrangement', cf. Gen 1:16 sdwr kwkby' 'arrangement of the stars', for MT hakkôkābîm, Num 28:2 lḥm sdwr ptwry 'the bread of the arrangement of my table', expanding MT laḥmî, and especially Lev 24:6,7 sdwryn (twice)...sdwr for MT ma^{ca}rākôt...ma^{ca}reket[2]; smwq' (m.s. det)/smwqh (f.s.abs.) 'red' (in Gen 25:30 and Num 19:2, respectively, for MT hā'ādōm/'^{a}dūmmā); ^{c}ybwr/^{c}ybwr' 'grain' (Gen 27:28,37, Num 18:27 [^{c}ybwr'], Deut 28:51, all for MT dagan[3]; p(y)qwdy' 'commandment(s)'.

a. Other forms:

Possibly qyṭwr/qyṭwr' in Gen 19:28, cf. qitol, above. One might also include here slq 'ascent' (= silluq?), in Gen 32:26, however cf. 32:24 slyq (but this may be slwq, with w/y confusion).

(1) With suffixes: ḥsdyy 'my shame' (=ḥissuday?); pqwdh 'her commandment' (Gen 3:22, but possibly the plural noun, with the 3fs suffix spelled defectively), pqwdyh 'her commandments' (Gen 3:24, and pqwdyyh!, Gen 3:15, therefore perhaps all should be interpreted as determined state plural).

6. qattul

A small class, attested only by inanimate objects. 'bwb' 'flute'; 'twnh/'twn'/'twn (construct) 'oven', including Gen 11:3, abbreviated 'twn`; ^{c}mwd/^{c}mwd'/^{c}mwd (construct) 'pillar'.

7. qittol

A small class, with no distinguishable semantic content.

a. Masculine Forms

gywryn 'strangers'; knwr' 'lute' (Gen 4:21, for MT kinnōr, and possibly in imitation thereof, cf. Gen 31:27 kynryn (= kinnārin?), also for MT kinnōr; ^{c}dnh/^{c}(y)dn'/^{c}dn and ^{c}dwny (constructs) 'appointed time', usually for MT mô^{c}ēd. At the same time, the MS translates lə^{c}ēt ^{c}ereb in Gen 8:11 and 24:11 by l^{c}dwny rmš' (the same translates lipnôt ^{c}ereb in Gen 24:63) and hērōnēk in Gen 3:16 by ^{c}dwnyk. Hence, it appears that these are two separate words with similar meanings, ^{c}iddānā 'appointed time' and ^{c}iddonā 'period', specifically 'menses' (the latter may be a Hebraism); rbwn 'lord'.

(1) Suffixed Forms: gywrykwn 'your strangers' (Exod 20:10); ^{c}dwnyk 'your (fs) periods'; rbwny 'my lord', rybwnyh 'his lord', rbwnh 'her lord', rbwnn 'our lord', rbwnyy 'my lords', rbwnyhw` 'their lord!' (Gen 13:7, thus abbreviated, referring to Abram, presumably pluralis excellentiae, cf. Hebrew '^{a}dōnā(y)w 'his lord').

b. Feminine Form

(1) With suffixes: rbwnty 'my mistress' (= ribbonəti), rbwntyk 'your (fs) mistress', rybwnyth! 'her mistress' (presumably = ribbonətah ⟶ ribbonitah), usually for MT gəbîrā + suffixes.

8. Unclassified

špwryn 'beautiful' in Gen 6:2 (= ?, probably a mistake for špyrn or even (masculine) špyryn 'beautiful' in špwryn ḥyzw 'nwn(?) 'they are beautiful of (?) appearance', for MT ṭōbōt (hēnnā). Or even perhaps the noun šuprā used in the plural. The subject, however, is f pl. Even so, the ḥyzw, based on the Hebrew text, appears to be an interpolation, which would account for the fact that špwryn is not in the construct state. The vocalization, is nevertheless, unclear).

B. Nouns of the Form qwtl

These include the following vocalizations: (qutālā:) qutāl; (qotəlā:) qotal; (quttālā:) quttāl; (qutelā:) qutel; (qutlā:) qótal, qətol, qətal (< *qutl).

1. qutāl

'wmn 'craftsman'; qwdš '(nose)-ring' (in Gen 24:22,= qudāš < qədāš, cf. Onkelos, e.g., Jastrow, "Dictionary," p. 1321, and the singular and plural determined forms, qdš'/qdšh and qdšy' for MT (han)nezem, hannəzāmîm); šwtpyn 'partners' (Deut 5:17 ff).

2. qotal

a. Masculine Forms

'wgr/'gr'(!)/'ygr (!construct) 'pile'. The form with -w- occurs in Gen 31:46, for MT gal. The -w- is clear, however 'ygr has been added supralinearly by a different hand. All other occurrences are on the base 'ygr, including Gen 31:47 'ygr śhdwt' for the MT Aramaic phrase yəgar śah[a]dûtā. In this case, one can postulate yəgar>'əgar → 'igar / → 'ogar ; 'wṣr' 'treasure'; gwzl 'young bird' (for MT gōzāl in Gen 15:9, and apparently in imitation thereof, since it is expanded in the Aramaic to gwzl br ywn; cf. suffix forms below); kwkbyn/kwkby'/kwkby (construct) 'star(s); [c](w)bdh/[c]bd (construct)/ [c]wbdyn 'deed(s)' (with -w- in the singular in Exod 20:10, without in Gen 44:15; the construct is in Exod 28:32; the plural form is in Gen 21:8,9 and 38:7).

(1) III-Weak Roots: s(w)gy (absolute and construct) 'largeness', cf. Onkelos səge: sagəyā, i.e., səge → soge with assimilation to the velar.

(2) Suffixed Forms: gwzlwy 'its young' (Deut 32:11, MT gôzālā(y)w); [c]wbdk 'your deed'/[c]wbdyy 'my deeds'/[c]wbdyk 'your deeds'/[c]wbdyhwn 'their deeds'.

b. Feminine Forms

'wrḥ/'(w)rḥ'/'(w)rḥ (construct)/'(w)rḥth 'way(s)'

(='oraḥ < *'urḥ, unmarked feminine noun in the singular), usually for MT derek (but for 'oraḥ in Gen 18:11 and 49:11, and in the plural, in the phrase pršwt '(w)rḥth 'crossroads', for MT (petaḥ) ᶜênayim twice in Gen 38); slt 'fine flour' (= solat?, feminine in Onkelos and in Hebrew, therefore also here?), in Gen 18:6 qmḥ dslt for MT qemaḥ sōlet, spelled also defectively, so the Aramaic may be in imitation of the Hebrew.

(1) Suffixed Forms: '(w)rḥy 'my way'/'rḥk 'your way'/'(w)rḥ(y)h 'his way'/'rḥkwn 'your way'/'wrḥtyˋ (Gen 6:12, thus abbreviated, for MT darkô) and 'rḥtyh 'his ways' (Deut 32:4, MT dərākā(y)w).

3. quttāl

Only slm(!) 'ladder' in Gen 28:12, for MT sūllām, also spelled defectively.

4. qutel

bwṣynyh 'lamps' (Lev 24:2); kwrsy{h} 'chair' (= kurse, Gen 28:12, with aural error -yh for -y, no Hebrew Vorlage)/kwrswwn 'chairs' (Gen 15:17) ᶜwlm 'young man'.

(a) Suffixed forms: ᶜwlymwy/ᶜwlymwhy 'his youths' (the latter in Gen 22:3), usually for MT naᶜārā(y)w, but also ᶜlmwy in Gen 14:14 for ḥᵃnîkā(y)w/ᶜwlymyhwn 'their youths'.

5. *qutl

The matres lectionis in this MS, as well as the comparative data in Onkelos, indicate that this well-represented segholate class may have developed into three separate vocalization groups in the absolute state. The forms rarely appear in the absolute or construct singular, however, so conclusions must be regarded as tentative. Many early mergings in Aramaic, together with some current assimilations, complicate the analysis, as does the confusion in this MS between w and y (e.g., Onkelos ᶜiqba = Neofiti ᶜwqbh 'end'. Is this velar assimilation or merely copyist confusion of w for y?). The majority of forms appear to be the expected qṓtal (vocalized thus in the absence of the vowel seghol in the Aramaic transcription); other forms are qətol and qətal.

a. Masculine Forms

(1) qutlā:qótal
'wrk` 'length' (Gen 6:15, thus abbreviated, possibly also for 3fs pronominal suffix)/'rkh 'its length' (3fs, Gen 13:17); ḥ(w)ṭr'/ḥ(w)ṭry' 'rod(s)'/ḥwṭry 'my rod'/ḥwṭrk 'your rod' (for MT maṭṭe/maqqal); ᶜwrb' 'raven'; q(w)dš'/qdšh 'holiness' (cf. qdš' 'nose-ring' in (B.1)qutāl, above); q(w)šṭ' 'truth' (without -w- only in Gen 17:1, usually in adverbial constructions bqwšṭ' 'in truth', e.g., Gen 5:22 or mn qwšṭ' 'in truth', e.g., Deut 13:15, 17:4)/qwšṭh 'his truth' (Gen 24:27).

(2) qutlā:qətol
tqph/tqwp (construct) 'strength'/twqpk 'your stength'.

(3) qutlā:qətal
rgz (absolute)/rwgz' 'anger' (abbreviated rwgz` in Gen 18:32)/rwgz(y)h 'his anger'.

b. Assimilated Forms
The following nouns are assimilated to the qutlā group in this MS, based on their appearance in Onkelos: ᶜwqbh 'end', 'future' (Gen 3:15); šwtp' 'seal-cord' (= šutpā<šatpā, cf. Onkelos, perhaps influenced by šwtp' 'partner', above)/šwtpk 'your (ms) seal-cord'.
Also included here are the plural forms (only) of gbr' 'man' spelled with a -w-, gwbryn/gwbry'/gwbryyh 'men' alongside the "expected" gbryn/gbry'/gbryy'. Approximately 50% of the plural forms are spelled with -w-, indicating assimilation of the vowel to the bilabial, however in none of the many singular forms is any assimilation indicated graphically (so gabrā:gəbar, but gubrayyā:gubrin?).

c. Feminine Forms
ḥkmh/ḥkmt' 'wisdom'/ḥkmthwn 'their wisdom' (in the phrase bs(w)gy ḥkmt'/ḥkmthwn 'in (their) great wisdom' for MT bəmirmā in Gen 27:35 and 34:13, cf. Onkelos for the vocalization ḥukmā); ḥwmṭh 'darkness' (Gen 15:17); nqbh/nqbth/nqbn'female(s)' (note the abbreviated forms nqb` in Gen 7:2 and

nwqbˋ in Gen 5:2). The absolute singular usually occurs in the Genesis phrase dkr wnqbh 'male and female'. For the determined, see Lev 27:7; ᶜrlt (construct) 'foreskin' (Deut 10:16)/ᶜrlt(y)h 'his foreskin' (e.g., Gen 17:25,26, Lev 19:23)/ᶜrltkwˋ 'your (mp) foreskin(s)' (thus abbreviated in Gen 17:11)/ᶜrlthwn 'their foreskin' (Gen 17:23), usually for MT ᶜorlā, etc.

An unmarked feminine is gwmryn 'coals', in Gen 3:24, gwmryn mbᶜrn 'burning coals'.

6. Unclassified Forms

There are two unusual feminine forms, when compared to Onkelos: kwrkwwn 'sheaves' (= kurikəwān?, cf. Onkelos kərikān, also feminine)/ kwrkwty 'my sheaves'/kwrkwtkwn 'your (mp) sheaves'; ᶜbydt' (sic) 'beasts of burden' (Gen 33:14, for MT hammǝlā(')kā). Onkelos has ᶜobadətā and this ᶜobidətā(?) presumably reflects copyist confusion with ᶜbydt' 'work'.

C. Nouns and Adjectives of the Form qtyl

Nouns and adjectives in this category are either of the type qattil, always spelled with -y-, with some possible exceptions, e.g., tqn, šlṭwy, and the feminine ybšt', which may all be interpreted differently (cf. also sgy'yn vs. sgyn); or of the type qətil (<passive participle) or qətel, also spelled with -y-, but with numerous exceptions. Due to the early merging in Aramaic of *qatal/qatil/*qatul with *qatl/*qitl/*qutl, many of these nominal forms are indistinguishable from the segholates (q.v), e.g., kəšar: kasrā; 'əbel: 'ablā, etc. For details, see the respective entries. Once again, the basis for comparison is the form as found in Onkelos.

1. qattil

a. Masculine Forms

zbydyn 'gifts' (cf. Onkelos zəbudin, therefore possibly w/y confusion here); ḥkym/ḥkym' (!construct plural)/ḥkymy''wise' (cf. Exod 28:3 for ḥkym' lyb' 'the wise of heart'); ḥmym 'warmth'; ytyr 'more; lqyšy'/lqyšy (construct plural) 'early-born' (Gen 30:42); sgy'/sgy'yn (rare)/sgyn (common) 'great' (cf. Gen 3:22 for sgy'yn); ᶜtyd/ᶜtydyn 'designated' ⟶ 'destined'

(+ participles or infinitives); ptyryn 'loaves' (Gen 18:6, 19:3, Lev 22:27); ṣdyq/ṣdyq'/ṣdyqyn/ṣdyqy' 'righteous'; qdyš (Exod 3:5)/qdyš' (Gen 38:25) 'holy'; qlyl (construct)/qlylyn 'a few'; qryb (construct) 'close' ⟶ 'relative' (Gen 29:14, Lev 18:6 + Gen 37:27 qrb bśrn for MT bāśār); qryr 'cold' (noun); rḥyq 'far' (= rāḥiq < *raḥḥiq); rṭyb 'fresh'; rkyk 'tender'; ršyᶜy' 'evil' (once abbreviated ršyᶜy' in Gen 4:8; šlyṭ/šlyṭ' 'commander' (cf. suffixed forms below); špyr 'good', but cf. also špr = šəpar; tnyny' 'giants'; tqn 'fitting' (presumably Onkelos taqqin, or else perhaps təqen); tqyp' 'strong' (Gen 31:42 and 53, for MT paḥad ('ābîw) yiṣḥāq).

(1) Suffixed Forms: dqyqyhwn 'their children'; qrybyhwn 'their relatives'; šlṭwy (!) 'his commanders' (cf. šlyṭ above).

b. Feminine Forms

ybšt' 'dry land' (= yabbištā ?, however cf. Jastrow, "Dictionary," p. 562, for alternate yabbaštā, or even yabbeštā); mryr' 'bitter'; ᶜmyqh 'deep'; qlyln 'a few' (note also the error in Gen 29:20 ywmyn qlyln 'a few days', for qlylyn); qrybh 'close'; špyr'/špyrt (construct) 'beautiful'; tqyph 'strong' (Gen 18:15, and tqyp' in Gen 27:34). An unmarked feminine is skyn' 'knife' (Gen 22:6,10, for MT hamma'ᵃkelet) No suffixed forms are attested.

2. qətil/qətel

a. Masculine Forms

'blyn/'blyh 'mourners'; bkyryh/bkyry (construct plural) 'first-born'; bᶜyr/bᶜyr' (bᶜyrh) 'cattle'; gzl (construct!)/gzylyn 'robbery (robberies)'; dbyr'/ dbyryh 'word(s) (in the singular, Gen 28:10; in the plural in Deut 4:9ff etc. ᶜśrty dbyryh 'The Ten Commandments'); dḥyl 'feared one' (Exod 15:2); zᶜyr/zᶜyr' 'small'; zqyq 'obligated' (probably the passive participle of root zqq 'to obligate', in Gen 30:30; cf. also Deut 9:21 zqyq ṭb'wt 'finely ground', MT ṭāḥôn hêṭēb, possibly passive participle of the same root, see Jastrow, "Dictionary," p. 410, and Levy, "Wörterbuch," p. 229; ḥbybh 'uncle' (Lev 10:4, MT dōd); ḥsyd' 'pious' (Gen 24:60, 28:12, 29:22, gbr' ḥsyd' 'pious man'); ymyn' 'right hand'; yqd 'burning' (Gen 38:25, cf. Onkelos yqyd, or else yəqad, but note the feminine yqydh/ yqydt' below); kšr/kšryn 'fitting' (cf. Onkelos kəšer, but also kəšar); mṣy^{c}h 'middle'; mšyḥ' 'Messiah'; nby' 'prophet'; npyš 'breathing (space)' Gen 32:17, for MT rewaḥ); ^{c}byṭ' 'saddle'; pryq 'redeemer' (Exod 15:2, but cf. prwq in (A.3.) qātol, above); ṣpyr (construct)/ṣpyr' 'he-goat'; rdydh 'veil'; rqy^{c} (construct)/rqy^{c}' 'firmament' (note also the error in Gen 1:17 rqy^{c}' šmy'); šbybyn 'sparks'; šlyḥyn 'envoys'; šl(y)m/šlmh/šlmyn 'perfect'; šmyn 'fat' (Lev 22:27); tlymyn 'twins' (Gen 49:5).

(1) Suffixed Forms: b^{c}yrk 'your (ms) cattle'/b^{c}yryh 'his cattle'/b^{c}yrhwn 'their cattle'/b^{c}yryhwn 'their cattle (pl)'; dbyry 'my words' (Deut 4:12, cf. dbry, Deut 4:10)/dbyrwy 'his words' (Deut 4:36); zbnn (?) 'our purchase' (or else perhaps zabbinān, Gen 31:15 ksp zbnn 'the silver of our purchase', for MT kaspēnû); yḥydk 'your (ms) only one' (Gen, Chapter 22); nḥyrwy 'his nostrils'; rdydh 'her veil'; šmynyhwn 'their fats' (Gen 4:4, spelled šmyny with hwn added in the margin in a different hand, for MT ḥelbēhen)

b. Feminine Forms

bkyrth 'first-born'; bsymh 'pleasant' (Gen 15:12 šnh bsymh 'pleasant sleep', for MT tardēmā, cf. Gen 2:21 šnh ^{c}myqh for MT tardēmā); bryt (construct) 'creation' (root b-r-', Gen 2:1); gzyrt (construct) /gzrt' 'decree'/'circumcision'; hpkt' 'destruction' (cf. Onkelos h^{a}pektā); zbynt (construct) 'that which is bought' (Gen 17:27); z^{c}yr'/z^{c}yrt' 'small' (note the unusual spellings in Gen 19:31 z^{c}rt', and 19:35 z^{c}yr't'! with internal 'aleph as mater lectionis for shewa mobile, cf. Chapter 2, Orthography, i.e., zə^{c}irətā ⟶ zə^{c}iratā); ḥbybh 'precious' (Gen 44:30, for MT qəšûrā!, cf. masculine ḥbybh 'uncle', above); yqydh/yqydth 'burning' (cf. yqd, above, Deut 29:22 and Gen 38:25, respectively)'; knyšt (construct)/knyšt' 'assembly'; lḥynth/lḥynt' 'concubine(s)'; nb(y)lh 'carrion', Lev 17:15, Deut 14:21; qbylt (construct) 'complaint' (Gen 6:13); škynh 'Shekinah' (cf. suffixed forms, below). An unmarked feminine is lbnyn/lbnyh 'bricks' (cf. Onkelos).

(1) Suffixed Forms: gzyrtyh 'his circumcision'/gzrthwn 'their circumcision'/gzyrtk 'your (ms) decree'; knyštyhwn 'their assemblies'; lḥyntyh 'his concubine' (Gen 22:4, and the same spelling for 'his concubines', Gen 32:22; note also lḥynty in Gen 25:6); ᶜbdtyh 'his work' (Gen 2:2, and cf. again in Gen 2:2,3, ᶜybydtyh 'his work', presumably ᶜabidteh ⟶ ᶜibidteh, all for MT məla(')ktô); qbyltyh 'its (i.e., Sodom's) complaint'/qb(y)lthwn 'their complaint'; škyntk 'your Shekinah'/škynt(y)h 'his Shekinah'.

D. Nouns and Adjectives of the Form qtl

1. Masculine

This classification includes all those nouns usually unmarked by the use of matres lectionis, the primary group being the segholates, i.e., those derived from PS *qatl, *qitl, and *qutl. Once again, the vocalizations offered here are based on the way these forms appear in Onkelos, given the unvocalized nature of Neofiti and the inconsistent use of matres lectionis. However, many of these words are inconsistent in Onkelos also, consequently comparative data are used where appropriate. Nonetheless, there remains a certain degree of arbitrariness regarding the citation of some of the forms.

None of the groups here is exhaustive. Rather, these groupings should be taken as representative, citing as they do many of the common words (and also most of the unusual ones). Once again, the analysis is based on Genesis, with frequent cross-checks and additional citations from the other Pentateuchal books. No attempt has been made to present a concordance of all

nominal forms that occur in the MS Neofiti 1. Where apparent overlap exists between these qtl forms and others, reference is made to the relevant sections, and the forms as presented there should be consulted.
The groups under consideration here are:

a. qatlā:qəṭal

This is the most common nominal form in the MS (derived from PS *qatal). In the absolute, it is indistinguishable from qitlā: qəṭal and qutlā:qəṭal (see below); given the inconsistent use of matres lectionis, the determined form is not always marked, consequently the classification of these three types depends most heavily on the Onkelos forms (usually as cited in Jastrow, "Dictionary," and Levy, "Wörterbuch"). The majority of the nouns in these classifications are masculine. Marked feminine forms of the types (1) qatlətā:qatlā; (2) qitlətā:qitlā; (3) qutlətā:qutlā are not heavily attested [the majority belong to group (1)], and are gathered at the end in separate classifications. Where an unmarked feminine form occurs (e.g., 'r^{c}' 'land', etc.), the gender is noted in the comments. Representative suffixed forms are also noted in the comments.

Singular Determined	Singular Absolute	Plural Determined	Plural Absolute	Gloss
---	'gr	---	---	'reward'
'dmh dm'(!)	'dm	'dmyyh	---	'blood'
'rk'	---	---	---	'length'
'r^{c}'	---	'r^{c}t'	---	'land'
'tr'	'tr	---	---	'place'
'gbr'	gbr	gbry(y)' gwbry' gwbryyh	gbryn gwbryn	'man'
---	grm	---	---	'bone'
dhb'	dhb	---	---	'gold'
wwldh	---	---	---	'child'
zhr'	---	---	---	'moon'
---	zr^{c}	---	zr^{c}yn	'seed'
---	ḥlb	---	---	'milk'
---	---	---	ḥmsyn	'violent acts'

Singular Determined	Singular Absolute	Plural Determined	Plural Absolute	Gloss
ḥmr'	ḥmr	---	---	'wine'
ḥql'	---	ḥqlyh	ḥqlyn	'field'
ḥtnh	---	---	---	'groom', 'son-in-law'
yldh	---	---	---	'birth'
yrḥ'	---	---	yrḥyn	'month'
yrk'	---	---	---	'thigh'
ksp'	ksp	---	---	'silver'
kpn'	---	---	---	'famine'
krkh	---	---	---	'city'
---	mḥr	---	---	'tomorrow'
---	mll	---	---	'word'
mšk'	---	---	---	'skin'
nhr'	nhr	nhryy'	nhryn	'river'
nḥlh	---	---	---	'valley'
npš'	npš	npšt'	---	'soul'
---	shd	---	shdy! śhdy!	'witness'
^{c}pr'	^{c}pr	---	---	'dust'
---	ṣ^{c}r	---	---	'pain'
ṣpr'	ṣpr	---	---	'morning'
---	---	---	qdmyn	'east', 'beginning'
---	---	---	qlpyn	'strips'
---	qmḥ	---	---	'flour'
qšt'	---	---	---	'bow'
rmš'	rmš	---	---	'evening'
r^{c}w(w)'	---	---	---	'favor'
---	---	---	śhryn	'moon'
---	ś^{c}r	---	ś^{c}ryn	'hair'
---	śrp	---	---	'Seraph'
šḥr'	---	---	---	'dawn'
---	špr	---	---	'choice'
---	tb^{c}	---	---	'teba-weight'
tr^{c}'	---	---	---	'door'

Comments:

'gr: Construct also 'gr; suffix forms 'gry, 'grk (and note Gen 31:8 'gryk 'your (ms!) reward').

'dmh: Construct 'dm; suffix forms 'dmyh, 'dmhwn; note especially Gen 38:25 dm'(!) dṣpyr' 'the blood of a goat'. Plural in Gen 13:13 špykwt 'dmyyh 'the spilling of blood'. Note the identity of form with the plural construct noun 'dmy 'price', e.g., Gen 21:33.

'r^{c}': Feminine noun, note the marked plural ending, but with suffixes, the "expected" 'r^{c}wthwn (compare Gen 26:3 with 10:5). There are numerous misspellings of the singular: ^{c}r'^{c} (Gen 22:18), 'r^{c}y' ('his land', Deut 11:3), 'r^{c}yh ('my land', Gen 30:25), 'r^{c}' for construct 'r^{c} often, abbreviations 'r^{c}\ and 'r\.

'tr': Occasional spellings 'trh, note the error 'rth in Gen 19:14. With suffixes, 'try, 'tryh, 'tryhwn (Gen 36:40).

gbr': See the note Assimilated Forms in Section 2, Nouns of the Form qwtl, (B.5.b), above.

grm: As the Reflexive Pronoun, see Chapter 6, Section 9. In the absolute, for MT ^{c}eṣem, see Gen 2:23; for suffixed forms, with the meaning 'bone', see grmy 'my bone', Gen 2:23, grmyy 'my bones', Gen 50:25.

wwldh: Construct wwld, twice in Gen 30:2, with suffix wldh 'her child', Exod 21:22 (for MT yəlādeyhā, but cf. the Samaritan and LXX cited in BHS, p. 121, wəlādāh). Cf yldh below.

zr^{c}: The singular means 'seed' (MT zera^{c}, numerous times); the plural in Gen 8:22 meaning 'seed-times', is for MT collective zera^{c} in the list zera^{c} wəqāṣîr, etc.; with suffixes, zr^{c}yhwn 'their seed'⟶'their progeny'.

ḥtn: With suffixes ḥtnk 'your son-in-law', Gen 19:12, ḥtnwy 'his sons-in-law', Gen 19:14. Cf. the feminine ḥtntyh (Deut 27:23), below.

yldh: In Gen 20:18 ptḥy yldh 'wombs', for MT collective reḥem, but cf. Exod 13:13 ptḥy wwld', for MT peṭer.

yrḥ: For MT ḥōdeš. Note the spelling yrt' in Gen 7:11, with ḥ/ṭ confusion, see Chapter 2, Orthography, and the abbreviation yrḥ\ dywmyn 'a month of days' (Gen 29:14).

yrk': Feminine noun. With suffixes yrky, yrkyh.

krkh: Possibly kərakkā, cf. Jastrow, "Dictionary," p. 669 and Levy, "Wörterbuch," p.387.

mll: Gen 34:3 mll dšlm 'word(s) of peace' only. Possibly malǝlā: mǝlal, cf. Jastrow, "Dictionary," p. 792, through usually one finds mylt' in Neofiti.

nhr: Note Gen 36:37 byny nhryy' 'Between-the-Rivers'= 'Mesopotamia', for the MT toponymn rǝḥōbōt hannāhār 'Rehoboth by the River'.

npš: Feminine noun, with marked feminine plural form.

shd: The plural form without -n is found once in Deut 5:20, spelled with ś, śhdy dšqr 'false witnesses' (based on MT ᶜēd šāw') and twice in a midrashic passage in Gen 38:25, wbᶜt tlt' shdy wl' 'škḥt ythwn...whb ly tlt' shdy w'nh mqyymh lk tlt' ṣdyqyn 'and she sought three witnesses and did not find them...and give me (my?) three witnesses and I will raise up for you three righteous men'. The second may be interpreted as 'my witnesses', although the first clearly can not. Perhaps both result from homoieteleuton with the following ws, due to a copyist confusion between -w- and final -n. The examples with suffixes are spelled with ś also: śhdy 'my witness' and śhdwy 'his witnesses', both also in Gen 38:25.

ṣᶜr: Note the form ṣᶜrwn 'their pain', Exod 4:31, for expected ṣᶜrhwn (cf. Gen 25:22)

qdmyn: Gen 1:1 mlqdmyn 'since the beginning' (MT bǝrē(')šît); Gen 2:8, 13:11 mn lqdmyn and Gen 3:24 mn mlqdmyn (!) 'at the east', both for MT miqqedem, (cf. Gen 25:6 qdmyyn 'east', MT miqqedem, and Deut 33:27 mlqdmyn 'since the beginning', based on the poetic MT 'ᵉlōhê qedem). Probably two separate idioms mlqdmyn and qdmyn that are confused in the MS due to the similarity of the forms.

b. qatlā:qátal

These are the segholates Tiberianized from Babylonian (<PS*qatl, and corresponding to Hebrew and occasional Biblical Aramaic forms mélek, etc.), transcribed thus due to the lack of the vowel seghol in the Aramaic transcription. Also included here are the II-guttural segholates, qatlā : qǝtel, usually spelled plene with -y- in Onkelos, though not necessarily so in this MS.

Singular Determined	Singular Absolute	Plural Determined	Plural Absolute	Gloss
'bn'	---	'bny'	'bnyn	'stone'
---	'lp	'lpyh	'lpyn	'thousand'
---	b^{c}l	---	---	'lord'
ḥrb'	ḥrb	---	---	'sword'
---	ṭ^{c}m	---	---	'taste'
---	---	ṭply'	---	'children'
ksp'	ksp	---	---	'silver'
---	krm	---	---	'vineyard'
lḥm'	lḥm	---	---	'bread'
mlk'	mlk	mlky(y)'	mlkyn	'king'
^{c}bd'	^{c}bd	---	^{c}bdyn	'servant'
---	---	psgyyh	---	'parts'

Comments:

'bn': Feminine noun; with suffixes, 'bnwy 'its (ms) stones'.

b^{c}l: Often in the idioms b^{c}l dbbw 'enmity', b^{c}ly dbb' 'enemies'. (Cf. Kaufman, "Akkadian Influences", p. 42). Most common with suffixes, b^{c}ly, b^{c}lh, etc.

hrb': Feminine noun.

ṭ^{c}m: Cf. Num 11:8 hwh ṭ^{c}myh kṭ^{c}m ššyn bdbš 'its taste was like the taste of pancakes with honey' (MT ṭa^{c}mô...ṭa^{c}am).

ṭply': Plural only. For MT haylādîm in Gen 33:5. With suffixes, translates MT ṭap + suffixes in Gen 34:29, ṭplyhwn, Gen 43:8, ṭplynn, Deut 1:39 ṭplykwn. (The more common translation for yeled etc. in the MS is ṭly' (or even occasionally bnyn), cf. Gen 33:5 where both ṭply' and ṭly' are used for haylādîm.

mlk': The singular and plural determined state is occasionally abbreviated mlk`/mlky`. Note the unusual spelling in Gen 26:1 mlk'hwn(!) dplšt'y 'the king of the Philistines', with א for shewa mobile, cf. Chapter 2, Orthography.

psgyyh: Once in Gen 15:11 for MT happəgārîm, and again in the same verse, abbreviated psgyy` in an interpretive expansion. Elsewhere MT peger = Neofiti pgr, e.g., Lev 26:30.

Other forms probably to be included here are dmkyh 'his bed', Gen 2:24 and hlṣyk 'your (ms) loins', Gen 17:6 and 35:11.

c. qātəlā:qātel

For the active participle, cf. Chapter 6, Verbs, Stem Forms.

d. qitlā:qətal

A common group of nominals, from PS *qatal/qital (cf. section (D.1.a) above). Once again, due to the inconsistent use of matres lectionis, the forms are based on Onkelos, however the Onkelos forms also vary considerably. Hence, a certain degree of arbitrariness is involved in assigning any given word to a given category.

Singular Determined	Singular Absolute	Plural Determined	Plural Absolute	Gloss
'lᶜ'(!)	---	---	---	'rib'
b(y)śr'	bśr	---	---	'flesh'
---	---	gzryy'	---	'sections'
dk(w)r'	dkr	dkryyh	dkryn	'male','ram'
---	---	---	dtyn	'sproutings'
z(y)mn'	zmn	---	zmnyn	'time'
---	---	---	zmryn	'songs'
ḥzw(w)h	ḥ(y)zw	---	---	'vision'
ḥlm'	ḥlm	ḥlmy'	---	'dream'
mṭr'	mṭr	---	---	'rain'
---	mšḥ	---	---	'oil'
---	ndr	---	---	'vow'
---	---	nksy'	nksyn	'goods'
syṭr'	sṭr	---	---	'side'
---	---	---	slᶜyn	'selas'
---	ᶜdr	ᶜdry'	ᶜdry(!)	'flocks'
ᶜśb'	ᶜśb	---	---	'grass'
---	---	---	ṣmḥyn	'plants'
---	qṭm	---	---	'ash(es)'
---	qṭp	---	---	'balsam'
---	šyᶜ	---	---	'cement'

Comments:

'lᶜ': Usually spelled thus, e.g., Gen 2:21,22 'lᶜ' mn 'lᶜwy 'a rib from his ribs', 'lᶜ' 'rib', but note in 2:21 a "mistaken" form ^{c}l' is "corrected" by repeating the word (cf. Klein, JSS, pp. 228-29), however this form seems to reflect the normal Onkelos ^{c}l^{c}', which is found in Gen 44:19 ^{c}yl^{c}' (for the same dissimilation, cf. also the verb 'r^{c} 'to meet' for Onkelos ^{c}r^{c}).

b(y)śr': The spelling byśr' is found in Gen 6:12. The word occurs often, also with suffixes.

dk(w)r': Spelled often with -w- meaning 'male', e.g., Gen 17:10, Num 31:17, etc., usually for MT zākār (and occasionally 'îš or ben), but also without -w- in the same circumstances. Spelled only without -w- meaning 'ram' for MT 'ayil/'êlîm.

dtyn: Gen 1:11,12 for MT deše' (also Deut 28:23), and Deut 32:2 dty ^{c}śbyh 'sproutings of grasses' based on MT poetic deše'...^{c}ēśeb (ditin < dit'in).

ḥzw(w)h: Spelled variously ḥzwh/ḥzwwh/ḥzww'. Absolute ḥyzw, e.g., Gen 24:16 špyrt ḥyzw 'beautiful of appearance', and note Gen 12:11 špyrt ḥzy (?), presumably ḥzw with w/y confusion.

nksy': Note the error spelling nknsyn(!) in Gen 15:14.

^{c}dr: Note the absolute plural ^{c}dry d^{c}n(!) 'flocks of sheep' (Gen 29:2, MT ^{c}edrê ṣō(')n), presumably an error due to haplography of the letters ^{c}d/d^{c} for the construct ^{c}dry ^{c}n (or else segholate, see section (D.1.e) below).

šy^{c}: i.e., šəya^{c}, Gen 11:3, for MT ḥōmer, Num 19:5, for MT (ṣāmîd) pātîl.

e. qitlā:qétal

Segholate type (< PS *qitl), cf. (D.1.b) above.

Singular Determined	Singular Absolute	Plural Determined	Plural Absolute	Gloss
'bl'	'bl	---	---	'mourning'
ḥsd'	ḥsd	ḥsdy'	---	'kindness'
yṣrh	yṣr	---	---	'inclination'
yrq'	---	---	---	'greens'
mlḥh	mlḥ	---	---	'salt'
sgdh(?)	---	---	---	'idol'
sdr'	sdr	---	sdryn	'arrangement'
spr'	---	---	---	'book'
---	---	---	pl'yn	'miracles'

Singular Determined	Singular Absolute	Plural Determined	Plural Absolute	Gloss
---	[ṣlm]	ṣlmy(y)h	---	'image'
qbrh	---	qbryh	qbryn	'grave'
rglh	rgl	---	---	'leg'
šmᶜh	---	---	---	'news'
šmš'	---	šmšyy'	---	'sun'
---	tbn	---	---	'straw'

Comments:

'bl: Cf. 'bylwtn 'our mourning', Deut 26:14.

ḥsd: Common with suffixes; for the plural, see Gen 32:10, for MT haḥᵃsādîm.

yrq': Deut 11:10, and in the construct, Gen 9:3 (the latter spelled with Hebrew vowels יְרַק). Note also Lev 14:37, the feminine plural adjective yrqn, qualifying šqᶜn 'green cavities', for MT yəraqraqqōt.

sgdh: In Onkelos this form is the abstract 'worship', however in Neofiti it occurs in Gen 11:4 wnᶜbd ln br'šyh sgdh 'and let us make for ourselves an idol at its head', cf. Pseudo-Jonathan, ad loc., sigdu and Fragment targum, ad loc., səgidu.

sdr': e.g., Gen 6:15, Exod 28:17. Common in construct, especially in Genesis chapter 1 in the idiom sdr ᶜbd br'šyt ywm... 'the order of the making of Genesis, day (number)..., and also in sdr dyn'/sdry dynyyh 'the order(s) of the judgement(s)', Gen 6:3 and Deut 5:31, respectively.

spr': Exod 17:14, and in the construct in Gen 5:1.

pl'yn: Exod 15:11, spelled plyyn in Exod 8:18.

ṣlmy(y)h: Possibly ṣalmayyā, cf. Onkelos. All occurrences of the singular ṣlm in this MS have been erased by the Catholic censor.

qbrh: Common with suffixes, e.g., qbryh, qbrynn, etc. For the plural, cf. Exod 14:11, and the toponym in Num 11:34 qbry š'lth 'The Graves of the Request', for MT qibrot hatta'ᵃwā

šmš': For the plural, cf. Gen 49:27 byny šmšyy' 'twilight'.

f. qutlā:qətol

A small group of nouns (< PS *qatul); in Aramaic

this group has by and large merged with those segholates from PS *qutl (section (D.1.g), below), as both are spelled qtwl in the absolute (when matres lectionis are used). So too in this MS, in which most of the forms are written defectively. Hence, the classification, while based on the forms in Onkelos, is also determined by comparative/historical considerations.

Singular Determined	Singular Absolute	Plural Determined	Plural Absolute	Gloss
q(w)šṭ'	---	---	---	'truth'
tqph	---	---	---	'strength'

Comments:

q(w)šṭ': Spelled qšṭ' in Gen 17:1.

tqph: Gen 18:1, btqph dywm' 'in the strength of the day'; also in the construct, tqwp rwgz(y)h 'the strength of his anger', e.g., Gen 27:45, Num 25:4.

g. qutlā:qótal

A small group of segholates, from PS *qutl.

Singular Determined	Singular Absolute	Plural Determined	Plural Absolute	Gloss
'wdnh	---	---	---	'ear'
ḥ(w)ṭr'	ḥṭr	ḥwṭry'	---	'rod'
kwtlh	---	---	---	'wall'
q(w)dš'	---	---	---	'holiness'
rwgz'	rgz	---	---	'anger'

Comments:

'wdnh: Exod 29:20; for the plural, Gen 35:4 'dnhwn(!) 'their ears' (MT 'oznêhem).

ḥ(w)ṭr': Spelled ḥṭr' in Gen 30:37, ḥṭr in Exod 4:2,4 and ḥṭry' in Gen 30:39.

kwtlh: Num 35:4, and the plural kwtly(!) dbyyth 'the walls of the house' (= kwtlyh?), Lev 14:37, 39.

q(w)dš': Variously spelled qwdš', qdš', qdšh.

rwgz': Abbreviated rwgz` in Gen 18:32.

2. Feminine

a. qatlətā:qatlā

The most common group of feminine form nouns (for the feminine active participle, see Chapter 6, Verbs, Stem Forms).

Singular Determined	Singular Absolute	Plural Determined	Plural Absolute	Gloss
'dmt'	---	---	---	'earth'
'm(h)t'	'mhh	---	'mhn	'handmaid'
bhtth	---	---	---	'shame
dḥlt'	---	---	---	'fear'
d^c^th	---	---	---	'knowledge'
ḥqlt<'>	---	---	---	'field'
[ḥtnt']	---	---	---	'mother-in-law'
---	---	---	nkswn	'sacrifices'
^c^qrt'	---	---	---	'barrenness'
rḥmt'	---	---	---	'love'
---	š^c^wwh	---	---	'wax'
š^c^t'	---	---	---	'hour'

Comments:

'm(h)t': Variously spelled, 'mht', 'mt' (Gen 16:8, 25:12), 'mth (Gen 21:10, 13); with suffixes also usually without -h-, but note Gen 30:4, 9, 10, 12 'mhth 'her handmaid' and also the error form in Gen 30:7, 'mhhth'.

dḥlt': Note the plural in Gen 31:30 meaning 'idols', dḥlty 'my idols' (MT 'ᵉlōhāy); elsewhere, the expected t^c^wt' etc. is found for 'idol'.

d^c^th: Especially in the idiom gnb d^c^t 'to deceive' (Gen 31:20,26), cf. Levy, "Wörterbuch," p. 182.

ḥqlt<'>: Only in Gen 23:17, ḥqlt<'> d^c^prwn 'Ephron's field', for MT śədе(h) ^c^eprôn; elsewhere, the masculine form ḥql is used (see section D.1.a above).

[ḥtnt']: Only with suffix, Deut 27:23, ḥtntyh 'his mother-in-law' (MT ḥōtantô).

nkswn: So in Gen 43:16. The apparent nksyn in Gen 31:54 is presumably the same, with w/y confusion (also possibly influenced by the more common nksyn 'goods'). The singular construct occurs commonly in the technical religious idiom nkst qwdšyn/qdyšyn 'holy sacrifices' (e.g., Exod 18:12,32:6, Lev 19:5).

š^{c}t' Common in compound conjunctions, usually for MT (bā)^{c}ēt, etc. and note Gen 28:10 š^{c}<w>y 'its hours', spelled š^{c}yy, with w/y confusion.

b. qitlətā:qitlā

A less well-attested group of nouns than qatlətā: qatlā.

Singular Determined	Singular Absolute	Plural Determined	Plural Absolute	Gloss
---	bq^{c}h	---	---	'valley'
brkt'	brkh	brkth	brkn	'blessing'
d^{c}th	---	---	---	'sweat'
	mšḥ'	---	---	'measure'
nṣbt'	---	---	---	'shoot'
nšm`	n(y)šmh	---	---	'breath'
^{c}glth	^{c}glh	---	---	'calf'
^{c}zqth	---	[^{c}zqy'(!)]	[^{c}zqyn(!)]	'signet-ring'
ṣdqth	---	---	---	'righteousness'
---	ṣwwḥh	---	---	'shout'

Comments:

mšḥ': Exod 26:2; construct in Gen 6:15,16, and note Num 13:32 mšyḥ'(!), either error for myšḥ' or else mišəḥā ⟶ mišiḥā.

nšm`: The determined is abbreviated in Gen 2:7, nšm` dḥyyn 'the breath of life'; the absolute is variously spelled, nšmh (Gen 7:15,22,9:3), nyšmh (Deut 20:16), nšwmh(!), in Gen 6:7.

^{c}zqth: Gen 38:18,25, for MT ḥōtemet; the masculine plural forms (Exod 25:12,14) translate MT ṭabbā^{c}ōt, hence presumably a different word.

c. qutlətā:qutlā

The only two words apparently belonging to this classification are also classifiable elsewhere, hence perhaps the grouping is not really attested in this MS.

yklh 'ability', Gen 4:13 *'yt ykl qdmk* 'you are able' (no *Vorlage*), Num 14:16 *lyt yklh qdmk* 'you are not able' (MT *mibbiltî yəkōlet*), but perhaps *yəkālā*.

ḥwṭrt' 'rods', Gen 30:37, for MT *hammaqlôt* (and influenced by its gender?), cf. the masculine singular and plural forms *ḥwṭr'*/*ḥwṭry'* (section (D.1.g) above).

E. Nouns and Adjectives of the Form *qtāl*

There is, of course, no indication of the length of the vowel in the second syllable of words of this type. However, based on comparative grounds, and especially Onkelos, these words in this MS must also have -ā-. The most common type is *qətālā*: *qətāl*, representative examples of which (again primarily from Genesis) are included below. Less common types follow.

1. *qətālā:qətāl*

a. Masculine Forms

Singular Determined	Singular Absolute	Plural Determined	Plural Absolute	Gloss
'lh'	'lh	---	---	'god'
---	---	---	dgnyn	'grains'
ḥmr'	---	---	ḥmryn	'ass'
ḥṣd'	---	---	ḥṣdyn	'harvest'
ṭyys'	---	---	---	'bird'
---	yqr	---	---	'honored'
ktb'	ktb	---	---	'writing'
---	lbn	---	---	'white poplar'
---	---	---	lwwṭn(!)	'curses'
---	msn	---	---	'shoe'
nḥš'	nḥš	---	---	'copper'
---	ny(y)ḥ	---	---	'rest'
^{c}bd'	---	---	^{c}bdyn	'deed'
^{c}nn'	^{c}nn	---	---	'cloud'
---	^{c}rd	---	---	'wild ass'
---	prn	---	---	'dowry'
qdš'	qwdš(!)	qdšy'	qdyšyn(!)	'ring'
qy(y)m'	qyym	---	---	'covenant'

Singular Determined	Singular Absolute	Plural Determined	Plural Absolute	Gloss
---	qyym	---	---	'enduring'
qrb'	---	qrbyyh	---	'battle'
---	---	---	ś^c ryn	'grains'
šbḥ'	---	---	---	'praise'
šlm'	šlm	---	---	'peace'
šrb'	---	---	---	'heat'
---	---	tyšy'	---	'he-goats'
tnn'	---	---	---	'smoke'

Comments:

ṭyys': Three times in a midrashic expansion on Gen 15:11, based on MT hā^c ayiṭ.

ktb': For the absolute, see Exod 32:16, Lev 19:28; also with the meaning 'Scripture', e.g., Gen 30:22, and note the spelling in Gen 35:9, ktbt, with h/t confusion, (see Chapter 2, Orthography, and Klein, JSS 19 (1974), p. 222).

lbn: Possibly also a segholate, i.e., ləban.

lwwṭn: In Gen 27:12, lwwṭn wl' brkn 'curses and not blessings'. Note Onkelos ləwāṭin, therefore possibly the feminine here is due to a copyist's mistaken imitation of the following feminine plural brkn (cf. lwwṭk 'your curses', Gen 27:13).

nḥš': For the absolute, Num 21:9; for the determined, Gen 14:23.

qdš': Note the absolute qwdš, presumably qədāš ⟶ qudāš with assimilation to the velar, and note also the plural qdyšyn (Num 31:50), either qədāšin ⟶ qədišin or, more likely, a copyist error based on the common qdyšyn 'holy'.

šlm': Note occasional Hebraisms, e.g., Gen 33:3 šlwmhwn 'their welfare', and also occasional plural forms, e.g., Gen 37:9, 23:7; šlmyy/šlmyhwn 'my/their welfare'.

b. Feminine Forms

There is a small group of feminine nouns belonging to this category:

'tnth: 'the (his?) she-ass' (Num 22:21)/'tnyn (Gen 12:16, 32:15); ^c llt' 'harvest'; ^c qrh 'barren'; ^c^lt'/^c^lh/^c^lwn 'offering' (Genesis Chapter 22, and Gen 8:20 for the plural).

2. qitālā:qitāl

A less common group of nouns than group (E.1) above, however still well attested (only masculine forms).

Singular Determined	Singular Absolute	Plural Determined	Plural Absolute	Gloss
'(y)ln'	'yln	'ylny'	'ylnyn	'tree'
'ymm'	---	---	ymmyn(!)	'day(-time)'
(')nš'	(')nš	---	---	'human being'
---	---	['sdy']	---	'pillows'
'yqr'	'yqr	---	---	'glory'
---	'tml	---	---	'yesterday'
lyšnh	lšn	---	---	'tongue'
---	symn	---	---	'sign'

Comments:

'(y)ln': Occasionally spelled 'ln' (e.g., Gen 3:11) and abbreviated 'yln` (Gen 3:17).

'ymm': Occasionally for MT yôm, though cf. the much more common ywm/ywmyn below. The normal Onkelos singular ymm' does not appear in Neofiti, but the plural ymmyn is the only form attested (cf. Gen 7:24).

['sdy']: Only occurs in the construct plural 'sdy r'š(y)h 'the pillows of his head', in Gen 28:11, 18 for MT məra'ᵃšōtā(y)w and in Gen 28:10 without Vorlage, but based on the following verse.

'yqr': Note the absolute 'wqr in Gen 3:21 with w/y confusion, and the variant spellings 'qryh (Gen 1:29), 'yqry` (Gen 1:17) and construct yqr(!), Gen 9:27.

'tml: Spelled thus Gen 31:2,4, Deut 4:42, but note Exod 4:10 'tmwl.

lyšnh: Spelled thus Lev 19:16; elsewhere, absolute lšn, e.g., Gen 11:1, Deut 27:8, but note occasional Hebraisms lšwn, e.g., Gen 31:47. Note the use of the singular for the plural in Deut 27:8, šb^c^ym (sic) lšn 'seventy tongues'.

3. qattālā:qattāl

Generally used for professional classes, however cf. also ḥbl', below (only masculine forms attested).

Singular Determined	Singular Absolute	Plural Determined	Plural Absolute	Gloss
---	---	[gzzy']	---	'shearers'
gnb'	---	gnby'	gnbyn	'thief'
dyyn	dyyn	dy(y)ny'	dyynyn	'judge'
---	dyyr	---	dywryn(!)	'dweller'
ḥbl'	---	---	---	'destruction'
ḥyyb'	---	ḥyybyh	ḥyybyn	'guilty'
srd'	---	---	---	'net-maker'
---	qyym	---	qyymyn	'enduring'
---	---	---	tgryn	'traders'

Comments:

[gzzy']: Only in the construct plural, Gen 38:12 gzzy ^{c}nh 'the shearers of the flock' (or else the active participle gāzəze), for MT gōz^{a}zê.

gnb': For the singular, see Exod 22:1; for the plural, see Gen 31:9, Exod 20:15.

dyyn': The plural is spelled dyny' in Gen 6:4, elsewhere all forms have -yy-, e.g., Gen 4:8, 18:25, Deut 16:18, but note the construct in Gen 19:9 lmhwy dyn dynynn 'to be judge of our cases' (MT wayyišpōṭ šāpōṭ), unless dyn = the active participle dāyen rather than the noun dayyān, with the spelling influenced by the following word dyn (= din).

dyyr: The absolute singular is in Gen 23:4, but cf. dywr in Gen 44:18. The plural also has two forms: dyyry ('r^{c}') 'the residents (of the land)', e.g., Gen 6:11, 10:25, etc. (and even spelled d'yry in Gen 11:9), plus with suffixes dyyryh 'its (fs) residents' (Gen 19:25, 36:20, etc.); but also dywryn (Deut 23:8). It is possible that the two examples spelled with -w- should be read dyyr/dyyryn, with w/y confusion, however cf. Jastrow, "Dictionary," p.297, for the existence of both forms.

srd': Gen 36:39, expanding the MT proper name maṭrēd (= sārādā < *sarrādā).

qyym: The singular occurs in the idiom ḥy wqyym 'living and enduring' (e.g., Gen 3:22, 24), and in the construct in the idom qyym kl ᶜlmyy' 'the one who endures forever' (e.g., Gen 16:14, 25:11, etc.). The plural occurs in ḥyyn wqyymyn, Deut 4:4

4. Other

There are isolated examples of other forms that must also have a long vowel in the second syllable:

qittālā: qittāl--'mr'/'mr/'(y)mry(y)'/'mryn 'lamb(s)' (but cf. the feminine forms 'mrh/'mrt'(pl), Lev 5:6 and Gen 21:29,30 respectively); gybr/gybry(y)' 'warrior(s)'. An adjectival form is ḥwwrt': ḥywr' (fs)/ḥwwryn (mpl) 'white' Gen 30:35, 37).

qutālā: qutāl -- ḥwlq': ḥwlq 'portion' (often, e.g., Gen 44:18, 48:22, and abbreviated ḥwl` in Gen 15:1). The form is also spelled without -w- in Gen 31:14, and in the plural, ḥlqyn (Gen 47:24)/ḥlqyhwn 'their portions' (Gen 14:24).

qetālā: qetāl -- ḥmr': ḥmr 'pitch' (Gen 6:14, 11:3, and 14:10, respectively).

F. Nouns and Adjectives Ending in -y.

The majority of the forms in this classification have two root radicals (usually from III-weak roots), however the following 3 (and 4) radical nominals contain a suffix -y.

1. Masculine Forms

'rᶜyyn 'lower': mpl, Gen 6:16, but note the masculine singular 'rᶜ', in Gen 1:6, presumably 'arᶜā for expected 'arᶜāyā, spelled thus under the influence of the common 'rᶜ' 'land'.

'ḥryyn 'last': mpl, Gen 33:2.

zhwry 'crimson thread': Absolute in Num 19:6, determined zyhwryh in Gen 38:28.

yḥydyy 'lone': ms in Gen 3:22, mpl yḥydyyn in Gen 22:10.

l(y)ly' 'night': Spelled lly' in Gen 1:5. The absolute lyly occurs in Gen 8:22, Exod 12:42 (the form in Gen 30:16 blyly hw' 'in that night' is presumably an error for lyly'). The plural lylw(w)n' can be seen in Gen 7:4,12.

n(w)kry(y)h 'foreign': Variously spelled, usually in the phrase pwlḥn' nwkryh 'foreign worship', including nkr'h (Gen 24:31), nwkr'h (Gen 26:35).
ᶜbdy 'servitude': Only in Exod 20:2 byt ᶜbdy 'the house of bondage' for MT bêt ᶜᵃbādîm, in which case this may be simply a defective spelling for ᶜbdyn, or else the Onkelos form ᶜbdw, with w/y confusion. The form ᶜbdy is not known in Onkelos.
ᶜrṭl'y 'naked': Masculine singular, Gen 3:10 (ᶜrṭlyy in Gen 3:11), masculine plural ᶜrṭlyn in Gen 2:25, 3:7.
qdmyy 'first': Gen 38:28, and note also the plural (?) qdmyyn meaning 'east', Gen 25:6.
rgly(y)n 'footsoldiers': Gen 33:1, Exod 12:37, Num 11:21.

For two root examples, cf. the following:
bhy' 'Bohu, 'void'; gdyyh/gdyyn/gdy(y)'(pl) 'kid(s)'; gylwy 'uncovering'; dkyh 'clean' (variously spelled, dykyh, dwky` in Gen 8:20); zwy 'angle' (Lev 24:12); zkyy'/zkyy 'innocent' (plural zkyyn and determined zkyy! in Gen 18:24, 28); ḥwy'/ḥ(y)wy 'snake' ṭly'/ṭly/ṭly(y)' (pl) 'young man'; mlyyn 'full' (fpl), Gen 14:10; nsy' 'sinew' (Gen 32:32); ᶜdwyyn 'menstrual periods' (Gen 18:12); ᶜ(y)ly' (ᶜl'h) 'upper'; pty(y)h 'its width' (Gen 6:15, 13:17); rby' 'lad'; šby 'captivity' (Exod 15:9); šmy(y)' 'heavens' (variously spelled, including šmyy`, Gen 15:1, and šmyMy!?, Gen 14:19, i.e., with final -m in the middle of the word, and -y added following it; note the construct šmy mrwm' 'the heavens on high', Gen 3:22); špy 'tranquil' (Num 23:3, MT šepî); šqyy' 'watering' (but note Gen 13:10 byt šqh!, in error for šqyh?); šrwyh 'its beginning' (Gen 11:1, and note the construct šrwy); thy' 'Tohu', 'waste'.

2. Feminine Forms

There are only two three-root radical nominals among the feminine forms: qdmyth and nkryyn. All the rest have two-root radicals.
bryyt' 'creations': Gen 7:23, but note the spelling bryytyh! in Gen 7:4, presumably an error for bryyth Note also the similar bryt šmy' w'rᶜ' 'creation of heaven and earth', Gen 2:1.

zk'h 'innocent': cf. the masculine singular and plural forms above.

klyyh 'destruction': Gen 18:21.

nkryyn 'foreign': cf. the masculine singular above.

slw(w)y 'quail': Apparently an unmarked feminine common noun (Exod 16:13, Num 11:26, 32, 21:6).

qdmyth 'past-time': Gen 13:4, 28:19, Num 10:13, Deut 9:18, 13:10.

qrt'(!) 'city': Absolute singular - qryh; determined plural - qryyt'; absolute plural - qryn (e.g., Exod 1:11). The construct singular is variously spelled: qyry/qry/qrwy (= Gen 19:29). With suffixes, cf., e.g., qrtyh/qrthwn.

rbyt' 'young woman': Note the error form rbyty in Gen 24:55, for rbyth, with y/h confusion, see Chapter 2, Orthography.

ššyn 'pancakes': Num 11:8, but cf. Exod 16:31 šyšyn. The Onkelos form is šašyān

G. Unclassified Nominal Forms

The nouns in this section are either of foreign origin, or else quadriliterals or quinquiliterals, however cf. ḥrk', ᶜlm', etc.

1. Masculine Forms

'rdᶜnyn 'frogs' (Exod 7:28 etc., spelled ᶜrdᶜnyy' in Exod 8:9); bdlḥ' 'bdellium' (Gen 2:12); bwṣynyh 'lamps' (Lev 24:2); glgly! 'wheels' (Exod 14:25, plural absolute and construct); drdryn 'brambles' (Gen 3:18, 4:16); zyqwqyn 'sparks' (Gen 3:24); zᶜ<z>wᶜ 'shock' (Gen 27:33, spelled in error zᶜwᶜ!); ḥrk' 'window (= ḥərakkā, cf. Onkelos; Gen 26:8; ṭlwpḥyn 'lentils' (Gen 25:29,34); ybrwḥyn 'mandrakes' (Gen 30:14-16, numerous spellings); kwkby'/kwkbyn 'stars' (i.e., kokab < *kawkab < *kabkab); kmst 'worthy' (Gen 20:16, 32:10); smqm<q> 'red' (Gen 25:25, spelled smqyn, in a corrupt verse); ᶜlm'/ᶜlm/ᶜlmy(y)'/ᶜlmyn 'world', 'universe' (= ᶜālam); prds/prdsyy' 'garden (see the spelling prdysy' in Gen 14:3); przl' 'iron' (Gen 4:22); ptgm'/ptgm/ptgmy' 'matter'; ṣw'rk, etc. 'your neck' (Gen 27:40, variously spelled ṣww'ryk, ṣw'ryh 'his neck', ṣwwryh, Gen 27:16, and the plural ṣw'ryhwn 'their necks', Num 31:50); rybwwdh '(her) appearance' (?), only in Gen 29:17, translating MT tō'ar; rbrby'/rbrbyn 'great' (as an adjective, but also with suffixes meaning 'chiefs', e.g., rbrbnwy, rbrbnyhwn, etc.; šyzbh 'that which is saved' (Gen 32:8); šlh<b>yn 'flames' (Gen 15:17, spelled šlhyn with -byn written in another hand); š^{c}bwd'/š^{c}bwd 'servitude' (Gen 27:40, Exod 14:13); špnyn 'turtle-dove' (masc. singular, Gen 15:9).

2. Feminine Forms

prnst' 'provision' (Gen 30:22); rb<rb>nt'/rbrbn 'great' (Gen 29:26, spelled in error rbbrnt'; rbrbn in Gen 12:17, mktšyn rbrbn 'great plagues'); š^{c}šw^{c}t (construct) 'smoothness' (Gen 27:16).

H. Nouns with Two Radicals

These nouns fall into three basic categories: ql, qyl, qwl. Among the nouns of the form ql, there are three types identifiable:

qəlā: qal (cf. Hebrew yād);
qallā: qal (cf. Hebrew ^{c}am);
qālā: qāl (cf. Hebrew qôl).

In addition, there is a limited number of non-classified forms.

Similarly, there are three types within the category qyl:

qilā: qil (cf. Hebrew dîn);
qaylā/qelā: qayil/qel (cf. Hebrew bayit);
qilla: qel (cf. Hebrew ḥēṣ).

In the category qwl, there are two types identifiable:

qulā: qul (cf. Hebrew šûq);
qolā: qol (cf. Hebrew yôm).

In addition, there are some isolated examples of a type qullā: qol, and two cases in which the -w- is consonantal.

1. The Form ql

a. Masculine - qəlā: qal::qəlayyā: qəlin

'^{c}yn 'trees' (Gen 6:14, but cf. Onkelos 'ə^{c}in or 'ā^{c}in); br'/br/bny'/bnyn 'son'; yd' 'hand', and for the plural, see construct ydy, suffixes ydyk, ydwy, ydynn, etc.; rm/rmyh 'high' (singular, Gen 39:14, plural, Gen 7:19).

Feminine - No forms attested (for brt', the feminine of br', see below).

b. Masculine - qallā: qal::qallayyā:qallin

'pyn 'face' (plural only, also construct 'py, and with suffixes 'pyk, 'pwy, 'pykwn, etc.); br'/br 'open space'; gb 'back' (singular in the compound preposition 'p ᶜl gb d- 'despite', plural in the compound preposition ᶜl gby 'on top of'); gdh 'luck' (Gen 30:11); gp 'side' (construct, Gen 22:17); ḥy(y)'/ḥy/ḥyyn/ḥyy' 'living (creature)', 'life' (plural only; for the absolute singular and plural, cf. ḥy wqyym, ḥyyn wqyymyn 'living and enduring'); ṭl' 'dew' (Gen 27:28,39); ym'/ymyy' 'sea' (for the plural, note Gen 1:22, but cf. 1:10 ymm', an error for ymy'); kwwy 'openings' (construct plural, Gen 7:11, 8:2); kp 'palm' (construct singular, and construct plural, kpy , Gen 20:5); ᶜm'/ᶜm(ᶜmm)/ᶜmy'(ᶜmmy')/ᶜmmyn! 'nation' (the forms ᶜmm/ᶜmmy' are only found in Gen 20:4,13 respectively; the only absolute plural form attested is ᶜmmyn, e.g., Gen 17:12,27, Exod 21:8); rb'/rb 'great' (for the plural, cf. rbrbyn in Section G, Unclassified Nominal Forms, above); śq' 'sackcloth' (Gen 37:34).

Feminine - The only forms attested are:
ḥyyt' 'midwife' (= ḥayyətā, Gen 35:17, 38:28); ḥyyt' 'animals' (= ḥayyātā, Gen 1:24, 25, 28, 9:2, etc.); rb'/rbt' 'great'.

c. Masculine - qālā: qāl::qālayyā:qālin
'tyn 'signs' (Gen 1:14); drh/dryn/dry' 'generation'; ḥl' 'sand' (Gen 22:17, 32:12); ṭb'/ṭb/ṭby'/ṭbyn 'good'; ql'/ql 'voice'.
Feminine - ṭb'/ṭbth 'good'; ᶜqt'/ᶜq' 'distress' (Gen 15:7, 22:14, and with suffixes, ᶜqty, ᶜqthwn); note also the unmarked feminine noun ᶜnh/ᶜn 'flock'.

d. Other
The following noun forms, for one reason or another, are not classifiable in the above three categories.

(1) Masculine Forms

(a) my(y)'/my(y)n 'water' (plural only, = mayā/mayin (?), however cf. the commonly occurring suffixed form mwy(!) 'its waters', i.e., mowi, in such idioms as mwy dmbwl' 'the waters of the flood', Gen 7:7, 10, 9:11, and mwy dym' 'the waters of the sea', Exod 15:19. This would necessitate postulating a change from mayowi ⟶ mowi, however one also finds forms such as Deut 29:10 myykwn 'your waters', presumably mayekon. However this same verse in Onkelos has mk! = māk. Note also Exod 7:19 mymyhwn 'their waters' (but here the MT has mêmêhem, hence this is probably in imitation of the Hebrew).

(b) mn/mnyn 'vessel(s)' (presumably mān/mānin, and never spelled with medial aleph). The singular is in Lev 11:33, the plural in Gen 24:53, Exod 11:2. For suffixed forms, cf. mnyy 'my utensils' (Gen 31:37) and for the construct, Gen 27:3, 31:37.

(c) mr' 'master' (presumably = mārā, cf. Exod 21:34, 22:7). Also singular construct mry in Gen 21:33, 25:27, 37:19, and with suffixes mryh, Exod 21:28, 29, 36, 22:11. For the plural, cf. the construct mry in Gen 14:13, 46:34, and with suffixes, mrwy 'its masters' in Exod 21:29.

(d) sb'/sb 'old' (= sābā/sāb?, cf. Onkelos sābā/sā(')bā, parallel to MT śāb?), Gen 10:4, 24:2.

(e) r^{c}y/r^{c}y' 'shepherd(s)' (= rā^{c}e/rā^{c}ayyā?), Gen 4:2, 28:10, and with suffixes r^{c}yy, r^{c}yk, r^{c}wy 'my, your, his shepherds', and note the Spelling r^{c}wwy (= rā^{c}owi) once in Gen 13:7.

(2) Feminine Forms

(a) ḥṭ'h 'sin (=ḥaṭ'ā/ḥeṭ'ā?), twice in Gen 10:9.

(b) brth/bnn/bnt' 'daughter(s)' (=bərattā/bənān/ bənātā, irregular, presumably as in Onkelos, feminine of br 'son'). Common also in the construct brt/bnt (=bərat/bənāt), and with suffixes brtyh, brtn, bnty, bntyh, bnthwn, etc.

(c) r^{c}yyh 'shepherdess' (=rā^{c}əyā, cf. the masculine r^{c}y above), Gen 29:9.

2. The Form qyl

a. Masculine - qilā: qil::qilayyā:qilin

byš'/byš/byšyy'/byšyn 'evil'; gyd' 'sinew' (Gen 32:32, twice, once misspelled through metathesis gdy'); gyryn 'arrows' (Exod 15:4); dyn'/dyn 'judgment', note also the plural dynynn 'our judgments', Gen 19:9, and the misspellings dyynyn, for dynyn, meaning 'arguments', in Gen 13:7,8, and dyyny 'my judgments', for dynyy, in Gen 26:5, cf. dyny 'my judgment', Gen 16:5, and note also Exod 21:9, dnhwn!; zyw(w)hwn 'their brightness' (Gen 4:5, 6); mynyh/mynh/mynhwn 'its (ms)/ its (fs)/ their type'; myt/mytyy' 'dead' (singular, Deut 14:1, plural Gen 19:26, 25:34, and note also mty, mtk, mtyh 'my/ your/ his dead', all in Gen 23:4, 6, 8, 11, 13, 15); nsy 'islands' (construct, Gen 10:5); nyr 'yoke' (construct, Gen 27:40); syt 'joint' (construct, Gen 11:4, 28:12, 17); qys'/qysyn/qysy(y)' 'wood', 'twigs'; šyryn 'songs'.

Feminine - There are limited feminine forms of this type attested:

byšt'/byš'/byšn 'evil'; tyrthwn 'their castles' (Gen 25:16); ksh 'fodder' (Gen 24:25, 32, cf. Onkelos); mytty 'my death' (Gen 27:2); sy^{c}' 'company' (Gen 26:26, 37:25).

b. Masculine - qaylā(qelā):qayil(qel) :: qaylayyā(qelayyā):qaylin(qelin)

There is no evidence to indicate whether the diphthongs in these words have been monophthongized: by(y)t' 'house' (common in compound expressions, byt knyšwt my',byt 'pyh, byt qwdš', etc.). The plural is attested, e.g., in Gen 25:27 bty mdrš' 'schoolhouses', Gen 30:13 bty knyšwt' 'synagogues', and with suffixes in Gen 17:12,13 btykwn 'your houses', however cf. Exod 1:21 btym! (for MT bāttîm, therefore presumably in imitation thereof) and especially Exod 8:9 byty!? (for MT habbāttîm, = bete?); zynk 'your weapon' (Gen 27:3); zyt 'olive' (Gen 8:11, abbreviated zy`); hyl 'strength' (Gen 31:29, cf. also hyyly 'my strength', Gen 31:6); ^{c}y(y)n' 'spring' (common, and in place names such as ^{c}yn dyn' and ^{c}yn gdy tmry', Gen 14:7); ᶜyn/ᶜyynyh 'eye(s)' (the singular in Lev 24:20, the plural in Gen 3:6; note also Gen 29:17 ᶜyny dl'h 'the eyes of Leah', presumably for ᶜyny l'h, and also Gen 38:25 ᶜyyny for ᶜyynyh 'her eyes'; also common with suffixes); ṣyd/ṣydh 'game' (Genesis, Chapter 27); qyṭ 'summer' (Gen 8:22); ryḥh 'smell' (Gen 27:27, and also construct ryḥ in the same verse).

Feminine - There is a limited number of feminine forms:

'ymtkwn 'your dread' (='ematkon?, Gen 9:2); ḥywh 'animal' (= ḥewā?, Gen 37:33, determined ḥywwt', Gen 37:20, construct ḥywt br' 'wild animals', Gen 31:39, plural determined ḥywt' in Gen 3:14, though possibly also the singular); ḥy(y)lwwt(y)h 'his hosts' (= ḥelwāteh?, Gen 21:22, 32, 26:26)/ ḥlwwthwn 'their hosts' (Gen 2:1).

c. Masculine - qillā: qel:: qillayyā: qillin

zyq'/zyq 'bottle' (Gen 21:14,15,19); ḥṭy(y)'/ḥyṭyn 'wheat' (=feminine noun, as in Onkelos?, Gen 30:14, Deut 8:8, 32:14; ḥn 'favor'; ṭl 'shade' (construct, ṭl šryty 'the shade of my roof', Gen 19:8); lbh 'heart', and common with suffixes, lby, lbk, etc., and cf. lbb in Section D, above); n(y)s'/nsy'/n(y)syn 'miracle(s)' (Gen 15:2, 21:8, 28:10, and note also nsy in Exod 4:21, for nsy'?; ᶜz/ᶜ(y)zy(y)'/ᶜzyn 'goat(s)'; syypyh 'ends' (Gen 23:9, bsyypyh ḥqly 'at the ends of his fields', for bsyypy ḥqlyh?); ryq 'empty' (Gen 37:24); š(y)ry'/šryn 'bracelets' (Gen 24:22, 30, 47). Also šyṭyn 'acacia wood' (Deut 10:3, feminine as in Onkelos?).

Feminine - The following common feminine forms are attested:

'št'/'š' 'fire'; 'tt'/'th 'woman' (spelled 'ytt' in Gen 3:1, 2, 4, 15, and with suffixes, 'tty, 'ttk, '(y)ttyh, etc.); gnth/gn' 'garden', and in the construct gnt ᶜdn 'garden of Eden' (Gen 3:24); mylh/m(y)ly'/m(y)lyn 'word(s)', 'thing(s)', with masculine plural ending, and with suffixes mlyy, mlyk, mlwy 'my/ your/ his words', etc.

d. Other

(1) Masculine

The following forms, usually spelled with -y-, do not belong in one of the above categories for a variety of reasons, and hence are grouped together in a miscellaneous category. b'r'/b'r/b'ry'/b'ryn 'well(s)' (= be(')r < bə'er, with aleph retained as an historical spelling). Note occasional spellings b'yrh, byr', etc.; feminine noun, e.g., b'r ḥwry, Gen 26:21,22, but cf. b'ryyt', feminine plural below; lyb' 'curds' (Gen 18:8, cf. Onkelos in Jastrow, "Dictionary," p. 695, Levy, "Wörterbuch," p. 405, but not in Sperber, "Onkelos," nor in Aberbach and Grossfeld, "Onkelos," ləwā'e, perhaps to be taken here as ləwā'e ⟶ ləwe = /ləve/ ⟶ /live/, and spelled thus in error by the medieval copyist); m^{c}yy' 'womb' (=me^{c}ayyā, plural only, Gen 30:2, and note the suffixed forms m^{c}yk, m^{c}y(y)h 'your/her loins', but cf. m^{c}k, Gen 3:14, and especially m^{c}h'(!) Gen 25:22); ^{c}yqy! 'sorrowful ones' (= ^{c}āyəqi?) in a midrash in Gen 38:25; pyry (singular)/pyryn 'fruit' (=pire/ pirin?), Gen 1:11, 12, 3:18, Deut 11:9, plus construct plural p(y)ry, and with suffixes prwy 'its fruits' (= pirowi?, Gen 3:6); ryš 'head' (Gen 32:26), and with suffixes r'šk, r'š(y)h, ryšyh, r'šh. For the plural, cf. the construct r'šy (Gen 2:10, 25:3) and ryšy (Gen 8:5).

(2) Feminine

b'ryyt' 'wells', an alternate feminine plural form found only in Gen 26:18, cf. b'r etc. in the masculine forms above; s'yn 'seahs' (= se'in, sə'in?), Gen 18:6; ^{c}ṣh/^{c}ṣn 'advice' (= ^{ca}ṣā/^{ca}ṣān?), Gen 29:22, Gen 15:11, Exod 1:10; qyymt'/qyym'(!) 'pillar' (= qimā?, or perhaps qāyəmā, cf. Onkelos, spelled only thus, apparently due to confusion with qəyāmā 'convenant', often in Genesis, e.g., 28:10, 18, 22, 35:14, 20, etc.); qynyyn!

'laments' (= qinyān?, cf. Onkelos qinin, the spelling here possibly due to a copyist's confusion with the more common qinyān 'possessions', Gen 4:22; šnh 'sleep' (= šənā?, Gen 2:21, 15:12), and with suffixes šnty, šntyh; šyr' 'meal' (= šerā?, only in Gen 26:30, perhaps an error for the expected šyrw, cf. Gen 19:3, 21:8, 29:22); tynh/t'ynyyh/t'nyn(tynyn) 'fig(s)', cf. Onkelos tə'enā/tenā, spelled with aleph in Num 13:28, Deut 8:8, without in Gen 3:7, Num 20:5. For the same phenomenon, cf. r'šh/ryš, b'rh/byr'.

3. The Form qwl

a. Masculine - qulā: qul:: qulayyā: qulin

ḥwṭ 'thread' (construct, Gen 14:23); ṭwb' 'goodness' (construct ṭwb in Gen 27:28, 39, and with suffixes, cf. ṭwbwy 'his goodness'⟶ 'blessed', used predicatively in Gen 38:25 ṭwbwy kl 'nš 'blessed be every man'); ṭwr'/ṭwry' 'mountain(s)' (= ṭurā/ṭurayyā, but note the plural forms ṭwwryn/ṭwwry (construct), i.e., ṭawrin, Deut 11:11, Gen 10:30, respectively, and also in Onkelos, cf. Jastrow, "Dictionary," p. 526); lwḥh/lwḥyn 'tablet(s)' (= luḥā/luḥin, Exod 26:19, 20, but cf. also lwwḥyn in Deut 10:1, 3, i.e., ləwāḥin?, cf. Jastrow, "Dictionary," p. 696); lwz 'almond' (Gen 30:37); mwš 'feel' (construct, Gen 27:22); nwny' 'fish' (Gen 1:26, plural nwnwy 'its fish', Gen 1:28, 9:2); nwr'/nwr 'fire', e.g., Gen 3:24, 38:25; p(w)m' 'mouth' (Gen 29:2 etc., and with suffixes pwmh/pmh 'her mouth', Gen 8:11, 24:57); rwḥ 'wind', 'spirit'; rwmh 'its (fs) height' (Gen 6:15, abbreviated rwm̀); šwq' 'market'. Feminine - qwltyk/qwlth 'your/ her jug' (= qultik/qultah, e.g., Gen 24:14, 15, etc., and spelled qltk in Gen 24:43); šwmh 'mark' (Gen 30:35).

b. Masculine - qolā: qol:: qolayyā: qolin

zwg 'mate' (cf. Onkelos zog or zug, Gen 2:18, 20, and with suffixes zwg(y)h 'his mate', Gen 1:27, 7:9, 35:9); ḥwbyn 'guilty', and with suffixes ḥwbyy/ḥwbyhwn 'my/ their guilt', Gen 4:13, 15:16; ywm'/ywm/ywmy'/ywmyn 'day(s)'; mwt' 'death'

(Gen 21:16); swph 'end' (Gen 19:26, and common in construct swp, e.g., Gen 4:3); ᶜwp' 'bird(s)', and common in construct ᶜwp; twr/twry(y)'/twryn 'bull'/'cattle', e.g., Lev 16:3, Gen 18:8, 32:5, and note the error form ṭwry'(!), a medieval copyist aural confusion for twry' (MT habbāqār).

Feminine - ḥwbty/ḥwbthwn 'my/ their guilt' (Gen 31:36, 18:20); ywnh/ywn (= yonā/yon, e.g., Gen 8:11, 15:9, but see ywwnh in Gen 8:8, 9, 10, 12, i.e., yawnā?, cf. ṭwr' and lwḥh in (3.a) above (apparently not known in Onkelos); twr' 'cow' (Num 19:2).

c. Other

gwb'/gwb/gwby'/gwbyn 'pit(s)' (= gubbā/gob, Gen 37:22ff, Exod 21:33, Gen 27:30, Num 21:22, respectively); gwryk 'your arrows' (= gurāk?, Gen 27:3, but cf. Gen 49:23 gyryy', therefore probably here also girak, with w/y confusion); hwny 'my condition' (Gen 33:14, = honi, həwāni, hawwāni?, cf. Jastrow, "Dictionary," p. 339); ḥwby/ḥwbk/ḥwbyh 'my/ your/ his bosom' (Exod 4:6, 7); kwbyn 'thorns' (= kubbin/*kob, plural only attested, Gen 3:18, 4:16, Exod 22:5, spelled kwkyn with b/k confusion, see Chapter 2, Orthography); lwb(!) 'plane-tree (= lub? Gen 30:37, but Onkelos ad loc. has dlwb, hence probably also here, in a dittographic error, i.e., ḥṭr' dlbn rṭyb wdlwz wd<d>lwb 'rods of fresh poplar, and of almond, and of plane-tree'); swsy'/swswn/swswwth 'horse(s)' (= susyā/suswān/ suswātā, Gen 49:17, Exod 15:1, 14:9, respectively, and also the plural construct swswwt, Exod 14:23); rwwh 'his appearance' (with consonantal -w-, presumably reweh, Gen 39:6); t'wmyn 'twins' (plural only in the MS, = tə'omin/tə'umin, in Gen 25:24, but spelled twmyyn? in Gen 38:27, possibly an error of metathesis for tywmyn, which would reflect the Onkelos təyomin/təyumin < tə'omin/tə'umin, as in the former. Note that the Hebrew is also unstable, tômîm in the former, tə'ûmîm in the latter); twpyn 'drums' (= tuppin/*top, Gen 31:27). The following feminine noun can also be classified under a miscellaneous heading: 'wmh/'(w)my(y)'/'wmyn

(= 'ummā/'ummayyā/'ummin, with masculine plural suffix, and note the determined singular 'mt', i.e., 'ummətā, Gen 15:14).

I. Gentilics

This section includes most examples of those nouns that are the names of ethnic groups or members thereof. It also encompasses classes, e.g., lywwyh/lywwyy' 'Levite(s)', and professional and regional groups, e.g., srqyy 'Saracens' and mdynḥ'y 'Orientals'. In the MS Neofiti 1, these gentilic nouns occur in three situations: (1) for an MT gentilic name, e.g., mṣryyh 'the Egyptian', for MT hammiṣrî; (2) expanding an MT toponym, e.g., lhbyy' 'the Lehabites', for MT ləhābîm (these are usually masoretic place names with plural endings, but cf. also 'dwm'y 'the Edomites', for MT 'ᵉdôm); (3) interpretive "modern" renderings of masoretic gentilics, e.g., šlm'y 'the Salmites', for MT haqqênî 'the Kenite'. The nominal inflexion is as follows:

Masculine

	Absolute	Determined	
Singular:	ᶜibray	ᶜibrāyā	'Hebrew'
Plural:	ᶜibrāyin	ᶜibrāye	

Feminine

Singular:	miṣriyā	miṣritā	'Egyptian'
Plural:	[not attested]	miṣrāyātā	

The spellings of the above forms is most varied. The following forms are attested:

Masculine

Singular Determined	Singular Absolute	Plural Determined	Plural Absolute	Gloss	Hebrew Vorlage
		'dwm'y 'dwmyy		'the Edomites'	'^{e}dôm
'mwryh		'mwr'y 'mwry`		'the Amorite(s)'	hā'^{e}mōrî
		'ntwky		'the Antiochenes'	haḥ^{a}mātî
		'rwwdyy'		'the Arvadites'	hā'arwādî
'rm'h 'rmyyh				'the Aramaean'	hā'^{a}rammî
		'rtwsy'		'the Orthosians'	hassînî
		grgš'y (drǧsyy!, Gen 15:21)		'the Girgashites'	haggirgāšî
		zymryy'		'the Zimarites'	haṣṣəmārî
ḥywwyh ḥywwy'		ḥwwy' (Gen 10:17) ḥwwyy (Exod 3:8) ḥywyy (Exod 3:17)		'the Hivite(s)'	haḥiwwî
		ḥwwryy' (Gen 14:6)		'the Haurites'!	haḥōrî
ḥwwrnyh (Gen 36:20) ḥwwrny` (Gen 36:21)				'the Hauranite'!	haḥōrî
ḥytyy' ḥytyyh ḥty(y)h		ḥtyy ḥyt'y ḥt'h (Gen 23:5)		'the Hittite(s)'	haḥittî bənê ḥēt bənôt ḥēt
		ybwsy' ybwsyy		'the Jebusites'	haybûsî

Masculine

Singular Determined	Singular Absolute	Plural Determined	Plural Absolute	Gloss	Hebrew Vorlage
yśr'lyyh (Lev 24:10,11)				'the Israelite'	hayyisrə'ēlî
kn^{c}n'h		kn^{c}n'y(y) kn^{c}ny' kn^{c}nyy kn^{c}y'! (Gen 10:18) kn^{c}n^{c}'y!? (Gen 24:3, 28:1,6,8)		'the Canaanite(s)'	hakkəna^{ca}nî kənā^{c}an
		kslwḥy'		'the Casluhites'	kaslūḥîm
		lhbyy'		'the Lehabites'	ləhābîm
		lwdy'		'the Ludites'	lūdîm
lywwyh (Exod 4:14)		lywwyy' lywwyyh lyw(w)yy (Lev 25:32,33) lwyy(Num 3:12)		'the Levite(s)'	hallēwî halləwiyyim
mdynyh (Num 10:29)		mdyyny(y)	mdyynyn (adj., Gen 37:28)	'Midianite(s)' 'Midianite'(adj.)	hammidyānî midyān hammədānîm midyānîm(adj.)
		mdynḥ'y (Gen 15:19)		'the Orientals'	haqqadmōnî
		mw'byh mw'byy		'the Moabites'	mô'āb
mṣry(y)h	mṣr'y (Gen 39:1)	mṣr'y mṣry(y)h (Exod 3:8)		'the Egyptian(s)'	hammiṣrî
	mṣryy (Exod 2:11)			'an Egyptian'	miṣrî
		mṣryy (Exod 3:17)			hammiṣrîm
		nptwḥyy'		'the Naphtuhites'	naptūḥîm

Masculine

Singular Determined	Singular Absolute	Plural Determined	Plural Absolute	Gloss	Hebrew Vorlage
		sdwmy'		'the Sodomites'	no Vorlage
		spry'		'the Sepharites'	səpārā (directional)
		srqyy	srqyn (*)		(hay)yišmə^{c}ē(')lîm
^{c}bryy' ^{c}br'(!) (Gen 39:17)	^{c}bry(y) (Exod 2:11)	^{c}bry'	^{c}bryyn (Exod 2:13)	'the Hebrew(s)' 'Hebrew'	hā^{c}ibrî ^{c}ibrî (^{c}ibrîm) bənê ^{c}ēber
^{c}dwlmyyh		^{c}dwlmyy		'the Adullamite' 'an Adullamite'	(hā)^{ca}dūllāmî
		(bny) ^{c}mwnyy		'(sons of) the Ammonites'	bənê ^{c}ammôn
		^{c}mlqy'		'the Amalekites'	hā^{ca}mālēqî
		^{c}nmyh		'the Anamites'	^{ca}nāmîm
		^{c}rqy'		'the Arkites'	hā^{c}arqî
		plšt'y plyšty'		'the Philistines'	pəlištîm
		pryzy' pryzy(y)		'the Perizzites'	happərizzî
		ptrwsy'		'the Pathrusites'	patrūsîm
		qnyz'y		'the Kenizzites'	haqqənizzî
		qpwdqy'		'the Capadocians'	kaptōrîm
		šlm'y(šlmyy) (Gen 15:19, Num 24:24)		'the Shalmites'	haqqênî

Feminine

Singular Determined	Singular Absolute	Plural Determined	Plural Absolute	Gloss	Hebrew Vorlage
yśr'lyth (Lev 24:10				'the Israelite'	hayyiśrə'ēlît
kwšyth (Num 12:1)	kwšyh (Num 12:1)			the 'Cushite' 'a Cushite'	hakkūšît kūšît
kn^{c}nyth (Exod 6:15)				'the Canaanite'	hakkəna^{ca}nît
mdynyth (Num 25:6)				'the Midianite'	hammidyānît
mṣryth/ mṣryt' (Gen 16:3, 21:9, 25:12)	mṣryy' (Gen 16:1)	mṣryyth (Exod 1:19)		'the Egyptian(s)' 'an Egyptian'	hammiṣrît miṣrît hammiṣriyyōt
		^{c}bryyt' (Exod 1:15,16,19)		'the Hebrews'	hā^{c}ibriyyōt

(*)Gen 37:25, written srqyn srq^{c}yn!., which is apparently the normal method in this MS of deletion, i.e., read srq^{c}yn, in which case, perhaps error of c for ', i.e., srq'yn?

NOTES

[1]For the full particulars of the data, see Golomb, *A Grammar of the Aramaic in Codex Vatican Neophyti 1 (Genesis)*, Ph.D. dissertation, Harvard University, 1978.

[2]Note should also be taken of *sydwryh*, presumably = *siddurayyā*, meaning 'blindness' in Gen 19:11, emended by Díez Macho to *sy<n>wryh* to better render MT (*bas*)*sanwērîm*. However, in view of the biblical Hebrew *hapax legomenon* in Job 10:22 *'ereṣ ^{c}ēpātā kəmô 'ōpel ṣalmāwet wəlō' sədārîm*, usually translated 'a land of darkness, like darkness, the shadow of death, *without any order*', this may be a genuine Semitic idiom for 'blindness'. Further militating against Díez Macho's emendation is the spelling with *-y-*, since a form such as **sinwer*(*îm*) is unattested in any language. The Job passage might then be rendered 'a land of darkness, like darkness, the darkness of death, *not that of blindness*'.

[3]Note also the same spelling in Gen 1:14, presumably also = ^{c}*ibbur*, meaning 'passing', in *lmqdš<'>* *bhwn* ^{c}*bwr* *śhryn* *yrḥyn* 'to sanctify by them the passing of moons (and?) months', paraphrasing MT (*wəhāyû*) *ləyāmîm* *wəšānîm*.

CHAPTER 8
VERBS

A. Inflection

1. Tense Forms

In a targumic text, the appearance of any given verbal tense is often conditioned on the tense used in the Hebrew base text. In particular, the Targum usually follows the Hebrew in the matter of the use of the perfect tense, less so with the imperfect (which is often translated into the Aramaic by a participial form, or, commonly, by a compound tense of 'to be' + participle). However, other factors must also be considered, e.g., intentional mimicking of Hebrew, "archaizing," interpretive translation, misinterpretation of the Hebrew, and the like. A discussion of the many complexities of the targumic verbal conventions is out of place in a grammatical study such as this, however for two syntactic questions, see Chapter 9, Syntax. In this section, the different forms attested are described and discussed, with examples provided for each section. No attempt has been made to provide an exhaustive list of all attested forms in the entire MS, but rather to provide paradigms with selected examples.

The tenses are as expected: perfect, imperfect, imperative, infinitive, participles. There is no independent jussive attested, with the exception of the verbs 'to be' and 'to live' (see below, Section 3.J). In general, the use of these tenses in this MS conforms to expected Aramaic norms; there are, however, numerous error forms, where one finds perfect for imperfect, imperfect for perfect, and these must be considered by and large as copyist visual or aural errors (see Chapter 2, Orthography). There is considerable variation in forms, especially due to the variable use of the *matres lectionis* *w* and *y*. The classification of the different verbal classes in this MS must await an independent detailed study, however when variant forms are attested they are noted below.

The participial forms occur either in isolation or compounded with the verb 'to be' (in all finite and infinite verbal forms), or also occasionally with attached pronominal suffixes (e.g., Gen 26:22 tqpynn 'we are strong', Num 13:32 ᶜbrynn 'we are passing'), however cf. Dalman, "Grammatik," pp. 230, 234-5. Participles also occur in the construct state (e.g., Gen 4:21 tpśy knwr' 'those who hold the lyre'), the determined state (e.g., Exod 15:6,9 śn'h 'the enemy'), or with suffixes (e.g., Exod 20:5 śn'y/ śn'yy 'my enemies'). The active and passive participles of the D and C stems are spelled identically, as are the D and C stem infinitives (see below).

2. Conjugations

The following conjugations are attested in the MS: (a) a base stem, referred to here as the G stem; (b) an "intensive" stem, referred to as the D stem; (c) a causative stem, referred to as the C stem; (d) two medio-passive (with occasional reflexive meanings) stems, corresponding to the G and D stems, referred to here as the Gt and the Dt stems (for the Ct, see below); (e) other rarer forms.

a. The vowel classes that characterize the G stem in Aramaic are, by and large, not distinguishable in this MS due to the unvocalized nature of the text. There are many examples of a G stem stative type verb written plene with y, among both the strong and the weak verbs, but all are also attested spelled without y, usually much more frequently, e.g., dḥl/dḥyl, nsb/nsyb.

b. The D stem is indistinguishable from the G stem in the perfect and imperfect (many G stem imperfects are spelled yqtl), however infinitives and participles of the D stem are marked by prefix m-. Furthermore, even if marked forms are not available for a given lexical item, many are identifiable as D stem on either comparative grounds (e.g., brk 'to bless', šmš 'to serve', šbḥ 'to praise') or due to the existence of contrasting pairs (e.g., ᶜbr G 'to pass'/ᶜbr D 'to be pregnant', ᶜtr G 'to be rich'/ᶜtr D 'to make rich'). Nevertheless, some are still open to interpretation, e.g., *šlḥ* translates both MT *šālaḥ* and *šillē^{a}ḥ* in the MS, and hence it could be either G or D stem. Similar considerations hold for the Gt and Dt stems.

c. In the C stem, the preformative of the perfect tense is always *'-*, never *h-*. The forms of the imperfect are not always spelled *yqtyl*, i.e., with medial *y*, hence they are often indistinguishable from the G (and D) imperfect. Similarly, the spelling of the C stem infinitive and participles is also generally indistinguishable from the D stem counterparts, and while many are obviously C stem on comparative grounds, there are many whose interpretation is unclear (however, a glance at both Jastrow and Levy reveals that this is the common situation throughout Middle Aramaic).

d. The perfect prefix of the Gt/Dt stems is *'t-*, with occasional spellings *'yt-* (e.g., Gen 21:6 *'ytqbl*, etc.), never *ht-*, however there are occasional unusual error forms, e.g., Gen 22:18 *htbrkwn*, Gen 34:9 *ht^{c}rbw*, where the sense of the text demands an imperfect. In all forms, the Gt is indistinguishable in spelling from the Dt, and individual items can only be assigned based on comparative grounds, or on the existence of a G or D stem base verb. There are also rare error forms with syncope of the *'-* of the prefix *'t*, e.g., Gen 8:4 *wštdkt* 'and it came to rest', probably to be explained as simple copyist error. In the Gt/Dt stems, there is the expected sibilant metathesis (e.g., Deut 18:10 *yštkḥ*, Gen 15:17 *'stdrw*); sibilant metathesis with partial assimilation (e.g., Gen 22:18 *'zdmn*, Num 24:24 *yṣṭrpwn*), and full assimilation to dentals (e.g., Num 22:25 *'dḥqt*, Gen 31:49 *nṭmr*, Exod 22:9 *ytbr*, however cf. occasional learned copyist error forms such as Deut 19:5 *wyzdḥp* in error for *wtdḥp*, see also Chapter 2 *Orthography*). Less commonly, one finds other medio-passive stems spelled without the *-t-*, presumably reflecting full assimilation to the first root consonant, familiar from Babylonian Talmudic Aramaic (e.g., Exod 5:12 *'bdrwn* 'they were scattered', MT wayyāpeṣ, Gen 32:19 'šlḥt 'it has been sent', MT šəlûḥā, and others).

In the strong verbs there are very few obviously Ct forms attested, however, cf. Exod 21:29 where the MT wəhûᶜad is translated by the explicitly spelled (and imperfect!) wyt'shd! 'and it will be (!) made known', based on the C stem 'shd (cf. Onkelos ad loc., wə'ittashad); similarly, Lev 27:29 yt'prš 'he will be set aside', MT yoḥoram, based on the C stem 'prš (cf. Onkelos ad loc., yittaḥram). However, elsewhere the spelling is inconclusive, e.g., Lev 4:10 ytprš 'it will be separated', MT yûram (cf. Onkelos ad loc., mittapraš).

e. The most widely attested of the rarer stems is the Š (and occasional Št), found in the following verbs: šzyb, škll, šlhp, šᶜbd and the tertiae infirmae verbs šyṣy and šlhy (see below, and cf. Kaufman, "Akkadian Influences," pp. 104-105, 123-124).

There are also three roots found in intensive stems spelled with -w- ("Poᶜel", "Ithpoᶜel"), sbr, rqn and tqp (see below), and occasional geminate stems spelled with -w- ("Polel", "Ithpolel"), e.g., mᶜwrr 'stir up' (Deut 32:11), nrwmmnh 'we will extol him' (Exod 15:12), mšwṭṭn 'scanning' (Gen 22:10) and 'tbwnnw 'consider!' (Deut 32:7). For details, see below.

B. Strong Verbs

1. The G Stem (Paradigm A)

a. The situation in the MS concerning the G stem vowel classes is most complex, with considerable mixing of the classes; this is exacerbated by the inconsistent use of matres lectionis. However, this situation is familiar from other contemporary Middle Aramaic dialects, and especially so in the language of Onkelos. There are numerous examples of a stative perfect written plene with -y-, however all verbs so attested are also found unmarked, usually much more frequently. The following strong verbs are found marked (at least once) with -y- in the perfect: dḥyl, zbyn, ḥkym, ḥpyr(!), ^{c}byd, pqyd, qṭyl, qryb, šlym, tqyp. Numerous other examples are found in the weak verbs, for which see below.[1] These examples from the strong verbs are as expected; cf. Dalman, "Grammatik," pp. 206 ff.

The spelling of the 1s suffix is distributed evenly between -t and -yt, and note also occasional error(?) forms such as Gen 44:18 'mry 'I said'. There is no indication of gender distinction in the second person singular (however there are some rare 2ms D stem "archaic" forms spelled -t'!, e.g., Gen 35:9, 'lpt', Gen 18:15, 19:21, ml(y)lt', ; note also other rare forms, e.g., Gen 20:9, ḥṭ'n'. Occasionally, the 2m and 2f singular is spelled -yt, e.g., Gen 26:10, ^{c}bdyt (ms), Gen 3:13, ^{c}bdyt (fs), apparently the resolution of the final consonant cluster (or, with this verb, an error of metathesis for ^{c}bydt).

The 3fpl form is rarely distinguished from the 3mpl, but when so, it is spelled -n, e.g., Gen 19:8 ḥkmn, Gen 33:6 qrybn. There are also 3 pers. pl. forms ending in -wn, with the suffix extended from the imperfect, e.g., š'lwn, Gen 26:7 (3mpl), ^{c}bdwn, Exod 1:17 (3fpl). Few 2fpl forms are attested in the MS, but those found appear to be identical to the 2 mpl, e.g., Exod 1:18 ^{c}bdtwn, Exod 2:20 šbqtwn.

Apart from the anomalous ḥṭ'n', the 1pl is spelled qtlnn. There are some examples of a suffix -ynn that from context cannot be interpreted as compounded participial forms, ^{c}brynn, Num 13:32, kbšynn, Deut 2:34, šm^{c}ynn, Gen 42:21, Deut 5:24, presumably ^{ca}barenan/ kəbašenan/ šəma^{c}enan with the suffix extended from nearby tertiae infirmae verbs, namely ḥmynn, Num 13:32, šyṣynn, Deut 2:34 ḥmynn, Gen 42:31, Deut 5:24 respectively. Note also rare error forms such as 'šthynwn and ḥzrnwn! in Gen 43:10, perhaps influenced by Hebrew -nw and by the adverb kdwn in the same verse.

b. In the imperfect too there is considerable confusion of vowel classes -- numerous plene spellings with -w- with occasional defectively spelled doublets, e.g., 'ḥzwr (Gen 18:14) vs. 'ḥzr (Gen 18:10), in addition to many verbs not marked by mater lectionis at all, but presumably of the u-imperfect type. The only verbs unequivocally assignable to the a-imperfect class are tertiae gutturalis, e.g., tšlḥ (Deut 15:13), and it should be noted that there are some mediae gutturalis spelled with -w-, e.g., yš'wl (Num 27:21), yrḥwm (Deut 7:13). The only strong verb spelled with -y- in the imperfect is ^{c}bd, e.g., '^{c}byd (Gen 31:43), t^{c}byd (Gen 6:16, 18:5), see Dalman, "Grammatik," pp. 216ff.

The 2fs is not common, but when found is spelled -yn, e.g., tdḥlyn (Gen 21:17, 35:17), t^{c}bdyn (Gen 20:13, spelled t^{c}bdwn with w/y confusion). In the 1s, there are occasional spellings such as '^{c}ybr 'let me pass' (Deut 2:27) with -y- to mark the shewa mobile, so 'a^{ca}bar ⟶ 'a^{c}əbar ⟶ 'a^{c}ibar?, however, cf. '^{c}br (Gen 30:32) and Dalman, "Grammatik," p. 218 (and also Chapter 2, Orthography, above).

There is no gender distinction marked between the 3 pers. pl. masc. or fem., nor between the 2 pers. pl. masc. or fem., e.g., yšlṭwn 'they will rule' (Gen 16:12, 3 fpl), tqṭlwn 'you will kill' (Exod 1:16, 2 fpl), however cf. occasional feminine plural forms preserved in, e.g., D stem yshdn 'they will witness' (Gen 30:33) and elsewhere. There are some prefixes spelled plene with -y-, e.g., nyṭrw<d> (Gen 3:22, abbreviated at the end of the line).

c. In the G stem imperative, there are some masc. sing. forms spelled with -w-, e.g., ḥzwr, ṭrwd, kpwt, nkws, but most are spelled simply without mater lectionis, e.g., dbr, ḥkm, ^{c}bd, qrb, etc. The fem. singular has ^{c}bydy (Gen 18:6), alongside ^{c}bdy (Gen 16:6) and ḥzry (Gen 16:9), but cf. the mpl ḥzwrw! (Deut 5:30), and also šlwṭw and tqwpw, as well as tqypw and kbyšw (= w/y confusion?). As can be seen, the situation is confused with the imperatives, and while in general they appear to belong to the same vowel class as the imperfects, the lack of a mater lectionis is in no way significant, and each lexical item should be examined independently. Again, there is no gender distinction between masc. and fem. plural forms, e.g., šm^{c}w (Gen 4:23, fem. pl.).

d. Most G stem infinitives are spelled without -w-, mqtl, however cf. e.g., msbwl (Gen 4:13) mṭrwd (Gen 20:18), mzbwn (Deut 2:6), mdḥwl (Deut 4:9, but mydḥl in Deut 10:12), etc. For other spellings of the prefix with -y-, see, e.g., mydḥwp (Deut 6:19). Again, absence of a mater lectionis is not significant, nor does there appear to be any connection between the spelling of the infinitive and that of the imperfect, e.g., mḥzr, mšbq, mšlṭ, etc. Occasional forms spelled without m- appear to be either copyist error (e.g., Gen 19:33 dmkh, cf. the parallel verse in 19:35 mdmkh 'her lying down') or else imitation of a Hebrew form (e.g., Gen 23:6 mlqbr 'from burying' MT miqqəbōr, cf. Gen 23:8 mqbr 'to bury'). However, other stems also lack the prefix on occasion, e.g., D stem lqbl', Exod 15:12.

The infinitive can also occur with pronominal subject suffixes, e.g., m^{c}rqk 'your fleeing (Gen 35:1), mšm^{c}hwn 'their hearing' (Gen 20:8), and much less commonly, with pronominal direct object suffixes, e.g., mqṭlyh 'to kill him' (Gen 37:18, MT lah^{a}mitô), cf. Chapter 9, Syntax.

e. While the ideal form of the masc. sing. active participle is spelled qtyl, in fact the defective spelling qtl occurs at the rate of approximately 8:1. While one does find such isolated forms as rḥyš 'creeping' (Gen 7:8), the preferred spelling rḥš occurs no less than eight times in Genesis, and cf. rḥym (Gen 37:3,4)/rḥm (Gen 29:20), etc. (The form pryq 'redeeming' in 'lh pryq, Gen 17:8, 28:21, may be rather the noun prwq, i.e., pāroq, cf. Lev 26:45 'lh prwq, or else w/y confusion for pryq.) There are also many examples of roots ending in either -r or a guttural, presumably, then, of the type qātal, e.g., ^{c}br 'passing', ptḥ 'opening', šm^{c} 'hearing', etc.

The fem. sing. active participle is predominantly spelled qtlh (approximately 10:1 over the spelling qtl'). For the fs used in the construct, cf. the common phrase npqt brh 'whore', literally 'she who goes out into the open' (e.g., Gen 38:21).

Some masc. plural forms are spelled with -y-, e.g., ḥkymyn 'knowing' (Gen 29:5), rḥyṣyn 'trusting' (Deut 28:52), i.e., presumably ḥākəmin→ ḥākimin, rāḥəṣin→rāḥiṣin, since they cannot be passive participles by context. These are also construct forms, e.g., tpśy knwr' 'those who hold the lyre' (Gen 4:21), plḥy ṭᶜwwth 'those who worship idols' (Deut 3:29), etc.

The fem. plural is ideally qtln, but generally it has been replaced by the masc. plural, cf. npqn 'going out' (Gen 24:11), slqn 'going up' (Gen 41:5), but more commonly slqyn (Gen 41:2ff, and others), npqyn (Gen 24:13), qrbyn 'approaching' (Num 27:1), etc.

The participle occurs most commonly as a compound tense with either finite or infinite forms of the verb 'to be', often for an MT imperfect or participle. For full discussion, see Chapter 9 Syntax.

There do not appear to be any compound participles of the type qtyln', qtylnn, etc. familiar from Babylonian Talmudic Aramaic. In Section A.(i) above, it was suggested that such forms as ᶜbrynn, kbšynn, etc. are perfects with suffix -ynn extended from tertiae infirmae verbs. All the examples cited did indeed have such weak forms in the same verse, but there are also examples without, e.g., Gen 26:22 tqpynn 'we have become strong' (MT pārînû). It is doubtful that these are compound participial forms, since (1) there are no examples from other conjugations; (2) unattached examples of participle + personal pronoun are common, e.g., ydᶜ 'nh 'I know' (Num 22:6), ḥkymyn 'nn 'we know' and ḥkymyn 'twn 'you know' (both in Gen 29:5), etc.

f. The passive participle of the strong verb occurs frequently, e.g., ktyb 'written' (Deut 9:10), šmyᶜ 'heard' (Exod 2:24), etc., and in the determined state brykh 'the blessed one' (Gen 24:31, 26:29). There are occasional defectively spelled forms, e.g., h' slm qb^{c} 'a ladder was fixed' (Gen 28:12).

The feminine singular is usually spelled qtylh, rarely qtyl', e.g., qby^{c}' (Gen 28:12), and note also š'lh 'borrowed' (Num 22:30), and others. For the construct, see Gen 17:27 zbynt ksp 'that bought with silver'.

The masc. plural (ktybyn, Deut 9:10, ḥšybyn 'considered', Exod 16:7, rby^{c}yn 'crouched', Gen 29:2, etc.) also has determined forms, e.g., qṭylyh 'the killed ones' (Gen 15:1, 34:27), construct forms, e.g., zbyny ksp 'those bought with silver' (Gen 17:23), and forms with pronominal suffixes, e.g., ḥbyšwy 'his bound ones' (Gen 39:20).

Feminine plural forms are not common -- ideally ending in -n, more commonly in -yn, e.g., zqypn 'raised' (Gen 29:17, Exod 17:12), msyryn 'handed over' (Gen 30:22), štylyn 'planted' (Num 24:6).

There are also uncommon passive participles of the form qtwl, e.g., ṭ^{c}wnyn 'loaded' (Gen 37:25); pswl/pswlh 'blemished' (Gen 49:2 but cf. psyl in the parallel verse Deut 6:4, hence perhaps a case of w/y confusion?); ḥtwm 'sealed' (Deut 32:34, MT ḥātūm), etc.

2. The D Stem (Paradigm B)

a. The spelling of the perfect of the D stem is by and large not distinguished from that of the G stem. Occasional spellings with -y- are found, e.g., qṭylw (Gen 49:6), zbynw (Gen 25:33), zbyn (Gen 25:33), bryk (Gen 14:9, cf. brk, Gen 24:1), šmyšt (Gen 19:33, cf. šmšt, Gen 19:35), but the overwhelming majority are spelled "defectively," e.g., qdš (Exod 19:14), qrbt (Exod 4:25), srbtwn (Deut 1:26), etc.

There are occasional error forms, usually of metathesis, e.g., Gen 30:17 ^{c}bryt 'she became pregnant', for ^{c}byrt; also Gen 37:28 zbn' 'they sold', for zbnw; Gen 19:36 ^{c}bryn 'they became pregnant' (for ^{c}byrn?).

b. Most imperfect forms are also spelled without -y-, but cf. e.g., Gen 4:14 yqṭyl 'he will slaughter' (MT yahargēnî), Lev 6:14 tqryb 'you will offer' vs., e.g., Lev 6:15 yqrb 'he will offer',

Lev 20:17 yqbl 'he will receive', Exod 22:4 yšlm 'he shall make restitution', Lev 5:18 ykpr 'he shall make atonement', etc. For quadriliteral imperfects, cf. e.g., Lev 27:33 ypšpš 'he shall search', Exod 15:17 t'ḥsn 'you shall cause them to possess', Exod 23:8 yṭlṭl 'it shall remove', Gen 11:7, Exod 14:13, 14 n^{c}rbb 'let us confound', but cf. Deut 7:23 y^{c}rbwb(!) 'he will confound' (= y^{c}rbyb, with w/y confusion?), and note also Exod 14:13, 14 nlwly, nlwwly 'let us shout' (presumably w/y confusion for nlwlw = nəlawlew for nəlableb, cf. Jastrow, "Dictionary," p. 689).

For the 3 fpl imperfect ending in -n, cf. Gen 30:33 yshdn, Deut 31:21 y'r^{c}n, etc. vs., e.g., Gen 30:13 yšbḥwn.

c. Most D stem imperatives are in the masc. sing and again most are spelled without -y-, e.g., brk, zbn, qbl, qrb, šmš (all occurring frequently). For forms spelled plene, cf. e.g., ḥšyb 'reckon' (Gen 23:15), z^{c}yr 'make small' (Num 23:7) and qbylw 'listen' (Gen 38:25 and often). Feminine forms are rare, however cf. Exod 15:12 qbly 'accept' (twice) and note Gen 19:34 šmš!, clearly a copyist error for šmšy in the phrase ^{c}wly wšmš(y) 'enter and serve' (MT bō'î šikbî). No fem. plural forms are found.

d. The spelling of the D stem infinitive is divided approximately evenly between mqtlh and mqtl'. There are occasional forms without the prefix m-, e.g., Gen 9:15 lḥbl' 'to destroy', Exod 15:12 lqbl' to receive', always with the preposition l- (not exclusive of m- however, cf. Exod 8:25 lmšqrh 'to lie', lmšlḥ' 'to send forth'). There are also copyist errors such as Gen 28:12 lmbśry 'to bring good news' with y/h confusion (i.e., י for ה, cf. Chapter 2, Orthography).

It is not certain whether the construct (qdmwt 'to meet' ⟶ 'towards' (e.g., Exod 19:17) should be interpreted here as a D stem infinitive (with Dalman, "Grammatik," p. 227), or as an independent nominal form.

e. The active participle is as expected, however there are no masc. sing. forms spelled with -y-. All are spelled mqtl, e.g., Gen 27:29 mbrk 'bless', Num 32:25 mpqd 'command', and determined state, Exod 4:25 mḥblh 'the destroyer'. There are some unusual forms, e.g., Deut 4:8 ('nh) sdr! '(I) order'; Gen 12:3 mbrkk (ytk) 'blesses (you)' (presumably an error of dittography, probably influenced by the Hebrew məbārəkeykā, and cf. mbrk in the identical idiom in Gen 27:29; Gen 21:9 mghk 'laugh' for mgḥk with h/ḥ confusion.

Note the fem. sing. participle with the direct object suffix in Gen 38:25 mprsyyh 'divulge him' (presumably məparsəyeh < məpārəsā + eh), and also the masc. plural determined state mšbḥy' 'those whose praise' (Gen 32:27). The fem. plural forms are spelled with -n, e.g., Gen 26:35 mgḥkn 'laugh', mqbln 'receive', the masc. plural -yn, e.g., Lev 24:12, Num 21:15 mqṭlyn 'kill', Gen 49:27 mqrbyn 'offer', mplgyn 'divide', etc.

f. The passive participle is always mqtl, e.g., Gen 4:8 mdbr 'lead', Gen 24:13, 43, Num 22:34 $m^{c}td$ 'placed', Exod 12:9 mhbhb 'roasted', mbšl 'cooked', Deut 4:25, 27:15 mrḥq 'abominable', etc. In Gen 28:17, Exod 19:11 (and elsewhere) one also finds mzwmn(yn) 'prepared', but cf. Exod 19:15, 33:31 mzmn(yn) (and especially Exod 15:17 mwzmn?!, see 3(f) below).

The fem. sing. has $m^{c}brh$ 'pregnant' (Gen 38:25) and for the determined state, cf. mprnqth 'the delicate woman' (Deut 28:56).

The masc. plural is, e.g., mšbḥyn 'praised' (Num 24:6), mqdqdyn 'striped' (Gen 30:39, 31:12), $m^{c}rbyn$ 'mixed' (Deut 22:11), and in the construct mzmny (^{c}m/ qhlh) 'those chosen (out of the people/community)' (Num 1:16, 16:2).

Note the unusual mpqdym 'commanded' (Gen 13:7, no Vorlage, apparently in imitation of Hebrew forms); and also Gen 27:15 mšbḥyyn! (?). There are no fem. plural forms found.

3. The C Stem (Paradigm C)

a. As mentioned above, the C stem perfect prefix is always '-, never h-. All examples of the 3ms noted were of the type 'qtl, never 'qtyl, e.g., 'prš 'he separated' (Gen 30:40), etc., however there are occasional 3mpl forms spelled with -y-, e.g., 'qdymw 'they arose early' (Gen 24:22), 'rgyzw 'they caused anger' (Deut 32:30), and note Deut 32:16 'k^{c}wsw! 'they roused to anger' (presumably 'k^{c}ysw with w/y confusion). The 3fs is occasionally abbreviated, e.g., 'sḥn` 'it supported' (Gen 13:6, root ḥsn?), 'šlm` 'she completed' (Gen 24:19).

The 1pl suffix is -nn, e.g., Gen 26:32 'škḥnn 'we found', but cf. 'rgzn! 'we caused anger' (Deut 32:31, perhaps an error of haplography for 'rgznn).

b. The C imperfect is not well represented. Few of the attested forms are spelled with -y-, and hence they are indistinguishable from those G and D stem imperfects written yqtl. Examples cited are from verbs attested clearly as C stem elsewhere: yṣlḥ (Gen 24:40), tšlm (Deut 20:12, or D?) 'šb^c (Gen 24:3), yšlmwn (Gen 24:19, or D?), tqdmwn (Gen 19:2), nškḥ (Gen 47:25). Problematic is the C stem of root ḥzr spelled apparently with -w- , e.g., 'ḥzwr (Gen 24:5, 28:15), tḥzwr (Gen 24:8), either due to w/y confusion, or copyist confusion with the commonly occurring G stem, or most probably a combination of both.

c. In the C imperative also, most forms are spelled without -y-, however the stem is generally poorly attested. In the ms one finds, e.g., 'dkr 'call to mind' (Lev 22:27), 'nhr 'lighten' (Gen 38:25), 'qrb 'bring near' (Gen 27:25), 'šlm 'complete' (Gen 29:27); in the fs, 'rkyny 'incline down' (Gen 24:14); in the mpl, 'dkrw 'remember' (Deut 32:7), 'mtynw 'wait' (Gen 19:18), and note 'ṣn^{c}wn(!) 'retain' (Gen 42:33, with suffix extended from the imperfect. In this case, this may however be a case of mimicking the ending -wn found three more times in this verse, 'twn, mnkwn, btykwn).

No fpl forms are attested.

d. The C stem infinitive is usually spelled mqtlh (slightly less so mqtl'), i.e., indistinguishable from the D stem infinitive, e.g., mprš' 'to divide' (e.g., Gen 1:4), mḥzrh 'to restore' (e.g., Deut 24:13), etc. Note the y/h confusion in lmškḥy (Gen 27:20, and cf. D stem lmbśry above). The construct form in Exod 36:6, Num 18:19, etc., 'pršwt 'offering' may be a C stem construct infinitive, however cf. other forms of the noun 'pršw (Num 18:14), 'pršwth (Exod 36:3), 'pršwty (Num 18:8), and note also, e.g., 'nhrwth 'illumination' (Num 4:9), 'ḥsnwtk 'your possession' (Exod 15:17), etc.

e. The C stem active participle is also rarely marked with -y-, hence indistinguishable from the D stem forms. For the ms, see mḥzyr 'return' (Gen 20:7) vs. mḥzr (Gen 44:18), mdkr 'remember' (Gen 41:9), mśhd 'testify' (Deut 32:46), mmtyn 'wait' (Gen 27:41), mśby^c 'satisfy' (Gen 30:22), etc. For the mpl, see mzry^{c}yn 'produce seed' (Gen 1:11) vs. mzr^{c}yn (Gen 1:12), mškḥyn 'find' (Gen 19:11), mḥzyryn 'return' (Gen 29:3), mqdmyn 'advance' (Gen 49:8).

The fs and fpl are problematic, as the only examples in the MS have the prefix '-', Gen 16:8 w'n byt 't 'škḥh kbytyh d'brm 'and where is the house that you could find like Abram's house' (no Vorlage) and Gen 19:15 wyt trtyn bntk d'škḥn 'and your two daughters that are here', (MT wə'et-šətê bənōteykā hannimṣā'ōt), explicable only as an error of א for מ. No other feminine forms are available.

f. The only C stem passive participles attested are Exod 15:17 mwzmn 'prepared' (but cf. D stem, Section 2(f) above, perhaps an error of metathesis for mzwmn) and especially mḥlṭ'/mḥlṭh 'declared leprous' (Lev 13:11, 51, 52, for MT nôšenet and mam'eret).

4. The Medio-Passive Stems (Paradigm D)

a. As mentioned previously, there is no orthographic difference between the Gt and the Dt stem, and individual lexical items must be assigned on comparative or synchronic grounds. The prefix is always 't- (with occasional plene spellings 'yt-, e.g., 'ytqblt Gen 15:1, 'ytknš Gen 5:27, etc.). The spelling 'tqtyl is only attested in 't^{c}byd 'it was done' (Exod 2:4, for MT imperfect!), 't^{c}bydw 'there were made' (Exod 14:13), etc. There is also a number of medio-passive perfects spelled without -t-, presumably reflecting full assimilation to the first radical of the root, e.g., 'knyš 'he was gathered' (Gen 5:20), 'bdrwn 'they were scattered' (Exod 5:12), 'dbqtwn 'you adhered' (Deut 4:4, cf. Jastrow, "Dictionary," p. 278), among others. In the 3 masc. and fem. plural perfect there are isolated examples of the imperfect suffix -wn extended to the perfect, e.g., 't^{c}bdwn 'they were made' (Deut 32:31), 'ytpthwn 'they (eyes, fpl) were opened' (Gen 3:7). For the 3fpl endings in -n, see 'tpr^{c}n 'they (our hands) were revenged' (Deut 32:27).

For the very few Ct forms attested in the ms, see section A.2(d) above, and see the I-Aleph, II-w/y, and Geminate verbs below.

b. The stem vowel is marked with -y- only in very few of the many attested 3ms imperfect forms, however cf. ytpsyl 'it will be rejected' (Gen 22:10), ytqtyl 'he will be killed' (Exod 22:18), vs. ytqtl (Exod 21:29, Num 35:16, etc.).

For forms with metathesis and/or dental assimilation, cf. yštb^c 'he has sworn' (Lev 5:24), yzdrqwn 'they will be thrown' (Exod 19:13), tzdhrwn 'you will be careful' (Deut 4:15), etc. Note also tbdqwn 'you will be tested' (Gen 42:15), and ytqp 'he shall be strong' (Num 24:7, or else G stem), and cf. the perfect in section (a) above.

The 3mpl has occasional error forms, e.g., ytknšw 'they will be gathered' (Gen 34:30, for ytknšwn) and yt^{c}bd! 'they will be done' (Exod 33:16, subject nsyn wpl'yn 'miracles and wonders').

The 3fpl has both endings, -wn (from the 3mpl) and -n, cf. ytpršwn 'they will be separated' (Gen 25:23, subject tryn(!) mlkwwn 'two kingdoms') and ytpr^{c}n 'they will be revenged' (Deut 33:7, subject ydwy 'his hands').

c. There are few medio-passive imperative forms attested, none in the fem. pl. Masc. sing. 'zdhr 'take care', masc. pl. 'zdhrw occur frequently (e.g., Gen 31:24, Exod 10:28, Deut 4:9, 8:11), but note Exod 23:21 'zdhrwn! One also finds 'stkl 'look' (Gen 15:5), 'štb^{c} 'swear' (Gen 21:23+), 't^{c}td 'be ready' (Deut 5:31), etc.; in the masc. pl., 'tgrw 'trade' (Gen 34:10), 'tknšw 'be gathered' (Gen 49:1), and note Exod 14:13 't^{c}<t>dw 'be ready' (spelled 't^{c}dw!). The only fem. sing. form attested is 'sṭ^{c}ry 'be troubled' (Gen 16:9).

d. Medio-passive infinitives are also not widely attested, but those found are as expected, e.g., mtḥmdh 'to long for' (Gen 31:30), mstkl' 'to look at' (Gen 3:6), mt^{c}bd' 'to be done' (Gen 20:9, 34:7), mtqṭl 'to be killed' (Gen 26:11+), mtnḥmh 'to be comforted' (Gen 37:35), mštlḥ' 'to be sent' (Exod 4:13+), msṭ^{c}rh 'to be troubled' (Num 12:16), etc.

The infinitive occurs often translating an MT cognate infinitive, e.g., Exod 22:18 mtqṭlh ytqṭyl 'he shall surely be killed', and note the same in Gen 26:11 spelled mytqṭl(!) ytqṭl (MT môt yûmāt).

e. Medio-passive participles are as expected, e.g., masc. sing. mtnks 'being sacrificed' (Gen 22:10), masc. pl. mtr^{c}myn 'murmured' (Exod 16:8), fem. sing. mt^{c}brh 'become pregnant', fem. pl. mtknšyn! 'being gathered' (Gen 37:7, subject = kwrkwtkwn 'your sheaves'). For metathesis and/or assimilation, cf. mstkl, msṭrpyn, mzdbn, and mdbryn(!) 'being led' (Deut 33:3).

5. Intensive Stems with -w-

There are remnant forms in Neofiti of the stems usually called "Poel", "Ithpoel", "Polel", and "Ithpolel". The majority of the attested verbs belong to the first two categories, and all these are found with three verbal roots only, tqp, rqn, and sbr.

Poel

Perfect:	twqpt	'I made strong' (Gen 17:20)
	twqpt	'you made strong' (2 ms, Gen 19:19)
	rwqn	'he emptied' (Gen 31:9)
	rwqn<w>	'they despoiled' (Exod 12:36, spelled rwqnn with w/final n confusion).
Imperfect:	'twqp	'I will make strong' (Gen 12:2, 17:2,6)
	ttwqp	'she shall seize' (Deut 25:11)
	yrwqn	'he shall empty' (Num 24:17)
	trwqnwn	'you (pl) shall despoil' (Exod 3:22).
Imperative:	tqwpw	'be strong' (masc. pl., Gen 1:28, MT pərû).
Infinitive:	mswbr'	'to endure' (Gen 45:1, MT ləhit'appēq, Exod 12:39, MT ləhitmahmē^{a}h, and note Gen 49:4 mswbryh! no MT).

Ithpoel

Perfect:	'twqp	'he seized'? (Exod 4;4, for twqp?)
	'twqpw	'they seized'? (Gen 19:15, 16, for twqpw?).
Imperative:	'twqp	'be strong' (masc. sing., Deut 31:7, 23, MT ḥ^{a}zaq)
	'twqypw	'be strong' (masc. pl., Deut 31:6, MT ḥizqû)
	'twqpw	'be strong' (masc. pl., Deut 12:23, MT ḥ^{a}zaq).

Polel

Imperfect:	yrwmm	'he will lift up' (Gen 40:13, MT yiśśā')
	nrwmmnh	'we shall praise him' (Exod 15:2, MT 'anwēhû, with direct object suffix).

Participle:	m^{c}wrr	'stir up' (Deut 32:11, based on MT poetic yā^{c}îr)
	mšwṭṭn	'scan' (fem. pl., subject 'eyes', Gen 22:10, no MT).

Ithpolel Imperfect:	ytrwmm	'it shall be exalted' (Num 24:7, subject fem. mlkwtyh!, cf. 24:8 and Deut 32:3 for cognate noun rwmmw[th]).
Imperative:	'tbwnnw	'consider' (masc. pl., Deut 32:7, bînû).

6. The Š/Št Stems

The Š prefix is not a productive causative prefix in Aramaic, and so too in Neofiti, as its limited attestation demonstrates. It occurs on the verbs šzyb, škll, šlḥp and š^{c}bd in the strong roots, and šyṣy and šlhy in the weak (both tertiae infirmae, q.v.).[2]

Only a partial paradigm is attested.

Š Stem Perfect:	šlḥpt	'you have changed' (masc. sing., Gen 31:41)
	šlḥp	'he has changed' (Gen 31:7, 48:14)
	šyzb/šzyb	'he saved' (Exod 2:19, Exod 12:27, Gen 37:21)
	škll/šklyl	'he perfected' (Gen 1:1, 2:22, Deut 20:5)
	š^{c}bydw	'they enslaved' (Exod 1:13)
	škll<w>	'they perfected' (3fp, Exod 15:7, spelled šklly with w/y confusion).
Imperfect:	'šyzb	'I will save' (Exod 6:6)
	tškll	'you shall perfect' (masc. sing., Gen 6:16)
	yš^{c}bdwn	'they will enslave' (Gen 15:13, 14).
Imperative:	šyzb	'save' (masc. sing., Gen 32:11).
Infinitive:	mšyzb'/mšyzbh	'to save' (Gen 18:1, 32:2, 37:22).

Active Participle:	myšyzyb	'one who saves' (masc. sing., Deut 32:39)
	mšyzyb	'one who saves' (masc. sing., Deut 28:29).
Passive Participle	mš^{c}bd	'enslaved' (masc. sing., Gen 25:23)
	mšw^{c}bd!	'enslaved' (masc. sing., Gen 27:40)
	mšyzb'	'the one saved' (masc. sing. determined, Gen 14:13)
	mšyzbh	'it is delivered' (fem. sing., Gen 15:11).

Št Stem

Perfect:	'štzbt/	
	'štyzbt	'it was saved' (3fs Deut 2:36, Gen 32:31)
	'štyzbwn	'they were delivered' (3mpl, Gen 15:17).
Imperfect:	'štyzb	'I will be saved' (Gen 19:20)
	yštyzb	'he will be saved' (Deut 23:16)
	yšt^{c}bdwn	'they will be enslaved' (Gen 27:29).
Imperative:	'štyzb	'be saved' (masc. sing., Gen 19:17 (x2), 19:22).
Infinitive:	mšt^{c}bd'	'to be enslaved' (Gen 40:12)
	mštyzb'	'to be saved' (Gen 19:19).
Participle:	mšt^{c}bd	'enslaved' (Gen 9:25, 26, 27)
	mšt^{c}bdyn	'enslaved' (Num 12:12).

C. Weak Verbs

1. Primae Infirmae -- I-Aleph (Paradigm E)

a. For the G stem, the verb 'kl 'eat' is taken as the paradigm, however the forms cited apply to other verbs such as 'gr 'hire', etc. (For 'zl 'go', 'mr 'say' and 't' 'come', cf. section I below.) Forms in the derived conjugations are not well attested; in this discussion, as for all the weak verbs, only attested forms found in the MS are cited. The remaining elements of the paradigm can usually be inferred.

b. The presence of the letter <u>aleph</u> in the imperfect and infinitive is to be understood as a morphological spelling based on the perfect, e.g., <u>t'kl</u> vs. <u>tykl</u>. The spelling of the stem vowel of the imperfect shows some variation, and the use of <u>matres lectionis</u> is not consistent within a given root, e.g., <u>tykwl</u> vs. <u>tykl</u>. No general conclusions can be made solely on the spelling in the MS, however, and any discussion of vowel classes must take comparative considerations into account.

Plural forms are by and large poorly attested, however cf. <u>t'klwn/n'kl</u> with <u>aleph</u>, <u>tyklwn</u> without, and note <u>ylpwn</u> 'they will learn' /<u>tlpwn</u> 'you will learn' (Deut 4:10/5:1) in the G stem.

c. The derived conjugations are also poorly attested, however cf. D stem <u>t'rś</u>(!) 'you will betroth' (Deut 28:30), <u>y'r^{c}wn</u> 'they will meet' (Deut 31:17), <u>m'rsh</u> 'betrothed' (Exod 22:15) for forms spelled with <u>aleph</u>, and also the medio-passive perfects and imperfects cited. Note also the "archaic" spelling of the suffix in <u>'lpt'</u> 'you have taught', three times in a midrash in Gen 35:9 (twice abbreviated <u>'lpt`</u>), and the unusual use of <u>aleph</u> in the 3fs suffix <u>'t'sy't</u> 'she was cured' (Num 12:16, vs. <u>'t'syt</u>, Num 12:15).

In the C stem, the perfect has <u>'klt</u>! 'I fed' (Exod 16:32, MT <u>he'^{e}kaltî</u>) alongside expected <u>'yykl</u> 'he fed' (Deut 7:3, 8:3, 32:13, Lev 22:27, but <u>'yykwl</u>! again in Lev 22:27). C stem infinitives are spelled with prefix <u>mw-</u>, i.e., they are assimilated to the I/<u>y</u> verbs (q.v.).

2. <u>Primae Infirmae</u> -- <u>I-y/w</u> (Paradigm F)

a. This is the most well attested of the primae infirmae groups, especially so in the G stem. There is considerable intermixing between vowel classes, and presumably also assimilation to verbs I-<u>Aleph</u>, I-<u>n</u>, and possibly II-<u>w</u> (as in Onkelos). The following representative verbs are attested:

Perfect	Imperfect	Imperative	Infinitive
yl(y)d (yəled)	yld (yellad, yelid?)	—	m(y)ld (melad?)
yd^{c}(yəda^{c})	yd^{c} (yidda^{c}?)	d^{c} (da^{c})	m(y)d^{c} (midda^{c}, meda^{c}?)
—	y(y)rt (yerat)	yrtw (yartu)	myr(w)t (merat, merot)
ykyl (yəkel)	yk(w)l (yikkol)	—	mkl (mikkol?)
yhb (yəhab)	—	hb (hab)	—
ytyb (yəteb)	—	tb (tib)	—
yqd (yəqad?)	yyqwd (yiqqod)	—	—
—	y(y)ṭ(y)b (yeṭib)	—	—

As can be seen, a complex situation is complicated even further by a lack of certain forms, and by the inconsistent use of *matres lectiones*.

(1) The imperfect of *yld* is never spelled with internal *-y-*, hence it is impossible to determine whether it is vocalized *yəlid*, as in Onkelos (presumably assimilated to the II-*w* group) or perhaps *yillad* (< I-*nun*). The spelling of the infinitive *mld/myld* would admit either *millad* (< I-*nun*) or *melad* (< I-*Aleph*, as in Onkelos).

(2) The imperfect of *yd^{c}* is presumably *yidda^{c}*, infinitive *midda^{c}* (or *meda^{c}*?), assimilated to I-*nun* (or I-*Aleph*).

(3) There is no example of the perfect of *yrt* (= *yryt*, i.e., *yəret*, as in Onkelos?); the imperfect is presumably *yerat* (spelling *yyrt*, < I-*Aleph*). There are two examples of the imperative, both masc. plural *yrtw* (Deut 1:8, 21) and *yrytw* (Deut 9:23). The latter is problematic, and might be explained as *yarətu* → *yaritu*, i.e., with *-y-* for vocalic shewa, rather than as *yaretu*. Similarly problematic is the infinitive spelling *myrwt* (Deut 4:5). Based on Onkelos, one expects *merat* (= spelling *m(y)rt*?); the form *myrwt* may represent assimilation to I-*n* (cf. *mpwq*). It is not possible to determine whether the

spellings m(y)rt are "defective" or whether both vocalizations are to be admitted in Neofiti.

(4) The spelling of the various forms of ykl is not consistent. The perfect is spelled either ykyl (= Onkelos) or ykl, and note also Gen 36:7 3fs yklyt!, presumably an error of metathesis for ykylt; the imperfect is spelled ykwl (= Onkelos) or ykl (cf. nykl, Num 13:30, nkl, Gen 24:50, etc., i.e., $<$ I-nun), and note also Gen 19:19, 22 'wkl!, perhaps a Hebraism, Gen 31:35 'kyl, perhaps w/y confusion for 'kwl, and Deut 7:17 'ykl, perhaps w/y confusion for the Hebraism (?) 'wkl. The only example of the infinitive is Num 13:30 mkl (MT yākôl, = mikkol?).

(5) The perfect yhb is found in a suppletive paradigm with the imperfect ytn, but cf. imperative hb/hby/hbw (= hab, etc.).

(6) There are no examples of the imperfect of ytyb, however cf. imperative tb/tby/tbw (= tib, etc.); the verb is less commonly used in Neofiti than šrh 'to sit', 'to dwell'.

(7) The perfect yqd (e.g., Exod 3:2), imperfect yqwd (e.g., Gen 38:25 nyqwd) may belong to the same class as ykyl/ykwl, i.e., perfect yəqed, however no forms spelled with -y- are found in the MS.

(8) The verb yyṭyb only occurs in the imperfect (cf. also MT yîṭab), spelled yyṭb, yyṭyb, tyṭb, tṭyb.

b. In the derived conjugations, only three forms are found in the D stem. However, the C stem is very well attested, and preserves most distinctions between verbs originally I-w (e.g., yld, ysp, ykḥ, ybl, yqd, yd^{c}) and those originally I-y (e.g., ynq, yṭb). Some mixing does seem to occur, but this may reflect w/y medieval copyist confusion rather than paradigmatic assimilation.

Verbs originally I-w have -w- in all forms, e.g.,:

Perfect: 'wl(y)d (Gen 5:3, 5 and often), 'ws(y)pw (Gen 37:5, 8), 'wkḥ (Gen 21:25, Deut 1:1), 'wbylw (Gen 50:13), 'wqdt (Deut 9:21), 'wd^c(y)t (Exod 6:3, spelled 'wd^{c}t with -y- added supralinearly);

Imperfect: ywld (Gen 17:20), twsp (Gen 4:12), ywkyḥn (Gen 31:37, with w/ final n confusion for ywkyḥw), twqdwn (Deut 7:5), twd^c (Exod 18:20), twzp (Deut 24:10), ywqr (Deut 5:16);

Imperative: 'wbylw (Gen 42:19);

Infinitive: mwldh (Gen 17:7), mwqrh (Num 22:37);

Participles: mwl(y)d (often), mwqd (Lev 16:28).

Verbs originally I-y are less commonly attested, e.g.,:

Perfect: 'yyṭb (Gen 12:16), 'yynyqt (Gen 21:7);

Imperfect: 'yyṭb (Gen 32:12);

Imperative: --;

Infinitive: myyṭybh (Gen 32:12, Deut 6:24, but cf. Onkelos meṭābā, hence perhaps influenced by the imperfect?);

Participles: myynqth 'her nurse' (Gen 24:59, with pronominal suffix), myynqyn (fpl, Gen 32:15, for MT mênîqôt).

However, the picture is complicated by numerous "unexpected" forms, cf.:

Perfect: 'wnqt (Exod 2:9, w/y confusion for 'ynqt?);

Imperfect: 'yqr/'yyqr (Num 24:11, 22:7, cf. mwqr', Num 24:11, and others), ysp (Gen 30:24, but the MT has the defectively written yōsēp, also spelled ysp), nwṭb (Num 10:29, and cf. also 'wṭb, Gen 32:9, w/y confusion for nyṭb/'yṭb?);

Imperative: 'wnyqy/'yybyly (both in Exod 2:9, cf. 'wnqt above, and also 'wbylw, Gen 42:19);

Infinitive: myqrh (Num 22:17, cf. mwqrh, Num 22:37, therefore perhaps w/y confusion).

c. The medio-passive stems in the I-w/y verbs generally distinguish a Ct stem, based on the existence of a C stem, e.g.,:

Perfect: Ct - 'twtbt (Gen 32:4, 1s, Gen 21:23, 2ms), 'twtb (Gen 20:1, etc.), 'twtbw (Exod 6:4), vs. Gt/Dt - 'tylyd (Gen 4:18, etc.), based on G stem yld, 'tyḥmw (Gen 30:30, etc.), based on D stem yḥm, and especially 'twwkḥt in Gen 20:16 with consonantal w;

Imperfect: Ct - ttwqd (Gen 38:24), ytwqd (Lev 19:6), ytwspwn (Gen 49:26), vs. Gt/Dt - ytyhb (Gen 4:1), based on G stem yhb, 'tyqr (Exod 14:17), based on G stem yqr, and note ttyybbwn (Num 10:7), ytldwn (Gen 8:17, perhaps yittilədun written defectively, or else a copyist spelling error), and ytwd^{c} (Exod 33:16, with w/y confusion for ytyd^{c}, or else a Hebraism?, cf. Jastrow, "Dictionary," p. 565);

Imperative: Ct - 'twtb (Gen 26:3), vs. Gt/Dt - 'tyldwn (Gen 9:7);

Infinitive: Ct - mtwqdh (Gen 38:25), mtwtbh (Gen 12:10);

Participles: Dt - mtylp (Gen 21:20).

3. Primae Infirmae -- I-n (Paradigm G)

a. There are very few examples of a stative perfect type in the G stem of I-n verbs. The spellings nsyb, nsybt, nḥyt occur infrequently, and most perfect forms are of the type nsb, nḥt, and also ntl, nṭr, nks, nsk, npḥ, npq, etc. (The spelling npwq(?) occurs in Gen 27:30, either w/y confusion for npyq or, more likely, influenced by the accompanying cognate infinitive mpwq.) There are three attested 1pl perfect suffixes: nsbnn, 'we took' (Deut 3:4, cf. kbšnn in the same verse); nṭln(!) 'we travelled' (Deut 1:19, cf. hlknn in the same verse?); and nṭlynn 'we travelled' (Deut 2:1, cf. kwwynn/'pqnn(!) in the same verse, and cf. Section 2.A(i) above).

b. All three historical vowel possibilities are attested in the imperfect:

a - ysb (common), 'ṭr (Num 23:12, but note nṭwr, Deut 6:25?);
i - ytn (occasional);
u - ypwq (Exod 21:3,4, 'ḥwt (Gen 37:35), nṭwl (Gen 33:12), ykws (Lev 4:24), but note the occasional defective spellings of the last group -- tpq (Exod 21:3, 22:5) and ypl (Exod 19:21), and cf. also the infinitives below.

In I-nun verbs, the prefix is occasionally spelled plene, e.g., tyḥwt (Gen 26:2), tysb (Gen 24:4,7,38), tykswn (Lev 19:5), etc.

c. Imperatives of the verbs spelled with -w- in the imperfect are usually similarly spelled, e.g., ṭwl (Deut 3:27), pwq (Gen 8:16, 31:13), ḥwtw (Gen 42:2), however cf. ṭl (Gen 31:12), pq (Gen 27:3), ṭlw (Deut 2:24, vs. ṭwlw, Deut 1:7,40). For verbs whose imperfect has the vowel a, cf. sb, šq (Gen 27:26), sby (Gen 18:6), sbw (Exod 12:21). There is no imperative of the verbal root ntn (cf. yhb in Section 3.B above). As all other G stem imperatives of the I-nun group are formed by omitting the first root consonant, it is likely that nksw 'sacrifice' in Exod 12:21 is in fact a D stem imperative, however cf. Levy, "Wörterbuch," Vol. II, p. 110, and Jastrow, "Dictionary," p. 911.

d. The situation with the infinitives parallels that of the imperfects: myṭwr (Deut 24:8)/mṭwr (Gen 2:15) but myṭr (Deut 4:2); mpwq (Gen 27:30) but mpq (Num 12:12), and cf. mḥt (Gen 43:20) and mykws (Gen 22:10). Roots in which -w- is not expected include: mšb 'blow' (Gen 3:8), mysb (Gen 4:8, 30:15, etc.), mytn (Gen 15:2,7, etc.)/ mtn (Gen 4:8,12). For the infinitive with pronominal suffixes, see Gen 35:18 bmpqh dnpšh 'at the going out of her soul' (MT bəṣē(')t napšāh).

e. Most masc. sing. active participles are spelled without -y- in the second syllable, e.g., nḥt, nṭl, nks, npq, etc., but cf. npyq (Exod 20:13). The plural has nḥtyn (Gen 43:20 etc.), nplyn (Num 11:26), npqyn (Num 21:15), etc. in the absolute, nzly' 'flowing' in the determined (my' nzly' 'flowing waters', based on MT poetic nēd nōzlîm), and nsby 'taking' (Gen 19:14) and npqy 'leaving' (Gen 9:10, 34:24) in the construct. The only fem. sing. form attested is also construct, npqt br/brh/br' 'whore' (usually for MT qədēšā, e.g., Gen 38:15,21,22). There is only one passive participle, fs construct nsybt gbr 'taken by man' (Gen 20:3, Deut 22:22, MT bəᶜūlat bāᶜāl).

f. In the D stem imperfect, infinitive, and participles, the first root consonant is preserved: ynšy 'he will forget' (Gen 27:45), ynṭr 'he will guard' (Gen 28:20), 'nṭr 'I will guard' (Gen 28:15), tnskwn 'you (pl) shall pour libations' (Exod 30:9), ynbḥ 'he shall bark' (Exod 11:7), tnšwn 'you (pl) shall forget' (Deut 25:19); mnḥmh 'to comfort' (Gen 35:9, 37:35), mnšqyh 'to kiss' (Gen 31:28 - written at the end of the line, with -yh added later, by a different hand, i.e., read mnšq̀, abbreviation for mnšqh); mnṭr 'keep' (Gen 37:11), mnṭryn 'keep' (Gen 27:40), mnšb' 'blow' (Gen 1:2); mnṭlyn 'exalted' (Num 24:6).

g. The C stem perfect, imperfect, and imperative are written either with or without -y- in the second syllable (the first root consonant is always assimilated), e.g.,:

Perfect: 'pyq (Exod 19:17) vs. 'pq (Lev 19:36);
Imperfect: ypyq (Deut 24:11) vs. npq (Num 20:10);
Imperative: 'pyqw (Gen 38:24) vs. 'pqw (Gen 45:1).

The perfect form 'wḥtw 'they brought down' in Gen 39:1 is problematic. In the same verse one also finds the C stem passive perfect form hwnḥt 'he was brought down', translating the MT hûrad (spelled hwrd). Further on the verse reads 'ᵃšer hôrīdūhû (spelled hwrdhw) and it is this that is translated 'wḥtw for 'ḥtw [= 'a(ḥ)ḥetu], clearly under pressure of the MT form, combined with the prima infirmae possibility of the I-y stem in -w-.

Alongside expected mnhr' 'to give light' (Gen 1:15,17) and msbh 'to give (as a wife)' (Gen 29:19,22), one also finds some problematic C stem infinitival forms. The infinitive of root nḥt occurs once in Gen 37:24 as nḥth, once in Gen 49:23 as mḥty, presumably both copyist errors for expected mḥth (y/h confusion is known elsewhere in the MS, not so m/n confusion); the root nsb occurs twice (Gen 29:17, 34:30) as mysb' (for expected msbh); and npq has one example (Exod 22:28) of mypqh (for mpqh).

For a C infinitive with pronominal suffix, see Exod 3:12 'pqwtk 'your bringing forth' (MT hôṣî'ᵃkā).

The C stem active participles attested are: ms - mḥt (Gen 7:4)/mḥyt (Num 22:32), mqp (Gen 2:11,13); mp - mnhryn (Gen 1:15); fp - mpqn (Num 24:6). Passive participles are: fs - mqph (Gen 15:17, Num 19:15); fp - mqypn (Deut 3:5), presumably maqqəpān ⟶ maqqipān, with -y- representing vocalic shewa; mp - mnṭlyn (Num 24:6), and mp det. mnṭly' 'the exalted ones' (Exod 15:21); fs det. mnṭlth.

h. The medio-passive stems are poorly attested:

Perfect:	'tnsybt (Gen 38:14);
Imperfect:	ytnzr (Num 6:12), ytnsk (Num 28:7);
Infinitive:	mtnḥmh (Gen 37:35);
Participles:	mtnḥm (Deut 32:36), mtnks (Gen 22:10), mtnṭlyn (Num 23:24).

4. Media Infirmae -- II-w/y (Paradigm H)

a. While the G stem II-w/y perfects are not well attested, examples are found of both original a-perfect verbs, e.g., qm/qmt/qmw and original i-perfect verbs, e.g., myt/mytt/mytw. Special note should be taken of the following unusual forms:

(i) mwtnw! (Exod 16:3, copying MT mûtēnû);

(ii) mtynn(!) 'we died' (Num 20:3, cf. Onkelos, ad loc., Sperber, "Onkelos," p. 256, mytn', and cf. also Babylonian Talmudic Aramaic, e.g., drynn, Margolis, "Lehrbuch," p. 51, Epstein, "Grammar," p. 89, and cf. active participles, below);

(iii) the error form w'bytw(!) 'and they spent the night' (Gen 31:54) for expected wbytw (presumably a dittographic error with the preceeding verb w'klw rather than C stem or medial aleph, cf. the imperative, below);
(iv) and the error form w'zl 'and it became worthless' (Gen 16:5) for expected wzl (by confusion with the common w'zl 'and he went'). Note also Gen 22:19 qmn 'they (mp) arose," for qmw with w/final n confusion.

b. Most imperfect examples found are with original u stem vowel, e.g., 'ᶜwṣ 'I will advise' (Num 24:14), tšwᶜ 'you will plaster' (Gen 6:14), tṣwmwn 'you (pl) will fast' (Lev 16:29), yqwmwn 'they will arise' (Exod 20:15), etc., however there are occasional i-imperfects, e.g., tbyt 'it (fs) shall spend the night' (Deut 21:23), nbyt 'we shall spend the night' (Gen 19:2). Forms such as ydynwn 'they will judge' (Gen 31:53) should be seen as due to w/y confusion, probably complicated by the presence of the common noun dyn (cf. ydwnwn, Exod 18:22). Note the unusual forms tmtwn, spelled defectively (Gen 3:4) and tyqwm (3fs, Lev 19:16, Num 31:50), with plene prefix. The 3fpl is attested in yḥwsn 'they shall (not) have pity' (Deut 25:12, subject ᶜyynykwn 'your eyes').

c. In the G stem imperative, all but the fpl forms are attested, but note lwwṭ(!) 'curse' (Num 22:6, cf. lwṭ, Num 22:11), and also w'bytwn (w'ṣhwn rglykwn) 'and stay the night (and wash your feet)' (Gen 19:2, both the prefix and the suffix presumably due to dittography with the following imperative, and cf. the perfect, above).

d. The spelling of the infinitive is fluid, e.g., mlwṭ 'to curse' (Gen 8:21), mmwt 'to die' (Deut 2:16), mṣwd 'to hunt' (Gen 27:5), mqwm 'to arise' (Deut 10:8), but myqwm (Gen 4:10), myqm (Gen 31:35, Exod 17:16, Deut 9:2), mymt (Gen 2:17), mmt (Gen 20:7, 25:32), mdn 'to judge' (Exod 18:13), etc. It is not possible to determine whether the forms with -w- really represent an ideal spelling. The forms mmyt (Gen 3:4) should probably be taken as mmwt with w/y confusion; the problematic root *byt* 'to spend the night' has *mbt'/mbth* (Gen 19:8, 24:23, 25), presumably C stem for expected G stem (C stem usually meaning 'to keep over night', 'to postpone burial', cf. Jastrow, "Dictionary," p. 167, and cf. Onkelos *ad loc.*, *mbt*, Sperber, "Onkelos," Vol. I, p. 35).

e. Similarly, the spelling of the active participles fluctuates, e.g., *q'm/qym/qyym/q'ym*, and none can be determined as "ideal." There is one impossible fpl form, *qyym'* (Gen 15:12). Note the forms of *myt*: *m'yt* (Gen 20:3), *myt* (Gen 25:8,17), *myth* (Gen 30:1, 35:18), *myytyn* (Deut 5:25), *myytynn*/ *mytynn* (Num 14:2, MT *matnû*, though cf. the perfect, above), *mytn* (Num 16:29, mpl), *mytn* (Gen 33:13, fpl) -- the picture is complex and must await a comprehensive treatment.

There is one passive participle -- *lyṭ* 'cursed' (Gen 12:3, Num 22:16), but note *lwṭ* (Gen 9:25, with *w/y* confusion for *lyṭ*, and the impossible *lyyṭ* (Gen 27:29) in *m<n> dlyyt ytk yhwy lyyṭ* 'whoever curses you will be cursed', a copyist error by dittography with the preceeding active participle.

f. Forms in the derived conjugations are not well attested. The D stem is as expected; the C stem perfect has occasional defective spellings, e.g., *'qm* 'he raised' (Gen 30:38, 31:45, 33:20, 35:20), *'qmyt* 'I raised' (Gen 44:18). No defective spellings of the imperfect or imperative were noted, e.g., imperfect - *'qym* (Deut 18:18) *tnyp* (Exod 29:26), *ynyḥ* (Deut 25:19), *tqymwn* (Lev 26:1), *yzydwn* (Deut 17:13); imperative - *'tyb* (Gen 37:14), *'ṣytw* (Deut 27:9).

g. The medio-passive stems clearly distinguish between Gt/Dt on the one hand, and Ct on the other; this is especially to be seen in roots involving sibilant metathesis. Unfortunately, examples only exist in the perfect, imperfect, and participles, however the general scheme is clear.

	Gt/Dt	Ct
Perfect:		
	't^cyqt 'I am distressed' (Gen 27:46)	't^cr 'he awoke' (Gen 28:16)
	'yt^{c}yryt 'I awoke' (Gen 41:21)	'tnp 'it (ms) was waved' (Exod 29:27)
	't^cyr 'he awoke' (Gen 9:24, 41:7)	'tṭš 'it (ms) was plastered' (Lev 14:43)
	'tpyys 'he was appeased' (Gen 6:6)	
	'dyyn 'he argued' (Gen 31:36)	
	'tḥyyb 'he was guilty' (Lev 5:5)	
	'tlyṭt 'it (fs) was cursed' (Gen 5:29)	
	'yzdyyntwn 'you (pl) armed yourselves' (Deut 1:41)	
	'zdyynw 'they armed themselves' (Num 31:7)	
	'dy(y)nw 'they argued' (Gen 26:20, 26:21,22)	
	'tqymn 'they (fpl) were established' (Gen 15:1	
Imperfect:		
	ytqyym 'let it remain' (Gen 33:9)	yt'rq! 'it will be poured out' (Lev 21:10)
	ytḥyyb 'he will be guilty' (Lev 5:23)	ytdnwn 'they will argue' (Gen 6:3)
	ttqyym 'it (fs) will exist' (Gen 12:13, 19:20)	ytznwn 'they will be fed' (Gen 41:40)
	ntḥyyb 'we will be guilty' (Gen 37:21)	

Gt/Dt	Ct
ttnḥwn/ttnwḥwn! 'you (mpl) shall rest' (Exod 34:21, bis)	
ydyynwn 'they will quarrel' (Exod 21:18)	

Participles:

Gt/Dt	Ct
mtkwyn 'aiming' (Gen 3:15, ms)	mytkl 'measured' (Gen 38:25, root kwl)
mšytyr 'remaining' (Exod 17:16, ms)	
mštryyh! 'remaining' (Gen 32:8, with error of metathesis for mštyyrh, fs)	
mtkwwnyn 'aiming' (Gen 3:15, mpl)	
mtgyyryn 'sojourning' (Lev 16:29, mpl)	

The inconsistent use of the matres lectionis complicates the question of the vocalization of these forms, as does the small size of the sample. The forms spelled with -yy- can be safely assigned to Dt, e.g., 'itpayyas, 'iddayyənu, yitqayyam, yiddayyənun, mištayyar, mitgayyərin, however it is not clear that those spelled with one -y- are necessarily to be vocalized as Gt, e.g., 'it^{c}irit, 'itliṭat. Note also the doublets 'dynw/'dyynw and 'tqymn/ytqyym. Those forms spelled without -y- are taken as Ct, e.g., 'ittənāp, yittədānun, mittəkāl. The following are problematic: Exod 34:21 -- ttnḥwn/ ttnwḥwn, presumably both titnuḥun, or else tittənaḥun (Ct)/ titniḥun (Gt, with w/y confusion based on other forms of nwḥ). A Ct of this root is known, cf. Jastrow, "Dictionary," p. 886, as is a Dt (but no Gt); Lev 21:10 -- yt'rq, presumably Ct yittāraq from root ryq spelled with medial aleph to mark the vowel [ā].

5. Mediae Infirmae -- II-Aleph (Paradigm I)

a. These verbs are found in all stems, but only with the roots b'š 'to be evil', s'b 'to be old' (D stem 'to defile'), š'l 'to ask', 'to borrow'. The paradigms are not complete. The root š'r 'remain' only occurs in the D/Dt stems, and the spelling indicates that the verb has been assimilated to the II-w/y verbs (see Paradigm I for examples, and compare to Paradigm H). The root m'k 'to be humble' only occurs in Gen 35:9, but spelled in error 'mk! Note should also be taken of the copyist errors b^{c}š 'it was bad' (Gen 4:6) and mb^{c}š' 'to do evil' (Exod 23:2), both with ^{c} for '.

b. There are occasional perfect spellings with -y- indicating a vocalization šə'el, bə'eš, sə'ebu, e.g., Gen 19:1, Num 16:15, Gen 18:11, respectively. Otherwise, cf. š'ltwn (Deut 18:16), š'l (Gen 40:7), š'lw (Gen 37:7), etc. Note also sb! (Gen 25:8, analogous to the II-w/y perfects) and š'lwn! (Gen 26:7, with suffix extended from the imperfect).

c. All forms of the imperfect are spelled with aleph, and note especially Gen 32:17 yš'lwnk! 'he (sic) will ask you', presumably w/y confusion for yš'lynk, 3ms imperfect + direct object suffix joined by nun (MT šə'ēlkā).

d. In the imperative, only mpl š'ylw/ š'lw is attested (Deut 4:32, 32:7), presumably to be vocalized šə'elu. The only infinitive in the G stem in the MS is mš'l (e.g., Gen 37:10, 43:7); the active participles are also of this root: ms š'yl (Gen 32:29), mpl š'lyn (often), fpl š'lyn! (Gen 33:6).

e. The derived conjugations are poorly attested. All forms of the D and C stems are spelled with aleph (for šyyr, etc., see section (i) above). The D stem infinitive has ms'b' 'to declare unclean' (e.g., Lev 13:44, 20:25) and, with suffixes, s'bwthwn/ s'bthwn 'their uncleanness' (both in Lev 15:31); note also Num 24:1 mš'lyh(?). The only root attested in the medio-passive is s-'-b (for 'štyyr, etc., cf. section (i) above), e.g., 'st'bt

(3fs, Lev 18:25), *yst'b* (Lev 5:3, Num 6:12), *mst'b'* (Lev 15:32, 18:20), etc.

6. *Mediae Infirmae* -- *Geminates* (Paradigm J)

a. As in other dialects of Middle Aramaic, the geminate verbs occur both with contraction of the two identical consonants and also without contraction, e.g., *^{c}l*, *hn*, *^{c}lw*, *bzw*, *qlw* ('they grew small', Gen 8:11), but *bzzw* (Num 31:53, MT *bāzəzû*), *bzznn* (Deut 2:35, 3:7, MT *bāzaznû*/*bazzônû*, respectively), and note *bzwn* (Gen 34:27, with suffix extended from the imperfect, MT *wayyābōzzû*). So too for the active participles: *^{c}lyn* (Deut 11:29) vs. *^{c}llyn* (Gen 41:21, Deut 4:5), *zmmyn* 'grazing' (Gen 13:7), and construct *^{c}lly* (Gen 23:10, 18), determined *^{c}llyh* (Gen 7:16); and the infinitive *my^{c}wl* 'to enter' (Gen 19:31, Deut 9:1) vs. *mgzz* 'to shear' (Gen 31:19). The infinitive also occurs with nominative pronominal suffixes, e.g., *m^{c}lk* 'your entry', *m^{c}lh* 'his entry' (Lev 16:23).

The imperfect, imperative, and infinitive, as in other dialects, are characterized by the shift of the gemination to the first radical, evidenced in the spelling, e.g., *ygn* (Exod 12:23), *'bwz* (Exod 15:9), *tqṣwn* (Deut 25:12), *tḥgwn* (Exod 12:14, Deut 16:15); *^{c}wl* (ms), *^{c}wly* (fs), *^{c}wlw* (mpl); *my^{c}wl*, however cf. *mgzz*. Note especially Exod 22:8 *y^{c}l' mly tryhwn* 'the words of both of them will enter', for an unusual 3fpl imperfect form, and note also "defective" spellings, e.g., *y^{c}l* (Lev 16:23), *n^{c}wl* (Gen 20:13), and ms imperative *^{c}l* (Gen 30:3), and *tṣwrwn* 'you (pl) shall bind' (Deut 14:25, *tiṣṣarun* ⟶ *tiṣṣorun*?).

b. The D stem is well attested, especially for the verb *mlyl* 'speak'. The perfect is not usually marked as different from the G stem -- the spelling *mll* occurs approximately twice as frequently as *mlyl*, cf., e.g., *gpp* (Gen 48:10), *mšš* (Gen 27:22), *mllnn* (Exod 14:22), *mrrw* (Exod 1:14), *mllw* (Gen 34:13), vs. *mlylyt* (Gen 28:15), *mlylt'* (*sic*, Gen 18:5, 19:21, Num 14:17), *mlylw* (Gen 34:20, Deut 5:28), *ylylw* (Deut 1:22).

There are occasional "collapsed" forms in the imperfect and participles, e.g., *yglwn* (Gen 29:8), *mglyn* (Gen 29:3). The infinitive of *mll* is variously spelled, with numerous copyist errors: *mmllh*, *mmll'*, *mmlllyh* (*sic*, Gen 28:10), *mllh*/*mll'* (four times in Genesis), and note also *mgzllh*! (Gen 28:10, for *mgllh*, spelled with -*z*-).

c. The C stem perfect and imperfect are well attested: *'gn* (Gen 7:16), *'^{c}l* (Exod 40:21), *'^{c}lt* (2ms, Num 16:14), *'^{c}ltwn* (Deut 1:1), and with -*y*-, *'^{c}yl* (Gen 29:13, *'^{c}ylw* (Gen 19:10). Note the two error forms: *'wqlw* (Gen 8:8, apparently analogous to the I-*w*/*y* verbs) and *'^{c}yl* for *'ṭyl*! in Exod 40:21, copying *'^{c}l* at the beginning of the verse. The imperfect, imperative, and infinitive are usually spelled conservatively, e.g., *t^{c}l* (Exod 27:7, 40:4), *yy^{c}l* (Deut 6:10), *n^{c}l* (Num 32:17); *'^{c}l* (ms, Exod 4:6); *m^{c}l* (ms participle, Lev 18:3), however cf. *y^{c}yl* (Deut 11:29), *t^{c}yl* (Gen 6:19). There is no nasalization in the C stem, familiar from other dialects.

d. In the medio-passives, few forms are found, however it does appear that the language distinguishes a Ct stem, cf. Section A.2(d) above:

Gt/Dt:

'tnddt	'it (i.e., sleep) wandered' (Gen 31:40)
ytmll	'it will (not) be spoken' (Exod 20:19)
ythll	'it will be praised' (Gen 15:1)
'tqrrw	'refresh yourselves' (mpl imperative, Gen 18:4)
mtmllh	'to converse' (Gen 18:29)
mtwqrrh!	'to refresh himself' (Exod 7:15, perhaps for *mtqwrrh*, with -*w*- for a labialized vowel following the -*q*-?)
mtḥmm	'warming himself' (ms participle, Gen 18:1)

Ct:

't^{c}lw	'they were brought in' (Gen 43:18, Onkelos *ad loc*. *'itta^{c}alu*)
yt^{c}l	'it will be put in' (Lev 11:32, Onkelos *ad loc*. *yitta^{c}al*)

ytmswn 'they will be melted' (Lev 26:39, Onkelos *ad loc. yitməson*)

mt^{c}lyn 'brought in' (Gen 43:18, Onkelos *ad loc. mitta^{c}əlin*)

The form *'tw^{c}l* (Lev 16:27) is anomalous (Onkelos *ad loc.* = *'itta^{c}al*) and possibly a copyist error.

7. *Tertiae Infirmae* -- *III-h/Aleph* (Paradigm K)

a. All verbs originally III-*Aleph* are included in this group, although one does find occasional spellings in which the *aleph* is preserved, e.g., *br't* 'I created', *śn'twn* 'you (pl) hated', *qr'* 'calling', etc. However, one finds many more cases of III-*h* 3ms perfects spelled with *aleph*, e.g., *ḥm'*, *ḥz'*, *rb'*, etc., as well as occasional imperfects, e.g., *ytks'* (Gen 18:14), indicating that the spelling with *aleph* is generally arbitrary, and only occasionally morphologically based (cf. also *brh*, *qrh*, etc.).

In the perfect, the 1s suffix is usually spelled -*yt*, only rarely -*yyt* or -*t*, (on comparative grounds, one expects the vocalization -*et*). The 3ms has some examples ending in -*y*(!), e.g., *dry* 'he scattered' (Gen 11:8,9), *zky* 'he acquired' (Gen 25:10), possibly active participles or D stem perfects. Note also the verbs with consonantal -*h*, e.g., *tmh*/*tmht*/*tmhw* 'he/she was astonished/they were astonished' (Gen 17:17, Gen 18:12, Gen 43:33). The spelling of the 3mpl suffix -*wn* occurs approximately three times as frequently as the spelling -*w*, and note also the problematic forms *šrn* (Gen 11:31), presumably *w*/final *n* confusion for *šrw*, and *qr'n* (Gen 24:58), either defective spelling for *qəron*, or else *w*/final *n* confusion for *qr'w* (however there are no other examples in the MS of the G stem spelling -*'n* or -*'w*).

There are also isolated examples of a passive perfect: *gly* (often, possibly always a passive participle), *lṭyt* '(the serpent) was cursed' (Num 21:6), *glyw* '(hidden things) were revealed'

(Gen 41:45), rmyw '(thrones) were thrown (i.e., set up)' (Gen 15:17).

In the imperfect, the spelling indicating the final vowel as -y is the norm, -h/-' being occasional isolated examples. Similarly, the imperfect prefix is only rarely spelled plene with -y-, e.g., tyqry (Gen 16:11), nyšry (Gen 29:22). The unexpected form nšrwn(!) 'they will reside' (Gen 34:23) presumably results from copyist error confusing the prefix with that of the preceding 1 pl verb in the sentence, nt^{c}rb.

The spelling of the ms imperative usually ends in -y, with perhaps only 25% of the examples ending in -h, e.g., ḥmy 'see' (Deut 3:27), ^{c}ny 'answer' (Lev 22:27), etc., indicating a vocalization ḥəme, etc. No fem. sing. examples are found. In the plural, all masc. forms end in -wn, the fem. is represented by qryn 'call' (Exod 2:20), cf. the same spelling in Onkelos, ad loc. (Sperber, "Onkelos," Vol. I, p. 90).

The spelling of the infinitive is varied, including plene prefix (e.g., myḥmy, Gen 38:25). Most commonly, the final vowel is spelled -y (e.g., mḥṭy), rarely -h (e.g., mzkh, Gen 3:16); there are occasional spellings with aleph (e.g., mḥm', Gen 26:28, mḥṭ', (Gen 3:16). Note the aberrant forms mr^{c} 'to pasture' (Gen 37:12), followed by yt, hence probably due to homoieteleuton with the y-; and mbryh 'to create' (Exod 12:42), presumably a copyist aural error rendering mibre.

The active and passive participles are well attested.

Active:

Most ms forms are spelled with -y; occasionally one finds spellings with aleph (e.g., qr', Gen 2:19, šr' (Gen 24:37). In the fs, aleph seems to predominate, and note the spelling of štyyh in Deut 11:11.

In the mpl, the spelling -yy- is equally distributed with -y, whereas in the fpl, only three examples are found -- khyyn (Gen 27:1), ḥmyyn (Exod 1:16), and qryn (Num 25:2).

The following forms should be noted -- Exod 15:12, ym' hwh b^{c}h... 'r^{c}' hwwt b^{c}h (sic) 'the sea (did not) want... the land (did not) want'; Gen 37:16, r^{c}n 'shepherds' (cf. Gen 37:13 r^{c}yn), presumably rā^{c}an as regularly in Onkelos (cf. ad loc.); Exod 15:6, 9, śn'h 'the enemy', determined state participle with morphologically based aleph (= śānə'ā); Gen 37:4, the same root, mpl, is spelled snyn 'hating'; Exod 20:5, the same root occurs twice with 1st pers. pronominal suffix śn'y/śn'yy 'my enemies'.

Passive: All forms but the fpl are attested, e.g.,

ms - sny 'hated' (Deut 4:25), gly 'revealed' (Exod 2:25, plus many others; the same spelling also for 'exiled', Gen 4:12,14,16, etc.).

mpl - glyyn 'revealed' (Gen 18:21), špyn/šypyn 'friendly' (Gen 31:2,5).

fs - śny' 'hated' (Gen 29:31,33), construct ksyyt 'pyn 'covered of face' (Gen 38:15).

b. In the derived conjugations, most 1s perfect suffix forms are spelled -yt; less commonly one finds -yyt, e.g., pnyyt (Gen 24:31), 'šthyyt (Gen 32:4), problematic forms given the expected vocalization -it, but probably due to confusion with the G stem perfect suffix -et (itself, however, only rarely spelled -yyt!). Note also the error form šwyty! (Gen 27:37), for šwyyt(?), due to Hebrew influence? Noteworthy also are the spellings of the 3fs, usually -yyt, occasionally -yt; the 3mpl form tny'w! (Gen 26:32, cf. Onkelos, ad loc.), alongside the common kswn, qnwn, šwwn, etc.; the varied spellings of the 3fs medio-passive forms, 't'syt (Num 12:15), 'tr^{c}yyt (Gen 34:3, 8, 19), 'tmly't (Gen 6:11,13), 't'sy't (Num 12:16), 'ytmlyt (Gen 9:19); and the unusual gly 'he rolled(?)' (Gen 29:10, MT wayyāgel).

The imperfect paradigms of the D and the medio-passive stems are well-attested; the C stem lacks many forms. There are occasional spellings with aleph, some morphologically based, e.g., ttbr' (Gen 2:23), ttml' (Gen 16:5), but also ytks' (Gen 18:14). Note also the varied spellings of the -t- stem of root zkh: tzdky (Gen 24:8), yzdkyh (Exod 21:19), tzdkh (Gen 24:41). In the D stem, 'yšwwy 'I shall place' (Deut 18:18), 'yqry 'I shall incite' (Lev 26:22) are unusual plene spellings. The 3fpl is represented in the D stem by yṣdwn 'they will desolate' (Lev 26:22), subject ḥywwth 'animals', extended from the 3mpl, but in the C stem by yṭᶜyyn 'they shall lead astray', subject bnthwn 'their daughters' (Exod 34:16).

The imperatives and infinitives are numerous, and as expected. Noteworthy are the D stem ms 'dy 'sprinkle' (Num 8:7, root n-d-h), the C stem mpl 'šqw 'water' (Gen 29:7, for expected 'šqwn), and the D stem infinitive mṣwlyyh! 'to pray' (Gen 24:63, = məṣalloyeh?, cf. the derived infinitives of Babylonian Talmudic Aramaic). For infinitival forms with pronominal suffix, see 'ytbrywthwn 'their creation' (Gen 2:4).

In the derived stem active participial forms, all save the fs C stem, fpl C and -t- stems are found. The feminine and plural forms can be spelled with -yy- or -y-, neither predominating, e.g., mrbyh/ mrbyyh 'producing' (both in Gen 4:16), mṣlyyn 'praying' (Exod 1:19), mskyyn 'calculating' (Gen 18:21), mšqyn 'watering' (Gen 29:3).

The passive participles are less well attested, however see D stem mdmy (ms)/ mdmyh (fs) 'similar' (Gen 16:12, 3:24), and C stem mḥṭyn (mpl) 'delicate' (Gen 33:13).

c. One may include in this discussion the numerous forms of the verb šyṣy 'to destroy'/ 'štyṣy 'to be destroyed'; for a discussion of the origin of these verbs in Aramaic, see Kaufman, "Akkadian," pp. 104-5.

The following forms are found in the MS:

Š Stem		
Perfect:	3ms	šyṣy (Gen 7:23, 13:10, etc.)
		šyṣy' (Exod 9:25)
	1pl	šyṣynn (Deut 2:34)
	3mp	šyṣwn (Num 21:35)
Imperfect:	3ms	yšyṣy (Gen 32:11, Num 24:19, Deut 9:3, etc.)
	1s	'šyṣ' (Gen 18:28, 29, 30, 31, 32, etc.)
		'yšṣy (Gen 7:4)
		'yšyṣy (Lev 23:30)
		'šyṣh (Gen 6:7)
		'yšyṣ' (Lev 17:10)
	3mp	yšyṣwn (Gen 34:30)
	2mp	tyšyṣwn (Num 33:52, 53)
Infinitive:		mšyṣy' (Gen 8:21, 19:13)
		myšyṣyh (Gen 6:3)
		myšyṣy (Deut 1:1)
		šyṣy?: (Deut 9:19)
Participle:	ms	mšyṣ' (Gen 18:24, 28)
		mšyṣyy'? (Gen 18:23)
	mpl	mšyṣyyn (Deut 12:2)

Note also mšlhy 'weary' (Gen 25:29, 30)

Št Stem		
Perfect:	3mpl	'štṣwn (Gen 7:23)
Imperfect:	3ms	yštṣy (Gen 9:11)
		yštyṣy (Gen 6:17, Lev 17:9)
	3fs	tyštṣ' (Num 15:30)
		tštyṣy (Lev 19:8)
	2ms	tštyṣ' (Gen 19:15)
	3mpl	yštyṣwn (Exod 12:42)

8. The Verbs slq 'go up'/ hlk 'go'

a. slq

As in other dialects of Middle Aramaic, this verb is characterized by the assimilation of the middle radical -l- in the G and C stems, on the analogy of the assimilation of the n in I-n verbs, specifically the semantic opposite of slq, namely nḥt 'go down' (cf. ntn/lqḥ in Hebrew). In particular, the -l- is assimilated in forms with a prefix, i.e., G stem imperfect and infinitive, and all of the C stem. In the G stem imperative, the -l- is absent also by analogy to nḥt imperatives ḥwt/ḥwty/ḥwtw. See the table below for the collected forms.

The existence of a D stem (meaning 'to remove') is confirmed by the imperfect example tslq, Gen 18:3, l' tslq 'yqr škyntk m^{c}ylwwy ^{c}bdk 'may you not remove the glory of your Shekinah from upon your servant' (paraphrasing MT 'al-nā' ta^{ca}bōr mē^{c}al ^{c}abdekā). A corresponding medio-passive ('to depart', 'to be removed') occurs in a number of forms, all but the first translating a form of the N stem of root ^{c}-l-h:

Perfect:	'stlq 'he departed' (Gen 12:8, MT wayya^{c}ətēq) 'stlqw 'they departed' (Num 16:27, MT wayyē^{c}ālû)
Imperfect:	ystlq 'it will (not) be removed' (Exod 40:37, MT yē^{c}āle/ hē^{c}ālōtô)
Imperative:	'stlqw 'depart' (mpl, Num 16:24, MT hē^{c}ālû)
Infinitive:	bound form, b'stlqwt ^{c}nnh 'at the departure of the cloud' (Exod 40:36, MT bəhē^{c}ālôt he^{c}ānān)

Collected Forms:

	G Stem	C Stem
Perfect:		
1s	--	'sqt (Num 21:6)
2ms	--	'sqt (Num 16:13)
fs	--	--
3ms	slq/slyq (Gen 19:28, 32:35)	'sq (Exod 32:1)
fs	slqt/slyqt (Exod 2:23, 19:18)	'sqt (Gen 40:10)
1pl	slqnn (Gen 28:12, 44:24)	--
2pl	--	'sqtwn (Num 20:5)
3pl	slqw (Exod 13:18)	--

	G Stem	C Stem
Imperfect:		
1s	'swq (Exod 32:30)	'syq (Gen 30:22, 46:4) 'sq (Exod 3:11)
2ms	tysq (Exod 19:24)	--
3ms	yswq (Exod 12:42)	--
1pl	nsq (Gen 35:3)	--
	nswq (Num 20:19), Deut 1:41)	--
	nyswq (Num 13:30)	--
2pl	tsqwn (Num 13:17)	tsqwn (Gen 50:25)
Imperative:		
ms	swq (Gen 35:1, Deut 3:27, 32:49)	'sq (Exod 8:1)
fs	swqy (Num 21:17)	--
mpl	swqw (Num 13:17, Deut 1:21)	--
	swqwn! (Gen 44:17, Num 22:19)	--
Infinitive:		
	mswq (Num 13:30, 31)	'sq'! (Exod 3:17)
	mysq (Exod 19:24, Deut 1:26)	'sqwty! 'my going up'(?) (Deut 9:9, MT ^{ca}lōtî)
Participles:		
ms	slq (often)	msq 'that which brings up' (grh 'cud') (Lev 11:5)
mpl	slqyn (Gen 28:12, 41:2,3,5, Num 16:12,14, Deut 1:28)	msqyyh (det.) 'those who take up (money)' i.e., 'tax collectors' (Deut 28:42, MT haṣṣəlāṣal) msqy (construct) 'those who bring up' (msym! 'tribute') (Gen 49:15); 'those who bring up' (grrt' 'cuds') (Lev 11:4)

	G Stem	C Stem
fs	--	msqh 'that which brings up' (grrh 'its cud') (Lev 11:6)

In the G stem imperfect, the forms spelled without -w- should be noted (tysq, nsq); the mpl G stem imperative sqwn has the suffix extended from the imperfect; the C stem infinitives spelled with aleph are anomalous (the similarity between these forms and Babylonian Talmudic 'assoqe, spelled 'swqy, is minimal at best, cf. Epstein, "Grammar," p. 76).

b. hlk

Unlike the situation that prevails in other dialects of Middle Aramaic, in the MS Neofiti 1 this root does not occur in a suppletive paradigm with a medial weak root h-w-k, or the like, for the imperfect/infinitive. Of forty-four examples collected, the h is preserved in all forms of the verb. The use of this verb does appear to be restricted, especially when compared to the very common 'zl, but the data are not large enough to determine the exact relationship between the two verbs. Over half of the forms (23) occur in Leviticus, Chapter 13, dealing with the laws concerning leprosy, and 20 of these are translations of various forms of the MT root p-s-h 'to spread' (of a disease). The other three translate MT p-r-ḥ 'to break out' (of a disease), however, cf. e.g., Exod 9:9, 10 for MT p-r-ḥ translated by Aramaic p-r-ḥ. Of the other 21 forms collected, 17 translate a form of the G stem of MT h-l-k, two the medio-passive of MT h-l-k, and two occur in paraphrase. The forms translating h-l-k refer both to walking on a road (derek, e.g., Num 21:22), and also to following the way/laws of the Lord (e.g., Deut 10:21/ Lev 18:3); some are preceded by the verbs n-s-^{c}, q-w-m, ^{c}-l-h (e.g., Deut 1:19, Gen 35:3); others are used in the idiom hlk 'aḥ^{a}rê 'to follow after' (Gen 24:61).

However, the verb 'zl also occurs in all the same circumstances, and no distinction is readily apparent. It should be noted that, with one exception (Gen 24:61, fpl active participle hlkyn), all the collected forms are also open to interpretation as D stem forms, and perhaps this may provide fruitful ground for future investigation (note especially the infinitive/participles).

The collected forms are:

		Singular	Plural
Perfect:			
	1	hlkt (Gen 35:3)	hlknn (Deut 1:19)
	2m	--	hlktwn (Deut 1:31)
	f	--	--
	3m	hlk (Lev 13:5, 6, 32, etc.)	hlykw (Deut 8:4)
	f	hlkt (Gen 7:18, Lev 13:8, 20)	--
Imperfect:			
	1	'hlk (Lev 26:41, Deut 2:27)	nhlk (Gen 33:12, Num 20:17, 21:22)
	2m	--	thlkwn (Lev 18:3)
	f	--	--
	3m	yhlk (Lev 13:35)	--
	f	thlk (Lev 13:7, 22, 27)	--
Imperative:			
	masc.	hlk (Gen 13:17)	--
	fem.	--	--

Infinitive:

mhlkh (Lev 13:7, 27, 35 - cognate infinitive, cf. also the error form mhlk! in Lev 13:22)

lmhlkh (Lev 18:14, Deut 10:12, for MT lāleket)

		Singular	Plural
Active Participle:			
	masc.	mhlk (Gen 3:8, 24:42, 28:20, 30:36, 32:20)	mhlkyn (Gen 9:23)
	fem.	mhlkh (Gen 32:21, Lev 13:42, 57)	hlkyn! (Gen 24:61)

9. <u>The Verbs 't' 'come'/ 'zl 'go'/ 'mr 'say'</u>

a. <u>'t'</u>

The verb <u>'t'</u> occurs in both the G and C stems. The forms attested appear to represent the vocalizations as found in other Middle Aramaic dialects, e.g., Onkelos.

	Singular	Plural
G Stem		
Perfect:		
1	'tyt (Gen 24:42, Num 22:38)	'tynn (Gen 44:18) 'tyn' (Gen 44:18)
2m	'tyt (Num 22:37)	'tytwn (Gen 26:27) 'ty<t>wn (Gen 42:9, spelled 'tyhwn)
f	--	--
3m	't' (Gen 19:9, 39:16+) 'th (Gen 23:2)	'twn (Gen 12:5, Exod 2:17, 35:21, 22)
f	'tt (Gen 29:9)	'tyyn (Exod 2:18) 'tyn (Exod 2:16)
Imperfect:		
1	--	nyty (Gen 37:10)
2m	tyty (Gen 24:41) tyyty (Gen 27:31)	tytwn (Gen 49:18, 19)
f	--	--
3m	yyty (Gen 32:8, 11)	yytwn (Exod 18:22, 35:10)
f	tyty (Gen 24:39)	ytyn (Gen 49:26, subj. = <u>brkt'</u>) yytyyn (Deut 33:16, subj. = <u>brkyyt'</u>!)
Imperative:		
masc.	't' (Gen 31:44, 37:13, Exod 3:10) 'yth (Gen 4:8)	'twn (Gen 11:3, 4, 7+) 'ytwn (Exod 1:10) 'tw! (Gen 37:20, 27)

	Singular	Plural
fem.	'twy! (Gen 19:32, for 'tyy?, cf. Onkelos *ad loc.*, *'yt'*)	--

---

Infinitive:

myyty (Gen 37:10, Num 22:14, 16)
myty (Gen 24:5)
mytyh! (Gen 24:8, aural confusion of *-yh* for *-y*, representing the vowel /e/)
mtyyh! (Gen 35:16, error of metathesis for *mytyh*, or *-yyh* for the vowel /e/)

With suffixes:

mytyyh 'his coming' (Gen 35:9, MT *bō'ô*)
myytwy! 'my coming' (Gen 48:5, 7, MT *bō'î*, for *myytyy?*)

Active Participles:

	Singular	Plural
masc.	'ty (Gen 4:7, 8+) 't<y> (Gen 33:1, spelled *'t!*) 't'! (Gen 32:6) 'tyh! (Gen 26:26, cf. Infinitive above)	'tyn (Gen 15:1, 24:63)
fem.	'tyyh (Gen 16:8)	'tyn (Gen 32:3, subj. = *mšryn*)
	'ty' (Gen 37:25)	'tyyn (Gen 41:29, subj. = *šnyn*)
	'tyy' (Gen 29:6)	

C Stem

Perfect:

	Singular	Plural
1	'yytyt (Gen 31:39) 'yytt (Gen 33:11, 44:18)	--
2m	'yytt (Gen 20:9, 39:17, the latter with *-y-* added above)	'yytytwn (Num 20:4)
f	--	--

	Singular	Plural
3m	'yyty (Gen 4:3,4, 27:12,23 39:14+)	'yytwn (Exod 35:21,23, 24,27,29, 36:3+)
	'yty (Gen 2:19, 32:13, 37:2)	
f	'ytt (Exod 2:10)	--

Imperfect		
1	'yyty (Gen 27:12, 31:52)	--
2m	tyyty (Gen 27:10)	tyytwn (Gen 42:20, Exod 23:19, Lev 23:14)
	tyty (Exod 3:18, 18:19)	
f	--	--
3m	yyty (Gen 18:19, Lev 5:25, 13:2)	yytwn (Lev 4:14, 10:15)
f	tty (Lev 15:29)	--

Imperative		
masc.	'yyty (Gen 27:4,7,9,13)	'yytwn (Gen 42:34, Exod 32:2)
fem.	--	--

Infinitive

myytyyh (Gen 27:5, Exod 35:29, Lev 12:8)
myytyh (Lev 14:32)
myyth (Exod 36:5)

Active Participles		
m.s.	myyty (Gen 6:17)	--
	myty (Gen 26:10)	

b. 'zl

The perfect is inflected like the strong verb. The 3ms is always 'zl, with one exception, Gen 18:6, 'zyl! For other forms, cf. 2ms 'zlt (Gen 31:30), 3fs 'zlt (Exod 2:8), 3mpl 'zlw (Gen 14:11, 12, 24, etc., but note 'zlwn in Gen 37:12).

In the imperfect, the aleph of the root is never written (cf. 'mr, below, and other I-aleph verbs, above). The following imperfect forms are attested:

	Singular	Plural
1	'zyl (Gen 24:58, Exod 2:7) 'yzyl (Gen 24:56) 'zl (Gen 33:14, Exod 3:11)	nzyl (Exod 3:18) nyzyl (Gen 33:12, 37:17) nyzl (Gen 30:2, 34:17)
2m	tzyl (Gen 24:4) tyzl (Gen 24:38) tzl (Gen 28:15)	tzlwn (Gen 19:2) tyzlwn (Deut 6:14)
f	tzlyn (Gen 24:58)	--
3m	yyzyl (Gen 21:7, Exod 10:24)	yzlwn (Gen 15:1)
f	tyzl (Gen 24:55)	--

In the imperative, the aleph of the root is always present:

masc. sing.	'zl (Gen 22:2, Exod 3:16, Num 22:35, Deut 5:30, and often)
fem. sing.	'zly (Exod 2:8)
masc. Pl.	'zlw (Gen 29:7) 'zylw (Exod 10:24) 'yzylw (Exod 5:4, Num 22:13)

Infinitive

myzl (Gen 11:31, 31:30, Exod 3:19, Deut 29:17, and often)
mzl (Gen 12:5)

With Suffixes

myzlk 'your going', Exod 4:21, MT lektəkā)

Active Participles

masc. sing.	'zl (Exod 3:13, 19:19, and often)
fem. sing.	'zlh (Gen 16:8, 24:60)
masc. pl.	'zlyn (Gen 8:3, 5, 13:17, 37:25)
fem. pl.	--

---

c. 'mr

The inflection of the perfect of 'mr follows that of the strong verb, e.g., 2ms 'mrt (Gen 12:19), 3ms 'mr (Gen 29:19, 21, etc.), 3fs 'mrt (Gen 16:13, etc.)/'myrt (Gen 24:58), 3mpl 'mrw (Gen 26:28, etc.)/'mrwn (Gen 11:4); and note occasional error (?) forms such as 1s 'mry

(Gen 44:18, cf. Babylonian Talmudic Aramaic, e.g., Epstein, "Grammar," p. 35).

In the imperfect, one often finds forms in which the *aleph* is retained in the spelling, however forms spelled with -*y*- to indicate the prefix vowel *e* are more common, cf.:

	Singular	Plural
1	'ymr (Exod 3:13, Gen 24:14, spelled *'mr* with -*y*- added above) 'mr (Gen 22:2)	nymr (Gen 37:20) n'mr (Gen 44:16)
2m	tymr (Exod 3:16) t'mr (Exod 3:14)	tymrwn (Exod 3:18) t'mrwn (Lev 25:20)
f	--	--
3m	yymr (Num 5:19) y'mr (Exod 22:8, Deut 5:27)	yymrwn (Deut 4:6) ymrwn (Gen 12:12) y'mrw! (Exod 3:13) yy'mrwn (Deut 31:17)
f	tymr (Gen 24:14, 44)	--

The remainder of the attested forms are predictable: imperatives and participles inflect like the strong verb, e.g.,

masc. sing. imperative:	'mr (Exod 6:6), but note also 'mwr! (Deut 1:42, 5:30)
fem. sing. imperative:	'mry (Gen 12:13, 20:13)
masc. sing. participle:	'mr (Exod 2:14, 3:13)
masc. pl. participle:	'mryn (Gen 18:5, 9, etc.), but note also 'mrn! (Gen 26:32, 34:14, perhaps copyist errors influenced by the spelling of *'škḥnn* and *'nn* later in the respective verses).

Note also the participle + pronominal suffix(?) in Gen 26:28, *'mrynn* (but more likely a perfect with irregular suffix extended from the *tertia infirma* verb in the same verse, *hmynn*; cf. Section B.1.a, above, where the examples from the strong verbs are cited).

fem. pl. participle: 'mryn! (Gen 31:14, subj. = rḥl wl'h, Exod 2:19, subj. = daughters of Reuel)

The infinitive is never spelled with aleph, and is most commonly used as the common noun "word," e.g., Gen 4:23 mymryh dpwmy 'the word of my mouth', etc. Note the "defective" spelling mmr (rarely, e.g., Gen 21:22).

10. The Verbs hwh 'be'/ ḥyh 'live'

a. hwh

The verb hwh occurs commonly translating the forms of the MT hāyā; in predicate usage; in compound tenses with the participle of another verb.

The most common attestation is in the phrase whwh 'and it happened', usually for MT wayhî, e.g., Gen 39:19, whwh kd šm^{c} rybwnyh 'and when his lord heard' (MT wayhî kišmō^{ac} '^{a}dōnāyw), however it also occurs in passages that have no Hebrew Vorlage. Whether this is solely a translation idiom or indeed reflects natural Aramaic usage cannot be determined. For an example of predicate usage, see, e.g., Gen 3:1, wḥwy' hwh ḥkym mn kl ḥyyt' 'and the snake was cleverer than all the beasts' (MT wəhannāḥāš hāyā ^{c}ārûm mikkōl ḥayyat haśśāde), and many others. For a discussion of compound verbal forms, see Chapter 9, Syntax, below).

The 3ms perfect form occurs most commonly, and the spelling hwh occurs approximately at the ratio of 6:1 over the spelling hwwh. Note also occasional error spellings of hw' for hwh (confusion with hw' 'he'), e.g., Gen 1:5 whw' rmš whwh ṣpr 'and it was evening and it was morning' (elsewhere in Genesis Chapter 1 always spelled whwh/ whwwh).

There are numerous examples of variation in spelling and usage with the perfect of hwh, e.g., singular for plural (Gen 5:14, 27:15 hwh/hwwh for hww); masculine for feminine (Gen 15:17, 39:5, the Hebrew 3ms, with fs subject, is faithfully translated into Aramaic as hwh; Gen 35:18, myth hwh 'she was dead', for hwt, with h/ṯ copyist confusion); errors for hwh (Gen 6:9, 31:42); w/y confusion (Gen 26:35, 41:53, hwyn for hwwn?); z/w confusion (Num 10:31 hzynn for hwynn), etc.

The attested forms in the perfect are:

	Singular	Plural
1	--	hwynn (Num 13:33, 31:50, Deut 6:21, etc.) hwwynn (Exod 16:3, Num 31:50) hwwnn! (Num 13:13, probably w/y confusion, cf., hwynn in the same verse) hwyn'! (Num 12:12, in the compound hwyn' mšt^{c}bdyn 'we were enslaved')
2m	hwwt (Gen 26:10)	hwytwn (Exod 23:9) hwwytwn (Exod 22:20)
f	hwwyt (Gen 24:60)	--
3m	hwh (Gen 1:2, etc.) hwwh (Num 7:9, etc.) hw'! (Gen 1:2, Deut 5:7) hww'! (Deut 4:46)	hwwn (Gen 5:4, and often) hww (Gen 2:25, 4:8, 13:7, 14:5) hwn! (Gen 4:10, 14:17, with w/final n confusion for hww?) hwwwn! (Exod 15:12)
f	hwwt (Gen 1:1, and often) hwt (Gen 19:26)	hwwyyn (Gen 22:10, twice, subj. = ^{c}yynwy; Gen 29:17, subj. = ^{c}yny dl'h [sic]) hwyn (Gen 26:35, subj. = wives of Esau, see below; Gen 41:53, subj. = šny śb^{c}n') hwwn (Gen 26:35, subj. = wives of Esau, see above; Gen 29:20, subj. = šnyn; Exod 1:5, subj. = npšwt') hwh! (Gen 15:1, subj. = mṣwwn)

The spelling and usage of the different imperfect forms show considerable variation, including occasional "plene" spellings of the prefix, e.g., nyhwwy (Gen 34:16); stem vowel sometimes spelled with -h in the singular (overwhelmingly spelled -y, and note also thww'!, 3fs, Gen 9:2); masculine singular for feminine singular, e.g., yhwwy (Gen 26:28, MT təhî); and learned and copyist error, including the unique lhwwn (Gen 8:21, no Vorlage, cf. Babylonian Talmudic Aramaic), the copyist aural error yhby (Gen 9:11, i.e., reflecting the medieval pronunciation /yihve/, hence written b for w), and yhwwn (Gen 34:31 for 3ms yhwwy, probably due to y/final n confusion.

The unusual 3fpl thwwn (Gen 21:30) is apparently the result of an interpretation of the MT 'et-šeba^{c} kəbāsōt tiqqaḥ...ba^{ca}bûr tihye-llî lə^{c}ēdā 'the seven ewes you shall take...that it (!) may be a witness for me', as yt šb^{c}ty 'mrt tsb...mn bgll dthwwn ly lshdw 'the seven ewes you shall take...that they (you?) may be a witness for me', i.e., thwwn perhaps based on MT thyh.

As with the verb ḥyh 'live' (see below), there are also examples found of a "short" imperfect of hwh, however the motivations for its usage are not immediately apparent, e.g., Gen 9:14 yhy = yəhe, for the MT converted perfect wəhāyā; Gen 3:5 (w)thwn, pointed in the MS וְתֶהֱוֹן, but perhaps = təhon, or else defective spelling for tihwon (cf. the spelling lhwn in Biblical Aramaic); and Exod 27:1 mrb^{c} yhy mdbḥ' 'the altar will be square' (MT rābû^{ac} yihye hammizbē^{a}ḥ).

The attested forms in the imperfect are:

	Singular	Plural
1	'hwy (Gen 17:8, 31:3) 'hwwh (Gen 26:3)	nhwy (Gen 27:12, 44:18) nhwwy (Gen 38:23) nyhwwy (Gen 34:16)
2m	thwy (Gen 3:14, 4:12) thwwy (Gen 4:12, Exod 22:24) thwh (Gen 3:14)	thwwn (Lev 19:2, Deut 7:26) thwn! (Gen 3:5, 34:15)

	Singular	Plural
	tyhwy (Gen 4:12, Num 10:31)	
	tyhwwy (Gen 14:23)	
2f	--	thwwn (Exod 1:16)
3m	yhwy (Gen 1:3)	yhwwn (Gen 3:15, 27:40)
	yhwwy (Gen 16:12, Exod 22:22)	lhwwn! (Gen 8:21)
	yhwh (Gen 18:18)	
	yhwwyy! (Exod 22:23)	
	yhywwy! (Num 9:14)	
	yhby! (Gen 9:11)	
	yhy! (Gen 9:14)	
f	thwy (Gen 3:17, 4:7)	yhwyn (Gen 41:27)
	tyhwy (Num 12:12)	yhwwyyn (Gen 44:36)
	thwwy (Gen 17:16)	yyhwwyyn! (Deut 21:15)
	tyhwwy (Gen 11:4)	thwwn! (Gen 21:30)
	thww'! (Gen 9:2)	

The remaining attested forms of the verb <u>hwh</u> are:

<u>Imperative</u>:

masc. sing.	hwh (Gen 17:1)
	hwwy (Gen 27:29, Exod 3:14)
masc. pl.	hwwn (Exod 19:15)

<u>Infinitive</u>:

mhwy (common, e.g., Num 31:50)
mhwwy (occasional, e.g., Gen 17:7, 18:11, 12)
mhwh (rare, e.g., Gen 18:18)

<u>Active Participles</u>:

masc. sing.	hwy (e.g., Gen 21:20)
	hwwy (e.g., Exod 3:14)
fem. sing.	hwwy' (Exod 9:3)
masc. pl.	hwyn (Gen 11:3)
	hywn! (Gen 26:35, an error of metathesis compounded with <u>w/y</u> confusion, for hwyn)
	hwwyyn (Lev 22:27)
fem. pl.	--

The participial form hwy occurs often for MT wayhî, and one might offer the preliminary suggestion that it is used in clauses that are subordinate to a main verb, or in temporally subordinate clauses, cf., e.g., Gen 21:20 whwy YYY ^{c}m ṭly'...whwy mn mtylp mrmy bqšt' 'and the Lord was with the child...and he became one of those expert at shooting with a bow' (MT wayhî '^{e}lōhîm 'et-hanna^{c}ar...wahyî rōbe qaššāt); Gen 29:13 whwy kdy šm^{c} lbn...wrhṭ 'and this is what was happening when Laban heard...that he ran' (MT wayhî kišmō^{ac} lābān...wayyāraṣ); Gen 43:2 whwy kdy 'šlmw lmykl...w'mr 'and this is what happened when they finished eating...that he said' (MT wayhî ka'^{a}šer killû le'^{e}kōl...wayyō(')mer).

Both the ms and the fs participles of this root occur with the 1s personal suffix -nh/ -n', and while the examples are not numerous, a preliminary statement may be made concerning the use of this idiom, and its contrast to both the simple perfect and the compound of perfect hwh + participle. All examples save that in Gen 31:40 are followed by the participle of another verb (possibly also excepting kmst, Gen 20:16). The examples collected are:

(1) ...'ylw yhbt kl mh dy ly l' hwynh kmst... '...if I gave everything I had, I would (still) not be worthy...' (Gen 20:16);

(2) ...kl ḥd' mnhwn dhwwt ^{c}rqh mn mnyynh 'nh hwynh mšlm yth...'nh hwyn' mšlm ythwn '...every one of them that would flee from the flock, there I was replacing it...there I was replacing them' (Gen 31:39);

(3) hwyn' b'ymm' 'kl yty šrb'...'There I was, in the daytime the heat devoured me...' (Gen 31:40, MT hāyîtî bayyôm '^{a}kālanî ḥōreb...);

(4) 'nh k^{c}n hwynh m^{c}td byn mymryh dYYY wbynykwn 'There I was standing between the word of the Lord and you' (Deut 5:5, MT 'ānōkî ^{c}ōmēd bên YHWH ûbênêkem);

(5) ḥmyt dl' hwynh yldh wnsbyt lhgr...'I saw that I was not going to give birth, so I took Hagar...' (fem., Gen 16:5);

(6) mbśr hwwyn' ... wl' mn swp dhwyn' tb^{c} ^{c}lk mn qdm YYY hwwyn' mṣly ^{c}lk...'There I was being notified...and not finally that I was making petition for you from before the Lord, there I was praying for you...' (Exod 10:29).

As can be seen from the suggested translations, this form indicates duration of action in the past, with the added feature of first person reportage. In other words, this form is used whenever the narrator wishes to create a "picture" of his/her action in the past and convey that action as ongoing. Contrast this with the conditional and other uses of the compound verbal forms with hwh + participle (see below, Chapter 9, Syntax), e.g.,

Gen 26:10 'ylw šmš ḥd mn ṭly' ^{c}m 'ttk whwwt myyty ^{c}lynn ḥwbyn rbrbyn 'if one of the young men had had intercourse with your wife, then you would have brought great sins upon us', or

Gen 44:18 h' mn zmn' qdmyy' d'tynn lwwtk hwwyyt 'mr ln...'now, from the first time that we came to you, you have been (continuously) saying to us...', and also contrast with the simple past, also in Gen 44:18,

h' bzmn' qdm'h d'tyn' 'mrt ln...'now, the first time that we (or perhaps better, 'I') came, you said to us...'

b. ḥyh

Few forms are attested, and those are mostly 3ms perfect ḥyh, occuring in genealogical formulae, cf. especially Genesis Chapter 5 and 11, wḥyh PN x šnyn 'and PN lived x years'. Note the occasional spelling ḥyyh, e.g., Gen 25:7 (and also the abbreviated form ḥy` in Gen 11:21).

The imperfect is a little better represented:

2ms	tḥy (Gen 20:7, 27:40)
3ms	yḥy (Gen 3:22, 17:18, Lev 18:5, 25:36, Num 12:12)
	yyḥy (Deut 8:3)
3fs	tyḥy (Exod 1:16)
1pl	nḥy (Gen 42:2)
2mpl	tyḥwn (Deut 4:1)
3mpl	yyḥwn (Gen 19:26)

As can be seen, all forms found are "short" imperfect forms; the prevelance of "plene" prefix spellings would indicate a vocalization yeḥe, teḥe, teḥon, hence presumably also neḥe.

The other forms attested are mpl imperative ḥywn (Gen 42:18, MT wiḥyû) and possibly the ms active participle, Num 21:9 (whwwh ḥyy 'then he would live' (= ḥāye?, MT wāḥāy), or else the common adjective (?) ḥy, spelled with -yy for the diphthong.

There is one rare C (D?) stem participle form, Deut 32:39 mḥyy 'bring to life' (based on MT poetic ʾaḥayye); this idiom is usually expressed in the MS by the D stem qyym, e.g., qyymtwn (Exod 1:18, Num 31:15), qyymt (1s, Num 22:33), qyymwn (Exod 1:17), tqyymwn (Exod 1:22, 22:17), nqy(y)m (Gen 19:32, 34), imperative qyymw (Num 31:18), and many more examples.

VERBAL PARADIGMS

Strong Verbs

G Stem

	Singular	Plural
Perfect		
3m	qtl/ qtyl	qtlw/ qtylw
f	qtlt	qtln (qtlw)
2m	qtlt	qtltwn
f	qtlt	qtltwn
1	qtlt/ qtlyt	qtlnn/ qtlynn
Imperfect		
3m	yqtwl/ yqtl	yqtlwn
f	tyqtwl/ tqtl	yqtlwn
2m	tqtwl/ tqtl (tqtyl)	tqtlwn
f	tqtlyn	tqtlwn
1	'qtwl/ 'qtl ('qtyl)	nqtwl/ nqtl
Imperative		
masc.	qtl/ qtwl	qtlw/qtylw
fem.	qtly/ qtyly	qtlw
Infinitive		
mqtl/ mqtwl		
Active Participle		
masc.	qtl/ qtyl	qtlyn
fem.	qtlh/ qtl'	qtlyn!/ qtln
Passive Participle		
masc.	qtyl	qtylyn/ qtwlyn!
fem.	qtylh	qtyln/ qtylyn!

VERBAL PARADIGMS

Strong Verbs

D Stem

	Singular	Plural
Perfect		
3m	qtl/ qtyl	qtlw/ qtylw
f	qtlt/ qtylt	qtlyn (?)
2m	qtlt	qtltwn
f	qtlt	--
1	qtlt/ qtlyt	qtlnn
Imperfect		
3m	yqtl/ yqtyl	yqtlwn
f	tqtl	yqtln/ yqtlwn
2m	tqtl/ tqtyl	tqtlwn
f	--	--
1	'qtl	nqtl
Imperative		
masc.	qtl/ qtyl	qtlw/ qtylw
fem.	qtly	--
Infinitive		
	mqtlh/ mqtl'	
Active Participle		
masc.	mqtl	mqtlyn
fem.	mqtlh/ mqtl'	mqtln
Passive Participle		
masc.	mqtl/ mqtwl!	mqtlyn
fem.	mqtlh/ mqtl'	--

VERBAL PARADIGMS

Strong Verbs

C Stem

	Singular	Plural
Perfect		
3m	'qtl	'qtlw/ 'qtylw
f	'qtlt	--
2m	'qtlt	'qtltwn
f	--	--
1	'qtlt/ 'qtlyt	'qtlnn
Imperfect		
3m	yqtl	yqtlwn
f	--	--
2m	tqtl (tqtyl)	tqtlwn
f	--	--
1	'qtl ('qtyl)	nqtl
Imperative		
masc.	'qtl	'qtlw
fem.	'qtyly	--
Infinitive		
	mqtlh/ mqtl'	
Active Participle		
masc.	mqtl/ mqtyl	mqtlyn/ mqtylyn
fem.	'qtlh?!	'qtln?!
Passive Participle		
masc.	--	--
fem.	--	--

VERBAL PARADIGMS

Strong Verbs

Gt/Dt Stems

	Singular	Plural
Perfect		
3m	'tqtl/ 'ytqtl/ 'tqtyl	'tqtlw/ 'ytqtlw
f	'tqtlt	'tqtln/ 'ytqtlwn!
2m	'tqtlt	'tqtltwn
f	--	--
1	'tqtlt	'tqtlnn
Imperfect		
3m	ytqtl/ ytqtyl	ytqtlwn/ ytqtlw!
f	ttqtl	ytqtln/ ytqṭlwn
2m	ttqtl	ttqtlwn
f	--	--
1	'tqtl	ntqtl
Imperative		
masc.	'tqtl	'tqtlw
fem.	'tqtly	--
Infinitive		
	mtqtl'/ mtqtlh	
Participle		
masc.	mtqtl	mtqtlyn
fem.	mtqtlh	mtqtlyn!

VERBAL PARADIGMS

Weak Verbs

PRIMAE INFIRMAE (I-Aleph)

	Singular				Plural			
	G	D	C	-t-	G	D	C	-t-
Perfect								
3m	'kl	'sy	'yykl/ 'yykwl	't'bl/ 't'kl	'klw	'r^{c}w		
f	'klt			't'syt/ 't'sy't!				
2m	'klt	'lpt'!						
f	—							
1	'klyt/ 'klt	'lpyt	'klt					
Imperfect								
3m	yykwl/ykl y'kl			yt'kl	ylpwn/ yyklwn	yylpwn/ y'r^{c}wn		
f	tykwl/ t'kl			tt'kl/ tt'sy	—			
2m	tykwl/ tykl/t'kl	tlyp/ t'rś			tlpwn/ t'klwn/ tyklwn			
f	—				—			
1	'kwl/ 'ykwl/'kl	'lp			n'kl			
Imperative								
masc.	'kl	mlp/ 'sy	'ykl					
fem.	—	—	—					
Infinitive								
	mykl	mlph/ mlp'	mwbdh					
Active Participles								
masc.	'kl/'kyl	mlp			'klyn			
fem.	'klh	—			—			
Passive Participles								
masc.	—	—	—		—			
fem.	—	m'rsh	—		—			

VERBAL PARADIGMS

Weak Verbs

PRIMAE INFIRMAE (I-y/w)

	Singular G	Singular D	Singular C	Singular -t-	Plural G	Plural D	Plural C	Plural -t-
Perfect								
3m	yhb/ytyb		'wl(y)d/ 'yyṭb	'tylyd/ 'twtb	yhbw/ylydw		'ws(y)pw	'tylydw 'tyḥmw/ 'twtbw
f	yhbt/ylydt		'wspt/ 'yynyqt 'wnqt!	'tylydt/ 'tyḥmt	ylydw/yldn			
2m	yhbt		--	'twwkḥt/ 'twtbt	--			
f	yhbt		--	--	yd^{c}tn			
1	yhbt/yhbyt		'wqdt/ 'wd^{c}⟨y⟩t	'twtbt	yrtynn!			
Imperfect								
3m	y(y)rt/yd^{c}/ yyṭ(y)b	ybm	ywld/ysp!	ytyhb/ ytwd^{c}!	yrtwn		ywkyḥn!	ytyldwn/ ytldwn!/ ytwspwn
f	tld		twsp	ttwqd	yldn		--	--
2m	tykl/td^{c}/ tyṭb/tṭyb		twzp	--	tyrtwn		twqdwn	ttyybbwn
f	tldyn		--	--	--		--	--
1	'yrt/'ld/ 'wkl/'kyl/ 'kwl		'wsp/ 'yqr/ 'yyqr!/ 'yyṭb	'tyqr	n(y)kl/ nyqwd		nwṭb!	--
Imperative								
masc.	hb/tb	ybm	--	'twtb	hbw/tbw/ yr(y)tw	--	'wbylw	'tyldwn
fem.	hby/tby	--	'wnyqy!/ 'yybyly!	--	--	--	--	--
Infinitive								
	mld/myld m(y)rt/ myrwt	--	myyṭybh! mwldh	mtwqdh				
Active Participles								
masc.	ykl/ykyl	mylp	mwl(y)d/ mld!	--	yhbyn	--	--	--
fem.	ytbh	--	myynqth (suff.)	--	yldn	--	myynqyn!	--
Passive Participles								
masc.	yhyb	--	--	mtylp	yhybyn	--	--	--
fem.	yhybh	--	--	--	--	--	--	--

VERBAL PARADIGMS

Weak Verbs

PRIMAE INFIRMAE (I-n)

	Singular				Plural			
	G	D	C	-t-	G	D	C	-t-
Perfect								
3m	nsb/nsyb	nḥm/nsy	'syb/'ḥt	--	nsbw	--	'pqw/'pyqw 'qypw/'wḥtw!	
f	nsbt/nsybt	--	'sbt	'tnsybt	--	--	--	
2m	nsbt	--	'pqt	--	npqtwn	--	--	
f	nsbt	--	--	--	--	--	--	
1	nsb(y)t	--	'sbt/'pqyt		nsbnn/ nṭln!/ nṭlynn!	--	'qpnn	
Imperfect								
3m	ytn/ysb/ ypwq	ynbḥ/ ynšy	ypyq	ytnzr/ ytnsk	ytnwn/ ysbwn	--	ypqwn/yhtwn	
f	tsb/tpq!	--	tpq	--	ypqwn	--	--	
2m	ttn/tyḥwt/ t(y)sb	--	--	--	tkswn/ tykswn	tnskwn	tḥtwn	
f	--	--	--	--	--	--	--	
1	'tn/'sb/ 'ḥwt	'nṭr	'pyq	--	nsb/ntn/ nṭwl	--	npq	
Imperative								
masc.	sb/ṭwl/ṭl!	--	'pq/'pyq	--	pwqw	--	'sbw/ 'pyqw/'pqw	
fem.	sby/ṭwly	--	--	--	--	--	--	
Infinitive								
	mysb/mšb/ mpwq/ myṭwr/mṭwr/ mṭr	mnhmh	mnhr'/ msbh/ mqph/ mypqh!	mtnḥmh				
Active Participles								
masc.	npyq/nḥt	mnṭr	mḥt/mḥyt/ mqp	mtnḥm	nplyn/ nsby(const) nzly' (det)	mnṭryn	mnhryn	
fem.	--	mnšb'	--	--	--	--	mpqn	
Passive Participles								
masc.	--	--	--	mtnks	--	mnṭlyn mnṭly' (det)	--	mtnṭlyn
fem.	nsybt const)	--	mqph/ mnṭlth(det)	--	--	--	mqypn!	--

VERBAL PARADIGMS

Weak Verbs

MEDIAE INFIRMAE (II-w/y)

	Singular				Plural			
	G	D	C	-t-	G	D	C	-t-
Perfect								
3m	qm/myt	qyym	'qym/'qm!	't^{c}r/ 't^{c}yr/ 'tpyys	qmw/mytw	qyymw	—	'dy(y)nw/ 'zdyynw
f	qmt/mytt	—	—	'tlyṭt	—	—	—	'tqymn
2m	—	qyymt	'qymt	—	—	—	'zydtwn	'yzdyyntw
f	—	—	—	—	—	qyymtwn	—	—
1	—	qyymyt/ qyymt	'q(y)myt 'rymt	't^{c}yqt/ 'yt^{c}yryt	mtynn!	šyyrnn	—	—
Imperfect								
3m	ymwt	—	yqym	ytqyym/ yt'rq!	ymwtwn/ ydwnwn/ ydynwn!	yqyymwn	yzydwn	ytdnwn/ ydyynwn
f	tmwt/tbyt	—	—	ttqyym	yḥwsn	—	—	—
2m	tmwt	—	tnyp	— tmtwn!	tmwtwn/	—	tqymwn	ttn(w)ḥwn
f	—	—	—	—	—	—	—	—
1	'mwt	'qyym	'qym	—	nmwt/nbyt	nqyym	—	ntḥyyb
Imperative								
masc.	qwm	—	'qym	—	qwmw	qyymw	'ṣytw	—
fem.	qwmy	—	—	—	—	—	—	—
Infinitive								
	myqwm/ myqm/mqwm/ mmt/mmyt!/ mmwt!	mqyymh/ mqyym'	mqm'/ mmth					
Active Participles								
masc.	qy(y)m/ q'(y)m	mqyym	mṣyt		qyymym	mdyynyn	—	
fem.	qyymh/ qy(y)m'	mqyymh	—		qyymn/ qyym'!	—	—	
Passive Participles								
masc.	lyṭ/lwṭ!/ lyyṭ!	mṣyyr	—	mytkl/ mtkwyn	—	mzyynyyn!	—	mtkwwnyn
fem.	—	—	—	—	—	—	—	—

VERBAL PARADIGMS

Weak Verbs

MEDIAE INFIRMAE (II-Aleph)

	Singular				Plural			
	G	D	C	-t-	G	D	C	-t-
Perfect								
3m	š'l/š'yl	s'b/šyyr	'b'š	'šty(y)r	s'ybw/ š'(y)lw š'lwn!	s'bw	'b'šw/ 'š'lw	'štyyrw
f	—	—	—	'st'bt/ 'štyyrt	—	—	—	'štyyrn
2m	—	—	'b'št	—	š'ltwn	—	'b'štwn/ 'byštwn	—
f	—	—	—	—	—	—	—	—
1	s'byt/s'bt	—	—	—	—	šyyrnn	—	—
Imperfect								
3m	yb'š	ys'b/yšyyr	—	yst'b	yš'lwn	ys'bwn	—	yštyyrwn
f	tb'š	—	—	tst'b/ tštyyr	—	—	—	—
2m	—	—	—	—	tb'šwn	—	—	tst'bwn/ tštyyrwn
f	—	—	—	—	—	—	—	—
1	—	—	—	—	nb'š	—	—	—
Imperative								
masc.	—	—	—	—	š'(y)lw	—	—	—
fem.	—	—	—	—	—	—	—	—
Infinitive								
	ms'l	ms'b'/ mš'lyh?	mb'š'	mst'b				
Active Participle								
masc.	š'yl	—	—	—	š'lyn	—	—	—
fem.	—	—	—	—	š'lyn	—	—	—
Passive Participle								
masc.	—	ms'b/mšyyr	—	—	ms'byn	—	—	—
fem.	—	ms'bh ms'b'	—	—	—	—	—	—

VERBAL PARADIGMS

Weak Verbs

MEDIAE INFIRMAE (Geminates)

	Singular				Plural			
	G	D	C	-t-	G	D	C	-t-
Perfect								
3m	^{c}l	mlyl/ mll	'gn/ '^{c}yl	'tw^{c}l?	bzw/bzzw! bzwn!	mllw/ mlylw	'^{c}ylw/ 'wqlw!	't^{c}lw
f	^{c}lt	mllt	--	'tnddt	^{c}lw	--	--	--
2m	--	ml(y)lt'!	'^{c}lt	--	--	mlltwn	'^{c}ltwn	--
f	--	--	--	--	--	--	--	--
1	^{c}lyt	mlylyt	--	--	^{c}lynn/ bzznn	mllnn	--	--
Imperfect								
3m	y^{c}l/ ygn	--	y^{c}yl/ yy^{c}l	yt^{c}l/ ytmll	y^{c}lwn	yglwn!	y^{c}lwn	ytmšwn
f	ty^{c}wl	--	--	--	y^{c}l'!	--	--	--
2m	ty^{c}wl/ t^{c}wl	tmll	t^{c}yl/ t^{c}l	--	ty^{c}lwn/ tbzwn/ tṣwrwn!	tmllwn	--	--
f	--	--	--	--	--	--	--	--
1	'y^{c}wl/ '^{c}wl	'mll	--	--	ny^{c}wl/ n^{c}wl	--	n^{c}l	
Imperative								
masc.	^{c}wl/ ^{c}l!	mlyl/ mll	'^{c}l	--	^{c}wlw	--	--	'tqrrw
fem.	^{c}wly	--	--	--	--	--	--	--
Infinitive								
	my^{c}wl/ mgzz	mmllh/ mmll'/ mllh!/mll'!	--	mtmllh/ mtwqrrh!				
Active Participle								
masc.	^{c}lyl	mmll	m^{c}l	mtḥmm	^{c}lyn/ ^{c}llyn	mgššyn/ mglyn!	mṭlyn	mt^{c}lyn
fem.	--	mmll'	--	--	--	--	--	--
Passive Participle								
masc.	ḥlwl!	--	--	--	rṣyṣyn	--	--	--
fem.	--	--	--	--	ṣryrn	--	--	--

VERBAL PARADIGMS

Weak Verbs

TERTIAE INFIRMAE (III-h/Aleph)

	Singular				Plural			
	G	D	C	-t-	G	D	C	-t-
Perfect								
3m	ḥmh/ḥm' ṫmh	sgy	'šqy	'tgly/ 'ytgly	ḥmwn/ bnw	sgwn/ tny'w!/tmhw	'qnwn	'tglwn
f	ḥmt/qr't ṫmht	sgyyt/ sgyt	'šqyyt	'(y)tglyt/ 'tgly'y/ 'tglyyt	khn/ dlyyn	mlyyn	'šqyyn	—
2m	ḥmyt	sgyt	--	'tglyt/ 'tglyt'!	bnytwn/ śn'twn!	nysytwn!	'šytwn	--
f	sṭyt	--	--	'tksyt	--	--	--	--
1	ḥmyt/ḥmt! ḃr't/ḃryyt	sgyt/ sgyyt!	—	'tglyt/ 'tglyyt	ḥmynn	kwwynn	—	'štlynn
Imperfect								
3m	yšry/ yklh/ybr'	ysgy	—	ytgly/ ytks'!/ yzdkyh!	yḥmwn/ nšrwn!	--	yšqwn	ytglwn
f	tšry	tsgy	--	ttgly/ ttbr'!	--	yṣdwn	yṭ^{c}yyn	--
2m	tqry	tsgy	--	ttgly	tšrwn	tsgwn	tšhwn	--
f	tyqry	—	—	--	--	—	—	--
1	'ḥmy/ 'bnh	'sgy/ 'sg'/ 'yšwwy!	'sqy	'tgly	nḥmy/ nbnh/ nyšry/nbr'	nsgy	nšqy	ndḥy!
Imperative								
masc.	šth/šty	tny	'dy	--	śrwn	tnwn	'sḥwn/ 'šqw!	'dkwn!
fem.	--	--	--	--	qryn	tnyyn	'šqyyn	--
Infinitive								
	mbny/mzkh myḥmy/mḥṭ'	mtnyyh/ mṣlwyyh!	msgy'/ mṣḥyh/ mšqyyh	mtḥmyy'/ mtmnyh				
Active Participle								
masc.	qry/qr'/ śn'h(det)	mgly/ mksh	mšqy/ msgy'!	mtqry	śryn/ šryyn	mknyyn	mskyyn/ mšqyn	mtḥmyn/ mthnyyn
fem.	šryh/pty' štyyh	mrby(y)h	—	mṣṭpyyh	khyyn/ qryn	mṣlyyn	—	--
Passive Participle								
masc.	gly	mdmy	--	--	śpyn/ šypyn!	—	mḥṭyn	--
fem.	śny'/ ksyyt (cons)	mdmyh	--	--	--	--	--	--

NOTES

[1]The following weak verbs are found spelled (at least once) with -*y*- in the perfect: *'zyl*, *'myr'*, *hpyk*, *ylyd*, *nḥyt*, *nsyb*.

[2]For the origin of these verbs in Aramaic, see Kaufman, "Akkadian Influences," pp. 104-5, 123-4, and see also Dalman, "Grammatik," p. 200.

CHAPTER 9

SYNTAX

In most respects, the syntax of the Aramaic of Targum Neofiti resembles other examples of Middle Aramaic. Hence, this study will not describe all features of the syntax of the language, but rather reference should be made to already existing (however deficient) published descriptions of other dialects, manuscripts, etc. For a similar decision, see Levy, "Language," pp. 187-215, however his resolution of the problem of discussing syntax without a comprehensive analysis of the language is "to limit the comments to brief statements on various phenomena" which are "idiomatic to Aramaic" and wherein Neofiti differs from the Hebrew it is translating. This present study, by contrast, provides an in-depth analysis of four important features of Aramaic, two verbal and two nominal.

Levy's statement (p. 187) that "Aramaic syntax, especially in the later periods, is fairly loose" is difficult to understand. The features isolated here are both unique to Aramaic (in contradistinction to biblical Hebrew) and central to a description of and adequate comprehension of the language of this MS. The language is by no means "loose," as shall be obvious from the discussions below; nor is it necessary to view the Targum solely as a "translation" of the Hebrew, and hence as copying the syntax of biblical Hebrew, although this indeed occurs. More than this, one can also identify probable attempts to mimic biblical Hebrew syntax even in midrashic inserts or expansions, where there is no exact correspondence in the Vorlage, and these phenomena should be accounted for in a complete description of the syntax of Neofiti. However, Neofiti also differs very often from the biblical Hebrew word order, etc., and such occurrences must also be marked. This is especially so in the discussion of compound verbal forms and the use of the predicate adjective, below (for a complete discussion of the latter phenomenon, see Golomb, "Predicate Adjective").

PART ONE
Features of Verbal Syntax

SECTION A
Compound Verbal Forms

This discussion is based on a collection of some 143 examples of compound verbal forms taken from the book of Genesis, and cross-checked with over 100 examples culled from the other four books of the Pentateuch. The term "compound verbal forms" refers to a form of the verb hwh 'be' in the perfect, imperfect, imperative, infinitive, or participle, followed by one or more participles of another verb. Other "compound" forms, such as ᶜtyd + infinitive and swp + infinitive are not discussed in this present format.[1]

The unusual first person form hwyn' + participle has been discussed above, Chapter 8, Verbs, Section C.10.a.

In all cases where Neofiti uses a form of the verb hwh + participle, the option of the simple perfect, imperfect, etc. was also open to the "translator," hence the question of the motivation for using the compound form must be addressed. In the MT, one finds such compound Hebrew forms rarely (only 6% of the total Genesis sample are based on a form of hāyā + participle, see Table 1, line 1), hence one cannot accuse the targumist of intentionally mimicking the Hebrew.[2]

By contrast, over one-third of the Genesis sample are to be found in passages that have no Hebrew Vorlage, or are used in midrashic expansions of the Hebrew text, and as such, this represents an important body of information concerning the use of these forms (see Table 1, line 4; it should also be noted that over half the examples of imperfect of 'be' + participle are found in passages that have no masoretic Vorlage). Finally to be noted is that nearly one-quarter (22%) of all the examples in the sample (25% of the examples of the perfect and 11% of the examples of the imperfect) translate an MT participle, and the appearance of such a form in the MT is clearly enough justification to suggest to the "translator" that he use the compound verbal form in his work (see Table 1, line 2).

We shall first look at the largest group in the sample, examples of perfect hwh + participle, and we shall examine this group with respect to the four suggested lines in Table 1, i.e., what does the form translate. Then we shall briefly look at the smaller groups (imperfect, imperative, infinitive, and participle), and finally conclude with some general remarks arising out of the discussion.

TABLE 1

Sample from Genesis Showing Relationship between Hebrew Base Text and Aramaic Compound Verbal Forms

Hebrew Base Text	Total of Compound Verbal Forms in Sample		Compound Verbal Forms of Type: Perfect hwh + Participle		All other Compound Verbal Forms	
1. Compound of hāyā + participle	6%	(8)	6%	(6)	5%	(2)
2. Simple participle	22%	(32)	25%	(27)	14%	(5)
3. Other:	38%	(55)	40%	(42)	35%	(13)
Perfect	9%	(13)	11%	(12)	3%	(1)
Converted Imperfect	13%	(19)	18%	(19)	--	
Imperfect	9%	(14)	6%	(6)	22%	(8)
Converted Perfect	1%	(1)	--		3%	(1)
Infinitive	4%	(6)	3%	(3)	8%	(3)
Other	1%	(2)	2%	(2)	--	
4. No Hebrew base text (midrash or expansion of a Hebrew term)	34%	(48)	29%	(31)	46%	(17)
TOTAL	100%	(143 cases)	100%	(106 cases)	100%	(37 cases)

1. The use of a compound verbal form in early biblical Hebrew is limited, and usually describes continuing or repeated action in the past or future, depending on whether it is used with a form of *hāyā* or of *yihye*.[3] The expansion of this form in mishnaic Hebrew is one of the more notable features distinguishing it from the earlier language. In mishnaic Hebrew it also denotes repeated action, the simple imperfect being restricted to the modus, and the simple perfect to the preterite.[4] In the Aramaic of Targum Neofiti, the compound perfect can also indicate repeated or habitual action in the past, consequently, on those few occasions where the Hebrew has a compound, the Aramaic mimics it (see above, Section 1.A, and refer to line 1 of Table 1).

2. The appearance of a simple participle in the MT (Table 1, line 2), while not necessitating a compound form in the Aramaic, clearly provides a "trigger" to the "translator" to use one, should its appearance not totally violate the clear meaning of the Hebrew, and should the understanding of the Hebrew admit of a durative sense. Often this contains a nuance of meaning not found in the Hebrew, and this presumably provided an opportunity for exegetical comment. For instance, example (1):

(1) ...wḥšwk' prys ^{c}l 'py thwm' wrwḥ drḥmyn mn qdm YYY *hwh* (sic) *mnšb'* ^{c}l 'py my' (Gen 1:2 *wəḥōšek* *^{c}al-pənê* *təhôm* *wərûaḥ* *'ᵉlōhîm* *məraḥepet* *^{c}al-pənê* *hammāyim*) '...and darkness was spread over the face of the abyss and a spirit of love from before the Lord *was blowing* (better '*began to blow*') over the face of the water'.

In this case, two exegetical comments are apparently made: (1) the insertion of the passive participle *prys* where none is used in the Hebrew; and (2) the ingressive, durative nature of the compound form *hwh* (*sic*) *mnšb'*. The participle *prys* appears to indicate the perfective aspect in the past, in this case following *w'r^{c}'* *hwwt* *thy'* *wbhy'* 'and the earth was empty and formless,' and the compound form, based on the MT participle *məraḥepet*, provides the "translator" with the opportunity to comment that the 'spirit of love' had indeed begun its motion and was continuing to move.

A similar case can be seen in (2):

(2) wnhr hwh npq mn ^{c}dn lmšqyyh yt gnt' wmn tmn hwh mtprš wḥzr...(Gen 2:10 wənāhār yōṣē' mē^{c}ēden ləhašqôt 'et-haggān ûmiššam yippārēd) '...and a river used to go out from Eden to water the garden and from there it would split and return...'

Whereas the Hebrew participle actually describes a present state of affairs (from the narrator's point of view), the Aramaic now has become a statement of duration in the past. For the Hebrew indeed is part of a general description in Genesis Chapters 1 and 2 that is characterized by the use of participles, in an apparent attempt to offer the reader a glimpse of the creation of the world. In a sense, the writer of the Hebrew is telling his audience what "he sees," what the Garden "looks" like. By contrast, the Aramaic has replaced this with a factual description of an on-going past event, with no indication that this is a present-day phenomenon.

The compound form is also used to describe a state of affairs obtaining during the action of the main verb, as can be seen in (3) and (4). Here the parallel to the use of the participle in biblical Hebrew is clear.

(3) ...w'tgly mmryh dYYY ^{c}l 'brhm bmšry ḥzwh whw' hwwh ytyb btr^{c} mšknyh btqph dywm'...(Gen 18:1, part of a midrash based on the MT wayyērā' 'ēlā(y)w YHWH bə'ēlōnê mamrē' wəhû' yōšēb petaḥ-hā'ōhel kəḥōm hayyôm) '...and the word of the Lord was revealed to Abraham in the Valley of the Vision while he was sitting at the door of his tent during the strength of the day...'

(4) wḥzrw w^{c}lw l^{c}yn dyn' hy' rqm wqṭlw yt kl tḥwmhwn d^{c}mlqy' w'p yt 'mwry' dhwwn šryyn b^{c}yn gdy tmry'...(Gen 14:7 wayyāšūbû wayyābō'û 'el-^{c}ên mišpaṭ hî' qādēš wayyakkû 'et-kol-śədē(h) hā^{ca}mālēqî wəgam 'et-hā'^{e}mōrî hayyōšēb bəḥaṣəṣōn tāmār) 'And they turned back and entered the Spring of Judgement, that is Rekem and massacred all the territory of the Amalekites and also the Amorites who were dwelling (at the same time) in Ein-Gedi of the palm trees'.

In both these examples, the participles yōšēb/hayyōšēb are translated by compound verbal forms, and describe a state of affairs that obtains during the action described by the main verbs wayyērā'/wayyāšūbû/wayyābō'û.[5]

3.a. The compound perfect of hwh + participle also translates an MT perfect (or converted imperfect, especially in certain set phrases), see Table 1, line 3. The sentences below offer instructive examples to compare the use of the simple perfect with the compound form; in particular, the nonperfective, durative use of the compound form is apparent, and this is especially true with the stative verbs, e.g., rḥym in example (5):

(5) wyśr'l hwh rḥym yt ywsp mn kl bnwy 'rwm br sybw hwh lyh wᶜbyd ly<h> prgwd mṣyyr (Gen 37:3 wəyiśrā'ēl 'āhab 'et-yôsēp mikkol-bānā(y)w kî-ben-zəqûnîm hû' lô wəᶜāśā lô kətōnet passîm, cf. also 37:4 for the same idiom) 'And Israel was enamored of Joseph more than all his sons because he was a son of old age to him, and (so) he made him a colored cloak'.

The translation 'was enamored of' is offered in an attempt to convey both the stative nature of the verb and the durativeness of the compound form. Compare this nonperfective use of hwh rḥym with the perfective use of the simple perfect in (6):

(6) wrḥm yṣḥq yt ᶜśw 'rwm mn ṣydyh hwh 'kyl wrbqh rḥmt yt yᶜqb (Gen 25:28 wayye'ᵉhab yiṣḥāq 'et-ᶜēśāw kî-ṣayid bəpîw wəribqā 'ōhebet 'et-yaᶜᵃqōb) 'Now Isaac loved Esau because he was (in the habit of) eating from his hunt, but Rebecca loved Jacob'.

This case is especially interesting, as the Aramaic masculine rḥm translates a converted imperfect, whereas the feminine rḥmt translates a participle! How is the Hebrew to be understood, and how the Aramaic? In the context of the preceding verse, clearly the Hebrew verb wy'hb here means 'to love better than', 'to prefer', i.e., the Hebrew verses read: (27) 'Now the youths grew up, and Esau became a man proficient in hunting, a man of the open country, but Jacob was a quiet man, (preferring to) sit around (the) tents. (28) Now Isaac preferred Esau, because game was to his taste (lit 'in his mouth'), but Rebecca (continued to) love Jacob.' (The use of the participle 'ōhebet indicates the on-going nature of the action in the past, i.e., continuing affection, in contrast to the emotion attributed to Isaac, namely that of making a preferential choice betwen the two youths.)

The Amamaic has altered the verses and the scene somewhat. Verse 27 now reads: 'Now the youths grew up, and Esau was a man proficient in hunting, a man (who was) lord of the fields, and Jacob was a man perfect in good work, dwelling in the Academies (bty mdrš'). This is then followed by verse 28, in which not only is the contrast between the brothers made evident, but also the competition between the parents. For the emotion attributed to both in the Aramaic is the same: Isaac loved Esau, Rebecca loved Jacob, and we are (of course) to understand that this is because of their different employment: Esau is still the hunter, but Jacob now no longer mopes around the tents, but is a scholar in the (talmudic) Academies![6]

Compound forms translating MT perfects generally express the durative, nonperfective aspect of the verb, e.g.,:

(7) wyd^{c} 'wnn 'rwm l' lšmyh ytqrwn bnyh whwh kd hwh ^{c}lyl lwwt 'tt' d'ḥwy hwh mḥbl ^{c}wbdwy ^{c}l 'r^{c}' dl' mqm' bnyn lšmh d'ḥwy (Gen 38:9 wayyēda^{c} 'ônān kî lō' lô yihye hazzāra^{c} wəhāyā 'im-bā' 'el-'ēšet 'āḥîw wəšiḥ(ḥ)ēt 'arṣā ləbiltî natan-zera^{c} lə'āḥîw)

'Now Onan knew that her children would not be (allowed to be) called by his name and it happened that, when he would enter into his brother's wife, he would destroy his works upon the ground, so as not to raise up children in his brother's name'.

This durativeness is particularly apparent with other verbs of motion, e.g., hwwn mhlkyn in (8):

(8) wnsb šm wypt yt 'sṭlyth wšwwn ^{c}l ktp tryhwn whwwn mhlkyn lbtrhwn wkswn yt ^{c}ryth d'bwhwn w'pyhwn hpykw lbtrhwn w^{c}ryth d'bwhwn l' ḥmwn (Gen 9:23 wayyiqqaḥ šēm wāyepet 'et-haśśimlā wayyāśîmû ^{c}al-šəkem šənêhem wayyēlkû '^{a}ḥōrannît waykassû 'et ^{c}erwat '^{a}bîhem ûpənêhem '^{a}ḥōrannît wə^{c}erwat '^{a}bîhem lō' rā'û)

'And Shem and Japheth took the cloak and they placed it on both their shoulders and (then) they went walking backwards and they covered their father's nakedness, and they turned their faces behind them and (so) they did not see their father's nakedness'.

Here, the compound form used for the verb of motion is "embedded" in a whole sequence of other verbs, all in the simple perfect (the Hebrew sequence is composed of all perfects): 'they took', 'they placed', 'they covered', 'they turned', 'they did not see'. In clear contrast, the durative nature of the one action in the past, viz. 'they were walking' must be expressed by the compound verbal form.

The compound perfect hwh + participle is also used in conditional expressions, as in (9) and (10):

(9) ...'ylw šmš ḥd mn ṭly' ᶜm 'ttk whwwt myyty ᶜlynn ḥwbyn rbrbyn (Gen 26:10...kimᶜaṭ šākab 'aḥad hāᶜām 'et-'išteka wəhēbē(')tā ᶜālênû 'āšām) '...if one of the youths had used your wife then you would have brought great sins upon us'.

(10) 'n kdyn hwh 'mr qrḥyn yhwh 'gryk hwwt yldh kl ᶜnh...(Gen 31:8 'im-kōh yō(')mar nəqūddîm yihye śəkārekā wəyāldu kol-haṣṣō(')n...) 'If he would say thus: "The white-spotted will be your wages," (then) all the flock would bear...'

The same idiom expresses iterativeness, in (11):

(11) wśry 'tth d'brm l' hwwt yldh lh... (Gen 16:1 wəśāray 'ēšet 'abrām lō' yāldā lô..., and cf. also Gen 30:1) 'And Sarai the wife of Abram had not been bearing children for him...'

Finally, the formulaic idiom hwh mwlyd (variously spelled) occurs nine times in Genesis Chapter 5 and eight times in Genesis Chapter 11 in the set genealogical phrase whyh PN_1 mn btr d'wyld yt PN_2 ( ) šnyn wbhn bšnyh hwh mwlyd bnyn wbnn 'and PN_1 lived after he had begotten PN_2 ( ) years, and in those very years he was (continually) begetting sons and daughters', translating the MT wayyôled by the durative compound form; compare this form to the perfective 'wlyd (used as a pluperfect), and note that neither the Hebrew hôlîdô nor wayyôled is marked for durativeness, whereas the Aramaic must make the distinction between the act of begetting one child and that of begetting numerous children over a period of years.

3.b. While most of the examples in line 3 of Table 1 translate a MT perfect or converted perfect, there are some examples that translate either an MT imperfect, or an infinitive, or another nominal form. The examples below are representative of the Genesis sample; the same categories identified above for the use of the compound form are to be found in this current group also, i.e., conditional, durative, etc. The question is rather what is to be found in the Vorlage that required the "translator" to translate an imperfect by a compound perfect of hwh + participle.

For the comments concerning the nature of the narrative of Genesis Chapters 1 and 2, and hence the explanation of the use of the form hwh mtprš wḥzr 'it would split and return' (for MT yippārēd) in Gen 2:10, see above, example (2).

In example (12), the compound form expresses an iterative idea, (translating the Hebrew imperfect), and it is preceded by a (future) participle, qr' (= qāre).

(12) ...w'yty ythwn lwt 'dm lmḥmy mh hw' qr' lyhwn wkl mh dhwh 'dm qry lyh... (Gen 2:19...wayyābē' 'el-hā'ādām lir'ôt mah-yiqrā'-lô wəkol 'ᵃšer yiqrā'-lô hā'ādām...) '...and he brought them to Adam to see what he will call them, and whatever Adam would call it,...'

Example (13) shows habitual action in the past, expressed in Hebrew by an imperfect, in Aramaic by the compound form.

(13) 'n kdyn hwh 'mr... (Gen 31:8 'im kōh yō(')mar...) 'if he would say this...' cf. example (10) above.

This compound form occurs a number of times for a pair of MT inifinitive absolutes, used adverbially with a verb of motion; see examples (14), (15) and (16).

(14) wšlḥ yt ᶜwrb' whwwh npq wḥzr npq wḥzr ᶜd dy... (Gen 8:7 wayšallaḥ 'et-hāᶜōrēb wayyēṣē' yāṣō' wāšôb ᶜad...) 'And he sent forth the raven and it continually went out and back, out and back, until...'

This example clearly demonstrates the frequentative nature of the compound form, and eloquently captures the sense of the adverbial use of the Hebrew infinitives (see Gesenius, "Grammatik," p. 358, § 113s); so too in the following two examples:

(15) wmy' hwwn 'zlyn wḥsryn ^{c}d... (Gen 8:5 wəhammayim hāyû hālôk wəḥāsôr ^{c}ad...) 'And the waters kept on gradually diminishing until...' (see verse 3 for the use of the perfect with this same idiom: wḥzrw my' m^{c}ylwy 'r^{c}' 'zlyn wḥs<r>yn wḥsrw my' lswp m'h wḥmšyn ywmyn 'And the waters gradually receded from upon the earth and the waters had diminished by the end of one hundred and fifty days').

(16) wtqp gbr' whwwh 'zl wtqp ^{c}d zmn dy tqp lḥd' (Gen 26:13 wayyigdal hā'îš wayyēlēk hālôk wəgādēl ^{c}ad kî-gādal mə'ōd) 'And the man became powerful and he kept on growing powerful until such time as he had become very powerful'.

The final two examples (17) and (18) show the use of the compound form to translate an MT nominal form. In the former, the nominal is in a sense an equivalent of a perfect; in the latter, the adjective in the MT (ra^{c}) is expanded in an exegetical comment describing the evil that was done.

(17) ...whwwn b'pwy kywmyn qlylyn mn rḥmt' dhwh rḥm yth. (Gen 29:20 wayyihyû bə^{c}ênā(y)w kəyāmîm '^{a}ḥādîm bə'ah^{a}bātô 'ōtāh) '...and they were in his face as a few days because of the love with which he was loving her'.

(18) whwh ^{c}r bkwrh dyhwdh ^{c}bd ^{c}wbdyn byšyn qdm YYY wmyt bmymr mn qdm YYY (Gen 38:7 wayhî ^{c}ēr bəkôr yəhûdā ra^{c} bə^{c}ênê YHWH waymītēhû YHWH) 'And Er, the first born of Judah, used to do evil deeds before the Lord and he died at a command from before the Lord'.

3.c. Nearly one-third of the examples of perfect hwh + participle in the Genesis sample occur in passages that have no Hebrew base text, i.e., either in midrashic passages or in verses which expand a single word or phrase in the MT. Hence this group of examples is particularly valuable since there is generally no "interference" from the Hebrew base, and we are dealing solely with an Aramaic idiom, see Table I, line 4.

As expected, these forms display the same semantic range as those described in sections 2 , 3.a, and 3.b above; these examples, however, are often in longer passages, and hence the use of the compound perfect can be easily appreciated, and contrasted with that of the "simple" forms in the same passages. The main function of this form is to express the durative aspect of the verb in the past, and this gives rise to a number of nuances (not always clear from a translation) such as iterativeness, inchoativeness, frequency, etc. One use in particular is to express a kind of continuous or progressive pluperfect, e.g., example (19):

(19) w^{c}br 'brm ^{c}d 'trh škm w^{c}d mšryh (sic) ḥzwwh wkn^{c}ny' ^{c}d k^{c}n hwwn šryyn b'r^{c}' 'And Abram moved on to the place Shechem and to the Plain of the Vision, and up until now the Canaanites had been dwelling in the land' (Gen 12:6).

This formulation is based on the MT wəhakkəna^{ca}nî 'āz bā'āreṣ, and see also the same idiom in Gen 14:5 (w'mtnyh dhwwn šryyn bgwwh qrth 'and the powerful who had been dwelling in the midst of the city', for MT wə'ēt hā'êmîm bəšāwēh qiryātāyim). However, compare this with Gen 13:7, which is a midrash based on an MT text containing the participle yōšēb: l' tnṭwn lkn^{c}ny' wpryzy' ^{c}d k^{c}n 'nwn šryyn b'r^{c}' 'do not turn aside to the Canaanites and the Perizzites; so far they are (continuing to) dwell in the land'.

The compound form also expresses a habitual action in the past (20), or continuous action in the past (21):

(20) whwwn kl dyyry<h> d'r^{c}' lšn ḥd wmmll ḥd wblšn byt qdšh hwwn mšt^{c}yn dbh 'tbry ^{c}lm' mn šrwyh 'Now all the residents of the earth were one language and one speech, and they used to converse in the language of the sanctuary in which the world was created from the beginning' (Gen 11:1). Note especially the contrast between the compound form and the simple perfect ('tbry) used for a single action in the past.

(21) ...whw' hwh qyym ^{c}lyhwn tḥwt 'yln' whwwn mtḥmyn hyk 'klyn whyk štyn '...and he was standing over them under the tree and they were giving the appearance of eating and drinking' (Gen 18:8). This verse is based on the MT wəhû'-^{c}ōmēd ^{ca}lêhem taḥat hā^{c}ēṣ wayyō(')kēlû, and in both the Hebrew and the Aramaic the first part of the verse is in the perfect. The compound form is also common in past tense modal expressions, usually to be translated by auxiliaries such as 'would', 'could', 'might', etc., e.g.,

(22) ...'yln d^{c}th dkl mn *dhwh* *'kl* mnh yd^c lmpršh byn ṭb lbyš '...the tree of knowledge from which anyone who *might eat* will know how to distinguish between good and evil' (Gen 2:9, 17, both based on MT *^{c}ēṣ* *hadda^{c}at* *ṭôb* *wārā^c*).

Note the normal use of the participle *yd^c* for the assured, non-modal future, 'will know'.

The following two examples (23) and (24) both come from longer midrashic passages, and contain numerous examples of the compound, especially in contrast to the use of "simple" verbal forms.

(23) *wnṣb* 'brhm prds bb'r šb^c *wyhb* *bgwyh* l^{c}wbry' *whwwh* kd *'kylyn* *wštyn* *hwwn* *b^{c}yn* lmytn byh...*whwh* *'mr* lhwn mn d'mr whwh ^{c}lm' *'twn* *'klyn* *wl'* *hwwn* *z^{c}yyn* mn tmn ^{c}d zmn *dhwh* *mgyyr* ythwn *wmylp* ythwn...*wplḥ* *wṣly*... 'And Abraham *planted a* garden in Beesheba and *gave* within it food for the passers-by; and it *happened* that, while *eating and drinking, they would attempt* to give him...and *he would say* to them: "From he who said and the world was *you are eating*," and *they would not move* from there until *he would convert* them and *teach* them...and *he worshipped and prayed*...' (Gen 21:33). In this text, the compound forms express the habitual past, and contrast clearly with the simple perfects that precede and follow them. Note also the participle (*'kylyn*) used for the continuous present.[7]

(24) ḥmšh nsyn 't^{c}bdw ^{c}m 'bwnn y^{c}qb...ns' qdmy' *'tqṣrw* š^{c}wwy dywm' w<ṭ>m^{c}t šmš' dl' b'šwn' mn bgll *dhwh* dbyr' *mtḥmd* bmmll<h> ^{c}myh...wnys' rby^c'h 'bn' *dhwwn* kl r^{c}y' *mtknšyn* lmgllh yth m^{c}lwy pwm' db'rh *wl' hwwn yklyn*...wnys' ḥmyš'h...*ṭpt* b'rh *wslyqt* b'pwy *whwwt* *ṭyyph* ^{c}śryn šnyn kl ywmyn *dhwh* *šry* bḥrn 'lyn ḥmyšty nsy' *'t^{c}bdw* ^{c}m 'bwnn y^{c}qb bzmn' dy *npq* mn b'r šb^c lmyzl lḥrn 'Five miracles *were worked* with our father Jacob...The first miracle: the hours of the day *were shortened* and the sun *set* before its time because the Word *was desirous* of speaking with him...And the fourth miracle: the stone which all the shepherds *were in the habit of gathering* in order to roll from off the mouth but *were not able*...And the fifth miracle: the well *overflowed*

and came up at its mouth and it (continued) overflowing for twenty years, all the days that he (continued) to dwell in Haran. These five miracles were worked with our father Jacob when he went forth from Beersheba to go to Haran' (Gen 28:10).

Once again, the compound forms contrast with the "simple," and the durative aspect of the former is apparent: progressiveness (hwh...mtḥmd); habit (hwwn...mtknšyn); iterativeness (hwwt tyyph, hwh šry). The unreal nature of these events is stressed since, in the targumic narrative, they have not yet occurred. This summary midrash occurs at the beginning of Jacob's journey (the first miracle takes place in the next verse, Gen 28:11) and the event at the well will not be recounted until Gen 29:2-10.

4. Other forms of hwh + participle

While the majority of compound verbal forms comprise the perfect of hwh + participle, there are occasional examples of other forms. Most of these are the imperfect of hwh + participle, however there are also examples of imperative, infinitive, and participles of hwh + participle, so that an entire paradigm of the compound verbal forms may be identified.

As expected, the one unifying characteristic of all these forms is that they are marked for durativeness. This allows the form to accrue to itself other aspectual nuances, such as incohativeness, habitualness, frequency of action, etc., as have been extensively catalogued in the discussion of the perfect compound forms above.

4.a Imperfect of hwh + participle

Just as the perfect compound forms indicate a variety of aspectual phenomena relative to the past, the imperfect forms have a similar function relative to the future. The following examples are drawn primarily from passages which have no Hebrew *Vorlage*, or which are expansions of a single MT word or phrase.[8]

(25) ...kd yhwwn bnyh nṭryn 'wryyt' w^{c}bdyn pqwdyyh yhwwn mtkwwnyn lk wmḥyy<n> ytk lr'šk wqṭlyn ytk wkd yhwwn šbqyn pqwdy<h> d'wryt' thwy mtkwyn wnkt ytyh b^{c}qbh wmmr^{c} ytyh... '...when her children shall be (continually) observant of the Law and

performing its commandments, they shall (continually) be taking aim at you and striking you on your head and killing you; but when they shall be abandoning the commandments of the Law, (then) you shall be taking aim at and wounding him in his heel and making him ill...' (Gen 3:15).

In this example, as in many others, the compound form is used to describe a future, prophesied state of affairs, one in which, if such-and-such shall be done, then so-and-so will follow, but if not, then the reverse will take place. One might freely translate this passage by such paraphrase as: "as long as her children continue to observe the Law, then..." The imperfect compound forms primarily record such continuing future action (either in this kind of implied conditional or not), and the contrast with the simple imperfect (used for the modus), and the simple participle (used for the plain future) is clear in (26):

(26) w'mrwn 'twn wnbnh ln qryh wmgdl wr'šh mty ^{c}d ṣyt šmy' wn^{c}bd ln br'šyh sgdh wntn ḥrb' bydyh wtyhwwy ^{c}bd<'> lqblyh sdry qrb' qdm ^{c}d l' ndry ^{c}l 'py kl 'r^{c}' 'And they said: "Come, let us build for ourselves a city and a tower, whose top shall reach to the heights of the heavens, and let us make for ourselves an idol on top of it, and let us put a sword in its hand so that it shall be able to wage war (lit. "make battle lines") against him lest we be scattered over the face of all the earth"' (Gen 11:4, based on the MT imperfects nibne, wәna^{ca}śe, and nāpôṣ).

The ingressive nature of this compound is most apparent in example (27). This is one of the four appearances of the midrash of the four cases brought for decision to Moses (the others are at Num 9:8, 15:34, and 27:5), and while each occurrence is slightly different in its phraseology, all four use compound imperfects to express a nuance of undertaking an action, the result of which can have unforeseen consequences (in this instance, e.g., putting an innocent man to death and consequently being ashamed):

(27) dn ḥd mn 'rb^{c}h dynyn dqmw qdm mšh...btryn mnhwn hwh mšh zryz wbtryn mnhwn hwh mšh mtyn...lmlph ldyynyh dqyymyn btr mšh dyhwwn zryzyn bdyny mmwnh wmmtynyn bdyny npšth dl' yhwwn qtylyn bpry^{c} yt mn

dḥmy lyh lmtqṭlh bdynh dylmh dyštkḥ lh zkw mn zwy ḥwry bdynh dl' yhwwn bhtyn lmymr... 'This is one of four cases that arose before Moses...in two of them Moses was hasty and in two of them Moses was slow...in order to teach the judges who will exist after Moses that they should always be hasty in fiscal cases and they should delay in capital cases, so that they should not undertake the killing in haste of someone whom it is permissible to kill in law, lest acquittal be found for him from another angle in the law, so that they should not have to be ashamed to say...' (Lev 24:12).[9]

Other aspectual nuances are apparent also, e.g., inchoate action in (28):

(28) kd yhwwn ^{c}nny' prsyn ^{c}l 'r^{c}' wtthmy qšt' b^{c}nn' 'When the clouds (begin to) break up over the earth, then the bow may be seen in the cloud' (Gen 9:14, based on the MT bə^{c}anəni ^{c}ānān ^{c}al-hā'āreṣ wənir'^{a}tā haqqešet be^{c}ānān).

4.b Infinitive of hwh + participle

Compound infinitival forms, while not common, are well enough attested that the general circumstances of their use are clear. These forms either translate an MT infinitive, when the "translator" understands the action of the Hebrew verb to be an on-going action, or else they appear in passages with no Hebrew Vorlage, in which the durative aspect of the verbal action is required. In both sets of examples, the compound infinitive often follows a finite verb which is itself inchoative or ingressive, e.g., šrw 'they began' in Gen 4:26, ḥzrw 'they changed' in Gen 44:18.

Examples which translate or are based on an MT infinitive include:

(29) ...w'dm ^{c}d kdwn l' 'tbry lmhwy plḥ b'r^{c}' '...and Adam had not yet been created to work (i.e., continually) on the land' (Gen 2:5, MT ... wə'ādām 'ayin la^{ca}bōd 'et-hā'^{a}dāmā).

(30) ...w'šry ytyh bgnt' d^{c}dn lmhwy plḥ b'wryt<'> wlmṭwr pqwdyh '...and he placed him in the garden of Eden to be striving (continually) in the Law,

and (consequently) to keep its commandments' (Gen 2:15, MT ...wayyannîhēlû bəgan-^{c}ēden lə^{c}obdāh ûləšomrāh). Note that the second infinitive in the Aramaic is simple, hence to be understood as consequent on the (frequentive) action of the first infinitive.

(31) ...bkdyn šrw bny 'nš' lmhwy ^{c}bdyn lhwn ṭ^{c}wn wmknyyn ythwn bš<m> mmrh dYYY '...then men had begun to be making idols for themselves and to be calling them by the name of the word of the Lord' (Gen 4:26, MT ...'āz hûḥal liqrō' bəšēm YHWH).

Examples in passages with no Hebrew Vorlage include:

(32) ...wmn dḥṭ' wqṭl lhbl ḥzrt lmhwy mrbyh qdmw<y> kwbyn wdrdryn '...and after he had sinned and killed Abel, it (the earth) changed to become (one) producing thorns and thistles before him' (Gen 4:16).

(33) ...wkdwn ḥzrw dynk (sic) lmhwy mdmyyn ldynwy dpr^{c}h rbk... '...and now your judgements have changed to become similar to the judgements of Pharaoh your master...' (Gen 44:18).

(34) ...wzmn bnwy lmhwy mṣlyyn w'mryn... '...and he appointed his sons to be (continually) praying and saying...' (Lev 22:27).

4.c Imperative of hwh + participle

Given the narrative nature of most of the pentateuchal text, the number of durative imperatives to be found is unremarkably small. Two examples are found in one version of the Decalogue only, namely Exodus 20:8 and 20:12, and they are both passive participles. Whether this is the only type of compound imperative expression possible cannot be determined considering the paucity of examples, however both verbs commonly use these passive participles in an "active" sense.

The two cases are:

(35) ^{c}my bny yśr'l hwwn dkyryn yt ywm' dšbt' lmqdš<'> ytyh 'Oh my people, the children of Israel, be mindful (continually) of the Sabbath day to sanctify it' (Exod 20:8, MT zākôr).

(36) ^{c}my bny yśr'l hwwn zhyryn gbr byqryh d'bwy wb'yqrh d'ymyh... 'Oh my people, the children of Israel, be watchful (constantly), each man for the

honor of his father and for the honor of his mother...' (Exod 20:12, MT kabbēd).

4.d Participle of hwh + participle

Again, examples of compound participial forms are not especially common, but they do occur frequently enough to enable general guidelines to be enunciated. Clearly, these forms also express durative, habitual, or frequent action, however the scarcity of examples make it difficult to pinpoint the motivations for use, and also to ascertain the differences between these compound forms and others, e.g., the compound perfect forms.

Some cases translate an MT participle, when it refers to action contemporaneous with a main verb (37), or when that action also describes another state of affairs (38).

(37) ...wmll ᶜmhwn lmymr ...wyzbn ly yt mᶜrt kpylh...wᶜprwn hwy šry bgw bnwy dḥt wᶜnh ᶜprwn ḥtyyh... '...and he spoke to them, saying: "...let him sell me the cave of Kephelah..." Now Ephron was dwelling (at that time) among the sons of Heth, so Ephron the Hittite answered'... (Gen 23:8-10, MT waydabbēr 'ittām lē(')mōr... wəyittēn-lî 'et- məᶜārat hammakpēlā ... wəᶜeprôn yōšēb bətôk bənê ḥēt wayyaᶜan ᶜeprôn haḥittî...).

(38) wqmt rbqh wrbyth wrkbyn ᶜl gmly' whlkyn btr gbr' wnsb ᶜbd' yt rbqh w'zl: wyṣḥq hwy 'ty mn byt mqdš' (sic) dšm rbh...whw' hwh šry b'rᶜ' drwm' 'And Rebecca and her maidens arose, mounting camels and following after the man, and so the servant took Rebecca and departed. Now (at the same time), Isaac was coming (= 'on his way') from the sanctuary of Lord Shem...for he had been dwelling in the south country' (Gen 24:61-62, MT wattāqām ribqā wənaᶜᵃrōteyhā wattirkabnā ᶜal-gəmallîm wattelaknā 'aḥᵃrê hā'îš wayyiqqaḥ hāᶜebed 'et-ribqa wayyēlak: wəyiṣḥāq bā' .. wəhû' yōšēb bə'ereṣ hannegeb).

This example uses two participles in the Hebrew, bā' and yōšēb, dependent on the perfects in the previous verse: Rebecca "arose," "rode," and "followed." Now, while this was happening, Isaac was on his way north, because he was normally to be found dwelling in the south. In the Aramaic, this contemporaneity is expressed by a compound participle, hwy 'ty, and the perfect-in-the-past, "he had been dwelling," by the compound perfect hwh šry.

This compound participial form also translates an MT imperfect (39) and a perfect (40).

(39) ...wšwy y^{c}qb yt ḥwṭry' qdm ^{c}nh ...wblqyšy ^{c}nh l' hwy mšwy... '...and Jacob placed the rods before the flock...but with the first-born of the flock, he used not to put (them)...' (Gen 30:41-42, MT... wəśām ya^{ca}qōb 'et-hammaqlôt $lə^{c}$ênê haṣṣō(')n ...ûbəha^{ca}ṭîp haṣṣō(')n lō' yāśîm...).

(40) wqnwn byh 'ḥwy w'bwy hwy mnṭr yt ptgm' 'And his brothers were jealous of him, but his father was keeping note of the matter' (Gen 37:11 wayqan'û-bô 'eḥā(y)w wə'ābîw šāmar 'et-haddābār).

This unusual use of the perfect šāmar in the MT is what Joüon, "Grammaire," calls "quasi-statif" (p. 295), in which the perfect of non-stative verbs denoting mental activity expresses an apparent stative condition. Examples are rare in narrative, and are confined mostly to poetic passages, see Joüon, pp. 295-297 for references. The only other case he cites using the verb šāmar is in Jer 8:7, in which this verb is used in parallel to the more commonly occurring $yāda^{c}$ 'to be in a state of knowledge about something': gam-$ḥ^{a}$sîdā baššāmayim $yād^{c}ā$ $mô^{ca}$deyhā wətōr wəsîs $wə^{c}āgûr$ šāmərû 'et-^{c}ēt bō'ānā $wə^{c}$ammî lō' $yādə^{c}û$ 'et mišpaṭ YHWH 'Even the stork in the heavens knows her appointed times, and the dove and the swift and the thrush keep the time of their coming, but my people do not know the judgement of the Lord?' In Gen 37:11, the targumist clearly did understand this rare usage, and translated accordingly by a durative form: w'bwy hwy mnṭr yt ptgm' 'but his father was keeping the matter in mind'.

There are also some examples of compound participles found in passages that have no Hebrew Vorlage, and these are especially explicit in expressing the habitual (41, 42) and continuous (43) aspects of the action of the verb.

(41) whwwn swrbnyn wmpḥn rwḥ wmgḥkn bpwlḥn' nwkr'h *wl' hwyn mqbln* 'wlpn... 'And they were rebellious and haughty of spirit, acting licentiously in foreign cultic practices, *nor would they accept* instruction...' (Gen 26:35).

Here and in the following case, the habitual nature of the verbal action is stressed. It should also be noted that the form *hwyn* is fem. pl. active participle, to be vocalized *hāwəyān*, cf. also example (43), below.

(42) ^{c}dn dtdkr ln qrb<n>ynn mh *dhwwyyn* *mqrybyn* wmtkpr ^{c}l ḥwbynn... '(This is) the time when you should remember for us our sacrifices which *are being offered*, so that atonement shall be made for our sins...' (Lev 22:27).

This is the beginning of a very long midrash which recounts three of the sacrifices of the patriarchs as a prelude to explaining why the Hebrew states that three specific animals are to be sacrificed. The participial *hwwyyn mqrybyn* is understood here as masc. pl. participle of *hwh* + masc. pl. C stem passive participle, i.e., *hāwayin maqribin* (< *maqrəbin*), with *-y-* spelling the vocalic shewa, as often in this MS. It should be noted that the English translation of the *editio princeps* does not translate the verse thus, rendering the imperfect *tdkr* by a past tense, "you remembered(!)" and the participial form as "we used to offer."

Continuity of action is expressed in the final example (43):

(43) w^{c}yny<h> dl'h *hwwyyn* *zqypn* bṣlw...wrḥl *hwwt* y'yh... 'And Leah's eyes *were* (constantly) *raised* in prayer...but Rachel *was* fair... (Gen 29:17).

This is the passive participle *zəqipān*, fem. pl. agreeing with 'eyes', and consequently *hwwyyn* is to be understood also as fem. pl. active participle, *hāwəyān*.

5. Concluding Remarks

The contrast between the various compound forms and those termed here "simple" is dependent on an aspectual opposition. The compound forms are marked for durativeness, the other forms unmarked.

The basic uses of the different forms can be summarized thus:

perfect - past; preterite; pluperfect.

imperfect - future modus (precative, imperative, jussive, etc.).

participle - future; present continuous; describes a state of affairs contemporaneous with the action of a main verb, when that main verb is either perfect (e.g., Gen 13:17), or non-perfect (e.g., example 19).

compound perfect - durative action in the past; habitual, iterative, etc.; unreal conditions in the past; describes a state contemporaneous with the action of a main verb, when that main verb is in the perfect (e.g., example 3).

compound imperfect - durative action in the future; habitual, iterative, etc.; unreal conditions in the future.

compound participle - durative action in the present; habitual, iterative, etc.; describes a state of affairs contemporaneous with the action of a main verb, when that main verb is a compound verb (37, 38).

As can be seen, there are three forms available for expressing a state contemporaneous with a main verb, i.e., that function which is fulfilled by the participle in biblical Hebrew: the compound perfect, the compound participle, and the simple participle. In these three forms there is an opposition between forms which can be used when the main verb is perfect and those which cannot be used when the main verb is perfect. Within both groups, there is a further opposition between compound verbal forms (= durative) and simple verbal forms (= non-durative), see Tables 2 and 3:

TABLE 2

The Forms Used for Expressing Contemporaneous State in Targum Neofiti

Main Verb is Perfect		Main Verb is Non-Perfect	
State = Compound Perfect or Simple Participle		State = Compound Participle or Simple Participle	
Durative	Non-Durative	Durative	Non-Durative
State = Compound Perfect	State = Simple Participle	State = Compound Participle	State = Simple Participle

This opposition between the durative and non-durative aspects of the verb is a key element found throughout the entire verbal system, along with a tense opposition between past and non-past:

TABLE 3

The Tense System in Targum Neofiti

	Durative	Non-Durative
Past	Compound Perfect (hwh + participle)	Perfect ($p^{c}l$)
Future	Compound Imperfect (yhwh + participle)	Participle ($p^{c}yl$)
Present	Compound Participle (hwy + participle)	Participle ($p^{c}yl$)
Modus	Imperfect ($yp^{c}l$)	Imperfect ($yp^{c}l$)

The opposition between past and non-past is clear in the non-durative aspect ($p^{c}l$ vs. $p^{c}yl$) and hence one might postulate a similar state of affairs in the durative (hwh + participle vs. non-hwh + participle), even though the past is not explicitly marked. One other consideration in this regard might be the number of examples (see Table 1), since 75% of the samples are indeed found to be of the compound perfect, however further study, in addition to comparisons with other dialects, is necessary before final conclusion can be drawn.

SECTION B
Expression of the Direct Object

There are four ways to express the direct object of a transitive verb employed in the MS: yt, l-, Ø, and by pronominal suffix attached to the verb. While the choice of means is often dependent on the Masoretic Vorlage, the motivation for the use of one form over another in untranslated or paraphrastic passages is not immediately clear.

1\. yt: The most common expression of the direct object is yt. It usually translates MT 'et, e.g., Num 13:21 wslyqw wylylw yt 'r^{c}' 'and they went up and spied out the land' (MT wayya^{ca}lû wayyāturû 'et-hā'āreṣ), and examples throughout the MS. There are also examples of slavish following of the Hebrew, even to the point of mistranslation for MT 'et = 'with', e.g., Gen 39:2 whwh YYY yt ywsp 'and God was (with) Joseph' for MT wayhî YHWH 'et-yôsēp.

For examples translating multiple direct objects with 'et, see, e.g., Lev 14:9 wyhwy bywm' šby^{c}yh yspr yt kl ś^{c}ryh yt r'šyh wyt dqnh wyt gbyny ^{c}yyny (sic) 'and on the seventh day he shall shave all his hair, his head, his beard and (his) eyelashes' (MT wəhāyā bayyôm haššəbî^{c}î yəgallaḥ 'et-kol-śə^{c}ārô 'et-rō(')šô wə'et-zəqānô wə'et gabbōt ^{c}ênāyw, and especially the example in Gen 21:10, where the Aramaic adds 'et missing in the Hebrew, ṭrwd yt 'mt' hdh wyt brh 'expel this handmaid and her son' (MT gārēš hā'āmā hazzō(')t wə'et-bənāh).[10]

The particle yt also translates other MT prepositions, e.g., lə-, depending upon the semantics of the individual Aramaic verb, e.g., Gen 29:13 wqpp yth wnšq yth 'and he embraced him and kissed him' (MT wayḥabbeq-lô waynaššeq-lô).

The particle yt is used distinctively in this MS in technical translation idioms following passive verbal forms in euphemistic contructions to avoid anthropomorphisms. The "subject" of these constructions is usually God, but can also be angels (cf. Gen 31:12), and even human beings, when the Hebrew has the N stem of root yld + 'et (Gen 4:8 and 21:5). Examples are usually found with šmy^{c} 'heard' and gly 'revealed', cf. Gen 21:17 wšmy^{c} qdm YYY yt qlyh dṭly' 'and the boy's voice was heard before the Lord' (MT wayyišma^{c} '^{e}lōhîm 'et-qôl hanna^{c}ar) and Exod 4:31 gly qdmwy yt ṣ^{c}rwn (sic) 'their distress was revealed before Him' (MT rā'ā 'et-^{c}onyām).

Similarly, in Gen 31:12, the subject is an angel, 'rwm gly qdmyy yt kl mh dlbn ^{c}bd lk 'because all that Laban is doing to you is revealed before me' (MT rā'îtî 'ēt kol-'^{a}šer lābān ^{c}ōśe lāk). There are two examples in Genesis which mimick the unusual Hebrew construction of N stem of root yld followed by the direct object marker 'et: 4:18 w'tylyd lḥnwk yt ^{c}yrd 'and Irad was born to Enoch' (MT wayyiwwālēd laḥ^{a}nôk 'et-^{c}îrād) and 21:5 bzmnh d'tyld lh yt yṣḥq bryh 'when Isaac his son was born to him' (MT bəhiwwāled lô 'ēt yiṣḥāq bənô).

Finally, yt is used with pronominal suffixes, either translating MT 'et + suffixes, e.g., Gen 29:19 yth (twice) 'her' (MT 'ōtāh), Gen 50:26 ytyh 'him' (MT 'ōtô), and even uncommon MT forms, e.g., Exod 29:35 ytk 'you' (MT 'ōtākāh), etc., or, more commonly, for MT pronominal suffixes affixed directly to a transitive verb, e.g., Num 22:33 wḥmt yty 'tnth 'and the ass saw me' (MT wattir'anî hā'ātôn), Gen 27:4 mn bgll dy tbrk ytk npšy 'so that my soul may bless you' (MT ba^{ca}bûr təbārekəkā napšî), or Gen 29:13 w'^{c}yl yth lgw byytyh 'and he brought him into his house' (MT waybî'ēhû 'el-bêtô).

2. l- See the complete discussion under Chapter 3, Prepositions, l-, above. As indicated, for every example with l-, counter examples of yt in similar situations can be found. However, the fact that the direct object of many of these verbs is a proper noun seems to be significant.

The verb ḥm' 'to see' does seem to occur in a number of the examples, cf. Gen 28:12, Num 21:34 cited above, and also Num 24:17 ḥmy 'nh lyh 'I see him' (MT 'er'ennû). However, in a selective sample of some forty chapters of Genesis, there were thirty eight examples of ḥm' + direct object. Of these, 28 used yt, eight used Ø, one used l-, and one (Gen 21:16) used b, mimicking the Hebrew bə-. Of the 28 examples with yt, no less than 20 were copies of a Hebrew 'et, two translated a Hebrew verb + pronominal suffix, and six were used in paraphrastic or midrashic passages. All eight examples of Ø copied a Hebrew verse using Ø, and the one example of l- was in a midrashic passage. Clearly, when viewed in this perspective, the use of l- as the mark of the direct object is secondary at best, and certainly restricted to a limited number of examples.

3. Ø: Even more limited are the examples where no object marker is used. These occur overwhelmingly in passages where the MT also has no marker, e.g., Gen 27:40 wtprwq nyr š^{c}bwd' m^{c}lwy ṣww'ryk 'and you shall remove the yoke of servitude from upon your neck' (MT ûpāraqtā ^{c}ūllô mē^{c}al ṣaww(')ārekā), or Gen 30:31 'n t^{c}bd ly ptgm' hdn 'if you do this thing for me' (MT 'im-ta^{ca}śe-lî haddābār hazze). However, there are some instances where the MS has Ø where the MT has 'et, cf. e.g., Gen 24:52 whwh kd šm^{c} ^{c}bd' d'brhm mlyhwn 'and when Abraham's servant heard their words' (MT wayhî ka'^{a}šer šāma^{c} ^{c}ebed 'abrāhām 'et-dibrêhem), Gen 24:64 wnṭlt rbqh ^{c}yynh 'and Rebecca raised her eyes' (MT wattiśśā' ribqā 'et-^{c}ênêyhā) and Gen 30:26 'rwm 't yd^{c}t plḥny 'because you have known my work' (MT kî 'attā yāda^{c}tā 'et-^{ca}bōdātî). For examples without Vorlage, cf. e.g., Gen 13:7 r^{c}wy d'brm hwwn zmmyn b^{c}yrhwn 'Abram's shepherds used to muzzle their cattle' and Gen 27:40 yhwwn mšwyyn nyr mṭwlhwn ^{c}l

sw'rk 'they will place the yoke of their burden on your neck', etc.

4. Pron. Suff.: The most limited group of examples are those in which a pronominal suffix is attached directly to a finite verb. Some of the examples attested are: Gen 32:18 'rwm y^{c}r^{c} ytk ^{c}św 'ḥy wyš'lwnk(!)[11] lmymr ... 'when my brother Esau meets you and they(!?) ask you, saying ...' (MT kî yipgoškā ^{c}ēśāw 'āḥî wišə'ēlkā (sic, see Biblica Hebraica Stuttgartensia, ad loc., p. 52); Gen 30:22 'rb^{c} mptḥn d'ynwn msyryn byd rbwn kl ^{c}lm' YYY wl' msrn l' lml'k' wl' lśrp '(there are) four keys which are passed over into the hand of the master of all the world, the Lord, and he did not pass them over, neither to an angel nor to a seraph' (no MT); Exod 4:21 wt^{c}bdynwn qdm pr^{c}h 'and you shall do them before Pharaoh' (MT wa^{ca}śîtām lipnê par^{c}ōh, cf. the example in Exod 15:2, and also the same form in Onkelos, Sperber, "Onkelos," Vol. I, ad loc., p. 95; cf. also Dalman, "Grammatik," p. 310); and in the Song of the Sea, Exod 15:2 dn hw' 'lhn wnšbḥynyh 'lh 'bhtn wnrwmmnh 'this is our god and we shall praise him, the god of our fathers and we shall extol him' (MT ze 'ēlî wə'anwēhû '^{e}lōhê 'ābî wa'^{a}rōməmenhû).

Clearly these are frozen, literary forms; the question, however, why they are employed where they are is one perhaps not totally admitting of an answer. One might account for the forms in Gen 32:18 and Exod 4:15 by an appeal to Onkelos; however, this will not explain the other two forms. One might account for msrn in Gen 30:22 as part of an intrusive midrash which presumably has a different provenance, whereas the forms in the famous Song of the Sea clearly owe their appearance to the very similar forms in the Hebrew Vorlage. However, the retention of just these forms in these verses is undoubtedly due to non-linguistic reasons.

PART TWO
Features of Nominal Syntax

SECTION A
The Use of the Predicate Adjective

One notes in the Targum Neofiti two kinds of nominal sentence word order: one where the Subject precedes the Predicate (SP) and one where the predicate is fronted, with the addition of a pronominal "copula" acting as a Pronominal Anticipation of the Subject (PAS).[12]

It is important to note that there are no examples of sentences where the Subject is fronted and then followed by the "copula", i.e., SAP does not exist. The following examples are representative:

SP

(1) ^{c}wbdyhwn byšyn 'their deeds are evil' (Gen 6:3).

(2) dhb' d'r^{c}' hhy' ṭb 'the gold of that land is good' (*z^{a}hab hā'āreṣ hahî' ṭôb*) (Gen 2:12).

(3) qrt' hdh qrybh 'this city is close' (*hā^{c}îr hazzō(')t*) *qərōbā*) (Gen 19:20).

(4) b'ryyn mlyyn ḥmr 'wells full of pitch' (*be'^{e}rōt ḥēmār*) (Gen 14:10).

PAS

(5) zk'h hy' tmr klty myny hy' m^{c}brh 'Tamar my daughter-in-law is innocent; by me is she with child' (Gen 38:25).

(6) ṭb' hy' 'wryt' lplḥy (*sic*) b^{c}lm' hdyn hyk pyry 'yln ḥyy' 'the Law is good for those who serve it in this world just like the fruits of the tree of life' (Gen 3:24).

(7) (wḥmh ^{c}św 'rwm) byšn 'nwn bnthwn dkn^{c}n^{c}'y (*sic*) b'pwy dyṣḥq 'bwy '(and Esau saw that) the daughters of the Canaanites were evil in the sight of Isaac his father' (*rā^{c}ōt bənôt kənā^{c}an bə^{c}ênê yiṣḥāq 'ābîw*) (Gen 28:8).

(8) h' z^{c}yr' hy' d' dy nsbt yt b^{c}ly w't b^{c}y' lmysb yt ybrwḥ<w>y dbry 'is it a small thing that you have taken my husband? Would you (also) take away the mandrakes of my son?' (*hamə^{c}aṭ qaḥtēk 'et-îšî walāqaḥat gam 'et-dûdā'ê bənî*) (Gen 30:15, and cf. Num 16:9, 13 for the same idiom).

SAP

(9) * ^{c}wbdyhwn 'ynwn byšyn.

(10) * qrt' hdh hy' qrybh.

These last do not exist in the language of Neofiti.

It is suggested here that sentences (5) - (8), i.e., PAS, be interpreted as "cleft sentences," in which the predicate is highlighted by preposing it.[13] The cleft sentence, by setting the predicate off, enables this element to be contrasted, hence the common notion that the main function of this device is contrastive. However, when viewed in terms of the greater discourse unit, one sees a more subtle function.

Recent work on such syntactic devices as Left-Dislocation and Topicalization gives an interesting insight to this notion of the contrastive nature of cleft sentences, especially since this work deals primarily with discourse units. Most of the examples we are examining come from so-called midrashic passages, i.e., long, story-like textual interpolations that are perhaps the closest thing to a discourse that can be found in an ancient text. Even those examples that are taken from exegetical passages can be understood in terms of discourse units since the difference is generally one of degree, not kind, and one can only understand such an explanatory expansion of a holy Hebrew text in terms of conscious didactic intent. Ellen Prince[14] theorizes that such devices as Topicalization are used to signal features of the organization of the discourse. The text is a set of instructions for the construction of a discourse model, and information is added by what she calls 'incrementation,' the most common form of which is 'forward incrementation.' Prince hypothesizes that speakers provide clues in their syntactic (and other) choices to the arrangement of the pieces of information. In particular, Topicalization indicates that a change of direction in the incrementation of pieces of information is required. I would suggest that clefting be understood in a similar manner. As a matter of fact, most of the examples discussed here occur towards the end of a midrashic passage; those that do not are to be found towards the beginning. In this case, clefting can be viewed as an isolating feature, one that sets off one piece of information from the rest of the story. Now, this piece is invariably the main point or the moral of a particular discourse, and hence it appears to show up as a contrast to the rest of the discourse.

A brief analysis of the examples (5) - (8) will provide clarification.

(5) zk'h hy' tmr klty myny hy' m^{c}brh (Gen 38:25).

This sentence occurs towards the end of a long midrash describing the trial of Tamar, who is to be burned for harlotry. The scene builds in intensity, as Tamar's prayers to heaven are answered in the form of three witnesses (the signet, cord, and staff) in exchange for three just men who will be her descendants (Hananiah, Mishael, and Azariah). Her "eyes were enlightened" and she presents these three objects to the court. Judah at once ups and confesses, since "as a man measures, it will be measured to him." Hence, to avoid the fire of the world to come, he shall reveal his evil deeds: -- first he dipped his brother Joseph's cloak in blood and deceived his father; and now it is being said to him: "To whom this signet, cord and staff belong," by him is Tamar pregnant. Now the clefting device draws attention to the moral of the story: as regards Tamar, it is innocent that she is. This piece of information is isolated as the main point of the discourse, and hence provides the contrast that is so often described as being a part of the nature of cleft sentences: "As regards Tamar my daughter-in-law, she is innocent, and this is so because she is pregnant by me (and hence guiltless)." That this is the main point of the discourse, and hence to be highlighted by this clefting device, is reinforced by the fact that the story then ends abruptly with the anticlimactic addition: br<t> ql' mn šmy' npqt w'mrt trykwn zkyyn mn qdm YYY hwh ptgm' 'A bat qol (divine voice) came forth from heaven and said: You are both innocent; the affair is the doing of the Lord'.[15]

Note that the cleft sentence zk'h hy' tmr, the main point of the discourse isolated by this syntactic device, is followed by the non-cleft trykwn zkyyn -- that this is anticlimax, and quite possibly a later accretion to the original midrashic tale, is instantly apparent. If this were the main point of the story, then what value would there be in the telling?! It is the innocence of Tamar that is the main point of this story, and the dramatic effect of Judah's declaration is decidedly reduced by this apologetic after-thought.

(6) ṭb' hy' 'wryt' lplḥy (<u>sic</u>) b^{c}lm' hdyn hyk pyry 'yln ḥyy' (Gen 3:24).

This sentence is the last sentence of a long midrash on the Garden of Eden and Gehenna. Each is described, Eden for the just, Gehenna for the wicked: in Eden the just will eat of the Tree of Life, in Gehenna the wicked will be tormented by fire, and this will take place <u>^{c}l dy l' nṭrw mṣwth d'wryt' b^{c}lm' hdyn</u> 'because they did not observe the precepts of the Law in this world.' The moral of the story is now introduced by a cleft sentence, highlighting the predicate of the sentence. A change of direction is indicated, from one of simple forward incrementation of additional facts about Eden and Gehenna, to one that picks up the theme of (the Torah as) the Tree of Life that was introduced at the beginning of the midrash (and with which the Hebrew verse on which it is based ends): 'rwm <u>'yln dḥyyn</u> hy' 'wryyt' lkl mn dl^{c}y bh 'for it is <u>a Tree of Life</u> that the Law is for all who labor therein',

wnṭr pqwdyh hwy ḥy wqyym <u>k'yln ḥyy'</u> l^{c}lm' d'ty 'and whoever observes its commandments is going to be alive and enduring like <u>the Tree of Life</u> for the eternity to come.' And now the midrash closes with another cleft sentence, which explains the moral of the moral, as it were, i.e., the reason why the Law is the Tree of Life:

ṭb' hy' 'wryt' lplḥy (<u>sic</u>) b^{c}lm' hdyn hyk pyry <u>'yln ḥyy'</u>: 'It is good(ness) that the Law is for those who serve it in this world, just like the fruit of <u>the Tree of Life</u>'.

(7) (wḥmh ^{c}św 'rwm) byšn 'nwn bnthwn $dkn^{c}n^{c}$'y (<u>sic</u>) b'pwy dyṣḥq 'bwy (Gen 28:8).

This sentence too, even though it appears close to a verbatim translation of the Masoretic <u>Vorlage</u>, should be understood as an exegetical translation, since the use of the cleft sentence to isolate the predicate (and not merely preposing the predicate as would be were this a straight mimic of the Hebrew) provides the "translator" with the opportunity to comment on the episode.

Rebecca, in fear for the life of Jacob, deceives the aging Isaac into sending him away from Esau on the pretext that the Hittite women are not suitable wives. Isaac summons Jacob, blesses him, and sends him off to Padan-Aram. Now Esau has been observing all this and finally "puts two and two together;" he saw the blessing, saw Isaac send Jacob away for the express purpose of finding a wife, saw Jacob obey his father and his mother (vs. 7 <u>wšm^c y^cqb l'bwy wl'mh w'zl lpdn 'rm</u>). Then verse eight, introduced by <u>whmh ^cśw 'rwm</u> 'then Esau realized that', focuses upon the main point, the reason (according to Esau and the "translator") why Jacob was sent off, but Esau was not -- "it was evil that the daughters of the Canaanites were in the sight of his father and of his mother." Having finally realized why his two previous wives had not found favor in his parents' sight, and why Jacob had been sent off to his relatives, Esau (pathetically) tries to mimic Jacob and does the next best thing -- takes a wife from distant relatives, the Ishmaelites.

The fact that the <u>Hebrew</u> has a preposed predicate is what enabled (and presumably inspired) the "translator" to translate by the cleft sentence. It must be noted that a verbatim translation was <u>not</u> possible -- such sentences as <u>*byšn bntyhwn dkn^cn'y</u> do not exist in this MS. The "translator" could only translate either:

(i) <u>bnthwn dkn^cn'y byšn</u>, or

(ii) <u>byšn 'nwn bnthwn dkn^cn'y</u>, as he did.

The choice of translation (ii), while clearly dependent on the Hebrew work order, departs from it in plainly exegetical terms. The cleft sentence introduces a change of direction by isolating the moral of this episode, and explains, from Esau's point of view, the set of events that he had witnessed. It also refers back to Gen 26:35, and finally indicates for Esau the cause of his parents' dislike of his wives (although presumably the women were not evil in <u>his</u> sight). It may even hint at an ultimate cause for Esau's disinheritance, since the Rabbis would have felt that it was unfitting for a man married to idolators to receive his father's blessing, and hence Jacob's otherwise reprehensible deception of Isaac was justified.

(8) h' z^cyr' hy' d' dy nsbt yt b^cly w't b^cy' lmysb yt ybrwḥ<w>y dbry (Gen 30:15).

The Aramaic indeed both translates and effectively captures the mood of the Hebrew (<u>hamə^caṭ qaḥtēk 'et-îšî</u>, and it is this strongly sarcastic <u>Vorlage</u> that enables the Aramaic to utilize the cleft sentence to highlight the adjectival predicate <u>z^cyr'</u> 'small thing'. In the Hebrew, Leah's unexpectedly violent outburst appears to come as a shock, both to Rachel and indeed to the reader. The Aramaic "translator" effectively portrays the episode: Reuben brings mandrakes to

Leah, his mother, and Rachel asks Leah for some of them. The bitter sarcasm with which she is answered marks a sudden directional change in the incrementation of information. This statement of Leah's immediately becomes the focus of the entire incident: h' z^{c}yr' hy' d' 'is it an insignificant thing (that you think) that this is', dy nsbt yt b^{c}ly 'having taken my husband', w't b^{c}y' lmysb yt ybrwḥ<w>y dbry 'now do you want to take my son's mandrakes!?' It is this focus that then gives perspective to Rachel's equally bitter reply -- bgyn kdn yšmš ^{c}myk blyly' hdyn tḥwt <y>brwḥwy dbryk 'because of this, let him use you tonight in payment for your son's mandrakes'! (Hebrew lākēn yiškab ^{c}immāk hallaylā taḥat dûdā'ê bənēk).

This same idiom occurs twice in Num 16:9, 13, also for MT hamə^{c}aṭ, in the story of the death of Korah and his cronies. Here too the apparently "minor" discrepancies between the Aramaic and the Hebrew indicate conscious exegetical comment. The first use of h' z^{c}yr' hy' d' is at the beginning of Moses' major address to Korah and the "sons of Levi," and here the intent of the speech is to admonish them for desiring too much: 'is it an insignificant thing to you that the God of Israel has separated you', i.e., are you not satisfied with what you have been given? w'twn b^{c}yyn lmysb 'wp khnth rbth 'do you now want to take the High Priesthood also'? (MT ûbiqqaštem gam-kəhūnnā). Here the sin is explicitly stated. The second use of h' z^{c}yr' hy' d' is (mockingly) from the mouths of Dathan and Abiram: 'is it an insignificant thing that you brought us up from a land that produces good fruits, pure as milk and sweet as honey, to kill us off in the desert'? (MT hamə^{c}aṭ he^{ce}lîtānû mē'ereṣ zābat ḥālāb ûdəbāš lah^{a}mîtēnû bammidbār). They then proceed to ridicule Moses further, who is grieved, and commands the "contest" that is ultimately the undoing of the renegades. Again, the sarcasm of the Aramaic is much more pointed than in the Hebrew, and it is the cleft sentence used twice by either side of the dispute that is the fulcrum around which the scene revolves.

SECTION B

The Expression of the Genitive Relation

Aramaic has three possible expressions of the genitive, and the question of the relationships between them has long been a vexing one. While all the issues have not been resolved, it is possible to enunciate some guidelines for the choice of one form over another, at least in the Aramaic of this targumic MS, and to specify some environments in which one form or another is expected to appear.[16]

The three genitive constructions are here referred to as Type A, Type B, and Type C, and they are as follows:

Type A: bryh dywsp /bəreh dəyosep̱/ 'the son of Joseph', i.e., noun with anticipatory pronominal suffix + ḏ + noun

Type B: br' dywsp /bərā' dəyosep̱/ 'the son of Joseph', i.e., noun + ḏ + noun

Type C: br ywsp /bar yosep̱/ 'the son of Joseph, i.e., noun + noun (the "construct state")

One can identify a number of kinds of expression in which one type appears to be preferred over another; moreoever, when that "expected" type is not used, the replacement is invariably Type C. In summary, one finds:

1) Nouns indicating inalienable possession - Type A.

This is the case both with kinship terms (e.g., 'b 'father', 'm 'mother', etc.), and with other terms (e.g., byt 'house', yd 'hand', ywm 'day', etc.).

2) Common idioms - Type B

This category includes nouns used often enough in the text of Genesis so that potential patterns can be identified (e.g., 'lh' 'god', 'r^{c}' 'land', mlk' 'king').

3) Anthropomorphic avoidances - Type A or Type A + Type C

This is a small group of expressions usually used in paraphrase of the masoretic YHWH or '^{e}lōhîm (e.g., (šm) mmryh dYYY '(the name of) the word of God'). This group contrasts with other, non-formulaic expressions involving the name of God in which Type B is an acceptable form (e.g., ml'k' dYYY 'angel of the Lord', 'wrḥ' dYYY 'the way of the Lord').

4) Expansions of masoretic place names - Type B

This includes places such as pltywt' dqrt' 'the streets of the city', MT rəḥōbōt ᶜîr, ṭwr' dgbl' 'the mountain of Gabla', MT har śəᶜîr, etc., and this group contrasts with other exegetical translation formulae, in which a masoretic idiom or idioms had one acceptable rendering into Aramaic, and which departed from the Hebrew in plainly exegetical terms (e.g., 'twn nwrhwn dkśd'y 'the furnace of the fire of Chaldeans', MT 'ûr kaśdîm 'Ur of the Chaldeans'). This group usually has combined genitives of the form Type C + Type A, or simple genitives of Type B.

For details of the sample, reference should be made to Table 4 at the end of this section. The following discussion presents the data for each of the four groups enumerated above, all of which is drawn from the book of Genesis. Consequently, textual reference is made solely by chapter and verse number, without continual specification that the text referred to is Genesis.

1. NOUNS INDICATING INALIENABLE POSSESSION.

1.A Kinship terms.

The following kinship terms are discussed: 'b 'father', 'ḥ, 'brother', 'ḥh 'sister', 'm 'mother', 'mh 'handmaid', 'th 'wife', br 'son', brh 'daughter'. The semantics of kinship terms dictate that the possessor will always, of course, be a human being, or a group of human beings.

Most examples (91%) occur in passages with a masoretic Vorlage, usually a Hebrew construct form. The first four terms ('father', 'brother', 'sister', 'mother') occur a total of 31 times, all translating Hebrew constructs, and all translated by Type A genitives (e.g., 'bwhwn d-'; 'bwy d-; 'ḥwy d-; 'ḥtyh d-; 'ḥth d-; 'mhwn d-; 'mh d-. In this MS, final heh can represent the definite article, the 3ms pronominal suffix, or the 3fs pronominal suffix, hence some of these forms can be interpreted as determined, i.e., Type B, though this seems unlikely given the general preference of all kinship terms for Type A). With one exception, the five examples without Vorlage also use Type A.

1.A.1 '<u>Son</u>'/'<u>Daughter</u>'.

The situation concerning the very frequently occurring noun <u>br</u> 'son' (and also <u>brh</u> 'daughter') presents a complicated picture. In the singular, the form <u>bryh</u> <u>ḏ</u>- occurs three times, the form <u>brh</u> <u>ḏ</u>- five times, all for the Hebrew construct <u>ben</u>. These five spellings <u>brh</u> appear to consist of the 3fs suffix three times and the 3ms suffix twice, though of course all five could also be interpreted as the determined state. In the plural, Type A (<u>bnw(h)y</u> <u>ḏ</u>- 'sons of ...') occurs 40 times for the Hebrew plural construct <u>bənê</u>. The forms <u>brtyh d</u>-/<u>brth d</u>- 'daughter of...' occur six times for the Hebrew construct <u>bat</u>, and twice in a passage (34.31) that has no masoretic <u>Vorlage</u>. The determined state with <u>'aleph</u> (i.e., Type B) occurs with this noun only once, 36.10 <u>br' dᶜdh</u> 'the son of Adah', also for Hebrew construct <u>ben</u>. On the other hand, the Aramaic construct (Type C) is used, but in the following rather specific circumstances:

(a) expressions of age -- <u>br</u> <u>tšᶜyn</u> <u>wtšᶜ</u> <u>šnyn</u> 'ninety-nine years old' (17.1), <u>brt</u> <u>tlt</u> <u>šnyn</u> 'three years old' (15.9, Hebrew <u>məšūllešet</u>);

(b) expressions of membership -- <u>br</u> <u>byty</u> 'member of my household' (15.2), <u>br</u> <u>ᶜmy</u> 'member of my people' (19.38, translating the proper name <u>ben</u> <u>ᶜammî</u>), <u>br nš</u>(!) 'man', <u>gwzl</u> <u>br</u> <u>ywn</u> 'pigeon' (15.9), <u>ṣpyr</u> <u>br</u> <u>ᶜzyn</u> 'young goat' (37.31), <u>brt</u> <u>btw'l</u> 'the daughter of Bethuel' (24.47), <u>bny</u> <u>yśr'l</u> 'sons of Israel' (etc. 32.33), <u>bny</u> <u>'nš'</u> 'men', <u>gdyy'</u> <u>bny</u> <u>ᶜyzyy'</u> 'goats' (27.16, Hebrew <u>gədāyê</u> <u>hāᶜizzîm</u>), <u>bnt</u> <u>yśr'l</u> 'daughters of Israel' (30.13);

(c) compound kinship terms -- <u>br</u> <u>brh</u> 'his grandson', <u>br 'ḥwy</u> 'son of his brother', <u>br</u> <u>'ḥth</u> 'son of his sister', <u>brt</u> <u>'ḥwy</u> <u>drybwny</u> 'the daughter of the brother of my lord' (24.27), <u>bny</u> <u>bnyhwn</u> <u>dᶜm'</u> 'the sons of the sons of the people' (16.5).

In the case of these eight kinship terms, the preferred expression of the genitive relationship is this MS, either in passages with a masoretic <u>Vorlage</u> or without, is overwhelmingly Type A, Type B being restricted to six examples in three words, and Type C being restricted to 20 cases of the singular or plural of <u>br</u>, eight of <u>brt</u>. Many of these, however, occur in fixed idioms usually paraphrasing a particular Hebrew idiom.

1.B. Other terms.

There are six very common nouns used in expressions of inalienable possession which also occur exclusively or primarily in Type A, again usually fixed or formulaic expressions: 'pyn 'face', byt 'house', ḥyyn 'life', yd 'hand', ywm 'day', and šm 'name'. When these nouns do not occur in Type A genitives, the preferred expression of the genitive is then Type C. As was the case with the kinship terms, there are very few cases of Type B genitives with these words, when compared with Types A and C. Many of the occurrences of these nouns do not have a human possessor in the genitive relationship, as was the case with the kinship terms.

With these words, the preferred expression of the genitive relationship in this MS is Type A, with 62% of the examples (65 out of 105). Type B accounts for under 6% (six out of 105, two with the word byt, two with yd, one with ywm and one with šm). Statistically, Type C appears to have a much greater distribution than in kinship words (32%, or 34 out of 105 cases), but these include 15 used in phrases with the word 'py and 12 with the word ywm (especially ywmy ḥywy d- 'the days of the life of' for Hebrew yəmê.)

The most common of these nouns is byt 'house', and it occurs some 24 times in Type A and twice in Type B. Type C is used only in formulae, mostly in verses without Vorlage, or in idioms which expand a single word in Hebrew:

(a) without Vorlage -- lšn byt qdšh/qdš' 'the language of the sanctuary' (three times, plus 35.18 spelled lšwn!); byt mqdš' 'temple' (24:62 and 27.27); byt mdrš'/mdršhwn '(their) academy' (25.22 and 34.31); byt mr^c^y 'pasture' (13:7); byt tldwwty 'the house of my birth' (16.5);

(b) expansions of Hebrew -- byt mqdšy' 'temple' (28.22, paraphrasing the Hebrew bêt 'ᵉlōhîm); byt nhwr 'window' (6.16, Hebrew ṣōhar); byt špr 'best' (23.6, Hebrew mibḥar).

1.C Conclusion

The situation with nouns expressing inalienable possession is very clear -- Type A is overwhelmingly the preferred expression of the genitive. This is so in part because the possessor (or what Kaddari calls member B of the phrase) in such expressions is usually a human being (though not necessarily with expressions other than kinship terms, as we have seen). Of the sample of 179 examples of kinship terms, 81% are of Type A, 3% of Type B, and 16% of Type C. Of the sample of 135 non-kinship terms, 55% are of Type A, 6% of Type B, and 39% of Type C. When totalled together, the entire sample of 314 examples of terms used to express inalienable possession consists of 70% Type A, 4% Type B, and 26% Type C (see Table 4 below).

2. COMMON FIXED IDIOMS

2.A Common Idioms

There are a number of nouns in the MS that are used primarily in certain oft-recurring expressions. Certainly in the text of Genesis, such idioms as 'the god of...', 'the land of...', 'the king of ...', etc. appear often enough to enable certain conclusions to be drawn as regards the use of the idioms. The words included here in this section are 'lh' 'god', 'r^{c}' 'land', gnt' 'garden', hyyt' 'animals', mlk' 'king', nšmh 'breath', ^{c}bd' 'servant', ^{c}wp' 'fowl', ^{c}pr' 'dust', tr^{c}' 'door'. This list is by no means exhaustive; the words chosen merely occur frequently enough in the same or similar expressions to enable patterns to be determined. The immediate conclusion that can be drawn is that in these common expressions, Type B is not only an acceptable form, but indeed the overwhelmingly preferred expression of the genitive.

The three most common idioms, 'god', 'land', and 'king' can be taken as representative:

(i) 'god of...' -- 13 out of 25 Type B ('lh' d-). Moreoever, there are nine cases of 'lhh, some or all of which may be Type B (there is only one sure example of Type A, 'lhyh d'b' (31.42). There are also two cases of Type C, 'lh šmy' 'god of heaven' (28.3, 35.11).

(ii) 'land of...' -- 21 cases of Type B, 'r^{c}' d- (+ toponym); five cases of Type A, followed by ethnonym. Finally, there are also four definite occurrences of Type C genitives. Furthermore, there are no less than ten other occurrences of the determined 'r^{c}' (= ['ar^{c}a] used in a construct (nine of which translate the Hebrew construct 'ereṣ; one, 29.1 l'r^{c}' mdynḥ' 'to the land of the east' is for the Hebrew directive 'arṣā bənê qedem), and these are presumably all copyist errors for the construct 'r^{c} (= ['^{a}ra^{c}].

(iii) 'king of ...' -- 25 of 28 Type B; three of 28 Type A; no examples of Type C.

2.B Conclusion

There are ten common nouns dealt with in this section, comprising a total of 145 examples of the three genitives. Ninety-four (65%) of the cases occur with three nouns only, 'lh', 'r^{c}' and mlk'. Of the 145 cases, 16 (11%) are of Type A, 96 (66%) are of Type B and 33 (22%) are of Type C. When we examine the situation with the three most common nouns, however, the picture is even more striking: Type A comprises 11 cases (12%), Type B comprises 66 cases (70%) and Type C comprises 17 cases (18%). Even if we consider as Type A all those forms ending in -h, the situation is still one in which the predominant form is Type B [Type A would then consist of 29 cases (20%), Type B 83 cases (57%) and Type C 33 cases (22%)]. It becomes clear from these figures that when one examines nonformulaic occurrences of commonly recurring nouns the preferred expression of the genitive is overwhelmingly Type B; but in its absence Type C is used (see Table 4 below).

3. DEISTIC EXPRESSIONS

3.A Anthropomorphic Avoidances

One of the most characteristic uses of the genitive with d- forms (Types A and B) in the MS is in expressions referring to God, usually in euphemistic paraphrases to avoid anthropomorphism. The masoretic forms YHWH and '^{e}lōhîm are both translated by numerous expressions, primarily of Type A or of a combination of Type C followed by Type A. There does not appear to be any significant factor involved in the choice of which euphemistic expression translates which masoretic form, although (šm) mmryh dYYY '(the name of) the word of God' does occur more frequently. The formulaic nature of some of these specialized translation techniques is again apparent in the almost total lack of Type B genitives.

The expressions in this group are:

Type A -- mmryh dYYY 'the word of God' - 16 examples.
'yqryh dYYY 'the glory of God' - 5 examples.

Type B -- mymr' dYYY - 1 example (21.23).
šm' dYYY 'the name of God' - 1 example (24.6, but note also 3 cases of šmh dYYY, = Type A?).

Type C -- yqr škyntyh 'the glory of his Shekinah' (3.24 + yqr škynty in 9.27).

Type C plus Type A -- šm mmryh dYYY 'the name of the word of God' - 11 examples.
yqr škyntyh dYYY 'the glory of the Shekinah

of God' - 5 examples.

ql mmrh dYYY 'the voice of the word of God' - 2 examples.

Type C plus Type B - šm mmr' dYYY - 1 example (15.6).

3.B Other Terms

The fixed nature of the above formulae is dramatically highlighted when one examines the other expressions involving the names of God (again usually translating the masoretic YHWH or 'ᵉlōhîm) which do not appear to necessitate avoidance of anthropomorphism. In this group of expressions, Type B appears as an acceptable form.

Indeed, of the 16 expressions involving the names of God used other than in technical or religious formulae, only one is clearly of Type A, four are clearly Type B, and there are only combined forms of Type C (e.g., ṭwr mqdš' dYYY 'the mountain of the sanctuary of the Lord', 22.14, for Hebrew har YHWH). Unfortunately, this is a very small sample, and conclusions must be tentative. The situation is further complicated by the orthographic alternation alluded to previously, viz., the possibility of spelling the determined state with either 'aleph or heh, since eight of these genitive examples are spelled with -h, and could be interpreted as Type A or Type B. A final complication is the use of abbreviated forms, making it impossible to tell whether a Type A or Type B genitive is intended.

The expressions are:

ml'kh dYYY -- 'angel of the Lord' - 5 examples (all the rest occur only once).

ml'k' dYYY -- 'angel of the Lord'

dḥlth dYYY -- 'fear of the Lord'

dḥlt' dYYY -- 'fear of the Lord'

brykh dYYY -- 'blessed of the Lord'

gynt\` dYYY -- 'garden of the Lord' (abbreviated)

'wrḥ' dYYY -- 'the way of the Lord'

brktyh dYYY -- 'the blessing of the Lord'

rwgz' dYYY -- 'the anger of the Lord'

rwgz\` dYYY -- 'the anger of the Lord' (abbreviated)

There is also one Type C plus Type B:

ṭwr mqdš' dYYY -- 'the mountain of the sanctuary of the Lord'.

3.C Conclusion

The formulaic uses of deistic expressions indicate a preference for Type A (53%) or combinations of Type C plus Type A (34%), and there are less than 6% Type B genitives (three examples). In marked contrast, the non-formulaic expressions (even in the extremely limited sample available) do not have such restrictions. In this group, at least five out of the 16 (42%) are of Type B, and possibly as many as 13 out of 16. There is only one sure Type A, and one combined Type C plus Type B (see Table 4 below).

4. EXPANSIONS OF MASORETIC FORMS

4.A Exegetical Translation Formulae

One of the more striking characteristics of targumic language is the standard literary or exegetical expansion of various masoretic idioms or place names. Some of these are well-known interpretive renderings, such as 'twn nwrhwn dkśd'y 'the furnace of the fire of the Chaldeans' for 'ûr kaśdîm 'Ur of the Chaldeans', though others are less obvious expansions of a Hebrew base, e.g., yḥws tldwwtyh d- 'the genealogy of...' (for Hebrew tōlədōt, or zr^{c}yyt bn(y)k 'the families of your children' (for Hebrew zera^{c}).

This section contains a limited group of four exegetical expansion idioms, a regrettably small sample of only 26 examples, however the general system is clear. Seventeen of the 26 examples (65%) translate with a combined genitive idiom, nine with a simple genitive of Type A, B, or C. The idioms are 'twn nwrhwn dkśd'y, yḥws tldwwtyh d-, qhl knyšt 'wmyn ṣdyqyn, and zr^{c}yyt bnyk.

These idioms tend to be combined genitive forms, usually Type C + Type A:

Combined Forms - 65% (17)
- Type C + Type A - 42% (11)
- Type C + Type C - 19% (5)
- Type C + Type B - 4% (1)

Uncombined Forms - 35% (9)
- Type A - 4% (1)
- Type B - 19% (5)
- Type C - 12% (3)

4.B Expansions of place names

Many place names which are of the construct type in the Hebrew text are expanded in the Aramaic translation, usually by a Type B genitive. These at times reflect an interpretive rendering, at other times an apparent misunderstanding of the Hebrew place name.

When a Hebrew construct place name is translated into Aramaic, the preferred form again is a Type B genitive. Of 21 cases, 14 (67%) are of Type B, though perhaps the three spelled with -h could be considered Type A. These 14 examples also include one combined form of Type B followed by Type B, mdbr' db'rh dšb^{c}.

There are five cases (24%) of Type C, including one combined form of Type C plus Type C (^{c}yn gdy tmry') and only one sure case (5%) of Type A, and that is the prepositional phrase bgwwh dqrth 'inside the city'. Even if the three examples spelled with -h are considered as Type A, the situation still remains heavily weighted towards the Type B genitives, viz., Type A = 19%, Type B = 57% and Type C = 24%.

4.C Conclusion

This final section presents us with the data that are the most difficult to interpret, but at the same time the most tantalizing. For in these expansions of masoretic idioms we come face to face with the real essence of the targumic method. The interpretive exegesis (e.g., zr^{c}yyt bnyyk) is at once the most subtle and the most opaque of the translation methodologies. Yet it is clear that these are fixed translation idioms -- the "translator" was not at liberty to translate as he wished, but was obliged to render each "loaded" Hebrew term with its appropriate technical Aramaic equivalent, at once both translating and interpreting the biblical text.

There are a total of 46 idioms discussed in both sections 5.A and 5.B. Simple genitives of Type A, B, or C comprise 59% (27 cases) of the examples, combined genitives comprise 41% (19 cases). Once again the sample is regrettably small, however the general outline is clear. The exegetical expansion idioms, both translation formulae and place names, contain 39% (18 cases) Type B genitives (but 67% of the simple, uncombined genitive forms). As we have noted previously, the alternative to the preferred form is always Type C (15%, i.e., 7 cases, but 26% of the simple genitive form), one of which is a prepositional phrase.

As regards combined genitive forms, the preferred idiom is Type C plus Type A (11 cases, 24%, but 58% of the combined forms). Similarly, the alternative to the preferred idiom is Type C plus Type C (6 cases, 13%, but 31% of the combined forms). Finally, there is one example of Type C plus Type B, and one Type B plus Type B (see Table 4 below).

5. GENERAL

It is clear from this analysis that Type A genitives are 'marked', and occur in particular in expressions of inalienable possession and in euphemistic anthropomorphic avoidance. Type B is 'unmarked' and occurs in most "common" phrases. Type C is invariably the "second choice," though the motivations for its use are not immediately apparent.

Combined forms of these genitives are common, especially when translating highly technical religious idioms. In this case, combinations are usually Type C plus Type A or B (rarely Type C plus Type C or Type B plus Type B).

TABLE 4:

Statistical Summary of Genitive Forms
in Targum MS Neofiti 1 (Genesis)

	Type A	Type B	Type C
I.a. Inalienable Possession			
Kinship Terms	81%	3%	16%
Other Terms	55%	6%	39%
b. Common Idioms [a]	11%	66%	22%
II.a. Deistic Expressions			
Anthropomorphic Avoidance	53%	6%	4% [b]
Other Terms	6%	42% (>81%)	--- [c]
b. Masoretic Expansions	4%	39%	15% [d]

NOTES:

a. The three most common idioms, 'god', 'land', 'king', comprised Type A - 12%, Type B - 70%, Type C - 18%.

b. Combined genitives C + A - 34%.

c. Combined genitives C + B - 6%.

d. Combined genitives C + A - 24%; C + C - 13%; C + B - 2%; B + B - 2%.

NOTES

[1]Both these periphrastic forms are common in mishnaic Hebrew, as well as in Middle Aramaic, and the question of mutual influence is an open one, as is that of the direction of that influence. Cf. Segal, "Grammar," p. 167, and also Fink, "Aspects," p. 41 for the same phenomenon in "Maimonidean" Hebrew.

[2]When such a form does occur in the MT, it is always copied in the Targum, e.g., Gen 1:6 wyhwy mprš, MT wîhî mabdîl, Gen 39:22 hw' hwh ^{c}bd, MT hû' hāyā ^{c}ōśe, Deut 9:24 msrbyn hwytwn, MT mamrîm h^{e}yîtem, etc.

[3]See, e.g., Bergstrasser, "Grammatik," pp. 72-74, for examples.

[4]See Kutscher, "History," pp. 131-132.

[5]The Aramaic cannot translate these participles by simple participles, for, as in mishnaic Hebrew, the participle alone signifies either a present tense, or else an immediate or assured future. The following extracts from the midrashic insertion in Gen 38:25 concerning the trial of Tamar will serve to illustrate the use of both the simple participle and the use of the imperfect as modus: ...tlt ^{c}yyny (sic) bmrwmy' w'mrt...hb ly tlt' shdy w'nh mqyymh lk tlt' ṣdyqyn...kd nḥtyn bnwr' yqydt' wmqdšyn šmk qdyš'...w'nhrwn ^{c}yynh wḥmt ythwn...w'mrt lyh gbr' d'ylyn dylyh mynyh 'nh m^{c}brh w'nh 'p ^{c}l gb d'nh yqdh l' mprsyyh brm śhdy dbyny lbynyh hw' ytn blybyh lmyḥmy ythwn bš^{c}t' hdh wyprwq yty mn dyn' rb' hdyn... '...she raised her eyes on high and said: "...give me my three witnesses and I shall (surely) raise up for you three just men ...when they shall go down into the burning fire then they shall sanctify your holy name..." Then her eyes were enlightened and she saw them...and she said to him: "The man to whom these belong, by him am I pregnant and I, even though I shall burn, I shall not reveal him; but rather the (or 'my') witness that is between me and him may it allow his heart to see them at this time, and may it deliver me from this great judgement."...'

Here the participles mqyymh, nḥtyn, mqdšyn, yqdh, and mprsyyh all indicate the future; the participle m^{c}brh is stative, and hence describes her condition at the time of address. By contrast, the imperfects ytn are yprwq are both precative. The situation can at times be complicated when the Aramaic uses the imperfect to translate an MT imperfect, however cases such as this midrash are instructive and can be found throughout the MS. It should also be noted that the English translation in the editio princeps does not understand the Aramaic in this fashion and translates both as simple English futures: "will put" and "will deliver" (pp. 603-604).

6 In Hebrew, stative verbs (including 'hb) in the perfect express a present condition, e.g., 'āhabtā 'you are in love with' (Gen 22:2) or 'āhabtî 'I am in love with' (Exod 21:5), see Gesenius, "Grammatik," p. 321, 106g. This is not the case in Aramaic and this (mis?)understanding of the MT accounts for the (mis?)translation of, e.g., the above two verbs in the MS by the perfect: Gen 22:2 dbr k^{c}n yt brk yt yḥydk dy rḥmt yt yṣḥq... 'Take, therefore, your son, your only one, whom you have loved(?), Isaac...'; Exod 21:5 w'm mymr ymr ^{c}bd' rḥmyt yt rbny yt 'tty wyt bny lyt 'nh npq lḥyrwth. 'And if the slave actually says: "I have loved(?) my lord, my wife, and my children; I shall not go forth to freedom."'

7 It should be mentioned that the English translation in the editio princeps does not understand the Aramaic thus, and translates: "when they had eaten and drunk they wanted to give him...you have eaten...they did not move...until he had converted them and he used to teach them...and he worshipped and prayed..." (p. 550). However, the participles cannot be translated as perfects, nor can the compound forms be understood as punctual pluperfects, since the essence of both is the durativeness of the action expressed.

8 Many of the other compound imperfect examples, which either mimic a Hebrew compound, or translate an MT participle or imperfect, are made up of a compound of imperfect of hwh + passive participle. This unusual fact may be partially accounted for by the general development away from the use of separate passive verbal stems (Gt/Dt and Ct), and their replacement by various paraphrastic expressions. Examples of this are common: Gen 4:12 gly wmṭlṭl tyhwy qyn b'r^{c}' 'exiled and cast out will you be, Oh Cain, in the land' (MT nā^{c} wānād tihye bā'āreṣ, and cf. Gen 4:14 for a similar expression); Deut 28:29/33/34 thwwn...^{c}syyn wgzylyn/wthwwn...^{c}ṣn (sic) wrṣyṣyn/wthwwn mšg^{c}yn 'you will be oppressed and robbed'/'and you will be oppressed and crushed'/'and you will be driven mad' (MT wəhāyîtā...^{c}āšûq wəgāzûl/wəhāyîtā ^{c}āšûq wərāṣûṣ/ wəhāyîtā məšūggā^{c}); Gen 25:23 wrbh yhwwy mš^{c}bd qdm z^{c}yr' 'and the greater

shall be subjugated before the smaller' (MT wərab ya^{ca}bōd ṣā^{c}îr).

[9]The spelling of the participle qtylyn does not necessarily indicate a passive participle, and many active participles are spelled thus, with -y- to indicate a vocalic shewa, so qātilin < qātəlin.

[10]The Samaritan Pentateuch does have 'et, see Biblica Hebraica Stuttgartensia, ad loc., p. 29.]

[11]Cf. Sperber, "Onkelos," Vol I, ad loc., p. 53, for the form in Onkelos wyš'lynk, and also the variant form in other MSS wš'ylynk. One should probably also read the form here as wyš'lynk, due to w/y confusion, see Chapter 2, Orthography.

[12]This is a condensed version of a paper "Nominal Syntax in the Language of Codex Vatican Neofiti 1: Sentences Containing a Predicate Adjective," Journal of Near Eastern Studies, 42 No. 3, 1983, pp. 181-194.

[13]This device is familiar for other Aramaic dialects (and other Semitic languages). Examples and discussion can be found in Gideon Goldenberg, "Tautological Infinitive," Israel Oriental Studies I, 1971, pp. 36-85, and for full details, see H.J. Polotsky, Etudes de syntaxe copte, Le Caire, 1944, reprinted in his Collected Papers, Jerusalem, 1971, pp. 102-202.

[14]Cf. Ellen Prince, "A Comparison of Left-Dislocation and Topicalization in Discourse," University of Pennsylvania, MS.

[15]Not "They are both just," etc. as the English translation in the editio princeps states, p. 604.

[16]An expanded version of this section has appeared as "Nominal Syntax in the Language of Codex Vatican Neofiti 1: The Genitive Relationship," Journal of the American Oriental Society, Vol. 102.2 (1982), pp. 297-308. The data for this study were drawn solely from the text of the book of Genesis in the MS.

BIBLIOGRAPHY

Aberbach, Moses, and Bernard Grossfeld. Targum Onkelos on Genesis 49. Society of Biblical Literature Aramaic Studies, Number 1. 1976.

________ and Bernard Grossfeld. Targum Onkelos to Genesis. Center for Judaic Studies, Ktav, New York. 1982.

Bacher, W. "Targum." Jewish Encyclopedia, Vol. 12, 1906, pp. 57-59.

Bauer, Hans, and Pontus Leander. Grammatik des Biblisch-Aramäischen. Tübingen, Max Niemyer Verlag. 1927. Reprinted Georg Olms Verlag, 1969.

Baumgartner, Walter. Hebräisches und Aramäisches Lexicon zum Alten Testament. Leiden, Brill. Vol. I, 1967; Vol. II, 1974.

Bergsträsser, G. Hebräische Grammatik, Vol. II, Verbum. Leipzig, J.C. Hinrichs. 1929. Reprinted Georg Olms Verlag, 1962.

Berliner, Abraham. Raschi. Der Kommentar des Salomo b. Isak über den Pentateuch (Hebrew). Frankfurt a.M., J. Kauffmann. 1905.

Biblia Hebraica Stuttgartensia. Eds. K. Ellinger and W. Rudolph. Deutsche Biblestiftung, Stuttgart. 1977.

Bowker, John. The Targums and Rabbinic Literature. Cambridge, University Press. 1969.

Bravmann, M.M. "The Idea of 'Possession' in Linguistic Expression." Studies in Semitic Philology, pp. 357-373. Leiden, Brill. 1977.

Brockelmann, C. Semitische Sprachwissenschaft. Berlin/Leipzig, Göschen'sche Verlagshandlung. 1916.

Cohen, Gerson D. "Esau as Symbol in Early Medieval Thought." Jewish Medieval and Renaissance Studies, Vol. IV, 1967, pp. 19-48.

Coxon, Peter W. "The Syntax of the Aramaic of Daniel: A Dialectal Study." Hebrew Union College Annual, Vol. 47, 1977, pp. 107-122.

Dalman, Gustaf H. Grammatik des jüdisch-palästinischen Aramäisch. Leipzig, J.C. Hinrichs'sche Buchhandlung. 1894.

________. Aramäisch-Neuhebräisches Wörterbuch. Frankfort a.M., J. Kauffmann. 1901.

Díez Macho, Alejandro. Neophyti 1: Targum Palestinense. Consejo Superior de Investigaciones Cientificas. Vol. I, Genesis, 1968; Vol. II, Exodo, 1970; Vol. III, Levitico, 1971; Vol. IV, Numeros, 1974; Vol. V, Deuteronomio, 1978.

________. "Le targum palestinien." Exegese biblique et judaïsme, J.-E. Ménard (ed.), Strasbourg, 1973, pp. 14-77.

Epstein, Jacob N. A Grammar of Babylonian Aramaic (Hebrew). Jerusalem, Magnes Press. 1960.

Fink, David. "Aspects in the Mišne Tora." Hebrew Annual Review, Vol. 5, 1981, pp. 37-46.

Fitzmyer, Joseph. The Genesis Apocryphon of Qumran Cave 1: A Commentary. Rome, Pontifical Biblical Institute. 1966.

_______. Review of Neophyti 1, Tomo I: Genesis, by Alejandro Díez Macho (ed.). Catholic Biblical Quarterly, 32, 1970, pp. 107-112.

_______. Review of Neophyti 1, Tomo II: Exodo, by Alejandro Díez Macho (ed.). Journal of Biblical Literature, 91, No. 4, 1972, pp. 575-578.

_______. "The Languages of Palestine in the First Century A.D." A Wandering Aramean: Collected Aramaic Essays, Scholars Press, Chico. 1979, pp. 29-56.

_______. "The Phases of the Aramaic Language." A Wandering Aramean: Collected Aramaic Essays, Scholars Press, Chico. 1979, pp. 57-84.

Gesenius, Wilhelm. Hebräische Grammatik (Revised by E. Kautzsch), Leipzig. 1909. Reprinted by Georg Olms Verlag, 1962.

Goldenberg, Gideon. "Tautological Infinitive." Israel Oriental Studies, I, 1971, pp. 36-85.

Golomb, David. Targumno, Part I: Genesis. Berlin. 1932.

Golomb, David M. A Grammar of the Aramaic in Codex Vatican Neophyti 1 (Genesis). Ph.D. dissertation, Harvard University. 1978.

_______. "Nominal Syntax in the Language of Codex Vatican Neofiti 1: The Genitive Relationship." Journal of the American Oriental Society, Vol. 102.2, 1982, pp. 297-308.

_______. "Nominal Syntax in the Language of Codex Vatican Neofiti 1: Sentences Containing a Predicate Adjective." Journal of Near Eastern Studies, 42, No. 3, 1983, pp. 181-194.

Goshen-Gottstein, M.H. "The 'Third Targum' on Esther and Ms. Neofiti 1." Biblica, Vol. 56, No. 3, 1975, pp. 301-329.

Greenfield, Jonas. "Standard Literary Aramaic." Actes du premier congrès international de linguistique sémitique et chamito-sémitique, held in Paris, 1969, André Caquot and David Cohen (eds.). The Hague, 1974, pp. 280-289.

Grossfeld, Bernard. A Bibliography of Targum Literature. Hebrew Union College Press, Ktav, New York. Vol. I, 1972; Vol. II, 1977.

Grossfeld, Bernard. "The Relationship Between Biblical Hebrew ברח and נוס and their Corresponding Aramaic Equivalents in the Targum - צרק, אפך, אזל: A Preliminary Study in Aramaic-Hebrew Lexicogrphy." Zeitschrift für die Alttestamentliche Wissenschaft, 91, No. 1, 1979, pp. 107-123.

Haneman, Gideon. A Morphology of Mishnaic Hebrew (Hebrew). Tel Aviv, Texts and Studies in the Hebrew Language and Related Subjects, Tel Aviv University. 1980.

Hayward, Robert. "The Memra of YHWH and the Development of its Use in Targum Neofiti 1." Journal of Jewish Studies, Vol. 25, No. 3, 1974, pp. 412-418.

Hengel, Martin. Judaism and Hellenism. 2 Volumes, Philadelphia, Fortress Press. 1974.

Holladay, William L. A Concise Hebrew and Aramaic Lexicon of the Old Testament. Leiden, Brill. 1971.

Hyman, Aaron. Torah Hakethubah Vehamessurah, Part 1: Pentateuch. Tel Aviv, Dvir. 1979.

Jastrow, Marcus. A Dictionary of the Targumim, the Talmud Babli and Yerushalmi, and the Midrashic Literature. The Judaica Press, New York. 1975.

Joüon, P. Grammaire de l'hébreu biblique. Rome. 1923.

Kaddari, Menahem Z. "The Use of ד- Clauses in the Language of Targum Onkelos." Textus, Vol. 3, 1963, pp. 36-59.

________. "Construct State and dī-Phrases in Imperial Aramaic." Proceedings of the International Conference on Semitic Studies, held in Jerusalem, 1965, pp. 102-115. Jerusalem, Israel Academy of Sciences and Humanities. 1969.

Kasher, Menahem M. Torah Shelemah, Vol. 24: Aramaic Versions of the Bible. Jerusalem, American Biblical Encyclopedia Society. 1974.

Kasovsky, Hajim J. Concordance to Targum Onkelos (Hebrew). Jerusalem, Ha'ivri Press. 1935.

Kaufman, Stephen A. The Akkadian Influences on Aramaic. The Oriental Institute of the University of Chicago Assyriological Studies, No. 19, the University of Chicago Press. 1974.

Klein, Michael. "Deut 31:7, תבוא or תביא?" Journal of Biblical Literature, 92, No. 4, 1973, pp. 584-585.

________. "Notes on the Printed Edition of MS Neofiti 1." Journal of Semitic Studies, Vol. 19, No. 2, 1974, pp. 216-230.

________. "Elias Levitas and MS Neofiti 1." Biblica, Vol. 56, No. 2, 1975, pp. 242-246.

________."Converse Translation: A Targumic Technique." Biblica, Vol, 57, No. 4, 1976, pp. 515-537.

________. "The Translation of Anthropomorphisms and Anthropopathisms in the Targumim." Vetus Testamentum, Supplement, Vol. 32, Congress Volume, 1981, pp. 162-177.

Krauss, Samuel. Griechische und Lateinische Lehnwörter im Talmud, Midrash und Targum. Vol. I, Berlin, 1898; Vol. II, Berlin, 1899. Reprinted Georg Olms Verlag. 1964.

Kutscher, Eduard Y. "Studies in Galilean Aramaic" (Hebrew). Tarbiz, Vol. 21, 1950, pp. 192-205; Vol. 22, 1950-51, pp. 53-63, 185-192; Vol. 23, 1951, pp. 36-60. Reprinted by Academon, Jerusalem, 1969. Translated by Michael Sokoloff, Studies in Galilean Aramaic, Bar Ilan Press, Ramat Gan. 1976.

_______. "Aramaic." Current Trends in Linguistics, ed. Thomas A. Sebeok, Vol. 6, 1970, pp. 347-412.

_______. A History of Aramaic, Part 1 (Hebrew). Jerusalem, Academon. 1973.

_______. The Language and Linguistic Background of the Isaiah Scroll. Leiden, Brill, Studies on the Texts of the Desert of Judah, Vol. VI. 1974.

_______. A History of the Hebrew Language (ed. by Raphael Kutscher). Jerusalem, Magnes Press. 1982.

Le Déaut, Roger. La nuit pascale. Rome, Institut Biblique Pontifical. 1963.

Levy, B. Barry. The Language of Neophyti 1: A Descriptive and Comparative Grammar of the Palestinian Targum. Ph.D. dissertation, New York University. 1974.

Levy, J. Chaldäisches Wörterbuch über die Targumim. Koln, Joseph Melzer Verlag. 1959.

Lieberman, Saul. Greek in Jewish Palestine. New York, Jewish Theological Seminary of America. 1942.

_______. Texts and Studies. New York, Ktav. 1974.

Lund, Shirley and Julia Foster. Variant Versions of Targumic Traditions Within Codex Neofiti 1. Society of Biblical Literature Aramaic Studies, Number 2. 1977.

Margolis, Max. Lehrbuch der aramäischen Sprache. München, C.H. Beck'sche Verlagsbuchhandlung. 1910.

Martin, M. Fitzmaurice. "The Paleographical Character of Codex Vatican Neofiti 1." Textus, Vol. 3, 1963, pp. 1-35.

McNamara, Martin. The New Testament and the Palestinian Targum to the Pentateuch. Rome, Pontifical Biblical Institute. 1966.

_______. Targum and Testament. Shannon, Irish University Press. 1972.

Melammed, Ezra Z. Bible Commentators, Vol. I (Hebrew). Jerusalem, Magnes Press. 1975.

Miller, Jonathan Robert. A Grammar of the Type II Marginalia Within Codex Neofiti 1 with Attention to Other Aramaic Sources. Ph.D. dissertation, Boston University. 1979.

Muraoka, Takamitsu. "Notes on the Syntax of Biblical Aramaic." Journal of Semitic Studies, Vol. XI, No. 2, 1966, pp. 151-167.

Polotsky, Hans J. Etudes de syntaxe copte. Le Caire. 1944. Reprinted in Collected Papers, Jerusalem, Magnes Press. 1971.

Porath, Ephraim. Mishnaic Hebrew (Hebrew). Jerusalem, Bialik Foundation of the Jewish Agency. 1938.

Prince, Ellen. A Comparison of Left-Dislocation and Topicalization in Discourse. University of Pennsylvania. MS.

Rosenthal, Franz. A Grammar of Biblical Aramaic. Wiesbaden, Otto Harrasowitz. 1963.

Seeligmann, Isac L. The Septuagint Version of Isaiah. Leiden, Brill. 1948.

Segal, Moses H. "Misnaic Hebrew and its Relation to Biblical Hebrew and to Aramaic." The Jewish Quarterly Review, Vol. XX, 1908, pp. 647-737.

_______. A Grammar of Mishnaic Hebrew. Oxford. Clarendon Press. 1927.

Segert, Stanislav. Altaramäische Grammatik. Leipzig, Veb Verlag Enzyklopädie. 1975.

Sperber, Alexander. The Bible in Aramaic. Leiden, Brill. Vol. I, 1959; Vol. II, 1959; Vol. III, 1962; Vol. IVA, 1968; Vol. IVB, 1973.

Stenning, J.F. The Targum of Isaiah. Oxford. 1949.

Stevenson, W.B. Grammar of Palestinian Jewish Aramaic. Oxford, Clarendon Press. 1924.

Tal (Rosenthal), Abraham. "Ms. Neophyti 1: The Palestinian Targum to the Pentateuch." Israel Oriental Studies, IV, 1974, pp. 31-43.

_______. The Language of the Targum of the Former Prophets and its Position within the Aramaic Dialects. Tel Aviv, Texts and Studies in the Hebrew Language and Related Subjects, Tel Aviv University. 1975.

Weil, Gerard E. "Le codex Neophiti I: à propos de l'article de M. Fitzmaurice Martin." Textus, Vol. 4, 1964, pp. 225-229.

York, Anthony. "The Dating of Targumic Literature. Journal for the Study of Judaism," Vol. V, No. 1, 1974, pp. 49-62.

INDEX OF VERSES CITED

VERSE	PAGE
Exodus	
3:10	160,166
3:12	146
3:13	166,167
3:14	62,167,171
3:15	66
3:16	166,167
3:17	115,116,160
3:18	165,166,167
3:19	166
3:21	76
3:22	136
4:2	96
4:3	49
4:4	96,136
4:6	113,153
4:7	113
4:10	101
4:12	60
4:13	60,135
4:15	211
4:16	76
4:21	66,110,166,211
4:25	129,131
4:31	91
5:1	49
5:4	166
5:11	33,64
5:12	123,134
6:3	142
6:4	143
6:6	137,167
6:7	29,78
6:12	58
6:15	118
7:15	153
7:19	108
7:28	76,108
8:1	160
8:5	59
8:9	76,105,109
8:18	95
8:25	130
9:3	171
9:9	161
9:10	161
9:25	158
10:3	59
10:7	59
10:24	166
10:28	28,135
10:29	173
11:2	108
11:7	145
12:6	72
12:9	131
12:14	152
12:21	144
12:23	152
12:27	137
12:36	136
12:37	104
12:39	136
12:42	103,155,158,160
13:13	90
13:18	159
14:3	71
14:7	63
14:9	113
14:11	35,95
14:13	106,130,134,135
14:14	130
14:17	143
14:22	78,152
14:23	113
14:25	32,55,105
15:1	61,113
15:2	85,86,136,211
15:3	25
15:4	109
15:6	64,122,156
15:7	137
15:9	104,122,152,156
15:11	25,71,95
15:12	124,127,130,156,169
15:17	130,131,133
15:18	64
15:19	107
15:21	146
15:26	60
16:3	43,146,169
16:7	47,129
16:8	47,135
16:13	105
16:31	105
16:32	139
17:12	129
17:14	95
17:16	147,150
18:12	98
18:13	147

OTHER BIBLICAL VERSES CITED

THE ESSENTIAL T. S. ELIOT

THE ESSENTIAL
T. S. ELIOT

A CRITICAL ANALYSIS

H. L. SHARMA

S. CHAND & CO. (Pvt.) LTD.
RAM NAGAR, NEW DELHI-55.

S. CHAND & CO. (Pvt.) LTD.
H.O. : RAM NAGAR, NEW DELHI-55

Branches :

Fountain, Delhi
Mai Hiran Gate, Jullundur
Aminabad Park, Lucknow
102, Prasad Chambers, Behind
Roxy Cinema, Bombay-4
32, Ganesh Chandra Ave., Calcutta-13
35, Mount Road, Madras-2
Sultan Bazar, Hyderabad
Exhibition Road, Patna

Price : Rs. **25·00**

Published by S. Chand & Co. (Pvt.) Ltd., Ram Nagar, New Delhi-55 and printed at Rajendra Printers, Ram Nagar, New Delhi-55.

85472

In memory

of

my parents

PREFACE

Talking about T. S. Eliot has assumed the proportions of a new fashion. I concede that my rugged taste has been too rigid to acquiesce in this matter. Hence, when some of my colleagues had insisted on me to re-interpret the creative outreach of **T.S.E.** in some new perspective, I had brushed aside the whole idea as fantastic. Obviously, I did not want to venture into a task for which my reading, then, seemed inadequate.

The present book, however, is the by-product of my doctoral studies. I have attempted here a critical analysis of the mind and work of **T.S.E.** in all its essential facets. My chief endeavour has been to present a systematic study of the principles, methods, and achievements of a literary figure who has left an indelible influence on the thought, pattern and consciousness of our age. In fact, the book is a kind of literary-cum-biographical adventure, which I hope, may better the quantum of **enjoyment** and **understanding** of anyone who is seriously interested in the poetry and poetics of T. S. Eliot.

Amongst those who have made this book possible, my thanks are chiefly due to the publishers: S. Chand and Co., Delhi, for readily accepting the manuscript; to my teacher Dr N. Das Gupta to whom I owe much for my present academic interests; to Principal B. S. Mathur, for allowing me to make use of the college library; to Dr V. A. Sharma; Professor J. P. Jain and Professor Devendra Sharma 'Indra'; for reading the typescript and for suggesting valuable alterations, corrections and improvements; and to my wife for providing encouragement and criticism in the much needed directions, even more important, at the right moments.

It is not possible to record my indebtedness to previous writers. Suffice it to say that my creditors are more than I can specify and the liability beyond my discharge. I have always tried to acknowledge the sources of quotations and references I have made use of. I am really indebted to all the authors and publishers for permission to quote from their works in copyright. I also acknowledge that the opinions expressed in the book are entirely mine. As for the lapses, if any, I alone am responsible.

The title of the book should not be misconstrued. "Here, in a nutshell, is the kind of creative mind I understand **T.S.E.** to have been", is what it is intended to convey.

I confess to have invaded the territories of specialists without having the equipment of a specialist. Yet, I have never thought of competing with them. I shall deem my endeavours as amply rewarded, if the book helps in any way towards cultivating a better taste for the study of T. S. Eliot. Even otherwise,

What thou lovest well remains,
the rest is dross.

Delhi H. L. SHARMA
January 14, 1971.

ABBREVIATIONS EXPLAINED

C.F.	—	Compare.
F.Q.	—	Four Quartets.
O.P.P.	—	On Poetry and Poets.
S.E.	—	Selected Essays (1932 Edition).
S.P.	—	Selected Prose (Penguin Book).
S.W.	—	The Sacred Wood (Mathuen & Co. Ltd.).
T.S.E.	—	Thomas Stearns Eliot.
U.P.U.C.	—	The Use of Poetry and The Use of Criticism (Faber and Faber).
W.L.	—	The Waste Land.

CONTENTS

CHAPTER I

LITERARY CRITICISM BEFORE ELIOT

It is not easy to venture an all acceptable definition of literary criticism. The nature of its rudiments is varied and complex. The areas under its province have always been conditioned by factors which have differed from time to time. The general attitude of each age, the state of its literary development, the maturity of its creative genius, and above all the specific outlook of each of its major critics, go to determine its "own categories of appreciation."[1] The vogue of new assessments becomes more necessary, for the simple reason that no generation is interested in Art in quite the same way as any other.[2] Its more independent minds do not parrot the opinions of the last masters of criticism. They cater to the new demands made upon literature, stimulating thus, the process of re-orientation of the literary values.

The literature of criticism is not small or negligible. Its chief architects, from Aristotle onwards, have often been among the first intellects of their age.[3] Yet it is difficult to arrive at some consensus of an agreed code or set of fixed principles of criticism which may be presented with a view to evaluating the literature of all ages, and of all writers. Still, the basic fact remains the same: that literary criticism with some embarrassing exceptions is a single activity running through Plato to Eliot; that its history is the story of successive critics offering different answers to the same questions; and that while catering to the needs of their respective ages, the critics have

1. Eliot, T. S.—*The Use of Poetry and The Use of Criticism*, p. 109.

2. *Ibid.*

3. Richards, I. A.—*Principles of Literary Criticism*, p. 5.

also added something valuable to the tissue and fibre of the general critical thought. Allen Tate refers to the same assumption:

> "The permanent critics are the rotating chairmen of a debate, only the rhetoric of which changes from time to time."[4]

Wimsatt and Brooks subscribe to the same analogy:

> "The first principle on which we would insist is that of continuity and intelligibility in the history of literary argument."[5]

George Saintsbury, Atkins and Wellek also support the same view. George Watson, however, puts a dissenting note to the "kind of order"[6] these historians have seen.

In the light of this perspective, the total genre of literary criticism may be said to constitute one organic whole. May be, in the lengthy galaxy of critics, the extraordinary critics influenced the course better than the ordinary ones. But taken as a regular phenomenon of growth, the efforts even of the ordinary have got their due significance when screened through the "historical context."[7] Sidney's "Apologie" or Dryden's "Prefaces" might be timeless in as far as they continue to be of perpetual use to the critics of the future. But the value of Thomas Eliot's "Governour" or Pope's "Essay on Man" must not be underestimated, simply because they cease to exercise any ostensible impact beyond their contemporary setting. No serious student of literary criticism can afford to neglect the study of such treatises.

Literary criticism, in the now popular sense, may be regarded as "any formal discussion of literature"[8] which loosely implies three kinds of literary evaluation: the legislative, the aesthetic and the descriptive. Legislative criticism addresses itself more to the artist rather than to the audience. Its main function is to educate the would-be writer to do his job well,

---

4. Tate, Allen: Quoted by George Watson—*The Literary Critics,* p. 11.
5. Wimsatt & Brooks—*Literary Criticism,* p. vii.
6. Watson George—*The Literary Critics,* p. 11.
7. Eliot, T. S.—*To Criticise the Critic,* p. 17.
8. Watson George—*The Literary Critics,* p. 11.

and in accordance with the rules laid down in the standard works of Greek and Latin literature. Most of the sixteenth century criticism, barring that of Sir Phillip Sidney, and a large part of that of the classical age, fall under this category. Aesthetic criticism considers literature an independent art—an activity purely of the mind. It advocates that literature has an end in itself which is completely unfettered by religion, science, morality or politics. Its function is to probe into such psychological questions as the nature of the creative act, rather than the Platonic stress on the nature of poetic truth.[9] Sidney in the sixteenth century, Dryden in the seventeenth, and Addison in the eighteenth, represent this class of literary criticism. Later on, these subjects are treated more elaborately by Coleridge in the early nineteenth century, Pater and Wilde in the Victorian age, I. A. Richards and T. S. Eliot in the early twentieth century. Descriptive criticism is the youngest and the most popular of the three forms. It confines itself to the study of individual works vis-a-vis their objects, methods and efforts. This type of criticism has displayed a rare capacity of life and vigour of its own. Dryden's "Prefaces", and Ben Jonson's "Conversations", are some of the notable examples of this type of criticism. It may not base its conclusions on the norms suggested by legislative or aesthetic criticism. A large part of English criticism is influenced by this class of criticism.

Chronologically, the art of criticism in the West goes as far back as the fifth century B.C. It is closely connected with that great intellectual awakening which was heralded by Aeschylus, Sophocles, Euripides, Socrates and Aristophanes. The **'Frogs'** contains the first glimpses of the regular criticism of the Western World. Aristophanes, in this comedy, initiates for the first time, the most valuable discussion on such subjects as language, craftsmanship, morality and merit in art and literature. His inquiries help in the exploration of the hidden and the dormant in poetry and drama. Afterwards, the laurels of regular criticism are shared by scholars of the eminence of Plato, Aristotle and Longinus in Greece; Horace, Cicero and Quintilian in Rome. After Dante in the thirteenth century,

---

9. *Ibid.,* p. 14.

the Muse of literary criticism broadens its geographical base; crosses the frontiers of Italy; passes through France; and comes to England. The efforts of the Tudor Trio—Cheke, Ascham, Wilson—in the initial stages, and that of Sidney and Ben Jonson in the later decades of the 16th century, go a long way in laying the foundations of English literary criticism.

Renaissance Criticism, in its general complexion is eclectic and derivative. The Graeco-Roman classicists and Latin rhetoricians provide guidance and inspiration. The stress is on "the curb"—the necessity of submission to a code of conduct both on the part of the writer and the critic. Although obedience to the authority of the classical masters is freely prescribed yet the more intelligent favour the adherence to certain reservations. They advocate freedom and moderation in imitating ancient models, their style and technique. The achievement of Renaissance Criticism is five fold: first, it establishes the noble traditions of imaginative literature; second, it revives interest in the classics of antiquity; third, it ensures a dignified place for the poet; fourth, it prescribes for a regulated creativity based on the models of the ancients; and fifth, it advocates freedom to art and literature, in developing themselves in a natural way, as conditioned by local and indigenous tastes.

The Restoration period marks a new era in the realm of English criticism. It is known for catholicity of taste and broadness of outlook. Dryden, its main exponent, has rightly been called the father of English criticism. It is he who sets the fashion for its future course. His practical criticism has permanent value. He still occupies a unique position. He represents certain qualities that are of perennial interest to the students of literary criticism. He is free and unbiased in the display of critical spirit. He is ever alive to the native sensibilities. He blends in himself the rare qualities of imaginative sympathy, critical insight, and literary skill. His capacity to penetrate and see merits in all literary camps, irrespective of their affinities with diverse schools of thought, amply displays his flexibility in the matters of critical judgments. In an age of new influences of science and philosophy, Dryden shows a great sense of balance and propriety. He maintains an equilibrium between the local and the foreign; the old and the new; and the modern and the neo-classical. He is great in his own way.

The early eighteenth century shows the height of neo-classicism. This period is remarkable for the expansion and the diffusion of critical strain. The key to this temper lies in the maxim: "Follow Nature", which is interpreted by critics in more than one sense. It is important to point out that the impact of neo-classical traits in England was basically different as compared to the one felt in France and Italy. The most acceptable reasons for this difference are three: first, the influence of Shakespeare and other Renaissance dramatists; second, the patriotic liberalism of Dryden; and third, the wide popularity which Longinian "Concept of Sublimity" had acquired by this time. Even Pope—the uncompromising theoriser of neo-classical ideals—falls in line with the liberal traditions when he declares:

> "To judge of Shakespeare by Aristotle's rules is like trying a man by the laws of one country who acted under those of another."

At this stage, it appears advisable to take into account other factors also which are directly or indirectly responsible for the growing liberalism in the application of "those immutable laws of Nature". The influence of Reynold, Hobbes, Locke, Hartley, Beattie and Burke in this connection demands special mention. In the works of these and other men of letters of the age, we note an increasing emphasis on instincts as better and wiser guides than reason. As a result, the whole complexion of Aristotelian Theory of Catharsis undergoes a systematic re-interpretation. The concept of the "picturesque" in art as a distinctive merit, and its emotional appeal, are strongly advocated. The theory of the "Association of Ideas" further strengthens the philosophical base of Imagination as the fountain of great art. Lastly, the growth of scientific spirit and the development of historical consciousness weaken the notion of strict adherence to ancient names and authority. Art as such becomes more dynamic and is regulated by the standard and taste of the national genius.

Thus, the period starting with Dryden and ending with Dr. Johnson, marks an important epoch in the history of literary criticism. The reasons are abvious. First, it highlights an ever-increasing interest in literature and initiates serious discussion on its scope, form and functions. Second, it is rich, both in creative and critical output. Third—and the most significant of all—is the way in which the age, first pre-occupies itself and then wriggles out of the hotly-debated controversy of the ancients versus the moderns, or what is popularly known as the relative significance of "Authority" and "Autonomy" in literature. Ever since the middle of the seventeenth century, "reason" is the watch-word that sways the entire field of literary activity. But in the later half of the eighteenth century, romantic exuberance of the Elizabethans tends to assert itself once again. The change may be interpreted as a sort of systematic reaction against the unwarranted restrictions of the Augustan Age. Till we come to Dr. Johnson, Neo-classicism undergoes major decomposition owing to the pulls of disintegration from within, and the pressures of new ideas from without. The great Dictator hastens this process, though unconsciously, by prescribing certain postulates to the customary laws of Nature. But the disintegration of Neo-classicism is just the negative aspect of the whole literary atmosphere of this era. Even a coursory glance into the popular literary genres of this period would elaborate the view that substantive advances had been made in the directions of the Romantic Revolt which burst out in the early nineteenth century. It would be helpful to quote Atkins in this context who has summed up the whole critical history in the following words:

> "The truth is, therefore, that the real progress, the positive and lasting significance of these two centuries in critical history, lies not in the 'dissolving of Neo-classicism' but rather in the more enlightened conception of literary criticism that was gradually formed during that process, in the suggestive theories, its varied judicial methods and acute judgments, elements which more effectively than is sometimes supposed, prepared the way for the critical achievement of the 19th century."[10]

The publication of the preface to the Lyrical Ballads

10. Atkins—*English Literary Criticism,* p. 356.

marks the culmination of a new outlook in the development of English literary criticism. Romanticism is the name applied to the new change. The epithet 'romantic' had been in vogue in the continent since long but it assumed dimensional significance through the discussions of Schlegal and Madame de Stael. The two terms 'classical' and 'romantic' have come to stay as distinctive literary schools. Like romantic poetry, romantic criticism also has demonstrated its potentiality, homogeneity and profundity. It opposes all regimentation in literature that left nothing to freedom and Nature.[11] It evaluated a piece of art by its end rather than by its means. Whereas the neo-classical critics judged literature in the light of surreptitious standards such as social propriety or moral purity, the romantic critics started assessing poetry with regard to the poets' mind and its inner working. Coleridge propounds the theory of "willing suspension of disbelief"; Keats refers to the "negative capability of the poet"; Wordsworth speaks of the "tranquillised emotions", while Hazlitt theorises on "sympathetic identification". Till now, literary judgment is more a matter of knowledge than of "opinion." But the revolt unfolds new vistas not of reason, but of imagination. The gear is reversed. The foundations of a new aesthetics are laid where "knowledge" becomes subservient to "opinion" and impressions are made the vehicles of critical evaluation.

There is a fundamental difference between the new aesthetics and the preceding one. The renaissance criticism excepting that of Sidney in England, is mainly humanistic. It is preoccupied with linguistic and rhetorical bias. The Neo-classic criticism which succeeds it, does in no way prove itself better. The problems of language and style still dominate the minds of the critics. The worst of all, rules and not principles, dictate supremacy, authority and veto. The romantic aesthetics promises a new basis of appreciation. The whole conception of Beauty, its nature and sources undergo a radical change. Art and its appeal acquire new colours rooted deeply in psychology, philosophy and metaphysics. The pioneer of the new aesthetic outlook is the distinguished German trio—Lessing,

11. Kellett, E. E.—*The Whirligig of Taste,* p. 110.

Herder and Goethe. Later on Kant, Schlegel and Schelling embodied the whole philosophy and gave it a subtlety and depth of its own. The list will not be complete if we do not mention the name of Rousseau, to whom the whole romantic revolt stands in allegiance, for providing it an emotional respectability and a colourful originality. Equally significant in this connection is the impact that the changing political map of the continent has left on the human mind. The American War of Independence and the French Revolution aroused aspirations, unexperienced so far. They ignited new sparks of freedom and fraternity which in their turn generated a chain of reaction and even of revolt against the schackles of so called authority. The European Continent became surcharged with an indomitable spirit of inquiry and an unprecedented longing for independence. Art and literature also do not remain unaffected. As a result, the rules and regulations of Aristotle, Horace, Boileau and Le Bossu are questioned. Even the "cham of literature"—Dr. Johnson throws his weight against the ancients when he declares that "no man as yet ever became great by imitation."

The romantic aesthetics touches new horizons of evaluation. It is basically different from all other modes of criticism. In one sense, its primary source of inspiration is Longinus. The romantic criticism is distinguished by its own characteristics. First, it shows a shift from the "mimetic" to the "subjective and the expressive" criticism. Second, it probes into such metaphysical questions as "the origin and appeal of poetry." Third, it recognises the seminal principal of imagination, working at the core of each individual writer and his work. Fourth, it is impressionistic in form and character. Fifth, its very nature is fundamental and creative. Sixth, it is highly philosophical and abounds in psychological bias. Speaking negatively, it discards all linguistic and rhetorical considerations which we see persisting throughout the Renaissance and neoclassic techniques of criticism.

Wordsworth's position as a pioneer and leader of Romantic Revival is universally recognised. The bulk of his critical output is small. In his attack on poetic diction or in his definition of poetry, Wordsworth makes a powerful plea against what Read has referred to as the "wit-writing" of the 18th century. He is opposed to the neo-classical vogue of evaluating a work of art by the standards of the ancient models. He advances a new theory both about form and content of poetry and makes emotions the core of poetic perfection. His advocacy of powerful emotions either displayed spontaneously or tranquilised through a process of recollection, adds a new meaning to the metaphysical interpretation of poetry and its sources. The glaring pitfalls in his critical outlook are three: he lacks the depth of Coleridge; does not show much proportion and balance; and overstates the possibilities of his concept of "poetic diction." But with all his shortcomings, Wordsworth occupies an outstanding position in the new aesthetics of romanticism. His place is with Dante as far as he makes bold assertions on the problems of language and style.

Coleridge's place as a critic is far superior to that of Wordsworth, both in depth and originality. He may be considered the most shining luminary amongst the great critics, England has produced. Actually speaking, it is Coleridge who under the influence of German metaphysicians, gives to literary criticism a deep philosophical basis. His highest success lies in the fact that he makes criticism a science. Hence, psychology and philosophy now tend to bear great influence upon literary criticism. He explores new horizons—horizons that spring from the soul and impregnate the fountains of inspiration and creation. Coleridge's distinction between the twin terms of "Imagination" and "Fancy", and its further classification into Primary and Secondary Imagination, are the high marks of all his creative philosophy. He strongly protests against the earlier interpretations of "Imagination" which are nothing but mechanistic. "Fancy", according to Coleridge, is more of the nature of a mechanical operator. Its main function is to juxtapose the images. "Imagination" on the other hand has something more vital to perform. It is conceived as esemplastic power, underlying each organic perception. Its main function is to fuse all such images into an organic whole. In other words, the operation of Imagination lies in visualising all things as one, and one in all things. Moreover, Coleridge's aesthetic principles are closely related to his practical criticism. In the absence of this relationship, the bulk of his critical output would remain mere metaphysical abstractions. In his Shakespearian criticism, Coleridge adds new dimensions to the evaluation of drama and poetry. As a critic of fundamentals, Coleridge's place is by the side of Aristotle and Longinus.

Our assessment of the romantic aeasthetics would perhaps be incomplete without William Hazlitt. In fact, it is the trio comprising Wordsworth, Coleridge and Hazlitt that directs the new revolution in literary criticism in England. All the three have something to say to one another. In more than one sense, Coleridge remains the uniting-link between Wordsworth and Hazlitt. Virtually speaking, the current of thought running through Hazlitt's criticism shows flashes of Coleridgean metaphysics. It is the striking adeptness of the former that distinguishes him from the latter. Hazlitt may be said to be the fore-runner of Impressionistic creed of criticism. At his best, he displays a rare amalgam of gusto, impression and avocation. At his worst, he indulges in outbursts of personal affront and aspersion. Nevertheless, Hazlitt's criticism does reflect the soul and body of an art in its real perspectives of light, shade, and colour. Some of his reflections on individual poets and their works display his ability for mature judgments in the field of literary criticism. Hazlitt's sound artistic taste in prose may be considered one of the most outstanding features of his personality as a man of letters.

In the distinguished array of romantic criticism, the names of Lamb, Shelley, and Keats are equally important. They also have left indelible marks on the developing process of the new aesthetics. Lamb's critical writings are replete with the similar flashes of confidential and personal notes, as those of **Essays of Elia.** His dramatic criticism is unique. Unlike Hazlitt, Lamb is devoid of any feeling of affront and rancour. The appeal of his criticism lies in the pure genuineness of his impressions on the one hand and the honesty of their imaginative stress, on the other. Shelley's output as a critic is quantitatively scanty but its qualitative impact has been great. His reputation rests mainly on **Defence of Poetry.** The essay, by its very phrases and terms, echoes the influence of Coleridge on Shelley. Shelley's contribution to romantic thought lies in the fact that he platonises the theory of Imagination and lays stress on the necessary fusion of inspiration and imagination together as the essential basis of creative endeavour. Keats' criticism is substantially based on his own experience as a creative artist. Analytically speaking, the nature of his criticism is introspective. His emphasis on "negative capability" wherein he refers to the poet as the "most unpoetical having no Identity", displays his striking originality.

Looking lack at the course of criticism in England, the Romantic Revolt characteristically changes the nature of literary criticism. The battle between the two schools—the Neo-classical and the Romantic—was the battle not only of divergent techniques but also of different tastes. It was a battle between authority and autonomy. The whole of romantic aesthetics invokes inspiration from the German metaphysicians. Psychology and philosophy begin to dominate the creative and critical faculties of the artists. The guiding principle throughout the romantic period is the seminal concept of Imagination. It demonstrates unprecedented outbursts of emotional and imaginative frenzy. The majority of the outstanding critics interpret the principle of artistic creation in terms of imagination. Wordsworth and Hazlitt interlink passion with imagination; Coleridge interfuses feelings and imagination together; Shelley signifies the role of inspiration in the context of imagination; and to Lamb, only the impressions are the impelling soul behind every imaginative activity.

In the process of transition from the Romantic criticism to that of the Victorian period, we find once again, a major shift in the tone of literary values. The reasons are obvious. In the late thirties of the nineteenth century, when Queen Victoria occupied the throne of England, most of the Romantics had passed away. The emotional fervour of the early decades had also cooled down. The spirit behind romanticism, as was natural, had exhausted itself. The rise of democracy and the progress of Science aroused new aspirations, hopes and fears. The faith in God, man and church touched the lowest ebb. In the economic field, the world experienced the worst of depressions. The age may be called an age of contrasts in which authority compromises with autonomy; faith with freedom; wealth with want and culture with philistinism. Darwin's theory of Evolution and other positivist doctrines weakened the romantic influence. As a consequence, the hold of the German philosophers who had provided unstinted inspiration to the romantics, was further loosened. The venue of influence shifts to France and the French philosophy, with its stress on material reality, begins to attract the English mind. Religion and metaphysics cease to be the moving spirit and even the Biblical versions are freely challenged. The temper reflects a sort of protest against aesthetic and moral blindness.

The literary controversies of the Victorian period expose its very character in more than one sense. They bring on the surface, the serious concern of its men of letters with the ethical, aesthetic and intellectual problems of the day. Apart from other things, we find two divergent currents swaying the European Continent. England also does not remain out of the orbit of this development. One current is represented by scientists, historians and writers of the eminence of Darwin, Huxley, Mill, Macaulay and Herbert Spencer; all these and others display their ungrudging adherence to material well-being, scientific development and intellectual independence. The second current runs through the works of Arnold, Ruskin, Carlyle, Cardinal Newman, Pater, Symonds and Swinburne. Another distinctive feature of the Victorian literary perspective as compared with that of the Romantic age, is its varied and complex nature. The romantic scene is marked by the simplicity, and the directness of its light and shade. It is pure and harmonious. A certain set of aesthetic rules accompanied by an unrestricted stress on imaginative and emotional exuberance is more than enough to characterise the entire field of literary activity in the period of Revolt. But the colours of the Victorian perspective are not so simple to explain. They are not even homogeneous. They are complex and even show a sort of hybrid growth. Victorian literature and criticism reflect the same heterogeneous mass of complexity.

The graph of the chronological history of Victorian criticism shows a chequered development. It is marked by three different stages which, broadly speaking, correspond to three periods: the early Victorian; the mid-Victorian; and the later Victorian. The literary criticism in the early period is rich neither in quantity nor in quality. The only names worth mentioning are of Keble, Brimley and Dallas. Their standard of the critical output is mediocre, and sometimes even ordinary. Some of the prose-writers of this period occupy an outstanding place. The writers such as Carlyle, Macaulay and Mill, though mainly thinkers and historians, have something to say valuable, as critics too. The merit of the first two lies in their rhetorical vein and historical sense. Both of them give to Historical criticism a catholic colour and an appealing tone. Carlyle's individual contribution lies in his vision to liberate English criticism from its narrow privincialism and to give it an international perspective. The mid-Victorian criticism is more fertile in output and standard. It is brought up under the able stewardship of Arnold and Ruskin. Both the critics represent the general mood of Victorian compromise in their critical attitudes. They blend together the claims of Art and Morality. The criticism in the third stage shows signs of departure from that of the preceding ones. Pater and his followers declined to accept the moral claims of Art and declared aesthetic appeal as its primary consideration.

The genesis of the whole Victorian imbalance is governed by that basic reality which science and democratic consciousness displays by bringing critics closer to men and matters of the times. As the poets address themselves to society, so do the critics. They begin to think in terms of communicating to the people the "best"—whether written or thought of. But the travesty of the situation is that none possesses either the capacity or the wisdom of prescribing some standard for measuring the worth of art and literature. As a consequence, they grope in wilderness. The Romantics had explicitly discarded the authority of the rules without providing a uniform or universal alternative of artistic excellence. All the same the scientific mind of the Victorians made them love the classical poise and order minus the slavish rigidity of its application. Hence, in literature, criticism, and elsewhere, we find writers clinging to a line of compromise. The critics seek refuge under the garb of divergent theories.

The clue to the crucial problem is supplied in the biographical-cum-critical method evolved by the French critics, Taine and Sainte-Beuve. The former formulates his theory of literature as the product of three social forces, operating jointly as well as severally. He categorises them as the **race,** the **milieu** and the **moment.** In his opinion, the race of the writer to which he belongs, together with the milieu, the social atmosphere—wherein he is brought up, go a long way in casting his talent into particular moulds. Developed in this manner, the artist, on the spur of an opportune moment, is forced to exhibit his own creative powers. Taine recommends that in evaluating a particular author, all the three elements should be properly assessed by judicious critics. Saint-Beuve's method is almost similar to that of Taine. He also lays equal emphasis on race, country and the state of society a writer is born into. Besides this, he recommends that the writer's ancestory, his standard of education and the pattern of his youthful associations must also be analysed by the critic before any judgment is passed on his works. Sainte Beuve is seriously concerned about the adolescent period of the author. It is this period which is the most formative and hence, very significant in as far as it goes to develop the real personality of the writer. The French critic qualifies this phase in the life of the author as "the true date of his birth", which, if not ascertained properly and analytically, may lead to gross inaccuracies in the final assessment of his work.

The biographical-cum-critical method, as envisaged above, catered satisfactorily to the needs of the Victorian temper. It suggested a golden mean between the Neo-classical way and the Romantic creed. It promised a dispassionate and disinterested study of an author and his work. It abjured impressionistic judgment. The method greatly appeals to the Victorians because of its twin dividends: it introduced a new approach of objective criticism; secondly, it struck golden mean between classical authority and romantic autonomy. No wonder, if Arnold also readily subscribes to Sainte-Beuve and follows him closely.

Academically, Victorian Criticism flows into three powerful strains. The first is embodied in the critical writings of Carlyle and Ruskin. In one sense, it represents the Moral trends. The second springs from the line advocated by Pater, Oscar Wilde, Rossetti and Swinburne. This approach may be described as purely artistic. Arnold becomes an able exponent of the new direction. To elucidate the point further, it may be said that Ruskin and Carlyle try to harmonise art and morality. In their creative and critical works, they rise in favour of religion and morality and defend them against the onsloughts of science and skepticism. Pater and Oscar Wilde on the other hand, stress on the pleasure-giving quality of art and literature. They adhere to the view, that art in no case should be fettered to any ethical considerations. The two groups represent two different schools of thought. The former clings to the classical ideal of "Art for Life's" sake and the latter stands for the romantic principle of "Art for Art's" sake only. In its ultimate analysis, the difference between the two schools appears to be the difference of two distinctive ends of literature: Teaching and Pleasure. Arnold moves midway between the two ideals. His position is analogous to that of Dr. Johnson who wants "poetry to teach through delight."

Arnold's literary criticism should be viewed from a wider perspective—his social and cultural bias, manifesting itself in **Culture and Anarchy.** He qualifies criticism as "a disinterested endeavour to learn and propagate" what he calls "the best, that is known and thought in the world, and thus to establish a current of fresh and true ideas." The definition is of great significance. It clarifies in its various facets, the total attitude of Arnold's criticism. Arnold's critic has a threefold function to perform: duty in relation to his own person, society and literature. The first function consists in "learning the best"; the second, in "propagating it"; and the third, in "establishing a current of fresh and true ideas." The endeavour must be disinterested and must abjure all likes and dislikes on the part of the critic. The way the Arnoldian critic is to propagate is equally important. It should be so regular as to establish a sort of continuous flow of ideas which are not old and stale but fresh and true. The qualifications "fresh and true" link Arnold with the Aristotelian poetics. In his definition of poetry as criticism of life, Arnold shows the same Aristotelian affinity. But in elucidating his Grand style and the Touch-stone-method, the Victorian critic appears moving more towards Longinus than towards Aristotle. Nevertheless, Arnold displays great respect for the ancients. In his critical analysis, he is generally subscribing to the classical line. Finally, Arnold recommends "real estimate" in criticism, as against the Historical and the Personal estimates. He voices his disapproval of the historical method because of the danger of the shift of emphasis from the actual work to that of the history of the period, and the consequential misjudgments accruing therefrom. By personal estimate, Matthew Arnold means inferences drawn from literary works, merely on the basis of likes and dislikes, leading to a sort of impressionistic criticism of the arbitrary type.

Notwithstanding his drawbacks, Arnold is one of the greatest modern critics and perhaps the greatest of his own times. It is he who tries to set right the deplorable state of Victorian literature. Though he has great love for some of the romantics, yet he rules out their principles. He firmly affirms the need of studying the ancients and seeking guidance and inspiration from them. He is Aristotelian in more than one sense. His grestest achievement lies in curbing the unwarranted excesses of his age. Under the influence of Sainte-Beuve, he incorporates into English criticism, a new ideal and method. His denunciation of the Personal and the Historical estimate as well as his advocacy of the comparative criticism, point to one and the same end, viz., the need of a code or system in critical evaluation. But equally large is the list of sins attributed to Arnold. It has been alleged that he is more of an advocate than a critic. There are critics who openly brush him aside as propagandist, a salesman, and even an advertiser of literature. Some have talked of the inherent contradiction between Arnold—the romantic poet; and Arnold—the classical critic. In spite of such remarks, Arnold's position as critic is still very imposing. "He was", says Prof. Saintsbury, "if not the absolute reformer, the leader in reform, of the slovenly and disorganised condition into which Romantic criticism had fallen. The things which he had not, as well as those he had, combined to give him a place among the very first."

After Arnold, the Victorian criticism experiences new orientation. Under the legacy of the two outstanding thinkers, Kant and Gautier, the school of "art for art's sake" received a powerful impetus. Once again, Edgar Allan Poe in America, Baudelaire and Flaubert in France and Whistler, Pater, Oscar Wilde, Rossetti and Swinburne in England, become the outstanding protagonists of the new aesthetic school. Antagonised by the Victorian atmosphere, they took shelter under the light of art and thought for curing the malaise in terms of aesthetic principles. This cult of Beauty sways the England of the nineties, and its most devoted votaries are Pater and Oscar Wilde.

Pater evaluates literature in relation to delightful experiences in life. He divides it into two categories—imaginative and unimaginative. Imaginative literature in his opinion has something more to communicate than the mere transcription of bare facts. It presents not only the facts but the sense of facts also. Therefore, a writer whether knowingly or unknowingly engaged in depicting not only the facts but his sense of facts also, tends to become always an artist. Pater also distinguishes between good and great art. The only pre-condition he attaches to the goodness of art is the truthfulness of the "sense of fact." Great art, on the other hand, would depend on the nature of the ultimate end of "the sense of fact." In other words, it must have the power to ennoble and fortify people in what Pater calls the "sojourn here or immediately to the glory of God." It is in this context that T. S. Eliot names Pater as a moralist and not a mere aesthete. In stressing the dignity of the sense of fact, Pater is very close to the Longinian way of importing sublimity of thought into art as the first requisite of its greatness. In the matter of style also, Pater subscribes to the views of Longinus. Declaring sense of fact, the central theme of artistic greatness, he prescribes three means—diction, design and personality—of presenting it in all its charm and beauty. The personality which he calls the "soul in style" is a spiritual activity. It is the very life-breath of the writer's work. In other words, it is his very self that manifests itself through his art. Suffice it to say, it is "the man" in style.

Pater's basic position is clear. His main concern in literature is with sense of fact and style as the only medium of its communication. The primary function of the critic is to know what the first is and how has it been conveyed to the readers. Pater categorises the functions of the critic:—

> "to feel the virtue of the poet or the painter, to disengage it, to set it forth—these are the three stages of the critic's duty."[12]

This virtue of the poet is nothing but his "sense of fact" which may be latent in the content and form of his work. It is the first responsibility of the critic to unearth the same and discern its distinctive feature. Browning's virtue or distinctive quality lies thus in his optimistic philosophy, a faith in life-after-death and the resultant "Immortality" of the soul. But there may be much in his work that does not undergo this particular feature of Browning's quality. Therefore, the second duty of the critic is to disengage or separate his sense of facts from such alien elements. With the virtue thus alienated, the critic's function does not end. He has been left with the third duty to perform: he must set it forth, also for the advantage of his readers which means the critic should be able to locate and mention the source of that impression as also the background of its experience. Pater's critical method is regulated mainly by a thorough search of the delightful or the beautiful in the author—a search which finally demands from us an analytical study of the artist's sense of fact on the one hand, and his way of conveying it, on the other.

Literary criticism implies many modes of evaluation. The impressionistic method which Pater developed is not a new one. It was also tried by the early romantics. Long before them, even Longinus had expressed similar views. In fact, Pater in his analysis of sense of fact is indebted to Coleridge. His interpretation of style as an activity of the mind is Longinian in theory as well as in practice. No one before Pater had stressed so much on the pleasure-giving quality of literature. In his criticism, he tried to harmonise the beauty and delight

---

12. Pater—*Preface to Renaissance.*

within, with the beauty and delight without. Both Arnold and Pater may be said to have refined the lietrary taste of the Victorian era. Each one of them shares the success of redeeming English criticism from stagnation and raising it to a status which in its own way is worthy of respect and admiration.

Victorian criticism on the whole is characteristically diverse and complex. There appears to be a great measure of uniformity in the literary criticism of the preceding age. But in the Victorian period that singleness of approach is no more to be seen. There is heterogeneity everywhere, criticism being no exception. Something like pure criticism is not easily visible. Politics, History and Sociology often trespass into the frontiers of criticism. Generally speaking, three types of critics are available. They are the votaries of science, idealism and pure beauty. Historically, two new phenomena of this period have great significance. First, the periodical criticism becomes very popular. There is hardly any critic who is not actively associated with the one or the other of these periodicals. Second, it happens for the first time, that University men begin to devote themselves to the study of literary criticism.[13] As a result, the entire field of critical evaluation receives new academic significance hitherto unknown. In the last decades of the century the efforts of scholars such as Lord Leslie Stephen, Dowden, Stopford Brooke and Prof, Saintsbury are of considerable merit. Arnold and Pater show distinction of promise and performance. Both have something valuable to say on the theoretical as well as practical nature of criticism. Barring their endeavours, Victorian criticism is barren and deficient. It gives, more than once, an impression of paucity.

The change of century ushers in an era of a "New Spirit". From the early nineties, a transition is visible which becomes more evident in the very wake of the twentieth century.[14] The Queen is born in one world; she dies in another. This period is summed up in what Decker calls an evolution from "a

---

13. Ellis Havelock—*The New Spirit.*
14. Jackson Hal Brook—*The Eighteen Nineties.*

dogmatic to an experimental spirit."[15] His full assessment runs as follows:

> "Between the Coronation and Diamond Jubilee, Victorian life had passed from an agricultural to an industrial economy; from an aristocratic to a middle-class-proletariate society; from a fixed and static to an evolutionary science; from an authoritarian to a relative theology: and generally, from a dogmatic to an experimental spirit."[16]

Prof. A. C. Ward qualifies the new spirit as the spirit of "Interrogation." Love of investigation and experiment now replaces the Victorian attitude of acceptance, compromise and complacency. It prescribes a vigorous examination of the accepted canons of evaluation in life and literature to see whether or not they stand the test of scrutiny. "Interrogation before Acceptance" is the new slogan. Question:Examine: Test, are the watchwords of the "new spirit."[17] The new era of Inquiry is surely propitious for the healthy growth of the critical talent but it is unfortunate that between Pater and Eliot, none is there among the English men of letters who can be classed with the highest creative or critical genius.

In the dawn of the new century, the twin impact of Arnold and Pater is clearly discernible. The spirit of "high-seriousness" of the former as also the "impressionistic zeal" of the latter still haunt the realm of the Edwardian and the Georgian literature. Another important aspect of this period is the further development of academic criticism in England. Scholars and historiographers such as George Saintsbury, Walter Raleigh, Oliver Elton, W. P. Ker and A. C. Bradley share laurels in exalting criticism to new academic heights. The early decades also register a remarkable beginning in the field of Textual Criticism. A long array of eminent writers devoted themselves to the study of classical texts and the determination of their authoritative versions. On the continental plane, various influences appear to be actively working—the influences which further bifurcated the trends of literary criticism in the first two decades of the century. The Arnoldian tradition is represented by the neo-Humanists. They may be said

15. Decker Clearance, R.—*The Victorian Conscience,* p. 175.
16. *Ibid.*
17. Ward, A. C.—*Twentieth Century Literature,* p. 6.

to be the conservators of order, restraint and discipline. In practice, they tend to oppoes two literary tendencies: Naturalism with the debased view of man, denying him free will and responsibility; and Romanticism, with its excessive cultivation of the ego and sympathy with comparatively unrestrained expression."[18] The Neo-Humanists, in the initial stage, include in America, the scholars of the eminence of Paul Elmer More and Prof. Irving Babbitt. T. E. Hulme's position is somewhat different, though he also is as vehemently opposed to "the softness and confusion of Romanticism."[19] The school of Neo-Humanism with its strong stress on morality has led to a charge of "ethical hyperorthodoxy."[20] Yet, many of them tried hard to synthesize "moral earnestness"[21] based on a rational concept of man's nature with "aesthetic sensitivity.[22] Another trend, equally potential, is that of the Imagists in France. This school represents the impulse towards concentration on technique and the precise presentation of visual images. The vocabulary was to be simple but exact; the verse experimental to the choice of the writer; and the subject matter completely free. The powerful exponents of this school are T. E. Hulme and Ezra Pound. Hulme is a staunch protagonist of "dry and hard" verse, capable of repudiating the softness of the Romantic poetry. His essential stress in poetry is on solid, clear and plastic images.[23] The Imagists offer examples of the close study of form. In fact, their theory and practice may be said to be the precursors of the Formalistic criticism of the thirties. Both Hulme and Ezra Pound, through their creative and critical originality, leave an indelible impact on the susceptible mind of T. S. Eliot.

The names of two thinkers require special mention here. They are Benedetto Croce and Sigmund Freud. Both of them

---

18. Scott Wilbur, S.—*Five Approaches of Literary Criticism*, p. 24.

19. *Ibid,* p. 25.

20 *Ibid,* p. 24.

21. *Ibid.*

22. *Ibid.*

23. Hulme, T. E.—*The Speculations.*

tend to direct criticism into new channels. One propounds the theory of "Expressionism", and the other advocates the concept of "Libido" in art. The Italian critic defines art as "intuition expression." He asserts that what the people understand by art is nothing but the vivid impression of the artist's mind. It is a sort of copy in words, colours or stones of those impressions which the artist experiences in an intuitive mood. True art consists in the externalisation of these "intuition-expressions." The purpose of the artist is to so illumine the reader or the audience as to induce in them the same impression which he has been able to experience himself. The basic incentive, according to Croce, behind all such literary processing, is the incentive of pleasure. The seamy or ugly aspects, being important constituents of nature, are bound to form an inseparable part of the artist's expression, irrespective of their being useful or otherwise. The primary significance lies in their expression. The names of Lascelles Abercrombie in England and of J. E. Spingarn in America fall in the line of Croce's earlier followers.

The influence of Sigmund Freud, in giving literary criticism, a psycho-analytical bias is remarkable. The complexion of the entire critical movement of the thirties is replete with the growing impact which the Freudian theory has left on the writings of the contemporary critics. The Austrian theorist deals with "Libido"—the unconscious mind. He believes that this "Libido" or what he calls the "sex urge" plays a dominant role in moulding human behaviour. If restrained or suppressed, the urge leads to neurotic effects. The only means of eroding neurosis, according to Freud, is by way of sublimating the sex in art and literature. In this way, art tends to become an expression of the artist's sub-conscious self. The novels of James Joyce and his critical writings establish a remarkable affinity with the Freudian psychology.

The present survey of the literary scene, operating by the turn of the century, amply demonstrates its characteristic diversity. George Watson rightly points out that the three decades between Arnold and Eliot (1890-1920) "defy useful generalization."[24] T. S. Eliot compares it to "a Sunday Park of con-

24. Watson George—*The Literary Critics*, p. 164.

tending and contentious orators."[25] The two powerful critical movements—the Aesthetic and the Moralistic—set in motion during the Victorian era, run almost simultaneously. The Aesthetes, the Arnoldians, the Expressionists, the Naturalists, the Neo-Humanists, the Impressionists, the Academicians, the Formalists and the Freudians—all are in the field. Some of them are vigorously active in throwing their full weight for the development of a new critical movement. No doubt, left to itself, the literary scene in the Edwardian and Georgian period is hardly convincing. Yet, the way different forces are at work, creates a sense of promise as against the feeling of paucity of Victorian age. Wilbur S. Scott's reflections, in this background are significant:

> "The main conditions necessary to the development of a critical movement by this time were in existence; release from the criteria of the past; a new body of creative writing worthy of critical attention; and a sense of excitement (not optimism, however) about the future of literature. Oddly enough, the first group of critics who gathered together with common ideals of examination and evaluation were not the *oficionados* of experiment, but the conservators of the Arnoldian tradition: the Neo-Humanists."[26]

And strikingly enough, one has not to wait for long. The void is filled by T. S. Eliot, the poet-critic of the highest rank. The publication of his first book—**The Sacred Wood**—in 1923, marks the beginning of a new era in the history of English literary criticism.

---

25. *Selected Prose,* p. 18.

26. Scott Wilbur, S.—*Five Approaches of Literary Criticism.* Introduction.

CHAPTER II

ELIOT—THE POET AND CRITIC IN MAKING

Thomas Stearns Eliot may best be called a "Literary Crusader."[1] It is impossible to "separate his work as a critic from his work as a poet."[2] It is futile and unprofitable, even to speculate how far or how fast he would have been recognised as a critic, had it not been for the impact of his early poems. Indeed, the numerous monographs, critiques and tributes, published during the last three decades are demonstrative of his legendary reputation.

The study of Eliot does not either begin or end with his work. His work as a whole has "its full meaning only in the larger context of the cultural tradition of Western Europe."[3] To understand the development of the critic in Eliot, is in fact, to understand not only the core of Western Culture, but an important part of Eastern Culture also. In this respect, the comments of D. E. Jones are significant.

> "In following up the allusions and references in or the implications of his work one is liable to find one reading anybody from Heraclitus to F. H. Bradley in the realm of philosophy or from Aeschylus to Anovilh in the realm of drama. One will almost inevitably go to the Divine Commedia, the Bhagwad Gita and the writings of St. John of the Cross. Eliot is a pathway into each, in that, not only does he provide the occasion for going to them but also an insight which makes them more meaningful to the present-day reader."[4]

Eliot's literary development is closely related to his family environment and the prevailing pulls and pressures of New

---

1. Lucy Sean—*T. S. Eliot and the Idea of Tradition,* p. 71.
2. *Ibid.*
3. Jones, D. E.—*The Plays of T. S. Eliot,* p. ix.
4. *Ibid.*

England traditions. The impressions and influences of his early life have much to say in the future make-up of his mind and personality. He is, in many ways, a typical product of "New England Puritanism in its decadence."[5] His work is no less than a "living and evolving organism",[6] springing always from an obsession with his early memories and experiences. All his works—creative and critical—tend to establish one growing impression—the search for the reality of "human situation"[7] and "the need for significance."[8] Circumstanced as he was, Eliot is zealously concerned with the quest for true "meaning" or "meaninglessness" hidden under the exterior aspect of things. As a consequence, he is always interested in the exploration of "spiritual recovery and integration."

Eliot was born on September 26, 1888, in St. Louis Missouri, a large industrial city. His father was president of an important business concern. His mother was a woman of keen intellectual interests. Both his parents were, however, descendants of New England families of the early settlements. The Eliot family, which was of Devonshire origin, goes back in America to Andrew Eliot (1627-1704) who, emigrating in middle life from East Coker, Somerset, was enrolled as a member of the First Church of Beverly, Massachusetts, in 1670.[9]

Eliot, in this way, inherited strong influences through the background of his parents. Their distinguished scholarship, outstanding commerical enterprise and puritan earnestness deeply touched the mental propensities of the pre-cocious child in his teen-age.[10] "The Boston mind" once so cheerful, now being full of the "sense of last things,"[11] was also imparted to his developing intellect. The "exhausting literary tradition";[12]

---

5. Hoskot, S. S.—*T. S. Eliot—His Mind and Personality,* p. 7.
6. *Ibid,* p. 7.
7. Lucy Sean—*T. S. Eliot and The Idea of Tradition,* p. 142.
8. *Ibid.*
9. Matthiessen, F. O.—*The Achievement of T. S. Eliot,* p. xix.
10. Brad Brook, M. C.—*T. S. Eliot,* p. 7.
11. Brooks Van Wyek, New England—*Indian Summer,* pp. 409, 414.
12. *Ibid.*

the "dissolving religious catholicity";[13] and the "decaying Jawry and Christian Science"[14] left an indomitable impact on the mind of Eliot.

Apart from this, the atmosphere in the family included the "extreme form of Protestant rationalism known as Unitarianism"[15] which Eliot himself qualifies as "Boston doubt: a scepticism difficult to explain......not destructive but dissolvent."[16] This Unitarianism, in his later life, formed an integral part of his temperament. In more than one way, it had a very salutary impact over his expanding intellectual horizons.

Addressing members of Washington University at the centenary of its foundation in 1953, Eliot himself referred to the general outlook of the family and disclosed:

> "The standard of conduct was that which my grandfather had set; our moral judgements, our decisions between duty and self-indulgence, were taken as if, like Moses, he had brought down the tables of the Law, any deviations from which would be sinful. Not the least of these laws, which included injunctions still more than prohibitions, was the law of Public Service......operating especially in three areas: the Church, the city, and the University......They were the symbols of Religion, Community and Education."[17]

It is apparent that the ethos of Eliot's family was highly moral and religious. The stress on strict adherence to the principle of subordinating personal and selfish interests to the general good of the community, might have gone a long way to mould the Humanist in Eliot.

The literary interests of T. S. Eliot, one may assume, were stimulated by his mother who herself was a distinguished writer. He received his early education in that preparatory department of the University which was named Smith Academy. The subjects, he was taught were the essentials: Latin and

---

13. *Ibid.*

14. *Ibid.*

15. Smidt Kristian—*Poetry and Belief in the Work of T. S. Eliot,* p. 2.

16. *Ibid.*

17. *American Literature and American Language,* Appendix, pp. 4-5.

Greek, together with Greek and Roman History, English and American History, elementary mathematics, French, German and English. At this stage, his interest in literature was scanty. He did not imbibe any liking for poetry, till at last, at the age of fourteen, he happened to pick up a copy of Fitzgerald's Omar which ignited in him "a new world of feeling." Eliot recalls that experience:—

> "It was like a sudden conversion; the world appeared anew, painted with bright, delicious and painful colours. Thereupon I took the usual adolescent course with Byron, Shelley, Keats, Rossetti, Swinburne.'"[18]

At the school, he came to know something of the classic poets of Greece and Rome, and he very much enjoyed reciting Homer and Virgil.[19]

Eliot entered Harvard University in 1906 and attracted attention as a writer of verse. It was about this very period that he read John Donne for the first time. He attended the lectures of George Santyana and Irving Babbit. In 1908, he read **The Symbolist Movement in Literature**, written by Arthur Symons which left an indelible impression on his mind and came to him as "a revelation and introduction to wholly new feeling."[20] Speaking of this book, he says, "It is one of those which have affected the course of my life." It was Symons who brought the young boy into literary contact with Laforgue, Rimbaud, Veraline and Corbiere, the French symbolists who radically changed his poetical aspirations.

He spent 1910-11 in Paris, studying French literature and philosophy at Sorboune. After returning to America, he continued the study of philosophy, again at Harvard. He also received some instruction in Sanskrit; read Patanjali's metaphysics; and experienced a "state of enlightened mystification."[21] It was exactly at this time that he began to read Dante with the help of a prose translation of **Divine Comedy**. In the year

---

18. Eliot, T. S.—*The Use of Poetry and the Use of Criticism*, pp. 33-4.
19. Eliot, T. S.—*The Music of Poetry*, p. 26.
20. *The Sacred Wood*, p. 5.
21. Pinto V de S—*Crisis in English Poetry*, p. 182.

1913-14, he was appointed as an assistant in philosophy at Harvard. In the following year, he was awarded a travelling fellowship and was in Germany during the summer before the outbreak of the war. In the following winter, he passed over to Merton College, Oxford, for pursuing his studies in Greek philosophy.[22]

The suggestiveness, idiom and technique of the French Symbolists had inspired new hopes for poetry in Eliot. Having no inclination for the rules of prosody, the classics did not materialise his desire to master verse-technique in English. There was, according to him, no poet either in America or in England who could "contribute to his own education."[23] The only recourse was to "poetry of another age and to poetry of another language."[24] It is in this context that Eliot's stress on Ezra Pound and Laforgue as "technical innovators"[25] is of particular significance. He acknowledges his debt to Jules Laforgue and the later Elizabethan dramatists when he says:

> "The form in which I began to write, in 1908 or 1909, was directly drawn from the study of Laforgue together with the later Elizabethan drama."[26]
>
> "He was the first"; says Eliot, "to teach him the poetic possibilities of his own idiom of speech."[27]

Speaking of Ezra Pound, Eliot summarizes the impact:

> "What is curious, is his complete and isolated superiority as a master of verse form. No one living has practised the art of verse with such austerity and devotion; and no one living has practised it with more success."[28]
>
> "I confess that I am seldom interested in what he is saying, but only in the way he says it."[29]

---

22. Matthiessen, F. O.—*The Achievement of T. S. Eliot,* p. xxi.
23. Ezra Pound—*Literary Essays*: *Introduction.*
24. *Ibid.*
25. Williamson George—*A Reader's Guide to T. S. Eliot,* p. 43.
26. Eliot—*Selected Poems of Ezra Pounds Introduction,* p. viii.
27. *Ibid.*
28. *Eliot—in the Dial.*
29. Smidt Kristian—*Poetry and Belief in the Work of T. S. Eliot,* p. 9.

It sounds paradoxical that Eliot learnt English verse technique from the French poets but the fact that Frenchmen did teach him the craft of verse, gives him another advantage. Obviously, Pound and Laforgue helped Eliot to "liberate himself from the manners exhausted by the Victorian poets and to introduce a new sense of rhythm"[30] into English Poetry.

Some other influences which are easily discernible on Eliot's early works are of the metaphysical poets of the seventeenth century, Baudelaire, Dante, T. E. Hulme, F. H. Bradley and Tristan Corbiere. T. E. Hulme's attack on the "liberal humanist tradition"[31] and his plea for a "dry, hard classical verse",[32] also had an important effect on him. Pinto rightly remarks:

> "Eliot has been to school with French Symbolists, not so much with Mallarme and Veraline, the two poets, who most influenced Yeats and his contemporaries, as with Jules Laforgue and Tristan Corbiere, writers who had evolved a peculiar technique based on the use of rhythms of colloquial speech, imagery drawn from contemporary life and sudden transitions from lyric intensity to terse ironic realism."[33]

The poets of the symbolist group wrote poetry of a different type as compared to that of the Georgian England. It was different in its methods. Its imagery was new and startling. It embraced new aspects of life and the peculiar feature of its imagery was that it worked "by association and juxtaposition and contrast of opposites."[34]

It was this poetry which infused new hopes into the mind of Eliot and it was such poetry, he was looking for. It explored for him a new method, suited to his sensibility. But Eliot had never been a theory-swallower. He followed the pattern established by the French poets, but not their multifarious theories. For instance, he perfected their technique and practised the method of "suggestion instead of statement",

30. Smidt Kristian—*Poetry and Belief in the Work of T. S. Eliot,* p. 9.

31. Pinto V de S—*Crisis in English Poetry,* p. 183.

32. *Ibid.*

33. *Ibid.*

34. Lucy Sean—*T. S. Eliot and The Idea of Tradition,* p. 152.

The Waste Land being the best specimen thereof. He did not adhere to Mallarme's dictum that poetry must always be allusive and never speak directly. **"Ash Wednesday"** and the **"Four Quartets"** signify the fact that direct statement can often form the highest poetry.[35]

Eliot's task was difficult. In the second decade of this century, he was almost alone. The vocabulary, imagery and mood of the Georgian poetry had worn out. Not only this, it had retained a tone ludicrously out of keeping with the time. The touch with life and its different modes had also been lost. The range of its expression, being limited as it was, could only be made to play a stock repertoire of old-fashioned songs.[36]

Eliot's answer to the poetic needs of the age can be best understood from his three contributions: **"Reflections on Verse Libre"; "Tradition and the Individual Talent";** and **"The Functions of Criticism."** These treatises, the **Summum Bonum** of his early criticism, may be interpreted as laying down the foundations of the whole theory of poetry.[37] His **"Reflections on Verse Libre"** brings him directly under the influence of Laforgue, Shakespeare, Webster and Tourneur.[38] He defines the verse libre in his introduction to Pound and qualifies it as having the capacity "to stretch, contract and distort the traditional measures,"[39] in vogue. The second essay **"Tradition and the Individual Talent,"** which may better be called "Eliot's poetic manifesto of 1919," connects him directly with Ezra Pound.[40]

Intellectually, Eliot was a composite product of Harvard, Paris and Oxford. Temperamentally, he was a mystic, given to literature and philosophy. He was also much influenced, then or later, by the prophetic instructions of the Bible and the esoteric teaching of Zoroaster, Buddha and Lao-Tzu. It is not sur-

---

35. Lucy Sean—*T. S. Eliot and The Idea of Tradition,* p. 152.

36. Lucy Sean—*Eliot and the Idea of Tradition,* p. 80.

37. *Ibid,* p. 82.

38. Williamson, *A Reader's Guide to T. S. Eliot,* p. 43.

39. *Ibid.*

40. Smidt Kristian—*Poetry and Belief in the Work of Eliot,* p. 23.

prising that he was also a student, almost a disciple of I. Babbit and G. Santayana.[41] Philologically, Dante, Baudelaire, Goethe, Bradley and Shakespeare are the writers who have inspired Eliot in his search for a new and effective mode of expression.

Dante inspired him in three directions: "developing and refining" the language of his nation, teaching the lesson of "width of emotional range" and "being European."[42] Eliot became interested in Dante and Shakespeare because both of them "gave" as he calls "body to the soul of language,"[43] the one more directly, and the other less consciously.

Eliot was influenced by Baudelaire because of latter's stress on "theological innocence,"[44] on the one hand, and imbibing in his outlook, what he calls "the sense of age,"[45] on the other. Baudelaire's business was not to "practise Christianity" but to "assert its necessity."[46] Eliot pays him the following encomiums:

> "The invention of language at a moment when French poetry in particular was famishing for such invention is enough to make of Baudelaire a great poet. Baudelaire is indeed the greatest exemplar in modern poetry in any language, for his verse and language is the nearest thing to a complete renovation that we have experienced. But his renovation of an attitude towards life is no less radical and no less important."[47]

According to Eliot, the true claim of Baudelaire as an artist is not that he found a superficial form, but that he was searching for a "form of life."[48] Eliot's own endeavours in this respect show a close affinity with the French poet. This "form of life" implies the fusion between the sordidly realistic and the phantasmagoric; the possibility of the juxtaposition of the matter-of-fact and the fantastic. Summing up the com-

---

41. Durrel Lawrence—*Key to Modern Poetry,* p. 134.
42. *Selected Prose*—Dante, p. 195.
43. *Ibid.*
44. *Selected Prose*—Baudelaire, p. 176.
45. *Ibid.*
46. *Ibid.*
47. *Ibid.,* p. 180.
48. *Ibid.*

mon characteristics of Dante, Shakespeare and Goethe, Eliot asserts three traits: Abundance, Amplitude and Unity.[49] It is important to note that the trio in question has left apparent marks on Eliot's poetic growth, as also on his critical development.

Philosophically speaking, Josiah Royce, F. H. Bradley, T. E. Hulme, Middleton Murry and Bergson have exercised considerable influence on the philosophic mind of Eliot. Royce was an extra-ordinary philosopher—a monist and post Kantian idealist. He held the whole universe to be a part of an all-comprehensive Mind, the **Logos** or the **Absolete.** According to him, loyalty was the greatest virtue of the individual, pushing him beyond himself and thus redeeming him for the complete life of reality. In its ultimate analysis, Royce's philosophy was voluntaristic which proclaims order and surrender as the supreme virtues of the individual to work out his salvation.

It was through Royce that Eliot began to take interest in Bradley. The books which made great impact on Eliot were: **Appearance and Reality; The Principles of Logic and Ethical Studies.** Bradley was a disciple of Hegel and Lotze and an ardent believer in the New-Idealism. He does not believe in individual immortality but thinks that individuality is only a passing phase of the final Reality or Absolute as he calls it. Bradley is less of a voluntarist and more of an intellectual. Both of the idealistic philosophies retain their impressions on the mind of Eliot throughout his lifetime, though with some variations.

"Excessive Caution" on the part of Eliot, in dealing with problems of individuality, consciousness and communication, are, according to Mr. Hugh Kenner, the direct result of his study of Bradley's system. Perhaps, even a greater and a far-reaching influence exercised by Bradley, lies in the analogy provided by "Tradition and the Individual Talent." Eliot's stress on the "reality of human situation" and his attempt to discover meaning of the past in tradition is part of his quest for

---

49. *On Poetry and Poets*—p. 213.

the individual to integrate himself with the infinite coherent unity of Reality.[50] This search of the "need of significance" in Eliot is an off-shoot of Bradley's theory of "finite centres." According to this theory, consiousness is contained in closed units, complete in themselves and yet united in the Absolute.

Eliot has praised Bradley for his porse which, according to him, is "excellent and persuasive."[51] He was equally impressed by "the catholic, universal and civilised qualities of his philosophy."[52] He had a liking for Bradley because of the dislike of the latter for extreme positions. According to Eliot, Bradley was a man of "vision and wisdom."[53] Eliot feels that scepticism and disillusion are useful for religious understanding and to that extent, Bradley "had a share too."[54] Eliot's quest for knowledge"; his stress on the "need of significance"; and his "concern with the human situation" may in one way, be interpreted as the corrolaries of Bradley's "theory of knowledge."[55] Eliot's use of the imperatives of "is and seems"; the emphasis on "now and ever"; and the references to "time and timeless" constitute the bulk of the philosophic probes of Eliot, which in their ultimate analysis, suggest his close affinities with the Bradleyan logic of **Appearance and Reality.** On the level of critical theories, propounded by Eliot, Bradleyan influence appears more remarkable. His advocacy of "extinction of personality in Art"; "Dissociation of sensibility" and "sensuous perception of thought" in ordinary experience and poetry are just the part of the same thought, expounded in **"Appearance and Reality."**

Equally significant is the Bergsonian influence on the making of the poet and critic in Eliot. The latter came to know of Bergson when he was studying at Paris in 1910-11. Eliot

---

50. Lucy Sean—*Eliot and the Idea of Tradition,* p. 140.
51. *Selected Essays,* pp. 406-7.
52. Smidt Kristian—*Poetry and Belief in the Work of Eliot,* p. 16.
53. *Selected Essays,* pp. 406-7.
54. *Ibid.*
55. Bradley, F. H.—*Appearance and Reality.*

was so much fascinated by the lectures of Bergson that he reached the venue, sometimes, even one and a half hours earlier than the scheduled time.[56] His early poetry amply displays the traits of Bergson's "conception of distinct qualities in a heterogeneous world." Bergson differentiates, as does Eliot, between two levels of consciousness: intuition and intellect and it is the first that gives experience of "Reality." According to him, consciousness results from the unison of "perception" and "memory." Perception is the surface reflection of the physical or the matter while memory is the synthetic manifestation of the "sub-conscious" or "life of the spirit." Memory in this context, represents something of an "entity" ever present in the process of evolution. It has no relation to the presentness or pastness of time. Different experiences in the life of each individual constitute what Bergson calls "the components of Memory" which in its turn is sorting, eliminating, arranging and regularising these experiences into an integrated whole. Bergson refers to this "organic pattern" as the **durre** of each individual.

Eliot's belief in "different leyels of consciousness"[57] shows remarkable affinity with the Bergsonian conception of **duree.** The "awareness" of Harry in **The Family Reunion** corresponds to Bergson's idea of "intuition"—the main constituent of consciousnness. There appears closeness of approach and resemblance in what Bergson describes as the concept of "Personal memory" and what Eliot terms as the "Historical sense."[58] The former sees memory as modifying the entire being of our past and present while the latter visualises a particular phenomenon in History which involves a perception, not only of the pastness of the past but of its present also. This "simultaneous order"[59] which, in Bergson, is the resultant product of "memory" at the human level, is practically synonymous with the country's "mind" which is the ultimate outcome of "tradition" on

---

56. Smidt Kristian—*Poetry and Belief in the Work of Eliot,* p. 163.

57. Eliot, T. S.—*UPUC,* p. 135.

58. *Selected Prose,* p. 23.

59. *Ibid.*

the national level. In this way, both Bergson and Eliot believe in the continuity of the moments of the past and the present, the major emphasis being on an order, directing as well as being directed, by the spirit of the past and the awareness of the present. Eliot asserts:

> "that the past should be altered by the present as much as the present is directed by the past."[60]

In their ultimate analysis, both Bergson and Eliot are philosophising the role of time in the context of human situation To Bergson, the absolute reality is the present, the past and the future, being intellectual abstractions only. The interminable past and the measureless future are the two facets of the same reality—The Present. Eliot's preoccupation with time displays his basic agreement with Bergson's interpretation of **duree.** Right from his earliest poems to **Four Quartets,** Eliot is developing the theme of Time in various forms. In one of his lyrics in 1905, he is advocating:

> If space and time, as sages say
> Are things that cannot be,
> The fly that lives a single day
> Has lived as long as we.

In Ash Wednesday he says:

> ". . . . I know that time is always time."

In Burnt Norton he stresses:

> Time present and time past
> Are Both perhaps present in time future,
> And time future contained in time past.
> If all time is eternally present
> All time is unredeemable.

In **The Waste Land,** the analysis of the concept of time is symbolised in three figures: Tiresias, Lithuanian woman and the Lady of "A Game of Chess." The first figure shows time as a sequence; the second, as a sort of cyclic repetition embodied by the seasons; and third, as a vast vagueness, unfettered by any direction or order.

Whatever may be the efficacy of the "time-concept"

---

60. Eliot, T. S.—*Selected Prose,* p. 23.

whether in Bergson or in Eliot, it is clear that, to start with, the former provides a plausible philosophy to the latter. But "To be conscious is not to be in time,"[61] does suggest a departure from the Bergsonian concept of **duree.** They show a growing concern with timelessness and imply an earnest desire for finding out the means of redeeming its unredeemableness. It is here that Eliot repudiates Bergson and his theories. Nevertheless, the fact remains that Bergson's philosophy has an exciting influence on the susceptible mind of T. S. Eliot.

Another literary figure and an eminent thinker who had exercised considerable influence on Eliot's work and personality, is T. E. Hulme. Though Eliot never met him, yet reaching London, he found that the literary atmosphere was surcharged with the impact Hulme had left on a coterie of brilliant writers and philosophers. Hulme was a disciplinarian and a classicist. He was a firm believer in the philosophy of "Original Sin" and the inability of man to be perfect:

> "A man is essentially bad, he can only accomplish anything of value by discipline—ethical and political. Order is thus not merely negative, but creative and liberating. Institutions are necessary."[62]

Hulme attracted Eliot, first on the literary plane. It was only after the publication of **Speculations** in 1924, that his religious views could cast an impression on Eliot. Immediately before finishing his doctoral dissertation on Bradley, some poets of the Imagist group had focussed Eliot's attention on the hollowness of the Georgian poetry as also on the need of creating a new style. They had aimed at restoring to poetry, its direct appeal to the senses, mainly to the sense of sight by using clear and visual images. The new style was to prune away unnecessary words and abstract terms. It was in this background that a handful of poems written by Hulme, not only made an indelible impression on Eliot but also suggested a model for the new style which Eliot also was in quest thereof.

---

61. *Burnt Norton.*
62. Hulme, T. E.—*Speculations.*

Hulme's poetic manifesto is clear from the following observations:

> "Poetry always endeavours to arrest you, and make you continuously see a physical thing, to prevent you gliding through an abstract process."[63]

He continues :

> "Plain speech is essentially inaccurate. It is only by new metaphors that it can be made precise."

Hulme is convinced that in poetry "the great aim is accurate, precise and definite description."

He asserts the necessity of a new instrument of poetic expression:

> 'We shall not get any new efflorescence of verse until we get a new technique, a new convention...."

These and other observations show a parallel development of thought in Hulme and Eliot.[64] Hulme's emphasis on concrete situation; his dislike for the abstract; his belief in the "dry classical spirit"[65]; and his earnest desire to recreate a new poetic expression, suited to the sensibility of his own age are pointers which establish Hulme's claim of influencing Eliot in many ways. They indicate the propriety of Eliot's advocacy of "fresh poetic experiment" as well as his reaction against the prevailing loose standards of taste and value. Eliot's efforts in this direction may be regarded as an indispensable part of an "emerging general state of mind."[66]

Speaking of Hulme in **The Criterion** in 1924, Eliot qualified him as "the fore-runner of a new attitude of mind which should be the twentieth century mind, if the twentieth century is to have a mind of its own."[67] "Hulme", he said, "is classical, reactionary and revolutionary; he is the antipodes of the eclectic, tolerant and democratic mind of the end of the last century."[68]

---

63. Hulme, T. E.—*Speculations.*
64. Mathiessen, F. O.—*The Achievement of T. S. Eliot,* p. 71.
65. *Ibid,* p. 33.
66. *Ibid,* p. 71.
67. *Criterion,* April 24, 1924.
68. *Ibid.*

According to Buckley, Hulme's influence is important in three respects. First, "his views impinged upon" Eliot and his generation; second, they are stated with "great fierceness and in an unpleasantly compulsive tone"; and third, they provide an "emphasis and terminology" both of which entered very early into Eliot's work.[69]

Hulme has also influenced Eliot's critical thought in another respect. The thinkers of the nineteenth century had developed what they called the "theory of continuity." They had tried to establish a relation between "the organic and the inorganic" on the one hand and "biology and religion," on the other. Hulme repudiated such relationship and challenged the existence of any continuity between man and nature. In his ultimate analysis, Hulme came to believe in an unbridgeable distance between "man and God" and hence, an "extreme discontinuity." Therefore, he began to advocate a literature alienated from "man, nature and life."[70]

Hulme seems to regard the doctrine of Original Sin as the guiding insight of Christianity and classicism. It holds, that man is "essentially bad."[71] Only discipline and order can recreate something through him. Hulme, in this context, is opposing Renaissance and Post-Renaissance art and literature, because it displays a disregard for the dogma of "Original Sin";[72] and shows an appraisal of new interest in "man, character and personality."[73] He refutes the cult of personality:—

> "The fundamental error is that of placing Perfection in humanity, thus giving rise to that bastard thing Personality, and all the bunkum that follows from it."[74]

Classicism then, paradoxically speaking, is a sort of scornful opposition of vitality, of Personality and of general acceptance of life. And it is here that Eliot's views correspond to that of Hulme. Being a classicist as also a subscriber to the

---

69. Buckley Vincent—*Poetry and Morality,* p. 90.
70. *Speculations.*
71. *Ibid,* p. 13.
72. *Ibid,* p. 25.
73. *Speculations,* p. 33.
74. *Ibid.*

dogma that "man is essentially bad",[75] Eliot directs his main attack on the cult of Personality and Emotion in his critical battle against the nineteenth century. To put it the other way, Eliot's theorising on Order and Impersonality in art appears to be a modified form of Hulme's position on classicism and his dogma of Original Sin. As for Hulme's influence on Eliot, David Daiches says something, very interesting:

> "For Hulme there is classicism (good) and romanticism (bad); abstract or geometrical art (good) and naturalistic art (bad); the religious attitude (good) and humanism (bad); belief in original sin (good); and confidence in man (bad); hard, clear, precise images (good); and the emotional and soft (bad); fancy (good); and imagination (bad); discipline (good) and self-expression (bad); dictatorship or at least royalism (good) and democracy (bad)."[76]

Suffice to note here that these are the collocations but they explain a great deal of the attitude of T. S. Eliot.

The brief survey of various influences on Eliot requires the mentioning of two more literary figures: Middleton Murry and Remy de Gourment. Murry, like Eliot, was a mystic. He struggled very hard to find out a foothold in faith. Eliot was fascinated by Murry when the latter was editing "Athenacum." Some of his earlier essays were written under the direct influence of Murry. But the influence left by Remy de Gourment on Eliot was far greater than of any other artist of the period. Eliot recognises his debt to the French critic who was the first to "bring to light"[77] the contribution made by the French symbolists. Gourment was a believer in Hedonist philosophy. He had a delicate sense for literary style and wanted a cosmopolitan type of culture to develop in Europe as against the narrow traditions, then prevailing. In the preface to **The Sacred Wood,** Eliot pays tributes to Remy de Gourment and acknowledges his debt to his critical writings.[78]

Three years—1919, 1922 and 1927—have played a very significant part in the early development of T. S. Eliot's liter-

---

75. *Selected Essays,* p. 393.
76. Daiches David—*The Present Age,* pp. 123-24.
77. Eliot, T. S.—*The Sacred Wood,* p. viii.
78. *Ibid.*

ary career. In 1919, he brings out his "poetic manifesto" by publishing **"Tradition and the Individual Talent"** and other essays. In 1922, appeared **The Waste Land**—the "poem of the age."[79] In 1927, he accepts the Anglican church and becomes a British subject. It is again in 1922, that the literary world finds a talented critic in Eliot who begins editing the famous literary review—The Criterion. The contacts which he has developed during his tenureship as editor of this review, lasting upto 1939, proved very fruitful to him. His critical writings diversified as they are, go a long way in estalishing the reputation of Eliot as a critic. Not only this, the change from 1919 to 1927 is, in itself, a great change. It marks a new era, a new promise and a new performance. In 1919, the critic in Eliot was referring to "the integrity and autonomy of poetry."[80]. In 1927, he started discussion on the problem of the "relation of poetry to the spiritual and social life of its time and of other times."[81]

The manner and the matter of Eliot's early poetry and criticism is not a mere accident. They are the echoes of the cumulative influence of the age, environment and education in which Eliot's sensitive, catholic and intellectual personality was developed. The greatness of his early poetry lies in the "vision of the age", he has pictured therein. The ordeal, he dedicated himself to, was not of a small magnitude. The falling literary standards had thrown out a challenge. The tone, temper and technique of poetry demanded a radical change. The rituals and rudiments of criticism needed re-orientation. Not only had Eliot understood the nature of the literary mission he was asked to accomplish, he had also shown the necessary will and training by studying closely to the works of Bradley, Laforgue, Pound, Baudelaire, Bergson and Hulme.

Moreover the poet and critic in T. S. Eliot was a simultaneous growth. His criticism and his poetry, his precept and

---

79. Leavis, F. R.—*New Bearings in English Poetry.*

80. Eliot, T. S.—*The Sacred Wood,* Preface.

81. Eliot, T. S.—*The Use of Poetry and The Use of Criticism,* Introduction.

his practice, are interdependent and complementary to each other.[82] "His earlier criticism", to put in Eliot's own language "is a by-product of his private poetry workshop."[83]

Speaking of the indispensability of Pound's critical writings, what Eliot spoke of him, holds equally true in his own case:

> "They began at a moment when they were very much needed: the situation of poetry in 1909 or 1910 was stagnant to a degree difficult for any young poet of today to imagine. Pound himself had a long way to go: and he has gone it."[84]

Eliot, in his literary criticism, may have been inspired by the triple mission he decided to work out: to review the past of literature; to set the poets and the poems in a new order;[85] and to correct taste.[86] However, George Watson has noticed three voices in T. S. Eliot, the critic:

> "These then, are the three voices of Eliot the critic: first, the youthful, exploratory enthusiasm of the Twenties, where, an almost ideal balance between poetic and critical activity is realised; second, an abortive career of social and religious advocacy in frankly obscurantist causes; and third, a bold but exhausted attempt to recover the creative urge, followed at once by denial and desperation."[87]

But irrespective of any such analogy, we should bear in mind the two basic aspects of Eliot's literary criticism: first, his criticism and poetry compose a single "oeuvre",[88] and second, his whole work, as he once noted of Shakespeare's, is in important respects, "one continuous poem."[89]

---

82. Brad Brook, M. C.—*C. F. B. Rajan's—Eliot*: *A Study by Several Hands.*
83. Eliot, T. S.—*On Poetry and Poets,* p. 106.
84. Eliot, T. S.—Introduction: *Literary Essays of Pound,* p. xiii.
85. Eliot, T. S.—*U.P.U.C. Arnold,* p. 108.
86. Eliot, T. S.—*Selected Prose,* p. 18.
87. Watson George—*The Literary Critics,* p. 195.
88. Eliot, T. S.—Introduction: *Literary Essays of Pound,* p. xiii.
89. Kenner Hugh—*T. S. Eliot*: *Collection of Critical Essays,* p. 13.

CHAPTER III

THE CRITIC IN THE TWENTIES

A simple codification of the principles and methods of T. S. Eliot's criticism is not possible. It is because, he is not a literary legislator in the sense Aristotle is considered to be. He does not even dictate as does Dr. Johnson. Unlike Sidney, Eliot does not theorise on the Cult of Poetry. His place is different. He is pre-occupied to create in criticism a new method, more as an initiator than as an inventor. The body of his literary opinions may be compounded from the scattered pronouncements of his prose writings. As a critic, Eliot has his own limitations. He is neither a theoretician of art nor a critic of fundamentals. His criticism is not purely academic; nor is it in any way dogmatic. His love for details; his precision in judgment; and his flexibility to change his mind and ground have rightly installed him at the position of "one of the best arbiters of taste"[1] of our present generations.

Before attempting to analyse the critical efforts of T. S. Eliot in the Twenties, we must bear in mind some of the salient features of his criticism. First, it is significant that in criticism as in poetry, Eliot is the first exponent to give expression to the spirit of his age. Second, what Eliot writes about poetry must be assessed in relation to the poetry he composes. Third, the impact of Eliot's criticism, as also of his poetry, is full of what Eliot himself spoke of Pound's criticism: the "historical perspective."[2] It is through **The Waste Land**, that the elite proclaims him "the poet of the age." And it is by means of

---

1. Smidt Kristian—*Poetry and Belief in the Work of T. S. Eliot,* p. 36.

2. Eliot, T. S.—*Introduction to the Literary Essays of Pound,* p. x.

Reflections on Verse Libre (1917); **Tradition and the Individual Talent** (1919); and **The Functions of Criticism** (1923); that the world became acquainted with Eliot's literary credo. This trio of prose essays forms the main plank of those principles and methods which he sets out to uphold in criticism. In them, we can visualise the whole content of his critical thought and practice. Fourth, it has been said that Eliot speaks with three voices in criticism:[3] the one representing the critic in the Twenties; the second coming out of the humanist in the Thirties; and the third signifying the sobriety of the rationalist in the last phase. But, whatever be the logic, there is still an underlying synthesis of the same outlook manifesting itself in each voice. His literary career possesses an essential unity.[4] In this context, it is of vital importance that Eliot's critical mind displays an organic growth of maturity, flexibility and understanding. In spite of some inconsistencies and contradictions in his opinions, there appears to be present, a well sustained and moderately defined current of values in the entire body of his criticism. The way Eliot modified his judgments in relation to Arnold, Milton and Kipling, amply substantiates this point of view. Fifth, Eliot's literary effort is directed by a firm belief in the "creative" and "critical" faculties, working simultaneously in the artist. He maintains that "there is a significant relation between the best poetry and the best criticism of the same period."[5] According to him, the age of criticism is also the age of critical poetry.

Lastly, Eliot is a critic of poise and order. He embodies a constructive attitude towards the problems of art and literature. He stands for the ideal of objective criticism of the work rather than of the writer. His efforts are directed to "bring the poet back to life." He means the poetry and not the man. No doubt, he spearheads the attack on the "old order" of the Victorian and Georgian literature, he has never

---

3. Watson George—*The Literary Critics,* p. 195.

4. Brooks Cleanth—*Eliot: Thinker and Artist.* C. F. Eliot—*The Man and His Work,* p. 316.

5. Eliot, T. S.—*The Use of Poetry and the Use of Criticism,* p. 30.

advocated disorder as was misconstrued and misinterpreted in certain quarters. In fact, he happens to be the teacher of a new order which envisages a stricter discipline as compared to that of the old order.

His opposition to Romanticism and Victorianism is inspired by the twin ideals of his literary criticism: objectivity and order. He voices his strong reaction against the gross emotionalism of the romanticists, their rule-lessness and sheer private judgments of "meeting by oneself in one's own house."[6] He is opposed to most of the Victorians because of their sense of complacency; love for status-quo; and lack of sensitiveness to poetic values. He carries a tirade against the Georgian literature because it is moribund, dead, and unrealistic. The whole climate of the period prior to him, rebounds with sterility and lack of reality, unprecedented before.

Eliot calls the romantic generation as "belonging to the numbers of the great heretics of all times."[7] He charges them on three counts. First, they failed to distinguish what Prof. Richards suggests in **Science and Poetry** "intuition of an emotion from an intuition by it."[8] Second, they philosophised their own poetic insight rather than used it. Third, their faults and limitations cannot be separated from their greatness. Eliot shows his dislike for "Keats' egotism",[9] but calls it "that of youth which time would have redeemed."[10] He blames Shelley for borrowing "shabby ideals"[11] and then "muddling them up with his own intuition."[12] He argues further that his positive dislike for some of Shelley's views "hampers enjoyment of the poems in which they occur."[13] "What complicates the problem still further"; says Eliot, "is that in poetry so fluent as Shelley's, there is a good deal which is just bad

---

6. Saintsbury—*A Short History of English Criticism,* p. 413.
7. Eliot, T. S.—*U.P.U.C.,* p. 100.
8. *Ibid,* p. 99.
9. *Ibid,* p. 100.
10. *Ibid.*
11. *Ibid.*
12. *Ibid.*
13. *Ibid,* p. 91.

jingling."[14] Finally, he alleges that Shelley is an "eighteenth century rationalist and a cloudy Platonist."[15]

Eliot refers to the criticism of Wordsworth and Coleridge as "the criticism of an age of change."[16] He calls the two critics "just as eighteenth century as anybody"[17] in their appraisal of John Donne, except that, where the eighteenth century critics spoke of lack of elegance, the Lake poets found lack of passion. He continues:

> "much of the poetry of Wordsworth and Coleridge is just as turgid and artificial and elegant as any eighteenth century diehard could wish."[18]

Eliot attacks the theory of "Willing suspension of disbelief" and asserts that though Coleridge points out an important fact, yet not "quite in the happiest terms."[19] He is of the opinion that if one is reading well, the question of belief and disbelief in the intellectual sense, never arises: He suggests:

> "If unfortunately, it does arise, either through the poet's fault or our own, we have for the moment ceased to be reading and have become astronomers, or theologians, or moralists, persons engaged in quite a different type of activity."[20]

He also raises strong objections against Poetry as "emotion recollected in tranquillity" and says, "it will not do to talk of, which is only one poet's account of his recollection of his own methods."[21] Speaking of the metaphysical interests of Coleridge in his literary criticism, Eliot qualifies it as "an affair of his emotions";[22] which, in its ultimate analysis, blurs critical faculty and directs Coleridge "into a metaphysical hare and hounds."[23] As a consequence, the centre of interest

---

14. Eliot, T. S.—*U.P.U.C.*, p. 91.
15. *Ibid.*
16. *Ibid*, p. 81.
17. *Ibid*, p. 72.
18. *Ibid.*
19. *Ibid*, p. 95.
20. *Ibid*, p. 96.
21. Eliot, T. S.—*The Sacred Wood*, preface, p. ix.
22. *Ibid*, p. 12.
23. *The Sacred Wood*, p. 13.

changes and the critic is lost in something else which can neither be the work of art; nor can it bring its enjoyment. According to Eliot, this is a great drawback in Coleridge which results from the "pernicious effect of emotion."[24] Hence, Eliot remarks that Coleridge is more philosophic than Aristotle but in the derogatory sense.[25]

Among the Victorians, it is Arnold who has to face the brunt of his attacks. He refers to Arnold as belonging to a "period of stasis."[26] Secondly, he lacks vision and imagination and "hardly looks ahead to the new stage of experience."[27] Thirdly, though he speaks of discipline, it is the discipline of culture and not the "discipline of suffering."[28] Eliot refers to the limited range of Arnold's poetic insight. He picks up one of his commendatory remarks for Burns which said, "no one can deny that it is of advantage to a poet to deal with a beautiful world", and retorts:—

> "But the essential advantage for a poet is not, to have a beautiful world with which to deal: it is to be able to see beneath both beauty and ugliness; to see the boredom and the horror and the glory."[29]

But Eliot adds:—

> "The vision of the horror and the glory was denied to Arnold but he knew something of the boredom."[30]

According to Eliot, Arnold's taste is not comprehensive. Arnoldian criticism of the Romantic poets, says Eliot, is "tinged by his own uncertainty, his own apprehensions and his own beliefs", and it is very much influenced by his own religious attitude.[31] Apart from this, Eliot objects to the Arnoldian method in criticism and alleges that it lacks the precision of Johnson and makes his critical judgments "too reflective, too

---

24. *The Sacred Wood,* p. 13.
25. *Ibid.*
26. Eliot, T. S.–*U.P.U.C.,* p. 103.
27. *Ibid.*
28. *Ibid,* p. 106.
29. *Ibid.*
30. *Ibid.*
31. *Ibid.,* p. 103.

ruminative to rise ever to the first-rank."[32]

At this stage, it appears necessary to correct a misgiving which may arise from the present discussion. Eliot is not all opposition to the Romantics and the Victorians. What he is opposed to, is their vagueness and emotionalism. He criticises the romantics because they are driven to judge by their fading inner lights alone. Naturally, Eliot given to objectivity and order as he is, exposes the sham in them.

Eliot's assessment of the preceding critics is not biased. His endeavours appear to be motivated by objective standards of critical thought and value. He is not against this or that critic. What he attacks is not the critic or the poet but certain inexactitudes latent in their works. If required, Eliot is generally liberal in his praise. He commends Wordsworth's theory of poetic diction;[33] appreciates Keats for "his occupations only with the highest use of poetry";[34] and calls Arnold "the most satisfactory man of letters of his age" whom he says, "we cannot afford to neglect."[35] He clarifies his own position:—

> "Each generation, like each individual, brings to the contemplation of art its own categories of appreciation, makes its own demands upon art, and had its own uses of art......Hence each new master of criticism performs a useful service merely by the fact that his errors are of a different kind from the last; and the longer the sequence of critics we have, the greater amount of correction is possible."[36]

Eliot's stress on the thorough study of the art of each generation and the relative utility of the errors of subsequent critics as a means of correction and qualification of literary values, brings us close to his theory of tradition. His essay on **"Tradition and the Individual Talent"** which was published in 1919, forms the **Locus classics** of his principles of literary criticism. Its basic theme runs through the entire body of his literary activity. This essay coupled with **"The Functions of**

32. Eliot, T. S.—*The Sacred Wood,* p. 43.
33. Eliot, T. S.—*U.P.U.C.,* p. 67.
34. *Ibid,* p. 102.
35. *Ibid.*
36. *Ibid.,* p. 109.

Criticism" brought out in 1923, solemnly declares the purpose, principles and methods he proposes to establish in literary criticism. Tradition with Eliot is not the maintenance of certain dogmas and beliefs. It has a wider meaning and significance. In fact, all his literary effort is deeply rooted in his ideas of tradition. These ideas are scattered through his writings, yet they present a unified thought and integral system. From the beginning till late in Eliot's career, the whole vision of life and literature is predominantly inspired by his own notions of tradition. For example, he says in **After Strange Gods:**—

> "What I mean by tradition involves all those habitual actions, habits, and customs, from the most significant religious rite to our conventional way of greeting a stranger, which represent the blood kinship of 'the same people living in the same place'."[37]

Here, Eliot does not mean a sentimental attitude towards the past. He neither favours, clinging to "unessentials" nor does he advocate hostility to "change." He is for the preservation of the real and the vital in the past. It is this vitality which, according to Eliot, must be maintained in order to stimulate life. In this context, tradition is not "feeling" only, but a concern of "intellect" also. The loss of such traditional values amounts to the loss of vitality, hence, of life. Therefore, he asserts: "By loosing tradition we loose our hold on the persent."[38]

In literature, as in the life of people, Eliot restates the same point:—

> "Tradition cannot be inherited, and if you want it, you must obtain it by great labour. It involves, in the first place, the historical sense, which we may call nearly indispensable to anyone, who would continue to be a poet beyond his twenty-fifth-year; and the historical sense involves a perception, not only of the pastness of the past, but of its presence; the historical sense compels a man to write not merely with his own generation in his bones, but with a feeling that the whole literature of Europe from Homer and within it, the whole of the

37. *After Strange Gods,* p. 18.
38. *The Sacred Wood,* p. 62.

literature of his own country has a simultaneous existence and composes a simultaneous order."[39]

Eliot has made important observations. He says that literary tradition is not a matter of inheritance. Only the persistent efforts can obtain it. A maturer poet must imbibe in him the "historical sense"—the life breath of tradition. It is this sense of history which interconnects the past, the present and the future. The historical sense again paves the way for a close intercommunion or interfusion between the classics on the one hand, and the literature of the writers' own country, on the other. It broadens the mental horizons of the artist; functions as a sort of discipline for him; and stimulates a process of creative activity—genuinely novel, highly artistic and completely objective. In the ultimate analysis, this sense of the pastness of the past as also of its presentness—the very essence of literary tradition—makes the artist feel the current of the whole of a literature which is essentially "one" and steadily "living." As a result of this feeling, the "creative" as well as "critical" genius strives for perfection in literary standards and values.

In **The Music of Poetry**, published in 1942, Eliot repeats the same assertion:—

"Concern with the future requires a concern with the past also; for in order to know, what there is to be done, we need a pretty accurate knowledge of what has been done already and this again leads to the examination of those principles and conditions which hold good always."[40]

The true sense of tradition in this respect is, according to Eliot, a must for an artist aspiring to improve literary values of art which may vary from the technical to the fundamental. The programmatic interest in the future will naturally kindle in a conscientious mind, an urge for the pragmatic analysis of the past, opening thus, new vistas of critical efforts, patterns and mothods. But the most emphatic assertion for preserving tradition is made by Eliot in the introduction to **The Sacred Wood:**—

"It is part of the business of the critic to preserve tradition—

39. Selected Prose: *Tradition and The Individual Talent,* p. 23.
40. Eliot, T. S.–O.P.P.: *The Music of Poetry,* p. 26.

where a good tradition exists. It is part of his business to see literature steadily and see it as a whole; but this is eminently to see it not as consecrated by time but see it beyond time."[41]

Eliot is prescribing here, a code for the literary critic. He is asking the critic to preserve tradition and thus equip himself with the necessary artistic vision to elucidate any work of art. The knowledge of the past brings forth precise models and standards to serve as tools for making comparative study of the present ones. Another important task which the critic is expected to do is to correct and qualify literature of the present by means of his knowledge of the past.

This kind of organic vision of literature establishes a living relationship of the present artist with those of the past. He is brought in the company of the **dead** for the purpose of evaluation which cannot be made in isolation. Eliot says, that no poet or artist of any art has his complete meaning alone. His appreciation is the appreciation of his relation to the dead poets and artists. In order to evaluate him, we must set him for **contrast and comparison.** "I mean this", declares Eliot, "as a principle of aesthetic, not merely historical criticism."[42]

The declaration involves some fundamental implications: First, the artist is to be judged by the standards of the past. Second, it is going to be a "judgment", not "amputation."[43] Third, the judgment is not either final or for good, bad and worse.[44] Fourth, it is only a sort of comparison where two things are measured by each other. Lastly, the canons applied for measuring the artist must not be of the **dead** critics.[45] The emphasis on the word dead here, is of special significance.

But there are ambiguities which still remain unexplained. First, that Eliot talks of the standards of the past but does not refer to contemporary standards. Second, the judgment being not "final, good, bad or worse", appears a remote possibility. Third, the adjective **"dead"** qualifying the critics has

41. Eliot, T. S.—*The Sacred Wood*: Introduction, xv.
42. *Selected Prose,* p. 23.
43. *Ibid,* p. 24.
44. *Ibid.*
45. *Ibid.*

not been clarified. May be, Eliot is thinking of the changes in the types and standards of literature as a result of the changes in the sensibility of the age. What he suggests is perhaps this phenomenon which any critic must take into account. For instance, application of romantic canons in judging the Augustan literature, would be of no use.

Tradition, therefore, is the living spirit of critical activity. The important critic is always absorbed in the present problems of art. He is the person who assimilates in his thought and technique, the consciousness of the past. He must be conversant with the "main current",[46] flowing invariably even through ordinary reputations. According to Eliot, such grasp of the past empowers any critic to solve his present problems. It is in this sense, that the pastness of the past bears its direct impact on the present. Hence, Eliot comes to believe that a common and continuous strain of literary tradition is running through the veins of the Past, the Present and the Future.

In short, Eliot's final position, in the matter of tradition is that a concern for the future, generated by the present, necessitates a concern for the past. The standards of the past provide matter and manner for the present. The present is also engaged in a similar activity, though in a different way. In the form of new works of art, it is making its own contribution towards the heritage of the past. As a result, the pastness of the past also appears in a process of alteration—an alteration which each new work of art stimulates. Therefore Eliot comes to the general conclusion that the past should be altered by the present as much as the present is directed by the past.[47] This organic vision of great art as a whole is the resultant product of what Eliot repeatedly claims, the "living sense of tradition."

If, on the one extreme, Eliot stresses on the indispensability of Tradition, on the other, he strongly voices his opposition to the preponderance of individualism. In his essay,

---

46. *Selected Prose* (Penguin), p. 25.
47. S.P., p. 23.

"Tradition and the Individual Talent", Eliot develops what is popularly known as The Impersonal Theory of Art:—

> "The poet must be aware that the mind of Europe—the mind of his own country—a mind which he learns in time to be much more important than his private mind—is a mind which changes, and that this change is a development which abandons nothing enroute."[48]

He continues:—

> "The poet must continue to develop his consciousness of the past throughout his career" which means "a continual surrender of himself as he is at the moment to something which is more valuable."[49]

He goes on:—

> "The progress of an artist is a continual self-sacrifice, a continual extinction of personality."[50]

He concludes:—

> "It is in this depersonalisation that art may be said to approach the condition of Science."[51]

He repeates:—

> "There is accordingly something outside of the artist to which he owes allegiance, a devotion to which he must surrender and sacrifice himself in order to earn and to obtain his unique position."[52]

In the extracts quoted above, Eliot has made some very significant observations. He demands from the poet an awareness of the mind, viewed not from a limited perspective, but from a broader one. He prescribes that the poet must aim at something higher to which his efforts must be directed all his life. He must develop in him, an ever increasing consciousness of the past and his personal emotions must be objectified entirely therein. This depersonalisation of the artist, according to Eliot, is the pre-requisite of art that is natural, concrete and real.

---

48. S.P., p. 24.
49. *Ibid,* p. 25.
50. *Ibid.*
51. *Ibid.*
52. *Ibid.*

Eliot lays stress on two aspects of his Impersonal theory of poetry: first, the conception of poetry as a living whole, viz., the relation of one poem to other poems by other authors; secondly, the relation of the poem to its own author. He advocates that honest criticism and sensitive appreciation is directed not upon the poet but upon his poetry. He pours scorn over the knack of fact-finding in contemporary criticism; "inquiring into the number of times giraffes are mentioned in the English novel." He denounces in categorical terms that "the discovery of Shakespeare's laundry bills would not be of much use to us." Biographical satistics can be of some advantage but they can never be literary criticism. Eliot's position in the early stages is one of reaction and re-assessment. He reacts to the vogue of romantic emotionalism and condemns the Historical and the Biographical types of literary criticism. His concern for impersonality in art is the immediate result of his concern for reassessment. In order to clarify his position, he uses the oft-repeated analogy of the catalyst:—

> "The mind of the poet is the shred of platinum. It may partly or exclusively operate upon the experience of the man himself; but the more perfect the artist, the more completely separate in him will be the man who suffers and the mind which creates."[53]

The word "emotion", occurring so frequently in Eliot's criticism is, in fact, very baffling. Eliot, from the beginning, is against the poetry of emotions. He calls emotions recollected in tranquillity an "inexact formula."[54] It is his search for "human significance", that stimulates his interest in ordering of the emotions. He is opposed to the emotions exercising a despotic hold over human action. He wants to depersonalise them.

In the process of depersonalisation or objectification of emotion, it is the intellect which holds the key:—

> "The poet's mind is a receptacle for seizing and storing up numberless feelings, phrases, images, which remain there until all the particles which can unite to form a new compound are present together."[55]

53. S.P., p. 26.
54. *Ibid*, p. 29.
55. *Ibid*, p. 27.

The new compound as pointed out by Eliot is to result in what he qualifies as "the new art emotion."[56] Its final emergence will take place by a process of spontaneous fusion, which the poet's mind regulates like a catalyst. According to Eliot, "great variety"[57] is possible in the process of transmutation of these emotions.

But he emphatically declares that the greatness of the fusion does not lie in the intensity of the emotions—the components—but in the "artistic process, the pressure so to speak under which the fusion takes place."[58] The intensity of such an artistic pressure appears to involve question of technique, which in Eliot's view is never "conscious."[59] It results from some ecstatic mood alienated from the sphere of reason. Eliot cites the example of Keats:—

> "The Ode of Keats contains a number of feelings which have nothing particular to do with the nightingale, but which the nightingale, partly perhaps because of its attractive name, and partly because of its reputation, served to bring together."[60]

Certainly the genesis of Keats' feelings is like parallel lines meeting at infinity. The riddle is not possible to explain. To Eliot, it is a sort of concentration which does not happen "consciously or of deliberation."[61]

Eliot's emphasis on depersonalisation of emotions in poetry is born, perhaps, out of a deep skepticism and distrust for individual personality. In this respect, he might have been influenced by Hulme's doctrine of original Sin and man's inability to reach perfection. Eliot acknowledges this fact when he says:—

> "the point of view I am struggling to attack is perhaps related to the metaphysical theory of the substantial unity of the soul: for my meaning is, that the poet has, not a "personality" to express, but a particular medium, which is only a medium and not a personality."[62]

56. S.P., p. 29.
57. *Ibid,* p. 27.
58. *Ibid,* p. 25.
59. *Ibid,* p. 29.
60. *Ibid,* p. 27.
61. *Ibid,* p. 29.
62. *Ibid,* p. 27.

In this medium, different permutations and combinations are regularly formed out of impressions and experiences of the poet. Eliot is of the opinion that even "very ordinary experiences may find their place in poetry",[63] while the important ones remain negligible. And impressions, significant from the point of view of man in the poet, may be of little or of no importance for the poet in him.

Eilot's "Impersonal Theory of Art" does not envisage a total negation of emotions in poetry. What he is after, is a process of their objectification. The significance of a poet does not lie in the nature or the variety of his personal emotions. His personal emotions may be simple, crude or flat while the emotions in his poetry will be a complex affair. Eliot is against hunting after novelty of emotions in poetry. He explains:—

> "The business of the poet is not to find new emotions, but to use the ordinary ones and in working them up into poetry, to express feelings which are not in actual emotions at all."[64]

In fact, he is propounding what he qualifies as "a new art emotion", which in its very nature is impersonal.

And this impersonality, according to Eliot, cannot be achieved unless the poet surrenders himself wholly to the work, which he proposes to do. He concludes:—

> "Poetry is not a turning loose of emotion, but an escape from emotion; it is not the expression of personality, but an escape from personality."[65]

Which means that Eliot stands for the neutralisation of personal emotions rather than their total negation or erasion. He wants their ordering through an artistic process, so that their despotic effects in human actions are brought under control. In their depersonalisation, he visualises the birth of a "now art emotion"—the fusion of emotion and feeling directed by the mind. But his repeated obsession with "extinction of personality" as a pre-condition of great art, takes him to an extreme that is hardly tenable. It is a position from which

63. *Ibid.*
64. S.P., p. 29.
65. *Ibid,* p. 29.

Eliot had to retreat in his later criticism.[66] He had to reconcile himself to a moderate point of view.

Eliot's re-interpretation of emotion and its function in poetry leads us directly to his study of the Metaphysical poets and the Jacobean dramatists. He praises these poets and dramatists by expounding the theory of "Dissociation of Sensibility." He accounts for the verbal and sensuous abundance of the Elizabethan and Jacobean dramatists and the metaphysical poets through the invocation of feeling and sensibility. According to Eliot, they possess a mechanism of sensibility, powerful enough to devour any experience. He compares them to Dante, Cavalcanti and Cino. He laments the decline of this sensibility in the Seventeenth century and says:—

> "In the seventeenth century a dissociation of sensibility set in from which we have never recovered."[67]

The loss, he specifically characterises, is that "with the language becoming more refined, the feeling became more crude."[68] Referring to Tennyson, Browning and Donne, Eliot elaborates the same theme. The first two are poets and they think; but they do not feel their thought "as immediately as the odour of a rose."[69] On the other hand, Donne to Eliot is an intellectual poet. A thought to him was an experience, which modified his sensibility. Eliot praises the "massive music of Donne";[70] and feels that Johnsonian criticism against him must be broken up. Besides, these poets—Donne, Crashaw, Vaughan, Herbert, Lord Herbert, Marvell, King and Cowley—in all their difference of kind and degree, be rehabilitated, in their true perspective.[71] Eliot registers one of the most successful pleas in the court of literature when he declares that the metaphysical poets, at their best "are in the direct current of English poetry."[72] According to him, the

66. *Ibid,* p. 186.
67. *Selected Prose,* p. 111.
68. *Ibid.*
69. *Ibid,* p. 110.
70. *Ibid,* p. 114.
71. *Ibid,* p. 113.
72. *Ibid.*

adjectives such as "quaint", "obscure" and "eccentric" should not be used to describe their qualities. The modern poets, he suggests, must follow the line and example of the metaphysicals. Eliot sounds a note of caution:—

> "Those who object to the 'artificiality' of Milton or Dryden, sometimes tell us 'to look into our hearts and write.' But that is not looking deep enough; Racine or Donne looked into a good deal more than the heart. One must look into the cerebral cortex, the nervous system and the digestive tracts."[73]

Eliot's concept of "dissociation of sensibility" is further clarified by his remarks that "the poets in the sentimental age thought and felt by fits and reflected."[74] Eliot feels that the process of unification of sensibility which started with the Elizabethans and the Jacobeans; and which was continued by the Metaphysicals, could not be carried further by the succeeding generation of poets. The result was that the poets grew less comprehensive, less allusive, and more direct. They could neither force, nor dislocate, even if necessary, language into their meaning. They grew unbalanced and started ruminating. It is in this context that Eliot's resurrection of the metaphysical poets and his insistence to copy their mode and pattern, are of great importance.

Thus, Eliot's appraisal of the Metaphysicals, in the light of sensibility highlights one of the significant aspects of his early criticism—the role of intellect in the process of poetry. Eliot lays emphasis on the merging of the intellect with the senses. The intellectual poet is able to feel his thought immediately. He is capable of a "direct sensuous apprehension of thought, or a recreation of thought into feeling."[75] According to Eliot, the moment, a poet begins to ruminate, his thoughts are divorced from his feelings. Sensibility to Eliot is obviously something in which feeling and thought are used as "dual and inseparable agents not only of perception but also of poetic creation."[76] A poem in this way tends to be a precise way

73. *Ibid.*
74. *Ibid,* p. 111.
75. *Ibid.*
76. Buckley Vincent—*Poetry and Morality,* p. 102.

of feeling and thinking. The function of the poet is to bring the resources of feeling, thought and language to bear on his subject in such a way as to present an actuality. Therefore, Eliot stresses on the need of separating the man from the artist, because, in that case, the chance of emotion entering in an undisguised form, and distorting or deflecting the feeling, would be very meagre. Eliot assigns a primary place to thought and feeling in the process of poetry while emotion, though important as the subject of poetry, has no say in the artistic process of its shaping. The role of emotion in this sense is secondary, disguised and dormant. The importance of the artistic process is two fold: first, to dramatise emotions; and second, to externalise them, by making them surrender before sensibility, "acting as judge and maker."[77] The description of such artistic process is contained in his famous analogy on the "Objective Correlative."

> "The only way of expressing emotion in the form of art is by finding an 'objective correlative'; in other words, a set of objects, a situation, a chain of events, which shall be the formula of that particular emotion; such that when the external facts, which must terminate in sensory experience, are given, the emotion is immediately evoked. If you examine any of Shakespeare's more successful tragedies, you will find this exact equivalence; you will find that the state of mind of Lady Macbeth walking in her sleep has been communicated to you by a skilful accumulation of imagined sensory impressions..... The artistic inevitability lies in this complete adequacy of the external to the emotion and this is precisely what is deficient in Hamlet."[78]

The whole passage shows Eliot's concern for doing away with the adverse effects of emotion in poetry. He does not want it to manifest itself in a direct way. He aims at its dramatisation or objectification, to be achieved by the power of feeling. Emotion in this context ceases to be an agent of creation and becomes the compound of a poem. It is a set of objects, a situation, or chain of events, which shall reflect in a concrete manner, the image of a particular emotion. This image again shall be invoked through the sensory experience

77. *Ibid,* p. 106.

78. Selected Prose, Hamlet, p. 102.

and in terms of feeling. Thus feeling has to embody, a sense of emotion, a sense of language and a sense of actuality of life and its significance. A correlative or symbol—an object, situation or event—of this type can express an objective observation in terms of a subjective experience and a general truth in terms of subjective truth. The emotion is made concrete or idolised in a different way than that experienced by the poet. The triumph of Samson Agonistes lies in Milton's complete success in finding there a dramatic situation that would externalise his own emotions and give them universal stature.[79] Hamlet is an artistic failure because the essential emotion of the play—the feeling of a son towards a guilty mother—could not be objectified. Eliot, therefore, makes a categorical declaration:—

> "In the character Hamlet, it is the buffoonery of an emotion which can find no outlet in action; in the dramatist it is the buffoonery of an emotion which he cannot express in art."[80]

The objectification of emotion appears to involve three stages: first, the actual experience; second, the attitude of the poet formed out of that and similar experiences; and third, a universalised outlook representing the spirit of the age. The second and the third stages are marked by personal and general attitudes respectively. In many poems, when both the attitudes appear, they exhibit double meanings. The surface displays the objectified meaning, but at the bottom, there lies "the meaning which is generalised while still belonging to the poet."[81] **The Waste Land** in this respect incorporates meanings at both the levels. It shows a sense of general disillusionment on the one hand, and the poet's personal feelings, on the other.

In his concept of objective correlative, Eliot appears to have been influenced by the visual imagery of Dante, the precise descriptions of Hulme, and the condensed expressions of Ezra Pound. The expression such as:—

---

79. Matthiessen, F. O.—*The Achievement of T. S. Eliot,* p. 58.

80. Seletced Prose, (Penguin), p. 103.

81. Smidt Kristian—*Poetry and Belief in the Work of T. S. Eliot,* p. 42.

"I have measured out my life with Coffee spoons" shows a close affinity of Eliot with Pound's definition of an "Image" as "presenting an intellectual and emotional complex in an instant of time."[82] This amalgam of intellectual and emotional complex, corresponds to Eliot's notion of "emotional equivalent of thought" as the main concern of the poet. Eliot, on the one extreme, is against emotions exercising an undue hold on the poet; but on the other, he is equally hostile to over-intellectualisation in poetry. In fact, he deems poetry a presentation of thought and feeling by means of "events in human action, or objects in the external world." Eliot's remarks about the Metaphysicals being engaged in the task of finding out "verbal equivalent for states of mind and feeling"[83] explain his position vis-a-vis the concept of objective correlative. The reference to "states of mind and feeling" suggests that Eliot is minimizing the interplay of pure emotion, personal to the poet,[84] which ultimately brings us back to his Theory of Impersonality in art.

All of Eliot's literary theorisation, in the beginning, is idealised by a missionary desire for what he declares in the essay **"The Functions of Criticism"** (1923) as "the correction of taste."[85] He dissects not only the body of criticism but operates the critic also. He acknowledges, that it is difficult to eject impostors from the domain of criticism, which is no better than "a Sunday park of contending and contentious orators."[86] He prescribes that in order to justify his existence, the critic should discipline his personal "cranks and prejudices."[87] He eulogises that the end of criticism is the "elucidation of works of art." Elucidation is not interpretation in the ordinary sense of the word. In Eliot's version, legitimate interpretation is "merely putting the reader in possession of

82. Matthiessen, F. O.—*The Achievements of T. S. Eliot,* p. 61.
83. Selected Essays, p. 248.
84. Brooks Cleanth—*Literary Criticism,* p. 669.
85. *Selected Prose* (Penguin), p. 18.
86. *Ibid.*
87. *Ibid,* p. 19.

facts, which he would otherwise, have missed."[88] He is against any such method, or mode of interpretation, which prejudices the mind of the readers. He advocates presentation of simple kind of facts about a work—its conditions, its setting, its genesis—to develop right liking. Eliot shows his dislike for cheap critical literature, which in the long run, corrupts literary standard and taste. He is opposed to the supply of literature of "opinion and fancy",[89] but exhibits an extraordinary interest in furnishing facts of a piece of art. He asserts:—

> "And any books, any essay, any note in Notes and Queries, which produces a fact even of the lowest order about a work of art is a better piece of work than nine-tenths of the most pretentious critical journalism, in journals or in books."[90]

The reasons, he gives, are two-fold: first, the multiplication of critical books and essays vitiates taste for reading about works of art instead of reading the works themselves; second, they may supply opinion but do not educate taste."[91]

In the same essay—**The Functions of Criticism**—Eliot qualifies comparison and analysis as the chief tools of the critic. These tools, he observes, must be handled with care. They need only "the cadavers on the table" as against interpretation requiring "to produce parts of the body from its pockets."[92] But Eliot is emphatic to make a declaration as to the use of cadavers. "The ancients", he says, "open the gates as guides, not commanders."[93] He implores us to give Aristotle and others their dues, to the extent they inculcate interest for making further discoveries of truth. They suggest and enforce a method of comparison and analysis, which if repeatedly applied to the original, sharpens objectivity; enhances competency; and broadens insight and understanding.[94] The classics, in this context, open new vistas of art and reassert its values. They educate taste: both critical and creative.

88. S.P., p. 20.
89. *Ibid.*
90. *Ibid,* p. 19.
91. *Ibid,* p. 20
92. *Ibid.*
93. Eliot, T. S.–U.P.U.C., p. 48.
94. *Selectd Prose,* p. 32.

Criticism, then, is more a matter of taste than merely a set of hard and fast rules. Taste implies insight and perception which may vary from critic to critic. It depends upon the sensibility of the individual critics, which, according to Eliot, must be developed through a process of experience and discipline, spread over to a long span of time and labour. Again, this process of experience is not merely the "sum of the experiences of good poems."[95] Its first requisite is its "ability to select a good new poem and to respond properly to a new situation."[96] Secondly, it involves organisation of all such experiences in poetry. Eliot says:—

> "There is not one of us who is born with, or who suddenly acquires at puberty or later, an infallible discrimination and taste. The person whose experience is limited is always liable to be taken in by the sham or the adulterate article."[97]

Then, the critical sense, in Eliot's view, is the amalgam of "an innate and developed taste."[98] A limited experience is liable to lead to immature judgments. It would adversely effect the critic and his criticism. Therefore, Eliot offers an integrated plan for the development of taste in poetry.[99] He makes certain generalisations on the basis of his own experience. He feels that the majority of children up to say twelve or fourteen, are capable of a certain enjoyment of poetry. At or about puberty, a small minority of them shows a craving for poetry. At the age of nineteen or twenty—a time of rapid assimilation—the poem or the poetry of a single poet invades the youthful consciousness and assumes complete possession. The final or the mature stage of enjoyment of poetry comes when one ceases to identify oneself with the poet; and becomes aware of one's critical faculties. The poem, at this stage, has "its own existence",[100] apart from the reader, who is able now to distinguish between various degrees of greatness in poetry.

---

95. Eliot, T. S.–U.P.U.C., p. 18.
96. *Ibid,* p. 18.
97. *Ibid.*
98. Lucy Sean–*Eliot and the Idea of Tradition,* p. 50.
99. Eliot, T. S.–U.P.U.C., p. 32.
100. U.P.U.C., p. 32.

Eliot is of the view, that recommending poetry, uncongenial to the degree of maturity in the readers, would be of no use. It would "deaden their sensibility" to poetry and confound the genuine development of taste with its sham acquisition. He states the same point in a categorical manner:—

> "that to have better 'taste' in poetry than belongs to one's state of development, is not to 'taste' anything at all."[101]

Eliot's concern for preserving tradition and correcting taste is motivated by one and the same desire for "setting the poets and poems in a new order."[102] Through his endeavours, he envisages the creation of new poets and critics. Eliot's stress on the development of taste vis-a-vis the continuity of literature and its essential greatness is part of the critic's business to see the "literary past" as a whole. In this context, tradition and taste appear to be the two facets of the same coin. Eliot strikes a balance between the two, when he says:—

> "One function of criticism is to act as a kind of Cog regulating the rate of change of literary taste, when the Cog sticks and reviewers remain fast in the taste of a previous generation, the machine needs to be ruthlessly dismantled and reassembled; when it slips and the reviewer accepts novelty as a sufficient criterion of excellence the machine needs to be stopped and tightened up."[103]

It means that the faults of either of the extremes—the "antiquation of the old" and the "eccentricity of the new"—tend to obstruct the development of taste, which must be properly cultivated and regulated by persistent and conscious efforts of the critics. He reiterates:—

> "The true literary mind is likely to grow slowly but surely and positively, provided it is given more comprehensive and more varied diet; is educated under greater experience of men and ideas; and is subjected to a broader knowledge of facts."[104]

The foregoing account would amply reveal that Eliot's criticism in the twenties is inspired and directed by what Arnold lacks—"the maker's point of view."[105] Eliot's endevaours at

---

101. *Ibid,* p. 36.
102. *Ibid,* pp. 108-109.
103. *Selected Prose,* p. 216.
104. *Ibid,* p. 218.
105. Eliot, T. S.–U.P.U.C.: Arnold, p. 108.

this stage are the endeavours of a literary "advocate."[106] Dissatisfied as he is, by the sham, the impure and the artificial trends of the Georgian literature, he takes up the problem of establishing an "order."[107] In poetry, he sets himself to evolve out a "form."[108] In criticism, he tries to build up a relevant code of "aesthetic principles."[109] But, both of his creative and critical faculties form part of the same crusade.

Eliot's harping on the study of the past is accentuated by his desire to establish a "literary order",[110] in the perspective of tradition. Tradition, in this sense, assumes the role of a custodian of all those values which he proposes to expound. In the initial stages it amounts to a sort of obsession with him. He attributes the unreality of the contemporary literature, to the loss of sense of Tradition. Perplexed by the problems of the present, he brought the forces of the past to bear upon their solutions. Interested in the development of taste, Eliot foresees the use of tradition in preventing "antiquation" or accepting "novelty" as the only criterion of excellence. What he aspires to achieve through tradition, is to make use of the past to direct the development of the present, as also to judge its perfectness. Moreover, the sense of tradition, as he envisages, brings forth all literary activity as one "organic whole",[111] which when screened from time to time by major critics, reorients the whole complexion of the past also. As a rule, Eliot's theory of Tradition as a means of collective artistic perfection is contestable. It bears a strong resemblance to the "catholic idea of a universal church."[112] Prima-facie it may sound plausible but is certainly imperfect, if put into practice.

But the discipline of tradition vis-a-vis the talent of the artist, which Eliot so ardently puts forth in the twenties,

---

106. Eliot, T. S.—*To Criticise the Critic,* p. 16.
107. Eliot, T. S.—*The Sacred Wood,* p. 49.
108. *Ibid,* p. 63.
109. *Ibid,* p. 49.
110. *Ibid.*
111. Eliot, T. S.—*The Sacred Wood,* p. 49.
112. Lucy Sean—*Eliot and the Idea of Tradition,* p. 16.

suggesting even the "total extinction of personality", has undergone considerable modifications. He theorises on the impersonality of art with the zeal of a missionary. The theory starts with the aim of neutralising human emotions, but gets so involved as to become confused, complicated and complex. On the one hand, he considers poetry an "escape from emotions." On the other, he sees it, as the "transmutation of human suffering"—suffering met on the personal level, but presented on the general or universal one. Eliot, in this respect, blows hot and cold in the same breath. He is vacillating between continuity and discontinuity in art. Therefore, his concept of impersonality is no more a virtue than tradition is. Paradoxically speaking, the virtues in either theories—Tradition and Impersonality—are valuable to the extent they are personalised and lived.[113]

On another count, where the theory of Impersonality does not hold water, is Eliot's concept of "a new art emotion."[114] Eliot refers to the "significant emotion having its life in the poem."[115] But the "new art emotion" and the "significant emotion" are merely the part of the poem. In case, the personal emotions are too strong to control, they are sure to creep up and have their say in the poem, jeopardising in this way, the process and product of depersonalisation.

Apart from theorisation, Eliot's criticism of the twenties is equally significant in other respects. His essays: **The Perfect Critic; Imperfect Critics** and **Homage to Dryden,** contain some of the fine specimens of literary appreciation. In the first two essays, Eliot has attacked the Impressionistic Edwardian School of Arthur Symons, Charles Whibley and others.[116] His pre-occupations with the Shakespearian and Jacobean dramatists in search of a suitable "form of poetic expression"[117]

---

113. Buckley, Vincent—*Poetry and Morality,* p. 113.
114. Selected Prose, p. 27.
115. *Ibid,* p. 29.
116. Eliot, T. S.—*The Sacred Wood,* p. 17.
117. *Ibid,* p. 63.

are very important. Moreover, it is in this period that he explores the possibility of reviving the "poetic drama."[118]

Eliot's literary credo in his early career seems sometimes slightly ambiguous and apparently contradictory. Maybe, the lapses are there. But, they are the lapses of an over-zealous advocate of certain principles in criticism. It is the enthusiastic idealist of the Twenties who prepares the prospectus but in the decades that follow, the maturing humanist prunes away its unnecessary parts.

---

118. Eliot, T. S.–*Ibid.*, p. 60.

CHAPTER IV

THE CRITIC IN THE THIRTIES

Eliot comments:—

> "So far as I can judge", "from quotations and reprints in anthologies, it is my earlier essays which have made the deeper impression."[1]

He attributes this to two causes: first, the dogmatism of his youth; and second the implicit defence at his hands, of the poetry he and his friends were writing then. Both the causes, he asserts give his criticism, "a kind of urgency the warmth of appeal of the advocate which his later, more detached criticism cannot claim."[2] He confesses:—

> "I was in reaction not only against Georgian poetry but against Georgian criticism; I was writing in a context which the reader of today has either forgotten or has never experienced."[3]

The confession is significant. It is illustrative in as far as it provides valuable clues to Eliot's mind and its working. The extract, being part of a convocation lecture delivered at the University of Leeds in July 1961, throws a searching light on the nature and scope of his early criticism. In the same lecture, he asserts:—

> "In reviewing my own early criticism, I am struck by the degree to which it was conditioned by the state of literature at the time at which it was written as well as by the stage of maturity at which I had arrived by the influences to which I had been exposed and by the occasion of each essay."[4]

---

1. Eliot, T. S.—*To Criticise the Critic,* p. 16.
2. *Ibid.*
3. *Ibid.*
4. *To Criticise the Critic,* p. 16.

The assertion is valuable. Eliot is subjecting his early criticism to his stage of maturity and various other influences. It shows that he is conscious of his occasional flaws and faults. He sums up:—

> "I hope that what I have said today may suggest reasons why, as the critic grows older, his critical writings may be less fired by enthusiasm, but informed by wider interest and one hopes, by greater wisdom and humility."[5]

These excerpts from Eliot's convocation lecture are categorically self-explanatory. Distanced as they are, from his earlier essays, by more than four decades, they provide a sort of integral continuity to the entire genre of his critical endeavour. In spite of the fact that during this long span of time, Eliot has been shifting emphasis from one aspect of literature to another, his criticism appears essentially of a piece. The essence of his growing position remains the same. He has never ceased to demand from the poet a sort of self-surrender to the judgment of an objective presence in history.[6] It is merely the conception of this presence, that indicates some change, sometimes.

Eliot's criticism in the thirties is marked by a new strain, the glimpses of which are discernible in his introduction to the 2nd edition of **The Sacred Wood** in 1928 and the essay **"Baudelaire in Our Time"** published in the same year. Eliot himself acknowledges that in between 1920 and 1928, he has come to give weight to an additional problem: "that of the relation of poetry to the spiritual and social life of its time and of other times."[7] To understand fully the implications of the "additional problem" suggested herein, it is necessary to follow the basic position which Eliot has taken earlier.

His early criticism is marked by a characteristic stress on "impersonality" and "order" in art. The whole critical effort is moulded through the conception of poetry having an "autotelic character." He emphasizes on the "reality" and "autonomy" of poetry. He is not prepared to bestow it with any

---

5. *To Criticise the Critic,* p. 26.
6. Buckley Vincent—*Poetry and Morality,* Introduction.
7. *The Sacred Wood*: Introduction, p. x.

other status either equivalent of or substitute for something else. Poetry is conceived as a process where the mind of the poet is just a medium. Operating through feeling and being directed by the course of tradition, the poet thus creates, what Eliot thinks, impersonal art, consistent with the highest standards of the past.

Poetry, purely as a process, envisaged by Eliot, suggests two requirements: first, its autonomy, and second, "continual extinction of Personality." This assessment is based on the relation of the poet to his poetry. He is explicitly silent on the moral reality of poetry. Eliot in the initial stages is measuring "poetic intactness in its own terms."[8] and in nothing else. He deliberately avoids moral judgment or prescription. The reasons are obvious. He is simultaneously engaged in critical as well as creative practice. As such his main interest for the time being is to create a coterie of intelligent readers and followers. In **The Sacred Wood**, therefore, he points out some critical guide-lines, which closely bear upon his own creative practice.

Moreover, Eliot's view of morality may be called "inadvertent-didacticism."[9] The reality of a poem (and hence its moral stature) is connected with the reality which the poet investigates; and that reality is largely the actuality, the immediacy, of his own emotions. It is in this context that Eliot prefers the reality of emotions of the poet to the reality of the external world, as poetic subject. The emotions for him assume a primary place while the external world remains secondary. His stress on their dramatisation, apart from artistic considerations is full of didactic strain. It is on account of two reasons: First, the self-investigation of the poet into his own emotions, being pervaded by good and evil, is always moral and spiritual. Second, the reality confronting the poet ceases to be personal, the moment it is dramatised. It tends to be the reality of a permanent state of human mind.

With this synoptic discussion of the basic view of Eliot in the beginning, the gradual shift in his position by the end

8. Eliot, T. S.—*The Sacred Wood,* Preface, ix.
9. Buckley Vincent—*Poetry and Morality*.

of the twenties can be easily understood. By 1926, he has begun to erect into an "open standard"[10] the notions that lie behind his criticism of Arnold and P. E. More in **The Sacred Wood.**[11] He criticises Arnold's denition of poetry: "criticism of life" as "shallow, provincial and lacking seriousness."[12] He prefers the poetry of Dante to that of Shakespeare because of "illustrating a sober attitude towards the mysteries of life."[13] He praises Baudelaire for "seeing truly"[14] into his own condition and goes to the extent of finding him "primarily occupied in religious values."[15] He stresses, for the first time, on the "socio-spiritual"[16] aspect of poetry. He declares in unequivocal terms:—

> "On the other hand, poetry as certainly has something to do with morals, and with religion, and with politics perhaps, though we cannot say what."[17]

The declaration, though conditioned by "we cannot say what", marks the end of a process of transition—transition from a purely poetic process to a religio-socio-literary order. In **Religion and Literature,** Eliot makes an important statement:—

> "Literary criticism should be completed by criticism from a definite ethical and theological standpoint. In so far as in any age there is common agreement on ethical and theological matters, so far can literary criticism be substantive. In ages like our own, in which there is no such common agreement it is the more necessary for Christian readers to scrutinize their reading, especially or works of imagination, with explicit ethical and theological standards. The 'greatness' of literature cannot be determined solely by literary standards; though we must remember that whether it is literature or not can be determined only by literary standards."[18]

---

10. Buckley Vincent—*Poetry and Morality,* p. 134.
11. Eliot, T. S.—*The Sacred Wood,* p. 43.
12. *Ibid.*
13. S. W., Introduction, 1928, Ed. p. x.
14. Eliot, T. S.—*Essays Ancient and Modern,* p. 67.
15. *Ibid,* p. 68.
16. Eliot, T. S.—*The Sacred Wood,* Introduction, p. viii.
17. Eliot, T. S.—*Selected Prose,* p. 31.
18. *Ibid.*

This is perhaps, the most controversial statement, ever made by Eliot. May be, the shift in his position is the result of his allegiance to catholic Christianity; or it may have been brought by the compulsions of the international crisis the world was facing in the beginning of the thirties. But it is important to recall, that the critic in Eliot, in the early twenties, speaks with the singleness of purpose—the purpose of a literary enthusiast. The thirties experience an additional strain: he speaks with a different voice. It is the voice of a humanist.

Before initiating a detailed study of Eliot's criticism of this period, it is necessary to point out some of its important features, as compared and contrasted to those elucidated earlier. In the first place, an evaluation in terms of impersonality is the key note of Eliot's early criticism. But, from 1932 onwards, he is less concerned with the emphasis on impersonality of art. His main endeavour gradually assumes a new complexion. He starts exposing and censuring the eccentricities of different poets. Secondly, the epistemological interest of the early period is radically transformed into the metaphysical one, in the thirties. Thirdly, in **The Sacred Wood**, the stress is on the poet as "medium", being directed by tradition but in turn, may be very slightly, modifying the tradition itself. In **After Strange Gods** the stress is shifted from the play of "medium" to that of "tradition."[19] The poet's sensibility, now, is to be judged by the extent to which it is enlightened by tradition. Fourthly, the animus of tradition is asserted as part and parcel of Christian morals and philosophy. Fifthly, greater emphasis is made on "orthodoxy of the sensibility" which conceives, controls and classifies emotions, but does not aim at probing their reality. The emotions in this way are made subservient to orthodoxy of the sensibility which means, moral reality is a precondition before emotions are fully and successfully actualised. No doubt that the sensibility of the poet is stressed as a guarantee to ensure impersonality; yet the emphasis is on its orthodox character. It implies not that sensibility which is directed by the general wisdom of the community, as stated in Eliot's early criticism, but the one, actualised in the Christian sense of good and evil.

---

19. Bickley Vincent—*Poetry and Morality,* p. 143.

Sixthly, there is now greater stress on analysing human life more minutely than was done or suggested in the Twenties The general attitude centres round a new criterion: "to see life steadily and see it whole."[20]

Lastly, even if the literary values seem to remain the same, the stress which at one time is on "poetic process" as custodian of those values, is shifted to ultimate sanctions and considerations.

We must guard against one misunderstanding, which is likely to arise out of the comparative summary we have presently made. It should not be gathered that the critic's moral interests have increased overnight. The real position is that the moral emphasis which had been dormant and passive till the end of the 2nd decade, becomes more explicit and pronounced.[21] Moreover, insistence on moral values shows a rising graph, even to the degree of "disproportionateness."

In **After Strange Gods** and the essay "**Religion and Literature**" Eliot becomes explicitly interested in finding ways and means to protect sensibility from degenerating and corrupting influences of eccentric writers. He begins to affirm impersonality in a negative way. He is passing censures on the personal whims and idiosyncrasies of the poets and the writers. His concern shows a sort of negative didacticism in as far as he reveals the misuses of personality. The censures he passes on Hardy and his novels display the extent of anger he has nourished against such fiction which "affects behaviour."[22] He attacks Hardy on six counts: his powerful personality "uncurbed by any institutional attachment"; extreme "emotionalism"; lack of "objective beliefs"; obsession for "self-expression"; his "indifference even to the prescripts of good writing" and finally, the peculiar use that he makes of the landscape for purposes of "self-absorption."[23] He comments:—

"In consequence of his self-absorption, he makes a great deal

20. Eliot, T. S.—*The Sacred Wood,* p. 47.
21. Eliot, T. S.—*Elizabethan Dramatists.*
22. Eliot, T. S.—*Selected Prose,* p. 35.
23. *Ibid,* p. 185.

of landscape; for landscape is a passive creative which lends itself to an author's mood. Landscape is fitted too for the purposes of an author who is interested not at all in men's minds, but only in their emotions; and perhaps only in men as vehicles for emotions."[24]

Eliot's attack in the whole passage is directed against too much a "personal view of life." Hardy's self-absorption and self-indulgence are at the root of his exploitation of the landscape. The "vehicles of emotions" referred in the passage, mean to Eliot, the vehicles of his "private emotions", which display an inherent moral and spiritual flaw. "This extreme emotionalism", he asserts, "seems to me a symptom of decadence."[25] It amounts to "deliberately releasing emotions of his own at the cost of the reader.[26] Eliot's position is clear. He attacks Hardy for his imbalance, resulting in his weak moral sense. His extreme emotionalism, and sheer self-indulgence show the lack of what Eliot demands from the writer, an "orthodox sensibility."

We have discussed Eliot's notion of "dissociation of sensibility" in the preceding chapter. Sensibility to him, is obviously something in which feeling and thought are used as dual and inseparable agents not only of perception but also of poetic creation. In the changed circumstances, after his allegiance to Catholic Christianity, Eliot's demand from the writers of orthodox sensibility has assumed wide significance and has even earned unfavourable comments. He has not fully explained anywhere what he actually means by the use of the appended adjective: "orthodox." Whatever meaning "orthodoxy" has come to retain, is the result of its uses that the critic has made in different contexts.

For instance, Eliot says:—

"We are not concerned with the author's beliefs, but with orthodoxy of sensibility and with the sense of tradition, our degree of approaching that "region where dwell the vast hosts of the dead."[27]

---

24. S.P., p. 185.
25. *Ibid.,* p. 185.
26. Eliot, T. S.—*After Strange Gods,* p. 56.
27. *Ibid,* p. 28.

He continues:—

"The artistic sensibility is impoverished by its divorce from the religious sensibility, and the religious by its separation from the artistic."[28]

He declares:—

"Aesthetic sensibility must be extended into spiritual perception, and spiritual perception must be extended into aesthetic sensibility and disciplined taste before we are qualified to pass judgment upon decadence or diabolism or nihilism in art."[29]

He links Tradition and Arthodoxy, together:—

"Tradition by itself is not enough; it must be perpetually criticised and brought up-to-date under the supervision of what I call orthodoxy."[30]

He demarcates their functions:—

"A tradition is rather a way of feeling and acting which characterizes a group throughout generations; and (that) it must largely be, or that many of the elements in it must be, unconscious; whereas the maintenance of orthodoxy is a matter which calls for the exercise of all our conscious intelligence. The two will therefore considerably complement each other."[31]

All these stray references suggest, by implication, Eliot's stand vis-a-vis orthodoxy and tradition; the nature and extent of their functions; their relationship and relative value in art and literature. While Eliot defines tradition as "rather a way of feeling and acting", he evades defining orthodoxy and refers only to its functioning on a conscious plane. The extracts cultivate an impression, that to Eliot, sensibility—artistic, religious and aesthetic—is all one and unified activity. What he means by orthodoxy of sensibility is that it is primarily an ethical quality. It is this quality in an outstanding writer which makes him feel and read about human life and its external realities in a way wherein moral implications get precedence over their other counterparts. In poems or novels, where emotions are the subject matter, the orthodoxy of sen-

---

28. Eliot, T. S.—*Notes Towards the Definition of Culture,* p. 26.
29. *Ibid,* p. 30.
30. Eliot, T. S.—*After Strange Gods,* p. 62.
31. *Ibid,* p. 29.

sibility, would function, not only through the reality of such emotions, but also through their relationship with an entire set-up of life. Hence, any literary work of merit ought to contribute positively towards the revelation of some human condition. But how and in what balance the contribution is to be measured? Eliot's answer, perhaps, is: through the sanction of morals as reflected in the Christian sense of good and evil.[32] He refers to Baudelaire and Joyce as highly ethical because they display a desirable degree of "orthodoxy of sensibility." The reason is apparent. Both of them are engaged in portraying the essentially limited nature of man and his condition.

Tradition and orthodoxy have been shown as related to each other. Tradition is considered in terms of something hypothetical. It is orthodoxy which is to preserve, control, judge and supervise tradition. It means that tradition is being assigned now a secondary role—secondary in the sense that it has been brought under the supervision of orthodoxy. Eliot does not hesitate to confess in **After Strange Gods** that "tradition by itself is not enough"; as also that, "orthodoxy and tradition are complementary to each other." This is a position quite different from the one taken by Eliot in **The Sacred Wood.** He is explicitly silent there as to such a role of orthodoxy. Moreover, his early view is marked by the stress on the poet as "medium." In the later view, the stress shifts from the value of the medium to that of tradition—tradition which is distinctly guided by the moral tests of Christianity.

The incorporation of the concept of orthodoxy into the realm of aesthetics as an authoritative factor, basically affects Eliot's position with regard to the functions of criticism. In **The Sacred Wood,** he stresses on the autotelic nature of art; visualises poetry as a process; and declares the purpose of criticism as "elucidation of works of art and the correcton of taste." But, in **The Use of Poetry,** (calling it his eccentricity) he gives the verdict that the study of aesthetics should be guided by sound theology.[33] In the same way, he makes another

32. Buckley Vincent–*Poetry and Morality,* p. 126.

33. Eliot, T. S.–U.P.U.C., p. 150.

important declaration on "the poet's vital concern with the social 'uses' of poetry." In 'Religion and Literature' the assertion becomes more emphatic:—

> "Literary criticism should be completed by criticism from a definite ethical and theological standpoint......In so far as in any age there is common agreement on ethical and theological matters, so far can literary criticism be substantive. In ages like our own, in which there is no such agreement it is the more necessary for Christian readers to scrutinize their reading, especially of works of imagination with explicit, ethical and theological standards. The greatness of literature cannot be determined solely by literary standards; though we must remember that whether it is literature or not can be determined only by literary standards."[34]

The assertion amounts to a declaration of principle. Eliot prescribes "completing literary criticism by definite ethical and theological standpoint." He has exhorted Christian readers to scrutinise works of imagination on the touch-stones of ethical and theological standards. The underlying purpose is their protection from corrupting influences. Finally, he refers to the "greatness of literature" but makes only a negative statement: it cannot be determined solely by literary standards. With what other standards then, the greatness of literature shall have to be determined, Eliot does not specifically mention. That perhaps, is cleverly left suggestive under the cover of rhetoric. It may be inferred that Eliot in this way is appending, in the thirties, an additional and radically different criterion to his literary criticism as against that substantiated earlier in the twenties. Eliot's new emphasis introduces a new element in determining the value of art. It leads to a kind of evaluation which we may term as socio-religious criticism. It raises other complexities, as well. How far the core of such theological standards can be justified as a part of literary criticism? In what way and to what extent Christianity and its standards are relevant to the realm of literary criticism? These are questions which bring us directly to an important issue—the issue of poetry and belief, which at present is not our concern. There has been an honest feeling, not only amongst the critics of Eliot but also his ad-

34. Eliot, T. S.—(*Religion and Literature*) *Selected Prose,* p. 31.

mirers that too much of socio-religious bias has tarnished his critical faculty. This may be true to a certain extent. But, in **The Use of Poetry and The Use of Criticism,** he has ably penetrated into the fibre and tissue of pure literary criticism. He has spoken with the same fare and flavour of the early period. The subject of the book is the "varying conceptions of the use of poetry",[35] that the poets themselves have provided in their criticism, during the last three centuries.

Eliot envisages poetry and criticism closely related to each other. He sees the two strains—the critical and the creative—working together. In fact, the appropriate time for the functioning of criticism is the one when poetry "ceases to be the expression of the mind of a whole people."[36] He censures those who treat the two strains as opposed to each other:—

> "Nevertheless, those who as if criticism were an occupation of decadence, and a symptom if not cause, of the creative impotence of a people, isolate the cricumstances of literature, to the extent of falsification, from the circumstances of life."[37]

He lays stress on close examination of the history of criticism, not merely as a "catalogue of successive notions" about poetry but as a "process of adjustment"[38] between poetry and the world. This he says would lead to the learning of criticism and poetry. He asserts:—

> "I only affirm that there is significant relation between the best poetry and the best criticism of the same period."[39]

Speaking on the structure and anatomy of a poem, he says:—

> "Any radical change in poetic form is likely to be the symptom of some very much deeper change in society and in the individual."[40]

While appreciating Wordsworth, he further develops the same idea:—

---

35. Eliot, T. S.–U.P.U.C., p. 32.
36. *Ibid,* p. 22.
37. *Ibid,* p. 21.
38. *Ibid.*
39. *Ibid,* p. 30.
40. *Ibid,* p. 75.

"It is Wordsworth's social interest that inspires his own novelty of form in verse and backs up his explicit remarks upon poetic diction."[41]

Demanding from the poet the communication of precise meaning in a poem, he denounces the looseness of the Romantic poets:—

"But poetry has as much to learn from prose as from other poetry; and I think that an interaction between prose and verse like the interaction between language and language, is a condition of vitality in literature."[42]

Some of Eliot's rhetorical phrases, which have gained wide currency in the domain of criticism, are directly inspired by his general outlook towards life and the imperfectibility of man. For example, commenting on Arnold's definition of poetry as "criticism of life", he gives his popular comment:—

"But the essential advantage for a poet is not, to have a beautiful world with which to deal: it is to be able to see beneath both beauty and ugliness; to see the boredom and the horror and the glory."[43]

The same outlook regarding man as limited and transient make him say:—

"Pure artistic appreciation is to my thinking only an ideal, when not merely a figment and must be, so long as the appreciation of art is an affair of limited and transient human beings existing in space and time."[44]

Eliot does not see criticism as divorced from life and society. In his view, each age demands different things both from poetry and criticism.[45] Each new artist and master of criticism is required to cater to the demand of their own age. "There is" says Eliot "for each time, for each artist, a kind of alloy, required to make the metal workable into art."[46] As for the critic, he performs a useful service merely by the fact that his errors are of a different kind from the last, leading

41. U.P.U.C., p. 74.
42. *Ibid,* p. 152.
43. *Ibid,* p. 106.
44. *Ibid,* p. 109.
45. *Ibid,* p. 141.
46. *Ibid*, p. 109.

in this way, to greater amount of correction. Hence, Eliot declares:—

"The uses of poetry certainly vary as society alters, as the public to be addressed, changes."[47]

The sociological interest, which Eliot evinces in poetry leads him to a sort of didacticism:—

"The rudiment of criticism is the ability to select a good poem and reject a bad poem; and its most severe test is of its ability to select a good new poem, to respond properly to a new situation."[48]

It is this very interest again, which makes Eliot proclaim Wordsworth superior to Landor. He states in categorical terms a new principle:—

"And in estimating for ourselves the greatness of a poet we have to take into account also the history of his greatness. Wordsworth is an essential part of history: Landor only a magnificent by-product."[49]

Eliot's assessment of Arnold contains some of his most significant and universally accepted pronouncements. They are the fine pieces of pure literary criticism. For example, his concept of **Auditory Imagination** is the best and the noblest contribution of this period. Apart from this, his re-iteration of critic's duty "to review the past of literature, and set the poets and the poems in a new order"[50] gives a new colour to the complexion of his literary criticism. In the same essay, he makes another equally important observation pertaining to the responsibility of the exhaustive critic. It is: to bring to light and thus to focus interest on the literary greatness of poets, hitherto regarded as minor ones. The passage is worth-quoting and runs as follows:—

"The exhaustive critic, armed with a powerful glass, will be able to sweep the distance, and gain an acquaintance with minute objects in landscape with which to compare minute objects close at hand."[51]

---

47. U.P.U.C., p. 150.
48. *Ibid,* p. 18.
49. *Ibid,* p. 88.
50. *Ibid,* p. 108.
51. *Ibid.*

He reasserts the question of order and deems it necessary on the part of more independent critics to accomplish this task:—

> "The majority of critics can be expected only to parrot the opinions of the last master of criticism; among more independent minds a period of destruction, of preposterous over-estimation and of successive fashions takes place, until a new authority comes to introduce some order."[52]

Criticising Arnold for the lack of virtues of poetic style, Eliot makes one of the most laudable of pronouncements on "auditory imagination":—

> "What I call the 'auditory imagination' is the feeling for syllable and rhythm, penetrating far below the conscious levels of thought and feeling, invigorating every word; sinking to the most primitive and forgotten, returning to the origin and bringing something back seeking the beginning and the end. It works through meanings, certainly, or not without meanings in the ordinary sense, and fuses the old and obliterated and the trite, and current, and the new and surprising, the most ancient and the most civilised mentality."[53]

Eliot defines "auditory imagination" as "a feeling for syllable and rhythm." It is not an ordinary feeling. It must have two attributes: first, to penetrate, far below into the conscious level of thought; and second, to invigorate each word, used by the poet. Such a feeling, to Eliot, works through meanings certainly, or not without meanings in the ordinary sense. But its main functions in either case is to fuse together every type of mentality—the old, the new, the most ancient and the most civilized.

Eliot's rhetorical phraseology has made the contents of the passage, somewhat difficult to understand. What he means, is the appropriate use of diction, not only in its pure literal meaning, but also in its emotional context. The stress on the syllable and rhythm not only as conceived, but felt also, means that the poet must incorporate into his poetry, the quality of music—music which moves the readers even on an un-

---

52. U.P.U.C., p. 109.
53. .*Ibid,* p. 118.

conscious plane. Again, the musical stress should not be taken to mean, mere melody separated from the actual meaning or sense of the poem. Melody is just one of its component parts and nothing more than that.[54] Lastly, the underlying purpose behind such an imaginative activity of the poet is to appeal people of every intellectual standard and taste, the common and the uncommon, alike.

It is in this context that Eliot implores the poets to approach the avenues, provided by the common speech. "The music of poetry", he says, "is the music latent in the common speech of its time." He further clarifies the position and reaffirms:

> "Of course, we do not want the poet merely to reproduce exactly the conversational idiom of himself, his family, his friends, and his particular district; but what he finds there is the material out of which he must make his poetry. He must, like the sculptor, be faithful to the material in which he works; it is out of sounds that he has heard that he must make his melody and harmony."[55]

The conversational idiom, so to say, is to furnish material to the poet, out of which, he is to recreate his poetic diction. His function is that of a sculptor. It means, he is to recast, reconstruct and if need be, reshape the words, accounting of course, for the sounds, which he himself has heard. This done, the poet can bring melody and harmony into the poem. We should guard against one misunderstanding which is likely to arise and that is, that his insistence on the pattern of sound should not be taken to mean a pattern, separated from the sense in any way. In his view the two patterns are indissoluble and one.[56] The musical quality springs from both the elements—sound as well as sense—one illiterative and the other, perceptive. To put it in another way, this indissoluble harmony of sound and sense, constitute what Eliot calls "the music of a word." He explains:—

> "The music of a word is, so to speak, at a point of intersection: it arises from its relation first to the words immediately pre-

54. Eliot, T. S.—*On Poetry and Poets,* p. 31.
55. *Ibid,* p. 32.
56. *Ibid,* p. 33.

ceding and following it, and indefinitely to the rest of its context; and from another relation, that of its immediate meaning in that context to all the other meanings which it has had in other contexts, to its greater or less wealth of association."[57]

Which means that the poet must concentrate on the sense of rhythm and the sense of structure. He must be very cautious about the most appropriate use of a word, its contextual meaning and associational significance. His ear must be sensitive to the tones and overtones of words as his mind is to the association of ideas and images. The poet, in nutshell, must be a craftsman in the use of words.

The foregoing discussion reveals that the feeling for rhythm and syllable, the capacity to create verbal melody out of common speech, the emotional width of vocabulary and the discriminatory power to make its appropriate use are the main qualities which constitute "auditory imagination" in the poet. There may be poets who struggle to bring the language of poetry nearer to that of the common speech, as also those who attempt to create for poetry a more elaborate diction unfettered by colloquial speech. Auditory imagination may show itself in either way.[58] Chaucer and Spenser, display this faculty in abundance. Pope, though a great artist, is yet very poor in this respect. It is by virtue of "auditory imagination" that Shakespeare excels and surpasses all other English poets. He plays in the great ocean of words as buoyantly as "Cleopatra's dolphins."[59] Eliot's own praise of Shakespeare for the same qualities is significant:—

"The recreation of word and image which happens fitfully in the poetry of such a poet as Coleridge happens almost incessantly with Shakespeare. Again and again, in his use of a word, he will give a new meaning or extract a latent one; again and again, the right imagery, saturated while it lay in the depths of Shakespeare's memory, will rise like Anadyomene from the sea."[60]

---

57. O.P.P., p. 33.
58. Gardner Helen—*The Art of T. S. Eliot,* p. 5.
59. *Ibid,* p. 6.
60. Eliot, T. S.—U.P.U.C., p. 147.

Eliot, at this stage, touches another important aspect of literary value—the question, what is poetry? In the introduction to **The Use of Criticism,**[61] he makes a cursory review of the whole question. He does not furnish any "academic definition" of poetry but examines its various aspects in relation to what he calls "the experience and appreciation of poetry."[62] Eliot views the entire perspective of the question from a definite angle. He affirms that the poet communicates an experience—experience which is not ordinary and personal but composite and impersonal, ordered out of many experiences of the poet. But the reality of the poem he asserts is not simply the reality of what the poet is trying to express or convey his own experience of writing it. It is not even the experience of the reader or of the writer as a reader. He states that the poem's existence is somewhere "between the writer and the reader." Hence, "a poem is not just either what the poet "planned" or what the reader "conceives."[64]

In his essay on Dante, written in 1929, Eliot says that the experience of a poem is the experience of a moment and of a life time. The experience of a moment is unique and may be of shock, surprise or terror. As one outgrows, majority of such experiences remain only on a subconscious plane, forming part of a larger whole of experiences. But there may be some poems which impart experience of a long time—experience that cannot be erased. In this connection, Eliot quotes Dante's poems as examples. What Eliot implies may be best elaborated from his references to Shakespeare.

> "Shakespeare too was occupied with the struggle—which alone constitutes life for a poet—to transmute his personal and private agonies into something rich and strange, something universal and impersonal."[65]

He continues:—

> "the great poet, in writing himself, writes his time."[66]

---

61. U.P.U.C., Introduction.
62. *Ibid.*
63. *Ibid,* p. 30.
64. *Ibid,* p. 31.
65. Eliot, T. S.—*Selected Prose,* p. 29.
66. *Ibid.*

He concludes:—

> "Thus, Dante, hardly knowing it, became the voice of eighteenth century; Shakespeare hardly knowing it became the representative of the end of the sixteenth century."[67]

Eliot, in all these references, is repeating the same assertion that a poet, no doubt, is communicating his own experiences, but they are ordered in such a way as to appear impersonal and universal. The poem, thus, is embodying a "new-art-experience" and the poet is making conscious efforts towards this end. His greatness lies in his power of transmuting personal experiences into something "rich and strange, something universal and impersonal." Such a poet becomes the representative of his age, not knowingly, but unknowingly because in writing himself, he writes his time.

Reverting back to the fundamental nature of poetry, Eliot reaffirms that the question "what is poetry issued quite naturally from our experience of our poems."[68] But this experience is not of the same type, or of the same standard, even in the case of a single poem. It may vary from reader to reader. The reason lies in one's standard of maturity and sensibility. It is here that Eliot favours "wide and increasingly discriminating reading."[69] Such study would develop the sensibility of readers and in turn would check them, being taken in by the "sham and adulterate in its own time."[70] He makes another observation which is equally significant. According to him, the experience of poetry, as it develops in the conscious and more mature person, is not merely the sum of the experiences of good poems:[71] it is more than that. It requires alteration and modification through a process of organisation of those experiences which he calls "education in poetry."[72] An adolescent reader experiences a sort of passing infatuation for a certain kind of poetry. The reason for this is not merely that the

---

67. S.P., p. 29.
68. Eliot, T. S.–U.P.U.C., p. 19.
69. Eliot, T. S.–*Selected Prose,* p. 37.
70. Eliot, T. S.–U.P.U.C., p. 18.
71. *Ibid.*
72. *Ibid.*

sensibility at this age is keener than maturity. What happens is a kind of inundation, or invasion of the undeveloped personality by the "stronger mind of the poet."[73] But in the course of time, and with an advanced age, maturity and multiplicity of his poetic experiences, the element of enjoyment, according to Eliot, is enlarged into appreciation, adding thus, a new dimension of intellectual intensity or feeling. He refers to this as the second stage in our understanding of poetry.[74] At this stage, one is no longer interested in the selection or the rejection of poems but becomes engaged in a different process—the process of organisation. Eliot's reorganisation—alludes to the third stage of appreciation wherein the reader is involved in something new in poetry which he comes across in the form of a new pattern of poetry. Now the poem assumes wide proportions and has its own existence apart from the reader. As a result, the reader becomes equipped with a faculty to distinguish between various degrees of greatness in poetry.[75]

Enumerating difficulties, which account for the unintelligibility and obscurity in poetry and hence, for the hindrance caused in the way of its proper appreciation, Eliot says forthrightly that the chief use of the "meaning of a poem in the ordinary sense may be "to satisfy one habit of the reader and to keep his mind diverted and quiet."[76] In his opinion, the poem, irrespective of its meaning, leaves its impact on the seasoned reader.[77] He cites his own example:—

> "The more seasoned reader, he who has reached in these matters, state of greater purity, does not bother about understanding; not, at least, at first. I know that some of the poetry to which I am most devoted is poetry which I did not understand at first reading; some is poetry which I am not sure I understand yet: for instance Shakespeare's."[78]

What Eliot implies by these remarks is the natural character of poetry. He is against every sort of superfluity. He

---

73. Eliot, T. S.—*Selected Prose,* p. 37.
74. *Ibid,* p. 49.
75. Eliot, T. S.—U.P.U.C., p. 34.
76. *Ibid,* p. 151.
77. *Ibid,* p. 152.
78. *Ibid.*

suggests to all readers of poetry to "take the poem as they find" and implores the poets to "write as they can." Any studied attempt to compose poetry or forced effort to discern meanings in a poem is, unwanted. Eliot feels that it is not possible for the reader to translate into words, the experience of poetry. It can be done only to a partial degree. Even if a person knows a poem to be good, still, he may not be able to explain its reasons. But, to critics, he declares categorically:—

> "In order to analyse the enjoyment and appreciation of a good poem; the critic must have experienced the enjoyment and he must convince us of his taste."[79]

Since 1932, Eliot's criticism shows a greater concern for highlighting the literary misuses of personality, as against the earlier one, where the stress is on the positive value of impersonality. We have already discussed the critics' period of transition from **The Sacred Wood** to **After Strange Gods** and some of its far-reaching implications. Barring his essay on Yeats, in 1940, Eliot is continuously exposing the cult of personality. In his assessment of **The Age of Dryden; Words-Worth; Coleridge; Shelley; Keats** and **Arnold,** he is attacking the same point.

Eliot calls Wordsworth and Coleridge, "the two most original poetic minds of their generation."[80] He shows his dislike of Coleridge for too much metaphysical interests and criticises him, for "the sudden, fitful and terrifying kind of inspiration",[81] he suffered from. He discusses the poet-critic vis-a-vis two main points: first, Coleridge's doctrine of fancy and imagination; and second, where both made a common cause together—the Theory of Poetic Diction.

In Eliot's view, the theory of poetic diction—the stress on the very language of men implied a kind of "revolt against a whole social order."[82] He feels that any radical change in

79. U.P.U.C., p. 17.
80. *Ibid,* p. 70.
81. *Ibid,* p. 69.
82. *Ibid,* p. 25.

poetic form is likly to be the symptom of some very much deeper change in society and the individaul.[83] He believes that Wordsworth's occupation is not simply with "the reform of the language." Instead, he was pre-occupied with "its very revolution."[84] He also affirms that the language of Wordsworth is artificial, turgid and no more capable of naturalness than that of Pope."[85] As far as the theory of poetic diction goes, Eliot declares that "no serious critic could disapprove."[86]

Eliot shows his disagreement with Wordsworth's definition of poetry and says:—

> "It will not do to talk of 'emotions recollected in tranquillity', which is only one poet's account of his recollection of his own methods."[87]

Eliot does not agree with Coleridge's distinction between Fancy and Imagination:—

Coleridge has defined:—

> "The Primary Imagination I hold to be the living power and prime agent of all human perception, and as a repetition in the finite mind of the eternal act of creation in the finite I am."[88]

> "The Secondary Imagination, I consider as an echo of the former......It dissolves, diffuses, dissipates in order to re-create......"[89]

> "Fancy has no other counters to play with, but fixities and definities. The fancy is indeed no other than a mode of memory emancipated from the order of time and space."[90]

Eliot joins hands with Prof. I. A. Richards[91] to point out the baffling complexities of the passage and contends:—

> "There is so much memory in imagination that if you are to distinguish between imagination and fancy in Coleridge's way

83. U.P.U.C., p. 75.
84. *Ibid,* p. 26.
85. *Ibid.*
86. *Ibid,* p. 74.
87. Eliot, T. S.—*The Sacred Wood,* p. ix.
88. U.P.U.C., p. 77.
89. *Ibid.*
90. *Ibid,* p. 77.
91. Richards, I. A.—*Principles of Literary Criticism,* p. 191.

you must define the difference between memory in imagination and memory in fancy; and it is not enough to say that the one "dissolves, diffuses and dissipates" the memories in order to recreate, whilst the other deals with fixities and definities."[92]

He criticises Coleridge for his theory of "willing suspension of disbelief" and states that the latter, no doubt, "was noting an important fact, but not quite in the happiest terms."[93] He assigns two reasons for this; first, one is not aware of a disbelief; and second, if so, none is voluntarily suspending it.

Eliot, in his final analysis refers to the criticism of Wordsworth and Coleridge as the criticism of an age of change.[94] In his view, the best in Coleridge's criticism seems to come "from his own delicacy and subtlety of insight as he reflected upon his own experience of writing poetry."[95] He feels that of the two poets as critics "Wordsworth knew better, what he was about."[96] He assigns him the highest place because of "the critical insight which Wordsworth displays in his poetry and in his Preface",[97]—the insight which he qualifies as symptomatic of a "profound spiritual revival."[98] He praises the two critics for what he finds in them, "the expression of a totality of unified interest."[99]

The concluding line in the lecture on Arnold is highly instructive. It may be taken as a key to the working of Eliot's mind during the early thirties. Therein, Eliot refers to a new phenomenon—a phenomenon which not only in the case of Arnold but also in his own case, is amply borne out by relevant facts. He concludes:—

"A man's theory of the place of poetry is not independent of his view of life in general."[100]

---

92. Eliot, T. S.–U.P.U.C., p. 79.
93. *Ibid,* p. 95.
94. *Ibid,* p. 81.
95. *Ibid,* p. 80.
96. *Ibid.*
97. *Ibid.*
98. *Ibid.*
99. *Ibid,* p. 81.
100. *Ibid,* p. 119.

Eliot does not see eye to eye with Arnold when the latter inter-relates Poetry, Life and Morals.[101] Arnold's assertion: "A poetry of revolt against moral ideas is a poetry of revolt against life", in Eliot's view, "is going to upset and disturb literary values."[102] According to him, the statements such as, "Poetry is the reality, philosophy the illusion" display Arnold's obsession to "find out a substitute for religious faith."[103] Eliot continues the attack and says:—

> "To ask of poetry, that it gives religious and philosophic satisfaction, while, deprecating philosophy and dogmatic religion, is of course to embrace the shadow of a shade."[104]

He criticises Arnold's definition of poetry as "criticism of life":—

> "No phrase than 'criticism of life' can sound more frigid to anyone who has felt the full surprise and elevation of a new experience of poetry."[105]

He reacts at the other counterpart of the definition—the prefix—and ridicules the very idea:—

> "At bottom: that is a great way down; the bottom is the bottom. At the bottom of the abyss, is what few ever see, and what those cannot bear to look at for long; and it is not a criticism of life."[106]

Arnold's whole literary outlook, according to Eliot, is conditioned by his own mental make-up. First, he is neither a reactionary nor a revolutionary.[107] Secondly, his notion of life is not so deep.[108] Thirdly, being conservative, he tends to become a reformer. Fourthly, to use his own phrase Arnold "did not know enough."[109] And lastly, he was not Dryden or Dr. Johnson; he was an Inspector of Schools and became Pro-

101. U.P.U.C., p. 103.
102. *Ibid,* p. 116.
103. *Ibid,* p. 113.
104. *Ibid,* p. 118.
105. Eliot, T. S.—*The Sacred Wood,* p. ix.
106. *Ibid.*
107. *Ibid,* p. 103.
108. *Ibid.*
109. Eliot, T. S.—U.P.U.C.; Arnold, p. 104.

fessor of Poetry. The resultant effect is that "the use to which he puts poetry remains limited." In the words of Eliot, Arnold became so conscious of what, for him, poetry was **for,** that he could not altogether see it for what **it is.**"[110]

And this is perhaps the border line between Eliot and Arnold separating them in their creative and critical efforts. Prof. F. O. Matthiessen has focussed our attention on the same point:—

> "The chief difference separating in quality both their criticism and verse is suggested in Eliot's remark that Arnold's poetry has little *technical interests.*"[111]

Eliot alludes to another vital weakness in Arnold. He criticises Arnold for defining criticism as "a disinterested endeavour to view the best that is known and thought in the world." He contends:—

> "The 'disinterested endeavour to know' is only a prerequisite of the critic, and is not criticism, which may be the result of such an endeavour."[112]

He continues:—

> "Arnold states the work of the critic merely in terms of the personal ideal, an ideal for oneself—and an ideal for one self is not disinterested."[113]

Eliot's whole criticism of Arnold is streamlined from a particular angle. Arnold is too academic and sometimes personal. His poetry displays "little technical interest."[114] He tells us little or nothing about his experiences of composing poetry.[115] Arnold, unlike Eliot, shows no concern with poetry from a "maker's point of view"[116]—the view, which in Eliot, is the starting point of all his critical activity.

Eliot praises Tennyson for the excellence of technical interest which he found lacking in Arnold. He affirms that

---

110. U.P.U.C., p. 118.
111. Matthiessen, F. O.—*The Achievements of T. S. Eliot,* p. 7.
112. Eliot, T. S.—*The Sacred Wood,* p. 43.
113. *Ibid.*
114. *Ibid,* p. 105.
115. *Ibid.*
116. *Ibid,* p. 108.

Tennyson's "variety of metrical accomplishment is astonishing."[117] Tennyson displays three qualities—abundance, variety and competence—which, according to Eliot, are seldom found together, except in the "greatest poets."[118] He considers Tennyson's technical competence masterly and satisfying and refers to "In Memoriam" as "the most unapproachable of all his poems."[119] He calls the poem unique and full of great poetry, known for its economy of words and a universal emotion related to a particular place.

In Eliot's view, "In Memoriam" is a religious poem, but for reasons, different to those assigned by the contemporaries of the poet. They had regarded the poem as a message of hope and reassurance to their rather fading-christian-faith. Eliot asserts that it is not religious because of the quality of its faith, but because of the quality of its doubt. Its faith is a poor thing but its doubt is a very intense experience.[120] Eliot feels that in Tennyson, one comes across a sort of an interesting compromise between religious attitude and belief in human perfectibility. According to him, Tennyson was not complacent towards the fundamental changes, which Industrialization and the rise of mercantile calsses, aimed at. Justifying the poet for the spirit of "In Memoriam" Eliot states an important literary point:—

> "It happens now and then that a poet by some strange accident expresses the mood of his generation, at the same time that he is expresing a mood of his which is quite remote from that of his generation."[121]

Eliot analyses the whole temperament of the poet as also of the age. In his opinion, the poet's feelings were more honest than his mind. The age was such that had no hold on permanent things—on permanent truths about man, God, life and death. The poet also stirred about with his time and became confirmist. The best he could do was to hold fast

117. Eliot, T. S.–*Selected Prose,* p. 166.
118. *Ibid.*
119. *Ibid,* p. 169.
120. *Ibid,* p. 172.
121. *Ibid,* p. 170.

to his "unique and unerring feeling for the sounds of words."[122] Eliot foresees an intimate relation between the surface of words, on the one hand, and their deep significance, on the other. Peeping through its innocence, one can discern its inmost depths—to the abyss of sorrow. Hence, he declares:—

> "Tennyson is not only a minor Virgil, he is also with Virgil as Dante saw him, a Virgil among the Shades, the saddest of all English poets, among the Great in Limbo, the most instinctive rebel against the society in which he was the most perfect confirmist."[123]

The lecture on Yeats,[124] delivered by Eliot, before the Friends of the Irish Academy in 1940, occupies a privileged place in the development of Eliot's literary criticism. The reasons are: first, it contains some of his best critical observations; and second, in this very lecture, Eliot improves upon his earlier views vis-a-vis "extinction of personality," in art. The improvement, appearing as it does in the wake of a period, wherein Eliot had displayed so much interest in censuring the use of personality, assumes greater significance. The passage, being of much import, is quoted at full length:—

> "Now among all the poems in Yeats' earlier volumes, I find only in a line here or there that sense of a unique personality which makes one sit up in excitement and eagerness to learn more about the author's mind and feelings. The intensity of Yeats' own emotional experience hardly appears. We have sufficient evidence of the intensity of experience of his youth, but it is from the retrospections in some of his later work that we have our evidence."[125]

Eliot has criticised the earlier poetry of Yeats for the lack of what he calls that "sense of unique personality", which generates in the mind of the reader, a process of an excited curiosity for knowing something more of the mind of the author. He has shown his instinctive appreciation for his later poetry—poetry, which incorporates in it, the greater expression of his personality. This is a stand quite different to the one, Eliot has been advocating for the last 20 years. In

---

122. S.P., p. 173.

123. *Ibid.*

124. *Ibid,* p. 186.

125. *Ibid,* p. 189.

"Tradition and the Individual Talent", he has emphatically stood for "a continual extinction of personality."[126] While appreciating Yeats, he seems to have realised the flaw in his earlier position. He readily confesses his fault and gives a better interpretation of his idea of personality.

But Eliot is also alive to the implied contradiction in his new position. He comments:—

> "It may seem that, in giving as a reason, for the superiority of Yeats' later work, the greater expression of personality in it, I am contradicting myself."[127]

He offers his own explanation:—

> "It may be that I expressed myself badly or that I had only an abolescent grasp of that idea—as I can never bear to re-read my prose writings."[128]

Without commenting on the tenability of the explanation, let us pass on to what Eliot thinks now, "the truth of the matter":[129]

> "There are two forms of impersonality: that which is natural to the mere skilful craftsman and that which is more and more achieved by the maturing craftsman."[130]

But the most significant point is the one he advances by way of an elaboration of the second type of impersonality:—

> "The second impersonality is that of the poet who, out of intense and personal experience, is able to express a general truth; retaining all the particularity of his experience, to make of it a general symbol."[131]

In spite of the present shift, Eliot's stress on impersonality as a principle, still remains uncontestable. It is sometimes difficult to characterise his basic attitude. He starts theorising about impersonality in relation to human emotions, and gets himself involved in its complications. He sees poetry as a release from interior oppressions as also a vehicle of their

---

126. S.P., p. 25.
127. *Ibid,* p. 189.
128. *Ibid.*
129. Eliot, T. S.—*Selected Prose,* p. 189.
130. *Ibid,* p. 189.
131. *Ibid.*

dramatisation. He wants discontinuity of life with art and advocates its continuity as well. In his present stand, he harps on impersonality but visualises a state where the poet is expected to retain all the particularities of his "own experience." The correct position, which Eliot is advocating in 1940, appears to be a sort of golden mean established between the ideal of impersonality on the one extreme and a total extinction of personality, on the other. His stress is the same but its nature is revised. The impersonality, as envisaged now, is not the earlier one, totally divorced from the personal experiences of the poet, but one where the poet is expected to retain the identity of his own experience. Perhaps, Eliot by now, has come to realise that an absolute negation of personality is not possible. It may be a laudable aim but its virtual achievement is negatived by many practical limitations that are beyond human control.

Another important observation of equal intrinsic worth which Eliot makes in his discussion of Yeats' personality is the exclusive passion and integrity with which he serves the end of art. Commenting on the literary influence of Yeats, he says:—

> "Yeats' would not have this influence, had he not become a great poet; but the influence of which I speak is due to the figure of the poet himself, to the integrity of his passion for his art and his craft which provided such an impulse for his extraordinary development."[132]

Eliot is introducing here a new dimension of art. He links the integrity of the passion within the poet to the impulse of his development without. The impulse for continual development, therefore, provides to an artist, an incentive to care more for art than for his own reputation. It is in this context that Eliot asserts that "art was greater than the artist."[133] Yeats' success lies in the fact that he served the Muse with an unconditional zeal and interest. He became unquestionably the master but always remains the contemporary. That accounts for the secret of his influence and popularity.

Eliot suggests that an artist ought to develop in himself

---

132. S.P., p. 187.
133. *Ibid.*

the habit of hard work and concentration. Supported by what he specifically mentions "the force of character", he can proceed like Dickens to such masterpieces as "Bleak House", which the author could bring out even in his middle age.[134] By "the force of character", Eliot means the character of the "artist as artist."[135] It is a kind of moral and intellectual "excellence."[136] Again, it is in this context—the context of continual development of the artist—that Eliot demands an exceptional honesty and courage from such artist to "face any change."[137] Otherwise, most men either cling to their experience of youth, turning their works into "insincere mimicries"[138] or leave their passion behind, forcing them to write merely "from the head."[139] Therefore, Eliot while discussing Yeats—a poet, displaying continuity of purpose and personality—displays a new method of critical evaluation. The directions he provides, are important:—

> "Where, there is the continuity of such a positive personality and such a single purpose, the later work cannot be understood, or properly enjoyed, without the study and the appreciation of the earlier; and the later work again reflects light upon the earlier; and shows us beauty and significance not before perceived. We have also to take account of the historical conditions."[140]

It means that Eliot is recommending here, the evaluation of the work of a major writer as an organic whole. In his view, it cannot, and should not be assessed piece-meal. The different periods of its creation, their historical sequence and the relative state of maturity of the author, must also be taken into account, in order to attain, full, rightful and objective evaluation of the artist. By "historical conditions", Eliot indirectly suggests literary environment seen through the perspective of history. He cites the example of Yeats, who was born

134. S.P., p. 187.
135. *Ibid,* p. 187.
136. *Ibid,* p. 191.
137. *Ibid.*
138. *Ibid.*
139. *Ibid.*
140. *Ibid,* p. 192.

into the end of a literary movement. Yeats has before him absolutely no tradition of verse-play. He has to struggle very hard. His early attempts, even though imperfect as they appear, are in Eliot's view "more permanent literature than the plays of Ibsen or of Shaw."[141] It is through him, that the idea of the poetic drama is kept alive, which to Eliot, is the starting point of our greatest debt towards him. Where does this point end, Eliot does not know: Until, perhaps when drama itself ends. The concluding part of Eliot's discussion of Yeats is significantly instructive, in as far as it de-limits the artist's mental poise in relation to various literary trends, in which he is to work. He reiterates:—

> "Born into a world in which the doctrine of "Art for Art's sake" was generally accepted, and living on into one, in which art has been asked to be instrumental to social purposes, he held firmly to the right view which is between these, though not in any way a compromise between them, and showed that any artist, by serving his art with entire integrity, is at the same time rendering the greatest service he can to his own nation and to the whole world."[142]

We have discussed at length the development of Eliot's literary criticism in the thirties. The discussion reveals certain broad and salient features. There is a systematic shift from the epistemological interest to that of the metaphysical one. A new socio-religious strain is appended. The stress on autonomy of poetry is shifted to its ultimate sanctions and considerations. The concept of Tradition, vis-a-vis, poet as "medium" is reoriented. A new code of orthodox sensibility,—dictated and guided by Christian morals—is introduced.

To try to give judgment on whether or not Eliot's critical faculty suffered on account of his socio-religious bias, appears unwarranted for the purpose of present chapter. The bias, its Christian character in particular, has been deprecated even by Eliot's own admirers. Whatever the case may be, in the years that follow, we see him laying a much greater emphasis on this aspect.

---

141. S.P., p. 193.
142. *Ibid.*

Nevertheless, Eliot's sharp and critical mind has displayed, even in this period, some of his best and profoundest ponderings into the realm of literary criticism. **The Use of Poetry and The Use of Criticism** may be recognised as the ablest treatise of the period. His criticism of Coleridge's theory of Imagination; his support to Wordsworthian concept of diction; and his appreciation of Tennyson's artistic perfection, are some of his noble contributions. But his plea of auditory imagination is, perhaps, the noblest of all.

It must be remembered that in Eliot's criticism, the literary values remain basically the same. Rather, they appear to be unaffected. His emphases on the sovereignty of poetry; theory of Tradition; and Impersonality of art remain constant.

The discussion on Yeats incorporates a policy of revision in Eliot's view of impersonality. The revised view displays much balance and deeper understanding of the whole issue. He sees literature in a new perspective. The complexion of impersonality in art undergoes a radical change. Though intrinsically the concept remains the same, yet its contents are not to remain completely divorced from author's personality. The aim, now, is not their depersonalisation but universalisation. In Eliot's development as a critic, Yeats' evaluation marks the end of an era as also the beginning of a new one. It is the end, since Eliot begins to see literature in a new perspective. It is the beginning, because it provides a key to the understanding of the maturing phase of his literary criticism.

CHAPTER V

THE LAST PHASE

In passing through the forties and entering into the evening of Eliot's life, we reach the last phase in the development of his literary criticism. As already stated, the address on Yeats, in 1940, wherein he modifies his former stand on extinction of personality, marks the beginning of a new era—the era of greater maturity and objectivity in art and in its evaluation. Now, he does not speak with that adolescent enthusiasm of the earlier period. His critical writings become marked by wider interest, greater wisdom and deeper understanding.

Looking back at his own critical output in 1961, Eliot refers to its lapses with a sense of humility, unprecedented perhaps in any of the major critics:—

> "There are errors of judgment, and what I regret more, there are errors of tone: the occasional note of arrogance, of vehemence, of cocksureness or rudeness, the braggdocio of the mild-mannered man safely entrenched behind his type-writer. Yet I must acknowledge my relationship to the main, who made those statements, and in spite of all these exceptions, I continue to identify myself with the author."[1]

The confession has been made publicly. It amply shows that Eliot is alive to the adolescent nature of his views, expressed earlier. He even goes a step further and declares with an equal degree of modesty that there are statements the meaning of which he no longer understands.[2] In spite of this, Eliot's acknowledgment that he continues to identify himself with the author, demonstrates his character which he so ardently advocates for the Artist, in his appreciation of Yeats.[3] All such

---

1. Eliot, T. S.—*To Criticise the Critic,* p. 14.
2. *Ibid.*
3. Eliot, T. S.—*Selected Prose,* p. 191.

confessions vindicate the sincerity and integrity, working behind the critic in Eliot.

Before taking up a detailed discussion of the literary criticism of the last phase, let us clearly understand, first of all, its general nature. Its complexion, in the main, is socio-religious. The moral strain, which the thirties appended to Eliot's critical approach, gets further emphasis and strength. The reason is, not that, Eliot has embraced Christianity, but because he sincerely feels the inevitability of the approach itself. He explains:—

> "In our own day, the influence of psychology and of sociology upon literary criticism has been very noticeable. On the one hand, those influences of social discipline have enlarged the field of the critic, and have affirmed, in a world, which otherwise is inclined to depreciate the importance of literature, the relations of literature, of life. But from another point of view, this enrichment has also been an impoverishment, for the purely literary values, the appreciation of good writing for its own sake, have become submerged when literature is judged in the light of other considerations."[4]

The passage, once again, registers an important confession. Eliot agrees that divergent interests which a critic has to cater to in modern times, have impoverished "purely literary values." The Socio-psychological context has no doubt widened the area of criticism but it has surely eclipsed its purity. Eliot does not suggest any way out of the impasse, thus created. He simply explains the circumstances and says that the conditions under which literature is judged simply and naturally as literature and not another thing, no longer prevail.[5] In his view, for such normal judgments to be given by the critic, a settled society, definite public, limited number of reading class and a small minority, capable of taste and discrimination are essential. Moreover, such class or people ought to have faith in themselves and the area of differences—political, social, religious or otherwise—must be small.[6] The modern society, as it stands

4. Eliot, T. S.—*On Poetry and Poets,* p. 191.
5. *Ibid.*
6. *Ibid.*

divorced from one or all of these conditions, cannot claim to have criticism which is pure and simple in the normal sense. Making a categorical statement on the point, in 1961, he reiterates:—

> "I have suggested, also, that it is impossible to fence off literary criticism from criticism on other grounds; and that moral, religious and social judgments cannot be wholly excluded."[7]

He continues with the same force:—

> "That they can, and that literary merit can be estimated in complete isolation, is the illusion of those who believe that literary merit alone can justify the publication of a book which could otherwise be condemned on moral grounds."[8]

Eliot's position is more than clear. He takes for granted that moral, social and religious judgments are part of literary criticism. They cannot be wholly excluded. He censures those who think in terms of pure literary criticism. In his view, it is nothing but an illusion. He goes as far as to state that literary merit alone, cannot justify the publication of a book. While accounting for that, its moral aspect is also a pre-condition.

In discussing Yeats, Eliot raised an important literary principle—the continuity of the personality of the artist[9]—which is equally applicable to Eliot's own development. Raising the point, he had pleaded for the evaluation of such writers and their works, not in terms of their isolated periods, but as an integral whole. The reason he assigned was that each period has a relative and a subterranean role to play in flowering the latent faculties of the artist. The same holds true of Eliot also. A piece-meal study of his criticism is neither possible; nor can it lead to its objective and full understanding. Whatever he initiates, pronounces or develops in his early career, cannot be properly followed, in case, it is divorced from the subsequent modifications he has gone to make. Similarly, his latest criticism, again, is in direct sequence of that, what he proposes to accomplish in the beginning. For the purpose of

---

7. Eliot, T. S.—*To Criticise the Critic,* p. 25.
8. *Ibid,* p. 26.
9. Eliot, T. S.—*Selected Prose,* p. 192.

a comprehensive study of Eliot's literary criticism, what is needed, is a total approach. Maybe, his critical activity is spread over to more than four decades of voluminous production, yet it stands as one piece and looks like an organic whole.

But we must guard against the misgiving that Eliot, at the very outset of his career as a literary critic, had sketched out a design for a massive critical structure and also that, he spent the rest of his life, filling in the details and colours. Eliot himself removes such a misunderstanding.[10] He classifies his own essays into two categories: Essays of generalisation and appreciations of individual authors. He feels that it is the latter category which seems to have the best chance of retaining some value for the future.[11] Speaking of the value of his own phrases—phrases that gained so much of currency—Eliot makes an important point:—

> "But I prophesy that if my phrases are given consideration, a century hence, it will be only in their historical context, by scholars interested in the mind of my generation."[12]

The reference, to "the historical context", is significant. It is not the same thing which Eliot elaborates as "historical sense" in his essay on **"Tradition and Individual Talent."**

The twin phrases stand divided by a distance of forty-two years. In his essay on Yeats, Eliot has referred to historical conditions in which an author or a critic carries his way through. But, what Eliot actually means by the term "historical context" has been fully explained by him in his essay on **Johnson as Critic and Poet.**[13] He has asserted that in appraising the judgments of any critic of the past, one needs to see him in the context of that age, to try to place oneself at his point of view. It involves a difficult task for the interplay of imagination. The success Eliot feels can be only partial and not complete because of so many factors—the modifications of taste, the changes in sensibility and the state of literature—which might have come to stay in between the intervening

10. Eliot, T. S.—*To Criticise the Critic,* p. 14.
11. *Ibid,* p. 18.
12. *Ibid.*
13. Eliot, T. S.—*On Poetry and Poets,* p. 162.

period of the critic and that of the present reader. He cites his own practice of indicating the original date of each essay in order to remind the reader "of the distance of time that separates the author when he wrote it from the author as he is today."[14] What Eliot means, is the role of contextual aspects: the ever-changing maturity of the author; the temporal exigencies occasioned by each essay; and various other influences to which the artist remains exposed and which ultimately condition the final culmination of every creative activity.

In Eliot's view, instead of censuring a critic of the eighteenth century, "for not having a modern, historical and comprehensive appreciation"[15] one must look at him with a sympathetic attitude—an attitude broadly analogous to that of the same period. He agrees that Johnson's point of view is quite different from that of ours. Still, he affirms its positiveness which requires a "vigorous effort of imagination to understand.[16] With this attitude, even certain peculiarities of a critic like Dr. Johnson would acquire new measures of objectivity and appreciation. In this way, the sensibility of an age fettered as it is, with the standards of taste, maturity and capacity of a people, always gives the type and quality of literature they deserve. Any appraisal of a critic of the past, therefore, must be made in accordance with the spirit, sensibility and standards prevalent at the critic's own times rather than that of the person who sets out for evaluation.

Eliot contends that the sensibility of any period in the past is always likely to appear to be more limited than our own.[17] He describes Dr. Johnson's failure to understand rhythm and diction "not through lack of sensibility but through specialization of sensibility."[18] He even goes to the extent of qualifying it as "religious sensibility."[19] According to Eliot, Johnson's deafness of ear stimulated indirectly his sharpness of sensibility to "verbal beauty" in place of "verbal melody."

14. Eliot, T. S.—*To Criticise the Critic,* p. 14.
15. Eliot, T. S.—*On Poetry and Poets,* p. 164.
16. *Ibid.*
17. *Ibid,* p. 166.
18. *Ibid,* p. 168.
19. *Ibid,* p. 177.

Developing his plea further, Eliot emphatically says that within his time, within his range, Dr. Johnson had "as fine an ear as anybody."[20] He passes on to an important generalization and refers to the nature of sensibility in a particular age which may be quite different to that of the preceding or the succeeding age. This difference is of vital significance because it would regulate the whole complexion of a critic's activity. Eliot reduces the area of difference to mere "emphasis on sound or on sense." Elaborating still further the same argument, Eliot makes an important distinction between Dr. Johnson's sensibility and that of the moderns. He says:—

> "We forgive much to sound and to image, he forgave much to sense. And to exceed in one direction or the other is to risk mistaking the ephemeral for the permanent."[21]

Eliot's position is worth noting. He is striking a balance between incantation and meaning. Sound and sense, though abstractions, are required to produce their effect in unity. To separate them altogether, means "mistaking the ephemeral for the permanent." "The greatest poetry", he asserts, "passes the most servere examination in both the subjects,"[22] which ultimately brings us to the study of diction in poetry.

Perhaps, no other critic than Eliot has so much furthered the cause of poetic diction. From the very beginning, when he wrote **"Reflections on Verse Libre"**, in 1917, he had implored the poets "to hold up to the standards of prose",[23] which comes very near to Ezra Pound's axiomatic exhortation that "poetry ought to be as well written as prose." No doubt, that it is Wordsworth who initiates the debate on "poetic diction", but his own practice in his poetry is often divorced from his own theory. On the other hand, it is Eliot who not only theorises on the diction in poetry but demonstrates also through his poetic practice, the efficacy and the utility of the outlook he so ardently espouses.

---

20. O.P.P., p. 169.
21. *Ibid.*
22. *Ibid,* p. 169.
23. Eliot, T. S.—*To Criticise the Critic,* p. 189.

Eliot believes that any radical change in poetic form is likely to be the symptom of some very much deeper change in society and in the individual.[24] In his view, Wordsworth was occupied not merely with "reform of language but with revolution of language."[25] He considers it mandatory that "poetry must not stray too far from the ordinary everyday language."[26] In his essay on **"Goethe as The Sage"**, he goes as far as to reiterate:—

> ".....the true sage is rarer than the true poet; and when the two gifts, that of wisdom and that of poetic speech, are found in the same man, you have the great poet."[27]

And regarding poetic speech, he affirms:—

> "Whether poetry is eccentual or syllabic, rhymed or rhymeless, formal or free, it cannot afford to lose its contact with the changing language of common intercourse."[28]

Eliot is putting premium on the language of common intercourse. His stress is on conversation, which is to provide the poet all the avenues needed for what he refers to as "music of poetry." This is exactly what Dante and Goethe have done for their languages. The same was done by Oldham, Waller, Denham, and Dryden. Even Wordsworth aimed at something similar to do. Any poetry, expected to arouse a feeling of excitement and a sense of fulfilment, must have according to Eliot, such a relation to the speech of its own time as to acclaim from the listener or reader, the general comment: "that is how I should talk if I could talk poetry."[29]

Eliot's whole approach to the issue of poetic diction appears to coincide with his theory of Auditory Imagination. He looks at poetry from a particular angle. He subscribes to the view that while poetry attempts to convey something beyond what can be conveyed in prose rhythms, yet it remains all the same, "one person talking to another."[30] More-

---

24. Eliot, T. S.—U.P.U.C., p. 75.
25. *Ibid,* p. 26.
26. Eliot, T. S.—*On Poetry and Poets,* p. 29.
27. O.P.P., p. 207.
28. *Ibid.,* p. 29.
29. *Ibid.,* p. 31.
30. *Ibid.*

over, he feels that this is just as true if one sings it; for "singing is another way of talking."[31] The same approach makes him jump to another important statement that extreme differences of opinion between respective critics of poetry arise because of "difference of ear."[32] By ear for poetry, he means an immediate and unified effect of rhythm and diction—both "implying each other."[33] Eliot goes on to assert that the acceptability of a poem and a further interest into its various aspects, depend directly on the favourable impression of rhythm and diction, which again derive their strength from the music of words, latent only in the common speech of the time.[34] In this way, Eliot re-emphasizes the relative worth of colloquial speech. He proceeds with the belief that a spoken language has the inherent potentialities of providing a new poetic medium. Major poets polish and perfect it in one direction or the other so as to give it a new lease of life for the expression of "new objects, new feelings and new aspects."[35]

Closely related to Eliot's conception of poetic diction is his oft-quoted statement that "genuine poetry can communicate before it is understood."[36] What the statement implies is again the musical virtue of poetry. Communication, in this way, is nothing but a preliminary experience, which a reader enjoys at first from a poem. Its meaning at this stage is not essential. It would follow only, if the poem is accepted, otherwise not. Its acceptance, Eliot contends, depends on the musical virtue of the verse which "clothes the absurdities in grandeur, and makes all acceptable."[37] In his view, a poem has its own existence. At the first instance, it is more an experience than a meaning. Hence, Eliot denounces the heresy of paraphrase and suggests that only a part of the mean-

---

31. O.P.P., p. 31.
32. *Ibid.,* p. 167.
33. *Ibid.*
34. *Ibid.,* p. 31.
35. Eliot, T. S.—*The Sacred Wood,* p. 15.
36. Eliot, T. S.—*Essays Ancient and Modern,* p. 200.
37. Eliot, T. S.—*On Poetry and Poets,* p. 167.

ing can be conveyed in this way. It is, because a poet is occupied with frontiers of consciousness beyond which, "words fail, though meanings exist."[38] Not only this, a poem may appear to mean very different things to different readers, and all of them may be different from what the author thought he meant. Eliot raises another point:—

> "If we are moved by a poem, it has meant something, perhaps something important, to us; if we are not moved, then it is as poetry meaningless."[39]

Apart from its rhetorical strain, the assertion is valuable in as far as it prescribes a new basis of evaluation. But Eliot, as is usual with him, neither qualifies the capacity of a poem to "move"; nor does he explain its constituent elements. Whether this experience is the same thing that Longinus has elaborated in **"On the Sublime"**, is not easy to ascertain. The context, in which the reference occurs, confirms four impressions: first, Eliot is highlighting the value of auditory profuseness of a poem; second, he is interpreting potery in terms of experience; third, he assigns a primary role to communication and secondary one to understanding; and fourth, the meaning of a poem is not something which exists apart from its musical virtue. In fact, what Eliot suggests is not a discount on meaning but a sort of premium over experience. He deals with the subject on the psychological level. The first requisite of the poem is to move the reader. If it fails to do so, it has no reason to exist. It means, the poem has not been accepted.

Communication and understanding in this sense are two distinct activities. Though they imply each other, yet the two may not function at one and the same time. Unless some ground is prepared by the former, the latter's operation is of no material advantage. It will not be out of place, if we quote Eliot's own experience. He explains that in understanding a piece of prose in a foreign language, he had to be sure of the meaning of each word, and grasp the grammar and its syntax. But in poetry, the case was quite different. It so

38. O.P.P., p. 30.
39. *Ibid.*

happened, that even if, he did not either construe or translate a piece of poetry, the same conveyed something immediate, vivid and unique—something he could not put into words and yet felt that he understood.[40] And on learning that language better, he found that it was not an illusion but something that was really there. Therefore, he re-asserts:—

> "So in poetry you can, now and then penetrate into another country so to speak, before your passport has been issued or your ticket taken."[41]

As already pointed out, Eliot is vehemently opposed to the heresy of paraphrase. He has discussed the subject at length. The core of his arguments is that the experience of poetry like any other experience is only partially translatable into words. He subscribes to the view of Prof. I. A. Richards that it is never what a poem **says** that matters, but what it **is.**[42] Its different interpretations may be partial formulations of one thing and the ambiguity may be due to the fact that ordinary speech cannot always communicate everything to the extent the poet desires. A poem may mean more than that. Sometimes, it may contain even "much more than the author is aware of."[43] Eliot is equally against "the diversion of attention from the poetry to either the poet or the knowledge of its springs."[44] The biographical details he argues, may be necessary for the full knowledge of the poet but are totally irrelevant to our understanding of his poetry.[45] The revelation of various springs from which the poem got its life is not necessarily a help towards its understanding. His plea is, that too much information about the origins of the poem may even break the contact of the reader with it.[46] Referring to his own explanatory notes on **The Waste Land,** Eliot calls them, "the remarkable exposition of bogus scholarship."[47] He denounces

---

40. O.P.P., p. 24.
41. *Ibid.*
42. Eliot, T. S.–U.P.U.C., p. 18.
43. Eliot, T. S.–*On Poetry and Poets,* p. 31.
44. *Ibid.*
45. *Ibid.*
46. *Ibid,* p. 112.
47. *Ibid,* p. 109.

the practice on the ground that it "stimulates the wrong kind of interest among the seekers of sources.[48] He does not feel the necessity of any light upon the poem beyond the radiance shed by the poem itself.[49] The reasons are obvious. Eliot pleads for understanding of "poetry as poetry",[50] and nothing else. Secondly, he maintains that in all great poetry something remains unaccountable, however complete might be the knowledge, either of the poet or the springs of his poems. It is that "what matters most."[51] Thirdly, with the making of the poem, something new happens, something which, in Eliot's view, cannot be wholly explained by "anything that went before."[52]

Eliot does not treat enjoyment and understanding as separate activities.[53] In his view, both are interdependent. He believes that we do not fully understand a poem unless we enjoy it. It is equally true that we do not fully enjoy a poem unless we understand it. The critic's duty, in his opinion, is to help his readers to understand and enjoy.[54] But he warns them not to place isolated emphasis on either of the two. He feels that an emphasis in the extreme would profit no body. An all out reliance on understanding would detract into mere explanation and too much stress on enjoyment would divert one to fall into the subjective and the impressionistic.[55]

He asserts:—

> "Thirty-three ago, it seems to have been the latter type of criticism, impressionistic, that had caused the annoyance I felt, when I wrote on *"The Function of Criticism."* Today, it seems to me that we need to be more on guard against the purely explanatory."[56]

---

48. O.P.P., p. 110.
49. *Ibid.*
50. *Ibid.*
51. *Ibid,* p. 112.
52. *Ibid.*
53. *Ibid,* p. 115.
54. *Ibid,* p. 116.
55. *Ibid.*
56. *Ibid,* p. 118.

The admission made by Eliot is valuable. It is not an admission of a mere fact only. It also embodies a general principle of aesthetics. It takes us to his oft-repeated generalisation that criticism will reflect from age to age the things that the age demands.[57] But let us shed the misconceived notion that Eliot is all opposition to factual information pertaining to the poet and his age. He concedes that such knowledge may be necessary but only as a "preparatory" help to lead one to the "door of understanding."[58] He asserts that we must find our own **way in.**[59] Then, it is our own sensibility, intelligence and maturity which would pave the way for such understanding.

In his discussion on Dante,[60] Eliot focusses attention at an important matter—the sources of new poetry. He acknowledges that from Baudelaire, he learnt first the "poetic possibilities" of the more sordid aspects of the modern metropolis: of the "possibility of fusion between the sordidly realistic and the phantesmagoric, the possibility of the juxtaposition of the matter of fact and the fantastic."[61] Referring in the same context to the combined influence of Baudelaire and Laforgue, he says that through them, he realised that his own adolescent experience of an industrial city in America could form the "material for poetry."[62] As a result, he thought of turning "the hitherto impossible, the sterile and the intractably unpoetic",[63] into the sources of new poetry. His final generalisation, in this respect, touches an important literary aspect:—

> "That, in fact, the business of the poet was to make poetry out of the unexplored resources of the unpoetical; that the poet, in fact, was committed by his profession to turn the unpoetical into poetry."[64]

---

57. Eliot, T. S.–U.P.U.C., p. 141.
58. Eliot, T. S.–*On Poetry and Poets,* p. 117.
59. *Ibid.*
60. Eliot, T. S.–*To Criticise the Critic,* p. 126.
61. *Ibid,* p. 126.
62. *Ibid.*
63. *Ibid.*
64. *Ibid.*

Eliot expects from the poet to have what he himself calls the "creative eye."[65] A poet must respond properly to each new situation. In his view, a poet is committed to satisfy two obligations: first, to explore the resources of the unpoetical; and second, to make their use in carving poetry out of them. The task of the poet is to help the people comprehend the incomprehensible. He must incorporate into his poetry what he refers to as "the illusion of a view of life."[66] It is for this view, that he praises Dante, Shakespeare, Sapho, Baudelaire and Goethe. He visualises an underlying similarity of approach in Goethe's "healthiness" and Baudelaire's "morbidity."[67] He claims them as men with restless, critical and curious mind—men who understood and foresaw a great deal. The "health" and "melody" they present respectively, is symbolic of the "sense of the age." It is this understanding and fore-sight which gives them power to explore and exploit the unpoetical into poetry. It is the negation of this understanding that brings rebuke to Matthew Arnold through his oft-quoted imploration that a poet must be able to see beneath, both beauty and ugliness; to see the boredom and the horror and the glory."[68] In other words, Eliot is asking the poet to endure the contradictions of human life and depict them so analytically as to present them as part of essential "truth" about "man and the universe." It is this quality which endears Baudelaire to Eliot. He commends his great strength which he qualifies as strength "merely to suffer."[69] The way Baudelaire analyses his own suffering implies for Eliot, the possibility of a "positive state of Beautitude."[70]

> "Indeed, in his way of suffering is already a kind of presence of the supernatural and of the superhuman. He rejects always the purely natural and the purely human; in other words he is neither naturalist nor humanist."[71]

---

65. Eliot, T. S.—*The Sacred Wood,* p. 77.
66 Eliot, T. S.—*Selected Prose,* p. 51.
67. *Ibid,* p. 176.
68. Eliot, T. S.—U.P.U.C., p. 106.
69. Eliot, T. S.—*Selected Prose,* p. 177.
70. *Ibid.*
71. *Ibid,* p. 178.

Baudelaire, that way, accomplishes something rare and unique. He turns the unpoetical into poetry. The personal at his hands tends to become impersonal. Like a great poet Baudelaire in writing "himself" writes his "own times",[72] a feature so apparent in Dante and Shakespeare, where both are skilfully metamorphosing their personal emotions and feelings.

Before embarking on this chapter, it has been specifically mentioned that Eliot's literary criticism in its last phase is marked by an approach more objective and practical than that of the earlier periods. Now, the critic in Eliot, is always prepared to reconcile or even to accept the viewpoints he had himself vehemently opposed. He acknowledges his own faults and foibles and asks other critics also to "make similar confessions."[73] That, he feels, would stimulate a healthier and much desirable outlook in them. A single statement such as the one that "we cannot escape personal bias in discussing the subject of literary criticism",[74] shows the extent to which, Eliot has withdrawn himself from his former stand.

Looking back at Eliot as the author of "total extinction of personality" in 1919, none could imagine him allowing discount for personal bias, in 1961. But, it may be added that the shift in position has surely enhanced his stature as a critic. It has also appended the much needed degree of plausibility to his theory of Impersonality. Quoting the case of Lady Chatterly,[75] Eliot re-affirms that in literary criticism there are other standards besides that of "literary merit" which cannot be wholly excluded.[76] By "other standards" he surely implies moral, social and religious judgments. All the same, we must bear in mind certain points, pertaining to the stress of his moral strain. In the first instance, though Eliot is out and out a didactic critic, yet his didacticism is never explicit.

---

72. S.P., p. 53.
73. Eliot, T. S.—*To Criticise the Critic,* p. 11.
74. *Ibid,* p. 25.
75. *To Criticise the Critic,* p. 25.
76. *Ibid.*

Secondly, the moral stress in him is not an innovation either of the thirties or of the forties. Even **The Sacred Wood** provides ample indications of his moral concern. Lastly, the nature of this concern is of a particular pattern which should be thoroughly studied.

Eliot's whole outlook is impregnated by Hulme's doctrine of Original sin. The central insight of this philosophy regards man as a limited creature, given to inherent badness. Perfectibility for him is out of reach. He can only accomplish anything of value by discipline—ethical and political. Institutions, therefore, are necessary. Order, in this context, becomes constructive, "liberating and creative." This explains Eliot's concern for a poetry, presenting the illusion of life, set in a particular background. He wants poetry to exhibit the human condition and its significance. It ought to be an actual report of this condition. The genuine duty of the poet is to investigate this actuality from within and from without. Eliot feels that the moral stature of a poem is directly and proportionately connected with the findings of such an investigation. On the personal plane, it is the reality of his own emotions, but on the general human level, it implies a moral and spiritual reality. It is moral and spiritual because it involves a struggle of good and evil, in relation to a permanent human state. It is this emphasis in Eliot which not only responds to the artistic needs, but also becomes the spectrum of an ever increasing ethical concern.

Taken in this light, the moral impact of poetry lies mainly in exhibiting man's metaphysical status. Life, therefore, tends to appear nothing but a mere trial, being carried out under juxtaposed conditions—conditions which none can escape. The business of the artist is to help the people "comprehend the incomprehensible."[77] The extent of his greatness will vary according as he is able to depict the metaphysical reality within or behind the merely human.[78] It is for this reason that he declares Mr. Joyce "the most ethically orthodox of the more eminent writers";[79] praises Baudelaire for his "theo-

77. Eliot, T. S.–*The Sacred Wood.*
78. Vincent Buckley–*Poetry and Morality,* p. 152.
79. Eliot, T. S.–*After Strange Gods,* p. 38.

logical innocence";[80] calls Dante "the greatest religious poet";[81] and refers to Tennyson's In Memoriam a "religious poem"; "not because of its faith but because of the quality of its doubt."[82] He denounces Hardy for his powerful personality uncurbed by any "institutional attachment" or by submission to any "objective beliefs."[83] In fact, the artistic and the ethical concerns in the criticism of Eliot are not separate entities. His evaluation of literature in terms of order, tradition, impersonality and orthodox sensibility, apart from aesthetic considerations, is inspired by the motives of ethical values.

The rehabilitation of Milton and Byron by Eliot is a matter of great importance in the realm of literary criticism. The case of Milton, in particular, is of greater significance. It is on account of three reasons. In the first instance, it calms down an unnecessarily prolonged controversy wherein much heat has been generated. Secondly, it reassigns to Milton, his due place in the hierarchy of the great poets and technicians of the language. Thirdly, in the rehabilitation of Milton, we see Eliot, unhesitatingly withdrawing his earlier adverse observations made against Milton, in 1937.[84]

But, before we take up the issue of Milton, let us consider what Eliot himself has to offer by way of explanation in regard to the alleged recantation of his earlier opinion. He says:—

> "But when I wrote my first essay on Milton, I was considering his poetry as poetry and in relation to what I conceived to be the needs of my own time; and when I wrote my second essay on Milton I did not intend it to be, what Desmond MacCarthy and others took it to be, a recantation of my earlier opinion, but a development in view of the fact that there was no longer any likelihood of his being imitated and that therefore he could profitably be studied."[85]

It is not our concern here to doubt the genuineness of

80. Eliot, T. S.—*Selected Prose,* p. 176.
81. *Ibid,* p. 95.
82. *Ibid,* p. 172.
83. *Ibid,* p. 184.
84. Eliot, T. S.—*On Poetry and Poets,* p. 138.
85. Eliot, T. S.—*To Criticise the Critic,* p. 24.

the justification which Eliot has offered through his explanation. Eliot does not regard the second essay[86] as a recantation of his earlier views. Instead, he thinks it to be a sort of development. The reason he forwards is the possible unlikelihood of his being imitated. As for the views expressed in the first essay, Eliot's position is that he was considering his poetry as poetry and in relation to the needs of his own time—the needs which Eliot has left here undefined. But from a close study of the second essay on Milton, these needs as per Eliot's assessment may be summarized. First, the verse should have the virtues of prose. Second, its diction should become assimilated to cultivate contemporary speech before it is brought up to the elevation of poetry. Third, the subject matter and imagery of poetry should have close affinity to the realities of modern life. Fourth, the poet should incorporate the unpoetic into his poetry and should explore the possibilities of using new words, phrases and expressions such as never used in poetry. In Eliot's view, the study of Milton vis-a-vis these tenets, being of no help, "was only a hindrance."[87]

In the first essay on Milton, Eliot levels against the blind poet, mainly the charge of "peculiar kind of deterioration to which he subjected the language."[88] He recognises Milton's greatness but criticises him for his bad influence. He asserts that there is more of Milton's influence in the badness of the bad verse of the eighteenth century than of anybody's else.[89] The key passage runs thus:—

> "And it appears a good deal more serious if we affirm that Milton's poetry could only be an influence for the worse, upon any poet whatever. It is more serious, also, if we affirm that Milton's bad influence may be traced much farther than the eighteenth century, and much farther than upon bad poets: if we say that it was an influence against which we still have to struggle."[90]

The last sentence provides ample clues to Eliot's criticism

---

86. Eliot T. S.—*To Criticise the Critic.* p. 146.
87. Eliot, T. S.—*On Poetry and Poets,* p. 160.
88. *Ibid,* p. 138.
89. *Ibid.*
90. *Ibid,* p. 139.

of Milton. He confesses himself that in passing these strictures, "he failed to draw a threefold distinction";[91] first, that an influence has been bad in the past; second, that the influence can always be bad; and third, that the contemporary situation being such, Milton as a master should be avoided. Eliot argues that he is no longer prepared to make either of the first two assertions because of the fact that they have no meaning if detached from the third.[92] The exigencies of the contemporary situation have already been discussed. Referring to the bad influence of the poet, Eliot himself exonerates Milton by saying that the burden, if any, lies with the poets who were influenced, rather than with the poet whose work exerted the influence.[93] As far the influence in the remote future, he questions its validity on the ground that none can be certain as to what "good" and "bad" influences would **mean** in that future.[94]

Another reproach against Milton occurs in the essay on **The Metaphysical Poets,** wherein Eliot has alleged:—

> "In the seventeenth century a dissociation of sensibility set in, from which we have never recovered and this dissociation as is natural was due to the influence of the two most powerful poets of the century, Milton and Dryden."[95]

To this reproach also, Eliot answers himself and affirms that to lay the burden on the shoulders of Milton and Dryden was a mistake.[96] He reiterates:—

> "If such a dissociation did take place, I suspect that the causes are too complex and too profound to justify our accounting for the change in terms of literary criticism."[97]

The foregoing review of Eliot's position in relation to Milton would indicate the direction of what Eliot's critics consider "a recantation of his earlier opinion" and what Eliot

---

91. O.P.P., p. 151.
92. *Ibid.*
93. *Ibid,* p. 151.
94. *Ibid,* p. 152.
95. Eliot, T. S.–*Selected Prose; The Metaphysical Poets,* p. 111.
96. Eliot, T. S.–*On Poetry and Poets,* p. 153.
97. *Ibid.*

regards it as a sort of "development."[98] Irrespective of its genesis, nature or qualification, the revaluation has enhanced the stature of Milton and has added to the integrity of Eliot.

Agreeing with most of the criticism of Milton by Dr. Johnson in **The Lives,** Eliot sums up the final assessment of Milton in the following words:—

> "I repeat that the remoteness of Milton's verse from ordinary speech, his invention of his own poetic language seems to me one of the marks of his greatness. Other marks are his sense of structure, both in the general design of *Paradise Lost* and *Samson,* and in his syntax; and finally, and not least, his inerrancy, conscious or unconscious, in writing so to make the best display of his talents, and the best concealment of his weakness."[99]

The passage may be noted for its objectivity and frankness. It registers one of the best and the most factual recognitions of Milton's talents and his achievements. Now Eliot recommends to the poets without any reservation, to study Milton and refers to him, outside the theatre, as "the greatest master in our language of freedom within form."[100] In the context of discovering new and more elaborate patterns of a diction, already established, Eliot feels that poetry might learn much from Milton's extended verse structure. It might also avoid the danger of a servitude to colloquial speech and to current jargon. Milton can show, how to infuse the strongest music into poetry by the use of the appropriate words. Finally, Milton's example can inspire young poets to supplement knowledge of the literature of their own language, with knowledge of the literature and grammatical construction of other languages.[101] Then comes the final exhortation of Eliot, which says:—

> "It now seems to me that poets are sufficiently liberated from Milton's reputation, to approach the study of his works without danger, and with profit to their poetry and to the English language."[102]

---

98. *Ibid.*
99. O.P.P., p. 155.
100. *Ibid,* p. 160.
101. *Ibid.*
102. *Ibid,* p. 161.

The case of Byron's rehabilitation is quite different from that of Milton. In the essay on Byron, Eliot explains the reasons for writing on the younger romantic.[103] He expresses his dissatisfaction on the fact that no interpretation for Byron's verse has yet been offered. He refers to his own article as an attempt in that direction "to start that ball rolling."[104] In Eliot's view, the bulk of Byron's poetry is distressing in proportion to its quality. Moreover, one would suppose that he never destroyed anything. Eliot does not see anything, worthy of the name of Byron, in most of his shorter poems; but he appreciates his longer poems and goes to the extent of saying that he did something that no one else has "ever equalled."[105]

Eliot criticises Byron for his defective sensibility and imperceptiveness to the English word. He alleges that Byron unlike any other English poet of his eminence, "added nothing to the language, discovered nothing in the sounds, and developed nothing in the meaning of individual words."[106] Referring to his intermittent philosophizing and its failure to leave any impact, Eliot affirms that it is not the weakness of the ideas but the schoolboy command of the language that makes his lines seem trite and his thought shallow.[107] But the greatest praise that Eliot bestows on Byron, is with regard to the last cantos of Don Juan. He places them at the head of Byron's works, for the simple reason, that the subject matter gave him at least an adequate object for a genuine emotion—the emotion for the hatred of hypocrisy.[108] He categorically declares that Byron's satire upon English society in the later part of Don Juan is something, for which, he could find no parallel in English literature.[109] In his last analysis, while commending Byron for his unusual frankness and a reckless raffish honesty, Eliot gives his own verdict:—

---

103. O.P.P., p. 193.
104. *Ibid.*
105. *Ibid.*
106. *Ibid,* p. 201.
107. *Ibid.*
108. *Ibid,* p. 205.
109. *Ibid.*

> "I do not pretend that Byron is Villon (nor, for other reasons, does Dunbar or Burns equal the French poet), but I have come to find in him certain qualities, besides his abundance, that are too uncommon in English poetry as well as the absence of some vices that are too common."[110]

In his interpretation of culture Eliot has carried "the argument to an important new stage."[111] His position in this respect is essentially traditional and conservative. The whole discussion is regulated by his confession of a pre-determined attitude towards life and letters. In fact, the kind of analysis he undertakes in **The Idea of a Christian Society,** or **The Notes towards the Definition of Culture,** forms the gamut of Eliot's own reaction to contemporary society and to the cross-currents of its social philosophies. Nevertheless, it initiates a valuable dialogue on an oft-repeated subject—the importance of art to civilization. Taken together, the two books offer a sort of renewed definition of culture, conceived in the context of various problems, peculiar to an industrial and democratic society.

Eliot does not envisage a programmatic development of art and culture. In his opinion, they cannot flourish in isolation. The nature of the organisation of society directly influences the standards of art and cluture. In a state of confusion, chaos and disintegration, no material and physical improvement is possible. He believes that in order to better the standards of art and culture, it is necessary that the socio-religious complex on which the organisation of society ought to be built, is strengthened. Art, to him, is the by-product of a genuinely healthy state of an organised society. Its falling standard is always a symptom of what Eliot qualifies as "some social ailment",[112] which requires a thorough investigation in case any substantial improvement in art and culture is sought for. He observes:—

> "The steady influence which operates silently in any mass society organised for profit for the depression of standards of art and culture. The increasing organisation of advertisement and propaganda–or the influencing of masses of men

---

110. O.P.P., p. 206.

111. Williams Raymond–*Culture and Society,* p. 224.

112. Eliot, T. S.–*The Idea of a Christian Society,* p. 39.

> by any means except through the intelligence—is all against them. The economic system is against them, the chaos of ideals and confusion of thought in our large scale mass education is against them and against them also is the disappearance of any class of people who recognise public and private responsibility of patronage of the best that is made and written."[113]

These observations are significantly valuable. They form part of Eliot's basic approach which runs through the entire body of his literary effort. In all his important theories—of Tradition, Poetry and Impersonality—Eliot has stressed the organic character of art and literature. His concept of the diffusion of culture is primarily based on the same view. He voices his strong opposition to Mannheim's theory of substituting **elite** for classes, for the simple reason that "it posits an atomic view of society."[114] Eliot advances four arguments in objecting to the theory of an **elite** society: first, its common culture will be meagre; second, it will imply a change of persons in each generation; third, it will not ensure general continuity beyond the particular specialities of the elite itself; and finally, it will lack the much needed social cohesion which has always been guaranteed by a class.[115]

Eliot's emphasis is different. He is a conservative and wants to retain the status-quo in society. He is not for an **elite** society but still favours governing social class with which he expects "the **elite** to overlap and interact."[116] Eliot is against the specialisms of the **elite**, but within the whole content of culture, he is prepared to make allowance for the special skills, if any. He voices his strong opposition to the notions of classless society and the demands for a national educational system. In liberalism, he predicts only the dividends of disorder. "Industrialism", he suggests, "would create not a society but a mob."[117] Nor does he like the practice of defining social ends in terms of Democracy, which according to

---

113. Eliot, T. S.—*The Idea of a Christian Society,* p. 39.

114. Eliot, T. S.—*Notes towards the Defintion of Culture,* p. 37.

115. *Ibid.*

116. Williams Raymond—*Culture and Society,* p. 237.

117. *Ibid,* p. 226.

him, "means too many things to mean anything",[118] at all. As such, neither of them—Liberalism and Democracy—can provide to society the necessary avenues for regulating its whole way of life.

Eliot views culture as an organic whole. In his opinion, the sense of culture lies in the whole way of life rather than in any of its fragmented aspects, howsoever important they might be. He says:—

> "Culture includes all the characteristic activities and interests of a people; Derby Day, Henley Regatta, Cowes the twelfth of August, a cup final, the dog races, the pin table, the dart board wensledale cheese, boiled cabbage cut into sections, beetroot in vinegar, nineteenth century Gothic churches and the music of Elgar."[119]

Any galaxy of "activities and interests" would be inexhaustive from Eliot's point of view. The list furnished by him categorises culture into the ways of sport, food, religion and a little of leisurely art. Another significant assertion, which Eliot makes regarding culture, is that left to itself, the Culture of a people does have its own categories or levels, which may vary from time to time. For instance, he clarifies:—

> "You cannot expect to have all stages of development at once......A civilization cannot simultaneously produce great folk poetry at one Cultural level and Paradise Lost at another."[120]

From various levels of culture, Eliot passes on to the discussion of different senses of culture. He differentiates in its three senses which may correspond to three types of development—"the development of an individual, of a group or class, or of a whole society."[121] Proceeding with his own analysis, Eliot makes an important suggestion:—

> "A good deal of confusion could be avoided, if we refrained from setting before the group, what can be the aim only of the individual and before society as a whole, what can be the aim only of a group."[122]

118. *Ibid.*
119. Eliot, T. S.—*Notes towards the Definition of Culture,* p. 31.
120. *Ibid,* p. 25.
121. *Ibid,* p. 21.
122. *Ibid,* p. 22.

The suggestion furnishes a plausible ground to Eliot for building up his defence of social classes in society. His argument is, that in a healthy society, the maintenance of a particular level of culture is to the benefit, not merely of the class which maintains it, but also to the society as a whole.[123] He goes as far back as the primitive society to justify his theory of classes. Eliot's contention is that the higher types exhibit "more marked differentiations of functions"[124] amongst their members than the lower ones. In his view, it is only gradually that the classes tend to develop, out of the inherent condition, the idea that some functions are "more honoured than others."[125] And further more, a stage is brought where the honour and privilege is given to the person not merely as "functionary" but as "member of a class."[126] In this way, even the class acquires a functionary position and assumes to protect "that part of the total culture of the society"[127] which is so vital to its own existence. Hence, Eliot jumps to the final conclusion, that the awareness of such historical growth and necessity of the theory of classes would prevent us from supposing that the "culture of a higher class is something superfluous to society as a whole."[128]

Any one, seriously interested in anthropology and sociology, would find it difficult to subscribe in full to the above generalisation which Eliot has made in **The Notes towards the Definition of Culture.** Although, Eliot's emphasis on different levels of culture provides a useful hypothesis to the idea of the "community of Culture"; yet his stress on social classes is fraught with grave and practical misgivings. His analysis of the theory of classes, no less than his conclusions, suffer from the lack of a dispassionate outlook.

Historically speaking, the theory exposes itself to an utter disregard of the economic factor. Again, to equate class with

---

123. Notes: p. 35.
124. *Ibid.*
125. *Ibid.*
126. *Ibid.*
127. *Ibid.*
128. *Ibid.*

function, as Eliot has done, is basically incorrect. It is obviously for three reasons. First, "a function has the tendency to turn into property." Second, it can be divorced from the property and as a result, its maintenance may become a new function itself, falsifying thus, the relevance of any consistent relationship between class and function.[129] Moreover, in the limited sense, all this may lead to an unequal social state where accumulation of wealth would become itself a function of the privileged few.

Eliot's concept of culture, when pursued to its logical reasoning, betrays a similar type of inconsistency. In his emphasis on Culture as "a way of life", Eliot has referred to two of its major components—conscious and unconscious. The large part of "a way of life", according to Eliot, is necessarily unconscious. In this sense, "a religion, moral code, a system of law, or a body of work in the arts", are just the conscious parts of culture. Its bulk comprises the unconscious part which is essentially vital for its distinctive and effective existence. But the classification Eliot has adopted, appears not only ambiguous but also irrelevant. We find that it is not possible to establish practical correspondence between "the conscious culture and the whole way of life."[130] The conscious culture when it asumes such proportion, as to become identical with the vested interests of a particular class, ceases to perform any positive function. Under these circumstances, it is always confusing to make distinction in, what we call the degree of conscious culture on the one hand and the degree of social privilege, on the other.

In our final discussion of Eliot's **The Notes towards the Definition of Culture,** we may say, that with all its glaring lapses of outlook and analysis, the contents therein have been very useful. In its totality, Eliot's attitude towards culture has certainly helped in furthering understanding in many directions. His theory of culture as "a whole way of life" reiterates the organic view of society. His criticism of the theory of **elite** has been really educative. His stress on different levels

---

129. Williams Raymond—*Culture and Society,* p. 232.
130. *Culture and Society,* p. 233.

of culture is of no less practical value. Eliot's bold assertion against the democratic diffusion of culture has positively led to a sort of rethinking on the subject. His stand against liberalism and industrialism has been valuably significant. Finally, Eliot's strong disapproval of reducing "the transmission of culture to a system of formal education" may be considered an enlightening attempt in the process of simplifying an issue, which has been a subject of hard controversy, right from the beginning of the Industrial society to the present day.

But this should not be construed to imply that whatever Eliot has said about culture is all tenable. His emphasis on class as against **elite** is misleading. His advocacy of a consistent relationship between "class" and "function" as also between "conscious culture" and the "whole way of life" is **prima facie** evasive. Besides, Eliot insists on Culture as a whole way of life, but does not consider it feasible to assess the whole system as a whole. In theory, "his insistence is on wholeness; in practice he tends to become fragmentary."[131] He voices his opposition to the emergence of elites but recommends the retention of a "governing social class", with which he contends, "the elite would overlap and even interact."[132] It is worthwhile to quote Raymond William's valuable comment on Eliot's approach towards Culture:—

> "If Eliot, when read attentively, has the effect of checking the complacencies of liberalism, he has also, when read critically, the effect of making complacent conservatism impossible."[133]

Ever since the publication of **The Sacred Wood**, Eliot may be said to have given serious thought to the possible revival of "Poetic Drama."[134] After Yeats, he is perhaps the only person who has endeavoured so hard for the rejuvenation of this craft. He has not only theorised on the art of poetic drama, but has also tried to transform the same into practice through the body of plays he has written. We should bear

---

131. *Culture and Society,* p. 238.

132. *Ibid.*

133. *Ibid.*

134. Eliot, T. S.—*The Sacred Wood*: *"The Possibility of Poetic Drama",* p. 60.

in mind that the interplay between theory and practice which is well up to the mark in Eliot's poems is very weak in his plays. Mr. Matthiessen rightly observes:—

> "Eliot's conception of drama, his belief in the need for poetic drama, still remain more in the realm of theory even in his own experiments, as well as in their limited effect on the general course of drama in our time."[135]

Even Eliot is conscious of the limitations of his own efforts when he acknowledges:—

> "It is one thing to discuss the rules of an art when that art is alive and quite another when it is dead."[136]

He regards his own endeavours as only the preparatory stage in the revival of modern poetic drama:—

> "The creation of any form cannot be the work of one man or of one generation of men working together, but has to evolve by the small contributions of a number of people in succession each contributing a little. Shakespeare himself did not invent suddenly."[137]

Hence, in Eliot's view, the creation of any form is not an ordinary pursuit of an isolated individual. It demands collective efforts of a number of persons belonging to successive generations.[138] He agrees that modern poetic drama is "still very experimental."[139] He expresses the hope that whatever has been achieved in this direction would serve as "foundations upon which others would come to build."[140] The verse drama interests Eliot for the obvious reason that it "provides an incentive towards further experiment and exploration."[141] He exhorts the coming writers to work in the selfless spirit of Yeats, who, he says, "cared more for the theatre as an organ

---

135. Matthiessen, F.O.—*The Achievement of T. S. Eliot,* p. 155.
136. Eliot, T. S.—*Dialogue on Dramatic Poetry.*
137. *The Need for Poetic Drama; The Listener,* Nov., 1936, p. 994.
138. *The Aims of Drama,* p. 7.
139. Eliot, T. S.—*On Poetry and Poets,* p. 33.
140. *The Aims of Drama,* p. 7.
141. Eliot, T. S.—*On Poetry and Poets,* p. 86.

for the consciousness of a people than as a means to his own fame or achievement."[142]

As early as 1923, Eliot holds the conception of poetic drama as an organic whole.[143] He comes to the realization that verse is not a mere decoration or trimming added to the play. The poetic drama is not prose drama with a top dressing of poetry.[144] On the other hand, the poetic pattern and the dramatic pattern must subsist together as "integral products of one act of imagination."[145] In genuine poetic drama, poetry and drama are organically interfused together. In fact, it is the theatre where "poetry must justify itself dramatically."[146] As Eliot explains it:—

> "The writer of poetic drama is not merely a man skilled in two arts and skilful to weave them together; he is not a writer who can decorate a play with poetic language and metre. His task is different from that of the '"dramatist" or that of the "Poet", for his pattern is more complex and dimensional. ....The genuine poetic drama must at its best, observe all the regulations of the plain drama, but will weave them organically into a much richer design."[147]

According to Eliot, a great poetic drama is an extension of sensibility. It has the power to furnish vistas for exploring new horizons of thought and feeling. Eliot becomes deeply engrossed in the study of Elizabethan and Jacobean drama simply because it had demonstrated such potentialities. These dramatists could forge together all the elements required for the full flowering of the dramatic art. They expanded the range of fancy to its farthest extremes and wove it into the woof of complete verisimilitude. In the words of D. E. Jones, they were able to move smoothly from the one extreme to the other, in the same play "from the earthiness of the rude

---

142. Eliot, T. S.—*Selected Prose,* p. 187.

143. *The Nation and Athenaeum*; as quoted by Matthiessen, p. 158.

144. Jones, D. E.—*The Plays of T. S. Eliot,* p. 7.

145. Matthiessen, F. O.—*The Achievement of T. S. Eliot,* p. 156.

146. Eliot, T. S.—*On Poetry and Poets,* p. 72.

147. Eliot, T. S.—Introduction to G. Wilson Knight's—*The Wheel of Fire,* p. xix.

mechanicals to the ethereality of the fairies, from Caliban to Ariel."[148]

Eliot praises Shakespeare and other dramatists of the period. In his opinion, their plays are poetic, not because of touchstone passages of beautiful description or profound philosophy. The appeal of their poetry, on the other hand, lies in something else—the whole conception. With the disappearance of this conception, under the impact of science and industry and the break, which the closure of theatres, in 1642, brought in the tradition of poetic drama, the craft suffered a set back. The prose drama in the seventeenth century becomes divorced from human reality while poetic drama caters to the sheer bombast and heroic. As Eliot remarks:—

> "To create a form is not merely to invent a shape, a rhyme or rhythm. It is also the realization of the whole appropriate content of this rhyme or rhythm. The sonnet of Shakespeare is not merely such and such a pattern, but a precise way of thinking and feeling."[149]

Eliot's stress on "a precise way of thinking and feeling", provides a key to the understanding of all his creative endeavours in poetry as well as in drama. Poetic drama, he concedes, is better suited for "presenting feeling by a statement of events in human action or objects in the external world."[150] He argues that poetry alone is "the mode in which reality is experienced most profoundly."[151] It has the power to reproduce its various levels—sensuous, intellectual, psychological, social and spiritual—upon which the wheel of life moves forward. It is poetry which transforms the expression of drama into something more "complete and dramatic."[152] Therefore, Eliot contends:—

> "It is in fact the privilege of dramatic poetry to be able to show us several planes of reality, at once."[153]

He goes on:—

> "Everybody knows that there are things that can be said in

148. Jones, D. E.—*The Plays of T. S. Eliot,* p. 3.
149. Eliot, T. S.—*The Sacred Wood,* p. 63.
150. *Ibid,* p. 65.
151. Eliot, T. S.—U.P.U.C., p. 153.
152. Ronold Peacock—*The Art of Drama,* p. 225.
153. The Aims of Poetic Drama—Adam C. F. Jones: *The Plays of Eliot,* p. 15.

music that cannot be said in speech. And there are things which can be said in poetic drama that cannot be said in either music or ordinary speech."[154]

The assertion is significant. It incorporates a new element into the framewrok of poetic drama. Eliot's conception of a verse play involves a "musical pattern."[155] A playwright in verse, according to Eliot, "must work like a musician as well as like a prose dramatist."[156]

He does not agree with the general view expressed in literary circles that the failure of dramatists in the nineteenth century or earlier, was due to lack of their theatrical experience. He, however, gives his own verdict:—

"It is not primarily lack of plot, or lack of action and suspense, or imperfect realization of character or lack of anything of what is called "theatre", that makes these plays so lifeless: it is primarily that their rhythm of speech is something that we cannot associate with any human being except a poetry reciter."[157]

He expresses the same view about modern drama:—

"It is the rhythm so utterly absent from modern drama, either verse or prose and which interpreters of Shakespeare do their best to suppress."[158]

He concludes:—

"The ideal medium for poetry, to my mind, and the most direct means of social usefulness for poetry is the theatre."[159]

He continues:—

"For the simplest auditors there is the plot, for the more literary the words and phrasing, for the more musically sensitive the rhythm and for auditors of greater sensitiveness and understanding a meaning which reveals itself gradually.... sensitiveness of every auditor is acted upon by all these elements at once, though in different degrees of consciousness."[160]

---

154. *The Listener,* p. 994, Cit. by Jones, *The Plays of Eliot,* p. 14.
155. *Ibid.*
156. *Ibid.*
157. Eliot, T. S.—*On Poetry and Poets,* p. 31.
158. *The Nation and Athenaeum* (*quoted*) *Mathiessen, The Achievement of T. S. Eliot,* p. 156.
159. Eliot, T. S.—U.P.U.C., p. 153.
160. *Ibid.*

As in poetry so in drama, Eliot's first efforts were directed at revitalizing the rhythms and idioms of dramatic verse. By the end of the twenties, he had succeeded in performing the feat for the non-dramatic poetry. He was able to discover, create and develop a form of poetry, best suited to his own needs. But the theatre posed quite different problems. In the first instance, modern drama had lost the tradition in poetry. Secondly, the element of self-consciousness about dramatic poetry was lacking. Thirdly, naturalistic prose was the dominant theatrical medium. Fourthly, the loss of artistic conventions had persistently developed certain prejudices against dramatic poetry and its conscious enjoyment.[161] Fifthly, to the extent that the nineteenth century confined poetry to the closet, it also, in Eliot's view, impoverished drama.[162] Lastly, the lack of moral and social conventions also stood in the way of the poetic drama. In the absence of some common and well defined standards to measure what Jones refers to as "the significance of man's actions", it was but natural for poetic drama to face oblivion.

Eliot's efforts to revive poetic drama are marked, from the beginning, by full awareness of all these problems. He starts from one of his strongest convictions, that a verse form widely current in the past, even if renewed, cannot cater to the needs of the present. He expresses his genuine doubts if the Spensarian stanza, the Popean couplet or the Don Juan form of verse can serve any useful purpose. He has no hesitation in acknowledging the fact that blank verse for drama would be anything more than a poor imitation of Shakespeare. Eliot observes:—

> "The problem for us, therefore, is to get away from Shakespeare....That is not so easy. I have found in trying to write dramatic verse, that however different a metre from blank verse I was working with, whenever my attention was relaxed, or I have gone sleepy or stupid, I will wake up to find that I have been writing bad Shakespearean blank verse; and I had to scrap the lot and start all over again."[163]

---

161. Jones, D. E.—*The Plays of T. S. Eliot,* p. 21.

162. Matthiessen, F. O.—*Achievement of T. S. Eliot,* p. 157.

163. Eliot, T. S.—Radio talk quoted by Matthiessen: *Achievement of T. S. Eliot,* p. 158.

He concludes:—

> "Hence, we have to make use of suggestions from remote drama, too remote for there to be any danger of imitation such as Everyman and the late medieval morality and mystery plays and the great Greek dramatists."[164]

Long before, he modelled his **Sweeney Agonistes,** Eliot was convinced of the necessity of devising a new form out of the colloquial speech.[165] He had also expressed similar views in **The Sacred Wood:—**

> "The Elizabethan drama was aimed at a public which wanted *entertainment* of a crude sort but would stand a good deal of poetry; our problem should be to take a form of entertainment and subject it to the process which would leave it a form of art. Perhaps the music hall comedian is the best material."[167]

Sweeney Agonistes may be said to have initiated that "process." Eliot sub-titles its scenes as "fragments of an Aristophanic melodrama", but the source of conversational verse is much nearer at hand. The play stands out as the most important experiment in the development of Eliot's dramatic art. The reasons are obvious. First, it introduces colloquial rhythms and diction into poetic drama. Second, it deals with an aspect of the contemporary world. Third, it parodies the popular song of the Jazz era.[167] Fourth, Eliot shows by implication, that any hope for the revival of poetic drama is associated much more with the "robust entertainment" of the lower class than with that of the morally corrupt middle class which has been badly affected by the lifeless mechanisms of standardized cinema.[168]

Looking back at the efforts which Eliot has consistently made in reviving the art of drama, one may safely say that the promise of **Sweeney Agonistes** has been more than fulfilled. Besides, in between "Sweeney" and "Ash Wednesday" there has taken place a radical change. He has not lost his fondness for music hall as a dramatic medium. But the content

---

164. Matthiessen—*Achievement of T. S. Eliot,* p. 158.
165. Eliot, T. S.—*Introduction to Savonarola.*
166. Eliot, T. S.—*The Sacred Wood,* p. 70.
167. Jones, D. I.—*The Plays of T. S. Eliot,* p. 28.
168. Matthiessen, F. O.—*Achievement of T. S. Eliot,* p. 158.

of his plays irrespective of the medium, has become altogether different.[169]

The changing pattern of Eliot's dramatic themes is important. Considered as a literary problem, it may not sound logical. But the problem of reviving poetic drama is not purely literary. It is something more; and that perhaps, none can better understand than Eliot himself. He had rightly perceived that the revival of this dead art would involve the necessary pre-condition of the "wholeness of outlook"—an outlook which could comprehend and comprise all aspects of human life. It is the ever growing consciousness of this wholeness of outlook which marks all his dramatic and non-dramatic poetry since **Ash Wednesday**. The shift is not sudden. It is born out of a consistent point of view. As Eliot explains:—

> "For it is ultimately the function of art imposing a credible *order* upon ordinary reality, and thereby eliciting some perception of an order in reality, to bring us to a condition of serenity, stillness and reconciliation; and then leave us, as Virgil left Dante, to proceed toward a region where that guide can avail us no farther."[170]

Eliot's later poetry and his plays exhibit, to an ample degree, his efforts towards the formulation of "a credible order" which he deems so necessary for the purpose of art. How far has he been able through his plays to achieve this ideal is a question, yet too early to answer.

Criticism in the last phase of his literary career is important in many respects. His rehabilitation of Milton has greatly added to his prestige as a critic. His essays on "**Drama and Poetry**"; "**There Voices of Poetry**"; "**The Music of Poetry**"; and "**Johnson as a Critic and Poet**", taken together, would still place him by the side of the greatest of the literary critics. "**To Criticise the Critic**", is an honest attempt of the critic in Eliot to analyse his own art in the perspective of his literary career, spread-over to more than four decades. In the realm of social criticism also, the last phase is no less significant. **The**

---

169. Brown E. Martin—*Eliot, The Man and His Works,* (ed.) Allen Tate, p. 118.

170. Eliot, T. S.—*On Poetry and Poets,* p. 87.

Idea of a Christian Society; The Notes towards the Definition of Culture; The Social Function of Poetry; and **Virgil and the Christian World** are illuminating essays. His observations on contemporary society and even more, his concern for the future of society, especially in relation to religion and culture, may be considered of great value to the modern concept of society and anthropology. John Hayward rightly remarks:—

> "There is perhaps inevitably, an element of didacticism in his later essays and addresses, which is not wholly disguised, though it is mitigated by Mr. Eliot's characteristic method of exposition, by cautious stages of definition, doubt, reservation and qualification to the final affirmation."[171]

The Idea of a Christian Society—an essay which generated much heat and controversy—does not formulate a definite programme or plan. It distinguishes rather a Christian idea of society from other ideas "with which it has become entangled."[172] The book is revealing in as far as it provides some positive basis to the understanding of Eliot's enthusiastic bias of Christian Humanism. As he declares:—

> "A Christian education would primarily train people to be able to think in Christian categories."[173]

This is, what his later poetry in general and plays in particular, have been "unobtrusively doing."[174]

---

171. Hayward John—*Selected Prose,* p. 12, Introduction.
172. Williams Raymond—*Culture and Society,* p. 226.
173. Eliot, T. S.—*The Idea of a Christian Society,* p. 28.
174. Jones, D. E.—*The Plays of T. S. Eliot,* pp. 214-15.

CHAPTER VI

ELIOT AND OTHER CRITICS

Let me confess, that I feel myself diminished at the very idea of making a comparative study of Eliot and his contemporary critics. The subject, difficult as it is, seems no less embarrassing. It reminds me of an important dictum that to see his **maestro,** Dante had to "lift his eyelids a little higher."[1] Surely, the dictum states a significant principle but does not solve the problem. It will sound too arrogant to look up to Eliot and his contemporaries to claim scholarship. Yet, through these pages, a humble attempt has been made to determine the comparative nature of Eliot's literary criticism, in relation to that of Richards, Leavis and other critics of the Formalistic School.

We would like to initiate our discussion with some of the moving tributes which some of the contemporary writers have paid to Eliot after his death. **Ezra Pound,** his guide, friend, and philosopher recommends:—

> "Let him rest in peace. I can only repeat, but with the urgency of fifty years ago: READ HIM."[2]

John Crowe Ransom has expressed similar feelings:—

> "We must re-read him, and think a long time about his achievement, and about how the parts cumulated into a whole; thinking as precisely as we could possibly think about something intangible, in order to say what he had meant to English letters. His writings had already been committed to the public domain, but suddently we had become the executors who must appraise the state."[3]

---

1. Tate Allen—*Post Script*: *Eliot*: *The Man and His Work, p.* 389.
2. Tate Allen (ed.)—*Eliot*: *The Man and His Work,* p. 89.
3. Eliot—*The Man and His Mission,* p. 133.

Bonamy Dobree strikes a personal note of affection:—

"By his being he commanded respect; by his response to one's own being he nurtured the profoundest and most lasting affection."[4]

Allen Tate eulogises with a sort of spiritual candour:—

"One dies everday one's own death; but one cannot imagine the death of the man who was *il maestro di color che sanno.*"[5]

Cleanth Brooks highlights the literary aspect:—

"Few literary men in our history have so consistently related all their activities to a coherent set of principles. And the consistency of his various writings reflects the quality of the man. In a time of disorder, Eliot moved toward a restoration of order—toward the restoration of the order that poetry alone, perhaps can give."[6]

C. Day Lewis invokes the Muse of poetry:—

........"Now, supplying
Our loss with words of comfort, his kind ghost
Says all that need be said about committedness
Here in East Coker they have crossed
My heart again—*For us there is* only *the trying*
To learn to use words. The rest is not our business."[7]

Sir Herbert Read introduces a religious strain:—

"I do not presume to judge Eliot; I even tremble as I attempt to reveal some of the dimensions of his agony. But if in this context, I am to give any first allegiance to poetry (and I do not for a moment question the allegiance that a Christian poet must give to one whom Kierkegaard called "the unique person") it is not harsh to pretend that the poet can have any other life or kingdom but poetry."[8]

Perhaps, **I. A. Richards'** tribute is by far the most factual:—

"In talking of a writer we have known—and to those to whom he has mattered—how can we speak without feeling that he himself is by far the most important of the audience? As

---

4. Tate Allen (ed.)—*Eliot*: *The Man and His Work,* p. 88.
5. *Ibid,* p. 389.
6. *Ibid,* p. 316.
7. *Ibid,* p. 115.
8. *Ibid,* p. 37.

indeed he is, not in any supernatural or transcendent sense, but as represented here, now, in minds which are in a measure what they are through him, so that in their judgment and reflection he is alive. Of no one is this more true than *TSE*. In one degree or another we are all products of his work."[9]

In the context of these warm feelings, expressed by some of his closest associates, it appears desirable to point out that these tributes should not be taken as the expression of complete agreement with Eliot. In his essay on Yeats, Eliot himself has sounded a note of caution that "to be able to praise, it is not necessary to feel complete agreement."[10] But these expressions are certainly the token of this much of acknowledgment that Eliot and his work has a far greater relevance. His literary career is such that cannot be assessed in isolation. Any attempt to separate him from the wider literary or historical perspective is fraught with serious errors.

Looking back at the contemporary scene of literary criticism in the beginning of the Twenties, we experience the emergence of two major critics: T. S. Eliot and I. A. Richards. It is wrong to presume that either of them pioneered any school of criticism of which the other one is also a member. Although, both of them have lent their support in the development of what we know today as the New Criticism; yet each has maintained his own reservations on the subject.[11] Eliot has many times criticised I. A. Richards and his literary theories; while Richards also has more than once voiced his differences with T. S. Eliot.[12] The two critics, who have been jointly and severally responsible for directing literary criticism into new channels, right from the beginning of the twenties, hold identical as well as dissenting views on various aspects of English literary criticism.

It is not easy to summarize precisely their actual positions. Broadly speaking, the critical methods of Eliot and Richards may appear to be similar. To both of them, the critical process is the same: analysis, interpretation and evalua-

9. Richards, I. A.—*On T. S. E.: Eliot: The Man and His Work,* p. 1.
10. Eliot, T. S.—*On Poetry and Poets,* p. 262.
11. Eliot, T. S.—U.P.U.C., p. 149.
12. Richards, I. A.—*The Principles of Literary Criticism.*

tion. But, a close study of the details involved in the process, would show that there is much dissimilarity in the nature and scope of their respective methods. Apparently, we notice four differences. First, Richards being an adept analyst, brings out a more elaborate and comprehensive technique of verbal analysis. Second, being a teacher, he shows greater skill in the matter of interpretation. Third, Richards with his wider knowledge of science and technology, has given a scientific complexion to his verbal technique. Lastly, he has been able to provide to his technique a theoretical base, developed from his deep study and understanding of psychology. Eliot, on the other hand, is an analyst in the general sense. His interest and knowledge in psychology is not so profound. Moreover, he does not subscribe to Richards' theory of Value and Communication. Eliot's own observations, in this respect, are significant:—

> "Mr. Richards, like every serious critic of poetry, is a serious moralist as well. His ethics or theory of value, is one which I cannot accept; or rather, I cannot accept any such theory which is erected upon purely individual-psychological foundations."[13]

He explains the reasons of his disapproval:—

> "But his psychology of the poetic experience is based upon his own experience of poetry as truly as his theory of value arises out of his psychology."[14]

Eliot commends Richards' "discriminating taste in poetry", but warns:—

> "If on the other hand, you had no faith in the critic's ability to tell a good poem from a bad one, you would put little reliance upon the validity of his theories."[15]

Again, in the essay **The Modern Mind**, he pays a left-handed compliment to Richards' criticism:—

> "Even if his criticism proves to be entirely on the wrong track, even if his modern 'self-consciousness' turns out to be only a blind alley, Mr. Richards will have done something in accelerating the exhaustion of the possibilities. He will have help-

---

13. Eliot, T. S.–U.P.U.C., Introduction, p. 17.
14. *Ibid.*
15. *Ibid.*

ed indirectly to discredit the criticism of persons qualified neither by sensibility nor by knowldege of poetry from which we suffer daily."[16]

Eliot's disapproval of Richards' criticism is based on his own reaction against what he calls the "lemon squeezer school of criticism."[17] In fact, he directs his attack on the class-room-method of Richards' criticism, which the latter has propounded in his **Practical Criticism.**[18] Reacting indirectly to this technique, which he qualifies as the theory of Education, Eliot observes:—

> "The method is to take a well known poem, without reference to the author or to his other works, analyse it stanza by stanza and line by line, and extract, squeeze, tease, press every drop of meaning out of it that one can."[19]

The method "exhibits sincerity and singlemindedness",[20] but Eliot foresees three dangers. First, it may make us think that the poem has only one meaning.[21] Second, it may give rise to the legitimate speculation that this meaning is what the poet meant to mean. Third, such type of teasing and pressing the stanzas beyond their reasonable limits, may cause the poem to disintegrate in the mind of the readers.[22]

Apart from these objections, which Eliot enlists against the method of class-room criticism of Richárds, there are basic differences between the two critics on the problem of Value. Eliot's understanding of value is generally structural. He is asserting again and again close "interaction between prose and verse."[23] He affirms that in the writing of poetry, there is a great deal, which requires "conscious and deliberate"[24] efforts. He is always stressing the need of a suitable form, which

---

16. Eliot, T. S.—U.P.U.C., p. 123.
17. Eliot, T. S.—*On Poets and Poetry,* p. 118.
18. Richards, I. A.—*Practical Criticism.*
19. Eliot, T. S.—*On Poetry and Poets,* p. 118.
20. Lucy Sean—*Eliot and The Idea of Tradition,* p. 43.
21. Eliot, T. S.—O.P.P., p. 118.
22. *Ibid.*
23. Eliot, T. S.—U.P.U.C., p. 152.
24. Eliot, T. S.—*Tradition and Individual Talent, Selected Prose,* p. 29.

possesses "a precise way of thinking and feeling"[25]—the way the sonnet of Shakespeare showed that capacity. In short, Eliot stands for a well-knit "organisation"[26] of all the parts of a poem, fused together within the pattern of its structural unity—the sort of unity which Eliot was able to achieve in **Four Quartets.** Richards' concept of value is altogether different. It is not merely structural: it is mainly psychological. His concern is not so much with the poem itself, as it is with the reaction it brings in the mind of the reader. Pursued to its logical conclusion, the divergence in the two emphases assumes basic difference in the whole body of their literary criticism. Eliot foresees value in the poem itself while Richards explores it in the mind of the reader or the listener. This shift, from the object of art to the mind of its appreciator, plays a vital part in the whole theory and practice of Richards' literary criticism.

It has been pointed out that Richards' theory of Value is only a restatement of Aristotle's theory of Katharsis. In fact, the influence of Aristotle, Bentham, and Coleridge is clearly discernible in the poetics of Prof. Richards. For the purpose of a better understanding of Richards' view of Value, it is necessary to follow some of its meaningful features. We come across the first glimpses of his theory of Value in the **Foundations of Aesthetics**—a book which Richards wrote in collaboration with C. K. Ogden and James Wood. Later on, in the **Principles of Literary Criticism**; and **Science and Poetry,** Richards further develops the same concept. The **Aesthetics** provides a new definition of "Beauty" as "anything that excites emotions."[27] The book refers to the beautiful; and suggests a peaceful and pleasurable state of mind called **synaesthesis.** Richards explains that it is a state of "harmony and equilibrium for our impulses."[28] He contends that all impulses are not "naturally harmonious",[29] but a proper organisation of some

25. Eliot, T. S.—*The Sacred Wood,* p. 63.
26. Eliot, T. S.—U.P.U.C., p. 146.
27. Richards, I. A.—*Foundation of Aesthetics,* pp. 123-24.
28. Wimsatt and Brooks—*History of Literary Criticism,* p. 615.
29. *Aesthetics,* p. 75.

of them can bring us harmony.[30] It must be noted again that the organisation, as conceived by Richards in the fusion of these impulses, is quite different from that as suggested by Eliot.[31] Eliot's stress is on organisation in relation to the various parts of a poem; while Richards is talking of organising the impulses that are latent in the mind of a poet. In Richards' view, even the conflicting impulses must have their "free interplay"[32] in the process of producing a beautiful work.

But the most comprehensive statement on the Theory of Value is to be found in the **Principles of Literary Criticism.**[33] Richards observes that impulses often act in an imperceptible manner. They are sometimes not compatible to what he calls appetancies. It means that their organisation or systematization involves a large number of combinations and permutations, thus making organisation a subject for planned and conscious arrangement. But Richards warns:—

> "To guard against a possible misunderstanding it may be added that the organisation and systematisation of which I have been speaking in this Chapter are not primarily an affair of conscious planning or arrangements, as this is understood, for example, by a great business house or by a railway."[34]

In conclusion, Richards' position may be stated as: first, the synaesthesis "refreshes and never exhausts"[35]; second, the impulses may be organised by synthesis or by elimination but only the poetry emerging out of the former organisation or what he calls the poetry of "Inclusion" can be the greatest; third, the presence of irony may act as a sort of touch-stone in judging its greatness. He even declares that "fine irony is ever present in the best poetry."[36]

John Crowe Ransom does not agree with the conclusions of Prof. Richards. He has questioned the validity of the

---

30. Wimsatt and Brooks—*History of Literary Criticism,* p. 616.
31. Eliot, T. S.—U.P.U.C., p. 146.
32. *Aesthetics,* p. 75.
33. Richards, I. A.—*Principles,* p. 44.
34. Richards, I. A.—*Principles of Literary Criticism,* p. 57.
35. Richards, I. A.—*Aesthetics,* p. 77.
36. *Ibid.*

touch-stone of irony:—

> "My belief is that opposites can never be said to be resolved or reconciled merely because they have been got into the same poem or got into the same complex of affective experience to create there a kind of tension."[37]

Irony, according to Ransom, cannot be a "constant characteristic"[38] of good poetry. It only suggests failure to unify. He has equally criticised Eliot's notion of a poem as a "fusion of thought and feeling."[39] "Both the critics", Ransom asserts, "attempt to reconcile", what he considers "irrconcilables."[40] His contention is that "ironic poetry can represent only irresolution: that is, the oppositions produce an indecisive effect."[41] Ransom's attack on Richards is directed against contradictory elements in his theory and practice. First, that the poem is "susceptible to analysis."[42] Second, the psychological goings-on turn out to be "below the surface and out of sight."[43] Hence, Ransom concludes, that if the "poise" of the poem consists as Richards feels, it does in only the "response" of the readers as against relevant structure of the poem itself, then it becomes all the more useless to carry on its analysis in any form whatsoever.[44]

It is not easy to agree to all the observations of Ransom. The way he has questioned the propriety of the use of irony, does not sound as fully justified. Eliot's own position in this particular respect is somewhat analogous to that of Richards. He believes, that in poetry "heterogeneous ideas"[45] can be yoked together. He praises Marvell for what he calls "making of the familiar strange and the strange familiar."[46] He com-

---

37. Ransom, J. Crowe—*The New Criticism,* p. 95.
38. Richards, I. A.—*Principles of Literary Criticism,* p. 250.
39. Ransom, J. Crowe—*The New Criticism,* p. 183.
40. Wimsatt & Brooks—*History of Literary Criticism* (Quoted), p. 621.
41. *Ibid,* p. 622.
42. *Ibid,* p. 620.
43. *Ibid.*
44. *Ibid.*
45. Eliot, T. S.—*Selected Essays,* p. 243.
46. *Ibid,* p. 258.

mends the metaphysical poets for "amalgamating disparate experiences."[47] His argument that witty poetry is embodied "in the expression of every experience",[48] indirectly supports the view that wit calls for the fusion of the "potentially discordant"[49] elements—the elements which are necessarily present in a good poem. To quote some of the examples, the poetry, of Elizabethan dramatists in the 16th century; of Dante in the 13th; of Metaphysical poets in the 17th; and of Jules Laforgue and other symbolists in the present era, can be brought under this category, where disparate and discordant elements are effectively fused together.

In one more respect, Eliot shares his views with Richards. His theory of Poetry is equivalent to some version of latter's psychologistic theory.[50] Both of them agree that ordinary and artistic experiences are different. Moreover, an artistic experience comprehends greater complexity and inheres a wider scope. As to the sources of the poetic experience, both the critics have something common to suggest. For example, Eliot differentiates between the two experiences:—

> "The latter (ordinary man) falls in love, or reads Spinoza, and these two experiences have nothing to do with each other, or with the noise of the type writer or the smell of the cooking; in the mind of the poet the experiences are always forming new wholes."[51]

We quote a similar passage from Richards:—

> "The wheeling of the pigeons in Trafalgar Square may seem to have no relation to the colour of the water in the basins to the tones of a speaker's voice or to the drift of his remarks. A narrow field of stimulation is all that we can manage and we overlook the rest. But the artist does not, and when he needs it, he has it at his disposal."[52]

The two passages quoted above do not require further comment. They show, that in certain areas, Eliot and Richards

---

47. Eliot, T. S.—*Selected Essays,* p. 247.
48. *Ibid,* p. 261.
49. Wimsatt & Brooks—*History of Literary Criticism,* p. 621.
50. Ransom, J. Crowe—*The New Criticism.*
51. Eliot, T. S.—*Selected Essays,* p. 247.
52. Richards, I. A.—*Principles of Literary Criticism,* p. 185.

share each other's views. Nevertheless, the differences in them are basic. In this respect, let us bear in mind two important points: first, Richards has little to say on the phenomenon of poetic creation; second, he, from the very beginning, has endeavoured to maintain a careful distinction between the "emotional state produced in the reader (the state of synaesthetics) and the means used to produce this emotional state."[53] Eliot, on the other hand, has his own theory of the "poetic process"[54] and has always maintained that a "poem is a fusion of thought and feeling."[55]

On the question, whether art is expression or communication, Richards' stand is clear. He holds the view that communication is an integral part of poetry. He argues that "a great part of our experience takes the form it does, because we are social beings and accustomed to communication from infancy."[56] He goes as far as to suggest that all "supremely successful communication" involves a close and natural correspondence between what he calls "the poet's impulses and the possible impulses in his reader."[57] According to him, such a psychological correspondence becomes operative through the medium of language. He also forewarns against any "deliberate or conscious attempt to communication", because such an attempt is not going to be as "successful as the unconscious indirect method."[58]

Eliot's approach in this respect is different from that of Richards. He is not prepared to subscribe to the view that poetry is mere communication. "Communication", he says, "will not explain poetry."[59] He also appears to disagree with Richards' definition of a poem as "an artist's experience."[60] Eliot argues:—

---

53. Wimsatt & Brooks—*History of Literary Criticism,* p. 623.
54. Eliot, T. S.—*The Sacred Wood,* p. 53.
55. Eliot, T. S.—*The Selected Prose,* p. 112.
56. Richards, I. A.—*Principles,* p. 25.
57. *Ibid,* p. 29.
58. *Ibid.*
59. Eliot, T. S.—U.P.U.C., p. 138.
60. Richards, I. A.—*Principles,* p. 226.

"If poetry is a form of "communication", yet that which is to be communicated is the poem itself; and only incidentally the experience and the thought which have gone into it."[61]

He, however, agrees with Richards on two counts: first, that a poet wishes "to give pleasure to entertain or divert people";[62] and second, that any sort of planned or conscious attempt to design the communication is not to prove fruitful.[63] David Daiches' observations on the early phase of Richards' critical career are significant:—

"Richards' concern in his early phase of his critical career was to demonstrate the value of poetry by showing, how it arose from and communicated a state of psychological health, a finely balanced organisation of the nervous system which was a basic human problem."[64]

Naturally, if the poem is meaningful in communicating the "poet's valuable inner organisation",[65] as in Richards' view it is, then an investigation into the way it communicates, becomes necessary. It is with this view, that he takes up the study of semantics and considers the problem of meaning, language and its use in minute details. **The Meaning of Meaning**; the **Principles of Literary Criticism**; the **Philosophy of Rhetoric**; and **Practical Criticism** contain the various facets of the semantic principle, which Richards has elaborated. It is not possible here to discuss in detail the implications of this concept. But the whole case, which Richards has presented, may be studied in some of its broader outlines.

In the first instance, Richards makes out a point for the "symbolic or the referential"[66] use of language. Second, he differentiates between its "scientific and emotive"[67] values. Third, in determining what Richards calls the "meaning of meaning", he develops the psychological and contextual theory

---

61. Eliot, T. S.–U.P.U.C., p. 30.
62. *Ibid.*
63. *Ibid.*
64. Daiches David–*The Present Age,* p. 132.
65. *Ibid,* p. 132.
66. Richards, I. A.–*The Meaning of Meaning;* preface.
67. Richards, I. A.–*Principles,* p. 261.

of meaning.[68] The theory suggests that the words are symbols which signify their "full, proper and requisite meaning in that particular context."[69] Fourth, rhythm and meaning are inseparably related. "Poetic rhythm," says Richards, "influences and is influenced by meaning."[70] Fifth, he feels that metaphor is not merely "a grace or ornament or added power of langauge": it is its constitutive form."[71] Lastly, the semantic analysis such as that advocated by Richards appears to imply "value in complexity."[72] The semantic criticism lays stress on the organic structure of the parts of a poem wherein they happen to be so closely fused together as to make the totality of meaning possible, not on one level, but on various levels of the poem.

Barring Richards' classification of the language into scientific or emotive uses, Eliot's own practice in more than one sense, is not different from that of Richards. He, like Richards, supports the view that words have great power;[73] that rhythm and meaning are inseparable;[74] and that their "contexual background"[75] is no less important. Like any other semanticist, Eliot has closely stood by the "organic whole of the poem."[76] In fact, it is Eliot, who has emphasized, more than any one else, on the "musicality of words in their colloquial setting."[77] The sense of rhythm, according to him, is an indispensable part of the sense of structure.[78] As a rule, in the metaphorical and the ironic uses of language, Eliot's position is similar to that of Richards. But in its operative part, what Eliot wants the metaphor or irony to serve, is differ-

---

68. Richards, I. A.—*The Meaning of Meaning.*
69. *Ibid.*
70. Richards, I. A.—*Practical Criticism,* p. 229.
71. Richards, I. A.—*Philosophy of Rhetoric.*
72. Wimsatt & Brooks—*History of Literary Criticism,* p. 652.
73. Eliot, T. S.—*The Music of Poetry,* O.P.P., p. 26.
74. *Ibid.*
75. Eliot, T. S.—*"Auditory Imagination",* U.P.U.C., p. 118.
76. Eliot, T. S.—*The Music of Poetry,* O.P.P., p. 26.
77. *Ibid.*
78. *Ibid.*

ent from that what Richards wants them to constitute.[79] These, in Eliotian concept, are all aspects of dramatic presentation as distinguished from the "personal expression"[80] of the poet. It appears feasible to point out the significant shift in the earlier position of I. A. Richards. In the early phases of his criticial career, Richards had begun with the thesis, that words were "arbitrary signs."[81] But gradually, like Eliot, he arrives at the concept of a better organic impact of words.[82] In this respect, the observations of Wimsatt and Brooks are significant:—

> "Even a theorist like I. A. Richards, who began with the thesis that words were arbitrary signs, in the course of time proceeded toward a correction and modification of that thesis and in doing so came to argue for much more organic conception of words, finally arriving at the view that reality itself, as man can know it, is a symbolic construction: 'the fabric of our meanings, which is the word', is Richards' way of putting it in 1936."[83]

Apart from their literary significance, Richards' theories of Value, Communication, and Language have added new dimensions to some of the important issues, which the contemporary society is facing at present. Through these theories, both Richards and Eliot have been able to focus attention on such subjects as the relationship between "poetry and belief"; the contemporary "state of culture"; and the "social uses" which art, literature, and language can be put to. In this way, Eliot and Richards concentrate on directing their attack on the aesthetic notions of the Romantics. By the 1920s, there is an orthodox tendency of considering the "aesthetic experience in isolation",[84] which was vigorously attacked by the two critics. Eliot's attack is directed through his "re-emphasis on tradition and faith";[85] while Richards spearheads

---

79. Richards, I. A.—*Philosophy of Rhetoric.*
80. Wimsatt & Brooks—*History of Literary Criticism,* p. 675.
81. *Ibid,* p. 586.
82. Richards, I. A.—*Practical Criticism,* p. 232.
83. Wimsatt & Brooks—*History of Literary Criticism,* p. 584.
84. Williams Raymond—*Culture and Society,* p. 239.
85. *Culture and Society,* p. 239.

it from a different angle—the "social facts of language and communication."[86] He observes:—

> "We pass, as a rule from a chaotic to a better organised state by ways which we know nothing about. Typically through the influence of other minds. Literature and the arts are the chief means by which their influences are diffused."[87]

Pointing out the social use of the Psychological Theory of Value, Richards reaffirms its claim to regulate life and its standards:—

> "The conduct of life, is throughout an attempt to organise impulses so that success is obtained for the greater number or mass of them, for the most important and the weightiest set."[88]

Richards feels that the "thwarting of impulses"[89] in the individual as also in society leads to social disturbance and disorganisation. Hence, the problem of conduct is the problem of getting these impulses, adjusted and organised in a normal way. Value in this context assumes the role of order. What is psychologically effective in the case of an individual, becomes equally effective in relation to community and society. Thus, tensions—individual or social—if removed through the possible organisation of the impulses, would yield fruit and bring about a sort of sublimation in the entire conduct of life. The importance of art and literature lies in the fact that they offer convincing examples of such organisation. Therefore, Richards concludes that poetry is a "perfectly possible means of over-coming chaos."[90] He makes one of the oft-debated declarations:—

> "If this should happen a mental chaos such as man has never experienced may be expected. We shall be thrown back, as Matthew Arnold foresaw, upon poetry. Poetry, is capable of saving us......"[91]

---

86. *Culture and Society,* p. 239.
87. Richards, I. A.–*Principles,* p. 57.
88. *Ibid,* p. 46.
89. *Ibid,* p. 51.
90. Richards, I. A.–*Science and Poetry,* pp. 82-83.
91. *Ibid.*

Eliot strongly objects to this kind of Richards' assertion.[92] He resents "the intense religious seriousness of such an attitude towards poetry."[93] "What he proposes", Eliot affirms, "is nothing less than a regimen of spiritual exercises."[94] He continues:—

> "I only assert again that what he (Richards) is trying to do is essentially the same as what Arnold wanted to do: to preserve emotions without the beliefs with which their history has been involved. It would seem that Mr. Richards, on his own showing is engaged in a rear-guard religious action."[95]

In criticising Richards' statement: "Poetry is capable of saving us", Eliot, in fact, is criticising its "emotive vagueness"; its "blindness" to some of the relevant facts of modern life; and its suggestiveness of a religious terminology."[96] He is against the very notion of conceding to poetry any status, equivalent to that of a spiritual "Saviour."[97]

In closing our comparative analysis of Eliot and Richards, we may simply suggest that both of them have exercised considerable influence in their respective spheres. The former is the most influential of the "descriptive critics;"[98] and the latter is an "influential theorist"[99] of the century. Richards' criticism is affective rather than genetive. He has tried to interpret the value of literature in terms of its "after-effects"[100] on the reader's mind. It is but for him that semantics has become an "increasingly important aspect of modern criticism."[101] If Eliot, by his re-emphasis on Tradition, Impersonality and Order, comes very near to the classicists then Richards through his deep interest in psychology and syn-

---

92. Eliot, T. S.–U.P.U.C., p. 132.
93. *Ibid.*
94. *Ibid.*
95. *Ibid,* p. 135.
96. Buckley Vincent–*Poetry and Morality,* p. 30.
97. Eliot, T. S.–U.P.U.C.
98. Watson George–*The Literary Critics,* p. 196.
99. *Ibid.*
100. Wimsatt & Brooks–*History of Literary Criticism.*
101. Daiches David–*The Present Age,* p. 133.

aesthesis appears closer to the Romanticists. But irrespective of any such rigidity in their positions, the New Criticism owes much to their endeavours. It is through them that the literary criticism of today has acquired a scientific and psychoanalytical basis.

After I. A. Richards, the other major critic and contemporary of T. S. Eliot, is Dr. F. R. Leavis. His career as a critic may be said to have begun with the publication of the **"Scrutiny"**, in 1932. Watson calls him the most influential British-born critic of the century, "less original and more predictable."[102] Daiches finds in him the Arnoldian trait of "echoing the best."[103] Laurence Larner refers to him as a "child of I. A. Richards."[104] And there are some, who have qualified him as more "Eliotian than Eliot himself." Nevertheless, it is more correct to infer, that apart from Arnold, Dr. Leavis has been much influenced by "Eliot's earlier critical essays as also by the early Richards."[105]

We would like here to remove one misconceived notion. Dr. Leavis is not a verbal analyst of the line either of Richards or of his erstwhile disciple William Empson. Although, he relies too much on the "producible texts"[106]; yet for no other purpose than to see, what he calls **the thing** he finds himself "needing to say."[107] Perhaps, his position is "more original";[108] and his tone "more his own".[109] His critical method may be stated as:—

> "Dr. Leavis opposed a *prior* theorising about literature: criticism for him was a practical activity and properly consisted in the careful demonstration of the qualities of a work by a

---

102. Watson George—*The Literary Critics,* p. 208.

103. Daiches David—*The Present Age,* p. 136.

104. *Life and Death of Scrutiny—London Magazine*—(quoted) *The Literary Critics,* G. Watson, p. 208.

105. Daiches David—*The Present Age,* p. 137.

106. Leavis, F. R.—*Revaluation;* Introduction.

107. *Ibid.*

108. Daiches David—*The Present Age,* p. 137.

109. *Ibid.*

subtle blend of quotation, running commentary, and devices for communicating admiration or contempt."[110]

And the aim of his criticism is best contained in the first editorial of the **Scrutiny:—**

"The general dissolution of standards is a common place. Those who are aware of the situation will be concerned to cultivate awareness and will be actively concerned for standards."[111]

Taken together, the two statements may mean to suggest the critical credo of Dr. Leavis. He is interested in establishing new literary standards or what Daiches has called in "ruthless sifting of the little wheat of good and serious literature from the abundant chaff of triviality and shodiness......"[112] It is perhaps the same "ideal" which Eliot himself has qualified as the "sorting of certain books, certain essays, certain sentences, certain men, who have been "useful" to us."[113] In his method, Leavis is certainly "more relevant, more rounded and more complete"[114] than either of the two, Arnold and Eliot. He is always furnishing details of quotation and commentary, in order to carry the reader with him.

Obviously, this habit of critical procedure in Leavis may be due to the fact, that unlike Eliot, he is primarily a teacher. His criticism involves a particular conception of "critical education",[115] which at bottom, has always been moral. He displays a catholic disgust for mere "entertainment"[116] in literature. According to him, criticism is a very serious type of activity and the greatness of a work of literature consists in presenting a "genuine moral vision" of experience, communicated through a "fully particularised, and fully realised imaginative rendering of life."[117] In **The Great Tradition,** Leavis

---

110. Daiches David—*The Present Age,* p. 137.
111. *Scrutiny.*
112. Daiches David—*The Present Age,* p. 136.
113. *Selected Prose; The Functions of Criticism,* p. 19.
114. Buckley Vincent—*Poetry and Morality,* p. 158.
115. *Ibid.*
116. Daiches David—*The Present Age,* p. 137.
117. *Ibid.*

upholds the cause of three novelists: George Eliot; Henry James; and Joseph Conrad. He feels that the great tradition in English novel has been the tradition of a serious moral concern. He calls these novelists: "significant in terms of that human awareness they promote; awareness of the possibilities of life."[118]

Leavis' reference to "human awareness" is really significant. His own understanding of such an awareness is not negative. It implies an explicit positiveness for "the possibilities of life." It is at this point that Eliot and Leavis tend to differ in their approach towards moral values. Eliot in this respect represents the Hulme-Baudelarian tradition of morality. Leavis, on the other hand, looks forward to a literature, which explicitly brings out a victory of "life" over its sordid irritants—irritants which try to devitalise human energy. Eliot's appreciation of Baudelair's way of affirming life does not satisfy Leavis; for the simple reason, that the latter makes use of "negative emotions and attitudes"[119] in analysing, revealing and judging their negativity. His position is different. He stands for a positive affirmation of life—the kind of affirmation, which in one sense or the other, he happens to find in the novelists of **The Great Tradition.** But the affirmation of life Leavis envisages in a work of art, should in no case, be taken to mean an easy optimism towards life. It must involve a struggle, wherein its "radical and central" problems are "squarely faced."[120] The struggle within itself must be a struggle for the lived values of life. Art and literature, according to Leavis, further the emotional and spiritual health of the individual and community. What he really wants literature to achieve, is perhaps best explained in his own statement, where he defines the purpose of art as "serving the spontaneous—creative fullness of being."[121] His observations on Lawrence would clarify the point:—

118. Leavis, F. R.–*The Great Tradition,* p. 2.
119. Buckley Vincent–*Poetry and Morality,* p. 191.
120. *Ibid.*
121. Leavis, F. R.–*D. H. Lawrence, Novelist,* p. 172.

> "Lawrence stood for life, and shows in his criticism, tossed as it was, for the most part, in the most marginal way, an extraordinarily quick and sure sense for the difference between what makes for life and that which makes against it."[122]

Leavis' comparison of Eliot with Flaubert is equally suggestive:—

> "One may not have thought of comparing Eliot's creative work to Flaubert's, but Eliot's attitude to life is, not less than Flaubert's, one of distaste and disgust."[123]

In fact, Leavis is attacking on a particular point of view, or what he himself calls a cult of art that amounts to "religion",[124] and the directing spirit of which is the "rejection of life."[125] Leavis prescribes that the artist's purpose should be to help people in exploring the "profound energies and vast potentialities of life."[126] It is on this count, that he criticises Eliot for "standing-off"[127] from life. He finds in Eliot a sort of "sickness of spirit", which he argues, "is certainly not less intense"[128] than that of Flaubert. Again, he praises Hopkins, because his poetry presents a kind of "triumph of the spirit."[129]

It is not within the purview of our discussion to either refute or subscribe to what Leavis has to say on Eliot, in this particular respect. We have quoted certain extracts from Leavis to show, that the two critics, though committed to moral values of literature, have their respective limitations and differences of approach.

Again, on the problem of Impersonality in Art, Leavis' position is different from that of Eliot. He does not agree with the Eliotian view that the writer as artist is different from the writer as man who experiences. Leavis feels that impersonality lies in the effect of the work rather than in the

---

122. Leavis, F. R.—*The Common Pursuit,* p. 284.
123. Leavis, F. R.—*D. H. Lawrence—Novelist,* p. 25.
124. *Ibid.*
125. *Ibid.*
126. *Ibid,* p. 62.
127. *Ibid,* p. 26.
128. Leavis, F. R.—*New Bearings in English Poetry,* p. 182.
129. *Ibid.*

work itself. Hence, the deepest values of the artist, which are personal, cannot be separated from his art. Buckley's observations in this respect are important:—

> "The impersonality of art consists, for him, in having found, while remaining at the heart of human problems a point of rest from which to estimate one's values and to define one's own life, one's possibilities of full living, in relation to them."[130]

In this way, Leavis' concern in art is a concern for seeing the artist's "emotional" life as being "impersonalised."[131] According to him, an emotion which defines itself through the "actuality in the poem"[132] is an impersonal emotion. This again, is a position quite different from Eliot's concept of "extinction of personality"; or that of the poet moving away from the "whirlpool of his own emotions."[133] Leavis does not conceive impersonality in terms of depersonalisation of emotions—a situation completely divorced from the inner life of the poet. On the other hand, he envisages a point distanced though it may be from the poet: yet it must be subjected to the control of intelligence. What Leavis wants is perhaps an integration of the "emotional quality" with the "executory functions" of intelligence.

The whole process appears to imply five significant points: first, the emotions are universalized; second, their general importance to the community is explored; third, they are made subservient to an accepted code of living; fourth, they become the means of serving particular interests of the poet; and lastly these interests are basically moral.[134]

In this way, Leavis' concept of Art is a sort of amalgam of manifold interests. It requires a specialised interplay of thought, and emotional equality, where the interest in "human centrality" forms its basic tenet. Leavis, unlike Eliot, does not consider poetic activity a process of pure creation; nor does he subscribe to the Eliotian view that the "material of

---

130. Buckley Vincent—*Poetry and Morality,* p. 183.
131. *Ibid.*
132. *Ibid,* p. 174.
133. *Selected Prose,* p. 29.
134. Buckley Vincent—*Poetry and Morality,* p. 183.

the artist is not his beliefs as held, but his beliefs as felt."[135] He affirms that any creative impulse, howsoever strong, must necessarily form part of the poet's ethical concern, if it has to achieve the maximum results.

If we view the Doctrine of Impersonality from the "technical"[136] angle—the view Leavis has so often insisted upon—then, both the critics happen to hold identical opinions. Eliot as well as Leavis believes that there is an inherent relation between technique and the feelings and attitudes which it goes to depict. Both of them, in theory as also in practice, have focussed attention on technique in terms of the "sensibility it expresses." Eliot had stated categorically that the change of sensibility demanded a change of idiom"[137]; or that every vital development in language is a development of "feeling as well."[138] As for Leavis, he also expresses similar views:—

> "The technique that has mattered in our day is the outcome of an intense and highly conscious work of critical intelligence (which) necessarily preceded and acompanied the discovery of the new uses of words, the means of expressing or creating the new feelings and modes of thought, the new rhythms, the new versification."[139]

Paying tributes to Eliot, for "altering expression"[140] Leavis continues:—

> "Eliot's best, his important criticism has an immediate relation to his technical problems, as the poet in that moment in history was faced with altering expression."[141]

As critics, Eliot and Leavis have stood for bettering the literary standards. Both devoted themselves to the hazardous task with an unfaltering sense of dedication. Both of them have struggled very hard to expose the laxity of modern cri-

---

135. Eliot, T. S.—U.P.U.C., p. 136.

136. Leavis, F. R.—*T. S. Eliot's Stature as a Critic; Commentary*, November, 1958.

137. Eliot, T. S.—*Poetry in the 18th Century; From Dryden to Johnson.*

138. *Selected Prose.*

139. Leavis, F. R.—*T. S. Eliot's Stature as a Critic.*

140. Eliot, T. S.—*Selected Prose*, p. 154.

141. Leavis, F. R.—*T. S. Eliot's Stature as a Critic.*

ticism—academic as well as journalistic. They have endeavoured hard to revalue English literary tradition and have given new directions to the total genre of literary criticism. In more than one sense, their pursuits may be called common. Leavis himself confesses:—

> "The title of a late collection of essays, *The Common Pursuit* (1952), derives from Eliot's "The Function of Criticism", "one of those essays of Mr. Eliot which I most admire": "The critic ......should endeavour to discipline his personal prejudices and cranks-tares to which we are all subject—and compose his difference with as many of his fellows as possible in the common pursuit of true judgement."[142]

Such puritanical stress on discipline and dedication in the common pursuit of "true judgement" may be described as the meeting ground in the literary practice of the two critics. But discipline in this sense should not be taken to mean any rigid subscription to some stereotyped method or school of criticism. Both Eliot and Leavis are clear on this point. Leavis acknowledges:—

> "......to insist that literary criticism, is or should be, a specific discipline of intelligence is not to suggest that a serious interest in literature can confine itself to the kind of intensive local analysis associated with "practical criticism"—to the scrutiny of "words on the page", in their minute relations, their effects of imagery and so on: a literary interest is an interest in man, society and civilization and its boundaries cannot be drawn."[143]

Eliot also states the same point but from a different angle:—

> "The true literary mind is likely to develop slowly; it needs a more comprehensive and more varied diet, a more miscellaneous knowledge of facts, a greater experience of men and of ideas than the kind required for the practice of the other arts."[144]

The two statements, taken together, result in another common feature, which we discern in the comparative study of Eliot and Leavis: their literary interests converge with their interests in man, society and culture. In the scheme of their literary practice, the "cultural consciousness" occupies a very

142. Leavis, F. R.—*Preface to The Common Pursuit.*
143. Leavis, F. R.—*Scrutiny,* xiii, i, 78.
144. *Selected Prose,* p. 218.

significant place. The process of equating "culture" with "criticism" which Arnold initiated has been further accelerated by Eliot, Richards and Leavis. In fact, Leavis' interpretation of culture, has something common to Eliot as well as to Richards. In his stress on "literary minority"[145] as a means of keeping alive the literary tradition, he comes closer to Eliot. But, in suggesting that by "Culture", he means the "use" of a language upon which "fine living depends",[146] Leavis, in one sense, implies to support Richards in his theory of Communication. Leavis maintains that many of the "subtlest and most perishable parts of tradition" are contained in our literature and language.

On the level of culture, we find many similarities between Eliot and Leavis. Leavis' notion of "literary minority" is somewhat analogous to Eliot's theory of "social classes." Second, both have opposed the present role of press, platform, cinema and shallow literature. Third, they are deadly against the growing ills of the Post-Industrial-Society. Fourth, both of them have continuously attacked Marx for his dialectical materialism of a social alternative. Lastly, they agree that the old "organic community" is gradually disintegrating due to the compulsions of an Industrial society.

Before we wind up our present discussion, it appears advisable to refer to an oft-repeated charge against Eliot. Like many other critics, Leavis opposes the Eliotian dictum that "literary criticism should be completed by criticism from a definite ethical and theological standpoint."[147] Leavis' criticism of this dictum is based on two counts: intellectually, it being dogmatic, sounds irrational; practically, Eliot's own practice displays the tendency of "substituting theological considerations for literary rather than completing one with the other."[148] Leavis, in his own criticism, also stresses on the need of ethical standards but has nowhere said that "theological considerations are

---

145. Leavis, F. R.—*Mass Civilization and Minority Culture,* pp. 3-5.

146. Leavis,—*Mass Civilization and Minority Culture.*

147. *Selected Prose*: *Religion and Literature.*

148. Buckley Vincent—*Poetry and Morality,* p. 218.

necessary."[149] Without involving ourselves into further arguments we shall simply say that the position taken by Leavis is equally not so relevant. Bethal rightly points out:—

> "If the critic elects to take his stand on "ethics" without any philosophical examination of the matter, there will always be a chance that his ethics may consist of personal predilections or the assumptions of his own social group."[150]

In conclusion, we may suggest that Eliot and Leavis are both "moralists"[151] in one way or the other. Each of them finds the moral value "co-extensive with the artistic value"[152] of any work. Neither of them tries to replace "aesthetic values as a substitute",[153] for life. Lastly, they appear to be "preoccupied with almost similar problems",[154] that face life, literature and society. We refrain from determining the personal contribution, which Leavis has made to the cause of English literary criticism. We only refer to the quantum of success that **Scrutiny** has achieved under the able stewardship of Dr. F. R. Leavis:—

> "Richards wrote *Practical Criticism* but *Scrutiny* was practical and criticised. Cleanth Brooks wrote notes for a new history of English poetry but in essay after essay *Scrutiny* accumulated a new history in *extenso.* Burke and Ransom extended the boundaries of critical discussion but *Scrutiny* actually occupied the territory and issued new maps."[155]

The discussion on "Eliot and the formalistic critics" involves, first of all, the study of those essentials, which are generally attributed to the Formalists. In the words of Austin Warren:—

> "Modern critics limiting themselves to aesthetic criticism are commonly called "formalists"—sometimes by themselves, some-

---

149. Bethal, S. L.—*Essays on Literary Criticism and The English Tradition,* p. 13.

150. *Ibid.*

151. Buckley Vincent—*Poetry and Morality,* p. 18.

152. *Ibid.*

153. *Ibid.*

154. *Ibid.*

155. Bentley Eric—*Kenyon Review, Autumn,* 1946, quoted in *The Modern Age,* ed. Boris Ford, p. 360.

times (pejoratively) by others. As least as ambiguous is the congnate word "form." As we shall use it here, it names the aesthetic structure of a literary work—that which makes it literature. Instead of dichotomising "form-content" we should think of matter and then of "form", that which aesthetically organizes its matter. In a successful work of art, the materials are completely assimilated into the form: what was 'world' has become language."[156]

The formalistic criticism, then, aims first at the "aesthetic structure" of art. Second, it does not dichotomise "form" from "content." Third, to the "formalists" the matter precedes the "form." Fourth, it is the "form" which aesthetically "organises" the matter. Lastly, such an organisation is not to be superficial or ordinary: it must assimilate the matter into the form or what Warren calls a sort of transformation of the "world" into "language." Briefly speaking, the "dynamics of the aesthetic purpose"[157] is the only consideration with the formalists. According to them, it is this "purpose" that synthesizes the words, ideas and experiences of a poem into a kind of polyphonic relations."[158] In this way, a beautiful poem may become "manifoldly organised",[159] and thus embody "various levels of meaning, and pattern associations."[160] Eliot, though in a different context touches the same point. While referring to the plays of Shakespeare, he says:—

"For the simplest auditors there is the plot, for the more thoughtful the character and conflict of character, for the more literary the words and phrasing, for the musically sensitive the rhythm and for auditors of greater understanding and sensitiveness a meaning which reveals itself gradually."[161]

Eliot and the critics of the formalistic school have similar views on what Nietzsche and Richards formulate as the concept of "poetry of inclusion."[162] Diversity of the material; ambiguity in the language; and intensity in the use of irony and

156. Warren Austin—*Theory of Literature,* p. 241.

157. *Ibid.*

158. *Ibid.*

159. *Ibid.*

160. *Ibid.*

161. Eliot, T. S.—U.P.U.C., p. 153.

162. *Ibid.*

metaphor are some of the basic points, where the majority of the formalistic critics have generally voiced their agreement with the critical line of T. S. Eliot. As to the view of the "Formalists" that "form and content" should not be dichotomised, Eliot also holds almost the same view.[163]

Austin Warren has criticised the following dictum of Eliot:—

> "The view of life presented in a poem must be one which the critic can accept as coherent, mature and found on the facts of experience."[164]

He argues that the dictum in its phrasing "goes beyond any formalism."[165] He concedes that "coherence" is an "aesthetic" as well as "logical criterion";[166] but "maturity" and "truth to experience" are different things. One is psychological criterion, while the other is an appeal to worlds "outside the work of art."[167] His other observations are significant:—

> "Let us reply to Eliot that the maturity of a work of art is its inclusiveness, its awareness of complexity, its ironics and tensions; and the correspondence between a novel and experience can never be measured by any simple pairing off of items: what we can legitimately compare is the total world of Dickens, Kafka, Balzac or Tolstoy with our total experience, that is our own thought and felt "world."[168]

As a matter of fact, the formalistic criticism owes much to Eliot for its development. He may be said to have laid down the basis of this school of criticism. Guided by Pound, Hulme and other symbolists, Eliot stressed on the high values of art as "art", rather than art as "expression of social, religious, ethical or political ideas."[169] He strongly advocates the close study of the texts; puts forth the view of poetry

---

163. Eliot, T. S.—*Introduction to Ezra Pound.*
164. Eliot, T. S.—U.P.U.C., p. 96.
165. Warren Austin—*Theory of Literature,* p. 24.
166. *Ibid.*
167. *Theory of Literature*, p. 24.
168. *Ibid.*
169. Scott Wilbur, S.—*Five Approaches of Literary Criticism,* p. 179.

having "autotelic character";[170] develops the cult of impersonality; and warns the critics against their habit of what he calls "inquiring into the number of times giraffes are mentioned in the English novel."[171] He also pleads for moving away from the biographical details and other unnecessary facts, irrelevant to literature as such. In short, Eliot, from the beginning, shows his serious concerns to formulate a kind of criticism, which in concept and character, is entirely free from the exigencies of extrinsically historic, moral, psychological and sociological interpretations."[172] Later, the efforts of I. A. Richards and William Empson, further strengthen the formalistic approach, which in the wake of the thirties becomes so popular that it draws into its fold, such brilliant scholars as Wilson Knight, John Crowe Ransom, R. P. Blackmur, Allen Tate, Cleanth Brooks, Rober Penn Warren and Yvor Winters. Although, there exist considerable differences among them yet they are best recognised by their "common beliefs, attitudes and practices."[173] Robert Penn Warren's observations appear to sum up the position of the Formalists:—

> "Poetry does not inhere in any particular element but depends upon the set of relationships, the structure, which we call the poem."[174]

"Structure" in this sense holds the key to the entire complexion of the poem. It binds together, not superficially but organically, different elements that constitue the total poetic experience. It comprises not only the form but content also. Hence, to the formalist, the full meaning of the poem lies in the complete discernment of its structural implications, wherein both form and content are fused together for the artistic presentation of the poetic experience.

Doubtless to say that the formalistic approach has been regarded as one of the most influential methods of literary criticism. The other names which have acquired currency for

---

170. Eliot, T. S.—*The Sacred Wood,* p. 47.

171. *Selected Prose,* p. 19.

172. Scott Wilbur, S.—*Five Approaches of Literary Criticism,* p. 180.

173. *Ibid,* p. 184.

174. Warren, R. P.—"*Pure and Impure Poetry.*"

this method are: the aesthetic, the textual, the ontological or most frequently used the "new criticism."[175] As already stated, the critics belonging to the formalistic school have their own differences among themselves. But as soon as "the exposition of theory is abandoned, and the critical performance begins",[176] their inherent kinship is established. They may disagree in the matter of working out details, yet in their total outlook, there appears to exist a good deal of near similarity. All of them agree that a poem has an independent organism. Second, they regard poetry as a "valid source of knowledge" that cannot be communicated in terms "other than its own."[177] Third, they lay an unusual emphasis on the "relationships structurally present",[178] in the poem for any competent reader. Fourth, all of them prescribe a close study of the texts. Lastly, what most of them want to maintain, is that the poem is not only a cause or a potential cause of the reader's "poetic experience", but a specific, highly-organised control of the reader's experience, so that the experience is most fittingly described as—the "experience of the poems."[179] To the inquiry as to what the "new critics" have achieved on the practical plane, we quote here, a summary appraisal of William K. Wimsatt, who says:—

> "Impersonality, craftsmanship, objectivity, hardness and clarity of a kind, a union of emotion with verbal object, a norm of inclusiveness and reconciliation and hence a close interdependence of drama, irony, ambiguity and metaphor, or the near equivalence of these four—such ideas made up the neo-classic system as it worked its way into practical criticism about 1935 or 1940."[180]

Coming to the individual critics, we find that William Empson's contribution to the development of formalistic cri-

---

175. Scott, Wilbur—Five Approaches of Literary Criticism, p. 179.

176. *Ibid.*

177. *Ibid,* p. 181.

178. Warren Austin—*Theory of Literature,* p. 249.

179. *Ibid.*

180. Wimsatt & Brooks—*Literary Criticism: A Short History,* p. 731.

ticism has been very promising in the initial stages. His efforts in collaboration with that of Richards towards the investigation of meaning have led to the rise of the semantics—the science of signs and sign interpretations. His two major works—**Seven Types of Ambiguity** and **The Structure of Complex Words**—embody the whole of his technique of the verbal analysis. We must bear in mind that Empson did not invent any new technique. What he did, was: first, the systematization of the methods of verbal and structural analysis; and second, he popularised much of its "characteristic jargon"—"ambiguity", "irony" and "tension."[181] Eliot has criticised Richards and Empson for what he alleges, the "lemon-squeezer school of criticism."[182] Perhaps, on the figurative use of "irony" and the place of "ambiguity" and "tension" in a poem, both Eliot and Empson have almost similar views.[183] They have voiced their stern opposition to Richards' concept of "emotive use of language", though for reasons quite different to each other's.

R. P. Blackmur is another major critic, whose passion for "form" is known. He may be said to belong to the coterie of the more analytical of the aesthetic critics. In "**The Double Agent; Essays in Craft and Elucidation**", he has tried to apply analytical techniques as elaborately as I. A. Richards and William Empson have done. Blackmur's essay "**T. S. Eliot: From Ash Wednesday to Murder in the Cathedral**" shows the nature and degree of influence Eliot has left on him. Moreover, his catholic concern for the "meaningful expression in art",[184] again displays the same and oft-repeated Eliotian emphasis on the right use of words. His observations for example:—

> "Language is made of words and gesture is made of motion ......when the language of words most succeeds it becomes gesture in its words."[185]

---

181. Watson George—*The Literary Critics,* p. 206.
182. Eliot, T. S.—O.P.P., p. 113.
183. Wimsatt & Brooks—*Literary Criticism; A Short History.*
184. Blackmur, A. P.—*Language as Gesture,* p. 3.
185. *Ibid.*

give the impression that Blackmur is re-iterating that which Eliot had already affirmed in the essay on **"The Music of Poetry."**[186]

In more than one sense, Kenneth Burke's position is similar to that of Blackmur. Both share the view that the language of poetry may be regarded as "symbolic action."[187] In the words of Blackmur:—

> "Mr. Burke legislates; I would judge; the executive is between us."[188]

Both the critics have moved more and more to the Empsonian directions of minute analysis and dissection.

Kenneth Burke is a philosopher-cum-critic. He is basically an aesthete, but has tried to modify his position under the compulsions of social and political forces. **The Counter-Statement** may be considered a brilliant work on the study of poetry in which Burke has investigated into two major problems: the literary form; and the psychological aspects of aesthetics. In his later works: **Permanence and Change; An Anatomy of Purpose; The Philosophy of Form;** and **A Grammar of Rhetoric**, Burke has synthesized his concept of literature as pure art with his ideas of social and human values. It is a position, which if not anything else, is essentially Eliotic.

As a critic—Robert Penn Warren is as precise as one could wish.[189] He happens to be an eminent scholar, a successful teacher, a distinguished poet, an influencial critic and an able novelist. Politically speaking, Warren is a liberal; yet he professes to judge art on the ground of its inner integrity than on anything else. Warren stands for the poetry of "inclusion."[190] On the function of irony, his approach is perfectly consistent with that of Eliot and Richards.[191] His own

---

186. Eliot, T. S.—O.P.P., p. 26.
187. Blackmur, R. P.—*Language as Gesture*, p. 3.
188. *Ibid.*
189. Cunliffe Marcus (ed.)—*The Literature of the United States*, p. 335.
190. Wimsatt & Brooks—*Literary Criticism—A Short History*, pp. 646-47.
191. *Ibid.*

poetry bears testimony to the influences of the metaphysical poets. In Warren's view, the characteristic weakness of the "pure" poetry lies in what he calls the unwillingness to face up to the "other possible case."[192] The avoidance of any manifestation of "irony and witty intellection"[193] weakens rather than strengthens its appeal. Both Warren and Eliot appear to subscribe to the same point of view: Poetry in their opinion is an all "inclusive" art, which further imples that it must be "complex"[194] hence "difficult"[195] also. Warren's own observations on this point are significant:—

> "......The saint proves his vision by stepping cheerfully into the fires. The poet somewhat less spectacularly, proves his vision by submitting it to the fires of irony—to the drama of his structure—in the hope that fires will refine it. In other words, the poet wishes to indicate that his vision has been earned; that it can survive reference to the complexities and contradictions of reference. And irony is one such device of reference."[196]

The name of Cleanth Brooks is closely associated with R. P. Warren not only for the marked similarity of their critical approach, but also for their close collaboration in bringing out some of their major literary works. In **Understanding Poetry,** the two critics voice their strong disapproval of the "use of 'Poetry' for any purpose beyond itself."[197] Like Eliot, both of them are in favour of shunning all sort of historical and biographical details, being brought into the evaluation of a poem.

"Warren's accounts of **'The Ancient Mariner'** and Brooks' assemblage of analysis entitled **'The Well Wrought Urn',"** says Watson, "are strikingly indifferent to historical probability."[198] Brooks himself observes:—

"If literary history has not been emphasized, it is not because,

192. Warren, R. P.—*"Pure & Impure Poetry"*; Kenyon Review.
193. Wimsatt & Brooks—*Literary Criticism,* p. 646.
194. *Ibid,* p. 651.
195. *Selected Prose; The Metaphysical Poets,* p. 105.
196. Warren, R. P.—*"Pure and Impure Poetry."*
197. Warren & Brooks—*Understanding Poetry; Preface.*
198. Watson George—*The Literary Critics,* p. 221.

I discount its importance, or because I have failed to take it into account. It is rather that I have been anxious to see what residium, if any, is left, after we have referred the poem to its cultural matrix."[199]

The Well Wrought Urn shows Brooks' concerns with the methods in which a "great poem succeeds."[200] According to him, poetry such as that of the metaphysical poets, unites "apparent paradoxes"[201] by way of metaphor. The greatness of a poem lies, in this way, in the "balance or reconcilement" of opposite or "discordant qualities."[202] He concedes to art the highest values, and like other new critics, feels that the work of art exists "apart from everydayness."[203] In the appreciation of the metaphysicals, Brooks like Warren, is by the right side of Eliot.

The two distinguished scholars, who have done much for the cause of the New Criticism, are John Crowe Ransom and Allen Tate. Both belong to the Agrarian group and have remained for some time, closely associated with **The Fugitive**—a magazine of the Southern letters, wedded to the ideals of an agrarian economy and its allied aesthetic and socio-cultural values. They are neo-Aristotelians in the sense that in their critical thought, they dislike the "Platonic forms of literature",[204] which fail to bring out the required fusion, that one finds in the metaphysicals, Donne in particular. It may be said, that their approach in criticism is predominantly aesthetic or formalistic rather than "sociological, historical, psychological, economic or moral."[205] Ransom has vehemently criticised some of the current statements of T. S. Eliot.

Ransom's output—poetic and critical—is small, but "consistently distinguished."[206] **The New Criticism** is his standard

---

199. Brooks Cleanth—*The Well Wrought Urn; Preface.*
200. Cunliffe Marcus—*Literature of the United States,* p. 335.
201. *Ibid.*
202. *Ibid.*
203. *Ibid.*
204. *The Literature of the United States; Pelican Original,* p. 334.
205. *Ibid.*
206. *Recent American Literature; Little Field,* Adams & Co., p. 277.

work on the development of recent critical thought and its practice. Like any other formalist, he is deeply interested in the structure of poetry. He has developed his own view of good poetry which he contends, depends on the quality of "texure." His definition, that a "poem is a loose logical structure, having an irrelevant local texture"[207] has been received with mixed feelings in literary quarters. Ransom's explanatory observations, in this respect, are significant:—

> "By ontological insight the critic is to notice how particulars are a matter of texture, and universals of structure—and how both must be present in a poem as in a furnished house, in which the paint, the paper, the tapestry are texture."[208]

Ransom's theorisation on poetry is valuable. He feels that a poem consists of "structure" as well as "texture." He suggests that the structure is to be "loose" but "logical"; while the texture "irrelevant." He further argues, that though the texture is entirely irrelevant to the structure of the poem, yet it has its own share in moulding the poem by what he calls, the process of "impeding the logic or the argument." In this context, the irrelevance of the texture plays a vital role: it enhances the impact and incidence of logic by focusing on different aspects of reality with which logic cannot cope.[209] To put it in another way, what Ransom implies by texture, is perhaps what Winters has explained:—

> "feeling or emotion as existing independently of structure and yet in some obscure manner not wholly escaping from its presence."[210]

His own declaration points to the same direction:—

> "The more difficult the final structure, the less rich should be the distraction of the texture; and the richer the texture as we proceed towards the structure, the more generalised and simple may be the structure in the end."[211]

Ransom's whole position is not difficult to understand.

---

207. Ransom John Crowe—*The New Criticism,* p. 280.

208. *Ibid.*

209. Wimsatt & Brooks—*Literary Criticism; A Short History,* p. 626.

210. Winters Yvor—*In Defence of Reason,* p. 534.

211. Ransom, John Crowe—*The New Criticism,* p. 274.

The structure of a poem is not important in itself. It is important as a means to something else. It must justify its existence by catering to the psychological needs of the readers. On the other hand, the texture of the "perceptual impulses" is more important and it is through texture that they become gratified. Ransom states the same position, though in a paradoxical manner:—

> "The paraphrase of a poem is a fair version of the logical structure and since the paraphrase of even a fine poem usually reveals an undistinguished and common place argument, the structure is not the valuable element of the poem."[212]

In his theory of "structure and texture" Ransom seems to be nearer to Richards than to Eliot. He has tried to give it a cognitive complexion, yet the implications involved are no less simple.

Ransom objects to the immediate transference of emotions from the poet to the reader. Such immediacy, he feels, blinds the poet to the texture of the emotion. As against Eliot's theory of "Objective Correlative", Ransom holds the doctrine of the "Automatic Accuracy"[213] of emotions. According to him, emotions are motivated by some cause or object and are appropriate.[214] If the cognition of the object is sound, the emotion automatically becomes accurate. He observes:—

> "The specific quality of any emotion is all but indefinable in pure emotive terms, and that seems to be because the distinctness that we think of as attaching to an emotion belongs really to the object toward which we have it."[215]

Ransom virtually reverses Eliot's concept of "Objective Correlative" when he asserts:—

> "In short, the one automatic and sure method of identifying a feeling is to furnish an objective situation and say: Now imagine yourself in this situation. Under these circumstances I do not see why the critic needs to do more than talk about

212. Ransom, John Crowe—(quoted) *Literary Criticism;* Wimsatt and Brooks.

213. Winters Yvor—*In Defence of Reason,* p. 525.

214. *Ibid,* p. 524.

215. Ransom John Crowe—*The New Criticism,* p. 20.

the objective situations. The feelings will be their strict correlatives and the pursuit of the feelings will be gratuitous."[216]

Ransom also criticises Eliot's view of metaphysical poetry:—

"My belief is that opposites can never be said, to be resolved or reconciled merely because they have been got into the same poem, or got into the same complex of affective experience to create there a kind of tension."[217]

He feels that the two discordant experiences cannot be fused together. He asserts that in a pointed form of irony, the oppositions produce an "indecisive effect."[218] Such a device brings irresolution and strikes at the "structural unity"[219] of the poem itself. In fact, Ransom displays his dissatisfaction unsparingly against Eliot and Richards for advocating the "reconciliation" of what he thinks are "irreconcilables."[220]

Ransom has voiced his strong disagreement with Eliot on another fundamental point. The latter's affirmation that the poem has a "life of its own", is according to Ransom, "very nearly a doctrine of poetic automatism."[221] He contends that poet's function, being very important, he must exercise full control over the poem. Any slackness on that score is bound to result in serious derelictions of art itself.

We have tried here, to summarise in the span of our brief discussion, some of the distinctive features of Ransom's criticism in relation to that of Eliot. As it stands, Ransom thinks Eliot's criticism too psychologistic, too much concerned with affective experience and too little cognitive."[222] Both the critics have got their own differences—differences, which may be said to arise out of their respective approaches of literary

216. *The New Criticism,* p. 50.

217. *Ibid,* p. 95.

218. *Ibid,* p. 152.

219. *Ibid,* p. 95.

220. Wimsatt and Brooks—*Literary Critisim; A Short History,* p. 621.

221. Ransom, J. Crowe—*The New Criticism,* p. 152.

222. Wimsatt and Brooks—*Literary Criticism; A Short History,* p. 669.

criticism. Anyhow, we would like to quote two "recantations",[223] which Ransom has made about Eliot after his death. He says:—

> "The first time I scolded him for *The Waste Land,* with what I took to be its academic trick of recondite allusions on the one hand, and on the other hand, its want of a firm and consistent prosody, such as it seemed to require. I was mistaken about the allusions."[224]

He continues:—

> "My other unfortunate estimate of Eliot came when I wrote a harsh review of *Murder in the Cathedral.* I read the play at one sitting and wrote my piece the next day at another sitting. The trouble was that in that period, I was studying my Milton, and had a special liking for *Samson Agonistes* over all his other works. *The Murder* like the Samson was in Greek form of drama, but it seemed to me that the *Murder* was always running wild, and rejecting its form......But I was able after a little while to be reasonable and to reflect that the form of drama is subject to changes as soon as a new and able dramatist wants it so and that as a rule the new wine tastes better to his own public than the old."[225]

Allen Tate's concern with criticism is well known. He has been a teacher, editor, poet and critic. But, it is primarily as critic that he has distinguished himself in American letters. Tate may be regarded as one of the enthusiastic exponents of the "New Criticism." In his practical criticism, he has always laid great stress on the study of the text. He demands from the author a high degree of intellectual discipline; so that the personal in him is restrained at a reasonable distance. He believes in values and aspires for moral and emotional integrity.

Tate defines poetry as an "action rendered in its totality"[226]—an action which is prescriptive neither of means nor of ends. Like Eliot, he insists on its organic nature, where words, metaphors, similes, etc., join together for bringing out

---

223. Tate Allen (ed.)—*T. S. Eliot; The Man and His Work,* p. 133.

224. *Ibid.*

225. *Ibid,* pp. 134-35.

226. Tate Allen—*On the Limits of Poetry,* p. 113.

a cumulative effect. "The vision of the whole", Tate asserts, "is not susceptible of logical demonstration."[227] Hence, the poem is not a statement in the ordinary sense, that can be logically proved. As such, it cannot be subjected to external verifications. Its grasp may vary from one reader to the other, depending of course, on the imaginative competency of the readers. Tate also denounces the "belief that language itself can be reality, or by incantation can create a reality."[228]

Tate makes another significant point. He asserts that similes and metaphors should "grow out of the material"[229] and a poet must not impose them "from above." It implies: that a poet does not proceed in a pre-determined manner; that no manner, whatsoever, hinders the process of poetic creation; that the creation, while in the process of development, furnishes its own norms; and finally, that the poet reveals the very patterns inherent in his own experience. What Tate appears to confirm is that a poem, in its totality, is not a mere "subjective projection"—a notion, very similar to that of Eliot. Even imagination, though subtle, must obey some laws implicit in the human psyche, or what Tate suggests, "submit to analogy—analogy to the natural world."[230] Significantly enough, Allen Tate's position in respect of the poet's "fostering and nurturing the poem's life", on the principles of natural growth, seems analogous to the one Eliot has so consistenly held.

The name of Yvor Winters requires special mention. Though, his too much pre-occupations with moral values have made some critics[231] declare him, a critic of the moralistic school; yet his strict adherence to classical virtues and his strong advocacy of structural organisms, bracket him with the formalists—maybe, a formalist with some difference. Like Blackmur, Ransom and Tate, he also lays his fingers on form, but his approach is somewhat different. "Form", to Winters,

227. Tate Allen—*On the Limits of Poetry,* p. 113.

228. Tate Allen—*The Forlorn Demon,* p. 61.

229. Tate Allen—*On the Limits of Poetry,* p. 92.

230. Tate Allen—*The Forlorn Demon,* p. 78.

231. Scott Wilbur, S.—*Five Approaches of Literary Criticism,* p. 25.

is not mere architectonics of poetry; it embodies an ideal and a vision. As a critic, Winters shows a puritan interest in the study of the text. He has criticised Eliot's literary theories. "Eliot", he alleges, "is a theorist, who has repeatedly contradicted himself on every important issue that he has touched."[232] He further argues that "his intellectualism and his reactionary position are alike an illusion."[233] He criticises[234] Eliot's concept of art as "autotelic."[235] Commenting on the analogy of the catalyst which Eliot has propounded, Winters asserts:—

> "I should like to suggest that it describes more accurately the facts which Eliot appears to have in mind than does the theory of Eliot himself."[236]

He goes on:—

> "According to my view, the artistic process is one of moral evaluation of human experience by means of a technique which renders possible an evaluation more precise than any other."[237]

Winters contends that the feelings which art expresses should be "motivated by the artists' comprehension of his subject."[238] Moreover, it is on the "justness of the motivation",[239] in whole and in detail, that the value of art depends. But, "Eliot", says Winters, "prefers to assume emotion as initial."[240] Criticising Eliot's Theory of Objective Correlatives,[241] Winters affirms:—

> "This seems to me, I confess, a reversal of the normal processes of understanding human experience, and a dangerous reversal."[242]

---

232. Winters, Yvor—*In Defence of Reason; The Illusion of Reaction,* p. 460.
233. *Ibid.*
234. *Ibid,* p. 462.
235. *Selected Essays,* p. 19.
236. Winters, Yvor—*In Defence of Reason, p.* 464.
237. *Ibid.*
238. *Ibid.*
239. *Ibid.*
240. *Ibid.*
241. Eliot, T. S.—*Selected Prose,* p. 102.
242. Winters, Yvor—*In Defence of Reason,* p. 467.

Winters criticises Eliot, for what he reiterates as "giving primacy to the emotions."[243] "To take them as they come", he says, "is a dangerous practice."[244] It is not possible to control them in this way. The control over emotions requires the presence of a rational structure or what Winters calls "the formulable logic":[245] that is, the theme can be "paraphrased in general terms."[246] In Winters' view, if we express our emotions without understanding them, "we obviously have no way of judging or controlling them."[247] Hence, he launches another attack on Eliot:—

> "It is possible of course, as Eliot somewhere else remarks, to admire a poem deeply; without wholly understanding it but such admiration must rest on an understanding at least imperfect, and the idea that this admiration is adequate as compared with that which comes with full understanding is mere nonsense."[248]

Winters has criticised[249] Eliot's view, that "all poetry, even a lyric from the Greek anthology, is dramatic."[250] According to him, a "poem is a statement about an experience, real or imagined." Elucidating his point further, Winters says that it is an act of meditation or what he calls "the event plus the understanding of the event."[251] He voices his disagreement with Matthiessen who had interpreted dramatic element in poetry as "its power to communicate a sense of real life, a sense of the immediate present."[252] Winters alleges that Matthiessen is "merely indulging in incoherence."[253] The final attack on Eliot is based on:—

> "No matter how the doctrine of dramatic immediacy is understood, it is a doctrine which leads to illegitimate emotionalism;

243. *In Defence of Reason,* p. 469.
244. *Ibid,* p. 473.
245. *Ibid,* p. 31.
246. *Ibid.*
247. *Ibid,* p. 469.
248. *Ibid,* p. 473.
249. *Ibid,* p. 489.
250. *Selected Essays; "A Dialogue on Dramatic Poetry",* p. 38.
251. Winters, Yvor—*In Defence of Reason,* p. 489.
252. Matthiessen, F. O.—*The Achievement of T. S. Eliot,* p. 66.
253. Winters, Yvor—*In Defence of Reason,* p. 490.

> and understood as it appears in Eliot's practice, it leads to irrelevance and to incoherence as well."[254]

We may be allowed to point out here, some implicit confusion in the bold assertions of Winters. He appears to disregard "dramatic presentation", because it implies an abdication of the poet's control over his "statement" or what he himself refers to as "illegitimate emotionalism." But, Winters' own preference for the term "motive" vis-a-vis his definition of a poem as "statement" actually points to the same direction—"the mode of drama."[255] Cleanth Brooks rightly observes:

> "For if the emotions are "motivated", the emotion can only be inferred from the context of situation and action. It cannot be stated directly, and the paraphrasable matter that "motivates" it is not so much a "statement" as a dramatic situation—a narrative or a plot."[256]

Before we close our assessment of the Formalistic critics, we would like to mention some of the limitations these critics have suffered from. First, it has been generally felt that the majority of the formalists have tried to isolate the part of a poem from its whole. Second, they have stretched the technique of analysis to such rigid extremes that the very sense of the whole is eclipsed by the part. Third, they are so lost in the ontological formalities as to forget completely the poem in its totality. Lastly, there has grown a general feeling against most of the critics of this school, that they have neglected the values of literature to man as merely an "aesthetic being",[257] in favour of the analysis of form. But, with all its limitations, the formalistic movement has brought into its fold, some of the best critical talents available on either side of the Atlantic. As for its practical working, we give below the observations of R. C. Crane:—

> "Looked at broadly or from a distance, the movement exhibits a striking unity of spirit and method, as well as a re-

254. *In Defence of Reason,* p. 493.

255. Brooks Cleanth—*Literary Criticism; A Short History,* p. 675.

256. *Ibid.*

257. Scott, Wilbur, S.—*Five Approaches of Literary Criticism,* p. 182.

markable tendency to mutual admiration on the part of its adherents. Considered more closely, however, the apparent homogeneity of the "new criticism" is seen to be less complete than is often thought; and it is not hard to discover beneath the common preoccupation of these critics with "language", "symbol", and "meaning", at least two distinct ways, which are often associated in individual critics, of getting at the semantic nature of poetry and hence of defining the characteristic symbolic structures that condition its meanings and values."[258]

---

258. Crane, R. S.—*The Languages of Criticism and The Structure of Poetry,* p. 100.

CHAPTER VII

THE IMPACT OF ELIOT ON CONTEMPORARY CRITICISM

It is not too much to acknowledge that T. S. Eliot has left a considerable impact on contemporary criticism. But, its nature is such which defies every attempt of statistical assessment, the reason being three-fold: first, it is spread over a span of nearly fifty years; second, it is rhetorical and complex in character; and third, the critic in Eliot has shifted his own positions. It is in this context that Watson calls the influence "mysterious and indefinable."[1] Buckley interprets it in terms of a "new way of literary thinking of the past";[2] Luis Kronenberger of **The New York Times** qualifies it as an influence more of "style than of anything else";[3] and Sean Lucy sees it having a "decisive effect on the poetry of Realist Movement."[4] Irrespective of what different critics have said on Eliot, there exists a glaring unanimity on one distinctive feature of his literary criticism: it has turned upside-down the whole current of English literary criticism. It has won loud applause and yet its criticism is no less adverse. As a consequence, Eliot has exposed himself to a large number of opponents and disciples alike, who belong to every part of the globe.

Referring to the apparent shift of emphasis in the critical approach of Eliot, Watson has suggested the relevance of three voices in his criticism.[5] Biographically, the three voices cor-

1. Watson George—*The Literary Critics,* p. 178.
2. Buckley Vincent—*Poetry and Morality,* p. 87.
3. Brown, Francis—*Highlights of Modern Literature (Collection)*, p. 90.
4. Lucy Sean—*Eliot and The Idea of Tradition,* p. 150.
5. Watson George—*The Literary Critics,* p. 195.

respond to three distinct periods in the career of T. S. Eliot—the pre-Christian (1919-28); the post-conversion (1929-39); and finally, the last decades (1939-65). Literarily, the first decade is the most productive in as far as it reveals the intrinsic merit of the sixteenth and seventeenth century dramatists and poets. The second decade is marked by an unusual stress on the social uses of literature and the last decades highlight, once again, the renewal of Eliot's greater interest in dramatic and other critical issues. Chronologically, the first and the last decades synchronise with the best of Eliot's critical and creative endeavours, while the period in between them—the thirties—shows his pre-occupations, not so much with poetry and criticism, as with their ethical and theological uses. Vincent Buckley, while discussing the relative effect of this ethical concern, has made a pointed reference to the damage thus done to Eliot's critical faculty:—

> "He seems no longer capable of driving the scalpel of his finely discriminating intelligence into the very fibre and tissue of a literary work seen as a living whole; and he is too quick to take up questions (such as the theological orientation of a poet or a novelist) which are certainly important, but which in his hands come to seem the central ones and to overshadow others quite as important."[6]

As compared to other treatises, **The Sacred Wood** occupies a unique place. It forms the central core of Eliot's achievement as a critic. Some of its essays have come to stay as the un-official manifesto of his literary criticism. It is through these essays that Eliot rejects too much individualistic and liberal cults of Georgian criticism. The two essays: **Tradition and The Individual Talent;** and **The Functions of Criticism;** envisage a plan of some positive principles and methods. The originality of these essays does not lie so much in the doctrines formulated therein, as in their application to the immediate critical situation, which dominated the first two decades of the century. The first phase, in one way, may be said to aim at refining and modifying classicism, which by that time, had become "coarse and self-deviating."[7] It is important to note

---

6. Buckley Vincent—*Poetry and Morality,* p. 129.
7. *Ibid,* p. 87.

that Eliot's whole critical outlook at this stage, stands in direct reaction to the decayed romantic emotionalism of the Georgians. His three-pronged emphasis on the value of tradition; the extinction of personality; and the need for a more objective and factual criticism are the expressions of an unhidden longing for a criticism, which is substantively unemotional and impersonal. Sean Lucy in this respect makes out an important point:—

> "It was this need for an objective and factual literary criticism that found the most immediate popularity and support and which with the appearance of *The Sacred Wood* did much to **set a fashion that became known as the New Criticism.**"[8]

Examined through the contemporary setting, the point raised by Sean Lucy is very significant. May be, on the face of it, none would easily agree to share any such view that **The Sacred Wood** alone could set in motion the processing of a new mode of literary criticism; and yet **The Sacred Wood** stands monumental to the genius of Eliot. With its rhetorical brilliance, pontifical tone; intuitional emphases and an ever growing disregard of historical details, it may claim its humble share in stimulating, what later on, is known as **The New Criticism.**

Oddly enough, Eliot does not share the views expressed by Sean Lucy. In the **Frontiers of Criticism,** he disclaims the responsibility of "any critical movement which can be said to derive from myself."[9] For the sake of a better and deeper understanding of the issues involved, we quote the full extract:—

> "I have been somewhat bewildered to find, from time to time, that I am regarded as one of the ancestors of modern criticism, if too old to be a modern critic myself. Thus in a book which, I read recently by an author, who is certainly a modern critic, I find a reference to 'The New Criticism' by which he says 'I mean not only the American critics, but the whole critical movement that derives from T. S. Eliot.' I do not understand why the author should isolate me so sharply from the American Critics; but on the other hand I fail to see any

8. Lucy Sean—*Eliot and The Idea of Tradition,* p. 65.
9. Eliot, T. S.—O.P.P., p. 106.

critical movement which can be said, to derive from myself, though I hope that as an editor I gave the New Criticism, or some of it, encouragement and exercise ground in The Criterion."[10]

In the same essay, Eliot sounds a note of caution against indiscriminate use of the term "New Criticism" and the implications arising thereof:—

"A great deal has happened in literary criticism since this influential book—I. A. Richards' *Principles of Literary Criticism* 1925—came out; and my paper—*The Functions of Criticism,* 1923,—was written two years earlier. Criticism has developed and branched out in several directions. The term "The New Criticism" is often employed by people without realising what a variety it comprehends; but its currency does, I think, recognise the fact that the more distinguished critics of today, however widely they differ from each other, all differ in some significant way from the critics of a previous generation."[11]

The quoted extracts form part of "**The Frontiers of Criticism**", which was published in 1956. The very fact that the reflections on the terminology and the nature of "New Criticism" have been made by no less a person than Eliot himself, gives them an air of extraordinary relevance. Taken together, both the extracts throw some valuable light on how far Eliot has been responsible in popularising the mode of New Criticism. They also reveal something basic about the New Critics. They differ with each other yet have something common against the critics of Victorian and Georgian generations.

The origin of "New Criticism" may be said to date with the first decade of the century. In 1910, in his famous address, at Columbia University, Joel Spingarn was the first to use the term "New Criticism."[12] He started a serious dialogue on two important points: first, he rejected the hitherto practice of classifying literature into periods and groups; second, relying on the aesthetics of Croce, he demanded that each individual work of art be regarded in **itself.** The points then raised by Spingarn, developed later into a sort of controversy between the **Impressionistic** school of criticism and that of the **Formalists** in the thirties. But, it also made positive contribu-

10. O.P.P., p. 106.
11. *Ibid,* p. 104.
12. Scott, Wilbur S.—*Five Approaches of Literary Criticism,* p. 18.

tion to the contemporary setting of literary criticism of the Continent. Scott observes:—

> "Atleast in dismissing the professional tendency to categorise and to seek the moral significance of literature, Spingarn helped create an atmosphere congenial to artistic and critical experiment."[13]

The early beginnings of The New Criticism were made in England in the late twenties. The regular and formal examples of the first neo-critical analysis were furnished by Robert Graves and the American poetess Laura Riding, in their joint and "word-by-word collaborated" work: **"A Survey of Modernist Poetry."** In its own way, the book is full of original flashes of the critics and contains a cogent defence of post 1918 poetry. The authors adhere to the verbal and structural analysis of a poem. They stress on what they call the characteristic search for "the most difficult meaning." Later on, William Empson contributed notably towards the popular rise of the new school of verbal analysis, suffixing to it, the study of two additional aspects—psychological and semantic. The New Criticism spread to the United States in the late thirties and made great headway under the powerful patronage of such scholars as Kenneth Burke and John Crowe Ransom. The others, who also join the coterie of the new critics, are Richard Blackmur, Ronald Crane and Mortimer Adler. They may be called the Neo-Aristotelians, showing a very keen interest in language and its uses.

The position of I. A. Richards and F. R. Leavis needs separate mention. Although, the two critics have closely associated themselves with the school of New Criticism, yet each of them retains the individuality of his own particular view-point. It would be advisable to remove, at this stage, one current misgiving about Prof. Richards. He is supposed to have pioneered a School of Neo-criticism, of which, Eliot also is considered to be one of the members. "The dates alone", says Watson, "forbid such a notion: Eliot is the older man by five years; and his first and the best critical work, **The Sacred**

---

13. *Five Approaches of Literary Criticism.*

Wood appeared before Richards had published at all."[14] Equally mistaken would it be to construe, that Eliot prologued in one way or the other, what I. A. Richards published in **The Principles of Criticism,** in 1925. The latter has his own independent achievement as an aesthetician, which could have been made as readily, even if, "Eliot had never existed."[15] He is the pioneer of Anglo-American New Criticism of the thirties and forties. Richards provides a "ramshackle aesthetic"[16] to build upon and the examples of a criticism that is "practical rather than pedantically historiocist."[17] As a theorist, it is Richards, who colours the new technique of Verbal and Structural analysis, with a sound philosophy based on psychology and semantics.

F. R. Leavis is certainly a new critic, but with a difference. His criticism has an unquestionable imprint of contemporaneity. In one sense, Leavis may be said to be a genuine disciple of his twin masters—T. S. Eliot and I. A. Richards. In his passionate defence of "Values" he is perhaps more Eliotian than Eliot himself; while his adherence to the analytical techniques of practical criticism bring him closer to Prof. Richards. There are some who have regarded him as the British counterpart to the American New Criticism.[18] Leavis' position in some respect is analogous to that of Yvor Winters. Both of them "express the traditional concern for the moral ends of literature."[19]

Before discussing Eliot's actual contribution to the New Criticism it appears necessary that a synoptic summary of its salient features be taken up. The cult of "New Criticism" has a variety of meanings. It includes, the Neo-Humanists; the Moralists; the Formalists; the Analysts; and the Neo-classicists. It culminates into a mighty movement because of many factors—negative as well as positive—inherent in contempor-

---

14. Watson George—*The Literary Critics,* p. 196.
15. *Ibid.*
16. *Ibid.*
17. *Ibid,* p. 202.
18. *Ibid,* p. 208.
19. **Scott, Wilbur S.**—*Five Approaches of Literary Criticism.*

ary criticism. On its negative side, the movement is "reactionary", displaying a general contempt for the late nineteenth century values in art and literature. On its positive side, it introduces a new method and a new outlook. The adjective "new" however should not be construed strictly in the literal sense. It has always held for it, an air of "pleasing paradox."[20] Whatever tenets the new critics have prescribed are not new altogether. Nevertheless, in its totality, the New Criticism aims at a technique and a doctrine, which are basically original. Its underlying tenets are:—

(i) In the first instance, the work of art must be evaluated by itself; and as such, the social, moral and historical considerations should, in no case, be allowed to blur evaluation. These considerations may explain the circumstances or the motive behind the composition, but in no way, constitute the work itself. It is in this context that the new critics denounce historical and biographical criticism of the nineteenth century.

(ii) Second, the composition has an individual existence of its own or what Eliot phrases "something existing between the poet and his readers." "The evaluation or the judgment" argue the new critics "must concentrate itself on nothing but this fundamental reality."

(iii) Third, in New Criticism, the psychological aspect is always given a primary place in the process of creation. Its protagonists believe, that art itself implies transformation of particular states of mind of the artist. Hence, psychology being the main architect in the phenomenon of poetic creation, the critic also must attach due importance to psychology while evaluating a work of art.

(iv) Fourth, the new critics feel that the search for what Graves calls the "most difficult meaning" is the pre-requisite of objective assessment. They subscribe to the seminal doctrine that difficulty is the chief among the poetic virtues, and furthermore, it is always the most difficult meaning that is the most significant.

(v) Fifth, the new critic lays greater emphasis on un-

20. Watson George—*The Literary Critics.*

ravelling the ingredients of ambiguity and thus recommends a detailed study of the medium of communication. They suggest that the language should be analysed word for word and the meaning, rhythm, music, syntax, imagery, symbols and abstract nuances must be scanned properly to arrive at correct conclusions.

(vi) Sixth, in addition to the verbal analysis, the exponents of New Criticism are pre-occupied with the structural analysis of a poem. They feel, that in order to determine its internal growth, its inter-relation with the various parts; structure and form has to be closely analysed.

(vii) Lastly, the critics of the new school aim at the organic unity of the whole poem. As such, their stress on structure is, in fact, a stress on the determination of its total pattern. This pattern, according to them, has to correspond to a successful communication of the whole experience and not merely any part of it. It means that a poem must be one organic piece in as far as its total structure, experience, thought and emotions are concerned.

The method followed generally by the critics of the new school is the method of analysis—structural, verbal, symbolic and psychological. The structure of a poem with the neo-critics is not confined to its form only. It includes both content and form. It is in this spirit that Austin Warren and Rene Wellek refer to structure as "dynamic."[21] Justifying the emphasis of the new technique on structure O'Faolain has remarked:—

> "Men would turn to the poetry of exact expression of controlled sensibility, of limited but clear aims of a strict spiritual and emotional discipline and then set out to create a critical structure to define these reforms. This structure was the New Criticism."[22]

The inference drawn by the learned critic is hypothetical. It establishes an intimate relation between the creative urge, on the one hand, and the critical necessity, on the other. The

---

21. Warren and Wellek—*Theory of Literature.*
22. Quoted in *Five Approaches of Literary Criticism,* p. 19.

same hypothesis, if applied to the literary scene of twenties, appears to be perfectly valid. The New Criticism may be said to have corresponded to the pattern of the New Poetry, introducing which, Edwin Marsh has said:—

> "This Volume is issued in the belief that English poetry is now once again putting on a new strength and beauty."[23]

The strength and beauty mentioned by Marsh is the same what O'Faolain has suggested "the exact expression, controlled sensibility and disciplined emotions." It implies a change from the sheer emotionalism of the late nineteenth century poets to the exact, dry and hard poetry of the early twenties of the new century. Under the force of the changing literary patterns, critical values also undergo a process of new orientation giving rise to the development of a new movement in literary criticism.

We have already quoted at length the views of Eliot vis-a-vis the New Criticism. He stands rather loosely to the movement, part pioneer, part sceptic.[24] It would be incorrect to say that Eliot invents the new critical technique, which broadly speaking, is the product of an intellectual climate, wherein not one but many have their due shares. But let there be no doubt, that in criticism as in poetry, he is really the first "to give expression to the spirit of his time."[25] More than this, he provides a striking example to others by virtue of the power and penetration of his work. Commenting on the nature of Eliot's critical ideals, Sean Lucy has some valuable observations to make:—

> "Eliot's ideal criticism would be absolutely objective. This is clearly impracticable, as he admitted himself very early in the days but it remained the ideal of the new criticism. It was closely bound up with the idea of "the extinction of personality in poetry, and like this idea, was part of the expression of longing for a pure unemotional art of clean lines, in direct reaction to the decayed romantic emotionalism of the Georgians."[26]

---

23. *Five Approaches of Literary Criticism,* p. 19. (Quoted).
24. Watson George—*The Literary Critics,* p. 202.
25. Lucy Sean—*The Idea of Tradition,* p. 67.
26. *Ibid.*

The formal position of Eliot's criticism may be screened mainly through the three theories he has propounded: **The Theory of Impersonality; The Theory of Tradition** and **The Theory of Value.** In the first two, he throws his weight in favour of "tradition and order", restricting thus, the current tendency of romantic emotionalism in art. In the Theory of Value, he explains the creative process and lays down the criteria of "analysis and interpretation" for its objective elucidation. All the three theories add new dimensions to the contemporary vogue of literary criticism. They open new vistas. They reject the old modes and recommend the fresh ones. In asking critics to imbibe "the historical sense", Eliot discards the practice of biographical and historical criticism. In recommending "analysis and interpretation", as method of critical evaluation, he helps in popularising the technique of verbal analysis, which by the thirties is an article of faith with the new critics. In characterising a poem, as existing between the writer and the reader, Eliot provides to art an individuality that becomes the abiding creed of the New Criticism. But the key, to the assessment of Eliot's impact on contemporary criticism, finally lies in what may be summed up, as the principle of organic creation of art. He believes that the phenomenon of poetic creation involves a process of synthesis among feelings, sensations, emotions and thoughts, culminating into the totality of the artist's experience. Secondly, consequent upon this experience the organism of a poem should always exhibit harmony of its "inner perspective." Thirdly, its communication should be so processed as to result in a kind of synthesis of the appropriate idiom, rhythm and music of verse. This, in one sense, amounts to the same view, what Eliot calls "the Auditory Imagination" and what I. A. Richards has qualified as the "emotive use of language." Eliot's final position has been summed up by Vincent Buckley:—

> "What set him against Arnold is what set him against the Romantic century—the nineteenth. His total position is one of reaction against that century and an affirmation of a scheme of values to it."[27]

---

27. Buckley Vincent—*Poetry and Morality,* p. 88.

And the values Eliot affirms have done their job magnificently; the sham in the artist has been exposed; the dry hard verse in poetry has come to stay: the technique of new criticism has stirred imagination; the taste of the reading public—may be the elite only—has been regulated; and finally a variety of interests—moral, psychological and social—have been brought to bear upon the principle of literary criticism.

F. R. Leavis has adjudged the contemporary impact of Eliot from a different angle:—

> "It is not for nothing that Mr. Eliot's criticism has been directed mainly upon the 17th century. One might say that the effect of his criticism and poetry together has been to establish the 17th century in its due place in the English tradition."[28]

M. C. Bradbrook interprets the influence of Eliot's criticism in terms of taste rather than in anything else:—

> "The influence of Mr. Eliot as a critic must surely be noted rather in the history of taste than in the history of ideas."[29]

But Sean Lucy elaborates the same point, more rationally:—

> "In the realm of critical ideas Eliot's influence has been just as considerable as in the development of taste. His conception of true literary tradition (or perhaps a simplified form of this idea) is now, common currency as also are "pure criticism", comparison and analysis; the sensual experience of thought, the objective correlative; the fact that poetry should share the virtues of good prose, the necessity of discipline for good writing of any sort and many more ideas. They are not Eliot's inventions......but his influence in making them part of literary tradition in our day has been both seminal and formative."[30]

T. S. Eliot may rightly be regarded as representing a new "Literary Renaissance." True, that he does not appeal either as poet or as critic to any "great public."[31] But the fact is, when Eliot makes his debut in the early twenties, the "great public", still, suffered from moral and intellectual paralysis. It was

---

28. Leavis, F. R.—*New Bearings in English Poetry,* p. 199.
29. Bradbrook, M. C.—*Focus Three,* p. 119; *quoted* by Sean Lucy.
30. Lucy Sean—*Eliot and The Idea of Tradition,* p. 69.
31. *Ibid,* p. 70.

in a typical state of confusion. Nevertheless, Eliot does not write for this class. In fact, it is the minority, or what he himself calls the elite he cares to write for. As regards, what he has to say, he feels that the only jury of judgment is that of the "ablest poetical practitioners of his own time."[32] The difficulty is, that he demands prompt efforts and cooperation from his readers. Once given, Eliot is sure to delight, and possibly to broaden the horizons of one's understanding. English poetry of today and of tomorrow, is likely to have the same kind of relationship with him as the poetry of the later Romantics has had with Wordsworth and Coleridge."[33]

Discussing Arnold in **The Use of Poetry and The Use of Criticism,** Eliot has made a significant point, which may serve as key to the assessment of his own criticism and its various achievements. He says:—

> "From time to time, every hundred years or so, it is desirable that some critic shall appear to review the past of our literature and set the poets and the poems in order."[34]

The task of the critic, as envisaged in the statement, is very difficult. Such critics are rare, because in addition to an exceptional scholarship, it requires an unfettered mind, who can gear up enough power for interpretation, appreciation, and if need be imposition also. The whole of Eliot's literary career bears testimony to his being an exceptional critic of this category. It is now a matter of common knowledge that Eliot's single-minded devotion to literature with a view to reinterpreting its own values, has brought the old pattern of poets and poems under the spell of an evolutionary process. This evolution and the success it has achieved during its operation of 40 years or so, can be felt in the body of literary opinion and taste which it has cultivated in society. Without his exciting stewardship we might have been the poorer; for much that "we take for granted in our knowledge and enjoyment of the literature which satisfies our particular needs."[35] In this

32. Eliot, T. S.–O.P.P., p. 157.
33. Leavis, F. R.–*New Bearings in English Poetry.*
34. Eliot, T. S.–U.P.U.C., p. 108.
35. *Selected Prose;* Introduction, p. 7.

respect, his re-assessment of the Elizabethan dramatists; his rehabilitation of the Metaphysical poets; his judgments on Hamlet and Arnold; and his appraisal of Laforgue, Hulme and Baudelaire, have left considerable influence on the sensibility of the elite. John Hayward, the editor of the **Selected Prose,** rightly observes:—

> "Evidence of his imposing influence as a critic is perhaps most apparent in our appreciation of his own work as a poet and dramatist; for much of the satisfaction we derive from it is due to those very elements in the literature of the past which he has revalued, for his own profit as well as ours. It is indeed through knowledge of his criticism that we may often arrive at a clearer and deeper understanding of his poems and plays."[36]

He continues:—

> "I cannot indeed think of a critic who has ever been more widely read and discussed in his own lifetime; and not only in English but in almost every language except Russian, throughout the civilized world."[37]

Let there be no doubt in acknowledging the fact that Eliot has given to the literary world a critical **oeuvre,** which enforces a slowly changing conception not only of the "value of poetry but also of poetic values."[38] Moreover, there is a dialect of artistic development which has got its due acknowledgement in literary circles. Eliot is one of its prophets.[39] It is but for him that Ezra Pound, Hulme and Baudelaire are popularly discussed in literary circles, as having "the significance he attributed to them."[40] The influence Eliot has been able to cast upon contemporary literary scene shows that he was not a "mere individual in isolation."[41] One specific quality, which distinguishes him from his contemporaries, is that his writings—creative and critical—embody the general plight and consciousness of the age more than anybody's else.

---

36. *Selected Prose;* Introduction, p. 7.
37. *Ibid,* p. 10.
38. Buckley Vincent—*Poetry and Morality,* p. 89.
39. Lucy Sean—*Eliot and The Idea of Tradition,* p. 89.
40. Leavis, F. R.—*New Bearings in English Poetry.*
41. *Ibid.*

He could do this more effectively in that he was a critic as well as a poet.[42]

Looking at the nature of Eliot's criticism is like listening to a rather "dry-voiced lecture,"[43] to which one has to get used. His whole effort, though spreading over to a full span of more than four decades, and comprising not less than five hundred pieces of prose criticism, is bound together into "one whole work"[44] by an innate pressure of a specific outlook. What, at first sight, gives an impression of heterogeneous mass of "very varied length,"[45] on deeper examination, proves to be one synthetic growth. From the very start of his career as a critic, Eliot is seen trying hard to reconstruct a new place for the critic in modern society. His efforts have added a few more dimensions to the status of a literary critic.

Eliot has classified critics into six types.[46] They are: the Professionl Critic;[47] the Critic with Gusto;[48] the Academic and Theoretical Critic;[49] the Critic "whose criticism may be said to be a by-product of his creative activity";[50] the critic as Moralist and the Special Critic. The critics of first category—the professional—are those writers whose literary criticism is their chief and perhaps their only title to fame. They may be called—the "Super-Reviewers"[51] for some magazine or newspaper. Eliot includes in this type such critics as Sainte-Beuve, Paul Elmer More, Desmond MacCarthy and Edmund Cosse. He even goes to the extent of declaring that "the Professional Critic may be, as Sainte-Beuve certainly was, a failed creative writer."[52]

---

42. Leavis, F. R.—*New Bearings in English Poetry.*
43. Sean Lucy—*Eliot and The Idea of Tradition,* p. 63.
44. *Ibid.*
45. *Ibid.*
46. Eliot, T. S.—*To Criticise the Critic,* p. 11.
47. *Ibid.*
48. *Ibid.*
49. *Ibid.*
50. *Ibid.*
51. *Ibid,* p. 13.
52. *Ibid.*

The second type—the Critic with Gusto—is not called to the seat of judgment. He is rather the advocate of the authors he brings to light. They may be those authors who are sometimes forgotten or unduly neglected and ignored. The Critic with Gusto endeavours to foci our attention on such writers and makes us see merits and charms, where formerly, the same have not been found. According to Eliot, George Saintsbury and Quiller-Couch are the critics belonging to this class.[53]

The third type consists of the Academic and the Theoretical critics. They have been grouped together because Eliot feels that they range from the purely scholarly to the philosophical critics. It includes such names as W. P. Ker, I. A. Richards and William Empson. Dr. F. R. Leavis has been called the Critic as Moralist. The last category comprises those critics who are also tenants of an academic post and are likely to have made a special study of one period or one author.[54]

Eliot's ideal critic is the one whose criticism is the by-product of his creative activity. He prescribes three conditions for the entrance into this category: first, the candidate is known primarily for his poetry;[55] second, his criticism is distinguished[56] for its own sake; and third, it should not be merely such as to "throw light upon its author's verse."[57] Eliot mentions Dr. Johnson, Coleridge, Racine and Dryden under this type. The name of Matthew Arnold is also included in the list but with reservations.[58] "It is into this company", Eliot suggests, "that I must shyly intrude."[59] The other types of critics which Eliot have mentioned in his stray reference are:—the Technical Critic; the Historical Critic; the Philosophical Critic; and the Exhaustive Critic. The technical critic according to him is the one who writes to expound

53. *To Criticise the Critic,* p. 13.
54. *Ibid.*
55. *Ibid.*
56. *Ibid.*
57. *Ibid.*
58. *Ibid.*
59. *Ibid.*

some novelty or impart some lesson to practitioners of an art.[60] He can be called a critic only in a narrow sense. "The historical and the philosophical critics" says Eliot "had better be called historians and philosophers quite simply."[61] The exhaustive critic is the one who is able to "sweep the distance and gain an acquaintance with minute objects,"[62] with a view to comparing "minute objects" close at hand. In the essay, **The Perfect Critic,** Eliot has referred to an additional category of critics, viz., the Important Critic. He comments:—

> " 'An important critic' is the person who is absorbed in the present problems of art and who wishes to bring the Forces of the past to bear on these problems."[63]

As to the functions of criticism, Eliot's notions appear to be very much diffused. But given a deeper thought, there appears again a sense of underlying uniformity, right through his first essay—**The Functions of Criticism,** to the last one—**The Frontiers of Criticism.** Eliot's position, on the subject, is characteristically different to that of any other critic, coming before him. The functions he assigns to a major critic are fairly multifarious. First, the critic is to discover the nature of poetry as a branch of aesthetics. He is to probe into such fundamental question as to "what is poetry?"; or "how is it written?"[64] Second, he is expected to discriminate between "the living and the dead in literature."[65] Third, the critic must preserve tradition where a good tradition exists.[66] Fourth, he is to elucidate works of art and correct taste.[67] Fifth, he should promote understanding and enjoyment of literature.[68] Sixth, he must involve himself in the study of literature of the past and thus bring out models and standards

60. Eliot, T. S.—*The Sacred Wood,* p. 12.
61. *Ibid,* p. 16.
62. Eliot, T. S.—U.P.U.C., p. 108.
63. Eliot, T. S.—*The Sacred Wood,* p. 38.
64. Eliot, T. S.—U.P.U.C.; Introduction, p. 20.
65. Eliot, T. S.—*The Sacred Wood,* p. 47.
66. *Ibid,* Introduction, xv.
67. *Selected Prose,* p. 18.
68. Eliot, T. S.—O.P.P., p. 115.

to bear on Art of the present.[69] Lastly, the critic is to build up the organic concept of literature: to see it steadily and whole.[70]

Hence, the Eliotian critic is the repository of various literary interests. He is the preserver of tradition; the elucidator of art; the corrector of taste; the architect of poetic values; the regulator of a new order; and the exposer or the destroyer of the sham in art. In this way, we come to assume that for Eliot the critic is the guardian of literary values. It is his primary duty to synthesize the past, the present and the future in literature. He must see its past in terms of its present; he must see its present in terms of its past; and must help its real development in the future by bringing his total knowledge of the past in finding out solution to the present problem of Art and Literature.[71]

What Eliot aspires for is the provision of a proper literary environment which in his plan is "very largely an affair of the critic.[72] Unless this is achieved, it is hardly possible to achieve anything else. The creative writer and the man of letters have also to collaborate in achieving this ideal. Hence, a genuine critic should have the necessary requisites. He must possess, what speaking of Mr. Whibley Eliot has prescribed as the first essential of a perfect critic: the quality of showing interest in his subject and the ability to communicate an interest in it.[73] Besides this, he should imbibe what Eliot calls the "historical sense."[74] He should have the capacity and temperament to handle with care "the tools of comparison and analysis."[75] In order to justify his existence, he should endeavour to discipline his personal prejudices and cranks.[76] Not

69. Eliot, T. S.—*The Sacred Wood; Tradition and Individual Talent,* p. 47.

70. *Ibid.*

71. Lucy Sean—*Eliot and The Idea of Tradition,* p. 21.

72. *Ibid,* p. 17.

73. Eliot, T. S.—*The Sacred Wood,* p. 37.

74. *Selected Prose.*

75. *Ibid,* p. 19.

76. *Ibid,* p. 18.

only this, Eliot even goes to the extreme to suggest that the critic in question should compose his differences with as many of his fellows as possible.[77] It means that the critic should not suffer from the defects either of feeling or of intellect; and must display what Eliot qualifies as the "dissociative faculty."[78] This is necessary because according to him "the critic needs to be able not only to saturate himself in the spirit and the fashion of a time—the local flavour—but also to separate himself suddenly from it in appreciation of the highest creative works."[79] Thus, Eliot conceives criticism as an orderly field of "beneficent activity";[80] and considers it a place for "quiet cooperative labour."[81] Its chief aim is the common pursuit of "true judgement"[82]—judgement which in its totality ought to be impersonal and objective. He makes a solemn declaration:—

> "Honest criticism and sensitive appreciation is directed not upon the poet but upon the poetry."[83]

which in its ultimate analysis becomes an article of faith with the New Critics.

It has already been pointed out that in his post-Christian decade, i.e., the thirties, Eliot's literary criticism is specifically marked by an unprecedented emphasis on social and religious concern. It ceases to be purely literary and becomes bracketted with religious and moral judgments. Since then, he has been persistently justifying his zeal for moral values. He has stated in **The Use of Poetry and The Use of Criticism,** that pure artistic appreciation is "only an ideal."[84] He repeats the same point in **"To Criticise the Critic"**, when he asserts, it is impossible to fence off literary criticism from criticism "on other grounds."[85] Eliot's contention is that in order to under-

---

77. S.P., p. 18.
78. Eliot, T. S.—*The Sacred Wood,* p. 37.
79. *Ibid.*
80. *Selected Prose,* p. 18.
81. *Ibid.*
82. *Ibid.*
83. Eliot, T. S.—*The Sacred Wood,* p. 53.
84. Eliot, T. S.—U.P.U.C., p. 109.
85. Eliot, T. S.—*To Criticise the Critic,* p. 25.

stand great art, one must enter into all other interests of the artist.[86] He asserts:—

> "Literary criticism is an activity which must constantly define its own boundaries; also must constantly be going beyond them."[87]

He continues:—

> "We cannot get very far with Dante, or Shakespeare, or Goethe, without touching upon theology, and philosophy and ethics and politics."[88]

In the **Frontiers of Criticism,** he elaborates the same point:—

> "The difference, then, between the literary critic, and the critic who has passed beyond the frontier of literary criticism, is not that the literay critic is "purely" literary or that he has no other interests. A critic who was interested in nothing but 'literature' would have very little to say to us, for his literature would be a pure abstraction. Poets have their interests besides poetry—otherwise their poetry would be very empty: they are poets because their dominant interest has been in turning their experience and their thought (and to experience and to think means to have interests beyond poetry)—in turning their experience and their thinking into poetry. The critic accordingly is a *literary* critic if his primary interest, in writing criticism, is to help his readers to *understand and enjoy.* But he must have other interests, just as much as the poet himself; for the literary critic is not merely a technical expert, who has learned the rules to be observed by the writers he criticises: the critic must be the whole man, a man with convictions and principles and of knowledge and experience of life."[89]

The extract is very significant in as far as it explains an important aspect of Eliot's literary criticism. He is not prepared to recognise his critic as purely literary—a man in isolation. An Eliotian critic, on the other hand, is the "whole man"—a man with convictions and principles, and of knowledge and experience of life. Like the poet, the critic also must be a man of varied interests—interests which shall bear upon his criticism. Eliot feels that only **the** whole man would

---

86. Eliot, T. S.—O.P.P., p. 215.
87. *Ibid.*
88. *Ibid.*
89. *Ibid,* p. 116.

be the most appropriately equipped for helping the readers in what he maintains "understanding and enjoyment" as the essential function of criticism.[90] Eliot is prepared to express his gratitude to this type of critic because he has the capacity to "make him look at something he has never looked at before."[91]

Eliot has qualified his critic as a man of convictions and principles which raises an important issue, the issue of poetry and belief. It brings us back to one of his most controversial essays **"Religion and Literature"** wherein he has asserted that "literary criticism should be completed by criticism from a definite ethical and theological standpoint."[92] Suffice it to say that in 1923, Eliot has defined the functions of criticism as "the elucidation of art and the correction of taste." The "function" used in this specific context, implies "social utility." The actual process of criticism, then, may be inferred as "more-or-less" formal guidance of the reader to the "kind and quality of life embodied in a poem or novel."[93] It tends to be a matter of social and communal concern. Perhaps, Leavis is right in his oft-repeated emphasis that the "definition is so phrased as to elicit agreement, modification or enlightened dissent."[94] Whatever the case may be, even stray references such as these, to an ethical and theological standpoint are fraught with serious misgivings. After the publication of the essay, **"Religion and Literature"**, even Eliot's admirers have questioned the validity of this approach. His religious leanings have been hotly debated in literary reviews and periodicals. But Eliot has not yielded ground. In the **Notes on the Christian Society,** and **The Definition of Culture,** Eliot has re-iterated the same point of view. In 1961, he asserts once again:—

> "That literary merit can be estimated in complete isolation, is the illusion of those who believe that literary merit alone can justify the publication of a book which could otherwise be condemned on moral grounds."[95]

90. O.P.P., p. 115.
91. *Ibid,* p. 117.
92. Eliot, T. S.—*Selected Essays,* p. 388.
93. Buckley Vincent—*Poetry and Morality,* p. 215.
94. *Ibid.*
95. Eliot, T. S.—*To Criticise the Critic,* p. 26.

Observed closely, the nature of these assertions becomes clear. He envisages not one but two operations of the critical faculty.[96] The extracts quoted above contain an explanatory qualification which may provide a clue to the problem whether or not any ethical and theological standards are relevant to literary judgment? In the first extract from "**Religion and Literature**", his stress is on "completing" literary criticism with ethics and theology. In the second, the emphasis, though expressed negatively, remains the same: complete isolation in literary estimate is not possible. The rhetoric in both the uses is cleverly worded. It implies that Eliot himself appears to be more than conscious of the probable complications which these assertions are likely to arouse. Hence, in the first stage of the critical operation, he conceives of literary criticism as "purely literary"; while in the second, he aims at a supplementary **forward** point, suggesting a kind of criticism which may be called "socio-religious."[97] But the ambiguity does not lie in any sort of theoretical assertion. It arises out of its practical implications: Speaking theoretically there is no harm if literary criticism is completed by some ethical standpoint. The trouble is only on the practical plane. It arises when Eliot tries to substitute theological considerations for the literary rather than completing the one with the other.

In our discussion of Eliot's classification of critics, we have already pointed out that his ideal critic is the poet whose criticism is the by-product of his creative activity.[98] He is the critic who is particularly a poet. Eliot's whole critical attitude here reveals the close observance of a solemn principle, which he himself has explained in **The Use of Poetry and The Use of Criticism:—**

> "The critical mind operating in poetry may always be in advance to the critical mind operating upon poetry."[99]

Which means that the creative and the critical faculties are to work together in unison to produce the best possible

96. Buckley Vincent—*Poetry and Morality,* p. 217.
97. *Ibid,* p. 218.
98. Eliot, T. S.—*To Criticise the Critic,* p 15
99. Eliot, T. S.—U.P.U.C., p. 30.

results. They present merely the two directions of the same sensibility and are complementary to each other. Hence, the critic and the creative artist should frequently be the "same person."[100] This type of workshop criticism has its own merits and demerits. It is meritorious because it is indicative of the thinking process that goes into the formation of the poet's own verse.[101] It has also the advantage of being appreciated in relation to the poetry he has written.[102] But it has its serious limitations also. First, what is anti-pathetic to the poet, is "outside of his competence."[103] Second, the judgment of this critic may be unsound outside of his own art.[104]

By virtue of his promise and performance, Eliot "intrudes shyly into the company of his ideal critics."[105] His equipment as a critic is congruent with his equipment as a poet.[106] His early criticism is analogous to that of Ezra Pound;[107] like Pound, Eliot also directs his energies in the exploration of a suitable pattern of structure and language. Eliot's immediate object was to restore stability and fertility to the words. He is after the formation of a new structure or a verbal technique of poetry, expressive of a precise way of "thinking and feeling."[108] It is this "personal search",[109] as he himself refers to, that inspires him to study Shakespeare and other Elizabethan dramatists. It is with the same view that Eliot looks forward to the poetry of Laforgue, Ezra Pound, and other French symbolists. If he turns to the poetry of Donne and other metaphysicals, it is also with the same mission: to reconstruct a living form of poetry out of the "dust-bowl of modern speech."[110]

---

100. Eliot, T. S.–*The Sacred Wood.*
101. Eliot, T. S.–O.P.P., p. 106.
102. *Ibid,* p. 107.
103. *Ibid,* p. 108.
104. *Ibid.*
105. Eliot, T. S.–*To Criticise the Critic,* p. 13.
106. Rajan, B.–*Eliot: A Study by Several Hands,* p. 126.
107. Eliot, T. S.–O.P.P., pp. 106-107.
108. Eliot, T. S.–*The Sacred Wood,* p. 63.
109. Eliot, T. S.–O.P.P., p. 106.
110. Rajan, B.–*Eliot: A Study by Several Hands,* p. 127.

It would be admirable to mention that the exploratory interest which Eliot evinces in the local effects of the language, is the key to his earlier criticism. The fact, that he continues working on the special qualities of rhyme and rhythm, in the colloquial speech, enhances further its intrinsic value. It is through **The Waste Land** that Eliot promises a new start for English poetry.[111] **The Essay on Dante**[112] establishes his reputation in balancing together the twin interests of structure and language. Finally, passing through the concept of "Auditory Imagination"[113] his achievements in linguistic effects touch their virtual climax in **The Music of Poetry,**[114] published in 1942. To put it briefly, both structure and vocabulary had come to Eliot with all their richness and variety. He was able to evoke new patterns of feelings, new modes of experience and new techniques of modern sensibility. Let us acknowledge that if present-day practitioners are now using words very differently as compared to poets of the last age, it is mainly due to him.[115]

Before closing our discussion on the status and function of the Eliotian critic, it is necessary to clarify, what Eliot exactly means by "correction of taste."[116] It is in the essay **The Functions of Criticism** that he refers, for the first time, to this term. In the essays in **Poetry and Poets,** he further elaborates it and comes to consider the question: how far can the critic alter public taste for one or another poet or one or another period of literature of the past.[117] In this respect, the stray references occurring at various places, in **"The Essays"**,[118] are more than enough to provide the clues, to his understanding of the subject. Eliot's basic position is: that distinction

---

111. Leavis, F. R.—*New Bearings in English Poetry,* p. 95.
112. Eliot, T. S.—*Selected Prose.*
113. Eliot, T. S.—U.P.U.C.
114. Eliot, T. S.—O.P.P., p. 26.
115. Leavis, F. R.—*New Bearings in English Poetry,* p. 71.
116. Eliot, T. S.—*Selected Prose.*
117. Eliot, T. S.—*To Criticise the Critic,* p. 21.
118. *The Essays—Ancient and Modern.*

must be drawn between taste and fashion;[119] that fashion—the love of change for its own sake—is very transient;[120] that taste springs from a deeper source;[121] that it is either innate or inculcated;[122] that it is inextricable from the development of character and personality;[123] that the critic however cannot create taste;[124] that one's taste in poetry cannot be isolated from one's other interests and passions;[125] that it affects them and is affected by them; and must be limited as one's self is limited;[126] and finally, that the critic's own tastes and views alter in the course of his life time.[127]

Eliot's contention is that the changes in the tastes and views of critics may be the results of either of the two reasons: greater maturity and earlier decay.[128] He concedes, as in his own case, that the "degree of excitement and sense of enlargement",[129] which one experiences in his formative period, may not come afterwards. In the course of time, because of such changes, the critic would likely turn to other authors than those, offering him pure delight in the earlier stages. Eliot cites his own example:—

> "I turn more often the pages of Mallarme than those of Laforgue, those of George Herbert than those of Donne, of Shakespeare than of his contemporaries."[130]

But this should not be taken to suggest a "judgement of relative greatness."[131] It is quite natural that what best responds to the adolescent needs would be different to the needs

---

119. Eliot, T. S.—*To Criticise the Critic,* p. 21.
120. *Ibid.*
121. *Ibid.*
122. Eliot, T. S.—U.P.U.C., Introduction.
123. *Ibid.*
124. Eliot, T. S.—*To Criticise the Critic.*
125. Eliot, T. S.—U.P.U.C.
126. *Ibid.*
127. Eliot, T. S.—*To Criticise the Critic,* p. 22.
128. *Ibid.*
129. *Ibid.*
130. *Ibid.*
131. *Ibid.*

of the middle and later periods of a critic's life. In the case of Eliot, it is also worthwhile to note the impact of an additional factor: that his own taste had become affected by the exploratory nature of his early criticism. It is on this score that he explains away[132] "the much talked of reticence"[133] in his views on Milton. He refutes the charge that it was "a recantation of the earlier opinion",[134] and upholds it as a development in view of the fact, that there was no longer any likelihood of his "being imitated."[135]

As to the current queries of how far Eliot has been responsible for first discovering and then starting the vogue of "the early dramatists and the metaphysical poets",[136] he categorically replies "hardly at all—as a critic."[137] But as a poet, he is prepared to share the credit:—

> "As the taste for my own poetry spread, so did the taste for the poets to whom I owed the greatest debt and about whom I had written."[138]

The reason he spells out for the popularisation of this taste is more meaningful than the acknowledgment itself; "their poetry and mine were congenial to that age."[139] He re-iterates:—

> "It is one function of the critic to assist the literate public of his day to recognise its affinity with one poet or with one type of poetry, or one age of poetry rather than with another."[140]

We may be allowed to sum up our assessment of Eliot's contemporary influence with an important generalization made by M. C. Bradbrook:—

"However the arbitrament of general principles may uphold

---

132. Eliot, T. S.—*To Criticise the Critic,* p. 24.
133. Watson, George—*The Literary Critics.*
134. Eliot, T. S.—*To Criticise the Critic,* p. 24.
135. *Ibid.*
136. *Ibid,* p. 21.
137. *Ibid.*
138. *Ibid,* p. 22.
139. *Ibid.*
140. *Ibid,* p. 21.

the dignity of letters, it is by the example of his practice that a critic educates his public."[141]

Eliot's own example, more than anything else, substantiates forcefully the maxim expressed, herein. He has become a public institution.[142] By example of his own practice, Eliot has certainly created as well as educated his public. The immediate history of the literary taste is enough to record his astounding achievement. But more than that is what he has "enabled his generation to achieve for itself."[143]

141. Rajan, B.–*Eliot: A Study by Several Hands,* p. 119.
142. Leavis, F. R.–*New Bearings in English Poetry,* p. 177.
143. Rajan, B.–*Eliot: A Study by Several Hands,* p. 119.

CHAPTER VIII

CONCLUSION

Eliot's theoretical speculations are widely interspersed in his essays, lectures and broadcasts. Apart from **Tradition and The Individual Talent**; the most significant specimens of his sustained thinking are the essays on **The Metaphysical Poets; Religion and Literature; Hamlet; Baudelaire; Arnold; Milton; Yeats; The Music of Poetry** and **What Dante Means to Me.** They contain some of his finest critical reflections. **The Functions of Criticism; The Frontiers of Criticism**; and **To Criticise the Critic** incorporate elaborate statements, as to the nature of the vicarious responsibility the critic is entrusted with. The two essays, appearing in **The Sacred Wood: The Perfect Critic** and **The Imperfect Critic** are more negative than positive in their tone, and that, perhaps, explains for their deletion in **The Selected Essays,** published in 1932. **The Possibilities of Poetic Drama; The Three Voices of Poetry**; and **Poetry and Drama** embody his views on the probable revival of the verse drama in English. As regards to Eliot's social criticism, besides **The Use of Poetry and The Use of Criticism,** the twin treatises: **The Idea of a Christian Society**; and **Notes Towards the Definition of Culture** are the more authoritative. The first four lectures, published in **On Poetry and Poets,** take their place beside **Tradition and The Individual Talent.** "They are", says C. L. Barber, "the master-pieces of balanced generalisation about the literary process."[1]

In our chapter-wise discussion, we have already studied the different aspects of Eliot's criticism with all its theoretical and practical bearings. He has left behind an established legacy of certain well acknowledged principles of literary critic-

---

1. Matthiesen, F. O.—*The Achievement of T. S. Eliot.* (Quoted).

ism. His three theories: **Theory of Tradition; Theory of Poetry;** and **Theory of Impersonality** have gained universal recognition. His four phrases: **Dissociation of Sensibility; Objective Correlative; Auditory Imagination;** and **Sensuous Apprehension of Thought** have been widely debated. His pleas for the revival of poetic drama and the strenuous endeavours made by him in that direction have earned considerable applause in literary circles. It is no less an achievement that Eliot has been successful in "establishing the 17th century in its due place in the English tradition."[2] Again, it goes to his credit that he could construct a living form of poetry out of the "dust bowl of the colloquial speech."[3] As to Eliot's critical **oeuvre,** one can safely assert that it has enforced a new conception, not only of the "value of poetry, but also of poetic values."[4] The assessment of Mario Praz is highly substantive:—

> "He has been anyhow a leader of taste, a sower of faithful seeds, or whom, within the limits of his self-imposed task of reformer, one must admire both the earnestness and uprightness which have won him a universal esteem, and also the fundamental coherence even in his apparent or actually substantial contradictions."[5]

Eliot's **Theory of Tradition** may be interpreted as a revolt against what is called the too much "isolation of aesthetic experience"[6]—a practice which had become a "kind of orthodoxy"[7] by the 1920's. His concept of tradition implies respect for the established order, "in the sense both of authority and of form."[8] But, the order evoked by him is not something "dead or done with."[9] It is rather a living tradition as much **present** in the present itself, as the present is always a virtual part of the future. The pattern of tradition, thus en-

---

2. Leavis, F. R.—*New Bearings in English Poetry,* p. 199.
3. Rajan, B.—*Eliot*: *A Study by Several Hands,* p. 127.
4. Buckley Vincent—*Poetry and Morality,* p. 89.
5. Tate Allen—*T. S. Eliot*: *The Man and His Work,* p. 277.
6. Williams Raymond—*Culture and Society,* p. 239.
7. *Ibid.*
8. *Selected Prose;* Introduction, p. 11.
9. *Ibid, Tradition and the Individual Talent,* p. 23.

visaged, is the one in which "the existing monuments form an ideal order......complete before the new work arrives."[10] After the "supervention of novelty",[11] there is alteration and readjustment of "the relations, proportions, values, of each work of art toward the whole."[12] Hence, Eliot affirms that "the past should be altered by the present as much as the present is directed by the past."[13] In this way, the existing order is complete, only "within itself." In no case, it implies that any addition or modification is absolutely ruled out.

It is here, with regard to this particular aspect, that Eliot departs from the Augustan emphasis of tradition. The Augustans took tradition as immutable and complete in all respects, while Eliot's theory takes an altogether different view. The living tradition is continuously being modified, re-adjusted, added, or even altered by the appearance, so to say, of every new work of art. What Eliot asks of the poets is not the apish or passive acceptance of the past. He wants them to "develop or procure its consciousness",[14] in order to enlighten their own works. This consciousness or what Eliot calls the "historical sense"[15] would make the writer acutely conscious of "his place in time, of his own contemporaneity."[16] As a result, he will become fully aware of his literary environs as also of the nature of art he is expected to create. Eliot feels that the moment an artist becomes aware of the presence of the past, tradition would certainly help in solving difficulties and providing guide-lines for bringing out works wherein, dead artists "assert their immortality most vigorously."[17] Tradition, in this context, assumes the role of a repository of literary values. Its nature becomes positively classical in as far as it substitutes the "historical sense" in place of the "inner

10. Eliot, T. S.—*The Sacred Wood,* p. 50.
11. *Ibid.*
12. *Ibid.*
13. *Ibid.*
14. *Ibid.*
15. *Ibid.*
16. *Ibid.*
17. Eliot, T. S. *Selected Prose,* p. 22.

voice" of the Romanticists. The rule of sheer emotionalism goes and once again, discipline of objective authority is introduced. Eliot's basic contribution, which the **Theory of Tradition** highlights, lies in the fact that the writer is no more considered an "unacknowledged legislator" of the world. In fact, the sense of tradition places before him certain obligations, which as artist, he must fulfil in a judicious manner. Moreover, it is he, who not only preserves tradition, but if need be, also alters that which already exists. Eliot's concept of tradition does not imply anything, entirely new and original. It simply systematises that which critics have spoken from time to time. The Augustans had always stood for a stricter adherence to the rule of tradition; but still, none of them could evolve out a systematic theory. It is Eliot who not only theorises on the role of tradition but also develops through its tissues a new literary concept—the concept which regards all literature as an organic whole. It is because of this concept, followed by Eliot's own practice of bringing "the 17th century back to English tradition",[18] that even those writers who were once considered, minor and ordinary, have got their due places in the annals of literary hierarchy. His own observations on this point are significant:—

> "There are new and strange objects in the foreground, to be drawn accurately in proportion to the more familiar ones which now approach the horizon, where all but the most eminent become invisible to the naked eye."[19]

Eliot's **Theory of Poetry** and **Theory of Impersonality** may be taken to mean as important corollaries of his **Theory of Tradition.** Both are significantly valuable in as far as they elaborate the "creative process" that goes to make a poem. Eliot tries to explain a poem and its composition in terms of "impersonal emotions."[20] His understanding of the whole "creative process" involves a two-tier working of the poet's personality. First, he must submit to the authority of poetic tradition.[21] Second, he should closely understand and follow

18. Eliot, T. S.–*Selected Prose,* p. 113.
19. Eliot, T. S.–U.P.U.C., p. 108.
20. *Selected Prose; Tradition and Individual Talent,* p. 23.
21. *Ibid,* pp. 22-23.

the literary heritage of his own people.[22] Such an interaction between the poet's mind and the mind of his own country would yield a poetic personality"[23] which, retaining a certain individuality, will be better equipped for the creative purposes of an impersonal art. Passing through such a graduated development, or what Eliot calls "the extinction of personality",[24] the poet becomes a medium "capable of relating"[25] the "accumulated wisdom of time"[26] to the problems of art, culture and socitey. Eliot asserts that the poet has not "a personality to express but a particular medium."[27] Moreover, it is this very medium which regulates the combination of poets' "impressions and experiences"[28] in such a way as to give an artistic appeal to the poem. Its perfection, according to Eliot, will proportionately vary with the quantum of impersonality the poet has been able to achieve through the interplay of tradition. Hence, he declares:—

> "the more perfect the artist, the more completely separate in him will be the man who suffers and the mind which creates."[29]

But in his essay on **Yeats,**[30] Eliot has appended a plausible modification. Now, he does not advocate his earlier notion of "total extinction of personality" of the artist. On the other hand, he adopts a mid-way course or a kind of golden mean. Nevertheless, there is no retraction from the basic concept of the "creative process." Only the stress is shifted from "depersonalization to universalization"[31] of "emotions and feelings",[32] which constitute the material for a poem. It may better be called a gradual immersion of the poet's personality into something, general and universal.

---

22. Eliot, T. S.–*Selected Prose,* p. 24.
23. Max Well, D. E. S.–*The Poetry of T. S. Eliot,* p. 23.
24. Eliot, T. S.–*Selected Prose,* p. 25.
25. Max Well, D. E. S.–*The Poetry of T. S. Eliot,* p. 23.
26. Eliot, T. S.–*Selected Prose,* p. 25.
27. *Ibid,* p. 27.
28. *Ibid.*
29. *Ibid,* p. 26.
30. *Ibid,* p. 189.
31. *Ibid.*
32. *Ibid,* p. 26.

The shift, mentioned above, together with the retractions on Milton throw some valuabe light on some basic aspects of Eliot's criticism. In the first instance, they show its empirical character; secondly, they display Eliot's "power to repent"[33]—the sure test of a critic's intellectual integrity and honesty; thirdly, they throw light on an important aspect of Eliot's literary criticism.

Eliot justifies the retractions on the grounds he has discussed in **The Music of Poetry**. He had stated therein that his critical method was that of a poet "always trying to defend the kind of poetry he was writing."[34] In **"Milton II"** he again refers to the same point by distinguishing between the interests of a scholar and that of a practitioner.[35] He goes as far as to define that the "scholar's interest is in the permanent, the practitioners in the immediate."[36] Eliot's contention is simple. He and his friends opposed Milton in the initial stages, as they felt that his influence would retard the process of bringing language back to the colloquial speech in which all of them were engaged as practitioners. The language having been brought back to the colloquial speech and the poets having been "sufficiently removed from Milton",[37] they can now afford to study his work "without danger and with profit to their poetry and to the English language."[38]

As for the phrases: **Dissociation of Sensibility; Objective Correlative**; and **Auditory Imagination,** Eliot's own observations, made in 1961, are significant. He acknowledges that they have been "useful in their time."[39] He feels that even if they go out of fashion completely";[40] they have served their turn as "stimuli",[41] to arouse critical thinking of others. But,

33. Rajan, B.—*The Overwhelming Question in T. S. Eliot: The Man and His Work* (ed.) by Allen Tate, p. 364.

34. Eliot, T. S.—O.P.P., p. 26.

35. Eliot, T. S.—*Selected Prose,* p. 125.

36. *Ibid.*

37. *Ibid,* p. 141.

38. *Ibid.*

39. Eliot, T. S.—*To Criticise the Critic,* p. 19.

40. *Ibid.*

41. *Ibid.*

his final affirmation is the most valuable as it embodies, again, one of the basic tenets of his literary criticism:—

> "But I prophesy that if my phrases are given consideration a century hence, it will be only in their historical context, by scholars interested in the mind of my generation."[42]

It means that the tenets he has tried to formulate and enforce have no "absolute validity in his eyes";[43] they are closely related to "historical circumstances."[44] In the first instance, as a critic, he does not belong to those who are temperamentally fit for bringing out legislation in the field of criticism. Secondly, even if he gives sometimes an impression of that type, it is only in relation to a specific class, category or generation of authors. In **The Frontiers of Criticism,** written in 1956, he elaborates the same principle:—

> "Thirty years ago, it seems to have been the latter type of criticism, the impressionistic, that had caused the annoyance I felt when I wrote on the *'Function of Criticism.'* Today it seems to me that we need to be more on guard against the purely explanatory."[45]

Eliot's final position in this respect is very convincing. The explanation he gives, is contained by his own assertion that "no generation is interested in Art in quite the same way as any other."[46] Each one has to cater to new problems, needs and tastes which makes "new assessments necessary."[47]

Much criticism has been levelled against Eliot's statement that a poem in some sense possesses a "life of its own."[48] Ransom and Winters have criticised Eliot for what they allege this as a "doctrine of poetic automatism."[49] Both of them feel that Eliot's affirmation implies an "**abdication** of poet's pro-

---

42. Eliot, T. S.—*To Criticise the Critic,* p. 19.

43. Praz Mario—*Eliot as a Critic in Eliot*: *The Man and His Work* by Allen Tate (ed.), p. 276.

44. *Ibid.*

45. Eliot, T. S.—O.P.P., pp. 117-18.

46. Eliot, T. S.—U.P.U.C., p. 109.

47. *Ibid.*

48. *Ibid,* Introduction.

49. Ransom, J. Crowe—*The New Criticism,* p. 152.

per responsibility."[50] They argue that since the poet is making an evaluation, he must remain "fully in control of his poem."[51] But such criticism of Eliot appears to be far-fetched. He has nowhere suggested the abdication of the poet's authority over his poem. Even in his essay on **Tradition and The Individual Talent,** where he develops the notion of "extinction of personality",[52] he does not fail to mention that a great deal in the writing of poetry must be "conscious and deliberate."[53] It virtually means that at no stage of a poem's development, the poet is to become passive or dormant; nor does it, in any way, suggest the lack of poet's direct control over the poem. Eliot's concept of "sensuous apprehension of thought"[54] fully endorses the same view. Brooks' remarks are significant:—

> "Eliot's metaphor about the poem's 'life' and his suggestion that the poet's primary task is to foster and nurture that life are not incorrigibly irrational. It is possible to argue that the poem like a growing plant, naturally grows toward the light and unless interfered with, tends to grow straight."[55]

Moreover, a pre-planned or over-emphasized control of the poet on the poem may obstruct its river-like natural march; may retard its continuous flow; and consequently, may pervert it to the unwarranted stagnancy of a mere dam. As a natural consequence of the stress on the poem having its "own life" most of the new critics tend to follow the vogue of treating art as "autonomous and self-explanatory."[56] They isolate the work of art and take it as a "thing **per se.**"[57] But Eliot has his own reservations on this point. His position is more rational as compared to that of the new critics. Accord-

---

50. Wimsatt and Brooks—*Literary Criticism: A Short History*, p. 676.
51. *Ibid*, p. 670.
52. *Selected Prose*, p. 25.
53. *Ibid*, p. 29.
54. *Ibid*, p. 113.
55. Brooks Cleanth—*Literary Criticism; A Short History*, pp. 676-77.
56. Gardner Helen—*The Business of Criticism*, p. 18.
57. *Ibid*.

ing to him, a work of art may "stand by itself",[58] but it does not necessarily have to "stand alone."[59] He is opposed to see literature stripped of all contexts. He condemns the practice of estimating literary merit in "complete isolation";[60] and refers to it as nothing else than "illusion."[61] He feels that literary criticism must "define its own boundaries"[62] and if need be, must go even "beyond them."[63] As to the position of the critic, Eliot affirms that he is "the whole man—a man with convictions and principles and of knowledge and experience of life."[64]

Eliot is basically opposed to any sort of infringement of the reader's rights vis-a-vis his aesthetic experience. He feels that the experience which a poem imparts to its reader is "conditioned by the individual's experience of life and art."[65] The function of the critic is to help the readers to "read for themselves and not to read for them."[66] He must honour their sensibility and should in no case thrust upon them his own theories. His primary interest is to help them to "understand and enjoy",[67] and he should so elucidate a work of art as to exert its full power. But Eliot thinks that any criticism can only "lead us to the door: we must find our way in."[68] It would naturally depend on our own "sensibility, intelligence and capacity for wisdom."[69] Hence, Eliot asserts that the meaning of a poem is "what the poem means to different readers."[70] He re-iterates that the job of the critic is to "set

58. Rajan, B.—*The Overwhelming Question in T. S. Eliot: The Man and His Mission* (ed.) by Allen Tate, p. 366.
59. *Ibid.*
60. Eliot, T. S.—*To Criticise the Critic,* p. 26.
61. *Ibid.*
62. Eliot, T. S.—*On Poetry and Poets,* p. 215.
63. *Ibid.*
64. *Ibid,* p. 116.
65. Gardner, Helen—*The Business of Criticism,* p. 17.
66. *Ibid.*
67. Eliot, T. S.—*On Poetry and Poets,* p. 116.
68. *Ibid,* p. 117.
69. *Ibid.*
70. *Ibid,* p. 113.

us face to face with and then leave use alone with it."[71]

Eliot's contribution to dramatic criticism—theoretical as well as practical—is equally significant. In this respect, he has made some valuable and basic assertions. He affirms that all poetry even a lyric from the Greek anthology is "dramatic."[72] "Poetry", he says, "must justify itself dramatically",[73] and as such, no play should be written in verse for which prose is "**dramatically** adequate."[74] In his view, the theatre is an "ideal medium"[75] for poetry. It can also serve as a "direct means"[76] of promoting its social usefulness for the obvious reason that it has the capacity to provide to its audience "several levels of consciousness."[77] Apart from Eliot's theorization about drama, his efforts for the revival of verse drama are no less important. May be, the interplay between his theory and practice is not as promising in his plays as it has been in his poems; yet, whatever he was able to achieve in the field of poetic drama, has already carved out a "preparatory"[78] base for its future progress and development.

Eliot's social criticism is very illuminating in as far as it throws a flood of light on some of the most relevant problems of contemporary society. His definition of culture as a "whole way of life"[79] provides sufficient clues to the understanding of his basic approach which is "organic rather than atomic."[80] His views on religion have been widely criticised. But, whatever he has theorized and advocated in this regard is certainly of great value to the modern concept of sociology and anthropology.[81] The very fact that Eliot does not sacrifice his artistic

71. Eliot, T. S.—*On Poetry and Poets,* p. 117.
72. Eliot, T. S.—*Selected Essays,* p. 28.
73. Eliot, T. S.—*On Poetry and Poets,* p. 72.
74. *Ibid.*
75. Eliot, T. S.— U.P.U.C.
76. *Ibid.*
77. *Ibid.*
78. Eliot, T. S.—*On Poetry and Poets,* p. 72.
79. Williams Raymond—*Culture and Society,* p. 235.
80. *Ibid,* p. 299.
81. *Ibid.*

and religious faiths to "easy popularity",[82] commands our respect, even if he is not able to "win our agreement."[83]

As to Eliot's critical method, we may simply assert that it is usually one of extracting assent than of provoking reaction or disapproval. His exposition is mostly marked by "cautious stages of definition, doubt, reservation and qualification to final affirmation."[84] In his earlier prose criticism, he is occasionally pontifical but his later essays and addresses reflect much of that rhetorical grace and cadence for which most of his critical writings have received general recognition. His style is devoid of metaphor and ornament. It is always replete with an unfailing sense of detachment—the first requisite of a major critic. His method in criticism may be called perfectly dialectical, which on its own, has established a new scientific order in revaluating English literary tradition. In this respect, Edmund Wilson's observations are significant:—

> "T. S. Eliot has undertaken a kind of scientific study of aesthetic values: avoiding impressionistic rhetoric and *a priorie* aesthetic theories alike, he compares works of literature coolly and tries to distinguish between different orders of artistic effects and the different degrees of satisfaction to be derived from them."[85]

According to Eliot, the best of his literary criticism consists of "essays on poets and poetic dramatists, who had influenced him."[86] It is the outcome of what he himself relates: "the prolongation of the thinking that went into the formation of my verse."[87] In fact, Eliot is a poet-cum-critic of the line and order of Dryden, Johnson and Coleridge. Their works, as also his own, amply display the convergence of two directions of sensibility—the creative and the critical. As such, Eliot's criticism can be fully appreciated only, when it is considered in relation to the poetry he has himself written.[88] His

82. Max Well, D. E. S.—*The Poetry of T. S. Eliot,* p. 212.
83. *Ibid.*
84. Hayward John—Introduction, p. 12.
85. Wilson Edmund—*Axel's Castle,* p. 115.
86. Eliot, T. S.—*On Poetry and Poets,* p. 106.
87. *Ibid.*
88. *Ibid.*

progress as a poet is congruent with his progress as a critic. Each re-animates the other.[89]

The exploratory nature of Eliot's studies of Laforgue, Baudelaire, Donne and other Shakespearian and Jocobean dramatists establish his claim to be an ardent adherent of tradition, of which, he has so powerfully spoken in his essay **Tradition and The Individual Talent.**[90] The interest he shows in these authors is not purely academic. It displays in him "the historical sense",[91] which, according to Eliot, is indispensable to anyone who would continue to be a poet "beyond his twenty-fifth year."[92] The study is also inspired by what he calls "personal search"[93] for a suitable style in poetry. His search for a new technique after the masters of the past, has other complexions also. It represents in him, what Pound has qualified as the "true Dantescan Voice."[94] In his Essay on Dante, Eliot affirms:—

> "To pass on to posterity one's own language, more highly developed, more refined, and more precise than it was before one wrote it, that is the highest possible achievement of the poet as poet."[95]

Which means that a major poet ought "to preserve, develop and even restore the health of language." His primary duty is to "give body to the soul of language."[96] No wonder, that Eliot's genius, great as it was, sets him forth to reconstruct the new language of poetry "out of the dust bowl of modern speech."[97]

Eliot's passion for restoring health of language is linked with another important aspect of his literary criticism. It

---

89. Rajan, B. (ed.) –*Eliot: A Study by Several Hands,* p. 126.
90. *Selected Prose,* p. 21.
91. *Ibid,* p. 22.
92. *Ibid.*
93. Eliot, T. S.–*On Poetry and Poets,* p. 66.
94. Tate Allen (ed.) –*Eliot: The Man and His Work,* p. 89.
95. *Selected Prose,* p. 95.
96. *Ibid.*
97. Bradbrook, M. C.–*Eliot; A Study by Several Hands,* p. 127; (ed.) B. Rajan.

exemplifies an important aspect of his poetic practice. In his essay "**Donne in Our Time**", Elilot has prescribed that a poet in his formative stage must idolize a specific poet or a specific school of poetry for his own guidance and training. To a large extent, Baudelaire was this poet for Eliot.[98] In precept and practice; in outlook and attitude; and in plans and performance both the poets give evidence of some common qualities. For Eliot, Baudelaire was more than a poet: he is an artist **par excellence**; not that, he found a superficial form but that, he was also searching for a "form of life."[99] Nevertheless, Eliot has his own reservations. In his later poetry, he outreached Baudelaire: Baudelaire sees the seamy side of life while Eliot has a faith to live on.

Before embarking on the actual achievement of Eliot's pattern of language, let us try to have some idea of what he expects from a poem to be. He feels that a poem has its own existence—an existence lying somewhere between the writer and the reader.[100] He is one with Prof. Richards who says, "it is never what a poem **says** that matters, but what it **is.**"[101] As to its logical function, the minimum he wants is its capacity "to move."[102] But he is not prepared to adjudge this capacity through the Arnoldian doctrine of "touch-stone" lines and passages.[103] On the other hand, the strength of a poem must grow out of "the whole poem" itself.[104] Eliot's remarks on **Grecian Urn** and **King Lear** clearly demonstrate the way he envisages the poem to develop as an organic whole.

On the structural plane, Eliot believes that "the poem comes before the form."[105] He insists upon the inner unity, which he calls unique to every poem, as against the outer unity,

---

98. Tate Allen (ed.)–*Eliot; The Man and His Work,* p. 300.
99. Eliot, T. S.–*Selected Prose,* p. 178.
100. Eliot, T. S.–U.P.U.C., p. 30.
101. *Ibid,* p. 17.
102. Eliot, T. S.–*On Poetry and Poets,* p. 30.
103. *Ibid.*
104. *Ibid.*
105. *Ibid,* p. 37.

which is only "typical."[106] In its practical aspects, the growth of language requires operation upon two stages—the exploratory and the developmental.[107] The first stage involves the poet in slowly adopting his form to colloquial speech;[108] while in the second stage, he should experiment with a view to making music out of the sense of structure and sense of rhythm.[109] It must be borne in mind that in the strict Eliotian sense, meaning is part of the structural pattern of a poem. It cannot be sequestered either from its structure or from its rhythm. As to the nature of this linguistic pattern, Eliot makes it clear:—

> "Our civilization comprehends great variety and complexity, and this variety and complexity, playing upon a refined sensibility, must produce various and complex results. The poet must become more and more comprehensive, more allusive, more indirect, in order to force, to dislocate if necessary, language to its meaning."[110]

The volume—**Prufrock and Other Observations,** records "the impression of a remarkable technique, already flexible and accomplished."[111] These early poems display the influence of Corbiere and Laforgue with Baudelaire in the background. The flexibility of the technique springs directly from the use of such devices as fluid metre, urban settings, literary allusions, ironic asides and intermingled nature of sense-impressions. The opening lines of **The Love Song** indicate the break from the old poetry wherein a mystifying situation is created by the use of colloquial language:—

> "Let us go then, you and I,
> When the evening is spread out against the sky
> Like a patient etherised upon a table;
>
> Let us go through certain half deserted streets,
> The muttering retreats;
> Of restless nights in one-night cheap hotels
> And Sawdust restaurants with Oyster-shells;

---

106. Eliot, T. S.—*On Poetry and Poets,* p. 37.
107. *Ibid,* p. 35.
108. *Ibid,* p. 36.
109. *Ibid,* p. 38.
110. *Selected Prose,* p. 112.
111. Ford Boris (ed.)—*The Modern Age,* p. 330.

In the room the women come and go
Talking of Michelangelo.[112]

The poem may particularly be noted for its effective use of "imagery" which is mostly drawn from the contemporary life. The thoughts are recreated into feeling, a feature he greatly admired in the poetry of the metaphysical poets. The imagery of the poem high-lights the directions, which Eliot is aspiring to give to the new technique. The way he conveys different states of the distressed mind of Prufrock is at once new and thrilling. The use of the visual expressions lends an extra-ordinary grace to the whole poem. To apprehend the state of agony through the image of the evening as "a patient etherised upon a table" or to experience the "lethargic animalism of life in the great city",[113] in the image of the yellow fog as "a sleepy cat that rubs its back upon the windows", are very exhilarating experiences for the lovers of poetry in the early decades of the century. The atmosphere of the poem is vague and uncertain but the images, which are diverse and diffused, give the poem a sort of distinctive colour. The half-audible images of "muttering retreats" and "talking women" are full of their own suggestiveness. Apart from imagery, Eliot has applied what he himself advocates the "method of contrast between fixity and flux as the very life of verse." Prufrock's environment comprises stable and hard objects, while the mood he depicts is vague and vacillating. He happens to face a serious problem but refuses to move forward to its logical solution.

The most fascinating aspect of **The Love Song** is its "power to move."[114] Its appeal does not lie in isolated lines, but the whole poem moves in one organism and whatever mood it has to communicate that grows out of the poem itself. The rhythm, structure, meaning, imagery, even syntax, all converge together to make it what it is. Being perfect, the poem

112. *Selected Poems*: Faber and Faber, p. 11.
113. Pinto V de S—*Crisis in English Poetry.*
114. Eliot, T. S.—*On Poetry and Poets,* p. 30.

displays a remarkable alikeness of content and form—a relevance which Eliot has so often stressed.[115]

For the full appreciation of the point raised here, it seems necessary to revert back to Eliotian acceptation of "reality" of a poem. As already stated, Eliot's approach in this respect is Baudelairian. Eliot sees in Baudelaire a new kind of "theological innocence."[116] The French poet's assertion that "it is better to do evil than to do nothing",[117] though paradoxical, marks for Eliot a new perspective of looking at poetic reality. Goethe and Baudelaire are great because both of them look into this reality—the plight of "human situation."[118] They understand and foresee a great deal and picture through poetry what is a "must" for a great poet—"the sense of the age."[119]

Seen in this light, **The Love Song of Prufrock** is a great poem. It is a landmark in English poetry. Not only does it depart from the conventional patterns but the poem also incorporates into its theme a new view of life: it depicts beatitude in terms of "the boredom, the horror and the glory",[120] of the contemporary urban life. Its most significant feature is the way Prufrock's irony is made to reflect on a general human predicament besides being directed against himself.[121]

"Portrait of a Lady"—the 2nd important poem of the selection—is also notable for its flexibility, control and precision. The movement of the verse is perfect. The tone is more subtle, and the technique promises a richer development. The atmosphere is dominated by the imagery drawn from the contemporary life.

The lines such as:—

Now that Lilacs are in bloom
She has a bowl of lilacs in her room.

---

115. *Selected Poems of Ezra Pound;* Introduction.
116. *Selected Prose,* p. 176.
117. *Ibid,* p. 183.
118. *Ibid.*
119. *Ibid.*
120. Eliot, T. S.–U.P.U.C., p. 106.
121. Ford Boris (ed.)–*The Modern Age,* p. 333.

And twists one in her fingers while she talks,
'Ah my friend, you do not know, you do not know
What life is, you hold it in your hands';
(Slowly twisting the lilac stalks)
. . . .
. . . .
I smile of course,
And go on drinking tea.[122]

show Eliot's power to "build up the perception of the profound significance",[123] on seemly trivial matters of life. The portrait of a woman, standing and looking at a typical way, is certainly an "expression of character."[124] As for its theme, the poem is not so much the **"Portrait of a Lady"** as the portrait of another uncertain Prufrock, adolescent rather than prematurely aged, but at the same time suspended between feelings of attraction and repulsion.[125]

The volume of 1917 may be said to concentrate on the sordid and dreary aspects of the modern urban life, portrayed in the background of "ironic gaiety and gusto."[126] As a whole, the poems satisfy the following criterion he has hinted out in **The Sacred Wood:—**

> "Any life, if accurately and profoundly penetrated is interesting and always strange."[127]

The next group of poems of 1920 is more serious. The essential attitude towards life is still unresolved. Eliot introduces yet another new pattern in these poems. In place of free verse, he substitutes the strict rhyming quatrains of Gautier. **Gerontion** is the most important poem in this selection. It may be noted, first, for its prophetic vision. Second, the speaker now is not a living character like Prufrock or the Lady: he is an impersonal symbol—Western civilization depicted in the form of an old man. Third, the poem is the first of its kind where Eliot tries to incorporate the idea of

---

122. *Selected Poems*: Faber and Faber.
123. Pinto V de S—*Crisis in English Poetry,* p. 186.
124. *Ibid.*
125. Williamson George—*A Readers' Guide to Eliot,* p. 71.
126. Pinto V de S—*Crisis in English Poetry,* p. 187.
127. Eliot, T. S.—*The Sacred Wood,* p. 81.

tradition into the central theme of a poem. Fourth, the concept of time in respect of its various contexts: of individual, society and eternity, is developed for the first time. Fifth, the poem records Eliot's recurrent theme of mixing "memory and desire", together. Lastly, **Gerontion** shows greater skill on the part of the poet, to develop still further the method of "sensuous apprehension of thought" or the technique of "dramatization of emotions" through "objective correlatives."

Gerontion is prefixed with an introductory quotation which shows a significant relevance to the impersonal and detached atmosphere of the poem. It runs:—

Thou hast nor youth nor age
But as it were an after dinner sleep
Dreaming of both.[128]

As against the personal nature of distress and disillusionment in the poems of 1917, the poet here probes life on a deeper level and questions "what it all come to."[129] The well sustained references to hollowness of life contained in the line "Thou hast nor youth nor age", serves as a key to the skeptical bearings of the poem. Naturally, the broodings of the old man as to the ultimate outcome of life, its meaning and its residue, assume a serious tone. The opening lines:—

Here I am, an old man in a dry month,
Being read to by a boy waiting for rain.[130]

generate a process of rethinking to be followed immediately by an amalgam of "memory and desire." The old man in his "dry month" waits for the elixir of "rain." In an atmosphere of barrenness, the very idea that it would never rain, stirs his feelings of despair and disappointment. He laments for the loss:—

My house is a decayed house
And the fur squats on, the window sill, the owner
Spawned in some estaminet.

---

128. *Selected Poems*: Faber and Faber, p. 31; Quoted from Shakespeare's *Measure for Measure*.

129. Leavis, F. R.—*New Bearings in English Poetry*, p. 72.

130. *Selected Poems*: Faber and Faber, p. 31.

But confesses:—

I an old man
A dull head among windy spaces.

What about his world? It is dry, barren and unproductive:—

Rocks, moss, stonecrop, iron, merds.

Despite all this, Eliot presents the man ruminating over the past memories of the spiritual rejuvenation:—

In the juvescence of the year
Came Christ the tiger

In depraved May,............

The last two phrases are fine specimens of Eliot's condensed expression. The poet in Eliot shows great skill in contrasting and fusing together, the diametrically different emotions and feelings. The passage is important in another respect also: it provides an example of Eliot's power to picture obscure states of mind through the medium of ordinary speech. The way "fear of life" hovers over the whole atmosphere of **Gerontion** brings it closer to the **The Waste Land**—the next best poem of T. S. Eliot.

The Waste Land was hailed as a great poem. Its symphonic character earned from no less a person than **Prof. I. A.** Richards, the title of "The Music of Ideas."[131] In the degree of technical achievement, the poem stands unrivalled in all its earlier counterparts. The method applied is mythical. The theme incorporated is the vision of a "devitalised world"[132]—a world completely devoid of spiritual values. The atmosphere of the poem is replete with the ever increasing sense of pity and terror of the contemporary society. It is in **The Waste Land** that Eliot makes free use of psychology, sexology and anthropology. The underlying idea is the sexual impotence which has been used as a symbol for the spiritual disintegration of the modern world. The plan of the poem presents a synthetic appearance of its five divisions—each distinguished from the other by the odd variety of the ironical contrasts. It is Tiresies—the legendary prophet of the

---

131. Richards, I. A.—*The Principles of Criticism.*

132. Pinto V de S—*Crisis in English Poetry*, p. 192.

Greeks—who synthesizes the various elements of **The Waste Land.** He may be described as the embodiment of the modern mind, "keen to observe"[133] but "powerless to act."[134]

The Waste Land is pictured with all the sordid aspects of the Grail legend. It is a dry and haunted place not easy to know or guess:—

> Son of man,
> You cannot say or guess, for you only know.
> A heap of broken images, where the sun beats,
> And the dead tree gives no shelter, the cricket no relief,
> And the dry stone no sound of water.

The poem records a great advancement in Eliot's basic method of contrast—a method which is so recurrent in his later poetry. **The Waste Land** depicts the sense of the age as seen through the Baudelairian angle.[135] Here the contrast is between two kinds of life and two kinds of death.[136] A life devoid of significance is death; while a death made for some sacrificial cause may be inspiring and life-giving. The fact that people in **The Waste Land** are no more able to discriminate between evil and good, supports the Baudelairian concept of reality as if they do not exist at all.[137] The opening lines:—

> April is the cruel last month, breeding
> Lilacs out of the dead land mixing
> Memory and desire, stirring
> Dull roots with spring rain.[138]

suggest the same analogy. In this section, the poet tries to develop the theme of longing for death. The people suffer from an ever lurking complex of death-in-life. They fear to live in reality. Hence, April—a time of mixing 'memory and desire' reminds us of the opening lines of **Gerontion** which

---

133. Pinto V de S—*Crisis in English Poetry,* p. 194.
134. *Ibid.*
135. Rajan, B.—*Eliot: A Study by Several Hands,* p. 8.
136. Brooks Cleanth; in *Eliot: A Study by Several Hands,* p. 8.
137. *Selected Prose,* p. 174.
138. *Selected Poems*: Faber and Faber, p. 51.

evoke emotional intensities of the highest order. Closely connected with this is the use of paradoxical symbols. If we take a surface view "they resist" what Brooks calls "equation with simple meaning."[139] But considered deeply, they render great help in simplifying the complexity of diverse experiences. For instance the lines:—

> You gave me hyacinths first a year ago;
> 'They called me the hyacinth girl.
> —Yet when we came back, late, from the Hyacinth garden,
> Your arms full, and your hair wet, I could not
> Speak, and eyes failed, I was neither
> Living nor dead, and I knew nothing,
> Looking into the heart of light and the silence.[140]

appear to reflect on a vision of beauty and goodness of life. The imagery used is sexual. Ordinarily, a forth-right experience of some joyous moments is conveyed. But, a little of deep study would suggest quite a contrary impression. Actually, the protagonist suffers from a state of "obscure vacuum." His eyes "failed" and he "knew" nothing. He felt as if "neither living nor dead"—a kind of typical death. There the experience, in its intensity, is an experience amounting to that of death. It hustles the protagonist to look into the "heart of light and the silence." The duality of such surface parallelism, subscribes to the basic method of the poem, where the poet is applying the principle of "complexity" to work out its effects. Again, the two sections—"**Death by Water**" and "**The Fire Sermon**"—form a contrast with each other. It is a contrast between the symbolism of **fire** and the symbolism of **water.** Cleanth Brooks rightly comments on its force "as a symbol of surrender and relief through surrender."[141] Similarly, the symbol of "**A Game of Chess**" implies two meanings: first, the game is used as a device to keep the widow occupied; while her daughter-in-law is being seduced;[142] second, the variety of the traditional environment, pictured in the room as contrasted with the "game of chess", symbolizes "the

---

139. Rajan, B.—*Eliot*: *A Study by Several Hands,* p. 24.
140. *Selected Poems*: Faber and Faber, p. 52.
141. Rajan, B.—*Eliot*: *A Study by Several Hands,* p. 24.
142. *Ibid,* p. 18.

inhuman abstraction of the modern mind."[143] It brings out the emptiness of life and stresses at its nothingness in a modulated way:—

> Nothing again nothing,
> 'Do you know nothing? Do you see nothing? Do you
> Remember nothing?'

In this way, the "forest of symbols" which **The Waste Land** abounds in, lends it a lustre of varied sense-impressions. On the contemporary level, the technique has pictured, in the form of a compendium, an urban background of the "Unreal City." On the metaphysical level, it has been able to comprehend spiritual disintegration of the modern mind. In applying the concept of sensory apprehension of thought, the poem may justly be called the "Poem of the Age". Its evidence lies in the very texture of its poetry.

At this stage, a casual reference to the allusive nature of **The Waste Land** appears necessary. The poem is overloaded with the recondite learning of Eliot. The literal quotations and abbreviated passages from the old authors are a part of the Eliotian technique of concentrated expressions. His erudite scholarship forms an essential feature of his "sensuous imagery."[144] May be, that the poem has its own limitations—limitations inherent in its very comprehensiveness, organisation and structure. Still, the fact is, that it is "genuine poetry" and "does possess the power to communicate before it is understood."[145] The absence of "notes" does not materially affect its movements. Irrespective of its allusive setting or symbolic expressions, **The Waste Land** is "obviously a poem."[146] It grows out of its own structure, and is a "self-subsistent poem."[147] The sense of its consistent impression conveyed in lines such as:—

> I think we are in rats' alley
> Where the dead men lost their bones.[148]

---

143. Rajan, B.—*Eliot: A Study by Several Hands,* p. 15.
144. Pinto de S—*Crisis in English Poetry,* p. 196.
145. *Selected Prose, Dante,* p. 94.
146. Leavis, F. R.—*New Bearings in English Poetry,* p. 94.
147. *Ibid.*
148. *Selectd Poems:* Faber and Faber, p. 55.

or

Who is the third who walks always beside you?[149]

or

Here is no water but only rock
Rock and no water.............[150]

has not been imposed: it has been revealed.[151]

Eliot's pre-occupation with "horror and boredom" of the decaying civilization is further continued in two other poems: **The Hollow Men**; and **Sweeney Agonistes.** The world of the first is similar to that of **The Waste Land.** It is inhabited by men who are "hollow"[152] and "stuffed."[153] Their voices are "dried", "quiet" and "meaningless." The poet pictures modern humanity as having no eyes. The vague optimism of the hollow men, to recover eye-sight after death, is categorically denounced:—

Sightless, eyeless
The eyes reappear.
....
....
The hope only
of empty men.[154]

At the end of the poem, Eliot strikes a gloomy note of irony and wit, which refers to the gruesome helplessness of modern civilization:—

This is the way the world ends
Not with a bang but a whimper.[155]

"Sweeney Agonistes" presents the venue of a London flat where two prostitutes entertain some officials. It is a satiric melodrama, composed in irony of the nursery rhymes. The theme is based on the Baudelairian concept:—

"That the sexual act as evil is more dignified, less boring,

---

149. *Selected Poems*: Faber and Faber, p. 65.
150. *Ibid,* p. 64.
151. Rajan, B.–*Eliot: A Study by Several Hands,* p. 34.
152. *Selected Poems*: Faber and Faber, p. 77.
153. *Ibid.*
154. *Ibid,* p. 78.
155. *Ibid.*

than as the natural life-giving cherry automatism of the modfern world."[156]

Sweeney's final declaration of "Life is Death" embodies another attempt of the poet to focus interest on the same human predicament, which one is given to understand through **The Waste Land** and other earlier poems.

In between **"Sweeney Agonistes"** and **"Ash Wednesday"**, there stands a new kind of poetry, comprising the **"Ariel Poems"; The Journey of the Magi; A Song for Simeon; Animula and Marina.** These poems are associated with the post-conversion era of Eliot. They show a shift in the stress which he has been laying since the beginning of his poetic career. It is a shift from the sordid discomfiture of the outer-world to the exigencies of the inner one. Now, may be, under the influence of Christianity, one marks a threefold change in the pattern of Eliot's poetry: first, it assumes a sort of religious complexion; second, it displays a feeling of withdrawal from the "nightmare visions of the modern world, that haunted the earlier poems";[157] and third, the style touches new heights of serenity and sublimity as against the ironic sting of the twenties.

Ash Wednesday may be considered the first major poem, embodying this change in stress and strain. A simple connotation of its title suggests that Eliot, now, is on the way to furnish some positive scheme of values. On Ash Wednesday is performed the ritual of anointing the fore-head with ashes,[158] while the priest recites:—

"Remember man, that thou art dust and unto dust thou shalt return."[159]

The atmosphere of the poem also registers an important shift. The dull horror of the "unreal city" has disappeared. Instead, the poet seems to pray in a place of solitude.[160]

And I pray that I may forget

---

156. Williamson, George—*A Readers' Guide to T. S. Eliot*, p. 195.

157. Pinto de S—*Crisis in English Poetry*, p. 201.

158. Matthiessen, F. O.—*The Achievement of T. S. Eliot*, p. 12.

159. *Ibid.*

160. Pinto de S—*Crisis in English Poetry*, p. 202.

These matters that with myself I too much discuss
Too much explain.

He appears in perfect humility:—

Desiring this man's gift and that man's scope
I no longer strive to strive towards such things.

In these lines, as in **"Prufrock"**, Eliot is turning his irony against himself. In both the poems, he has given dramatic expression to a whole complex state of mind.[161] The beauty of its expression lies in, what Eliot has himself suggested: the problem of "sincerity"[162] or "integrity"[163] for a poet. He has not expressed here that what he would like to feel or what he ought to feel, but that what he **does feel.** Both the poems dramatise the emotions of two individuals as felt under the pressure of some exalted moments. But in **Ash Wednesday,** the strain becomes remarkably different from that of "**Prufrock.**" The poet's humility, now, has so strengthened the fibre of his own life as to strike a radical improvement in the very tone of his poetry. As a result, even in his moments of temptation and perplexity, he does not adhere to "unrelieved blackness of hopelessness."[164] Instead, he longs for "an unexpected renewal of desire for life of the senses."[165] The symbol of the three leopards used in **Ash Wednesday** with all its terrifying impression is so managed that our principal reaction is a kind of "fascination with their beauty."[166] The passage is worth quoting:—

Under a junipar-tree the bones sang, scattered and shining
We are glad to be scattered, we did little good to each other
. . . .
. . . .
This is the land which ye
Shall divide by lot. And neither division nor unity
Matters. This is the land we have our inheritence.[167]

---

161. Matthiessen, F. O.—*The Achievement of T. S. Eliot*, p. 121.
162. Eliot, T. S.—*The Sacred Wood*, p. 137.
163. *Selected Prose*, p. 187.
164. Matthiessen, F. O.—*The Achievement of T. S. Eliot*, p. 121.
165. *Ibid.*
166. *Ibid.*
167. *Selected Poems*: Faber and Faber, p. 86.

One no more feels the ironic sting of any of the earlier three poems: **The Waste Land; Gerontion;** and **The Hollow Men. Ash Wednesday** does not echo the poet's "dread of death and dissolution."[168] It does not recall the hard gruesomeness suggested by the lines:—

> Oh keep the Dog far hence, that's friend to men
> Or with nails he'll dig it up again.[169]

In Ash Wednesday, even the very agents of dissolution no longer seem terrifying, but are "merged into the vision of death itself as the promised land."[170]

In the matter of technical accomplishment, the poem is perfect. On its first reading, one is captivated by its peculiar lucidity and translucency, which is not merely intellectual but poetic also. The second section affords some fine specimens of great poetry. For instance, the use of such imagery as the "three white leopards", the "brightness of scattered bones", the "cool of the day" and the "picture of the Lady", who

> ....is withdrawn
> In a white gown, to contemplation, in a white gown.[171]

create an extraordinary pure impression of whiteness[172]—an impression which may be classed as one of the rarest to be sought with sensuous effects of colour. Moreover, **Ash Wednesday** is equally superb in creating effects, purely through the rhythm of sounds.[173] According to Matthiessen, it has the best chance of appealing to an audience that could neither read nor write. He asserts:—

> "For Mr. Eliot has been able to summon up all the resources of his auditory imagination i nsuch a way that the Listener can begin to feel the rare force of what is being communicated and accept the poem as a kind of ritualistic chant long before his mind is able to give any statement of its meaning."[174]

---

168. Matthiessen, F. O.—*The Achievement of T. S. Eliot,* p. 118.
169. *Selected Poems*: Faber and Faber, p. 53.
170. Matthiessen, F. O.—*The Achievement of T. S. Eliot,* p. 118.
171. *Selected Poems*: Faber and Faber.
172. Matthiessen, F. O.—*The Achievement of T. S. Eliot,* p. 115.
173. *Ibid,* p. 114.
174. Matthiessen, F. O.—*The Achievement of T. S. Eliot,* p. 115.

If it is correct to infer that Eliot's early poetry "converges on **The Waste Land,** it is still more correct to qualify his later poetry as converging on **Four Quartets**[175]—the sequence of poems written in between 1939 and 1942. In detail and organisation, the poems may be called the masterpiece of modern English poetry.[176] None of the **four quartets** is half as long as **The Waste Land;** yet its musical pattern is far superior to that of the earlier poems. It establishes beyond doubt the claim of Eliot to have perfected a proper idiom out of the modern colloquial speech. It is through these poems that he works "too closely to musical analogies."[177] Each poem embodies what Eliot has called "the sense of rhythm and the sense of structure."[178] The form of the **Quartets** is one of Eliot's highest achievement:[179] it is subtler, more complex, and more controlled than the verse libre or irregular blank verse. Its measure shows an extra-ordinary poise, comprising lines of varying length. Opening lines of **The Burnt Norton:—**

> Time present and time past
> Are both perhaps present in time future
> And time future contained in time past.

exhibit an exemplary cadence affected jointly by the imposing rhythm, the studied repetition and the use of the key words. The "Abstract" used evocatively stresses the presence and reality of the eternal.[180]

The same cadence is felt throughout the passages in a longer line.

> There are three conditions which often look alike
> Yet differ completely, flourish in the same hedgrow;
> Attachment to self and to things and to person detachment
> From self and from things and from persons;
>
> (*Little Gidding*)

---

175. Pinto de S— *Crisis in English Poetry,* p. 204.

176. Ford, Boris—*The Modern Age,* p. 344.

177. Eliot, T. S.—*On Poetry and Poets,* p. 38 ; *The Music of Poetry.*

178. *Ibid.*

179. Pinto de S—*Crisis in English Poetry.*

180. Rajan, B (ed.)—*Eliot: A Study by Several Hands,* p. 81.

It suggests the "deliberateness of prose, but the effect of poetry."[181] The practice embodies Eliot's honest adherence to his own affirmation that "poetry has as much to learn from prose as from other poetry."[182] Significantly enough, the poetry involving "self"—the inconcrete—is specifically marked by a prosaic exactness. But, where the concrete is involved, the poetry becomes consciously inexact and evasive:—

> There they were, dignified, invisible
> Moving without pressure, over the dead leaves
> In the autumn heat, through the vibrant air.

The contrast inherent in the two passages is instructive. "Dead", is opposed to "vibrant"; and "invisible", is put against "dignified." Initially, such uses may not suggest anything substantial, or they may not take us very far, but the device involves an important principle of Eliot's literary criticism which he has elaborated in **The Music of Poetry.** It says:—

> "I know that a poem or a passage of a poem, may tend to realise itself first as a particular rhythm before it reaches expression in words and that this rhythm may bring to birth the idea and the image."[183]

In this way, phrases such as "autumn heat"; "Mid-winter spring";[184] "Soul's sap";[185] "Zero summer";[186] "conscious impotence";[187] or "dead water and dead sand"[188], all point to the one and the same direction: the rhythm helps to sustain what is suggested by the diction.[189] Even it stimulates the process of new ideas and new images. To quote another example, Eliot in developing the concept of time into movement, has used similar image: "at the still point of the turning world"; which in its own way opens a serious meditation on time.

---

181. Ford, Foris—*The Modern Age,* p. 345.
182. Eliot, T. S.—U.P.U.C., p. 152.
183. Eliot, T. S.—*On Poetry and Poets,* p. 38.
184. *Four Quartets*—Faber and Faber.
185. *Ibid,* p. 49.
186. *Ibid.*
187. *Ibid,* p. 54.
188. *Ibid,* p. 51.
189. Rajan, B. (ed.)—*Eliot: A Study by Several Hands.*

Perhaps our assessment of the **Four Quartets** would remain incomplete without referring to the following passage, where Eliot has produced a pathetic picture of the aftermath of an air-raid on London:—

In the uncertain hour before the morning
Near the ending of interminable night
At the recurrent end of the unending
After the dark dove with the flickering tongue
Had passed below the horizon of his homing.[190]

The lines record an indelible impact of war. They do not depict the accidents but their horrible "essence" is fully carried out.[191] Eliot catches the "nervous tension"[192] of the moment which is nowhere more, than when the dove unites the "pentecostal fire" and the "dive-bomber."[193] But the most thrilling aspect of the air-raid is the symbolic annotation of the enemy bomber—the drak dove. It is the bird that haunts the skies of London. The flickering tongue is the air-man's fire of destruction. The fellow warden Eliot encounters, reminds us of the Dantesque episode of the Holy Ghost. The "uncertain hour" assumes the form of an "intersection-time"[194] between London and Purgatory. Apart from its religious sanction, the whole symbolism signifies four major directions of the critical thought which Eliot has stressed from time to time. First, it reveals a personal experience which has left its definite marks on Eliot, but the poet in him has impersonalised the same into the poetry of the air-raid. Second, Eliot has not only turned sensation into thought but he has also made sensation universal. Third, though he speaks in the first person, yet in no way, obstructs the impersonal growth of **Four Quartets.**[195] Fourth, the appearance of the purgatorial spirit establishes a direct affinity of Eliot with Dante. Commenting that their mutual concern was speech, Eliot in one sense, reminds of an important tenet of his own criticism—

---

190. *Four Quartets*—Faber and Faber, p. 52.
191. Williamson, George—*A Reader's Guide to Eliot,* p. 229.
192. Ford, Boris—*The Modern Age,* p. 347.
193. Williamson George—*A Reader's Guide to Eliot,* p. 229.
194. *Four Quartets*—Faber and Faber, p. 51.
195. Ford, Boris—*The Modern Age,* p. 347.

the function of a major poet:

> Since our concern was speech and speech impelled us
> To purify the dialect of the tribe
> And urge the mind to aftersight and foresight.[196]

We may be allowed to touch some basic aspects of Eliot as an artist. In criticism as also in poetry, his work, like that of Shakespeare, is "one continuous poem."[197] All his endeavours, in more than one way, leave the impression of a man of "unified sensibility" given to evolve an impersonal order in the realm of imagination. The strain of thought which characterises Eliot's concept of Art is also akin to his understanding of life and its various problems. Both Art and Life in his outlook, tend to find "significance" in an organic whole. What he spoke of Dante, Shakespeare and Goethe, is also true in his own case. His poetry displays **Abundance, Amplitude** and **Unity**[198]—the three distinctive features which he prescribes for a major poet to become universal.

In the light of the diversified nature of his poetry, one cannot get very far with him, unless one touches philosophy, theology and psychology. His theological interests have deeply penetrated into his own poetry. From the very beginning, Eliot shows that as a poet he has "other interests"[199] to convey—the interests that are "beyond the bounds"[200] of poetry. Eliot has always objected to the tendency of centrifugal individualism in society. He is against the glorification of individual's role in any sphere, whatsoever. The view of man symbolised in the comparative myths of **The Waste Land** and **Ash Wednesday** reveals his doctrinnaire faith in the principle of Original Sin. To put in Miss Weston's assessment, an Eliotian man—the Heavenly Man, the Son of God—"though originally endowed with all power descends into weakness and bondage."[201] On can safely assert that theology and ethics

---

196. *Four Quartets*—Faber and Faber, p. 54.
197. Kenner Hugh—*The Invisible Poet.*
198. Eliot, T. S.—*On Poetry and Poets,* p. 215.
199. *Ibid,* p. 116.
200. *Ibid.*
201. Westen—Quoted in *"The Achievement of T. S. Eliot",* p. 134.

have filled the contours of Eliot's poetical strain, may be, with the colours highly unpalatable to some of the ardent lovers of his own poetry. We would like to clarify here one serious misapprehension about Eliot's ethical concerns: it is incorrect to associate the theological bias with his acceptance of Christianity in the late twenties. As early as 1921, Eliot is suggesting the presence of a superhuman pattern behind the human, when he comments:—

> "Marvell takes a slight affair; the feeling of a girl for her pet, and gives it a connection with that inexhaustible and terrible nebula of emotions which surrounds all our exact and practical passions."[202]

Moreover, Eliot's outright rejection of Arnold's theory of Poetry as "Criticism of Life";[203] his stress on the notion of "extinction of personality";[204] his emphasis on tradition as a sort of "consciousness of the past";[205] and finally his concept of "order", "orthodoxy", and "sensibility", all point to the one and the same aptitude—an aptitude which is fundamentally **ethical.** Eliot's concern with this aptitude underlies the significance of a high moral order that runs through his creative and critical efforts. According to Eliot, artistic and religious sensibilities should work in unison. The separation of the one from the other, impoverishes the artistic process.[206] His preference for Dante or Goethe to that of Shakespeare is inspired by the same concern. But there still remains one substantial difference between his earlier pronouncements and that of post-Conversion era. After his **"Essays on Baudelaire"**, in 1930, Eliot is less reticent to colour his attitude with Christianity than he seems to be at the earlier stages. His concern is obviously less explicit in **"The Love Song of Prufrock"** as it gradually develops in **The Waste Land; Ash Wednesday;** and **Four Quartets.** In fact, Eliot is full of an inadvertent note of didacticism. True, he may not always invoke the

---

202. Eliot, T. S.—*Selected Essays,* p. 300.
203. Eliot, T. S.—*The Sacred Wood,* p. ix.
204. *Ibid,* p. 53.
205. *Ibid,* p. 49.
206. Eliot, T, S.—*The Notes on The Definition of Culture,* p. 26.

mysteries of Christianity or openly preach for its practice. Still, there exists a dominant feeling that all his poetry, either directly or indirectly almost asserts "its necessity."[207]

This brings us close to the problem of belief in the poetry of T. S. Eliot. In fact, the key to its understanding lies in his view of life which he has sustained through the entire body of his own poetry. Strictly speaking, Eliot is neither a church artist nor does he preach religious dogmas. Still, the life-theme or the nature of spiritual reality he incorporates into poetry, is basically religious. The texture he has chosen is not religion but the way he interweaves it, "leads towards it, goes with it and comes with it."[208] He is certainly methodical in saying something about religion. All his poems from **Prufrock** to **Four Quartets** are religious in as far as they inhere a sort of a voyage from within the mind of the protagonist. Granted that **Ash Wednesday** and the poems succeeding it are explicitly more religious than the poems written earlier, yet the implicit religiosity of **The Love Song, Gerontion** and **The Waste Land** cannot be easily set aside. They also imply the verdict of a spiritual reality or depict to an ample degree what Eliot himself has declared in **After Strange Gods:—**

> "It is in fact in moments of moral and spiritual struggle depending on spiritual sanctions, rather than in those 'bewildering minutes' in which we are all very much alike, that men and women come nearest to being real."[209]

The earlier poems, in this sense, are the precursors of the later ones. They may not be poems of easy faith but they surely envisage the step-by-step forward development of the poet's experience. They voice, no less than the religious poems of the later period, the urge for belief and its relative importance in the superhuman order of the universe. They direct the mind of the poet from doubt, desperation and skepticism to acceptance, hope and enlightenment. Even **Prufrock** with all the agonies, fears, inabilities and indecisions of life, displays

---

207. *Selected Prose,* p. 177.

208. Barber, C. L.—*The Power of Development in The Achievement of T. S. Eliot,* p. 202.

209. Eliot, T. S.—*After Strange Gods,* p. 26.

an abiding sense for beauty, love and sympathy. In **Gerontion** the accents of fear and despair are deeper, but both the poems reveal the conditions of "being real" by the juxtaposition of circumstances which result from the absence of struggle on the moral plane. Both, **Prufrock** and **Gerontion** suffer on account of their inherent weaknesses. Both try to reach out to the meaningful context of life. They fail terribly: the one for his "inertness of will"; and the other for his "passivity." Prufrock passes from one mood to other, never settling down anywhere. He gropes in his own self-conscious isolation. Gerontion, on the other hand, makes his private dilemma merge with the group or society. But the way both of them surrender themselves to death, signifies the relevance of something, which, for all intents and purposes, confirms to a spiritual reality. It may be justly implied that "humanity is condemned to a living death, because it has disobeyed the eternal moral law and profaned the divine mysteries."[210]

The Waste Land also registers a similar type of religious authenticity. Eliot himself has scolded those who declared the poem as an expression of the "disillusionment of a generation."[211] According to Pinto, the poem is based on a very strong belief in original sin and the value of religion.[212] Cleanth Brooks sees "Christian material",[213] operating at the centre with the only difference that Eliot "never deals with it directly."[214] He has tried to explain the indirectness of the religious approach on three counts: first, that the form of the poem demands it; second, the poet's concern here, is not with the re-iteration of a faith—held and agreed upon, but with the rehabilitation of a system of beliefs—known but discredited; and third, he prefers to confine himself to the poet's business. The reason is obvious: he does not enforce the didacticism, which would have invited "stock responses" and as a consequence, would have marred the power of the poem as a "self-subsistent"

210. Pinto de S—*Crisis in English Poetry,* p. 198.

211. Eliot, T. S.—*Quoted* by Matthiessen: *Achievement of Eliot,* p. 106.

212. Pinto de S—*Crisis in English Poetry,* p. 198.

213. Rajan, B. (ed.)—*Eliot: A Study by Several Hands,* p. 35.

214. *Ibid.*

creation. On this method of indirection, Eliot himself has made an important observation:—

> "A poet may believe that he is expressing only his private experience; his lines may be for him only a means of talking about himself without giving himself away; yet for his readers what he has written may come to be the expression both of their secret feelings and of the exultation or despair of a generation. He need not know what his poetry will come to mean to others; and a prophet need not understand the meaning of his prophetic utterances."[215]

Suffice it to say that the "unconscious meaning" in Eliot's poetry is generally more important than the conscious one. In **The Waste Land** as also in his **earlier poems,** Eliot is dramatising or even juxtaposing the condition of a consciousness which in its logical conclusion moves towards the necessity of religion as "subtilized by Christianity."[216] The technical devices such as ironic gestures, references, allusions, parallelisms, contrasts, and paradoxes, all point to the same conclusion—the authenticity of the Christian **ethos.** In fact, Eliot from the very beginning, aspires for an "organisation in art, equivalent to the Christian organisation of society."[217] No doubt, **The Waste Land** incorporates allusions drawn from the none-Christian world, still, its web-like frame-work as a whole imparts the impression of the world of Christianity; while all its formal norms are deliberately kept at the back of the poem itself. For example, the narrative background of the "hyacinth girl" or of Madame Sosostris or of Albert is merely used as a sort of parallelism to the Christian background. The way the symbol of Buddha's Fire Sermon is juxtaposed to the Christian conditions, furnishes another example of the same device.

The end of the **Fire Sermon** explicitly points towards the Christian awareness:—

La La
To Carthage then I came
Burning burning burning burning
O Lord Thou pluckest me out
O Lord Thou Pluckest.[218]

---

215. Eliot, T. S.—*On Poetry and Poets,* p. 122.
216. Eliot, T. S.—*Essays Ancient and Modern,* p. 230.
217. Eliot, T. S.—*The Idea of a Christian Society,* p. 34.
218. *Selected Poems*: Faber and Faber, p. 62.

Presumably, the most significant acknowledgement of this awareness is contained in the admonition of the Thunder: "Datta", "dayadhyam" and "damyata", meaning "give, sympathise and control", respectively. The protagonist says:—

I have heard the key
Turn in the door once and turn once only
We think of the key, each in his prison
Thinking of the key, each confirms a prison
Only at nightfall, aethereal rumours
Revive for a moment a broken Coriolanus.[219]

The individual, locked in typical isolation, can release himself only "by self-surrender and by sympathy for others."[220] By referring to the modern man as a "broken Coriolanus", Eliot is voicing the present dilemma which the whole world is suffering from in the welter of a confused society. The story of Coriolanus states, that his tragedy was genuine. His pride alienated him both from man and God, bringing thus, his ultimate ruin. The "revival" of the "broken Coriolanus", or the "salvation" of the modern man, lies in the virtue of humility—the opposite pole of pride—which according to Eliot, is "the most difficult of the Christian virtues."[221] In this connection, Dr. Leavis' assessment of:—

"I sat upon the shore
Fishing, with the arid plain behind me."[222]

as "exhibiting no progression",[223] or the comment that the poem "ends where it began",[224] does not appear convincing.[225] It is true that the "thunder" brings no rain to revive the "Waste Land"; still, the striking note of the poem at the end involves an obligatory sense of Christian responsibility. Referring to the adverse effects of secularisation on modern civilization, it points out:—

---

219. *Selected Poems,* p. 62.
220. Matthiessen, F. O.—*The Achievement of T. S. Eliot,* p. 138.
221. *Selected Prose,* essay on Baudelaire, p. 174.
222. *Selected Poems*: Faber and Faber.
223. Leavis, F. R.—*New Bearings in English Poetry,* p. 87.
224. *Ibid.*
225. Brooks Cleanth—*A Study of Eliot,* p. 29.

London Bridge is falling down, falling down, falling down.[226]

And then the anxiety to restore order:—

"Shall I at least set my lands in order."[227]

clearly affirms an ever growing feeling of the Christian awareness and its much needed contribution towards society as a whole. Eliot's own observation on Christian faith is significant:—

> "I cannot see that poetry can ever be separated from something which I would call belief and to which I cannot see any reason for refusing the name of belief unless we are to reshuffle names together. It should hardly be needful to say that it will not be inevitably orthodox Christian belief, although that possibility can be entertained, since Christianity will probably continue to modify itself as in the past, into something that can be believed in."[228]

It is the presence of such an assurance and belief which has provided "Identity of Substance"[229] to all his poetry from **The Love Song** to the **Four Quartets.** Being essentially a lyrical poet, Eliot exhibits that "pious sincerity"[230] which is the first requisite of religious poetry. He is always faithful to his own "voices."[231] The poetry before **Ash Wednesday** expresses "not a self, but the struggle to find a self or do without a self."[232] The poetry in between **Ash Wednesday** and the **Four Quartets** is the poetry of withdrawal from the outer-world and of sojourn into the mysteries of the inner life as seen through the perspective of Christianity. The **Four Quartets** may be said to inhere the soliloquies of Eliot. The identity of substance in his poetry is marked by the integrity of his own feelings and impressions. As to his remarkable achievement in prosody, the observations of Ransom are significant:—

> "Somebody, by precept and example, had to bring into the music of poetry the grace and freedom which had arrived in

---

226. *Selected Poems*—Faber and Faber, p. 67.
227. *Ibid.*
228. *The Enemy;* January, 1927.
229. Blackmur, R. P.—*Language as Gesture,* p. 183.
230. Eliot, T. S.—*After Strange Gods.*
231. Eliot, T. S.—O.P.P., Three Voices of Poetry, p. 89.
232. Barber, C. L.—in *The Achievement of T. S. Eliot,* p. 210.

> the art of pure music many years before. Eliot was the man."[233]

Looking back at the plays of Eliot, one can safely make three assertions. First, the number of his plays is smaller in proportion to the voluminous nature of his dramatic criticism. Second, the plays remain no longer isolated successes, but proclaim the beginning of a movement.[234] Third, though small in number, they contain a wide variety, both of method and of success.[235] The entire body of Eliot's dramatic production comprises: **Murder in the Cathedral; The Family Reunion; The Cocktail Party; Sweeney Agonistes; The Confidential Clerk;** and **The Rock.** The first three works may be deemed as his major plays.

In **The Sacred Wood,** Eliot has attributed the failure of the past writers of poetic drama to their beginning at the wrong end: "They have" he says "aimed at the small public which wants poetry."[236] In making this statement, Eliot is referring to an important principle of dramaturgy. By "aiming at small public", the critic means to suggest their inability to satisfy various levels of consciousness of the audience. In **The Use of Poetry and the Use of Criticism,** he further develops the same idea, when he commends theatre as the "ideal medium" for poetry and a "direct means" of its "social usefulness."[237] Eliot's interest in drama sprouts mainly from his firm conviction of looking forward to drama as the "most socially relevant of the arts."[238] He rightly feels that if the plays do not draw and cater to an audience—of all categories—they fail "artistically as well as socially."[239] On the touch-stone of this social verisimilitude, the later comedies of Eliot, viz., **The Cocktail Party, The Confidential Clerk** and **The Elder States-**

---

233. Tate Allen (ed.) *Eliot: The Man and Work,* p. 134.
234. Williams Raymond—*Drama from Ibsen to Eliot,* p. 223.
235. *Ibid.*
236. Eliot, T. S.—*The Sacred Wood,* p. 70.
237. Eliot, T. S.—U.P.U.C., p. 135.
238. Gardner, Helen—*Comedies of T. S. Eliot, C. F., T. S. Eliot: The Man and His Work,* p. 160.
239. *Ibid.*

man are a great achievement in their own right. Helen Gardner rightly remarks that these plays catch the accents and the moral tone of what one may call "polite society"[240] in the post-war decade. As for his earlier plays, they, like his earlier poetry, picture a sense of life, at once sordid and gloomy: **Sweeney Agonistes** is a fragment of Aristophanic melodrama, **Murder in the Cathedral** is a religious tragedy; and **The Family Reunion** is a tragedy on the psychological plane.

Eliot's dramatic genius may be summarized in terms of "three important elements";[241] first, his emphasis on a "dramatic rather than a prose structure",[242] clearly discernible, in **The Waste Land**; second, his preoccupation with the "dramatisation of a consciousness", or the "dramtic realisation of a mind",[243] pictured through **Prufrock, The Lady** and **Gerontion**; and thirdly, his belaboured experiments in evolving out a suitable "dramatic speech",[244] such as the following:—

Death or life or life or death
Death is life and life is death.

(*Sweeney Agonistes*)

or

You know and do not know, what it is to act and suffer
You know and do not know, that acting is suffering
And suffering is action.

(*Murder in The Cathedral*)

As a poetic innovator, Eliot starts from the principle that language of poetry must be chosen from ordinary speech. The task of the poet is regulated by "the period in which he finds himself"[245] as also by "his personal constitution."[246] It may be in the nature of either "exploring the musical avenues of a language"[247] or "the catching up with the changes in colloquial speech."[248] The problem of speech, in this way, is

240. *Ibid.*
241. Williams Raymond—*Drama From Ibsen to Eliot,* p. 224.
242. *Ibid.*
243. *Ibid.*
244. *Ibid.*
245. Eliot, T. S.—*On Potery and Poets,* p. 35.
246. *Ibid.*
247. *Ibid.*
248. *Ibid.*

fundamentally related to the "changes in thought and sensibility."[249] Eliot feels that the Shakespearian blank verse, which had lost touch with the rhythms of the current speech, will not serve any purpose. Hence, he directs his energies towards the two main problems of dramatic technique: the discovery of "how people of the present day would speak, if they spoke verse";[250] and the realisation of a form to arrest, so to speak, the "flow of spirit at any particular point."[251]

Sweeney Agonistes is an experiment more in speech than in form. It is a successful embodiment of Eliot's attempts to order speech and its rhythms. **The Rock**—the critic's next play—is disappointing. The verse therein may be noted for its local effects. But, it is **Murder in the Cathedral** which earns for Eliot an assured place among the writers of verse drama. It has a completeness which springs from the "perfect matching of material and form."[252] The most conspicuous success in the matter of technical perfection comes from the device of the **Chorus,** designed to be recited by the women of Canterbury. The chorus is incorporated by the dramatist for a double purpose: first, like the Greek practice, it could mediate between the action and the audience; second, it could intensify the action by projecting its emotional consequences. Not only does he restore the "full throated chorus of Greek tragedy, but also enlarges its function in the light of the Christian liturgy.[253] Moreover, "chorus is choir—the articulate voice of the body of worshippers."[254] It takes the form of a "link between ritual and believers."[255] As it prays:—

> Forgive us, O Lord, We acknowledge ourselves as type of the common man
> Lord, have mercy upon us
> Christ have mercy upon us.[256]

---

249. Eliot, T. S.—*Poetry and Poets,* p. 35.
250. Williams Raymond—*Drama from Ibsen to Eliot,* p. 224.
251. *Ibid.*
252. *Ibid,* p. 227.
253. Jones, D. E.—*The Plays of T. S. Eliot,* p. 58.
254. Williams Raymond—*Drama from Ibsen to Eliot,* p. 228.
255. *Ibid.*
256. Eliot, T. S.—*Murder in the Cathedral,* pp. 87-88.

Murder in The Cathedral is not merely a dramatization of the death of Thomas Becket. It exhibits something more. It may be taken as a "deep and searching study of the significance of martyrdoms."[257] The greatest achievement of the play is its dramatic pattern—a pattern which "is the action"[258] and possesses a "formal design and beauty."[259] But it is nowhere imposed or contrived. It is a sort of formal movement, gradually springing through the basic relationships within the ritual. Its dramatic realization is made natural by virtue of three factors: the ritual tradition, and the pre-established affinity among the priests; the choir and the congregation; and third, the familiarity of the formal language, its rhythm and context. It is on account of these qualities that **Murder in the Cathedral** records a plausible achievement of Eliot, as a dramatist. F. O. Matthiessen hails the play as "the most sustained poetic drama in English since **Samson Agonistes.**"[260] The sustained action, however, is the resultant accrual of the form itself.

Before we proceed further, it appears necessary to refer to one of the basic features in literary principles of T. S. Eliot. He is never tired of emphasizing the role of tradition. In poetic as well as dramatic practice, he is invariably seeking guidance from the traditional values of the past. He begins with **Sweeney Agonistes** as a Aristophanic melodrama; models **Murder in the Cathedral** on the Greek form; and shapes **The Family Reunion** on the classical myth of Aeschylus. Even in his later pays, though the "borrowings are disguised"; yet he has not hesitated to base his plots on the "models of Greek tragedy."[261]

The Family Reunion is an important play in more than one respect: first, it marks Eliot's beginning of adopting Greek material to naturalistic form; and second, it is a drama of "contemporary people speaking contemporary language." Its

257. Jones, D. E.—*The Plays of T. S. Eliot,* p. 59.
258. Williams, Raymond—*Drama from Ibsen to Eloit,* p. 230.
259. *Ibid.*
260. Matthiessen, F. O.—*The Achievement of T. S. Eliot,* p. 176.
261. Jones, D. E.—*The Plays of T. S. Eliot,* p. 88.

setting and scenes are the familiar drawing rooms of naturalism. Its versification contains "firm yet infinitely flexible rhythms"—a distinctive feature which assumes the form of regular medium in all his subsequent play-writing. E. Matrin Browne feels that "of the modern plays, **The Family Reunion** is the one which has most lasting value."[262]

Eliot's last plays may be said to have been developed through his serious concern with the nature of society and culture he has dealt in **The Idea of a Christian Society** and the **Notes towards the Definition of Culture.** They are the outcome of the same mood which sprouted the poetry of **Four Quartets.** He attempts through these plays to project life and its problems in the background of his own experiences which he had acquired in multifarious vocations. In one way, they may be regarded as "foot-notes or exemplars",[263] to **Four Quartets.** The most striking merit of these plays is their "speakability."[264] Helen Gardner's final remarks are significant:—

> "Eliot's desire to create a transpicuous language as a vehicle for drama was fulfilled in what is best described as the heightened speech of these plays."[265]

Eliot's dramatic theory and practice has already processed a valuable phase in the revival of modern poetic drama. It is no mean achievement that he has sent drama back to its origins, inside the church. He has also pushed it forward to the commercial theatre. Irrespective of the fact, that some of his plays have been utter failures, Eliot's work is assured of a "permanent place in dramatic literature."[266] As to the general merit of his plays, we would like to close our assessment with the significant observations made by Bonamy Dobree:—

> "Their linking of the modern world with Greek tragedy is in itself of major importance—more than a mere matter of tradition. It is part of the statement that Eliot was constantly

262. Browne, E. Martin—*T. S. Eliot in the Theatre, C. F. Eliot—The Man and His Work,* p. 125.

263. Gardner, Helen—*The Comedies of T. S. Eliot, C. F. Eliot—The Man and His Work,* p. 162.

264. *Ibid,* p. 181.

265. *Ibid.*

266. Jones, D. E.—*The Plays of T. S. Eliot,* p. 215.

making as to the unchangeability of human nature and its problems. They are universal. Again, they are extremely actable, holding audiences as being based on contemporary actuality. In the end, Eliot evolved a masterly model of stage speech, telling to the hearers and easy for actors to say."[267]

In the end, we may conclude that Eliot's critical writings numerous and prolific as they are, have certainly cultivated a new method, a new taste, and a new standard in English criticism. The **New Criticism** and the **New Poetry** owe much to his endeavours. In theory, he can genuinely claim to have expanded the dimensions of literary criticism. In practice, he has restored "health to the language";[268] and has brought the "poet back to life."[269] In the totality of his efforts, Eliot may be said to have moved between the two important facets of literary criticism: **"What** is Poetry?"[270] and "Is this a good poem?"[271] The key to his literary achievements lies in the basic fact, that he not only understood but demonstrated also, the "relationship of life and letters in our time."[272] Perhaps, what he spoke of Yeats, in 1940, is true of Eliot also:—

> "He was one of those few, whose history is the history of their own time, who are part of the consciousness of an age which cannot be understood without them. This is a very high position to assign to him: but I believe that it is one which is secure."[273]

---

267. Dobree Bonamy—*A Personal Reminiscence, C. F.—T. S. Eliot*: *The Man and His Work,* p. 84.

268. *Selected Prose,* p. 65.

269. *Selected Essays,* p. 278.

270. Eliot, T. S.—U.P.U.C., Introduction, p. 16.

271. *Ibid.*

272. Hayward, John—*Selected Prose,* Introduction, p. 13.

273. Eliot, T. S.—*On Poetry and Poets,* p. 262.

SELECTED BIBLIOGRAPHY

HISTORIES

Atkins, J.W.H.—*English Literary Criticism*, 3 Vols.

Daiches, David—*Critical Approaches to Literature.*

Glicksberg, Charles—*Amercian Literary Criticism, 1900-1950*

Saintsbury, George—*A History of English Criticism.*
History of Criticism and Literary Taste in Europe, 3 Vols.

Scott, Wilbur S.—*Five Approaches of Literary Criticism.*

Spingarn, J.E.—*History of Literary Criticism in Renaissance*, 3 Vols.

Ward, A.C.—*Twentieth Century Literature.*

Watson, George—*The Literary Critics.*

Wellek, Rene—*History of Modern Criticism*, 4 Vols.

Williams, Raymond—*Drama from Ibsen to Eliot.*

Wimsatt, William, K. Jr. and Brooks Cleanth—*Literary Criticism : A Short History.*

STUDIES

Blackmur, R.P.—*The Language as Gesture.*
The Double Agent.

Bowra, C.M.—*The Heritage of Symbolism.*
The Romantic Imagination.

Bradbrook, M.C.—*T.S. Eliot.*

Brooks Cleanth—*The Well Wrought Urn* ; *Understanding Poetry* (with R.P. Warren).

Burke Kenneth—*Counter Statement.*
A Philosophy of Form.

Burtis & Wood—*Recent American Literature.*

Crane, R.S.—*Critics and Criticism : Ancient and Modern.*
The Languages of Criticism and the Structure of Poetry.

Daiches, David—*The Present Age.*

Decker, R. Clearance—*The Victorian Conscience.*

Drew, Elizabeth—*T.S. Eliot : The Design of His Poetry.*

Empson, W.—*Seven Types of Ambiguity.*
The Structure of Complex Words.

Ford, Boris (ed.)—*The Modern Age.*

Gardner, Helen—*The Business of Literary Criticism.*
The Art of T.S. Eliot.

George, A.G.—*T.S. Eliot : His Mind and Art.*

Graves Robert and Riding Loura—*A Survey of Modernist Poetry.*

Hayward, John (ed.)—*Selected Prose : T.S. Eliot.*
Hulme, T.E.—*Speculations.*
Hyman, Stanley, E—*The Armed Vision.*
James, Scott—*The Making of Literature.*
Jones, D.E.—*The Plays of T.S. Eliot.*
Lewis, C. Day—*The Poetic Image.*
Lucy, Sean—*Eliot and The Idea of Tradition.*
Matthiessen, F.O.—*The Achievement of T.S. Eliot.*
Maxwell, D.E.S.—*The Poetry of T.S. Eliot.*
Pinto, Vivian de Sola—*Crisis in English Poetry.*
Powell, A.E.—*The Romantic Theory of Poetry.*
Rajan, B. (ed.)—*T.S. Eliot—A Study of His Writings by Various Hands.*
The World's Body.
Ransom, John, Crowe—*The New Criticism.*
Santyana, George—*Poetry and Religion.*
Sitwell, Edith—*Aspects of Modern Poetry.*
Smidt, Kristian—*Poetry and Belief in the Work of T.S. Eliot.*
Sparrow, J.—*Sense and Poetry.*
Spender, Stephen—*The Destructive Element.*
The Constructive Element.
Stephenson, E.M.—*T.S. Eliot and the Lay Reader.*
Symons—*The Symbolist Movement in Literature.*
Tate, Allen—*Reactionary Essays on Poetry and Ideas.*
Tate, Allen (ed.)—*T.S. Eliot—The Man and His Work.*
Taupin, Rene—*The Classicism of T.S. Eliot : A Symposium.*
Unger, Leonard (ed.)—*T.S. Eliot : A Selected Critique,* New York.
Vincent Buckley—*Poetry and Morality.*
Vivos, Elisco—*The Objective Co-relative of T.S. Eliot.*
Walker, Hugh—*The Victorian Era.*
Warren Austin and Wellek Rene—*Theory of Literature.*
West, A.—*Crisis and Criticism.*
Williamson, George—*A Reader's Guide to T.S. Eliot.*
Williamson H. Ross—*The Poetry of T.S. Eliot.*
Williams, Raymond—*Culture and Society.*
Wilson, Edmund—*Axel's Castle.*
Wilson, Frank—*T.S. Eliot.*
Winters, Yvor—*The Anatomy of Nonsense.*
In Defence of Reason.
On Modern Poets.
Zabel, M.D.—*Literary Opinion in America.*

WORKS

ELIOT, Thomas Stearns, b. 1888. d. 1965.
Poetry :
Prufrock and Other Observations, 1917.
Poems, 1919.
The Waste Land, 1922.
Poems, (1909-25), 1925.

Journey of the Magi, 1927.
A Song for Simeon, 1928.
Animula, 1929.
Ash Wednesday, 1930.
Marina, 1930.
Triumphal March, 1931.
Collected Poems, (1909-23), 1936.
Old Possum's Book of Practical Cats, 1939.
East Coker, 1940.
Burnt Norton, 1941.
The Dry Salvages, 1941.
Little Gidding, 1942.
Four Quartets (the four above poems), 1943.
The Complete Poems and Plays, New York, 1952.

PLAYS

Sweeney Agonistes, 1932.
The Rock, 1934.
Murder in the Cathedral, 1935.
The Family Reunion, 1939.
The Cocktail Party, 1950.
The Confidential Clerk, 1954.

CRITICAL AND MISCELLANEOUS WRITINGS :

Ezra Pound, His Metric and Poetry, 1917.
The Sacred Wood—Essays on Poetry and Criticism, 1920.
Homage to Dryden, 1924.
For Lancelot Andrewes—Essays on Style and Order, 1928.
Dante, 1929.
Selected Essays, 1932.
The Use of Poetry and the Use of Criticism, 1933.
After Strange Gods—A Primer of Modern Heresy, 1934.
Elizabethan Dramatists, 1934.
Essays Ancient and Modern, 1936.
Milton I, 1936.
The Idea of a Christian Society, 1939.
The Music of Poetry, 1942.
The Classics and the Man of Letters, 1942.
What is a Classic ?, 1945.
Milton II, 1947.
Notes Towards the Definition of Culture, 1948.
Poetry and Drama, 1951.
The Three Voices of Poetry, 1953.
The Frontiers of Criticism, 1956.
On Poetry and Poets, 1957.
To Criticise the Critic, 1965.

LEAVIS, Frank Raymond, b. 1895.
Mass Civilization and Minority Culture, 1930.
New Bearings in English Poetry, 1932.
Culture and Environment (with Denys Thompson), 1933.
Revaluation, 1936.
Education and the University, 1943.
The Great Tradition, 1948.
The Common Pursuit, 1952.
D.H. Lawrence—Novelist, 1955.
Dr. Leavis edited *Scrutiny* from its foundation in 1932 until its closure in 1953.

RICHARDS, Ivor Armstrong, b. 1893.
Foundations of Aesthetics (with C.K. Ogden and Jas, Wood), 1921.
The Meaning of Meaning (with C.K. Ogden), 1923.
Principles of Literary Criticism, 1924.
Science and Poetry, 1925.
Practical Criticism, 1929.
Mencius on the Mind, 1931.
Coleridge on Imagination, 1934.
Basic English and Its Uses, 1943.

INDEX